Baptists, Jews, and the Holocaust

The Hand of Sincere Friendship

LEE B. SPITZER, PhD

Foreword by Reid S. Trulson

JUDSON PRESS
PUBLISHERS SINCE 1824
VALLEY FORGE, PA

Baptists, Jews, and the Holocaust: The Hand of Sincere Friendship

To contact the author, Dr. Lee B. Spitzer, please email him at lee.spitzer@baptistholocauststudies.org. For additional resources, visit www.baptistholocauststudies.org.

Interior design by Crystal Devine.
Cover design by Wendy Ronga and Hampton Design Group.

Library of Congress Cataloging-in-Publication data

Names: Spitzer, Lee B., author.
Title: Baptists, Jews, and the Holocaust : the hand of sincere friendship / Lee B. Spitzer ; foreword by Reid Trulson.
Description: Valley Forge, PA : Judson Press, [2017] | Includes bibliographical references.
Identifiers: LCCN 2017031726 (print) | LCCN 2017010387 (ebook) | ISBN 9780817081720 (ebook) | ISBN 9780817017828 (pbk. : alk. paper)
Subjects: LCSH: Baptists--United States--History--20th century. | Judaism--Relations--Baptists. | Baptists--Relations--Judaism. | Holocaust, Jewish (1939-1945) | World War, 1939-1945--Jews.
Classification: LCC BX6237 (print) | LCC BX6237 .S65 2017 (ebook) | DDC 261.2/60882861--dc23
LC record available at https://lccn.loc.gov/2017031726

Printed in the U.S.A.
First printing, 2017.

Contents

Foreword

Not since the end of World War II has the message of this book been timelier.

This week Philadelphia's leading newspaper bore a chilling front-page headline: "Something Bad Is Happening in Our Country." The photo accompanying the lead story showed people praying amid one hundred gravestones that had been toppled at Philadelphia's Mount Carmel Cemetery, a nearly two-centuries-old Jewish cemetery. The previous week, 170 tombstones had been overturned in a Jewish cemetery in St. Louis. In addition, Jewish community centers and day schools in thirty-three US states and two Canadian provinces had received bomb threats in just the first two months of 2017.

The newspaper's report on "a rash of anti-Semitism" is consistent with a broader trend in the United States and in Europe. The Anti-Defamation League's annual audit of anti-Semitic incidents reported that anti-Semitic incidents at US colleges and universities had nearly doubled from 2014 to 2015. The audit noted a dramatic rise in violent anti-Semitic assaults in the US. In total, reports of anti-Jewish incidents in 2015 increased 3 percent. A February 2016 CNN report concluded, "Anti-Semitism is thriving in Europe, so it was no surprise to hear the news last month of record-setting Jewish migration to Israel in 2015."

Dr. Lee Spitzer's *Baptists, Jews, and the Holocaust: The Hand of Sincere Friendship* reveals how Baptists responded to European anti-Semitism and the Holocaust in the 1930s and 1940s. The story is particularly timely in light of the reoccurring rise of anti-Semitism in the US and Europe today.

Although Baptists constitute the largest portion of US Protestants, little has previously been told of their response to the Holocaust and the hatred out of which it arose. Historical investigations by three earlier scholars had concluded that Baptists were largely silent about anti-Semitism and the persecution of Jews in Europe, implying that there was no story to tell. Those studies, however, bore several significant deficiencies that Dr. Spitzer's research has now corrected. Unlike the three shorter works, Spitzer's broadly scoped research examines Baptist actions on national, regional, state, and local levels as well as activity in home and foreign mission agencies. Spitzer's study is remarkably pan-Baptist, assessing the responses of Northern (now American), Southern, African American, Seventh Day, Swedish, and North American (German) Baptist Conventions, as well as documenting General Association of Regular Baptist, Baptist World Alliance, Baptist press, and Baptist ecumenical responses. His attention to African American Baptists, who identified as fellow sufferers with Jews, yields especially significant insight. By having ignored African American Baptists, the earlier scholarship had overlooked nearly 40 percent of US Baptists.

Context is crucial for accurate understanding. By placing the Baptist response in historical perspective, Spitzer corrects yet another deficiency of the earlier works. For instance, Spitzer reflects on the extent to which Baptist antiwar convictions after World War I influenced their response to European anti-Semitic acts. Similarly, the Turkish persecution of Armenians led to the Northern Baptists' first response to genocidal acts. Their strong appeals to the US government on behalf of the Armenians proved fruitless in halting the Armenian genocide and left Northern Baptists frustrated. As a result, the Northern Baptist Convention "entered into the Nazi era humbled and uncertain of how to actualize its peacemaking mandate when protests failed and evil prevailed" (p. 46).

Baptists, Jews, and the Holocaust is the first truly comprehensive assessment of the Baptist response to the repression and then persecution of Jews in the 1930s, culminating in the Holocaust. The book's subtitle, *The Hand of Sincere Friendship*, quotes British Baptist Dr. J. H. Rushbrooke, speaking at a 1935 London forum on anti-Semitism and the Nazi threat. On behalf of the Baptists, Rushbrooke offered Jewish brothers and sisters "a hand of sincere friendship." But how might such a hand be extended? Group actions such as official resolutions, petitions to government leaders, published articles, and solicited donations all played important roles. But Spitzer's meticulous research also yields the very human story of Baptist individuals in action—a story that neither ignores failures nor inflates achievements.

One center of action left unexamined by earlier scholarship was the activity of Baptist laywomen. Spitzer notes that the Woman's American Baptist Home Mission Society was "the sole Northern Baptist Convention–affiliated national agency to address in a practical manner the difficulties Jewish immigrants faced in fleeing Europe and beginning a new life in the United States" (page 169). Year to year from the East to West Coasts, more than five thousand Northern Baptist laywomen served Jewish refugees and immigrants through the society's Christian Friendliness ministry. Spitzer introduces ten specific women, such as Matilda Utecht, a Christian friendliness missionary for Rhode Island and Maine, to tell this worthy but unknown story. The women enacted "the most prophetic and practical rebuke to racial prejudice and anti-Semitism within the Northern Baptist Convention" (p. 178).

Baptists, Jews, and the Holocaust is a rich contribution to Holocaust studies as well as to Baptist, African American, and women's studies. It is the story of a great evil and the responses of a people of faith—from inadequate to courageous.

In light of contemporary global anti-Semitism, American Baptist International Ministries issued a 2014 Resolution on Anti-Semitism. Noting that anti-Semitism is wholly contrary to Jesus' teaching, it urges people "to reach out to Jewish neighbors and/or synagogues to build relationships of solidarity and to initiate mutual actions to confront anti-Semitic attitudes and actions."[1] Knowledge is power, but knowledge that does not lead to action is like a hand of sincere friendship that remains at one's side. The story of *Baptists, Jews, and the Holocaust* provides an informing and challenging incentive to Baptists and all people of goodwill to confront actively the anti-Semitism of our day.

Reid S. Trulson
Executive Director, retired
American Baptist International Ministries
March 1, 2017

Note

1. See https://www.internationalministries.org/download/55593-international-ministries-resolution-on-anti-semitism.

Preface

I was born in Brooklyn in 1957, during that peculiar and optimistic period of American life and culture that sought to forget the pain of the Nazi past even as we faced the prospect of nuclear war with communist Russia. We were stereotypical New York Jews, assimilated over four generations, progressively forsaking Hebrew and Yiddish for English, striving to achieve the American dream of economic success (with varying degrees of success), and trying to balance our deeply rooted sense of Jewish identity with the loss of traditional Jewish religious fervor and observance. My relatives never spoke of the Holocaust and its impact on our family in my presence, and even at the present time I am uncertain of how many of our forebears perished in pogroms, concentration camps, and persecutions that ravished Europe in the twentieth century.

As my family moved from Brooklyn to Far Rockaway, and then followed the Jewish exodus to the nondescript suburbs of Long Island, my personal awareness of the Holocaust slowly emerged by way of academic learning. I was a voracious reader. History, geography, politics, science, and philosophy were my favorite topics. However, I preferred to focus on the brief history of the modern state of Israel and its struggles with its Arab neighbors rather than on the Holocaust era. The silence of my family on that dark period reinforced my preference to pursue other areas of historical interest.

I converted to the Christian faith when I was fourteen years old in response to a recurring dream, and prompted by a private mystical experience that revealed its significance to my life, I became convinced that Jesus was the Jewish Messiah on Christmas Eve 1971. My teenage years were spent studying the Bible, devouring it from cover to cover more than half a dozen times before reaching my high school graduation. In my senior year, I felt led to forsake my dream of becoming an Ivy League–educated lawyer specializing in either constitutional or international law, to fulfill a call to serve the church as a pastor-teacher.

During seminary, I finally discovered my place in the perplexing world of Protestant Christianity. I was ordained as an American Baptist pastor in May 1981. In those years, I was so focused on establishing my vocational identity as a pastor and developing relationships throughout the fellowship of the American Baptist Churches USA that I ignored a question that popped into my consciousness from time to time: "How did American Baptists, my new spiritual family, respond to the Holocaust?" The personal acceptance I felt as a Jewish Christian lulled me into a comfortable and peaceful valley, and I did not feel the urge to explore whether my denominational family had a history of anti-Semitism or, as I hoped and assumed, a generalized attitude of acceptance, respect, and love for the Jewish people.

In April 1985, my sense of peace regarding Baptists and Jews was shattered by the announced travel plans of Ronald Reagan, the president of the United States, to Germany. As a pastor in Rhode Island and with the help of friends from that region's American Baptist Peacemakers, I organized a statewide campaign, asking President Reagan and Chancellor Helmut Kohl of West Germany to cancel the visit to the Bitburg cemetery, where Nazi Waffen-SS officers were buried, and replace it with a more appropriate symbol of American-German friendship. Some three thousand signatures were gathered, and the campaign was supported by the Christian and Jewish communities. However, one negative incident tempered my idealism.

At a meeting of the American Baptist Churches of Rhode Island, I waited my turn to speak and encourage delegates from all of our churches to sign and distribute the petitions in an effort to secure as many signatures as possible. I sat two-thirds of the way back in the sanctuary and overheard the conversation of two women in the pew in front of me. Unaware of my presence, one woman said, "Look, Rev. Spitzer is going to speak about his campaign against Bitburg." Her companion responded, "I don't trust and won't listen to anything he has to say." Startled, the first speaker asked, "Why not?" Her friend replied, "He's a Jew. You can't trust anything a Jew says." Minutes later, I was called to the pulpit, but I did not permit myself to look at the women who had been in front of me. I did not want to know their identities or to let their conversation diminish my love for the others who I knew did not identify with the anti-Semitic prejudice I had just overheard.

In my subsequent experience within the American Baptist world, I have only rarely encountered anti-Semitism. It usually takes the form of subtle criticisms regarding how good Jews are with money and negotiating good deals. More often, I have encountered various manifestations of an exaggerated philo-Semitism, in which people elevate my Jewish background to a semi-idolatrous appreciation. Most of my friends express a more nuanced attitude between the two extremes. They recognize and affirm that my Jewish background is an integral part of my personal journey and pastoral ministry.

In 2011 the question of the relationship between Baptists and Jews during the Holocaust roared back into my consciousness. I am not sure why; there was no precipitating event associated with its reemergence. As circumstances permitted, I probed what several respected American Baptist scholars and denominational leaders knew about this question, and each of them admitted that they did not possess a satisfactory answer. This provoked my curiosity, and a new intellectual journey soon consumed me.

It did not take me long to realize that scholarly attempts to answer this question were inadequate and incomplete. What I did not expect was to discover a fascinating and complex historical narrative, the threads of which would require me to visit archives throughout the United States, Europe, and Asia. This book represents the firstfruits of my journey into the Baptist past, as it relates to the Jewish people. It does not reveal everything I have discovered but rather focuses on how Baptists in the United States reacted to Jews in their midst, recognized the rise of Adolf Hitler and Nazi anti-Semitism, and responded to the unfolding of the Holocaust.

Acknowledgments

Numerous individuals and institutions have supported my research. I wish to express my deepest appreciation to my two professors, Professor Dr. Henk Bakker and Professor Dr. Parush R. Parushev, for their guidance and encouragement, resulting in my receiving a PhD in theology from Vrije Universiteit, in cooperation with the International Baptist Studies Center in Amsterdam, in September 2016. Special thanks to Dr. Deborah Van Broekhoven, executive director of the American Baptist Historical Society in Atlanta, Georgia; Dr. Taffey Hall, archivist at the Southern Baptist Historical Library and Archives in Nashville, Tennessee; Emily Burgoyne, library assistant at the Regent's Park College Library, University of Oxford; Rev. Nicholas J. Kerstan, director of education and history for the Seventh Day Baptist General Conference; and Rev. Dr. Reid Trulson, executive director of American Baptist International Ministries, for the extraordinary level of assistance each of you provided. Thanks to my colleagues throughout the country, who gave me access to primary source documents that have been invaluable to my research.

A manuscript of this length and complexity requires many eyes to perfect. Special thanks to Dr. Lois Spitzer, my wife and associate professor of education at Stockton University, and to Rev. Dr. Ann Borquist, International Ministries missionary in Southeast Asia, for their tireless editing services. Will you ever forgive me for the insane deadlines I imposed on you? Technology is both a godsend and a curse, and so I would like to thank Rev. Wesley Allen for his assistance with Scrivener and Word, and for the enthusiasm he has shown regarding this research. I would also like to express my appreciation for my editors at Judson Press, who have supported this project from beginning to end.

This project could never have been undertaken if it had not been for the support of my denominational family, the American Baptist

Churches of New Jersey (ABCNJ). With deep appreciation, I would like to dedicate this volume to my fantastic ministry team, ABCNJ's executive committee and council, and the region's churches and clergy. I am honored to serve such a wonderful fellowship!

One last thought: although they will never read the history I have chronicled in this book, I would also like to dedicate my research to the memory of our Jewish relatives who experienced the dark night of the Holocaust.

Lee B. Spitzer
April 30, 2017

INTRODUCTION

"The Hand of Sincere Friendship"

How did Baptists in the United States relate to Jews and respond to Nazi anti-Semitism and their persecution of the Jewish people during the turbulent era of 1933 through 1948 (from Hitler's rise to power to the establishment of Israel)?

In its 1942 Christmas Eve edition, *The Watchman-Examiner*, one of the most important Baptist weekly newspapers in the United States, published excerpts of a remarkable interfaith correspondence. Writing as president of the Baptist World Alliance (BWA), a worldwide fraternity of Baptist denominations that was numerically and organizationally dominated by Baptists from the United States, Dr. J. H. Rushbrooke sought to reassure Dr. J. H. Hertz, chief rabbi of England, that he could count on "the spontaneous and universal sympathy of Baptists with your people in the measureless suffering inflicted on them wherever the hand of their relentless foes can reach them." Though Rushbrooke was English, he cited a famous clause of the American Declaration of Independence while articulating core Baptist beliefs on human rights and freedom: "Through all our history, the members of my communion have been outspoken protagonists of the rights to life, liberty, and the pursuit of happiness, which as God-given belong to all men without distinction of race, creed, or color."

Rushbrooke recounted actions the Baptist World Alliance took at its two world congresses. In 1934, Baptists gathered for their world congress in Berlin and unanimously adopted a resolution condemning Nazi persecution of Jews: "This Congress deplores and condemns as a violation of the law of God the Heavenly Father all racial animosity, and every form of oppression or unfair discrimination against

Jews." He confessed that "nothing in my experience has moved me more deeply than to learn shortly afterwards that in some of your synagogues in Eastern Europe thanks had been given to God for this declaration." In 1939, the Atlanta congress affirmed the resolution and heard from "a distinguished Jewish visitor, Rabbi David Marx, who was warmly welcomed for his own and his people's sake." Reacting to the revelations of systematic extermination of Jews in Nazi concentration camps, Rushbrooke passionately reaffirmed Baptist support of the Jewish people:

> I BEG YOU in this time of your people's agony to rest assured of the continuing sympathy and indignation of the entire Baptist communion as we contemplate the ever growing wrong done to our brothers and sisters of your race and faith. With each passing week, the monstrous inhumanity of anti-Semitism stands out more clearly, as cruelty becomes yet more cruel and the torturers drag their victims from what were once countries of refuge. Yet we are also moved to a loftier appreciation of the dignity, courage, and patience with which God has endowed your people, as we contrast the spirit of the oppressed with that of the oppressor. The Jew, we know, will not perish from the earth; his way is not hid from his Lord, nor the justice due him passed away from his God. In writing thus to you, I know that I express the mind and heart of the Baptist people—the largest Free Church communion in the world. Even in lands whence its voice cannot be heard, it feels as I feel and prays as I pray that your people may be sustained under their suffering, and in the mercy of God granted ere long a happy issue from all their afflictions.

Dr. Hertz lamented the catastrophic predicament that Europe's Jews were facing: "Destruction, total and irretrievable, is overhanging Israel in Europe. A sentence of death has been pronounced upon the entire Jewish population on the Continent, and—by machine gun and poison chamber, by torture and famine—a million of my brethren have already fallen victims to the Nazi fury." He graciously accepted Rushbrooke's expression of Baptist solidarity, stating that "when multitudes of my brethren are daily consigned to slaughter, the sympathy and prayers of our countrymen strengthen our faith in humanity, and cause us hopefully to look forward to the victorious peace. Jewry will not forget the stand taken by the Baptist World

Congress at its Berlin meeting in 1934, and its courageous declaration against all racial persecution in the very citadel of Nazidom."[1]

Rushbrooke and Hertz had collaborated on religious freedom and human rights issues even before the Nazi era. On December 19, 1929, Rushbrooke participated in a public mass meeting sponsored by the Christian Protest Committee in London, protesting persecution of religious Jews and Christians in the Soviet Union. Appearing in front of some eight thousand people at the Royal Albert Hall, Rushbrooke noted that both Jews and Baptists were global religious communities with a significant number of adherents in both the Soviet Union and Great Britain.[2] In 1935, Rushbrooke spoke at a London forum sponsored by the Society of Jews and Christians on anti-Semitism and the Nazi threat. Armed with the 1934 BWA congress resolution on racialism and anti-Semitism, he confessed that Baptists were spiritually indebted to Jews. In appreciation, London's *Jewish Chronicle* published Rushbrooke's climactic offer of "the hand of sincere friendship" to the Jewish community, on behalf of all Baptists:

> "WHEN," SAID MR. Rushbrooke, "as spokesman of my own communion at Berlin, I condemned in that city 'the placing of a stamp of inferiority upon an entire race,' it was not merely as a Baptist, but in the name of all instructed Christians that I spoke, and when our Congress passed its resolution—unanimously, in Berlin—deploring and condemning 'as a violation of God the Heavenly Father all racial animosity, and every form of oppression or unfair discrimination towards the Jews,' we expressed a judgment that, while we would apply it to men of every race, carries with it that special application a unique warmth of sympathy and a unique strength of just resentment, evoked by the knowledge of recent and continuing oppression and suffering. To my Jewish brothers and sisters under such conditions I extend the hand of sincere friendship."[3]

"Do Baptists Care?"

Even as Rushbrooke proclaimed his desire to befriend the Jewish community in its time of crisis, others sought to rally the compassion of Baptists throughout the United States. Concern for people in need was a recurring theme in Baptist circles. Speaking in May 1933, just four months after Hitler's rise to power and weeks after the first anti-Semitic discrimination edicts were announced, the president-elect of the Rhode Island Baptist Convention, Charles W. Littlefield, closed his remarks by affirming "I would be friend of all—the foe, the friendless."[4] Rev. Guy Wimmer, president of Shurtleff College, spoke at the 1941 annual meeting of the Ohio Baptist Convention. He asserted, "When confronted by a problem of human need some reply, 'Who cares?', others say 'I care.' This last should be the attitude of every true Christian, for our God is a God of love. Christ asks us to share with Him in the matter of world redemption."[5]

Following the Allied victory, the war-ravaged nations of Europe and Asia called out for assistance and aid. Only a sacrificial and heroic response could make a difference in the lives of millions of refugees and displaced people across the globe. The Cooperative for American Remittances to Europe—CARE—emerged as the most significant nonprofit agency for responding to this need, offering twelve packages of food aid that individuals and churches could sponsor.[6] Mrs. Garrett Detwiler, the wife of the pastor serving the First Baptist Church in Matawan, New Jersey, composed these song lyrics to rally support for CARE efforts on behalf of displaced persons, many of whom were still languishing in camps throughout Europe:

Do Baptists care when they look today
  On a world filled with pains and grief?
Do the burdens press, and the cares distress?
  So they long to render relief?
Oh, yes, we care; God knows we care,
  Our hearts are touched with the grief;
When the days are weary, the long nights dreary,
  Our Saviour knows we care.
Do Baptists care when they look today
  On our brothers with naught to eat;
With no clothes to wear, and with heads bowed bare,
  And with bleeding unsandaled feet?
If Baptists care they will share through "CARE"
  With their brothers in distant lands;
Making burdens light, making cares seem bright
  Our's in Christ's, theirs in our's, joining hands.[7]

Baptist calls to care were not necessarily meant to assist non-Christians or even non-Baptists during the Nazi and World War II era. A 1947 CARE update pointedly focused on how Baptist chaplains made sure CARE packages were distributed specifically to German Baptists: "German Baptists stand desperately in need of help. . . . Dr. McCall suggested that Southern Baptists should have their package addressed to Baptist chaplains in Germany, in that these chaplains will then distribute the goods through German Baptist churches."[8]

The Baptist participation in the CARE relief campaign, which was often characterized by assisting Baptists and other Christians rather than supporting Jewish concentration camp survivors and displaced persons, raises serious questions. As the Nazis persecuted the Jews of Europe and the Holocaust raged during World War II, was the Baptist offer of friendship to Jews really sincere? Did Baptists throughout the United States reach out to Nazi victims through individual and corporate expressions of caring and compassion? Were Baptists in the United States truly concerned, or were they apathetic in the face of the persecution and attempted extermination of the Jewish people?

Were Baptists in the United States Silent?

The silence of individuals, communities, religious bodies, nations, and international organizations to the Holocaust is a dominant theme of Holocaust studies. Daniel Jonah Goldhagen argued:

> THROUGHOUT THE PERIOD of Nazi rule, as the government and people of Germany were subjecting the Jews of Germany and those of the conquered countries to an increasingly severe persecution that culminated in their physical annihilation, the German Protestant and Catholic churches, their governing bodies, their bishops, and most of their theologians watched the suffering that Germans inflicted on the Jews in silence. No explicit public word of sympathy for the Jews, no explicit public condemnation or protest against their persecution issued from any of the authoritative figures within the churches or from any of their ecclesiastical offices. Only a few lowly pastors and priests spoke out or, rather, cried out forlornly their sympathy with the Jews and, with it, their bitter reproach of the Church authorities for their silence.[9]

Were Baptists in the United States similarly guilty bystanders who quietly acquiesced to the Nazi persecution of the Jews? Three scholars have charged that white Northern and Southern Baptists were largely silent during all or part of the Holocaust era, while the perspective of African American Baptists has gone largely uninvestigated.

In his doctoral dissertation (1981) on the American mainline Protestant community's reaction to the Nazi persecution of the Jews from 1933 to 1941, William E. Nawyn surveyed the Northern Baptist Convention's responses in five paragraphs. Nawyn focused briefly on three themes: convention resolutions, the general council's Kristallnacht letter, and the denomination's response to the refugee crisis. He was critical of the timing of Northern Baptist response (implying a delay), characterized the responses as "mild," and implied that they were less significant because they were part of a larger set of resolutions. He could have just as easily, without doing any violence to the facts, judged that they immediately, forthrightly, and specifically responded to the initial Nazi persecution of the Jews and articulated a considered position consistent with the corpus of social justice pronouncements that represented the Northern Baptist social conscience. Nawyn reserved the final three paragraphs to address the issue of refugee resettlement, concluding that Northern Baptists lacked concern for Jewish refugees.

Nawyn's negativity toward the Southern Baptist Convention (SBC) is even more pronounced. In two paragraphs he charged that the Southern Baptist Convention "was totally silent from 1933 through 1941 on the subject of persecutions in Germany and the desperate needs of Jewish and Christian refugees." This is a conclusion that may be maintained only if one discounts the statements that were made by SBC national organizations and leaders that reported to the convention each year.[10]

E. Earl Joiner, a Southern Baptist historian, presented a paper, "Baptists and the Holocaust," to the conference on "Remembering the Future" in 1988. He claimed that Baptists in the United States were largely "ambivalent" to Jews due to their theological perspectives. After citing a few "modest" protests from the Northern and Southern Baptist Conventions, he provided examples of "praise and support for Hitler" by M. E. Dodd (Southern Baptist) and John W. Bradley (Northern Baptist), following the Berlin 1934 BWA congress.

He next turned to the theme of Baptist silence: "The most common Baptist response to Hitler's Germany and his repressive measures against the Jews, especially between the years 1933 and the early 1940s, was somewhere between the extremes of praise and protest. The most accurate word to describe this median seems to be *silence*. Their silence is especially surprising since in their early history they too were persecuted and harassed."

Focusing on the Southern Baptist Convention, Joiner offered a harsh assessment. They knew, or at least could have known, about the unfolding tragedy but did not speak out in any organized or significant manner: "Outside Germany, the most conspicuous examples of silence among Baptists were from the Southern Baptist Convention of the United States." Joiner suggested five reasons for Southern Baptist silence: a "narrow" understanding of social ethics that "ignored major issues of state morality," the priority of evangelism over social responsibility, racism, fear of communism, and Baptist concern for their own members in Europe.[11]

Robert W. Ross, in his oft-cited book, *So It Was True*, surveyed how the Protestant religious press in the United States covered the Nazi era and its persecution of Jews. He concluded that "the accepted view that the press had said little or nothing" was not true. The silence belonged to the recipients of the horrific news—the Protestant churches and their members. For Ross, this silence consisted of a cluster of inactions representing "failures" on the part of the American churches—the failure to permit the news to "persuade" them to intervene on a large-scale manner, a similar failure to unite in "concerted efforts" or even to engage in "modest actions," and a paradoxical failure to use military action to save Jewish lives during World War II. Furthermore, Ross asserted there was a failure to speak out of a sense of "moral passion." Following the discovery of the concentration camps, he observed: "The reaction was shock, horror, disbelief, or finding a prophetic meaning in the events, and it was silence. But there was no indignation or moral passion, words of moral outrage at such evidence of human degradation and utter disregard for human life."[12]

In March 1989, Ross presented a paper titled "Baptists, Jews, Nazis: 1933–1947" at the nineteenth annual Scholars' Conference on the Holocaust and the Church Struggle. Ross focused his research on the Northern and Southern Baptist Conventions, as well as the Baptist World Alliance. His objective was to "examine what was reported in the minutes of the meetings of these three Baptist organizations regarding the plight of the Jews in Germany under Hitler, and in Europe during the Nazi occupation." While much of the paper is devoted to the Baptist World Alliance congresses in 1934, 1939, and 1947, the Northern Baptist Convention receives slightly more than two pages worth of attention.

Ross cited the 1933 and 1934 convention statements, the former without comment and the latter with the judgment that the reference to Jews was "general" and not "specific" in nature. He characterized subsequent Northern Baptist Convention meetings (through 1944) as essentially silent on the issue. According to Ross, this pattern of Northern Baptist silence continued into the postwar years. Although revelations of Nazi concentration camps horrified the world, Ross charged that "the minutes of the General Council are silent. No mention is made of the plight of the Jews." Therefore Ross felt justified in passing harsh judgment on the Northern Baptist Convention because "the truth is plainly evident":

> AS REFLECTED IN its minutes, the Northern Baptist Convention had nothing official to say about what had happened or what was happening to Jews in Europe, victims of the Nazi regime. The silence speaks for itself. Comparisons can be made with other denominations and nonreligious groups; the silence remains its own commentary for Northern Baptists, now the American Baptist Churches of the USA.[13]

In a similarly cursory treatment of the Southern Baptist Convention, Ross agreed with Nawyn and Joiner that the denomination was silent in response to Jewish suffering. Ross acknowledged that a "brief mention of Jews appeared as a part of a discussion on International Relations" and that missionaries mentioned German Jews in their 1934 report. He also noted Jacob Gartenhaus's annual reports with their references to Nazi persecution of Jews but argued that there were years of "silence" in which Gartenhaus did not address the subject. Concerning the postwar period, Ross stated: "The minutes of the 1946 Southern Baptist Convention are interesting, simply because it seems as though WWII never happened. No mention is made anywhere of the conditions under which Jews were living in Europe, nor to DP's [displaced persons], refugees or to post-war problems for Jews."[14]

At the conclusion of his survey, Ross reiterated his judgment that the Northern and Southern Baptists did not express support for the Jews who suffered under Hitler's persecution: "What the minutes convey is a singular lack of concern for Jews under the Nazis. When direct action might have been possible early in the Nazi era, nothing was done. No effort to influence official policy by governments, contact agencies of the United States government or put pressure on the Congress in behalf of Jews was made. Intervention in behalf of Jews was not done, early or late."[15]

The negative assessments of Baptists put forth by Nawyn, Joiner, and Ross are susceptible to several lines of critique. All three historical investigations are brief, and two of the three do not cover the entire era. They ignore African American Baptists, who comprised approximately 40 percent of the Baptist constituency in the United States, as well as the immense amount of activity by Baptists on the regional, state, and local levels in relation to anti-Semitism and the persecution of Jews in Europe. The propensity toward minimizing any evidence that would negate their hypothesis about silence is intriguing. None of them places the Baptist response to Nazi persecution in historical perspective or offers an adequate explanation for the supposed silence on the part of Baptists. These deficiencies point to the need for a fresh assessment of the historical record in regard to Baptists in the United States, the Jewish people, and the Holocaust.

Baptists and American Culture

How do we situate the responses of the Baptists in the United States to the Holocaust in cultural and political perspective? Northern Baptists, particularly in the North and East, were comfortable with the Roosevelt administration and worldview, and they mirrored the president's perspective, concerns, values, and agenda—except when it came to committing US military forces to combat. Baptists never imagined that they could defeat Hitler or solve the problem of European anti-Semitism and Jewish persecution by themselves; they looked to both individual governments and their collective expressions (the

League of Nations, and after the war, the United Nations) to deal with the plight of the Jews.

In *A Baptist Democracy*, Lee Canipe explored how Baptist convictions regarding soul freedom and liberty merged with American political norms to create a sociopolitical position he referred to as "Baptist democracy" in the twentieth century. Three Baptists paved the way for this fusion of American patriotism and Baptist identity—the Northern Baptist social gospel advocate Walter Rauschenbusch, and two Southern Baptist giants, E. Y. Mullins and George W. Truett: "They made it plain; what America is to politics, Baptists are to religion—God's chosen way for humanity. Or, as George Truett put it in 1911, 'the triumph of democracy, thank God, means the triumph of Baptists everywhere.'"[16]

The fusion of Baptist convictions with American political democracy, particularly in the preaching of George Truett, is significant for our story. He was the most important Southern Baptist leader of the 1930s, as well as one of the key leaders within the Baptist World Alliance. Armed with Mullins's "axioms,"[17] Truett's persuasive powers guaranteed that Baptists all across the United States would oppose Nazi totalitarianism.[18] In a quieter way, Rauschenbusch's social gospel prepared Northern Baptists, and to a lesser extent, Southern and National Baptists, to yearn for a social order that reflected Christian values.

Thomas S. Kidd and Barry Hankins similarly credited this trinity of Baptist leaders for propelling Baptists from dissenting outsiders to a movement that, at least for the two European American (white) denominations, could be accepted as American insiders by the early twentieth century. They do not discuss how this transition affected Baptist responses to the Nazi persecution of the Jews or the Holocaust. Nevertheless, their core insight that Northern and Southern Baptists were becoming insiders within American culture helps us understand why there was such a correspondence between Baptist responses to the plight of the Jews and the responses of the government of the United States.[19]

David S. Wyman argued that American anti-Semitism, passivity, and reluctance to take concrete actions on behalf of Europe's Jews doomed them to their fate; if the United States and its allies, as well as private organizations, had mobilized, a significant number of persecuted Jews could have been delivered from the Nazi Final Solution.[20] Not all scholars accept Wyman's somewhat extreme thesis.[21] Like Wyman, Theodore S. Hamerow charged that anti-Semitism constituted the root cause for the passivity and ineffectiveness of Allied and American responses to the Holocaust.[22]

Although anti-Semitism did exist throughout the United States at that time and played a role in its politics, Richard Breitman and Allan J. Lichtman refute charges that President Franklin Delano Roosevelt was anti-Semitic. They argue that Roosevelt's political instincts guided him as he calculated what actions would enable his presidency to survive while meeting the pressing needs of a country facing both economic and international threats. Contending with isolationists and other antagonistic political foes, Roosevelt cared about the plight of the Jewish people suffering under Hitler's oppression, but he judged that other priorities took precedence over possible direct action on behalf of the Jews. In the 1930s, lifting the country out of the Great Depression and preparing the nation for the upcoming war took precedence over aiding refugees and permitting a higher level of immigration.

Following the outbreak of war, defeating the Nazis militarily took priority over destroying the concentration camps. Breitman and Lichtman stated, "FDR avoided positions that might put at risk his broader goals of mobilizing anti-Nazi opposition and gaining freedom to act in foreign affairs."[23] During the war years, military victory was paramount over all other concerns:

> FOR AMERICA AND Britain, the rescue of Jews, when considered at all, was far subordinate to the preeminent goal of winning the war and defeating the enemy by unconditional surrender. Some Allied officials even viewed rescue efforts as conflicting with those goals. The lack of an Allied military presence in most of Central and Western Europe until late in the war left most Jews in Nazi-controlled and influenced Europe facing near certain death.[24]

The same concern over priorities had an impact on Roosevelt's position regarding Jewish immigration to Palestine: "Despite his sympathy for Jewish aspirations in the Holy Land, FDR had to tread carefully on Palestine, weighing political priorities and competing interests such as military strategy during the war and good relations with Britain and oil-rich Arab states."[25] Roosevelt's strategy of prioritizing was disastrous for many Jewish victims of Hitler:

> THE STORY OF FDR and the Jews is ultimately a tragic one that transcends the achievements and failures of any one leader. Even if FDR had been more willing to override domestic opposition and twist arms abroad, he could not have stopped the Nazis' mass murder of some six million Jews. For Hitler and his followers, the annihilation of Jews was not a diversion from the war effort, but integral to its purpose. For America and Britain, the rescue of Jews, even if practical, was ultimately subordinate to the overriding priorities of total war and unconditional surrender of the enemy.[26]

Roosevelt cared, but perhaps not enough to transform his order of priorities. Similarly, Baptists in the United States were not by and large anti-Semitic, but they possessed a set of priorities in which the survival of the Jews was included but not at the top of their list. Baptists cared, but due to other overriding concerns, perhaps they did not care enough to make a more significant difference in the course of the Holocaust. But even if they cared more and acted with greater effectiveness, Baptists in the United States could not have prevented a fanatical European dictator from advancing his anti-Semitic agenda, as expressed in the Final Solution.

What Is Anti-Semitism?

Hubert Locke, cofounder of the Annual Scholars' Conference on the Holocaust and the Churches and retired University of Washington professor, observed: "It is the Holocaust, undoubtedly, which gives every Jewish person reason to fear any manifestation of prejudice toward Jewish people. But it is precisely the Holocaust that requires we make every effort to analyze and understand what is and is not anti-semitism."[27] Anti-Semitism is a difficult term to define precisely, but a clear and concise definition will help us evaluate whether Baptists in the United States exhibited anti-Semitic attitudes and actions.

In 2009, the US State Department published a report on anti-Semitism and adopted a working definition offered by the European

Center on Racism and Xenophobia in 2005: "Anti-Semitism is a certain perception of Jews, which may be expressed as hatred toward Jews. Rhetorical and physical manifestations of anti-Semitism are directed toward Jewish or non-Jewish individuals and/or their property, toward Jewish community institutions and religious facilities."[28]

Such an anti-Semitic perception necessarily involves an unfounded negative opinion of Jews as a collective people, as citizens, or as a religious entity, and its aim is to prejudice non-Jews against Jews. This creates a sense of alienation and estrangement that may facilitate expressions of hatred, such as discrimination (the denial of civil and political rights), ethnic cleansing (the removal or killing of minority populations from their geographical homes), and even the denial of the right of Jews to exist as a distinct community among or alongside other peoples. In its extreme, as represented by the Nazis, anti-Semitism perceives Jews as less than human, and thus not worthy of human rights or existence.

The term *anti-Semitism* owes its origin to Wilhelm Marr in 1873 and featured negative depictions of Jews based on the disputable concept of "race." Marr's conceptualization of race, as applied to Jews and others, went beyond the scope of "ethnicity" (the grouping of individuals based on social, cultural, or political common traditions) by ascribing a biological basis for distinguishing between populations of humans and then judging those distinctions according to Aryan myths.[29]

In the United States, both Jews and non-Jews struggled with the "Jewish problem," eventually leading to the incorporation of Jews into the white majority culture by the second half of the twentieth century.[30] Both Jews and Gentiles described the Jewish population as a race, indicating that referring to Jews in racial terms was not always anti-Semitic in and of itself. It simply identified Jews as a distinct people. Accordingly, it is appropriate to ask if Baptists understood anti-Semitism to be an example of race prejudice and to investigate if they opposed specifically anti-Semitic forms of race prejudice.

Leonard Dinnerstein charged that Christian evangelization is an integral aspect of Protestant and evangelical anti-Semitism.[31] However, Baptists in the period up to 1948 believed it was theologically and ethically consistent to engage in evangelical and social action witness to the Jewish community while practicing friendship with Jews, appreciating Jewish heritage,[32] and being against anti-Semitism in all of its political and social manifestations. Is it possible for Christians to evangelize Jewish people and invite them to adopt Christianity as their religion without being anti-Semitic? Dinnerstein made a valid point when it comes to the ideology of a "Christian America."[33] Like other mainline Protestants in the United States, Baptists espoused an understanding of American identity that assumed American democracy and Christianity were tightly woven together. They did not seem to appreciate how this perspective marginalized those who were outside of Protestantism.

From an African American perspective, Beverly E. Mitchell argued, "Western philosophical thought in modernity provided the intellectual support for racialism—the shared link between white supremacy and anti-Semitism."[34] Anti-Semitism should be understood as an example of racism, defined as "hatred, hostility, contempt, ill will, condescension, or prejudice against a certain group on the basis of race."[35] Racism targeting African Americans and anti-Semitism thus share descriptive similarities: "forced segregation from the larger society; familial separations; physical, emotional, and spiritual deprivations; the brutality of oppressors; the outrage of degradation; and the need to bear witness against dehumanizing conditions, . . . women's suffering, the agonizing transports to their place of subjugation, and the special humiliations found in being forced to dwell in one's own filth."[36]

This explains why African Americans felt a kinship with Jews suffering persecution. The Jewish experience of persecution in Europe mirrored the black experience in both the rural South and the urban north of America. Jews also recognized the similarity; Mitchell quoted refugee Georg Iggers's recounting of his move to Richmond, Virginia, in 1938: "I saw how blacks were treated there. They were being treated just like we Jews were being treated in Germany."[37] In like manner, Locke concluded: "In the final analysis, racism and anti-Semitism are of a single piece. Both are grounded in that strange worldview that requires identifying another group of humans to whom one can point as the pariahs of the earth."[38]

In light of the preceding discussion, my working definition of anti-Semitism for this book shall be: *Anti-Semitism is the expression of prejudice and animosity toward the Jewish people, collectively or individually, based on negative and false stereotypes, which may also then serve as the basis for unjust and discriminatory actions against Jews, leading to their political, social, or economic marginalization from a society, and in the extreme, individual physical harm, collective loss of freedom, or the threat of their destruction as a people.* In the 1930s and 1940s, the following examples were illustrative of anti-Semitism:

- Expressions of support for fascism, Nazism (National Socialism), and Adolf Hitler as a leader.
- Participation in acts of violence against members of the Jewish community (for example, Kristallnacht).
- Exclusion of Jews from membership in academic, vocational, and social institutions.
- Restriction of political, civil, and economic liberties and confiscation of private property.
- Explicit activity or passive/tacit approval of the ghettoization and movement of Jews to concentration camps.
- Religious attacks on Jews, such as branding the Jewish people as Christ killers.
- The promulgation of conspiracy theories (such as the *Protocols of Zion*).
- Assignment of blame and responsibility for prejudice and persecution on the victimized minority group.
- Opposition to assisting and welcoming Jewish refugees.

Like others, individual Baptists and Baptist organizations were tempted to express anti-Semitic prejudice in the 1930s and 1940s. However, when they were faithful to their foundational core convictions, they found the necessary theological and social resources to eschew anti-Semitism and express friendship toward the Jewish people.

Early Baptist Convictions and the Jewish People

From its inception, the Baptist movement has depended on a collection of theological, ecclesial, ethical, and political convictions to develop and maintain a sense of community. Baptists are a transnational, interracial, and multiethnic people bound together by a history flowing out of the more radical stream of the Protestant Reformation, a sense of global mission based on Jesus' Great Commission (Matthew 28:16-20), and a profound commitment to religious freedom and political liberty. With good reason, British Baptist historian Ian M. Randall characterized Baptist movements as "communities of conviction" and cited baptism of believers by immersion and freedom from governmental coercion as key early convictions.[39]

There is no single agreed-upon list of convictions to which every Baptist community subscribes,[40] but the following distinctives are characteristic of mainstream Baptist thought:

- adherence to the New Testament as the authoritative source of belief and life,
- respect for the Jewish Old Testament since it is also the Word of God,
- the soul freedom of the individual to determine one's own religious views and spiritual journey,
- baptism by immersion of individuals who can testify to a personal experience of God,
- the autonomy of the local church to determine its own beliefs, structures, ministries, and relationships,
- the associational principle, in which individuals and churches voluntarily enter into covenantal relationships with like-minded believers, churches, and organizations for fellowship and mission,
- public witness, including evangelism, cross-cultural missionary activity, and social ministries, and
- liberty, encompassing both a radical view of the freedom of the individual over and against the social order and the separation of church and state, so that the latter may not exercise coercive power over the former.

When Baptists come together for conventions and create resolutions, they seek to represent not only a biblical witness but a representative one as well, with the commonly understood caveat that no individual or church is bound by the statements passed. These are exercises in communal discernment, expression, and speech but are not binding in the sense of doctrine or even practice. The statements have value as representations of the evolving Baptist community's wisdom, perspectives, values, positions, and judgments at a given time.

Notes

1. "Persecution of the Jews: A Letter from the President of the Baptist World Alliance," *The Watchman-Examiner* (24 December 1942), 1261. This exchange is mentioned in Robert W. Ross, *So It Was True: The American Protestant Press and the Nazi Persecution of the Jews* (Minneapolis: University of Minnesota Press, 1980), 278.
2. "Religious Persecution in Russia," *The Jewish Chronicle* (27 December 1929), 22–23.
3. "The Evils of Arrogant Nationalism," *The Jewish Chronicle* (4 April 1935), 30.
4. *The 1933 Yearbook of the Rhode Island Baptist State Convention*, Minutes, 18.
5. *Proceedings of the 116th Annual Meeting of the Ohio Baptist Convention*, Minutes, 23.
6. *The Watchman-Examiner* (16 October 1947), 1042.
7. "Do Baptists Care?" *New Jersey Baptist Bulletin* (January 1948), 1.
8. "German Relief," *The Watchman-Examiner* (11 September 1947), 935.
9. Daniel Jonah Goldhagen, *Hitler's Willing Executioners: Ordinary Germans and the Holocaust* (New York: Vintage Press, 1997), 4–8, 436–37.
10. William E. Nawyn, *American Protestantism's Response to Germany's Jews and Refugees: 1933–1941*, Studies in American History and Culture (Ann Arbor: University of Michigan International Research Press, 1981), 36–37; see 212n32.
11. E. Earl Joiner, "Baptists and the Holocaust," a research paper presented at the International Conference on "Remembering for the Future," Oxford, England, July 10-14, 1988 (Jacksonville: Florida Baptist Historical Society, 1988), 1–12.
12. Ross, *So It Was True*, 292; see 286–300.
13. Robert W. Ross, "Baptists, Jews, Nazis: 1933–1947," in Alan L. Berger, ed., *Bearing Witness to the Holocaust, 1939–1989* (Lewiston, NY: The Edwin Mellen Press, 1991), 207–10.
14. Ibid., "Baptists, Jews, Nazis," 210–13, 218–19.
15. Ibid., "Baptists, Jews, Nazis," 222.
16. Lee Canipe, *A Baptist Democracy: Separating God and Caesar in the Land of the Free* (Macon, GA: Mercer University Press, 2011), 13.
17. See Edgar Young Mullins, *The Axioms of Religion* (reprint, Nashville: Broadman & Holman, 1997).
18. See Powhatan James, *George W. Truett: A Biography* (Nashville: Broadman, 1945); and Keith E. Durso, *Thy Will Be Done: A Biography of George W. Truett* (Macon, GA: Mercer University Press, 2009).
19. Thomas S. Kidd and Barry Hankins, *Baptists in America: A History* (Oxford: Oxford University Press, 2015). On Rauschenbusch, Mullins, and Truett, see 170–82.
20. David S. Wyman, *The Abandonment of the Jews: America and the Holocaust, 1941–1945* (New York: The New Press, 2007).
21. See, for example, Peter Novick, *The Holocaust in American Life* (New York: Mariner Books, 2000), 48–49.
22. Theodore S. Hamerow, *Why We Watched: Europe, America, and the Holocaust* (New York: W. W. Norton, 2008).
23. Richard Breitman and Allan J. Lichtman, *FDR and the Jews* (Cambridge, MA: The Belknap Press of Harvard University Press, 2013), 151.
24. Ibid., 324.
25. Ibid., 239. On the subject of Truman and Zionism, see Michael J. Devine, ed., *Harry S. Truman, the State of Israel, and the Quest for Peace in the Middle East* (Kirksville, MO: Truman State University Press, 2009).
26. Breitman and Lichtman, *FDR and the Jews*, 6–7.
27. Hubert G. Locke, *The Black Anti-Semitism Controversy: Protestant Views and Perspectives* (Selinsgrove, PA: Susquehanna University Press, 1994), 17.

28. United States Department of State, "Contemporary Global Anti-Semitism: A Report Provided to the United States Congress" (March 2008), 6; see http://www.state.gov/j/drl/rls/102406.htm, accessed 22 June 2016.

29. Gavin I. Langmuir, *Toward a Definition of Antisemitism* (Berkeley: University of California Press, 1990), 311.

30. Eric L. Goldstein, *The Price of Whiteness: Jews, Race, and American Identity* (Princeton, NJ: Princeton University Press, 2006), 1–7, 119–208.

31. Leonard Dinnerstein, *Antisemitism in America* (New York: Oxford University Press, 1995), xxviii; see 105–49 for his analysis of the period between 1933 and 1945.

32. See Basil Matthews, *The Jew and the World Ferment* (New York: Friendship Press, 1935), 63.

33. Dinnerstein, *Antisemitism in America*, 105.

34. Beverly E. Mitchell, *Plantations and Death Camp: Religion, Ideology, and Human Dignity* (Minneapolis: Fortress, 2009), ix. She further argues (56) that "anti-Semitism and white supremacy are two forms of racism with a common theological foundation."

35. Ibid., 81–82.

36. Ibid., 4–5.

37. Ibid., 7.

38. Locke, *Black Anti-Semitism Controversy*, 96.

39. Ian M. Randall, *Communities of Conviction: Baptist Beginnings in Europe* (Schwarzenfeld, Germany: Neufeld Verlag, 2009), v, 3.

40. For examples, see James William McClendon Jr., *Systematic Theology*, Vol. 1: *Ethics* (Nashville: Abingdon, 2002), 26–34; Walter B. Shurden, *The Baptist Identity: Four Fragile Freedoms* (Macon, GA: Smyth & Helwys Publishing, 1993), 5; William L. Lumpkin, ed., revised by Bill J. Leonard, *Baptist Confessions of Faith, Second Revised Edition* (Valley Forge, PA: Judson Press, 2011), 16–17.

PART ONE

Baptists and Jews Before the Nazi Era

The earliest leaders of the Baptist movement applied Baptist convictions of liberty and separation of church and state to other religious minorities, including Jews. Thomas Helwys believed that the "logic of religious freedom came out of Baptist principles" and advocated for "a truly tolerant society."[1] Three years after the establishment of the first Baptist church in Amsterdam (founded in 1609), Helwys proclaimed: "For men's religion to God is between God and themselves. The king will not answer for it. Neither may the king be judge between God and man. Let them be heretics. Turks, Jews, or whatsoever, it does not appertain to the earthly power to punish them in the least measure."[2]

Helwys also penned a less positive reference to Jews. Criticizing "seducers" who would lead Baptists astray, he cited Matthew 10:14 and asked, "But when will these men, according to this rule of Christ, shake the dust off their feet for a witness against Amsterdam or Leyden, cities which neither receive them nor the word they bring, any more than they receive Turks and Jews, and all sorts who come only to seek safety and profit?"[3] In this passage, Jews and Muslims signified marginalized people who were outsiders, outcasts, and undesirable in European Christian society's eyes.

In colonial America, Roger Williams similarly promoted a vision of an open and tolerant political society characterized by individual human rights and religious freedom, based on the Baptist understanding of soul liberty and the separation of church and state.[4] Williams advocated for a pluralistic society in which people of all religions would be tolerated and granted the right to participate fully in political matters, because "Christians, Jews, Muslims, and pagans were all capable of honoring tolerance as a condition of public discourse, whether they understood it in a context of a religious worldview or not."[5]

In 1652, Williams advocated for the full inclusion of Jews in British society. He called for "the civil magistrate to break down that superstitious wall of separation (as to civil things) between us Gentiles and the Jews, and freely (without their asking) to make way for their free and peaceable habitation amongst us." He warned that "the unchristian oppressions, incivilities, and inhumanities of this nation against the Jews have cried to Heaven against this nation and the kings and princes of it. What horrible oppressions and horrible slaughters have the Jews suffered from the kings and peoples of this nation, in the reigns of Henry II, John, Richard I, and Edward I, concerning which not only we but also the Jews keep chronicles?"[6]

Subsequently, Williams's democratic and egalitarian witness would become a cornerstone of US Baptist opposition to the rise of Nazism and Hitler's persecution of the Jewish people. One of the first Northern Baptist state convention resolutions against Nazism, passed by Michigan Baptists, relied on Williams's legacy: "Resolved, That our churches re-awaken interest in, and a keener appreciation for, the hard-won standards of religious and racial tolerance, exemplified in the thinking of the prophet Roger Williams, and in the practice of the Colonial community which he founded. . . . Resolved, That we do express our sympathies for the persecuted, both Jews and Christians, and that we take our stand in opposition to the popular Fascist tide."[7]

In 1940, an article was published in a number of Northern Baptist regional newspapers. Looking on with concern at the advance of the Nazi regime and perhaps anticipating that the United States might eventually be dragged into the war, the article expressed sympathy for persecuted people by invoking Williams's words:

> IN ROGER WILLIAMS' parable of the Ship of State he imagined a case where Papists and Protestants, Jews and Turks are embarked in one ship, "upon which proposal I affirm that all the liberty of conscience that I ever pleaded for turns upon these two things—that none of the Papists, Protestants, Jews or Turks be forced to come to the ship's prayer or worship, nor compelled from their own particular prayer or worship

if they practice any." Three hundred years after these words were written men were dying in European concentration camps because they craved a fraction of that religious liberty which Americans of all faiths have enjoyed for one hundred and fifty years.[8]

Notes

1. Ian M. Randall, *Communities of Conviction: Baptist Beginnings in Europe* (Schwarzenfeld, Germany: Neufeld Verlag, 2009), 24–25.

2. Thomas Helwys, *A Short Declaration of the Mystery of Iniquity* (1612), in *The Life and Writings of Thomas Helwys*, ed. Joseph E. Early (Macon, GA: Mercer University Press, 2009), 209.

3. Helwys, *Short Declaration*, 309. I am not asserting that this was Helwys's personal view but only that he felt comfortable employing the stereotype of the Jew as outsider in order to make his point against his opponents.

4. Annette Mosher, "Roger Williams: Conviction among the Convicted," *Baptistic Theologies* 6 no. 2 (2014): 47, 49–51.

5. James Calvin Davis, "A Return to Civility: Roger Williams and Public Discourse in America," *Journal of Church and State* 43, no. 4 (2001): 697.

6. Roger Williams, "The Fourth Paper Presented by Major Butler," in *On Religious Liberty: Selections from the Works of Roger Williams*, ed. James Calvin Davis (Cambridge, MA: Harvard University Press, 2008), 235–36.

7. *1933 Minutes of the Michigan Baptist Convention*, 52.

8. "The Baptist Idea of Liberty," *New Jersey Baptist Bulletin* (March 1940) National Supplement, 4. Williams's original statement may be found in his "Letter to the Town of Providence, January 1655," in *On Religious Liberty*, 278–79.

Chapter 1

Northern Baptists and Jewish Immigration

The American Baptist Home Mission Society (ABHMS) reviewed the history of Jewish immigration to the United States in its 1926 report. It noted that "five Jews were with Columbus." Jews faced persecution in New Amsterdam, and in colonial Rhode Island they found a measure of liberty and "built their first synagogue." The Revolutionary army featured "twenty Jewish officers." From the beginning, Jewish immigration was a feature of American history, but in the twentieth century it was a significant movement:

> IN 1825 THE number had grown to six thousand. In the century since then great numbers have come, and now approximately three million nine hundred thousand are scattered over the United States. In Greater New York there are one million seven hundred and fifty thousand. Warsaw, the next largest center, has three hundred thousand . . . One hundred and sixty cities in the United States have from one thousand to three hundred thousand of this race. Since 1880, three million three hundred thousand have come, and during the latter portion of that period mostly from Southern and Eastern Europe. Multitudes of them have abandoned their religion and many do not believe in God. A typical Jew said to one of our secretaries lately, "Yes, I am a Jew, but only on two days in the year."[1]

Northern Baptists responded to the coming of the Jews to America by expressing apprehension and concern. B. D. Hahn, a New Jersey Baptist, expressed his disdain for European immigrants by characterizing them as criminals and warning that "we stand at the mouth of this European sewer."[2] Rev. Samuel Zane Batten believed that the growing Jewish population constituted a fundamental threat to Protestant power and influence:

> THE PROBLEM OF the Hebrew in America is a recent one, though it promises to become a serious one. The Hebrews are in the main industrious and law-abiding, and many of them make good citizens. But unfortunately during the past decade they have been coming here by the thousands and have been flocking together into the cities. Last year some sixty thousand Hebrews came to America, and many of these were totally illiterate and wholly unskilled. There are Jewish colonies in all our cities and these people are almost impervious to Christian ideas. New York City has more Jews than Jerusalem or Alexandria ever had; in fact, one-fourth of all the people in that city are Jews. . . . We must be a Protestant nation. . . . We must assimilate, and Americanize and Christianize these immigrants who come to our shores.[3]

In 1904, Dr. E. E. Chivers lamented the "deterioration in the quality" of recent immigrant communities—Italians, Slavs, and Jews, which he called the "refuse of old-world civilizations."[4] However, his negative assessment was challenged by an engaging narrative about a Russian immigrant whose Jewish commitment declined after his arrival. Here was an intelligent Jew who even matriculated at the University of Chicago (affiliated with Northern Baptists); he was eager to learn and open to the changes America represented. Years later, he discovered that Christians revered the Jewish Bible. The moral of the story was clear: "This changed Jew is not easily to be won to Christianity, but he offers a fair chance of approach to a religion that is real and practical, that recognizes the fatherhood of God and the brotherhood of man. And there are thousands like him. What shall we do for them?"[5]

This question represented a change of heart among Northern Baptists. Contact with Jewish immigrants challenged stereotypes and prejudices and created an opening for Baptists to respect and listen to Jews. In January 1907, *The Baptist Home Mission Monthly* published "What the Jew Thinks of America" by David Blaustein. He chronicled the disappointment of Jews who immigrated to the United States "to be free and to enjoy equal rights."[6] These aspirations naturally would strike a chord in the hearts of Baptists, who espoused liberty and equality as core convictions. The editor of the *Monthly* felt compelled to add a humble rejoinder: "It would do us all good to have the immigrant's idea of us impress itself upon our minds. We must remember that we are not dealing with things, but with living beings who think and see and love and fear, and are human like ourselves."[7]

With fear removed, compassion toward Jewish immigrants could emerge. In January 1908, the *Monthly's* cover offered a portrait of an immigrant who "just arrived at Ellis Island from the Old World, faces a new world, a new life, a new year."[8] A feature article portrayed Jewish passengers to America in stereotypical fashion—the worried Jewish mother protecting her children, "shrewd" Jewish men bartering, and the lack of respect they received ("who as always since the destruction of Jerusalem receive the lowest place: in this instance on the lowest deck").[9] A follow-up article detailed Gentile persecution of Jews onboard the ship: "Poor Israel! God's own people, despised of men, not willing to recognize Jesus Christ as the Savior of the world. Who then will bring them the gospel of light, that alone can heal their wounded hearts?"[10]

The Northern Baptist response would take three forms—ministry to newly arrived immigrants at Ellis Island, Jewish evangelistic work targeting immigrant Jews in cities like New York, and the Christian Americanization women's movement. All three initiatives would exert an influence on how Northern Baptists responded to the plight of the Jews in the 1930s and 1940s.

Baptist Mission Work at Ellis Island

Approximately twelve million immigrants entered the United States through Ellis Island. Northern Baptist Howard B. Grose, writing in 1906, recognized that many of these immigrants were Jews: "Since the year 1881 not less than 750,000 Jewish immigrants have arrived at the port of New York alone. On Manhattan Island more than every fourth person you meet is a Jew. The Jews admitted at Ellis Island during the past five years outnumbered all the communicants in the Protestant churches in Greater New York."[11]

The Northern Baptist ministry at Ellis Island was the first organized social action ministry the Baptists sponsored that interfaced with Jewish immigrants to America. At Castle Garden and then Ellis Island, Northern Baptists served incoming immigrants alongside Protestants from other denominations. The Woman's American Baptist Home Mission Society (WABHMS) commenced work on behalf of European immigrants in 1884,[12] and in 1911 the society listed three female mission workers at Ellis Island: Miss Martha Troeck, Miss Minnie Nelson, and Mrs. M. C. Conversano.[13] In 1915, the society revealed that "the Home Missions Council has also recently appointed a Superintendent, who is a Baptist, to promote efficiency and economy and the missionary activities of many organizations having representatives at Ellis Island, and to co-operate with the authorities in the execution of plans for the protection and the welfare of the newcomers to our shores."[14] In 1918, Troeck resigned and Conversano also worked in Brooklyn among Italians.[15]

In 1920, the Social Service Committee applauded the Ellis Island ministry: "We should see that the immigrant is met at the point of entry by those who possess a right spirit and a willingness to help. The reports of the work being done at Ellis Island in this respect are most gratifying."[16] This welcoming ministry continued to flourish; in 1925, the WABHMS report declared: "Our missionary at Ellis Island has been granted a new nursery on the first floor near the detention room which has been well equipped and is a great comfort and help to the mothers with little children who are detained on the Island. The new room is much more convenient and because of its nearness to the detention room the mothers are more willing to leave their babies where they can have the care and attention they need."[17]

The Ellis Island ministry was highlighted at the 1927 convention,[18] but it is surprising that it was not emphasized to a greater extent throughout the decades of its existence. Fortunately, accounts of the ministry were published in several articles in *The Baptist Home Mission Monthly* (through 1910) and *Missions* (1911–1948). The February 1904 issue explored the immigrant experience upon entry to Ellis Island, and the necessity for Christian mission at this major portal of entry was affirmed. Drawings of mothers and children on the landing of Ellis Island and in the "Mother's Corner" served to emphasize the humanitarian need Baptists were addressing through the work of WABHMS.[19] In October 1907, an anonymous missionary shared several stories about how Jews and other immigrants received spiritual counsel at Ellis Island.[20] An article from March 1908 included a brief mention of Northern Baptist mission work: "Missionaries of our own and other denominations mingle freely among the immigrants, giving here a word of comfort or advice, there a tract or a New Testament, with Christian counsel if opportunity offers. An untold amount of good is being done."[21]

Michael Lodsin was one of the missionaries working for Northern Baptists in New York City and at Ellis Island. *Missions* published his updates periodically, and Jews were among the many nationalities Lodsin sought to influence on a spiritual level.[22] In 1913, Lodsin shared two instances in which Jews accepted Christ, and he then related an incident that took place in the Ellis Island detention hall: "A young Jew seeing me give Gospels to others in the detention room asked me why I did not give him one. I told him that we did not wish to press him hard as had been done in Russia, but if he cared for one he could obtain one when he returned to Russia in any mission for the Jews, as we are not permitted to give the New Testament or parts of it to the Jew. I handed him a book of Psalms, for which he was very grateful."[23]

It is unclear whether the restriction on providing Christian Bibles to Jewish immigrants was imposed by the Ellis Island administration, an agreement between Jewish and Christian agencies, the WABHMS, or personally by Lodsin. It may have been restricted to activities in the detention room, for Lodsin wrote: "A young Jewish girl asked me for something to read. I told her that I had nothing but the Gospels of Jesus and she said, 'That's right, I want the Gospel.'"[24]

The Baptist Home Mission Monthly consistently supported the work of Robert Watchorn, the commissioner for immigration at Ellis Island from 1904 to 1908, lauding his "humane spirit and Christian character."[25] The magazine praised him for his administrative prowess, fairness, wisdom, and sense of humanity.[26] Watchorn's autobiography also claimed that he "suffered from no trace whatever of anti-Semitism."[27] The Baptist editor who was so supportive of Robert Watchorn was Howard B. Grose.

In his 1906 book, *Aliens or Americans*, Grose expressed his conviction that American Protestants needed "to discern the supreme issues involved in immigration, recognize the spiritual significance and divine providence in and behind this marvelous migration of peoples, and so see Christian obligation as to rise to the mission of evangelizing these representatives of all nations gathered on American soil."[28] He surveyed the history of immigration, analyzed immigration policy, and described the various nationalities streaming through Ellis Island, including "refugee Jews."[29] In agreement with Watchorn, Grose believed Russian Jews came because of "hideous and savage" political persecution, while many refugees (both Jewish and Gentile) arrived in search of "fortune and freedom."[30] Grose praised the work of the United Hebrew Charities on behalf of Jewish immigrants.[31]

Russian Jewish immigrants received special attention from Grose. They preferred to settle in major cities (New York, Philadelphia, Boston, Chicago), enjoyed skilled work, were becoming estranged from traditional forms of Jewish religious observance and practice, excelled at education, and exerted great energy to overcoming poverty and achieving a measure of economic wealth and independence. In a more critical vein, Grose noted that most of the Russian Jewish immigrants were not open to Christianity, and thus he was ambivalent regarding their future as full American citizens:

> WITH DECENT ENVIRONMENT and a fair chance, the Russian Jew promises to become a good citizen, intellectually keen, commercially shrewd, professionally bound to shine. But that he would ever, except in rare instances imbibe the real American spirit or understand the American ideals is a question. At the same time, the Jews are believers in the principle of democracy, and in case of an issue arising on the separation of Church and State, would be found standing with American Protestantism for the religious liberties of the American people.[32]

Thirteen years later, the situation at Ellis Island had deteriorated, in part due to the Emergency Immigration Act of May 19, 1921. The Home Mission Society's Department of City and Foreign-Speaking Missions representative, David Nathaniel Boswell, visited Ellis Island to assess its impact on immigrants. His critical report specifically cited the "pitiful sight in the men's detention room . . . of five aged Russian Jews," delayed entry because of the act's quotas.[33] However, Grose, still editor of the magazine, defended the act while acknowledging the hardships it caused and "the strongest adverse sentiment" expressed by the Jewish community.[34]

Boswell focused on the "constructive agencies" active in Ellis Island in March 1922. Eighteen agencies (including WABHMS) cooperated in ministry to the immigrant families, and collectively they "make the immigrant feel that America is a land of loyal friendship." Boswell complained that kindergarten children could not be evangelized because of Jewish opposition to proselytism: "Religion is suppressed because of the antagonistic attitude of the Jewish people. An indirect method of religious instruction is given in which the non-Jewish children draw pictures of Bible characters, the model of which has been clipped from a magazine or secular book." He noted that the day nursery's WABHMS "nurse in charge" was performing an important service: "Since Ellis Island is the most strategic port of our country, Christian character at this gateway is very important. It is great opportunity which she has in taking these babies and caring for them, and at the same time giving instruction to the mothers. Many of the mothers are forced by necessity to neglect their children. . . . About fifteen babies are cared for each day by the nurse."

Boswell further noted that two Northern Baptist men were employed by non-Baptist agencies. Both men were linguistically gifted: one spoke sixteen languages, and the other fourteen. Both must have been involved in evangelistic ministries, because "the quarters designated to them have been set on fire several times by the Catholic and Jewish element on the Island. In spite of opposition the work is growing and has the full support of the new Commissioner of Immigration." Further friction between Jews and Christians was evident in regards to worship services. Catholics, Jews, and Protestants held services, but with a "stipulation" that "the name of Jesus Christ must not be mentioned." Boswell commented, "This condition I leave for your own analysis."[35]

City Missions in Jewish Communities (1896–1932)

Northern Baptists were well aware of the movement of Jewish immigrants through Ellis Island to the major metropolitan areas of the United States. In 1909 the Commission on the Relation of City Missions and Church Extension Societies noted the "great need for denominational aid in Eastern cities" to serve immigrant populations, using New York City as its example, "in which the Hebrews, Latin, and Slavic peoples predominate, the Jews alone outnumbering the American born of American parents."[36] The Home Mission Society's report asserted that evangelism among immigrants would prevent Northern Baptists from becoming "a diminishing factor in the forces of American Christianity" and noted how large the Jewish population had become in New York: "There are 1,062,000 Jews—the largest Jewish community in the world; fifteen times more than in Syria and Palestine, and about twenty times the population of Jerusalem. Can submerged Protestantism save these great cities and can it save itself from being run out?"[37]

Although the 1913 ABHMS report indicated that its mission work among Jews commenced in 1896,[38] Northern Baptists were engaged in city missionary work targeted toward Jewish populations prior to this date. The New Jersey Baptist Convention launched at least two mission projects prior to 1896: "Work was begun among Jewish immigrants at both Newark and Camden, in 1893 and 1894, respectively. Both of these had the greatest difficulty to survive, although they were given some financial aid by the City Mission Societies and the New Jersey Baptist Convention."[39] The Camden mission apparently was discontinued soon after its inception, but in 1910 the Newark work was still in existence, and an additional mission had been opened in Boston.[40] The Home Mission Society appointed a new missionary to Newark in February 1907, S. A. Hurwitz.[41]

While noting that in one city "Jews and Bohemians are utterly neglected," the commission outlined a policy in relation to such outreach to immigrants: "For the sake of establishing dynamic centers among foreign peoples, they should be organized into missions or churches under efficient leaders of their own nationality."[42] The Woman's Home Mission Society, accordingly, appointed an unmarried converted Jewish woman, Belle Chisakofsky, for service in New York City.[43] Her ministry budget in 1912 was $600 (approximately $14,000 in 2017, adjusted for inflation)—a not insignificant amount for the time for a one-person operation.[44] By 1916, however, she was reassigned to Wilmington, Delaware, to work among the "mixed-Slavic populations."[45] The WABHMS also appointed in 1914 another unmarried Jewish convert, Minnie Schulman, to work in Cleveland: "A graduate of our Training School of last June, a Russian Jewess, was appointed to work among her people in Cleveland and, as is usual in such work, she reports it necessary to win the confidence of the people before she can give the Gospel message."[46]

The City Commission believed that there was hope for Jewish missions to succeed because many of the Jewish immigrants were not becoming members of synagogues and "Jewish religious schools [were] reaching less than 25 per cent of the Jewish children of school age."[47] However, in 1920, with limited success in converting even nonreligious Jews to the Baptist faith, the commission lamented that in New York, the "greatest Jewish city" (in terms of population) posed a grave challenge to Baptists: "To interpret evangelical Christianity to Roman Catholics from all countries of the globe and to interpret it to Jews, who as yet fail to recognize that Jesus internationalized Moses, the Protestant churches of Greater New York have a task severer than that of the churches of any other large city of the nation."[48]

By the close of the decade, the ABHMS was pleased to report that the "work among Jews is progressing hopefully, with contributions over and above our budget and a request from several places that the Society cooperate in the establishment of new work in important and neglected fields."[49] The following year, the society announced that "a new Jewish work has been opened in Chicago, making three places where Baptists are engaged in mission work among these people: Buffalo—the House of the Prince of Peace; Boston—West End; and Chicago."[50]

By 1932, the new mission in Chicago was eclipsing the Buffalo mission:

> CHICAGO HAS NOW one of our best Jewish centers. A fine building was purchased during the year in a better residential community, and a program worked out to meet the need of a more advanced type of Jews. The results have been very interesting and satisfactory. Many Jewish families have enrolled, and a number of confessions of faith with subsequent baptism have followed. A particularly interesting feature of this work has been the open forum, conducted each week, with speakers from the University of Chicago, from Chicago churches, and also other men of ability and standing in the community. It has been the first contact with many of the neighborhood families, and leads to better acquaintance and closer fellowship, which we believe will bring many to

> Christ. There are several very promising openings for new Jewish work in our cities waiting for the Home Mission Society to come in. Lack of funds is holding us back.[51]

Two Home Mission Society–sponsored missions deserve special attention—the pioneering work of Leopold Cohn in Brooklyn (his was the work mentioned in the 1913 ABHMS report), and the Jewish mission in Buffalo. The 1896 date referred to the Jewish mission work initiated in Brooklyn by Cohn.

Leopold Cohn and the Brooklyn Mission

Rabbi Leopold Cohn emigrated from Hungary to the United States in March 1892, and in June, he accepted Jesus as his Messiah and was baptized.[52] By 1895, Cohn was seeking to establish a mission to the Jews in Brooklyn, and he shortly thereafter received support from a Northern Baptist pastor. Rev. J. T. Walker of the Bushwick Avenue Baptist Church "had never thought before of doing mission work among the Jews. When he realized its importance, he tried to help the cause in every way he could. He used to sing for us in the meetings and the audience enjoyed him very much."[53] The relationship between Cohn and the Northern Baptists in Brooklyn deepened when his wife "was baptized by the Rev. W. C. P. Rhodes, D.D., pastor of the Marcy Avenue Baptist Church," and he gained the support of a cadre of Baptist pastors and the American Baptist Home Mission Society in 1896.[54]

The ABHMS's commissioning of Cohn was consistent with Northern Baptist policy regarding ministry to immigrants—employ members of the immigrant target group to serve as a bridge to Baptist faith and American cultural values. He was officially appointed as an ABHMS missionary in April 1896.[55] Cohn's Jewish mission regularly was featured in *The Home Mission Monthly*. He shared testimonies of Jews who had accepted his evangelical invitations but rarely identified the converts by name. He often noted that missionary work among the Jewish people was exceedingly difficult and challenging.[56] In his inaugural article for Northern Baptist readers in *The Home Mission Monthly*, he addressed the issue of Christian anti-Semitism and how it hindered Jews from embracing Jesus as their Messiah—an enduring theme in Jewish-Christian missions:

> AS A RULE, the Jews had and still have the impression that Christianity is idolatry, because they have never seen true Christ-like life, but only Roman Catholic Christians who persecuted the Jews. In fact, the Jews here came to this country being driven out and cruelly treated by so-called Christians. They have found in Mohammedanism a toleration which was denied to them by Christians who regard killing or torturing a poor, innocent Jew as a service to Christ. Thus they have set before the Jews a false and distorted picture, a gross caricature of true Christianity.[57]

In July 1898, Cohn praised Baptists for their support on the occasion of his second anniversary as a missionary: "I do thank you, dear Dr. Morgan and the other brethren of the Society, with all my heart, for your kindness and practical sympathy toward this Gospel work among the Jews in Brooklyn."[58] Cohn's partnership with Northern Baptists lasted until 1907. He referred to the break in relations in general and relatively positive terms, but there are indications that the Home Mission Society tightened its accountability expectations, which Cohn was unwilling to accept. Cohn's desire for exclusive control over the Brooklyn mission was an ongoing issue.[59] It was therefore probably not coincidental that the denouement of the partnership involved both concerns.

Following his split with the Northern Baptists, Cohn's mission became interdenominational and evolved into one of the major independent American Jewish mission organizations, the American Board of Missions to the Jews.[60] From the perspective of the American Baptist Home Mission Society, the parting of ways represented a ministry disappointment, but this disappointment did not prevent the society from attempting to develop similar missions in other metropolitan localities.

The Buffalo Hebrew Baptist Mission

In the decades following Leopold Cohn's departure from the Northern Baptist fold, the American Baptist Home Mission Society struggled to make progress in sponsoring Jewish missionary work. In 1924, the Jewish mission in Buffalo, New York, was a rare bright spot:

> THE ONLY JEWISH Mission for which the denomination is responsible and whose work it supervises, is well housed and fortunately located

> in Buffalo, NY. The Mission attracts gifts from members of all denominations in the city who are especially interested in the conversion of the Jews, and occasionally members of churches in other parts of the land, hearing of this Mission, have designated gifts for its work. Mr. and Mrs. Machlin, themselves converts from the Jewish religion, are tactfully presenting the claims of Christianity to their neighbors and those who visit the Mission. The work is carefully supervised by Secretary E. Herbert Dutton and a local committee in Buffalo, and this Society makes an annual contribution for its work.[61]

In light of the Brooklyn debacle, it is interesting to note that the Home Mission Society emphasized the Baptist ties to the Buffalo Jewish mission and its accountability to the Buffalo Baptist Union and its secretary, E. H. Dutton. Dutton affirmed the close relationship between the mission and local Baptist leaders: "Our unique Hebrew mission continues to make friends and extend its influence. The work now moves forward with the hearty approval of our denominational leaders and the keen interest of all who are concerned for the evangelization of the Jews."[62]

The leader of the Buffalo mission was Abraham Benjamin Machlin, a Russian Jewish immigrant originally from Kiev, who after arriving in the United States, converted to Christianity in 1915 under the influence of Leopold Cohn.[63] The president of the Northern Baptist Seminary introduced Machlin to Baptist leaders in Buffalo, including Dutton and Rev. J. C. Massee, the pastor of the historic and influential Tremont Baptist Temple in Boston. The ABHMS agreed to commission Machlin to this work, and for several years, it was apparently successful.[64] In 1927, the Home Mission Society reported that "the Jewish Center, known as the 'House of the Prince of Peace' in Buffalo, has been placed on a foundation of better support, and plans are in progress to enlarge the work in other centers."[65]

In 1929, Jacob Bernheim was recruited to take over the Buffalo mission, as Machlin was called to launch the Albany Park Jewish mission project in Chicago. Writing for *Missions* magazine, Bernheim stated that the outreach was "the only Protestant Mission to over 25,000 Jews in Buffalo." He credited the Baptist Union as the sponsor of the mission and applauded Machlin for making "many friends among their neighbors and the business people of the community."[66]

This Jewish mission in Buffalo would survive into the 1930s, and in hindsight may be considered to be the most successful ABHMS Jewish project in the eastern part of the United States.

Friendship and Christian Americanization

A powerful denomination-wide Northern Baptist response to the challenge of immigration emerged in 1919—the Christian Americanization movement organized by the Woman's American Baptist Home Mission Society. The precursor to the Christian Friendliness mission that was fated to play a key role in the Northern Baptist response to the Nazi persecution of the Jews, Christian Americanization promoted assimilation into American society along with Christian indoctrination: "The great Americanization movement is sweeping over our country today. The heart of its message is the message of Jesus Christ. The Baptist denomination has not yet grasped the significance of the marvelous opportunities of this movement."[67]

The philosophy behind Christian Americanization was spelled out in the 1919 Report of the Committee on Bodies Using Foreign Languages, which made clear that "the most potent Americanization influence is contact with Christian personalities." The report stressed that Christian Americanization did not endorse "propaganda directed against any particular racial group, but [was] an attempt to overcome alienism and to achieve national solidarity" because "a great nation does not need to be of one blood, but it must be of one mind" and, as is stated later, "a common language."[68]

In 1920, the Committee on Social Service asserted that Americanizing immigrants involved teaching them to accept American political, social, ethical, and religious cultural norms, and to speak English. This was to be accomplished through relational means: "All this must be accomplished by actually coming into contact with the foreigner. We cannot deal with him at arm's length. While it is recognized that his habits of life oftentimes erect a barrier to our approach, for his sake and for ours we must find some way to overcome this barrier. We can do this in a measure by utilizing such of his race as have themselves become truly Americanized."[69]

Northern Baptists soon came to appreciate the opportunities assimilation ministries represented. Christian Americanization involved assimilation through friendship: "To go into homes of the new American women in democratic simplicity, as a friend to a friend" was the ideal, and would prove to be the key to the movement's growth and success throughout the 1920s and in a revised form, the 1930s and 1940s. Through this movement, the women of Northern Baptist churches interacted for the first time with their Jewish immigrant neighbors. One testimony said, "They have gone to the home of the Jewish woman, who said, as her baby took her lesson-leaf, 'Don't take that, baby, it's mother's life.'"[70]

Bertha W. Clark made it clear that Christian Americanization aimed to create a transformation of "attitude" in both Protestant Americans and the newer arrivals. Love of the foreigner would lead to the new immigrant loving the United States.[71] Therefore, Clark counsels, "Our attitude toward the foreigner must always be the human one."[72] Friendship constituted the environment to turn fears into hope, as this mission story about a Jew attending a WABHMS-promoted English class in Wierton, West Virginia, illustrated:

> ONE OF OUR English students, a Jew, attended the Sunday afternoon Bible class which meets in the church. After looking around he said, "Why there is nothing in here that would hurt anybody." Later he invited a Mohammedan to join our classes. The Mohammedan protested, "I cannot go there; it is a Christian Center." Our Jewish friend replied: "It makes no difference about your nationality or your religion. Everyone is welcome." What a wonderful opportunity to teach all nations.[73]

Opportunity became the buzzword among Northern Baptists as they recruited women to reach out to immigrants, including Jews. Churches in Brooklyn and Queens mobilized 142 volunteers in a concerted outreach to their multicultural neighborhoods, utilizing the slogan, "Just a Christian friend and neighbor!"[74] In contrast to the Ellis Island and Jewish evangelism movements, which required specialists, Christian Americanization relied upon the volunteer activity of laywomen in churches throughout the country. Each state convention and city society had a Christian Americanization ministry, usually lodged in the Woman's Department. In New Jersey, Mrs. A. H. Stanton served as chairperson of Christian Americanization. In 1932, she reported: "New Jersey surely has 'opportunity' knocking at her door. There is a great growing need. U.S. statistics and also Ellis Island report that one-sixth of all the New Americans who come to our shores come to New Jersey. The 1930 Census for New Jersey states: 'One-half of the population of New Jersey is First Generation American and over one-fifth foreign born.'"[75]

Notes

1. *Minutes of the 1926 Northern Baptist Convention*, American Baptist Home Mission Society Annual Report, 325–26.

2. Norman H. Maring, *Baptists in New Jersey: A Study in Transition* (Valley Forge, PA: Judson Press, 1964), 263–64. The quote is from the *Minutes of the 1892 New Jersey Baptist Convention*, 17–18.

3. "The New Problems of Immigration," *The Baptist Home Mission Monthly* (July 1903), 181, 184. See also the comments of R. W. Swetland, in Maring, *Baptists in New Jersey*, 263–64 (original source: *New Jersey Baptist Bulletin*, June 1914, 18–19).

4. "Immigration: A Peril and Opportunity," *The Baptist Home Mission Monthly* (February 1904), 43.

5. Philip Davis, "The New Environment: The Remarkable Story of a Young Jewish Immigrant," *The Baptist Home Mission Monthly* (December 1906), 444–46.

6. *The Baptist Home Mission Monthly* (January 1907), 26. See Miriam Umstadter Blaustein, ed., *Memoirs of David Blaustein: Educator and Communal Worker* (New York: McBride, Nast and Company, 1913).

7. Editorial Remarks, *The Baptist Home Mission Monthly* (January 1907), 26.

8. "The New Year," *The Baptist Home Mission Monthly* (January 1908), 1.

9. Anonymous, "From an Immigrant's Logbook," *The Baptist Home Mission Monthly* (January 1908), 15–21.

10. Anonymous, "From an Immigrant's Logbook," *The Baptist Home Mission Monthly* (February 1908), 50–51.

11. Howard B. Grose, *Aliens or Americans?* (1906; reprint, Lexington, KY: CreateSpace Independent Publishing Platform, 2015), 78.

12. *Minutes of the 1915 Northern Baptist Convention*, Woman's American Baptist Home Mission Society Annual Report, 797.

13. *Minutes of the 1911 Northern Baptist Convention*, Woman's American Baptist Home Mission Society Annual Report, 59. Nelson left the team within a year, according to the *Minutes of the 1912 Northern Baptist Convention*, Women's American Baptist Home Mission Society Annual Report, 116.

14. *Minutes of the 1915 Northern Baptist Convention*, Woman's American Baptist Home Mission Society Annual Report, 622.

15. *Minutes of the 1918 Northern Baptist Convention*, Woman's American Baptist Home Mission Society Annual Report, 752–53.

16. *Minutes of the 1920 Northern Baptist Convention*, Social Service Committee Report, 251.

17. *Minutes of the 1925 Northern Baptist Convention*, Women's American Baptist Home Mission Society Annual Report, 673.

18. *Minutes of the 1927 Northern Baptist Convention*, Program, 73.

19. Anonymous, "Entering the New World," *The Baptist Home Mission Monthly* (February 1904), 40–42.

20. Anonymous, "Sowing the Seed," *The Baptist Home Mission Monthly* (October 1907), 356–57.

21. R. T. C., "A Day at Ellis Island," *The Baptist Home Mission Monthly* (March 1908), 94.

22. "At Ellis Island," *Missions* (March 1911), 214; "In the Gates," *Missions* (January 1912), 76–77.

23. Michael Lodsin, "At America's Chief Gateway," *Missions* (May 1913), 386.

24. Ibid.

25. Editorial, "Concerning Immigration," *The Baptist Home Mission Monthly* (February 1908), 45–46.

26. Editorial, "A Model Gatekeeper," *The Baptist Home Mission Monthly* (March 1908), 91–92.

27. Herbert Faulkner West, ed., *The Autobiography of Robert Watchorn* (Oklahoma City: Kessinger Publishing, 2007), 108–9.

28. Grose, *Aliens or Americans*, 6.

29. Ibid., 9.

30. Ibid., 13, 17.

31. Ibid., 10, 39, 45.

32. Ibid., 68–79; the quote is from 80.

33. "The Immigration Situation at Ellis Island," *Missions* (November 1921), 608–12.

34. Editorial, "What Shall the United States Do about Immigration?" *Missions* (March 1922), 143.

35. Boswell, "Constructive Agencies at Ellis Island," Missions (March 1922), 144–46. For other examples of controversy regarding Christian missionary work at Ellis Island, see Vincent J. Cannato, *American Passage* (New York: Perennial, 2010), 136, 141.

36. *Minutes of the 1909 Northern Baptist Convention*, Report of the Commission on the Relation of City Mission and Church Extension Societies to the Northern Baptist Convention, 122.

37. Ibid., Report of the American Baptist Home Mission Society, 15–16.

38. American Baptist Home Mission Society, "The Society's Work among Our Foreign Populations," 644.

39. Maring, *Baptists in New Jersey*, 267. Maring's sources are the *New Jersey Baptist Bulletin* (March 1907), 4–5; (July 1907), 4; (August 1894), 8; and the *Minutes of the New Jersey Baptist Convention*, 1902, 61–62; 1906, 38–41 (see Maring's n. 102).

40. *Minutes of the 1910 Northern Baptist Convention*, Report of the American Baptist Home Mission Society, "Commission on City Missions," 181. The Boston mission was not mentioned in the 1911 report; see *Minutes of the 1911 Northern Baptist Convention*, Report of the American Baptist Home Mission Society, "Commission on City Missions," 147–48.

41. "Home Mission Appointments," *The Home Mission Monthly* (March 1907), 114.

42. *Minutes of the 1910 Northern Baptist Convention*, Report of the American Baptist Home Mission Society, "Commission on City Missions," 182.

43. *Minutes of the 1911 Northern Baptist Convention*, Report of the Woman's American Baptist Home Mission Society, 14, 60; see also *Minutes of the 1912 Northern Baptist Convention*, Report of the Woman's American Baptist Home Mission Society, 117; and *1913 Northern Baptist Convention*, Report of the Woman's American Baptist Home Mission Society, 801.

44. *Minutes of the 1913 Northern Baptist Convention*, "Northern Baptist Work among Foreigners in the United States," 189.

45. *Minutes of the 1917 Northern Baptist Convention*, Woman's American Baptist Home Mission Society Annual Report, 542.

46. *Minutes of the 1915 Northern Baptist Convention*, Woman's American Baptist Home Mission Society Annual Report, 765; see also 798.

47. *Minutes of the 1911 Northern Baptist Convention*, Report of the American Baptist Home Mission Society, "Commission on City Missions," 146. The same observation was made at the 1922 convention; see the *Minutes of the 1922 Northern Baptist Convention*, Report of the Committee on the Coordination of Baptist Bodies Using Foreign Languages, 150.

48. *Minutes of the 1920 Northern Baptist Convention*, Report of the American Baptist Home Mission Society, "Commission on City Missions," 211.

49. *Minutes of the 1929 Northern Baptist Convention*, Report of the American Baptist Home Mission Society, 302.

50. *Minutes of the 1930 Northern Baptist Convention*, Report of the American Baptist Home Mission Society, 584; see also 610–11.

51. *Minutes of the 1932 Northern Baptist Convention*, Report of the American Baptist Home Mission Society, 584; see also 354. This ascendency of the Chicago mission can be seen in the ABHMS financial commitment figures: "Boston, West End ($1,000); Buffalo, House of Prince of Peace ($900); Chicago, Albany Park Friendship House ($2,100), in *Minutes of the 1932 Northern Baptist Convention*, Treasurer's Report of the American Baptist Home Mission Society, 404.

52. Leopold Cohn, *The Story of a Modern Missionary to an Ancient People* (Orangeburg, NY: American Board of Missions to the Jews, 1908; republished 1962), 1, 19–27.

53. Ibid., 45.

54. Ibid., 49

55. "Home Mission Appointments," *The Home Mission Monthly* (May 1896), 185.

56. Leopold Cohn, "New York—Work among the Jews," *The Home Mission Monthly* (March 1897), 119–21; "Incidents in the Jewish Mission," *The Home Mission Monthly* (October 1897), 348–49. See also *The Home Mission Monthly* (February 1898), 73; (January 1901), 42–43; (May 1901), 142–43; (December 1903), 316–17.

57. Leopold Cohn, "New York—Work among the Jews," *The Home Mission Monthly* (September 1896), 318.

58. Leopold Cohn, "Work among the Jews," *The Home Mission Monthly* (July 1898), 240.

59. Yaakov Ariel, *Evangelizing the Chosen People: Missions to the Jews in America, 1880–2000* (Chapel Hill: University of North Carolina Press, 2000), 24, 30.

60. Cohn, *Story of a Modern Missionary*, 50, 61.

61. *Minutes of the 1924 Northern Baptist Convention*, Report of the American Baptist Home Mission Society, "Our Jewish Mission," 668–69.

62. Ibid., Report of the Buffalo Baptist Union, 729.

63. Helen B. Lyke, *The Faith of Abraham: The Biography of A. B. Machlin, D.D.* (Winona Lake, IN: American Association for Jewish Evangelism, 1962), 9, 11. While in Brooklyn, Machlin befriended Jacob Gartenhaus, who would become the foremost Jewish evangelist of the Southern Baptist Convention; see p. 24.

64. Ibid., 27–34.

65. *Minutes of the 1927 Northern Baptist Convention*, Report of the American Baptist Home Mission Society, "Our Jewish Mission," 489.

66. Jacob Bernheim, "Impressions of the Buffalo Hebrew Baptist Mission," *Missions* (March 1929), 192.

67. A. E. Jenks, "Christian Americanization," *Missions* (February 1920), 104–5.

68. *Minutes of the 1919 Northern Baptist Convention*, Report of the Committee on Bodies Using Foreign Languages, 143.

69. *Minutes of the 1920 Northern Baptist Convention*, Report of the Committee on Social Service, 249–51.

70. Jenks, "Christian Americanization," 105.

71. Bertha W. Clark, "American Attitude the Essential in Americanization," *Missions* (March 1921), 162. The same illustration was used in the WABHMS annual report; see *Minutes of the 1921 Northern Baptist Convention*, Woman's American Baptist Home Mission Society Annual Report, 746.

72. Clark, "American Attitude the Essential in Americanization," 163.

73. Editorial, "Race Relations in America," *Missions* (September 1924), 431.

74. Ida M. Cheesbrough, "Just Being a Neighbor," *Missions* (December 1927), 670.

75. A. H. Stanton, *New Jersey Baptist Bulletin* (April 1932), 5.

Chapter 2

Northern Baptist Resolutions about Jews before 1933

Following its organization in 1907, the Northern Baptist Convention turned its attention to the pressing problems of US society and the world at large. Through addresses, sermons, committee reports, and resolutions, the convention delegates sought to express convictions characterized by a social gospel–inspired concern for the poor, justice, and social equality. Though not doctrinally or legally binding on member churches, pastors, or individual Baptists, resolutions that were passed nevertheless represented a majority position at the time of the vote and carried some measure of weight. Resolutions received coverage in both religious and secular newspapers and were often sent to politicians for consideration.

In the tumultuous period between 1907 and 1933, Northern Baptists addressed a full range of sociopolitical issues. The convention devoted considerable attention to war and peace, assistance to European Baptists, the Armenian crisis, persecution of European Jews, and the evangelism of Jewish immigrants who came to the United States. Resolutions on these problems often made reference to historic Baptist convictions to justify the positions the convention espoused. This practice of relying on historic convictions set the stage for how the convention would address the rise of Hitler, the outbreak of a new world war, the Nazi persecution of the Jews, and the Holocaust.

World War I and Peace

While the United States was still officially neutral, Northern Baptists looked on as European nations battled one another during the first great world war of the twentieth century. At the annual convention in 1916, delegates expressed concern and anxiety regarding the conflict. The Resolutions Committee presented a resolution concerning European Baptists that elevated the peacemaking potential of the transnational Baptist movement: "It confuses our minds to think of them as divided by national boundaries and antagonisms into public enemies of each other; it makes us pray all the more earnestly that the great war may cease, and that the Baptists in the war-rent parts of the world may be the first to restore national friendships in the spirit of Jesus, our common Lord." Northern Baptists pledged to "extend to them our deepest sympathy and friendship, and answer their addresses and pleas with the pledge that we will do our part when the time comes for the healing of the nations, by renewed comradeship, by mediatorial service, and material help."[1]

This resolution represented the coming of age for the Northern Baptist Convention. The Baptist missionary enterprise had created a global fellowship that was inextricably bound to the great political events of the era and affected by the secular entanglements of nations. Resolution IX was the convention's first official peacemaking statement, and it contained sentiments that would become staples of later resolutions during World War II—the dedication to maintain fellowship with Baptists from both sides of the conflict, the exaltation of Baptist unity as opposed to nationalism, the desire for peace to be established (implicitly rejecting war as a means of international relations and problem solving), and the pledge to mediate and provide financial aid for Baptists in regions of conflict.

Northern Baptists then passed a resolution which for the first time indicated their willingness to aid Jews who were suffering at the hands of European Gentiles. Resolution XI urged "the members of our household of faith to continue their material contributions to the stricken countries of Europe and Asia, especially to the non-combatant populations of Belgium, Poland, Serbia, and Armenia, and to the Jews scattered abroad."[2]

In the early years of World War I, Northern Baptists supported the cause of neutrality.[3] The United States entered the war on April 6, 1917, and Northern Baptists expressed their support for the military efforts at their convention the following month. President C. A. Barbour noted that the "maelstrom of war has caught humanity in its swirling flood" and that this worldwide conflict "speaks in thunder tones of the infernal folly and crime of war as a factor in the life of humanity."[4] Barbour then unexpectedly declared that the war was also about personal liberty, freedom, and democracy, and accordingly, Baptists were compelled to display their loyalty by supporting the war effort.[5]

This duality was reflected in the resolution supporting entry into the military conflict: "Loving peace and abhorring war, having no selfish ends to seek, cherishing no bitterness or hatred toward any, and expressing our brotherly sympathy for our Baptist brethren in all the belligerent nations, at the call of country, and in response to the dictates of our own consciences, we dedicate ourselves to our just and righteous cause." They also processed the issue in light of Baptist core convictions: "In this struggle for the perpetuity and extension of democracy, Baptists, themselves belonging to a great religious democracy whose founders paid high price in persecution, exile, and martyrdom to secure civil and religious liberty, will be found second to none in loyalty and devotion."[6] Following the war, Northern Baptists embraced President Woodrow Wilson's dream of a League of Nations that would embody the Baptist core conviction of democracy: "We recognize in the Paris Covenant for the League of Nations a great step in the advance of a Christian civilization, and . . . we urge our people to use their utmost influence to secure its ratification."[7]

In 1921, the Social Services Commission spearheaded the convention's movement toward pacifism when it declared that the Bible looked forward to a time when war would be abolished.[8] The next year, Northern Baptists went on record as favoring the "abolition of war" because "war as a method of settling international disputes is barbarous, wasteful, and manifestly contrary to every Christian ideal and teaching."[9] Northern Baptists soon realized that their antiwar, antimilitaristic perspective needed to be accompanied by a more positive approach to international relations. In 1923, the convention passed a resolution calling for the rejection of isolationism, the establishment of a world court to operate alongside the League of Nations, and "an international conference to consider the whole economic and political situation in Europe."[10] They also established a Committee on International Justice and Good-will,[11] indicating that the leaders of the Northern Baptist Convention were committed to a postwar world order in which rational diplomacy and cooperation, a restraint on nationalistic ambition, and respect between people of goodwill would secure peace and justice among nations.

In 1924, the convention adopted a key phrase in its resolution against war, declaring that war "is contrary to the spirit and teachings of Jesus Christ."[12] By 1925, the antiwar resolution language had become standardized: "It is our conviction that war is contrary to the spirit and teachings of Jesus Christ, and that we declare our irrevocable determination to substitute the arbitration of law, reason, and conciliation for that of wholesale slaughter and to create some medium for the peaceable settlement of every national dispute."[13]

Alongside rejection of violent conflict between peoples and nations, the Northern Baptists sought to reimagine a world dominated by Christian values. Thus, the 1926 convention affirmed the "Golden Rule" as the preeminent social and political norm for governing relations: "Whereas, One of the important principles of the religion of Jesus is 'the solidarity of the human family' and such unity is constantly being frustrated; be it resolved, that we affirm our belief in the practice of the Golden Rule in social, racial, industrial, and international relationships."[14] In like manner, "World Peace" was introduced as a key component of the Northern Baptist political philosophy at the 1927 convention and was repeated when the convention voted in 1929 to "condemn modern war as contrary to the spirit of the Prince of Peace."[15]

The perspective forged by Northern Baptists in the 1920s dominated the Baptist debates about war following Hitler's rise to power and his rearmament of the German military. It would serve to guide, but also limit, the policy options Baptists could endorse as the Nazis threatened the peace of Europe, the independence of sovereign nations, and the existence of the Jewish people.

European Relief

Following the resolution passed in 1916 on European relief, Northern Baptists cooperated with the Baptist World Alliance (BWA) to assist European Baptists. The work was organized at a conference in London in July 1920 as a joint effort of Baptists in the United States, Canada, and Great Britain. The Northern and Southern Baptists each contributed financial aid of $166,666 per year. Almost one thousand orphans were supported, farm equipment and supplies were distributed, and the sick were cared for in France, Belgium, Poland, and Russia. Although the mission worked with affiliated Baptist groups, assistance was provided "for all who suffer, regardless of religious, political, or racial differences."[16] The last distinction may be a veiled reference to Jews.

The American Baptist Foreign Mission Society (ABFMS) took the lead role on behalf of Northern Baptists, and in 1922, delegates expressed their appreciation for their society's participation in the international relief effort.[17] The ABFMS acknowledged the impressive leadership provided by J. H. Rushbrooke, serving as Baptist Commissioner for Europe for the BWA. With his command of the German language, having lived in that country even as the First World War commenced, and enjoying relational ties throughout the continent, Rushbrooke was at the center of the postwar rebuilding efforts. He even entered the diplomatic arena, arguing for religious liberty rights for Rumanian Baptists—a lifelong priority for this Baptist statesman.[18]

The European relief initiative was cross-promoted with the Near East Relief program, designated for persecuted Christian minorities in Asia Minor. The joint offering date was set for January 21, 1923, but the donations received ($10,264.76) were "substantially less than the Near East Relief had anticipated, and was far below the amount required by the Foreign Mission Society, thereby necessitating a severe curtailment in its European relief efforts."[19] The Advisory Committee on Near East Relief projected that the 1923–1924 level of support would drop by 50 percent.[20] The lack of generosity on the part of Northern Baptists may have been prompted by several factors, including compassion fatigue, political isolationism, and a desire to focus on other issues. The lessons denominational leaders gleaned from this failure may account for their subsequent reticence to undertake large-scale campaigns for Jewish relief in the 1930s.

The Armenian Genocide

The Northern Baptist Convention's response to the Armenian genocide places the denomination's response to the Jewish Holocaust in historical perspective. The Ottoman Empire's assault upon its Armenian population, later characterized as the Armenian Genocide, commenced in April 1915. More than eight hundred thousand people were killed or removed from their homes over the ensuing years. The plight of the Armenians was highlighted in *Missions* in November 1915: "The concerted and carefully planned and cruelly executed attack upon the Armenians in Turkey surpasses in ferocity and thoroughness anything that has ever preceded in that country. . . . It is time the moral forces of the world found expression in protest against Turkey's atrocious procedure, calling upon Germany and Austria also to restrain their ally."[21]

Northern Baptists addressed this catastrophe during the 1916 convention by endorsing a fund-raising appeal from the Federal Council of the Churches of Christ in America and the American Committee for Armenian and Syrian Relief: "We urge Baptist churches everywhere to present this appeal for the relief of the stricken of Europe, and especially for the Armenian survivors. These, our brethren, are suffering through deportation and famine. The whole race is threatened with extermination, and is staggering under an unprovoked blow of heartless assassination."[22]

This 1916 resolution was the first Northern Baptist Convention (NBC) statement to respond to a genocidal act. The delegates saw the Armenian genocide as "unprecedented," recognized that it could lead to the "extermination" of a people, sympathized with strangers who nevertheless were of the same Christian faith, appealed for sacrificial giving, but did not name the aggressor. This omission was rectified at the 1917 convention, when the Resolutions Committee framed the genocide in religious terms and named its perpetrators: "In view of the appalling disaster that has, under Moslem misrule, overtaken our Christian brothers and sisters of Armenian and Syrian nationality in the near east, and in view of the imminent danger of starvation that threatens the survivors, we commend this cause to our churches as one of the most pressing for immediate relief if these imperiled fellow Christians are to be rescued."[23]

In 1920, the Northern Baptists, in a more politically focused resolution, continued to express their solidarity with the Armenian victims, adding to previous statements by invoking Baptist core convictions in support of the Armenian cause:

> INASMUCH AS THE heart of the Christian world has for generations been shocked and grieved by the atrocities committed by the Turks against the Armenians and other subject races. . . . This Convention

> expresses its heartfelt sympathy for the Armenians in their present defenseless and destitute condition, and calls upon our government to do everything in its power to secure for these long-suffering and heroic Christian people the free exercise of their rights to life, liberty of conscience and of person, and the pursuit of happiness.[24]

The 1920 resolution called for American governmental intervention, in recognition that private and religious humanitarian aid could not effectively address all dimensions of the situation. In 1921, Northern Baptists expressed concern for "the safety and welfare of the remnants of the Armenian people," fearing that "the enemies of the Armenians again may begin the policy of enslavement and extermination." The convention urged the United States to utilize "all just and honorable means to secure the lives and liberties of the Armenian people in their own and other countries."[25] This resolution surpassed its predecessor in its specificity regarding the actions the denomination expected the United States government to undertake. Both diplomatic and other means (implying military options) were proffered. Protection for the Armenians was not limited to their own country; as first mentioned in the 1920 resolution, the Armenians were viewed as a "people" and "race" as well as a political nation.

The 1921 resolution was extraordinary in that it entrusted the denomination's executive committee to take actions that might be necessary to further this cause. Progress in halting the genocide was limited, however, and the 1922 convention expressed its deep dismay and discouragement to the president and secretary of state of the United States:

> WE VIEW WITH profound pity and horror the extermination of the Christian peoples—Armenian, Greek, Syrian—now in progress at the hands of the Turks. At the conference at Versailles the United States was requested by the allied nations to assume a mandate for Armenia and to protect her faithful and heroic people. The Northern Baptist Convention makes a solemn protest against the ruthless starvation and massacre of the first nation to accept the Christian faith. We hereby petition our government immediately to adopt measures to secure united action on the part of the United States and European governments

> looking to the deliverance and security of imperiled Christian peoples in the Near East.[26]

Disappointment in the US government was highlighted again in 1923: "We record our horror at the unparalleled outrage suffered by the Armenians and other peoples at the hands of the Turks, and we deplore as a wrong against humanity the attitude of the Allied Nations, and especially America, for failure to protect these people from the despoiler."[27] The Committee on International Justice and Goodwill argued for "definite protest against any settlement of the Near East question on a basis of expediency or commercial advantage, and without some amends for tragic wrongs which have resulted in the persecution and practical destruction of the Armenian people, and the confiscation of their property."[28] In 1926, delegates approved a resolution arguing against any treaty with Turkey "which does not guarantee full religious liberty and freedom from persecution and make the necessary reparations in property, including the specific provision for the release and restoration of its Christian womanhood, now defenseless against atrocity and in need of the charity of the world."[29]

The Armenian crisis created a precedent for how Northern Baptists would respond to Germany's persecution of Jews, influencing the attitudes, strategies, and tactics the convention adopted in the 1930s and 1940s. Frustrated by its own inability to halt genocide and with governmental inaction, the Northern Baptist Convention entered into the Nazi era humbled and uncertain of how to actualize its peacemaking mandate when protests failed and evil prevailed.

Immigration and Racial Prejudice

While Northern Baptists looked on with grave concern, but from a geographical distance, at the plight of the Armenians in the Near East, the presence of Jewish immigrants fleeing persecution in Europe also caught the attention of the convention's leaders. In 1911, delegates recognized that European and Asian immigration was fueled by "religious persecution" that was "detrimental to the peace, progress, and prosperity of civilization." Accordingly, they appealed to President William Howard Taft "to consider the advisability of asking the nations of the world, either by treaty, by the Hague Peace Conference, or by calling an International Conference to secure religious liberty for people of every faith of the world."[30] Europe's Jews, among others, were no doubt subjects of the 1911 resolution. The first specific mention of Jews in need came in 1916: "Resolved, That we call upon the members of our household of faith to continue their material contributions to the stricken countries of Europe and Asia, especially to the non-combatant populations of Belgium, Poland, Serbia, and Armenia, and to the Jews scattered abroad."[31]

The 1925 Foreign Mission Society report recognized the global "menace of race prejudice" and indicated that "the most ominous sign on the world horizon is the apparent growth of race prejudice," fueled by technological advances that were "shrinking the world and making it one neighborhood." It concluded that only the missionary enterprise could supply a measure of hope to this scenario, since missionaries break down "the way of partition between Jew and Greek" and other ethnic and cultural divides.[32] Similarly, in 1926 the Committee on Interracial Relationships charged that the global trends regarding racism were also part of the American political and social landscape:

> THE FOREIGN RACES are crowding upon us in all city and country communities. . . . We have satisfied our consciences by establishing a very few missions or schools among the alien elements and working *for* them at arm's length. The result has been very few converts among Jews, Italians, or other foreign races, but a very large amount of sensitiveness and resentment at the snobbishness and feeling of caste of Christians, and a bitter attack from all the world on the hypocrisy of Protestant American Christians who profess to follow most closely in the footsteps of the Master, but who do not show that they have taken seriously the second command or the brotherhood of man and his substantial equality in God's sight.[33]

The statement indicated that Northern Baptists embraced the common assumption that Jews were a foreign race. In 1928, the Committee on Interracial Relationships affirmed the ABFMS belief that racially inspired prejudice was the most significant world problem, ominously warning that the "progress of humanity, the happiness of individuals as well as the well-being of states and nations, and even the very continuance of civilization itself, depend upon the proper solution of the difficulties which have their roots in this plane of interracial contacts. In racial prejudices and false nationalism are to be found the sources of such curses of the human race as wars, oppressions, and the exploitations by the stronger races of the weaker." The solution to the problem of racial strife was based on a trinity of basic Baptist convictions: "Only in the teachings of Jesus Christ, and in the common Fatherhood of God and the Universal Brotherhood of man which he reveals, is there a remedy for race antagonisms."

The committee offered specific recommendations for how Northern Baptists could promote a more racially just world. Baptists should cultivate "Christian comradeship with other races," especially those who spoke English, affirm that all races possess "equal rights, equal justice, and equal opportunities for advancement and happiness," and teach that "interracial fellowships transcend racial lines in commerce, literature, science, sports, and missions" in order to express "a spirit of world friendship." Furthermore, Baptists were to preach that "no race is in reality doomed to inferiority, but that we seek to recognize the divine image in whatever color or race it may be incarnated, and that we respect and cultivate the good qualities of every race and tribe and tongue." Rejecting all "racial antipathy" and "egotistical nationalism," Baptists were encouraged to "think of each race as an instrument in the great symphony of humanity" and work to "perfect each note and tune all the instruments together for the production of heaven's harmony of brotherhood and peace on earth and good-will among men."[34] Similarly, in 1929 the NBC passed a resolution that imagined a future in which all races would contribute to a much brighter future: "In a Christlike world, we believe the races of men should live in such relations as shall give fullest opportunity for the development of the lives of all individuals of every race and for their cooperation in Christian civilization."[35]

The 1928 recommendations and the 1929 resolution were consistent with the social outreach ministries Northern Baptists offered to Jewish immigrants and the evangelistic initiatives it spearheaded, but the delegates seemed to be unaware of two unanticipated consequences of their worldview—the marginalization of Jews as a distinct race (or people group) and the questioning of the validity of a Jewish

Israel deserving equal status among the nations. The racial vision of the Northern Baptists was emphatically Christocentric, and as such it apparently possessed no room for a race that did not accept Christ's teachings or lordship. Was conversion the sole pathway for Jews as a race to have an equal place among the peoples of the world? In fact, during the Nazi era, some Baptists would assert that the solution for persecuted Jews was to convert to Christianity.

The Christian civilization Northern Baptists were dreaming of was being severely tested, not by Jews but by a militantly atheistic communist Russia. The government's persecution of Russian Baptists[36] and other groups, including Jews, spurred protests in Europe and inspired the Baptist World Alliance to lobby for the welfare of its compatriots in that country. The 1930 ABFMS report noted that a broad interfaith coalition was united in protesting the anti-religion developments in Russia: "Of peculiar significance is the fact that all faiths, Jewish, Catholic, and Protestant, are united in this expression of protest against the anti-religious policy of Russia, recognizing in it a common menace to religion everywhere."[37] Meanwhile, in Germany, the National Socialist Party was beginning to gather strength. Would this broad coalition remain united and effective in countering this challenge to the Northern Baptist vision of a Christian civilization in which all races had a right to life, liberty, and the pursuit of happiness?

The Jewish Evangelism Controversies

Between 1925 and 1932, a series of controversies erupted regarding Northern Baptists' relationships with Jews immigrating to and residing in the United States. Jews, though remaining "loyal to the nationalistic traditions and ideals of their race, are yet in great numbers without a religion and are examining the claims of Christianity with ever-deepening interest." Jewish assimilation, it was hoped, would lead them to Christ: "The tendency to change their names or modify the spelling, for example from Gold to Gould, and the crucial issues that are the inevitable result of friendship and the mingling of the streams of educational, industrial, and social life . . . all prepare the soil of Jewish life for the seed of Christian truth."[38] Evangelistic ministries focused on the Jewish community had achieved limited results.

Should these ministries be abandoned? Or, should Northern Baptists pursue ecumenical relationships with Jews and seek their friendship? How would friendship affect evangelism ministries, and how would evangelism ministries affect the relationship between Northern Baptists and Jews?

The battle over these concerns should be understood as being a specific manifestation of the larger religious fault lines plaguing the Northern Baptist Convention in the 1920s. Fundamentalists and conservatives, on the one hand, and moderates and liberals on the other, were contending with one another on a host of issues, such as the nature of scriptural authority and revelation, science and miracles, exclusivity and inclusivity, the social gospel, the relationship between faith and politics, and organizational structure for the Convention. The relationship between Northern Baptists and Jews was processed in the context of contending visions of Baptist life and how its core convictions should be applied in the twentieth century.

At the 1925 Northern Baptist convention, the Committee on City Missions noted that there were four million Jews in the United States, with most residing in major metropolitan areas where Northern Baptists had a church presence. The question confronting Baptists concerned "how to spread a better knowledge of Jews and Judaism among Christians and a more sympathetic understanding of Christians and Christian purposes among Jews; and upon the double foundation of a better understanding and closer conformity to the spirit of both religions, to cultivate kindliness and good-will and substitute confidence and cooperation for suspicion and hate." The committee maintained that Baptists should encourage the "promotion of fellowship and understanding. . . . The finest contribution to human welfare which any man can make is the practice of kindness, fairness, and persistent good-will shown in speech, in conduct, in business, in society, in the church, in the school, and in the home."[39]

The message from the committee was unmistakable. Aggressive evangelism that might alienate Jews from their Baptist neighbors should be replaced by a relationally positive strategy that focused on mutual affirmation between different communities of people. "Good-will"[40] was to be stressed, so that friendships based on mutual respect might be established and promote harmony between Jews and Christians. Evangelism of Jews was not a priority; mutual tolerance and acceptance were preferred. Evangelism still had a lesser role, in those cases where religiously disaffected Jews were encountered.[41]

In contrast to the "good-will" initiative, the Resolutions Committee report included the sole resolution on Jewish evangelism ever to be passed by the Northern Baptist Convention. The resolution committed the convention and its agencies to continue and expand their evangelistic work aimed toward Jewish populations:

> WHEREAS, THE JEWISH race in this country is one of the largest unevangelized groups, and in view of the plain teaching of the Scriptures, it is the manifest duty of the Northern Baptist Convention to assume its share in the task of Jewish evangelization; be it
>
> *Resolved,* That the Convention recognizes its obligation to the Jewish people as in line with the Great Commission; and be it further
>
> *Resolved,* That the Convention requests The American Baptist Home Mission Society to make a special study of the opportunity for Jewish work and provide for the maintenance and extension of approved Baptist work among the Jews; and be it further
>
> *Resolved,* That we recommend that all Baptist contributions for Jewish evangelization be designated for denominational work and forwarded through denominational agencies.[42]

When delegates reconvened the following year, they affirmed the "Golden Rule" resolution,[43] which may be interpreted as a response from the moderates and liberals to the 1925 evangelism resolution. The 1926 ABHMS report contained a lengthy discourse on the history of Jews in America, hoped for "spiritual results" (Jewish conversions) and encouraged churches to conduct missionary work among Jews "as may be within their parish limits."[44]

The 1928 convention featured a series of forums, including one focused on Baptist ministry to Jews, presided over by Secretary E. H. Dutton of Buffalo. There were three presentations: "The American Jew Today" by Rev. A. G. Johnson, Michigan; "Protestantism's Approach" by Rev. A. B. Machlin, New York; and "The Contribution of Baptists" by Rev. J. M. Hestenes, Indiana; and concluding remarks titled "Our Next Steps" by Secretary F. A. Smith of New York.[45]

Also in 1928, the report of the Federal Council of the Churches of Christ (FCCC) announced that after "three years of effort by the

Committee on Good Will between Christians and Jews has led to the formation of an independent body entitled the National Conference of Jews and Christians, from which much good is expected."[46] This apparently created a stir, and at the 1929 convention, a committee was created to study whether Northern Baptists should remain affiliated with the FCCC.

The Committee on Relations with the FCCC submitted a lengthy report at the 1930 convention and addressed the Jewish question in a section entitled "The Work of the Council's Committee on Good-Will between Jews and Christians in Relation to Jewish Evangelization." It reiterated that the Good-will Committee was intended to "ascertain the causes of racial ill-will and to discover how these causes may be removed or modified" and promote "contacts between Jews and Christians in cities . . . to promote understanding and cooperation." Furthermore, the committee sought to discover areas in which Jews and Christians could cooperate and "so aid each other in human welfare and community benefits." It also was to function as a watchdog to "correct false and irritating statements and promote the spread of sound and proper information" and to counter prejudice through sharing "literature which will help shape a better public opinion." In bold print, the report concluded that "the work of the Federal Council's Committee on Good-Will Between Jews and Christians must never be interpreted as in any way discouraging or supplanting any policy that the denomination may adopt toward the evangelization of Jewish or other non-Christian groups."[47]

The report may be fairly interpreted as a compromise between the two camps of Northern Baptists, but it did not satisfy everyone. During the 1932 convention, fundamentalist leader William Bell Riley challenged the provision of funds for the FCCC; after debate, J. W. Brougher offered a resolution to give the FCCC $7,500 and the balance of $7,500 to the Home Mission Society for "evangelistic work among Jews." Riley withdrew his motion, and this compromise motion passed.[48]

Notes

1. *Minutes of the 1916 Northern Baptist Convention*, Resolutions Committee Report, Resolution IX, 216–17.
2. Ibid., Resolution XI, 217.

3. *Minutes of the 1915 Northern Baptist Convention*, Resolutions Committee Report, Section I, 253.

4. *Minutes of the 1917 Northern Baptist Convention*, President's Report, 22.

5. Ibid., 22–26.

6. Ibid., Resolutions Committee Report, Resolution III, 310.

7. *Minutes of the 1919 Northern Baptist Convention*, Resolutions Committee Report, Resolution VII, part 5, 294.

8. *Minutes of the 1921 Northern Baptist Convention*, Social Service Committee Report, 204–5.

9. *Minutes of the 1922 Northern Baptist Convention*, Resolutions Committee Report, Resolution II, "The Abolition of War," 181.

10. *Minutes of the 1923 Northern Baptist Convention*, Resolutions Committee Report, Resolution IV, "International Relations," 249.

11. Ibid., Committee on International Justice and Good-will Report, 252–53.

12. *Minutes of the 1924 Northern Baptist Convention*, Resolutions Committee Report, Resolution on "War," 252.

13. *Minutes of the 1925 Northern Baptist Convention*, Resolutions Committee Report, Resolution IV on "International Relations," Part (1), "War," 239.

14. *Minutes of the 1926 Northern Baptist Convention*, Resolutions Committee Report, Resolution II Social, No. 3, on the "Golden Rule," 161.

15. *Minutes of the 1929 Northern Baptist Convention*, Resolutions Committee Report, Resolution VI on "World Peace," 106.

16. *Minutes of the 1922 Northern Baptist Convention*, American Baptist Home Mission Society Report, "Relief Work in Europe," 530–35.

17. Ibid., Resolutions Committee Report, Resolution V, "European Relief," 182.

18. Ibid., American Baptist Home Mission Society Report, "Cooperation with Baptists in Europe" and "Service of Commissioner J. H. Rushbrooke," 528–29.

19. *Minutes of the 1923 Northern Baptist Convention*, Advisory Committee on Near East Relief Report, 76–77.

20. *Minutes of the 1924 Northern Baptist Convention*, Advisory Committee on Near East Relief Report, 220–21.

21. J. L. Barton, "A Stricken Race," *Missions* (November 1915), 386. In regards to the larger Protestant response, see William E. Nawyn, *American Protestantism's Response to Germany's Jews and Refugees: 1933–1941*, Studies in American History and Culture (Ann Arbor: University of Michigan International Research Press, 1981), 6–7.

22. *Minutes of the 1916 Northern Baptist Convention*, Resolutions Committee Report, Resolution X, 217.

23. *Minutes of the 1917 Northern Baptist Convention*, Resolutions Committee Report, Resolution VI, 313.

24. *Minutes of the 1920 Northern Baptist Convention*, Resolutions Committee Report, Resolution VIII, 268.

25. *Minutes of the 1921 Northern Baptist Convention*, Resolutions Committee Report, Resolution XX, "Armenian Welfare," 299.

26. *Minutes of the 1922 Northern Baptist Convention*, Resolutions Committee Report, Resolution III, "Armenia," 181.

27. *Minutes of the 1923 Northern Baptist Convention*, Resolutions Committee Report, Resolution IV, "International Relations," Section 2, 249.

28. Ibid., Committee on International Justice and Good-will Report, 253.

29. *Minutes of the 1926 Northern Baptist Convention*, Resolutions Committee Report, Resolution III, "International," Section 2, "Treaty with Turkey," 162.

30. *Minutes of the 1911 Northern Baptist Convention*, Resolutions Committee Report, Resolution X, 174.

31. *Minutes of the 1916 Northern Baptist Convention*, Resolutions Committee Report, Resolution XI, 217. Jews who had immigrated to American cities were discussed in the City Mission Commission report; see 144–48.

32. *Minutes of the 1925 Northern Baptist Convention*, American Baptist Foreign Mission Society Report, 428.

33. *Minutes of the 1926 Northern Baptist Convention*, Committee on Interracial Relationship Report, 168. Italics in the original text.

34. *Minutes of the 1928 Northern Baptist Convention*, Committee on Interracial Relationship Report, 87–89.

35. *Minutes of the 1929 Northern Baptist Convention*, Resolutions Committee Report, Resolution VII, "A Christlike World," Section 1, "Race Relations," 105.

36. See Heather J. Coleman, *Russian Baptists and Spiritual Revolution, 1905–1929* (Bloomington: Indiana University Press, 2005).

37. *Minutes of the 1930 Northern Baptist Convention*, American Baptist Foreign Mission Society Report, 397.

38. *Minutes of the 1924 Northern Baptist Convention*, Report of the American Baptist Home Mission Society, "State Conventions and City Mission Societies," 691–92.

39. *Minutes of the 1925 Northern Baptist Convention*, Report of the Committee on City Missions, "Work among Hebrews," 197.

40. Ibid., Report of the Federal Council of the Churches of Christ, "Christian Race Relations," 226, which states, "Within the past year another unique undertaking on behalf of racial understanding has been begun in the creation of a special Committee on Good-will between Christians and Jews, with an executive giving his full time to the work."

41. Ibid., Report of the Committee on City Missions, "The Polyglot and Foreign District," 208.

42. Ibid., Resolutions Committee Report, Resolution 3, "Jewish Evangelization," 239. The passing of this resolution was noted, without quoting it, in *Missions* (September 1925), 463.

43. *Minutes of the 1926 Northern Baptist Convention*, Resolutions Committee Report, Resolution II Social, No. 3, on "Golden Rule," 161.

44. Ibid., American Baptist Home Mission Society Report, 325.

45. *Minutes of the 1928 Northern Baptist Convention*, Program Agenda, 49, 82.

46. Ibid., Report of the Federal Council of the Churches of Christ, 74.

47. *Minutes of the 1930 Northern Baptist Convention*, Report of the Committee on Relations with the Federal Council of the Churches of Christ in America, 250–52.

48. *Minutes of the 1932 Northern Baptist Convention*, 91, 127–28.

Chapter 3

Southern Baptists and Jews Prior to 1933

In 1845, the Baptist movement in the United States suffered a division that has never been healed. Anticipating the political division of the country in the 1860s, Southern Baptists, unwilling to withdraw support for the slavery of African Americans, began their own foreign and domestic missions.[1]

The Birth of Concern (1846–1872)

One year later, in 1846, the Committee on New Fields of Labor for Foreign Missions presented a report featuring a lengthy paragraph on Jews and Palestine, which was adopted by the assembly. It recognized the role of the Jews as the Old Testament people of God, acknowledged a missionary call toward them, demonstrated ambivalence toward the restoration of Israel as a nation, and imagined a responsibility for mission work among Arabs as well. These initial considerations would become thematic of Southern Baptist perspectives regarding their relationship to the Jewish people for generations:

> THE COMMITTEE WOULD also suggest to the Convention, the propriety of making enquiries, through their Board, as to the practicability of establishing, at some future, yet not far distant time, a mission in Palestine, with reference, at least in part, to the spiritual benefit of the Jews. That interesting people are beloved for their fathers' sake, and faithful prophecy assures us that they are to be saved. Have Baptists, have Southern Baptists nothing to do, instrumentally, for their salvation? The number of Jews in Palestine at this time is considerable, and it appears to be rapidly increasing. . . . A Baptist mission in Palestine, if

> properly sustained, might be expected to extend its influence to others beside the Jews, and in time, to many surrounding regions.[2]

The 1846 report did not address the issue of Jews in the United States. This theme would be the subject of the first Southern Baptist national resolution on their Jewish neighbors, passed at the 1867 convention. On Saturday afternoon, May 11, 1867, Richard Furman, from South Carolina, presented the following sentence for convention consideration: "*Resolved*, That it is our duty, as Christians, to labor and to pray more earnestly for the conversion of the Jews." After remarks by other speakers, the resolution was adopted unanimously. Two days later, on the final day of the convention, a delegate from Mississippi, A. W. Chambliss, presented a second resolution which was also adopted: "Resolved, That this Convention deeply sympathizes with the views so ably expressed by Bro. R. Furman, of South Carolina, on the subject of the conversion of the Jews, and that Bro. Furman be requested to furnish a copy of his address for publication in some permanent form."[3]

The Jaeger Resolutions (1873-1900)

The eighteenth Southern Baptist convention, held in Mobile, Alabama, on May 8-12, 1873, passed the first set of comprehensive resolutions about Jews, on behalf of the Southern Baptists. Surprisingly, the resolutions were the result of a spontaneous and unplanned response to the message of a Jew.

On May 9, a motion was made and passed to invite a member of the host congregation, St. Frances Street Baptist Church, to speak to the assembly "on the subject of the conversion of the Jews to Christianity." The following day, Rev. Abraham Jaeger, a converted Jew and a former rabbi, "proceeded to address the Convention upon the importance of its engaging in labors for the conversion of the Jews to Christianity." In response, J. M. Wood of Georgia prayed "especially for the conversion of the Jews," and M. B. Wharton, a delegate from Kentucky, presented a resolution to appoint Jaeger "as a missionary to the Jews in this country." Wharton's proposal was immediately countered by an unrecorded substitute resolution by T. P. Miller from

Alabama, and "the resolution and substitute were referred to a special committee of five."[4]

On the last day of the convention, the report of the special committee was approved after Jaeger himself was given an opportunity to respond—possibly to decline respectfully the offer of a missionary position.[5] Miller read the committee's proposed resolution, which was approved:

> *RESOLVED,* THAT WE have heard with profound interest and sympathy the narration of the experience of Bro. Jaeger, and his address upon the subject of missions to the Jews.
>
> *Resolved,* That this Convention recognizes the comprehensiveness of the Great Commission, and the obligation to provide for the preaching of Christ to the Jews as well as to the Gentiles.
>
> *Resolved,* That should Bro. Jaeger now, or at a future time, be impressed with a sense of duty to preach Christ to his Jewish brethren, that this Convention pledges its sympathy, its prayers, and its active co-operation.
>
> *Resolved,* That we commend Bro. Jaeger to the fraternal regard of the brethren everywhere, and ask for him such Christian courtesies as may facilitate his labors in the cause of our Divine Master.[6]

Then, T. Harley, a delegate from Georgia, made a motion to adopt another resolution, which also passed: "Resolved, that we do gratefully remember this day our unspeakable indebtedness to the seed of Abraham, and devoutly recognize their peculiar claims upon the sympathies and prayers of all Gentile Christians, and we hereby record our earnest desire to partake in the glorious work of hastening the day when the superscription of the Cross shall be the confession of all Israel, 'Jesus of Nazareth, the King of the Jews.'"[7]

Two years later, the Southern Baptists revisited the subject of mission to the Jews. C. H. Toy offered a resolution, which passed after remarks by Jaeger and several other speakers. It affirmed that God had placed "a special call on Southern Baptists to make effort for the conversion of the Jews" and urged "the Home Mission Board . . . to inquire into the expediency of appointing, and if found practicable, to send out a missionary to the Jews, as soon as a suitable man can be found."[8] No suitable candidates were discovered, but in its 1877 report, the Foreign Mission Board did note that a Jewish mission was begun in Venice, Italy, in December 1876, with leadership provided by an independent missionary named Bellondi.[9]

At the 1882 convention, A. D. Cohen, a delegate from North Carolina, presented a resolution focused on "the present state of God's ancient people, the Jews, constituting an important part of almost every other nation among whom they mingle." He encouraged the Foreign Mission Board to create "missions to the Israelites in this and other countries; and if the proper men can be found, to appoint them to this special work; and that we commend the subject of Israel's conversion to Christianity to the prayers and effort of God's people everywhere."[10] Cohen's resolution was not voted on; instead, it was referred to committee.

In response, the Foreign Mission Board responded by asserting that all mission work may potentially engage Jews: "As to the resolution submitted to us regarding a mission to the Jews, we can only say that the Board will no doubt cheerfully expend any means and send any worthy men to such a mission as may come within their power. The Jews being scattered throughout all nations, in sending the gospel to those nations, we are practically sending it to these Jews, who constitute parts of those nations. There may be localities where separate missions to them may be established, such as our large cities; but even in these places much may be done by our settled pastors or missionaries engaged in such fields."[11] The perspective of the board seemed to be confirmed when it reported at length on the missionary recruitment of a Jew named Solomon Louis Ginsburg, in Bahia, Brazil, where many Jews lived.[12]

In these resolutions, the two dominant themes of Southern Baptist thought in regard to the Jews are outlined: appreciation and evangelism. Jews were esteemed for their place in the salvation history of God, and accordingly Christians owed them high regard—a positive statement representing a rejection of anti-Semitism. Second, Jews, like Gentiles, should embrace the soteriological claims of Jesus Christ and acknowledge him as their Messiah. It is of historical significance that the resolution was passed in response to the presentation of a Jewish convert, which eventually led to the calling of Jacob Gartenhaus to a national position in 1920.

Jews and the Southland (1900-1913)

A turning point in the history of Southern Baptists and Jews took place in 1906, when the convention received the report of the Committee on Cities and Foreigners. It recognized three global trends: "the spread of education, the extension of democratic government, and the growth of great cities" which had the potential to affect Protestant, and specifically Baptist, home missions. The growth in education and democracy met with their approval, but the rise of a metropolitan America was seen as a "most perplexing and most baffling problem."

Why? The committee was concerned that American cities were experiencing immigrant growth, especially from non-Protestant groups—"Roman Catholics, Jews and heathen." These Jews and others were "foreigners" and "enemies of the evangelical faith." The committee concluded that "patriotism and loyalty to Christ" required Southern Baptists to pay attention to transitions in America's metropolitan areas because "this social avalanche of foreigners, crowding our great cities, threatens our civic and religious institutions."[13]

World War I and Its Aftermath (1914-1919)

The United States entered World War I following Congressional approval of the declaration of war President Woodrow Wilson asked for on April 2, 1917. Southern Baptists met in convention in New Orleans from May 16-21, 1917, and learned from a select Committee on the Present Crisis on how the war was going to affect Baptist life and witness. They stressed the need for calm, affirmed the role of chaplains in ministering to military personnel, expressed sadness that war was necessary, and highlighted the Baptist core conviction of democratic liberty: "The cause of democracy is at stake. While we would not voluntarily claim for ourselves any superior devotion to this great cause, yet we cannot forget that democracy is peculiarly a part of our religion, that it is interwoven with all our common and cherished beliefs." A resolution was approved which affirmed the right of all religious peoples (including Jews) to practice their faith in military settings.[14]

Jewish communities throughout central and eastern Europe faced persecution following the conclusion of the First World War. Political uncertainties and transitions provided occasions for pogroms in Hungary, Poland, Ukraine, and Russia, while anti-Semitic organizations flourished during Germany's Weimar Republic. The Jewish situation was particularly dire in Poland. In November 1918, the Polish army committed atrocities against Jews in Lemberg over the course of several days, and in April 1919, Polish soldiers massacred thirty-five Jews in Pinsk. Jews also suffered in other cities: "Maurice Pate, an American relief official, depicted the situation in Kobryn, Poland: 'In a Jewish orphan home we found 200 children from two to twelve years of age in a most deplorable condition. . . . For the past two weeks the institution has not had a pound of bread. . . . All the children have is a thin barley soup.'"[15]

In an action that anticipated Baptist responses to Hitler's persecution of the Jews, Southern Baptists at their 1919 convention adopted a resolution proposed by F. W. Barnett in favor of an international conference to alleviate Jewish suffering:

> WHEREAS, DURING MANY centuries, in various countries of the globe, the driven, wandering Jews have suffered terrible persecutions and massacres, sometimes at the hands of professedly Christian nations . . . *Resolved*, That we, the Southern Baptist Convention, do hereby respectfully petition Woodrow Wilson, President of the United States, and other officials of our Government, as soon as deemed advisable, to intercede with the governments of Europe for an International Conference to consider the conditions of the Jews, and to adopt such measures as may deemed wise for their relief.[16]

The conference did not take place, but President Wilson pressed for limited religious, cultural, and linguistic rights for Jews in the Polish Minority Treaty imposed upon the Polish government in June 1919. The League of Nations had the authority to enforce the treaty's protective clauses. However, Hitler's rise to power led to its demise.[17]

Throughout the 1920s and 1930s, George W. Truett exercised increasing leadership influence within the Southern Baptist Convention and the Baptist World Alliance (serving as its president from 1934 to 1939). A master orator, he became one of the leading exponents of the blending of American democracy with Baptist core convictions.[18] Standing on Capitol Hill during the 1920 Southern Baptist convention meetings in Washington, DC, Truett delivered his most famous sermon, "Baptists and Religious Liberty," in which he proclaimed an essential union between American democratic ideals and historic Baptist core convictions on religious liberty and soul freedom:

> WE SHALL DO well, both as citizens and as Christians, if we will hark back to the chief actors and lessons in the early and epoch-making struggles of this great Western democracy, for the full establishment of civil and religious liberty—back to the days of Washington and Jefferson and Madison, and back to the days of our Baptist fathers, who have paid such a great price, through the long generations, that liberty, both religious and civil, might have free course and be glorified everywhere.[19]

Although Truett rarely referred to the Jewish community in his sermons, he affirmed that it was a historic Baptist core conviction that all people, and not just Baptists, deserved full religious and political freedom. Arguing that "toleration" of minorities is not a sufficient political or religious civic principle, Truett proclaimed that Baptists, as "champions of liberty, both religious and civil," must always advocate for "absolute liberty" as a "matter of principle." Furthermore, radical support for religious and political liberty was not to be understood as the peculiar doctrine of just Baptists in the United States but was universally proclaimed by the global Baptist movement on behalf of all humanity: "Our fundamental essential principles have made our Baptist people, of all ages and countries, to be the unyielding protagonists of religious liberty, not only for themselves, but as well for everybody else."[20]

Notes

1. For a contemporary Southern Baptist interpretation of the division, see *Proceedings of the Southern Baptist Convention*, held in Augusta, Georgia, May 8-12, 1845, 17–20.
2. *Proceedings of the Southern Baptist Convention*, held in Richmond, Virginia, June 10-15, 1846, 18.
3. *Proceedings of the Southern Baptist Convention*, held in Memphis, Tennessee, May 9-13, 1867, 19, 22. Richard Furman was the son of the South Carolina Baptist pioneer Richard B. Furman. See Joe M. King, *A History of South Carolina Baptists* (Columbia: General Board of the South Carolina Baptist Convention, 1964), 25.

4. *Proceedings of the Eighteenth Session of the Southern Baptist Convention*, held at Mobile, Alabama, on May 8-12, 1873, 19–20.

5. Abraham Jaeger apparently did not remain a Southern Baptist for long. He joined the Protestant Episcopal Church and served in the Tennessee and Ohio dioceses; according to the *Journal of the Proceedings of the Annual Convention of the Diocese of Ohio*, Jaeger transferred from Tennessee to Ohio on October 1, 1880 (12–13). From 1880 to 1883 he served on the faculty of the Kenyon Theological Seminary in Gambier, Ohio, as a professor of Hebrew, according to the *Gambier Catalogue of 1882*.

6. *Proceedings of the Eighteenth Session of the Southern Baptist Convention*, 35–36.

7. Ibid., 36.

8. *Proceedings of the Twentieth Session of the Southern Baptist Convention*, held at Charleston, South Carolina, on May 6-10, 1873, 25.

9. *Proceedings of the Twenty-Second Session of the Southern Baptist Convention*, held at New Orleans, Louisiana, on May 10-12, 1877, 47; *Proceedings of the Twenty-Third Session of the Southern Baptist Convention*, held at Nashville, Tennessee, on May 9-13, 1878, 58.

10. *Proceedings of the Twenty-Seventh Session of the Southern Baptist Convention*, held at Greenville, South Carolina, on May 10-14, 1882, 16.

11. Ibid., 34.

12. Ibid., Foreign Mission Board Annual Report, xxv–xxvii.

13. *Proceedings of the Fifty-First Session of the Southern Baptist Convention*, held at Chattanooga, Tennessee, on May 11-14, 1906, Committee on Cities and Foreigners Report, xxv–xxvii. In 1912, L. J. Ehrlich, a delegate from Georgia, "addressed the body in the interest of evangelism among the Jews." The minutes did not provide details of his speech. See *Proceedings of the Fifty-Seventh Session of the Southern Baptist Convention*, held at Oklahoma City, Oklahoma, on May 15-20, 1912, 80.

14. *Proceedings of the Sixty-Second Session of the Southern Baptist Convention*, held at New Orleans, Louisiana, on May 16-21, 1917, 100–102.

15. Zosa Szajkowski, "'Reconstruction' vs. 'Palliative Relief,' in American Overseas Work (1919–1939)," *Jewish Social Studies* 32, no. 1 (1970): 17.

16. *Proceedings of the Sixty-Fourth Session of the Southern Baptist Convention*, Atlanta, Georgia, May 14-18, 1919, 116. This resolution is quoted by Jerry Sutton, *A Matter of Conviction: A History of Southern Baptist Engagement with the Culture* (Nashville: B&H Publishing Group, 2008), 90–91, as an example of Southern Baptist conviction on religious liberty. He does not discuss it in terms of how Baptists related to Jews in particular. The text of the resolution, including the explicitly Christian references, is virtually an exact copy of Tennessee Senate Joint Resolution No. 70, which was passed on March 24, 1919. The resolution was also adopted by the State House of Representatives, and then signed by Tennessee Governor A. H. Roberts on March 25, 1919. See the *Public Acts of the State of Tennessee Passed by the Sixty-First General Assembly 1919*, 877.

17. Carole Fink, "The Paris Peace Conference and the Question of Minority Rights," *Peace and Change* 21, no. 3 (1996): 273–88.

18. See Lee Canipe, *A Baptist Democracy: Separating God and Caesar in the Land of the Free* (Macon, GA: Mercer University Press, 2011), 127–52.

19. George W. Truett, *God's Call to America and Other Addresses Comprising Special Orations Delivered on Widely Varying Occasions* (Nashville: Sunday School Board of the Southern Baptist Convention), 31.

20. Ibid., 33–34. The speech is also included in a later anthology: *George W. Truett, The Inspiration of Ideals* (Grand Rapids, MI: Baker Book House, 1950), 83–112.

Contemporary Impressions

Baptists and Jews in the Pre-Nazi Period

Influenced by Thomas Helwys, Roger Williams, and other early leaders of the Baptist movement, Baptists in the United States possessed a set of core doctrines and a historical legacy that strongly favored advocacy on behalf of persecuted minorities, regardless of race or religious affiliation. The Baptist core convictions of soul liberty, freedom, and separation of church and state provided a philosophical basis for affirming democracy over totalitarianism and human rights over persecution and oppression.

Northern Baptists had more opportunities than their Southern counterparts for contact with Jewish immigrants between 1880 and 1932. Jewish people pouring in by the hundreds of thousands congregated in cities where Northern Baptists historically were strongly represented on the local church level. Northern Baptist mission workers greeted immigrant Jews at Ellis Island. Beginning in 1896, the American Baptist Home Mission Society experimented with different ways to partner with Jewish converts demonstrating leadership gifts in order to evangelize in Jewish communities. The Christian Americanization movement, which can legitimately be criticized for its ethnocentrism, nevertheless represented a desire to relate to Jews and serve them according to the accepted wisdom of mainstream Protestant culture of the time.

Northern Baptist interaction with Jews between 1880 and 1932 sowed the seeds for a complex relationship with Jews during the Nazi era. Compassionate ministry and a desire to connect with Jewish immigrants had the potential to create friendships between Jews and Baptists and a reservoir of common understanding and mutual sympathy. To some extent, this indeed took place when Jews faced

Hitler's wrath. However, the relatively unsuccessful Baptist mission projects, coupled with prejudices operative within American Protestantism against Eastern European immigrants and Jews in particular, created a sense of distance between Baptists and the Jewish community. Baptists were frustrated over the resistance of Jews to convert and assimilate, which they saw as the epitome of the American ideal.

The organizational maturation of the Northern Baptist Convention, manifested in its willingness to address national and global political and moral issues, prepared Northern Baptists for the task of protesting Nazi totalitarian ideology and Hitler's persecution of the Jews in Germany and, later, throughout Europe. The Northern Baptist Convention's reaction to the Armenian genocide, a precursor to the Holocaust, appears to have set an unfortunate precedent regarding how Baptists would respond to future mass attacks against minorities. There was little Northern Baptists could do but pass resolutions and provide humanitarian aid; they had no means at their disposal to counteract effectively Turkish aggression. Righteous protest, coupled with the conviction that one was on the right side of the moral issues, was satisfying but ineffective in solving the problems addressed.

Following World War I, Northern Baptist enthusiasm for warfare, nationalism, and military expansion waned, and peace resolutions became a perennial feature of Resolutions Committee reports. This trend contained an unanticipated double-edged sword when applied to the Nazi challenge. Northern Baptists, in abandoning military intervention as a legitimate means of responding to aggression and oppression, found themselves left with only diplomatic negotiations as a tool of countering political evil.

Southern Baptists, especially in the more rural areas of the American South, may have had less opportunity for interacting with Jews, but there were important communities of Jews in Charleston, Atlanta, New Orleans, and Birmingham. The Southern Baptist Convention had a lengthy if sporadic history of expressing a desire for the evangelization of Jews, but it was more of a theoretical concern until Jacob Gartenhaus became the Home Mission Society's director of Jewish Evangelism in 1920 (Gartenhaus's ministry will be covered in chapter 14). Prior to the Nazi era, Southern Baptists had passed a resolution in 1919 expressing care for the welfare of European Jews, establishing a precedent that could potentially help inform their response to the Nazi activities.

In examining early Baptist expressions of support for the civic and religious freedom of Jews, we do not find any indication that the Baptists befriended or cared about Jews as people, but rather as a corporate representation of the outcast other. For many Baptists, Jews represented an extreme reflection of their own historical plight, a minority people striving for acceptance, freedom, and legitimacy. Baptists recognized the right of Jews and all others to live in a society that prized democratic values and toleration, but this was not necessarily accompanied by a desire for friendship on an individual level. This dichotomy would shape Baptist offers of support during the Nazi era, leading to an extensive series of sympathetic resolutions and other expressions of concern for Jews, without being accompanied by significant practical actions to alleviate Jewish suffering in Europe.

PART TWO

What Did Baptists Know about the Holocaust?

In the first half of the twentieth century, newspapers and periodicals (supplemented by radio, an important new medium) dominated the dissemination of news for the average American. President Franklin Delano Roosevelt received a collection of newspaper clippings on a daily basis. What did he and other informed Americans know about the Nazi persecution of the Jews? Holocaust historian and Emory University professor Deborah E. Lipstadt asserted that American inaction regarding Jewish persecution and the Holocaust cannot be blamed on a lack of knowledge about the Nazi anti-Semitic campaign, which was covered as it progressed by the American press. She also claimed that "an astonishing amount of information was available long before the end of the war. There was practically no aspect of the Nazi horrors which was not publicly known in some detail long before the camps were opened in 1945." This raises questions such as: "How did it [the press] transmit this news? Did it treat it as fact or rumor? . . . Did the press take Hitler's threats against Jews seriously? Did it consider them perhaps just bombastic rhetoric, or did it grasp that anti-Semitism was the keystone of Nazism?"[1]

American inaction regarding the plight of the Jews was facilitated by the misreading of Nazi anti-Semitism by the American press: "But the persecution of the Jews constituted only one small segment of the story of Nazi Germany and was never the central theme of the reports about the new regime." Lipstadt concluded: "Rarely was news of the persecution of the Jews handled by journalists, particularly by those who viewed the situation from the safety of the United States, as an inherent expression of Nazism. The failure to see Nazi antisemitism as a reflection of the fundamental principles of Nazism was to have important consequences for the interpretation and comprehension of the news of the persecution of European Jewry."[2]

While Lipstadt's research focused on secular newspapers, Robert W. Ross examined how religious newspapers and periodicals covered the persecution of Jews and the Holocaust:

> DID AMERICAN PROTESTANT Christians know what was happening to the Jews in Germany from 1933–1945? One way to attempt to answer this question is to turn to the American Protestant press to see how it reported events in Germany during the Hitler era. The use of religious periodicals to answer the question is based on two assumptions. The first is that, if the press did systematically report during the entire period what was happening to Jews in Nazi Germany, then Protestant Christians had this information before them. They could not claim that they had not been told. The second is that, if such reporting was not done, then Protestant Christians could later claim that they had not been told about the plight of the Jews in Nazi Germany.[3]

Baptists in the United States had their own extensive network of influential newspapers and periodicals. Although some were primarily concerned with internal denominational matters (events, programs, theological articles, and resources), most of them also published news articles and editorials about political, social, moral, and economic matters of importance to their readers. These periodicals also recommended books that addressed Jewish history and religion, as well as their struggles with anti-Semitism and, in particular, the Nazis. Unlike the secular press, these papers sought to bring Baptist convictions and beliefs into the conversation and thus had the potential of profoundly affecting how Baptists would respond to the Holocaust.

Notes

1. Deborah E. Lipstadt, *Beyond Belief: The American Press and the Coming of the Holocaust 1933–1945* (New York: The Free Press, 1986), 2–3, 4–6. See also Laurel Leff, *Buried by the* Times: *The Holocaust and America's Most Important Newspaper* (Cambridge: Cambridge University Press, 2005).

2. Lipstadt, *Beyond Belief*, 15.

3. Robert W. Ross, *So It Was True: The American Protestant Press and the Nazi Persecution of the Jews* (Minneapolis: University of Minnesota Press, 1980), 4. Ross makes sporadic mention of Baptist newspaper coverage of key events; see 53–56, 306–7.

Chapter 4

Missions—The Northern Baptist Official Voice

Missions served as the official voice of the Northern Baptist Convention. It was a monthly publication designed to advance convention programs and mission support, and therefore, it did not see itself as a forum for spirited debate and a diversity of views. The publication schedule and topic selection contributed to delays in responding to specific news events. *Missions* was tightly controlled by its editor, William B. Lipphard, who personally contributed many of the articles related to Germany, Hitler, and the plight of the Jews under Nazi rule.

From the Rise of Hitler to Kristallnacht (1933-1939)

In the November and December 1933 issues of *Missions*, Lipphard wrote an extensive two-part discourse titled "Hitlerism as I Saw It in Germany." In an attempt to be journalistically balanced, the November article documented the benefits of hitlerism and the follow-up article focused on the dangers of hitlerism. Like many other journalists, Lipphard rehearsed the humiliation of Germany after World War I and the economic disasters of the 1920s, and he contrasted that desperation with the industriousness and strength of the emerging Germany. He obliquely hinted at something nefarious when he admitted that Nuremberg was chosen for a Nazi convention "because it typified the purity of old Germany, undefiled with anything non-Aryan."

Hitler was portrayed as the center of all of German society, young and old alike: "He is glorified, idolized, almost deified. . . . He is almost worshipped as a god destined to lead the German people out of the despair of the post-war years into the radiance of a new day." Anticipating the second installment, Lipphard hinted that although the "achievements of his regime are legion," nevertheless, "its liabilities are equally formidable." He then listed five positive achievements for which he felt compelled to give Hitler credit and praise: the creation of "a new unified Germany," a "33% decrease in unemployment," the restoration of "law and order," saving "Germany from atheistic communism," and Germany's "new spirit" of "spiritual strength" and "confidence."[1]

The December 1933 issue acknowledged the outbreak of anti-Semitism in Germany, but in a manner that was hardly sympathetic to Jews. The lead editorial, "International Hypocrisy," portrayed Germany as a victim of international machinations, criticized the United States and other democracies for the demise of disarmament talks, and defended Germany's withdrawal from the League of Nations.[2] The first explicit reference to Jewish persecution appeared in the only article on Palestine to be found in the magazine from January 1933 through April 1936: "Thousands of Jews, persecuted in Germany, have in recent months migrated to Palestine." Due to Jewish emigration, "the country faces a serious racial and religious problem," as evidenced by "open hostility between Jew and Arab."[3]

Lipphard's analysis of the significance of Hitler and Nazism was the centerpiece of the December 1933 edition, and it illustrated the extent to which the Northern Baptist Convention leaders displayed bystander behavior as the Jews began to suffer persecution. He cited five "dangers" that had made the world apprehensive. Hitler had "abolished political democracy and representative government" and circumscribed "the freedom of the press and free speech." A "totalitarian" Nazi regime had "assumed control of Germany's religious life" and "by undue emphasis on the alleged German racial purity, and by fostering an intense nationalism, Hitlerism has undermined confidence in international cooperation."

Buried in the middle of his list was Lipphard's admission that "Hitlerism has inaugurated a reign of terror." Lipphard recognized that "thousands" of German dissidents had been "confined in immense concentration camps" and then admitted that the Nazi terror was specifically focused on German Jews. He did not converse with Jewish victims of Hitler's terror but instead interviewed non-Jewish

Germans who attempted to attribute violence against Jews to "irresponsible parties" or "persons pretending to be Nazis" but defended the "Nazi purpose to remove the Jew from the political and professional life of Germany."[4] He then reviewed a list of reasons offered by Germans in justification of their hatred of Jews:

> THE JEWS WERE said to have overrun the professions, especially law and medicine. They had come to occupy important positions out of proportion to their population. . . . It was claimed that Jews had profited greatly during the terrible inflation period. Moreover, through their strong position in the movies, the theater, literature and the press, the Jews were exerting an alien influence on German culture. This made it difficult to carry through the Nazi program for reawakened German nationalism. Again, more than 150,000 Jews from eastern Europe, far lower in standard of living that the older and more cultured type, had flocked into Germany in great numbers since the war. It seemed impossible to absorb them into the economic life of Germany, especially when the depression became so acute.[5]

Lipphard offered no refutation of the charges; he only meekly added a disclaimer: "In all this review of the Jewish problem in Germany, I am not defending the Nazi anti-Semitic program. I am merely reporting the reaction of Germans with whom I talked." Instead, he delivered a severe criticism of American racial prejudice: "It will be recognized that the race problem in Germany differs from that in America only in degree and not in kind. . . . In condemning Germany for her race prejudice, we are also condemning ourselves."[6] Lipphard's response to the dangers posed by Hitler's rise to power represented the antiwar and pro-diplomacy viewpoint of the Northern Baptist Convention's leaders, but he offered no practical support for Jewish victims. To add insult to injury, an editorial in the same issue noted "the recent outbreaks of Anti-Semitism in Europe have again drawn attention to the distribution of Jews throughout the world."[7] Instead of condemning anti-Semitism or expressing outrage or solidarity with Jews, the paragraph merely cited how many Jews lived in various places.

Charles S. MacFarland, the former general secretary of the Federal Council of the Churches of Christ (FCCC), wrote an article in the January 1934 issue recapitulating his one-hour interview of the German chancellor. Unlike Lipphard, MacFarland took the Jewish point of view into consideration, but he did not seem to grasp that Hitler's anti-Semitic campaign was central to his political program for Germany's future: "Take the Jewish situation. When he finds that the peoples of outside nations are protesting, he thinks to stop it by a boycott of German Jews, which, of course, simply intensified it. One wonders also why, in the Jewish situation, he did not have consultation looking toward a positive and constructive solution. . . . I am credibly informed that leading Jews, men of high standing, asked for a round-table conference and were refused. Refusal to consult is never justifiable."[8]

In 1934, the majority of *Missions* articles concerning Germany focused on the upcoming Baptist World Congress that was scheduled for August 4-10, 1934, in Berlin. J. H. Rushbrooke energetically pressured Baptists to support the Berlin congress, in spite of reservations expressed about safety and the propriety of meeting in a country with controversial policies, including the Nazis' anti-Semitic persecutions of 1933. A March 1934 editorial stated, "Baptists come from all over the world with their own historic insistence on religious freedom. To Berlin, with its 'Aryan paragraph,' Baptists come with the New Testament paragraph, 'neither Jew nor Greek, neither bond nor free . . . ye are all one in Jesus Christ.'"[9] Even though there was nervousness over the leading German Baptist, Dr. F. W. Simoleit, gaining the title of führer,[10] due to its association with Nazism, the Baptist World Alliance (BWA) argued that German Baptists, as hosts, would be severely disappointed if the congress was not held or moved to another venue.[11] Rushbrooke emphasized that 1934 was the one hundredth anniversary of the German Baptist movement.[12]

However, it was impossible to ignore Hitler.[13] Herbert Gezork, a German Baptist leader who defected to the United States in 1936,[14] provided a concise history of German Baptists in anticipation of the congress. He acknowledged the leading role of Julius Köbner, who "was by birth a Jew," in the formative years of the German Baptist movement, noting that this Jewish convert was the leading German Baptist "poet and hymn writer," for "scarcely a Sunday passes in which German Baptists do not sing at least one of Köbner's glorious hymns." He admitted that Baptists had to end their youth ministry work "as a result of political changes which have taken place in Germany during the past year." Contradicting himself, Gezork concluded his essay with what was to become a standard German Baptist assertion: "In the new Germany under the leadership of Chancellor Adolf Hitler, we have up until the present had full freedom to preach the gospel. Our work continues as in the past."[15]

The September 1934 issue of *Missions* quoted the Northern Baptist Convention resolution on the persecution of "Christian and Jewish" Europeans.[16] In October, Charles A. Wells's cartoon pictured the BWA congress as a tiny sweet bird singing a song of "love, tolerance, brotherhood and peace," although surrounded by cannons and a vulture labeled "intolerance."[17] Lipphard's review of the congress briefly referred to its report on racism and anti-Semitism, which stated, "We deplore the long record of ill-usage of Jews on the part of professedly Christian nations, and we declare such injustice to be a violation of the teaching and spirit of Christ."[18] In order to balance the implicitly harsh criticism of Nazi Germany, *Missions* also published an article on the struggles of American Jews. After chronicling how Jews were "prospering phenomenally in the United States," the article pointed out troubling news:

> A DISTURBING FACTOR in Jewish-American life is the rise of anti-Semitism. While we have not here the active persecution which has cast its blight over European lands, there is yet enough prejudice and social discrimination to furnish material for such explosive outbursts as those in the Dearborn Independent and the Ku Klux Klan. The duty of the Christian church is obvious. Anti-Semitism puts a veil between the Jew and Jesus. The church . . . must take an active part in exorcising prejudice and in creating good-will.[19]

In an endorsement of the annual Brotherhood Day for 1935 sponsored by the National Conference of Jews and Christians,[20] *Missions* continued to compare the United States with Germany in an unflattering way: "'There is far more anti-Jewish sentiment in the United States than in Germany,' President Lars W. Boe of St. Olaf College, Minnesota, is reported to have said on his return from Europe recently. 'If it ever breaks out here it will be far worse than in Germany because public opinion cannot be easily controlled.'"[21] The lead editorial in March 1935 claimed that an American delegate to the Berlin congress was embarrassed by the European critique of the lynching of African Americans in the southern states of the country and cited the *New York Post*: "Nothing in the annals of German, Italian and Balkan dictatorships is worse than the story revealed in the report of this lynching."[22] This issue also contained a brief article on Jewish refugees from Czechoslovakia and Poland who could not travel to Palestine.[23]

Missions published an excerpt from Rushbrooke's address at the 1935 Northern Baptist convention in which he revealed "that on Saturday following the Baptist World Congress in Berlin, the Jews of a leading city in Eastern Europe assembled in their synagogues and gave thanks to God for Baptists and their testimony. In this impressive manner they voiced appreciation of what Baptists had said in Berlin." Rushbrooke drew a lesson from the Jewish response: "Our attitude toward Jews, Negroes and other races, in the United States and in other lands, must exemplify what was said. Our insistence on religious freedom must include not only ourselves but also Catholics and all others with whom we may radically disagree. . . . Otherwise the Jews will have given thanks to God in vain."[24]

Missions' first feature article on Palestine and Zionism (April 1936) cited the Balfour Declaration,[25] noted the growth of the Jewish population in Palestine, and identified three "motives" of Zionism: patriotism (the desire for a homeland), religion, and "economic possibilities." Without mentioning Germany, it affirmed that "Zionism gives the Jew a refuge." The author confessed, "Zionism is a great movement. Any friend of the Jewish people and any friend of Palestine would wish it well." However, several "liabilities" were also listed, including friction with Arabs and the lack of religious belief of many settlers. Nevertheless, the article offered an essentially positive assessment of Zionism: "We can conclude that Zionism is filling a real need. There are hundreds of thousands of Jews in Europe who have suffered and are now suffering persecution. Their plight is desperate. It is imperative that a refuge be provided of them. They cannot come to America. As rapidly as possible they are being moved to Palestine."[26]

The "historic Baptist principle" of liberty was highlighted at the 1936 Northern Baptist convention, and *Missions* published President

James H. Franklin's attack against totalitarianism. The former Commissioner of the League of Nations for German Refugees, Dr. James G. McDonald, also spoke against German totalitarianism. He lifted up the "plight of German refugees, both Jews and Christians," and lamented the "colossal indifference of the Christian churches who assumed this was a Jewish problem, whereas it is really a Christian problem in that Jews and Christians are victims and the persecutors are so-called Christians." He condemned this as a "denial of the principle of liberty for which Roger Williams went into exile."[27] In an article covering the World Jewish Congress meetings, *Missions* quoted an unidentified Rumanian Jew, who asked, "Why do Christians permit this oppression to remain unpunished?" *Missions* responded: "In view of the remarkable address in St. Louis by Dr. James G. McDonald . . . some people are still wondering why the Northern Baptist Convention in its resolutions had nothing to say about this unchristian treatment of the Jews."[28]

Sympathy for Jews was a minor theme in *Missions* during 1937. In support of that year's Brotherhood Day, it opined, "The principle of justice for all, friendship among all, and understanding of all, transcends all difference in theology, variety in faith, and diversity in ritual . . . all who believe in God, whether Jew, Catholic, or Protestant, are equally concerned today over the threat of . . . the growth of the totalitarian state, the idea of prejudice and the menace of unbrotherliness."[29] *Missions* recommended *The Jews of Germany* by Marvin Lowenthal, which depicted Hitler's anti-Semitic persecution of Jews.[30] In September 1937, *Missions* reviewed Herbert J. Seligman's research on the growth of European anti-Semitism, noting that the German attacks on Jews were well-known and that "the plight of the Jew in Europe is more and more precarious." It also recognized that "America now harbors more than 800 centers of anti-Semitism and anti-Jewish propaganda."[31] The periodical furthermore reported that the Rockefeller Foundation had begun assisting German Jewish refugees.[32]

In its coverage of the 1937 Oxford Conference on Church, Community, and State, *Missions* noted some political intrigue when the representatives dealt with the report on "the Church and Community" and the issue of anti-Semitism: "The English version included the words 'anti-Semitism,' and the quotation from St. Paul, 'In Christ there is neither Jew nor Greek.' In the German translation both references were missing! Nobody could explain how that happened. The chairman, Sir Walter Moberly, assured all present, however, that it was purely an inadvertence, an unintentional oversight by the translator."[33] *Missions* reported that "W. M. Horton of Oberlin, Ohio, urged the Conference to speak out even more boldly on the dangers of anti-Semitism." The conference did call to the "church to preach the positive doctrine that the existence of different races is full of possibilities for the enrichment of human life and in particular must demonstrate the true community of people of all races within its own life."[34]

Lipphard returned to Germany and attended the Dusseldorf Exposition, where he discovered significant manifestations of German anti-Semitism, making it clear that "Jews are not desired": "Here was a display of anti-Semitic books, pitiful attempts by pseudo-scientific arguments on race purity, to rationalize the continued German persecution of the Jew. No longer brutal or spectacular, so as not to attract outside publicity, it nevertheless continues with undiminished vigor." Lipphard interviewed a Jewish man who claimed to have "little fear" of Nazi violence. However, Lipphard noted that in "numerous other ways the Jew is gradually being eliminated from German life. So the Jewish persecution under the Nazi regime remains one of the sad and unforgettable chapters in post-war German history."[35]

In the next issue, *Missions* observed that there were "five million Jews in Central and Eastern Europe who are absolutely not wanted. Hatred, injustice, and ill-will are driving them into exile." However, the journal could only encourage relief appeal donations and charge Northern Baptists to change American society:

> ALTHOUGH AS AMERICAN Christians we can do little to influence European governments in modifying their policies or in easing the relentless pressure, we can at least respond to relief appeals and thus in some measure ameliorate their terrible plight. Moreover we can resolutely seek to remove the causes of anti-Semitism which is ominously growing in the United States. Through personal example, teaching the younger generation, and the creation of Christian attitudes, we can check the antipathy against the Jew and thereby help bring on a new era of fellowship and cooperation.[36]

In a rare departure from the normative laser-like focus solely on Rumanian Baptist persecution (without regard for the Jewish plight in that country) that Rushbrooke and other Baptist leaders displayed,[37] *Missions* acknowledged that Jews were suffering under the anti-Semitism of the new Rumanian government: "Land now owned by Jews will be expropriated. All Jews naturalized after 1920 will be deprived of that citizenship. There are more than 1,200,000 Jews in Rumania. Nobody knows how many entered the country from Poland and Germany to escape Jewish persecution there."[38]

In the December 1938 issue of *Missions*, Lipphard recounted his summer visit to Germany in a rather ill-timed piece. Once again, he listed seven achievements Germany owed to Hitler's leadership: (1) "a new political unity," (2) the elimination of crime, (3) Germany's opposition to "atheistic communism," (4) "no unemployment," (5) the repudiation of the Versailles treaty, (6) Hitler's exposing of international disarmament "hypocrisy," and (7) Germany's "new spirit of pride." He then listed seven criticisms, and the third one, on Hitler's "reign of terror," mentioned anti-Semitism:

> AND THE HAND of oppression has fallen most grievously upon the Jew. The long, terrible, heart-rending story of five years of brutal anti-Semitism is too well-known to be repeated here. Charged with being anti-Nazi, anti-German, a degenerating influence in the theatre, the movies, the press, holding professional positions numerically far more than proportionately his population warranted, the Jew has been made the victim of a cruel campaign of extermination. The better class Germans are deeply sensitive over this anti-Semitism. They apologize for it, attempt to explain it and try to minimize its terrors and brutality. Yet neither explanation nor apology can remove the grim facts that the Jew, with systematic, calculated efficiency, is being eliminated.[39]

Missions' response to Kristallnacht appeared in January 1939, with the publication of a six-page article by Lipphard titled "The Wandering Jew—Where Can He Go Now?" In an attempt to place Kristallnacht in historical perspective, Lipphard rehearsed the history of European anti-Semitism from medieval times to the present. With the rise of Hitler in 1933, "an ever rising tide of anti-Semitism has been sweeping over the world." Lipphard pointed to a mass deportation of Jews to Poland and then focused on Kristallnacht:

> INHUMAN AS WAS this mass deportation in October, it was mild in contrast to the mob violence that swept across Germany in November. The world will not soon forget the orgy of frightfulness. . . . There is no need to repeat in detail the stories of damaged, gutted, destroyed or burned synagogues and of hundreds, perhaps thousands of Jewish shops smashed by organized bands of German youths, all of which was reported in the American press. . . . And yet the October deportations and the November violence are only spectacular incidents in the long story of Jewish persecution. After nearly six years of Nazi anti-Semitism, the position of the Jew in Germany today is extremely precarious.[40]

Lipphard stated, "What makes the plight of the Jew more tragic is that anti-Semitism is spreading through all Europe."[41] In response to such suffering, the world acted like passive bystanders. Referring to the failed Evian Conference,[42] he complained: "All recognized the gravity of the problem. Everyone talked sympathetically but nobody was prepared to do anything." Lipphard concluded, "And until an aroused Christian conscience supported by constructive Christian action removes the curse of anti-Semitism from our world, our civilization will be neither civilized nor Christian."[43]

World War II and the Holocaust (1939–1945)

Europe was rushing toward war. Following the 1939 Baptist World Congress in Atlanta, Rushbrooke expressed the hope that political divisions would not tear asunder the fellowship of Baptists (alluding obliquely to his wish that German Baptists would not be seen as enemies).[44] In November *Missions* once again published an ill-timed piece by Lipphard chronicling the anxiety of Europeans who clung to the hope that war could be evaded.[45] A positive review of Jacques Maritain's *A Christian Looks at the Jewish Question* appeared in the final issue of 1939.[46]

In its New Year editorial, *Missions* lamented "the concentrated brutality of a Nazi concentration camp, the new Jewish ghetto in what was once Poland."[47] The February 1940 issue highlighted the work of the Northern Baptist Christian Friendliness missionaries, who reached out to Jewish refugees.[48] Nevertheless, Lipphard, reporting on the National Study Conference on the Churches and the World Situation, admitted that Americans were not doing their share in embracing refugees. A workshop leader stated, "*All of American Protestantism had done less for Europe's war refugees than little Switzerland*."[49]

John S. Conning contributed the year's only major piece on the Jewish experience in America and anti-Semitism. Conning pictured American Jewry as prosperous, active, and eager to assimilate into American culture but faced with a loss of traditional spirituality. Acknowledging that "the most distressing aspect of Jewish life today is the virulent, ruthless, and persistent persecution of the Jews under the Nazi regime," Conning encouraged Christians to share the gospel of Jesus Christ with American Jews. However, "the greatest difficulty that churches have to face in a ministry to the Jews is the prevalence of anti-Jewish prejudice," which has "become endemic in various localities" and "is at work even in the churches of these communities." To counteract such prejudice, Conning called for reaching out to Jews in a spirit of friendship: "How many Jews in America through their association with Christians have come to think of Jesus as the source of kindness and sympathy and understanding?"[50]

In 1941, *Missions* refocused on the Jewish plight in Europe, noting the creation of the Warsaw ghetto:

> A SOLID WALL of concrete, eight feet in height, encloses the entire city area within which 500,000 Jews are compelled to live. This is race segregation unparalleled even in the Middle Ages. The wall surrounds more than 100 city blocks and closes off 200 streets and several street car lines. There are only 18 entrances. Every person entering or leaving must possess a special pass. The Germans claim that the wall was not built as an expression of anti-Semitism, but as a health measure to protect Poles and Jews from the pestilence likely to follow the war. The reader must form his own opinion as to the validity of that claim.[51]

Mainline Protestants struggled with how to balance opposition to Hitler's aggression and persecution of the Jews and their faith in reasoned diplomatic negotiations, peacemaking, and for some, pacifism.

Delegates at a Federal Council of Churches conference expressed opposition to war, recognized that appeasement had failed, and promoted "reconciliation" as the aim of Christian activism. They attempted to balance opposition to Hitler and support for the German people, and they issued a bland expression of caring for Jews: "We express as Christians our sympathy with the Jewish people in this hour of calamity for so many of their group in Europe. Christian attitudes toward the Jews should be a matter of primary concern for every Christian in every community."[52] Conrad Hoffman[53] had this in mind when he declared that "everywhere anti-Semitism has been on the march" and that "Hitler has declared it as his purpose to make all continental Europe '*Juden-rein.*' This threat menaces 2,000,000 Jews with exile or slow but sure annihilation." Hoffman worried about what might happen to the Jews in Palestine if Hitler gained control of the Middle East and called upon Protestants to support Jewish missions.[54]

In April 1941, *Missions* contrasted the clear loyalty of Palestinian Jews to Great Britain in its fight against Hitler with the Arab population's ambivalence: "One group is definitely pro-British. Another is definitely pro-Nazi, attracted by the nazi philosophy of national strength. By far the majority of Arabs are neutral . . . behind all of these contingencies remains the Jews' undying hope that the Balfour pledge will eventually be fulfilled."[55]

One of the practical ways for Northern Baptists to provide assistance to a small subset of Jewish and Christian refugees was to participate in a program to resettle exiled European professors in American colleges and universities. In a March 1942 article, an unidentified professor confessed, "One of the lights in my sky was the friendship of Baptist friends. I thank you from the very bottom of my heart for every kind word said and for every token of sincere friendship."[56]

The entrance of the United States into the war caused *Missions* to express opposition to the incarceration of Japanese Americans. It cited the Jewish experience under Nazism as an argument against this new and controversial policy:

> FOR THE PAST 10 years, ever since Hitler came to power, the American people with holy indignation have repeatedly damned the nazi practice of arresting and imprisoning Germans of Jewish origin. Now in

> these glorious United States it is proposed that we do likewise to Americans of Oriental origin. Everybody knows what happened in Germany. First directed against the Jew, the nazi policy by precedent eventually included everybody.[57]

In January 1943, *Missions* took hope in the possibility of five thousand French Jewish children finding homes in the United States who were "*left behind*" when their parents were deported to "concentration camps." It also admitted: "Unknown is the fate of the parents who were deported to Germany, Poland, and Eastern Europe following a recent round-up of Jews by the French police."[58] In the April 1943 issue, *Missions* warned that "measures of wholesale extermination" were decimating Europe's Jewish population:

> TEN YEARS AGO, in March, 1933, shortly after Chancellor Adolf Hitler had become master of Germany, the nazi party launched its anti-Semitic crusade. Throughout the centuries from the days of Pharaoh until now, the Jews have experienced many bitter persecutions; in all probability they have never before endured such horrible suffering as during the past decade. In every country conquered by Germany the same terrible persecution of the Jew has followed. . . . [The French Jew] can only hope that measures of wholesale extermination such as are reported from Poland will not be repeated in France.[59]

Missions characterized the anti-Semitic campaign of the Nazis, complete with concentration camps, as a "wholesale extermination" of Jews:

> TEN YEARS AGO there were about 600,000 Jews in Germany. Today the number is reported less than 60,000. Czechoslovakia's 170,000 Jews have been reduced to 35,000. In 1939 there was estimated to be 3,000,000 Jews in Poland. Three years of mass deportations, short rations, deliberate starvation, as well as outright massacres if the unbelievably horrible stories coming out of Poland have even a minimum basis in fact, have reduced the total to less than 2,000,000. How many Jews have died in Europe since naziism began persecuting them can never be even approximately calculated. An article in *The New Republic* estimates Jewish deaths at 2,000,000.[60]

In the face of such atrocities, *Missions* pressed for Britain to honor its "pledge to establish a Jewish national home in Palestine" and for Americans to "intensify efforts in behalf of friendly relations with the Jews" in the United States.[61] In March 1944, *Missions* noted that "260,000 European refugees had come here [to the United States] since 1933 when the Nazis in Germany began their ruthless campaign in Germany and eventually in all Nazi-occupied countries against Jews and others who opposed the Nazi totalitarian super-race philosophy," and criticized "ominous signs of rising anti-Semitism on the part of prejudiced Americans who too easily forget that their own ancestors came here from Europe to escape economic hardship, political oppression, and religious persecution."[62]

Zionism also received attention. On March 31, 1944, the British did not lift the "White Paper" ban on Jewish immigration to Palestine. *Missions* commented: "What Britain does in Palestine is legally none of America's business, but from a humanitarian point of view it is the world's business. Where else can the Jew go? How many Jews will the American people admit here? . . . Palestine seems the only solution."[63] *Missions* criticized both Britain for betraying its commitment to the Balfour Declaration and President Franklin Delano Roosevelt for his unwillingness to commit to further Jewish immigration: "If this war is really being fought for human liberation and freedom, it would be the last word in global irony and international injustice if the Jew who suffered most from nazi persecution should emerge after the war in more hopeless circumstances than before. The closing of Palestine on March 31st to Jewish immigration . . . means a moral victory for Hitler."[64] In June, *Missions* called for "unrestricted immigration of Jews to Palestine."[65] In December, the periodical quoted President Roosevelt's pledge to support "the establishment of Palestine as a free and democratic Jewish Commonwealth" and judged it to be "commendable."[66]

The Postwar Years (1945–1948)

The future of the Jewish people was still an unsolved problem a year later. The ravages of the Nazi era on the Jewish people were presented, raising a haunting question: "The return of the Christmas season again focuses attention on Palestine and the fate of Europe's Jews of whom there were about 6,000,000 before the war. Today only 1,500,000 survive. The others died of starvation and disease or were brutally massacred not only in the concentration camps of Germany but also in other lands where war conditions produced fertile soil for the spread of anti-Semitism. What is the fate of the survivors?" The only just solution seemed to be Palestine. In endorsing the Zionist dream, *Missions* cited global political consensus, past and present, and concluded: "The Jew seems to have every moral and legal right to live in Palestine. . . . there is probably no single international problem on which more people and organizations have gone on record than the admission of Jews into Palestine."[67]

Missions depicted the magnitude of the Holocaust graphically, reprinting a *New York Times* map of Europe detailing the "surviving Jewish population" in each country of Europe and then presenting the numbers in spreadsheet form. For the first time, the figure of six million dead was published:

> THE DECLINE IN Jewish population of Europe after six years of war thus reaches the staggering total of 5,719,100. Only a small fraction of these Jews migrated to Palestine or to the United States or other asylum countries to which the Jews sought to flee during the years of heartless Nazi antisemitism, which now seems to be infecting other European countries, notably Poland. Moreover, several hundred thousand Jews were "liquidated" in Germany during the six years of Nazism (1933–1939) before the war. The statistics thus confirm the terrible indictment against Naziism that during the 12 years from 1933–1945 more than 6,000,000 European Jews were annihilated in the most gigantic mass murder in history.[68]

In December 1946, *Missions* published a detailed article concerning the Palestinian situation, covering terrorism and violence, British unwillingness to put forward a solution, the political situation in the United States (including President Harry S Truman's position), and the Russian expansion into Middle East politics. The editorial endorsed the Zionist option for three reasons: "(1) More than 6,000,000 Jews were brutally exterminated during the years of Nazi anti-Semitism. (2) The Jews who survived have gone through [a] terrible ordeal and little has been done to alleviate their desperate condition. (3) The

Jews cannot remain in Europe." The editorial asked, "Where shall they go?"[69]

The November 29, 1947, United Nations vote to partition Palestine into Jewish and Arab states was acknowledged in the February 1948 issue. The article recognized the political challenges facing the Jews and Arabs and reminded its readers that Christians also had a vital interest in the future of the two-state solution.[70]

Notes

1. William B. Lipphard, "Hitlerism as I Saw It in Germany, Part 1" *Missions* (November 1933), 520–23.
2. Editorial, "International Hypocrisy," *Missions* (December 1933), 583.
3. "The German Language on the Streets of Jerusalem," *Missions* (December 1933), 584–85.
4. William B. Lipphard, "The Dangers of Hitlerism," *Missions* (December 1933), 586–89.
5. Ibid., 588.
6. Ibid.
7. Untitled editorial, *Missions* (December 1933), 610.
8. Charles S. MacFarland, "An Interview with Hitler," *Missions* (January 1934), 21. The article coincided with the publication of MacFarland's book, *The New Church and the New Germany* (New York: Macmillan, 1934), in which he characterized the Nazi political philosophy on race succinctly: "Honor resides in race and blood rather than solely in character and grace" (16). In a section on Karl Barth, he wrote, "The Aryan discrimination violates the super-racial principle of Christianity" (132). However, he still believed at that time that Hitler could be part of the solution for the church, as opposed to being the prime force behind the powers seeking to destroy it (148).
9. Editorial, "How Would You Have Decided?" *Missions* (March 1934), 135.
10. "A Visitor from the Land of Hitler," *Missions* (January 1934), 40: "Viewing matters from this distance, it seems like a distinct departure from Baptist democratic principles." The misspelling of the German word *Führer* (using a lowercase instead of a capital for the first letter) is found in the original text.
11. "The Fifth World Congress," *Missions* (January 1934), 2; "Are You Going to Berlin?" *Missions* (March 1934), 130. Simoleit's invitation was published; see "A Welcome from Germany," *Missions* (June 1934), 340.
12. J. H. Rushbrooke, "The Centennial of the German Baptists," *Missions* (April 1934), 214–15.
13. Hitler was even quoted by *Missions*: "We do not want to suppress any people's rights nor to suppress them, but the world must cease suppressing us. I am hoping the world will gradually realize that real friendship can be created only on a basis of equality and not of suppression"; "Remarkable Remarks," *Missions* (April 1934), 201. He was quoted a second time in the April 1936 issue, 203.
14. *The Watchman-Examiner* (8 June 1944), 558.
15. Herbert Gezork, "Yesterday and Tomorrow . . . for Baptists in the New Germany," *Missions* (May 1934), 294–95.
16. "What Will You Do with These Resolutions?" *Missions* (September 1934), 430.
17. "Brave Little Bird! A Cartoon on the Baptist World Congress," *Missions* (October 1934), 451.
18. "The World Fellowship of Baptists," *Missions* (October 1934), 469.
19. "The Jew in America," *Missions* (October 1934), 474.
20. See Victoria J. Barnett, "'Fault Lines': An Analysis of the National Conference of Christians and Jews, 1933–1948," PhD diss., George Mason University, 2012.
21. Untitled editorial, *Missions* (February 1935), 94.

22. Editorial, "We Don't Do That in Europe," *Missions* (March 1935), 135.

23. "The Wandering Jew in the 20th Century," *Missions* (March 1935), 137.

24. Editorial, "The Jews Give Thanks for Baptist Principles," *Missions* (October 1935), 477.

25. The Balfour Declaration was a brief letter from Arthur James Balfour, on behalf of the English government, to Lord Rothschild, dated 2 November 1917. The letter's support for Zionism inspired Jewish hopes for a homeland in Palestine.

26. Charles F. Banning, "Today and Tomorrow in Palestine," *Missions* (April 1936), 204–7.

27. William B. Lipphard, "The Historic Baptist Principle for Today," *Missions* (June 1936), 342–43.

28. "The Jew at Geneva Asks the Christian an Embarrassing Question," *Missions* (November 1936), 518.

29. "Jews and Christians Need Two Days for One Day's Observance," *Missions* (February 1937), 94.

30. "The Library," *Missions* (April 1937), 230. See Marvin Lowenthal, *The Jews of Germany: A Story of Sixteen Centuries* (Philadelphia: The Jewish Publication Society of America, 1936), 369–421.

31. "The Rising Tide of Prejudice against the Jew," *Missions* (September 1937), 390–91.

32. "Exiles from Germany Aided by the Rockefeller Foundation," *Missions* (September 1937), 391: "Of the 1,690 German teachers, professors and research workers who lost their positions, either because they were Jewish or had been married to Jews or because they held political and social views not in accord with Nazi philosophy, the Foundation aided 835 who are now employed in institutions in 46 countries."

33. William B. Lipphard, "The Christian Church in the Modern World," *Missions* (October 1937), 463. Italics in original.

34. Ibid. For the official report of the conference, see J. H. Oldham, *The Oxford Conference* (Official Report) (Chicago: Willett, Clark, 1937). *Missions* did not mention that Horton was a Baptist; for a listing of Baptists participants, see R. Birch Hoyle, "Oecumenical Conference at Oxford," *The Baptist Times* (29 July 1937), 573.

35. William B. Lipphard, "From Hitler's Fair to Hungary's Flagpole," *Missions* (January 1938), 11–12.

36. "Five Million Jews Not Wanted in Central and Eastern Europe," *Missions* (February 1938), 73. This friendship was in evidence when Jews attended the three hundredth anniversary of Baptists in Rhode Island; see Coe Hayne, "Three Hundred Years in Rhode Island," *Missions* (September 1938), 412–15.

37. See, for example, Rushbrooke's remarks at the 1938 Northern Baptist convention, as reported in *Missions* (June 1938), 351.

38. "Rumania Reopens Baptist Churches and Suppresses the Jews," *Missions* (March 1938), 141.

39. William B. Lipphard, "The Balance Sheet of Hitlerism," *Missions* (December 1938), 586–91.

40. William B. Lipphard, "The Wandering Jew—Where Can He Go Now?" *Missions* (January 1939), 12.

41. Ibid., 14.

42. The Evian Conference took place July 6-15, 1938, in response to the Jewish refugee problem created by Germany. Although delegations from thirty-two participating countries expressed sympathy for the Jews, no country committed to any plans for practical relief. Evian became a symbol of the passive bystander response adopted by Great Britain, the United States, and other nations. See Theodore S. Hamerow, *Why We Watched: Europe, America, and the Holocaust* (New York: W. W. Norton, 2008), 111–16.

43. Lipphard, "Wandering Jew,"16.

44. J. H. Rushbrooke, "Unshakable Unity Amid Overwhelming Calamity," *Missions* (October 1939), 490.

45. William B. Lipphard, "Just before Zero in Europe," *Missions* (November 1939), 520–27.

46. "The Library," *Missions* (December 1939), 611. See Jacques Maritain, *A Christian Looks at the Jewish Question* (New York: Longmans, Green, 1939).

47. Editorial, "The Dark New Year," *Missions* (January 1940), 7.

48. "Christian Friendliness Meets the Refugee," *Missions* (February 1940), 112–13, 126. On the work of these extraordinary missionaries, see chapters 4 and 9.

49. William B. Lipphard, "American Christianity in a Time of War," *Missions* (April 1940), 225. Italics in the original.

50. John Stuart Conning, "The Jew in America—What Will You Do with Him?" *Missions* (September 1940), 394–97.

51. "Race Segregation in Poland Now Complete," *Missions* (February 1941), 72.

52. William B. Lipphard, "Not War nor Appeasement but Reconciliation," *Missions* (February 1941), 84–87.

53. Hoffman served as secretary of the Presbyterian Board of National Missions in charge of Jewish work, and he was popular with Baptists. In 1941, Hoffman authored *The Jews Today: A Call to Christian Action* (New York: Friendship Press, 1941), in which he attacked anti-Semitism in both its global and domestic variations. He later published *What Now for the Jews? A Challenge to the Christian Conscience* (New York: Friendship Press, 1948). See also "The Christian Approach to the Jews," *The Watchman-Examiner* (11 October 1934), 1089.

54. Conrad Hoffman, "The Wandering and Wondering Jew," *Missions* (February 1941), 88–89.

55. "Jewish Loyalty to Britain and Arab Neutrality in Palestine," *Missions* (April 1941), 200.

56. Ruth G. McCrossen, "The Horrors of Nazi Europe Are behind Them," *Missions* (March 1942), 157–58. See Gabrielle Simon Edgcomb, *From Swastika to Jim Crow: Refugee Scholars at Black Colleges* (Malabar, FL: Krieger Publishing Company, 1993).

57. Editorial, "Is This the Beginning of Nazism in America?", *Missions* (September 1942), 422; the use of lowercase "nazi" instead of "Nazi" is in the original text. See also "Japanese Fiendishness and Nazi Brutality Compared with American Barbarism," *Missions* (March 1942), 161–62; "What Has Happened to America's Japanese?" *Missions* (November 1942), 533–38; "Does Relocation Center Really Mean an American Type of Ghetto?" *Missions* (February 1943), 99.

58. "America Becomes a Haven of Refuge for 5,000 Jewish Children from France," *Missions* (January 1943), 9. Italics in original text.

59. "Ten Horrible Years of Persecution of the Jew," *Missions* (April 1943), 204.

60. Ibid. Variant spelling of "naziism" is in the original text.

61. Ibid., 204–5.

62. Untitled editorial, *Missions* (March 1944), 164.

63. "Will the Doom of a People Be Sealed on March 31, 1944?" *Missions* (March 1944), 206.

64. "Was the End of March the Ides of March for the Jews?" *Missions* (May 1944), 270–71.

65. "What Will Happen to 2,000,000 People Who Have Lost Their Citizenship?" *Missions* (June 1944), 325.

66. "President Roosevelt Pledges Support to Jews in Palestine," *Missions* (December 1944), 546.

67. "What Is to Be the Fate of Europe's 1,500,000 Surviving Jews?" *Missions* (December 1945), 522–23.

68. "Map of Europe Showing the Surviving Jewish Population in Each Country" and "The Terrible Fate of the Jew after Twelve Years of Anti-Semitism," *Missions* (November 1946), 522–23.

69. "What Was Once the Holy Land Has Become the Terror Land," *Missions* (December 1946), 586–87. See also Lipphard's judgment: "The evil of anti-semitism has not been eradicated with the collapse of naziism," in "Unsolved Problems in Postwar Germany," *Missions* (December 1946), 588–89.

70. "The Long Awaited Fulfillment of a Jewish National Dream," *Missions* (February 1948), 74–75.

Chapter 5

The Watchman-Examiner

The Watchman-Examiner was a religiously conservative and evangelical Baptist newspaper that enjoyed a national readership. While friendly with the Northern Baptist Convention, it was not owned or controlled by the convention. It operated as a weekly newspaper, which permitted it to cover developing news stories more quickly and in greater detail than *Missions*. *The Watchman-Examiner* enjoyed positive working relationships with other Baptist newspapers from around the world, including *The Baptist Times* of London and *The Canadian Baptist*. The newspaper encouraged vigorous debates on controversial issues, and leading preachers and denominational personalities were invited to expound on issues facing the Baptist movement.

The Rise of Nazism and Jewish Persecution (1933–1938)

The first reference in *The Watchman-Examiner* to Hitler's persecution of German Jewry appeared in the March 30, 1933, issue, and it concerned an undated Boston ministers' meeting at which Dr. Samuel M. Lindsay commented on the "expulsion of the Jews from Germany under Hitler's dictatorship."[1] A week later, the paper's first editorial about the persecution of German Jews distinguished between the actions of the Nazi officials and the German people: "The ruling powers in Germany . . . are outdoing Russia in religious and social persecution. The Jews seem to be the particular objects of this bitter animosity. The German people as a whole cannot be held responsible. . . . It is the present government that is responsible."[2]

In June, *The Watchman-Examiner* published J. H. Rushbrooke's initial impressions of the Nazi political agenda. Rushbrooke was concerned with the rights and privileges of the German Baptists, but he ignored the plight of Germany's Jews. He admitted that there were Nazis within the ranks of German Baptists, but he expressed hope that Baptist leaders would not compromise "essential principles" or "loyalty to spiritual freedom and New Testament truth." Rushbrooke even imagined the possibility of Baptist support for Hitler: "There are elements in the policy of the present Government in Germany which command the strong support of Baptists, and the Reich will gain enormously if it adopts a policy of respect for the rights of the free evangelical communities."[3]

In contrast to Rushbrooke, *The Watchman-Examiner* noticed that the Jewish situation required close attention. It noted that "five hundred refugee German Jews had arrived in Palestine up to April 25, and many more are stated to be on the way."[4] On July 20, 1933, it published its second editorial on the subject, "Sympathy for German Jews." The paper criticized Germany's autocratic turn and the Nazis' "brutality and terrorism" against Jews: "A new law has been passed, which forbids Jews or those with Jewish family affiliations from holding office in the Reich, the states, municipalities or any other kind of public corporation or institution. This includes people who are connected by family ties with those of Jewish blood. This is supposed to affect between 2,000,000 and 3,000,000 people."[5] By August, the newspaper was worried about how the outflow of German Jewish refugees would be handled: "It is estimated that there are still 500,000 Jews in Germany. It is feared that these Jews will all be driven out and compelled to find residence in other countries of the world. Palestine may take 30,000 yearly."[6]

A third editorial reiterated *The Watchman-Examiner*'s strong political solidarity with Jews but added a new twist that differentiated this newspaper from the stand taken by the more mainstream and liberal contingents of the Northern Baptist Convention. The newspaper was uneasy with the good-will movement that sought to replace evangelistic outreach with ecumenical acceptance:

> THE HITLERITES ARE shamelessly persecuting the Jews. This return to medieval barbarism has aroused the indignation of the world. Nations and individuals are expressing their sympathy with the victims

> of this hatred in many ways. We are among those who sympathize most heartily with all movements to show the Nazis that intelligent people everywhere despise their attitude and methods. We cannot help but notice as a result of this sympathy, a recrudescence of the idea that Christians and Jews are fellow-religionists. This is unfortunate for it is fallacious. The Jews of the New Testament according to Christ needed the Gospel as much as the Gentiles. The Jews of the present day need the gospel as much as the Japanese, the Chinese, the Italians, the French, the English, the Americans or the Negroes. Judaism and Christianity are not on a parity. The Jew needs to be saved by the gospel of Jesus Christ. . . . The Hitlerites are treating the Jews abominably, but that does not lock the arms of Christianity and Judaism as co-religions.[7]

The fourth editorial of 1933, "Germany and the Jews," grudgingly admitted the validity of some anti-Semitic charges but nevertheless condemned Hitler's response to the Jewish situation in his country: "The whole world seems to be aroused over the persecution of the Jews by the Hitler government of Germany. There are many complications. No doubt it is true that the foreign Jews have been successful in Germany to the hurt of the native people. No doubt many of them have proved disagreeable. When all has been said, however, the method of the Hitlerites has been unjust and cruel."[8]

In the year's fifth and final editorial, *The Watchman-Examiner* contextualized the Jewish plight within the framework of nationalism. It was the paper's first recognition that anti-Semitism was not incidental to Nazi aims but central to its vision for the future of the German people:

> TO GET TO the heart of the problem that current nationalism presents to organized Christianity, let us consider the situation in Germany. By persuasion and force the Nazi (national) leaders have made Germany almost to a man a unified machine for nationalistic ends. What end or ends? The answer is racial supremacy. The Jews are persecuted, not because they are not Catholic or Protestant, but because they are Jews. It is not a matter of religion, but of race.[9]

The editorial also categorically rejected the Aryan paragraph, which prevented Jewish converts from holding pastoral positions within the German church: "Christianity knows nothing of the self-imposed superiority of one racial group over another; nothing of the greed and hatred that turns men into beasts athirst for blood."[10] In its January 4, 1934, issue, the paper noted Barth's famous "no" opposing "a church from which Jews are excluded."[11]

Most of *The Watchman-Examiner*'s coverage of Germany in 1934 concerned the Baptist World Congress in Berlin. It published a full-page article on the religious situation in Germany by Julius Janssen, who taught at the Hamburg Baptist Seminary. He claimed that German Baptists were enjoying freedom and only obliquely referred to a major November 13, 1933, meeting that featured a speech against the Old Testament by Dr. Reinhold Krause.[12] What Janssen omitted was that Krause explicitly stated, "Chancellor Hitler has taught us that we must be a racially pure people. . . . This principle must be applied to the church."[13] This was the first of several German Baptist attempts to entice the global Baptist community to Berlin while avoiding taking any stance on Nazi anti-Semitism.

The tentative program for the BWA congress was published in the February 22, 1934, issue. Although Rushbrooke had previously announced that the selection of Berlin was settled,[14] Illinois Baptist G. B. Hopkins wondered if meeting in Berlin would cause Baptists to lose their prophetic voice on the separation of church and state and other key issues. In light of Krause's views, Hopkins asked, "There are Baptist Negroes, Indians, Chinese, Japanese, Slovaks, and even Jews and people of every nation under heaven. Can all these be free to meet in common fellowship? Will delegates be allowed to quote the Old Testament?"[15] Two weeks later, the paper admitted it had been against Berlin as a site for the congress in 1933 and that "we are now receiving many letters declaring that the decision was a grave mistake."[16]

Rushbrooke, however, won the debate through tireless effort,[17] but not without having to respond to the charges and concerns. Baptist principles and discussion on controversial issues such as "racialism" would not be silenced.[18] F. W. Simoleit, on behalf of German Baptists, declared "members of all races coming to the congress will be welcome guests."[19] The paper even published a brief letter from Hans Luther, the German ambassador to the United States, welcoming Baptists to the forthcoming event.[20]

The congress went on as planned in Berlin from August 4-10, 1934, and *The Watchman-Examiner* covered the proceedings in a detailed series of articles. German representatives praised the leadership of Adolf Hitler, and John W. Bradbury quoted one German delegate, Rev. Henry Vieler, as stating that "whenever a race becomes a destructive force within the nation it is the duty of a government to take such measures as will put that race in its place"—an unmistakable justification of the Nazi mistreatment of the German Jews. Rushbrooke replied, "There are some elements of National Socialism with which we do not agree. We stand not for a section of the people, but for all."[21] Bradbury and other Baptist delegates were quite impressed with the new Germany and minimized the Jewish situation in light of the success of the congress: "It was a great relief to be in a country where salacious sex literature cannot be sold; where putrid motion pictures and gangster films cannot be shown. The new Germany has burned great masses of corrupting magazines and books along with its bonfires of Jewish and communistic libraries."[22]

In contrast, BWA President Clifton D. Gray prayed that the fifth congress would "send throughout the earth the voices of a thousand Luthers crying out against race bigotry."[23] *The Watchman-Examiner* reproduced the powerful address by M. E. Aubrey, the leading English Baptist opponent of Nazism and an ardent advocate for persecuted Jews:

> TYRANNIES HAVE HAD their day before but they have always gone down sooner or later, and they will go down again. . . . God treats all alike. Christ died for all. . . . We can hate and despise none whom Christ loved. Our duty is to serve all and to bless all—Greek and Barbarian, Gentile and Jew. In that sense we declare the equality of men and resist all those forces of the world that seek to raise barriers between races and between nations.[24]

In the afterglow of the congress, *The Watchman-Examiner* unwittingly contrasted the sadly ironic relationship between its speeches and resolutions, no matter how high sounding, and Baptist deeds. It honored Rushbrooke with the final word on the significance of the congress; the general secretary declared: "I am again astonished that anyone ever imagined that Baptists would shrink from speaking. These utterances have evoked wide response from outside our borders. The world knows that we are not ready to compromise on the freedom of the church, nor to condone anti-semitism, nor to abandon our witness and work for international peace. . . . We can hold up our heads and praise God that we did not miss our unique opportunity."[25]

But in the previous week's issue, the paper had noted: "A survey recently published in Berlin by the Central Welfare Committee of German Jews shows that 70,000 Jews have emigrated from Germany as a result of the Nazis anti-Semetic [*sic*] campaign. Another 120,000 Jews, under thirty years of age, will leave if they can find work abroad. . . . The rest will have to emigrate on the basis of their own resourcefulness."[26] In 1935 and 1936, *The Watchman-Examiner* repeatedly returned to this ongoing humanitarian crisis. The paper published a detailed overview of Zionism in its January 17, 1935, issue, which observed that "a new Palestine" is represented by a "transformation . . . being brought about by the Jewish immigrant from Europe and America."[27] The paper also noted that "Hebrew University at Jerusalem has added to its faculty 14 new professors from a group of renowned exiled German scholars."[28] In January 1936, the paper relayed an urgent appeal from the *Jewish Review* to resettle some "200,000" German Jewish emigrants.[29]

Although *The Watchman-Examiner* was sympathetic to Jews discovering a new life in Palestine, it did not believe that Zionism could cure their spiritual needs: "The solution of the Jewish problem is not Palestine, but Jesus Christ!"[30] True to its evangelical convictions, the paper published a speech by an Episcopalian bishop that criticized American Christians who were "not hospitable to Jews and do not want them in their churches."[31]

In its September 24, 1936, issue, *The Watchman-Examiner* reported on the growing reach of German anti-Semitism: "Austria's 250,000 Jews are watching with growing anxiety the spread of a new anti-Semitic campaign, close on the heels of this nation's pact of friendship with Nazi Germany. Some Jewish leaders hold to the belief Austria no longer is a safe harbor for their people, largely as a result of the Austro-German treaty and growth of the Nazi party in that country. Jewish communities were said to be swamped with applications for emigration to Palestine and other countries."[32] The paper reprinted an editorial from *The Baptist Times* of London, which criticized the Nazis: "Germany is still engaged in a desperate attempt to stamp out the Jewish element of her population."[33] It noted that Christian, as well as Jewish, refugees needed assistance, and then made a startling claim about who was caring for these Christians:

> WHEREAS THE JEWISH organizations have come generously to the relief of Jewish refugees, the Christian world has thus far done practically nothing for Christian refugees but, we must believe through ignorance of the facts, has left many of them to starvation or suicide. Most of the assistance that Christian refugees have received has come from Jewish sources thus far. But we cannot in good conscience leave it to our Jewish friends longer to care for these unfortunate Christian brethren and, indeed, in view of the burdens they are carrying in many parts of the world for their own people, they are not able, however well-disposed they may be, to do so.[34]

The plight of Jewish Christian refugees was highlighted further in April 1937.[35]

Also in April 1937, the newspaper declared, "If history teaches anything it is that the nations that have attempted to exterminate the Jews have in the end committed suicide."[36] It reported that "Germany's Jewish population has been reduced by 90,000 in the four years of the Hitler regime."[37] In the July 15, 1937, issue, a lengthy editorial lamented "racial, political or religious refugees nowadays are in a most pitiable plight," in part because "the League of Nations has not been able to solve the refugee problem." In Germany and elsewhere, "millions of Jews live under the threat of dire persecution."

Meanwhile, the BWA felt mounting pressure to speak out on the persecution of German Jews. In a press release, the executive committee continued to focus primarily on the difficulties Baptists were facing in Rumania, and then it noted that "attention was directed toward the restrictions upon religious freedom and the prevalence of repression and persecution in various countries." It recalled the 1934 resolution on church and state, which did not explicitly mention Jews, and then declared that "the entire Baptist communion throughout the world [was] resolutely opposed to religious repression of every kind, whether directed against Baptists or others, and it expresses the unwavering sympathy of all our people for the victims of persecution or repression whether belonging to our own or any other communion."[38] The plight of European Jews was not explicitly mentioned.

The Watchman-Examiner continued to be concerned with Zionism during the second half of 1937. In response to England's proposed partition plan, it asked, "Can it be otherwise than that in the restoration of Israel we are looking upon a racial movement under divine intervention?" The editorial answered its own question: "A Jewish state, with millions of Jews outside that state, will soon achieve remarkable power and international solidarity."[39] Just two weeks before Kristallnacht, the paper extolled the "ethnological miracle" of the Jewish people and eagerly anticipated the restoration of Palestine as a Jewish homeland.[40]

Unfortunately, Jews were destined to suffer before achieving the glorious Zionist future prophesied by *The Watchman-Examiner*: "Poland appears to be moving in the direction that is anti-Semitic. . . . The Polish government is planning the wholesale 'evacuation' of all Jews. The magnitude of the threat is startling."[41] In 1938, the newspaper broke ranks with the BWA on the plight of Rumanian Jews[42] and shared that "the new government of Rumania recently threatened to outlaw 800,000 Rumanian Jews."[43] It followed up with an editorial that increased the number of affected Jews to one million, curiously adding that "the situation is even more serious than it has been in Germany for there is lacking that element of moderation which has restrained the extremists there."[44] More than "3,000 Jews in the province of Burgenland" in Austria were "recently expelled from their homes by local Nazi organizations."[45] Even the persecution of Jews in the country of Ecuador received attention.[46]

The newspaper's sympathy for persecuted Jews did not prevent it from expressing criticism of American Jews. In reaction to reports that Jews were not accepting the validity of Jewish conversion to Christianity, the paper offered some "friendly advice":

> ANTI-SEMITISM THRIVES most where there are fewest Jews or where Jews maroon themselves as a segregated race. Jewish isolation has been generally charged—frequently for cause—to Gentile race prejudice; but Jews have not always cultivated the fellowship of their Gentile neighbors in an acceptable way. It is of little use for Jews in this country to cry out for tolerance and then for them to practice intolerance among

> themselves. . . . And no Jew should be persecuted by fellow Jews because God has come into his life through faith in Jesus Christ.[47]

The Watchman-Examiner's initial coverage of Kristallnacht was minimal. On November 24, it admitted that the "Jews are certainly having a terrible time in Central Europe."[48] It also reported that a Baptist pastors' conference in Knoxville passed a resolution protesting totalitarian persecution of Jews,[49] and an African American church in New York passed a resolution "denouncing the persecution of the Jews in Germany, and in addition, calling attention to the sufferings endured by Negroes in this country where lynch law prevails."[50] In Rochester and New York City, Baptists participated in protests; the Metropolitan Ministers Conference of New York passed a strong resolution, which emphasized core Baptist convictions as well as the idea of "the sacredness of human personality":

> AS BAPTISTS WHOSE forefathers have stood valiantly for the principles of religious liberties of all peoples and the separation of church and state and have always proclaimed the tenets which make for good will, toleration and the recognition of the sacredness of human personality, therefore be it resolved that this conference of Baptist ministers of Greater New York and vicinity go on record as deeply deploring the increased hatreds of races and express our sympathy for the oppressed and afflicted in Europe and call upon our people to exert every influence to prevent religious and racial antipathies and antagonisms of all kinds and under all considerations and circumstances.[51]

The paper responded more fully to Kristallnacht in an editorial on December 8, 1938, calling Jews "friends" while encouraging them to consider the messianic claims of Christ:

> THE TREATMENT ACCORDED Jews in Europe, and especially in Germany, has awakened in the hearts of truly Christian people everywhere a deep sympathy for these suffering people. One of the reactions in this country is to bring Jews and Christians into closer fellowship. For centuries Jews have suffered in lands reputedly Christian. This has developed a great prejudice in their hearts against organized Christianity. Their recent sufferings, however, have drawn forth from Christians

in this country such a strong denunciation of their persecutors that now they are coming to see that real Christians have no prejudice against them whatsoever on account of their race or religion. We cherish the hope that because of this display of sympathy and loving interest our friends the Jews will strive to learn what is the faith of Jesus Christ and the holy things for which he died and for which he lives eternally.[52]

The Watchman-Examiner argued that only the fulfillment of the Zionist dream of a Jewish homeland in Palestine could serve as a solution to the Jewish problem, calling alternatives such as Tanganyika and British Guiana laughable in the midst of "this racial tragedy."[53] In the last issue of 1938, the paper remembered, "The afflicted Jews have seen themselves increasingly persecuted during the year."[54]

The War Years (1939–1945)

As Europe continued its slow march to war in 1939, *The Watchman-Examiner* contrasted Christian internationalism and Nazi ideology. Southern Baptist Everett Gill wrote that although Jesus was a Jew, "he loved also men of all nations and races. He was not protagonist of 'race, blood and land.' He was an internationalist in both theory and practice."[55] The periodical observed that German Jews were filing into Italy but were faced with "new anti-Semitic laws requiring them to leave within six months."[56] Former president Herbert Hoover wrote: "Americans should and are expressing their indignation at the terrible outbreak of Jewish persecution in Germany and the assaults on Christian churches. . . . They are bringing to Germany a moral isolation from the entire world."[57] The paper published a graphic summary of Kristallnacht in its coverage of a Quaker visit to Germany:

WE FOUND THE agony of suffering almost greater than we expected. The "glass-breaking day"—November 10—had destroyed every synagogue in Germany, so that all corporate worship for Jews in that country was at an end. Nearly every Jewish shop, and many private homes, had all the glass on the street-front smashed and much of the property destroyed. Thirty-five thousand Jewish men were carried off to concentration camps, where most of them still were during the nine days of

> arctic cold and storm which enveloped Europe during our visit. It was a veritable reign of terror for those long-suffering people.[58]

The BWA's reticence to address Kristallnacht was challenged in an editorial entitled "Baptist Leadership and Our Historic Principles." The editorial acknowledged that "the impression has been created that our world Baptist leadership is merely paying lip service to our historic principles without effect." The editorial praised the Berlin congress, during which Baptists confronted unnamed "tyrannies."[59] Surprisingly, a week later *Mein Kampf* received mention. The reviewer paid little attention to the book's insistent anti-Semitism. Instead, he praised the work: "Mein Kampf is one of the most outstanding literary achievements of this century. Hitler has a particularly tenacious mind. He sticks to his principles and ideas until he has vindicated them according to his own processes of logic and unique concepts of justice."[60]

Meanwhile, the European outlook for Jews continued to appear bleak. "Fascism in Italy has revealed its compliance with the Germanic idea by passing its own Aryan law and launching an attack on Jews."[61] Regarding Christian anti-Semitism in Poland, Rumania, and Hungary, an editorial claimed, "European Baptists do not act so as to invite this stigma."[62] In truth, this could not be said of German Baptists. The paper mentioned that some 244,000 Jews had left Germany.[63] Jews were said to have been excluded from the 1939 Rumanian elections.[64]

The Watchman-Examiner covered the 1939 BWA congress in Atlanta in detail. Although the Nazi flag was on display as part of a gallery of flags, "officials of the Congress pointed out that there is no political or racial prejudice where Baptists get together."[65] British leader M. E. Aubrey attacked Hitler and Nazism, based on core Baptist convictions of liberty, democracy, and personality: "In America and England, where modern democracy was born, it sprang from the Christian religion as it was proclaimed in certain Christian churches. Their insistence on a man's right to freedom and a voice in the government of the community to which he belonged was based on a sense of human personality and had its roots in a definite religious experience. . . . Tyranny and evangelical Christianity cannot exist together."[66]

A German Baptist leader, Rev. Paul Schmidt, rejected Aubrey's interpretation and defended the experience of Baptists under Hitler, which he described as positive.[67] Similarly, another German Baptist delegate, Rev. F. Rockschies, said to three hundred German-speaking attendees: "We are convinced that the German Fuehrer has full confidence in the integrity of Baptists and their loyalty to the present government. With God almighty still in control of human affairs, and with Adolf Hitler, who has led the German people out of a desperate situation into unity and strength, our faith is in good hands."[68] German Baptist leaders who were permitted to travel internationally were unabashed Nazi loyalists and willing apologists for their government, even as it unleashed wave after wave of anti-Semitic attacks.

In contrast to the silence of German Baptists on Jews, Dr. J. W. Decker described the impact the victims of Hitler's governmental policies made on his heart during a trip to the Netherlands:

> OUR PASSENGER LIST is largely made up of Jewish refugees from the Nazi terror. In April we had seen this same tide of helpless and distressed people—men, women, and children—disgorging itself on war wrecked Shanghai, already burdened with an overwhelming refugee problem of its own. In our meeting, nothing stirred us more than a recital of the unspeakable suffering of the Jews in Germany today. Surely the plight of the Jew calls to America, the traditional haven of the oppressed, for pity and for action. Christians must lead the way in this and in vigilance against anti-Semitism in the United States itself.[69]

After war in Europe broke out in September 1939, Rushbrooke argued that it was morally right to fight against "injustice, oppression, persecution," while also asserting that the war should not harm relations between Baptists on either side of the conflict and that Germans were suffering. He also stated, "The Nazi theory has no room for the free man, and the Nazi practice crushes and dehumanizes."[70] Rufus Weaver, executive secretary of the DC Baptist Convention, was more forthcoming when he asserted, "The Jews have been in Germany the greatest sufferers."[71] *The Watchman-Examiner* sided with Weaver:

> BASED ON THE pre-war Jewish population of 3,200,000, the partition of Poland by Germany and Soviet Russia gave to the former about

> 2,000,000 Jews. Several hundred thousand are subsequently reported to have fled into the Soviet areas to escape Nazi terrorism. . . . Thus, about 2,300,000 Jews are now under Nazi rule. Indications are that they are not considered desirable citizens by either country. . . . Persistent reports give the impression that a special region for Jews is being established around Lublin in the southeastern part of Poland. Thousands of Jews from Vienna and the Bohemia-Moravia Protectorates have already been sent there. What this means in terms of broken families, breaking hearts, and bewildered lives is apparent. Unspeakable sorrow and misery is the lot of these exiled Jews. Emigration is still open to them, but there is no country to welcome them because they must go as penniless wanderers. Their only real hope is Palestine.[72]

In February 1940, Rushbrooke defended the BWA, asserting, "We have not been content to issue pronouncements." Several Baptist delegates to the Atlanta congress who could not return to Europe were relocated in the United States. Some Jewish refugees were assisted, "but not with funds of the Alliance, for its budget includes no provision for these special needs, but as a result of direct appeals to British Baptists." However, the BWA was able to process emergency funds for the German Baptist Union's mission in the Cameroons, where Rushbrooke's "beloved friend of many years" was the director.[73]

In April, the newspaper noted "the first act of the Danish Nazis upon German seizure of the country was to lay a heavy hand on Jews in Denmark.[74] J. C. Carlile, the outspoken editor of *The Baptist Times* of London, criticized the German Baptist silence on Jews: "The church [in England] could mind her own business, as she is said to be doing in Germany, which means that she is silent concerning concentration camps, the iniquitous treatment of the Jews, and the horrors of Poland."[75] At the Northern Baptist Convention meeting, Conrad Hoffman sought to raise funds for "Jewish and Christian non-Aryan refugees who seek to escape from Hitler's racial anti-Semitism." He posed a haunting question for the delegates: "What will the Baptist churches do?"[76]

Meanwhile, *The Watchman-Examiner* reported that the Jewish populations in several countries were under threat. In Holland and Belgium, "native Jews in those countries and the large number of refugees, some of them in transit, will receive no better treatment than in Germany or Poland. It is reported that the Lublin (Poland) ghetto plan is to be installed near Amsterdam and 160,000 Jews are to be moved there. Jews are also seized for forced labor in cleaning up the wreckage wrought by Nazi bombers."[77]

In October, *The Watchman-Examiner* reported that the aim of Hitler was "a Europe without Jews."[78] The newspaper provided statistics to assess the progress of Hitler's campaign: "Of the 650,000 Jews who lived in Germany in 1933, 200,000 have fled from Germany, 30,000 are in concentration camps, 20,000 have committed suicide, 8,000 have been murdered, and 90,000 have died."[79] At the beginning of 1941, the newspaper approvingly highlighted the aspirations of Jewish refugees to return to Palestine: "In the last eight years, 280,000 Jewish refugees have reached Palestine from Europe. The one hope in the bosoms of millions of Jews in Europe today is that they may reach the land of their fathers."[80]

In support of the annual Race Relations Sunday, the newspaper recognized that Hitler's *Mein Kampf* "made race the foundation of nationality" in which there "could be no Jewish parent or grandparent." The result had been devastating: "What anguish this theory of racial superiority wrought in countless thousands of human beings thus discriminated against is all too apparent."[81] The plight of Polish refugees was just one more illustration.[82]

Reflecting the paper's evangelical perspective, Jewish Christian evangelist Morris Gordin claimed that Nazi and communist persecutions were leading Jews in Poland to convert. In the United States, the assimilation of Jewish immigrants and the loss of traditional Jewish faith had created a similar spiritual hunger. He advocated for an evangelistic thrust by Christians, who should not succumb to a "satanic, anti-Jewish bias" that Jews cannot convert to Christianity.[83] As much as the newspaper supported the Jewish return to Palestine, it could also assert, "The tragedy of it is that so many Jews are pinning their hopes on Zionism and continuing to shut their eyes to their real Savior and Messiah, the Lord Jesus Christ."[84]

In May 1941, *The Watchman-Examiner* reexamined the Northern Baptist preference for pacifism and its opposition to military action even when diplomacy failed. In the face of Hitler's totalitarianism that was enslaving whole populations in Europe, the newspaper admitted: "Knowing these things, we cannot accept the modern pacifist's creed. There is no pacifism where tyranny conquers, except it be that of an enforced subjugation or a cemetery. To us it is a horrible thing that the souls and bodies of our fellow human beings shall be the chattels of a dictator's conquering might."[85]

Similarly, at the Northern Baptist convention, President E. J. Millington proclaimed: "There are things which are worse than war—slavery is worse, submission is worse; tyranny is worse; dishonor is worse, and the hope of the world . . . is the splendor of the human spirit."[86] Rev. Daniel Poling preached that "the Jew can stand persecution . . . but Christianity cannot live and fail to denounce it."[87] Jeanne Bradbury warned, "When the shadow of the swastika spreads over Europe, it carries with it the disease of anti-Semitism, a deadly virus which I trust we shall refuse to harbor."[88]

On September 11, 1941, the newspaper acknowledged that "from humanitarian considerations alone, the plight of millions of Jews the world around is most pitiable." The persecution of the Jews was of a different order than other nationalities undergoing oppression, and the editorial rejected the idea that the Jews deserved to suffer more than others due to their own shortcomings. Although in rejecting Jesus, the Jews collectively were "outside his providential protection," God was not to blame for their suffering. Satan was responsible for "the malice now being heaped on Jews." Therefore, Christians should stand in solidarity with the Jewish people, while also sharing "the gospel" with them.[89]

There may have been negative feedback to the editorial, for in the October 23, 1941, issue, the newspaper defended its position on anti-Semitism: "This paper hardly needs to state its position on anti-Semitism. It will be a sad day when the United States lends itself to the persecution of minorities as have the totalitarian countries of Europe. Many of our leading people are Jews, and our country owes a great debt to them for their loyalty and their generosity to all good causes. The Jews take care of the unfortunate of their own race and they do not become a public charity. Of course, we are against anti-Semitism in every form, and so are all right-minded people."[90]

As 1941 came to an end, *The Watchman-Examiner* twice referred to Nazi concentration camps. While Nazis had incarcerated "hundreds of churchmen" in the camps, Germans were manifesting signs of religious devotion: "There is widespread emphasis on the sacred rights of personality and the uniqueness of the Christian faith as over against the exaggerated nationalistic tendencies" of the Nazis.[91] Regarding Baptists in Norway, O. E. Anshus sadly stated that his country was a "land of blackouts and concentration camps."[92] At the beginning of 1942, the paper surveyed the state of persecuted Jewry throughout Europe:

> HOW PITIABLE IS the state of Jews in Europe. Singled out as the object of unspeakable hatred, large numbers of them are herded into limited property areas in Eastern Poland where typhus is daily taking its toll of death. In all countries under the blight of aggression, malice against Jews is fostered. In France, where Jews have enjoyed equality of opportunity for generations, they now exist under oppressive laws, their possessions are confiscated, and hostages are taken from among their number to be executed as reprisals for crimes with which they have had nothing to do. From the Middle Ages down to recent times, Holland has been an asylum for Jews and their citizenship there has been respected. Now, such horrible conditions are imposed that both Protestants and Catholics have cried out against the anti-Semitic measures of the Nazi administrators. Spain and Italy have only a comparatively small number of Jews, but even these helpless minorities tremble for their lives. Firing squads eliminating Jews are the daily order in certain Balkan countries. Such concentrated malice against the Jew is diabolical.[93]

The newspaper reported that "more than 1,000,000 Jews in Hungary are slowly being eliminated from the economic, cultural, and social life of the country. . . . It is estimated that 8,000,000 Jews are now under the control of Nazi Germany."[94] Concern for European Jews after Nazism's demise prompted *The Watchman-Examiner* to reaffirm the Zionist hope of the surviving Jews: "The Jews have an ancient moral claim to Palestine. . . . As the last World War ended in the designation of Palestine as the national home of the Jews—never completely realized as of yet—so, without doubt, the end of this war will see the Jews returning in large numbers to the land of their God-given heritage."[95]

By October 1942, the paper acknowledged that "more than 1,000,000 Jews have been killed or died as the result of ill treatment by the Nazis."[96] It was also very concerned about the Nazi insistence that the French "assist in the collection of Jews for deportation to the German Reich."[97] But it also sensed that the Christian faith was imperiled by the Nazi campaign against the Jews: "The attack in recent years upon the Jews is not solely a racial matter, it is religious. In their malice toward the Jews, the totalitarian nationalists have not hesitated to get rid of Jesus, because he was a Jew, as pertaining to the flesh."[98]

On November 28, 1942, Rabbi Stephen Wise revealed to the world that the Nazis were systematically exterminating the Jewish population of Europe. Soon afterward, Rushbrooke shared his correspondence with Rabbi J. H. Hertz with the readers of *The Watchman-Examiner*.[99] It stands as the clearest testimony of the Baptist leader's opposition to Hitler and anti-Semitism. On February 4, 1943, *The Watchman-Examiner* published Wise's assertion "that about half the 4 million Jews in Nazi occupied Europe have been slain."[100] By the end of September 1943, *The Watchman-Examiner* was reporting that five million Jews were dead.

In an editorial about Russian Jews seeking freedom of worship, it said: "The appeal [from the Jews] carries the statement that ten years ago the Jewish population of Europe numbered 8,300,000. This has been reduced by 5,000,000. In the whole of Continental Europe, embracing 24 countries occupied by the Axis, only 3,000,000 Jews remain alive."[101] As in the past, the newspaper's solution for the remaining Jews was emigration to Palestine: "Palestine remains the best hope of the suffering Jewish people. The Jews are the one race within the family of nations without a commonwealth located in a definite place. The Jews have a right to cherish the hope that Palestine will be made their national center in the post-war world."[102]

In December 1943, the newspaper once again reported on the situation in France, where "increasing numbers of Jews in the southern zone of France are being arrested and sent to the Drancy Concentration Camp, which is the jumping off place for deportation to Eastern Europe." The editors prayed for God to "intervene to shorten this horror and that succor may soon come to the afflicted."[103]

Three themes dominated the newspaper's coverage of the closing years of the war. First, *The Watchman-Examiner* occasionally reiterated its position on the right of the Jews to enter Palestine.[104] The paper quoted Chaim Weizmann on Zionism, adding that it wanted the Jews to accept Christ. The editorial concluded, "It is a supreme human consideration that the Jews should be given the land of Palestine as a suitable home in which they may dwell securely, and we trust, happily."[105] Following the war, the "sufferings of the Jews under the Fascist and Nazi tyrannies in Europe should compel the civilized world to demand that a Jewish commonwealth be established in Palestine."[106]

Second, the newspaper anticipated the plight of European Baptists who had been adversely affected by the war. It called for the BWA to prepare relief aid while acknowledging a tension existed between helping all people without distinction and the specific responsibility to help Baptists in particular. Assisting Jewish refugees was not mentioned while Baptist needs were amplified: "We would like to be sure that the Baptist minorities which have suffered so much in this war will receive the help and constructive relief they will surely need."[107]

Third, the paper pondered the future of Germany itself, imagining a post-Nazi Germany where the Christians who had suffered would provide a new generation of leadership; Jewish participation in the reconstruction of the country was unimaginable.[108] After the death of Hitler, it expressed anxiety regarding the level of participation of the German people in support of Nazism: "The rise of this man to power in Germany could never have taken place except with the support of many of the leading people of Germany. . . . It was with their consent that serious-minded, cold-blooded, and wholly inhumane Germans were permitted to exalt Nazism into a religion which proclaimed Hitler not only the Fuehrer of all Germans, but also their god."[109] This charge may represent an allusion to the reaction of the German Baptist leaders in 1933–1934. Did the editors recall the speeches of the German Baptist delegates at the Berlin congress, in which they enthusiastically endorsed Hitler and asserted that God had indeed sent him to Germany to deliver it from chaos?

Contact with German Baptists was slowly reestablished,[110] and the paper recalled that "we had a fine group of Baptists over there when the war began. We hope that many of them have been spared, for they were never so needed as at the present time."[111] Rushbrooke claimed, "Where the pressure was most terrible, the Baptists of Europe have remained faithful under intense suffering."[112] In contrast to Rushbrooke's rosy appraisal, Martin Niemöller was quoted as holding the German church responsible for supporting the Nazis.[113]

Lloyd A. Hollingsworth, an American soldier, published his personal research on German Baptists: "Before the United States declared war on Germany, we were told that the Nazis were not persecuting Baptists or the other Free churches that taught complete separation of church and state. I tried to investigate this fact and I believe it to be true . . . it appears that Baptists as a whole never supported the Nazi party to any extent or actively opposed it. As a result, the German government seems to have left the Baptist churches pretty much alone." But then the American admitted, "I am sorry to say that I have found no evidence to report where German Baptists took a firm stand against the persecution of the Jews."[114]

Europe, Zionism, and Israel (1946–1948)

During the postwar years, *The Watchman-Examiner* continued its coverage of the Jewish people's attempts to establish an independent homeland, Baptist relief and reconstruction in Europe, and how Baptists sought to relate to Jews. In general, the basic positions of the newspaper remained consistent.

The Watchman-Examiner published a major editorial titled "The Jewish Problem" in October 1945. It documented the calamity of the Holocaust: "While figures are confused . . . it appears that of the 8,000,000 Jews which formerly lived in Europe only approximately 1,500,000 to 2,000,000 remain." Among the survivors, "very few of them can return to the ghettos where formerly they may have lived," nor can they "remain forever behind barbed wire, nor is it right to keep them in concentration camps." The paper hoped that the establishment of a Jewish homeland would lead to a Jewish reconsideration of Jesus, which in turn could usher in a future where "anti-Semitism will be abolished."[115] Delays in opening Palestine to Jews were considered a "tragedy."[116]

Occasionally, the paper was critical of the Zionists and their use of terrorism.[117] It also expressed its displeasure concerning the chaos and militarization of the Arab and Jewish forces following the November 1947 United Nations action.[118] The paper clearly had reservations about the advisability of partition.[119] *The Watchman-Examiner* welcomed the independence of Israel with fear and trepidation because "the achievement of a Jewish state in Palestine is an awakening event for the whole world. The massed armies of the opposing Arabs create a threatening situation." It could not ignore the prophetic implications of the event: "There is before us an evident fulfillment of prophecy which enables the Bible student to know the line events of the immediate future will take. Israel cannot be restored except in the divine plan and purpose. If Israel is now being restored, then, as we interpret the Bible, history is rapidly approaching its climax."[120]

The Watchman-Examiner emphasized the plight of European Baptist displaced persons,[121] the reconstruction of Baptist church buildings through Germany and the rest of Europe, and the reestablishment of relations with Europe's Baptist unions.[122] The newspaper devoted much of its March 21, 1946, issue to the kind of polices Baptists should embrace as they ministered throughout Europe.[123] Rushbrooke stated the perspective of the Baptist World Alliance on this matter in April.[124] No mention of helping Jews can be found in these discussions.[125]

The Watchman-Examiner occasionally addressed the issue of whether Baptists aided Jews during the Holocaust. The anti-Nazi stance of the Dutch Baptists was celebrated.[126] Edith Traver asserted that the "Christian churches of Europe did not fail their Jewish countrymen during the years of persecution," but she covered only Holland and France, and the role Baptists played was not discussed.[127] Edwin Dahlberg, president of the Northern Baptist Convention, criticized German Protestants who were "content to preach our gospel message in a vacuum that takes no account of the political, economic, and racial sufferings of the people"—a charge that could easily be applied to the Baptists of that country.[128]

Rushbrooke, however, sought to reestablish ties with German Baptists and reintegrate them into the BWA. He minimized German Baptists' bystander behavior and past complicity with the Nazis:

> THE VERY FEW ministers who joined the Nazi Party—I did not learn more than four names—did so without sharing any of its anti-Semitism, anti-Biblicism, or anti-Christianity. . . . The truth is that the rarity of public protest on the part of the Baptists was due neither to cowardice nor a pro-Nazi trend, but to a "pietism"—of what we should call a "Plymouth Brother" type—which is characteristic of Germans. A defect assuredly—but not of the type sometimes alleged by outside critics!

> None of the Baptist ex-Nazis—however nominal was their membership of the Party—is now in the Executive Committee of the Union.[129]

The strategy of the German Baptist leaders in the postwar era was to portray themselves as victims, both of Nazism and the Allied bombing campaigns, and to seek reconciliation and aid from the global Baptist community. Rev. Jakob Meister, president of the Baptist Union of Germany, published an appeal in *The Watchman-Examiner* in March 1947. Without any reference to the destruction of the German Jewish community or the Holocaust, Meister opened his letter employing victim language: "Many of our brothers and sisters have in recent months shed more tears and endured more of want and pain than in the whole of their previous life." He then mentioned, "Gifts from America and other lands are warmly appreciated." He concluded: "We look forward with glad expectation to the World Congress in Copenhagen, and rejoice in the hope of seeing there once again many brethren from whom war has long separated us."[130]

Following the congress, *The Watchman-Examiner* published a second message from Meister, which expanded on the theme of German Baptist victimization. Without a single reference to the deaths of six million Jews at the hands of the German government, he wrote of the suffering of Christians: "Mountains of difficulties, sufferings, and needs which our prewar imagination never had dreamt of are towering before us. The terrors of the first world war appear like dwarfs when compared with the gigantic effects of the second world war. All disasters combined until now are only a snowball when compared with the avalanche of the present judgments of God."[131]

The postwar era ushered in significant sociological changes in the United States. The return of American soldiers led to a period of tremendous economic growth and prosperity, an expansion of the middle class, especially for Jews, and the continuance of the civil rights struggle of African Americans. *The Watchman-Examiner* reminded Baptists that many American Jews were not traditionally religious and thus should be offered the gospel.[132] The newspaper asserted that the United States is "a free country" in which Christians had the right to share their faith with their "Jewish neighbors, and do so without being regarded as proselyters."[133] It further asserted "narrowness and bigotry are not Christian qualities."[134] John Stuart Conning spoke glowingly about the faithfulness of Jews who converted to Christianity and then asserted that friendship of Christians was the key in the transformation of their spiritual journeys: "Jews almost universally testify that the main factor which led to their acceptance of the Christian faith was the friendly interest of some sincere and warm-hearted Christian. . . . Friendship is the alembic that can dissolve suspicion and prejudice and open the way for the Divine Spirit to work his miracle of grace."[135]

Notes

1. "Boston Ministers Meeting," *The Watchman-Examiner* (30 March 1933), 308.

2. Editorial, "Religious Persecution in Germany," *The Watchman-Examiner* (6 April 1933), 321.

3. J. H. Rushbrooke, "Germany: A Difficult Position for Baptists," *The Watchman-Examiner* (22 June 1933), 602.

4. *The Watchman-Examiner* (29 June 1933), 621.

5. Editorial, "Sympathy for German Jews," *The Watchman-Examiner* (20 July 1933), 697.

6. *The Watchman-Examiner* (24 August 1933), 811–12.

7. Editorial, "The Jews and the Nazis," *The Watchman-Examiner* (7 September 1933), 865. See also Editorial, "The Jews and Jesus Christ," *The Watchman-Examiner* (12 October 1933), 985.

8. Editorial, "Germany and the Jews," *The Watchman-Examiner* (19 October 1933), 1009.

9. Editorial, "Christianity and Nationalism," *The Watchman-Examiner* (7 December 1933), 1175.

10. Ibid., 1176.

11. *The Watchman-Examiner* (4 January 1934), 4–5.

12. He stated that Krause attacked the veracity of the Old Testament. Julius Janssen, "German Christianity and Baptists," *The Watchman-Examiner* (18 January 1934), 59. Krause was a leader in the German Christian movement; see John S. Conway, *The Nazi Persecution of the Churches 1933–1945*, 1st American ed. (New York: Basic Books, 1968), 51–54.

13. "Opposition to Semitism in German Church Again Voiced by Nazi Heads," *The Spartanburg Herald* (South Carolina) (16 November 1933), 3.

14. *The Watchman-Examiner* (4 January 1934), 2–3.

15. G. B. Hopkins, "Baptists and Berlin," *The Watchman-Examiner* (1 March 1934), 202.

16. Editorial, "About Going to Berlin," *The Watchman-Examiner* (15 March 1934), 265.

17. "The Oncken Centenary," *The Watchman-Examiner* (22 March 1934), 298, and "Baptists and Berlin" (29 March 1934), 330.

18. "Baptists and Berlin: A Statement on Behalf of the Baptist World Alliance," *The Watchman-Examiner* (12 April 1934), 394.

19. "A Letter from Germany," *The Watchman-Examiner* (12 April 1934), 395; see also "A Word of Welcome from German Baptists," *The Watchman-Examiner* (14 June 1934), 677. Will H. Houghton also encouraged visitors to come to Berlin, while never mentioning Jewish persecution; see "On to Berlin!" *The Watchman-Examiner* (31 May 1934), 632–33.

20. "An Invitation from the German Ambassador," *The Watchman-Examiner* (19 July 1934), 810.

21. John W. Bradbury, "Report of the Baptist World Alliance," *The Watchman-Examiner* (30 August 1934), 950. See Robert W. Ross, *So It Was True: The American Protestant Press and the Nazi Persecution of the Jews* (Minneapolis: University of Minnesota Press, 1980), 53–56.

22. John W. Bradbury, "Berlin Congress Reflections and Experiences," *The Watchman-Examiner* (13 September 1934), 996.

23. Quoted from Clifton D. Gray, "The Results of the Baptist Congress," *The Watchman-Examiner* (20 September 1934), 1021.

24. Quoted from M. E. Aubrey, "The Baptist Witness," *The Watchman-Examiner* (27 September 1934), 1043.

25. *The Watchman-Examiner* (1 November 1934), 1115–56. In 1935, Rushbrooke announced the German edition of the congress report, calling it more "journalistic"; see "A German Report of the Berlin Congress," *The Watchman-Examiner* (10 January 1935), 33.

26. *The Watchman-Examiner* (25 October 1934), 1132–33. The paper published a detailed overview of Palestine and Zionism in its January 17, 1935, issue (65–66), which observed that "a new Palestine" is represented by a "transformation . . . being brought about by the Jewish immigrant from Europe and America."

27. *The Watchman-Examiner* (17 January 1935), 65–66. See also *The Watchman-Examiner* (28 May 1936), 628-29; and York A. King, "British Justice and the Arabs in Palestine," *The Watchman-Examiner* (19 November 1936), 1283.

28. *The Watchman-Examiner* (28 March 1935), 322.

29. *The Watchman-Examiner* (23 January 1936), 85. Other appeals by the British were relayed in the April 2, 1936, issue (374) and the May 21, 1936, issue (599).

30. Editorial, "Instability of Jewish Christians," *The Watchman-Examiner* (23 April 1936), 475.

31. "The Church and the Jew," *The Watchman-Examiner* (23 July 1936), 861.

32. *The Watchman-Examiner* (24 September 1936), 1068.

33. "Is the World Going Mad?" *The Watchman-Examiner* (5 November 1936), 1218.

34. Robert A. Ashworth, "The Plight of Christian Refugees," *The Watchman-Examiner* (5 November 1936), 1221.

35. "Christian German Refugees," *The Watchman-Examiner* (15 April 1937), 439.

36. *The Watchman-Examiner* (1 April 1937), 357.

37. *The Watchman-Examiner* (20 May 1937), 581.

38. J. H. Rushbrooke, "Baptist World Alliance," *The Watchman-Examiner* (29 July 1937), 873–74. The BWA held meetings in Paris, Warsaw, and Germany, but *The Watchman-Examiner* did not mention any discussion of Jews at these meetings. See *The Watchman-Examiner* (26 August 1937), 955–56, 958; (2 September 1937), 978.

39. Editorial, "A Jewish State at Last," *The Watchman-Examiner* (2 September 1937), 984. See also Editorial, "The Dismembering of Palestine," *The Watchman-Examiner* (5 August 1937), 889; and Editorial, "The Palestine Dilemma," *The Watchman-Examiner* (3 March 1938), 203.

40. Editorial, "The Miracle of the Jew," *The Watchman-Examiner* (27 October 1938), 1148.

41. *The Watchman-Examiner* (7 October 1937), 1103.

42. As evidenced by, for example, Rufus W. Weaver, "The Fight for Religious Liberty," *The Watchman-Examiner* (27 January 1938), 83; and on Rushbrooke, *The Watchman-Examiner* (24 March 1938), 277; (20 October 1938), 1128.

43. *The Watchman-Examiner* (3 February 1938), 101.

44. Editorial, "Jews in Rumania," *The Watchman-Examiner* (24 February 1938), 177.

45. *The Watchman-Examiner* (26 May 1938), 566.

46. *The Watchman-Examiner* (2 June 1938), 598.

47. Editorial, "Friendly Advice to the Jews," *The Watchman-Examiner* (23 June 1938), 701. At the same time, the newspaper warned against prejudice in general and anti-Semitism in particular; see Editorial, "The Propaganda of Prejudice," *The Watchman-Examiner* (25 August 1938), 932.

48. *The Watchman-Examiner* (24 November 1938), 1238.

49. *The Watchman-Examiner* (1 December 1938), 1265.

50. *The Watchman-Examiner* (8 December 1938), 1286–87: "The congregation also raised funds to aid the cause of Jewish refugees."

51. Ibid., 1290–91; see also 1288.

52. Editorial, "Christian Sympathy for the Jews," *The Watchman-Examiner* (8 December 1938), 1295.

53. Editorial, "Where to Send the Jews," *The Watchman-Examiner* (22 December 1938), 1347–48.

54. Editorial, "1938," *The Watchman-Examiner* (29 December 1938), 1371.

55. Everett Gill, "Jesus and Nationalism," *The Watchman-Examiner* (5 January 1939), 11.

56. *The Watchman-Examiner* (26 January 1939), 83–84.

57. Herbert Hoover, "Justice for the Jew," *The Watchman-Examiner* (2 February 1939), 120–21.

58. Rufus M. Jones, "The Quaker Visit to Germany," *The Watchman-Examiner* (23 February 1939), 200.

59. Editorial, "Baptist Leadership and Our Historic Principles," *The Watchman-Examiner* (9 March 1939), 241. Rushbrooke is not quoted as mentioning the Jewish problem in an interview published in the May 25, 1939, issue (586).

60. *The Watchman-Examiner* (16 March 1939), 278. In a subsequent more critical review, the paper called the anti-Semitic manifesto "a most comprehensive collection of anti-Christian political philosophy"; Editorial, "Mein Kampf," *The Watchman-Examiner* (6 April 1939), 363.

61. Editorial, "Christianity and Ominous World Tensions," *The Watchman-Examiner* (23 March 1939), 297; see also A. H. C. Morse, "What Persecution and Depression Mean to Christians," *The Watchman-Examiner* (23 March 1939), 300: "There is persecution today: of Jews, in Germany and Italy."

62. Editorial, "Christian Refugees in Europe," *The Watchman-Examiner* (30 March 1939), 331.

63. *The Watchman-Examiner* (13 April 1939), 389.

64. *The Watchman-Examiner* (29 June 1939), 725.

65. *The Watchman-Examiner* (10 August 1939), 890.

66. Quoted in John W. Bradbury, "The Sixth Congress of the Baptist World Alliance," *The Watchman-Examiner* (10 August 1939), 914. The speech was reprinted later; see M. E. Aubrey, "Christianity and the Totalitarian State," *The Watchman-Examiner* (26 October 1939), 1170.

67. Bradbury, "Sixth Congress of the Baptist World Alliance," 898–99.

68. "More Gleanings from the Atlanta Congress," *The Watchman-Examiner* (17 August 1939), 923.

69. J. W. Decker, "A Week-End in Europe," *The Watchman-Examiner* (17 August 1939), 926. See also Editorial, "The Fate of the World's Exiles," *The Watchman-Examiner* (12 October 1939), 1119.

70. J. H. Rushbrooke, "Atlanta Hopes Disappointed: Atlanta Spirit Persists," *The Watchman-Examiner* (12 October 1939), 1123.

71. Rufus W. Weaver, "The World Crisis and Religious Liberty," *The Watchman-Examiner* (9 November 1939), 1218.

72. Editorial, "Suffering of Jews," *The Watchman-Examiner* (28 December 1939), 1392. For the situation on Lodz, Poland, see *The Watchman-Examiner* (25 January 1940), 76.

73. J. H. Rushbrooke, "Baptist World Alliance in Action," *The Watchman-Examiner* (29 February 1940), 202.

74. *The Watchman-Examiner* (25 April 1940), 438.

75. J. C. Carlile, "England's Second Thoughts on the War," *The Watchman-Examiner* (16 May 1940), 539.

76. Quoted in John W. Bradbury, "Report of the Northern Baptist Convention," *The Watchman-Examiner* (6 June 1940), 643–44.

77. Editorial, "The Unhappy Jew," *The Watchman-Examiner* (13 June 1940), 663. Luxembourg was next; see *The Watchman-Examiner* (1 August 1940), 829.

78. *The Watchman-Examiner* (24 October 1940), 1115.

79. *The Watchman-Examiner* (19 December 1940), 1308. The figures are from *The Jewish Missionary Magazine*.

80. Editorial, "Jews Going Home," *The Watchman-Examiner* (9 January 1941), 31.

81. Editorial, "Thoughts for Race-Relations Sunday," *The Watchman-Examiner* (30 January 1941), 105.

82. *The Watchman-Examiner* (20 February 1941), 170, 174.

83. Morris Gordin, "The Challenge of Jewish Evangelization," *The Watchman-Examiner* (20 March 1941), 276–77.

84. Editorial, "A Jewish Army," *The Watchman-Examiner* (3 April 1941), 321.

85. Editorial, "Is Pacifism the Solution?", *The Watchman-Examiner* (8 May 1941), 482.

86. Quoted in John W. Bradbury, "Report of the Northern Baptist Convention," *The Watchman-Examiner* (5 June 1941), 611. The speech was published in "The Lord God Omnipotent Reigneth," *The Watchman-Examiner* (12 June 1941), 644–46.

87. Daniel A. Poling, "The Christian in the Present Crisis," *The Watchman-Examiner* (19 June 1941), 668. Poling, though not originally a Baptist, served the Grace Baptist Church in Philadelphia and was highly regarded in Northern Baptist circles. A prolific author, he was also the editor of the *Christian Herald* magazine. Pro-Jewish and a Zionist, he had leadership roles in the Christian Council on Palestine and in Christian Endeavour.

88. Jeanne Bradbury, "Care for Casualties in a Suffering World," *The Watchman-Examiner* (17 July 1941), 762.

89. Editorial, "The Jewish Situation," *The Watchman-Examiner* (11 September 1941), 953.

90. *The Watchman-Examiner* (23 October 1941), 1090. However, in the next issue, the paper criticized an ecumenical service in which Christians helped dedicate a synagogue. It considered such interfaith activities "sentimentalism" and stated, "There is not a bit of antisemitism in our makeup, for we minister the Gospel of Christ to Jews at every opportunity, and so we exclude all ideas of bigotry"; *The Watchman-Examiner* (30 October 1941), 1119. See also Editorial, "Salvation for the Jew," *The Watchman-Examiner* (8 January 1942), 31; and Editorial, "An Anti-Prejudice Drive," *The Watchman-Examiner* (22 January 1942), 79.

91. Editorial, "Religious Conditions in Germany," *The Watchman-Examiner* (6 November 1941), 1143.

92. O. E. Anshus, "Baptists in Norway Carry On," *The Watchman-Examiner* (27 November 1941), 1218.

93. Editorial, "Jews in Europe," *The Watchman-Examiner* (15 January 1942), 56.

94. *The Watchman-Examiner* (12 February 1942), 149.

95. Editorial, "Jewish Immigration to Palestine," *The Watchman-Examiner* (13 August 1942), 801; see also Editorial, "Jewish Rights to Palestine," *The Watchman-Examiner* (8 October 1942), 991; George H. Gilmer, "Shall We Interpret Literally Prophecies Concerning Israel?" *The Watchman-Examiner* (8 July 1943), 651.

96. *The Watchman-Examiner* (1 October 1942), 963.

97. Editorial, "Deporting Jews from France," *The Watchman-Examiner* (15 October 1942), 1016; see also *The Watchman-Examiner* (29 October 1942), 1061. The Norwegian Christian protest is covered in Editorial, "Norwegian Christians Protest," *The Watchman-Examiner* (31 December 1942), 1279.

98. Editorial, "The Church in the War," *The Watchman-Examiner* (1 October 1942), 968–69.

99. "Persecution of the Jews," *The Watchman-Examiner* (24 December 1942), 1261. See introduction.

100. *The Watchman-Examiner* (4 February 1943), 100.

101. Editorial, "Russia and Jews," *The Watchman-Examiner* (30 September 1943), 933.

102. Editorial, "The Hope of Jewry," *The Watchman-Examiner* (29 July 1943), 717; Editorial, "Russia and Jews," *The Watchman-Examiner* (30 September 1943), 933. The figure of five million is astounding to find this early in the history of the Holocaust; even in *The Watchman-Examiner*, lower figures were cited later on; see Wayne Clark, "Racial Intolerance," *The Watchman-Examiner* (16 March 1944), 251, where he believed two million had died, with a possible additional two million to perish before the end of the war.

103. Editorials, "French Jews Suffering," and "Russia and Jews," *The Watchman-Examiner* (9 December 1943), 1173. For a prior report of Rumanian Jews arrested in Paris and sent to Drancy, see *The Watchman-Examiner* (28 January 1943), 78.

104. Editorial, "A Jewish National Home," *The Watchman-Examiner* (27 July 1944), 728.

105. Editorial, "Europe's Jews and Palestine," *The Watchman-Examiner* (10 May 1945), 453–54.

106. Editorial, "The Palestine Question," *The Watchman-Examiner* (28 June 1945), 623; see also Editorial, "Jews in Europe," *The Watchman-Examiner* (19 July 1945), 695.

107. Editorial, "Religious Liberty in Europe," *The Watchman-Examiner* (3 August 1944), 752; see also Editorial, "Baptist Reconstruction in Europe," *The Watchman-Examiner* (4 October 1945), 959; Editorial, "Baptist Reconstruction in Europe," *The Watchman-Examiner* (15 November 1945), 1104.

108. Editorial, "The Hope of Germany," *The Watchman-Examiner* (28 September 1944), 945.

109. Editorial, "The Process of Judgment," *The Watchman-Examiner* (10 May 1945), 454.

110. Editorial, "Europe's Liberated Churches," *The Watchman-Examiner* (9 August 1945), 767; Walter O. Lewis, "Baptist World Alliance News Letter," *The Watchman-Examiner* (16 August 1945), 803.

111. *The Watchman-Examiner* (12 July 1945), 666.

112. *The Watchman-Examiner* (19 July 1945), 691. Rushbrooke knew better, for he had been aware for years that the German Baptist leaders had capitulated to the Nazis. Rushbrooke did accurately report on Norwegian Baptist opposition to Nazism in *The Watchman-Examiner* (1 November 1945), 1051. See O. E. Anshus, "Baptist Convention in Norway," *The Watchman-Examiner* (22 November 1945), 1132–33.

113. Editorial, "Niemoeller Indicts Church," *The Watchman-Examiner* (8 November 1945), 1079.

114. Lloyd A. Hollingsworth, "German Baptists," *The Watchman-Examiner* (6 December 1945), 1178.

115. Editorial, "The Jewish Problem," *The Watchman-Examiner* (25 October 1945), 1032–33; see also John Stuart Conning, "Aspects of Modern Zionism," *The Watchman-Examiner* (3 October 1946), 1016–17; Walter L. Riley, "Great Prophecies Now Being Fulfilled," *The Watchman-Examiner* (18 December 1947), 1263.

116. Editorial, "The Palestine Tragedy," *The Watchman-Examiner* (7 February 1946), 129; see also Editorial, "Israel's Aspiration," *The Watchman-Examiner* (25 July 1946), 771.

117. Editorial, "Trouble in the Promised Land," *The Watchman-Examiner* (12 December 1946), 1251.

118. Editorial, "Unhappy about Palestine," *The Watchman-Examiner* (15 January 1948), 55–56.

119. George W. McPherson, "Divided Palestine," *The Watchman-Examiner* (25 March 1948), 305–6; Clinton N. Howard, "Partition of Palestine," *The Watchman-Examiner* (6 May 1948), 471–72.

120. Editorial, "Creation of Jewish State," *The Watchman-Examiner* (3 June 1948), 567. In a second editorial two months later, the newspaper observed, "The new state of Israel is born in travail and will survive only by the sovereign purpose of Providence"; *The Watchman-Examiner* (12 August 1948), 835.

121. Stanley I. Stuber, "Baptists Do Something Significant for Displaced Persons," *The Watchman-Examiner* (14 November 1946), 1165; see also A. Klaupiks, "What Are Displaced Persons?" *The Watchman-Examiner* (20 November 1947), 1168–70.

122. J. H. Rushbrooke, "Baptist World Alliance News," *The Watchman-Examiner* (10 January 1946), 42; Editorial, "An Example from Germany," *The Watchman-Examiner* (31 January 1946), 105; O. E. Anshus, "Baptist Minorities and European Relief," *The Watchman-Examiner* (7 March 1946), 228; Editorial, "Importance of European Baptists," *The Watchman-Examiner* (11 April 1946), 360–61; Walter O. Lewis, "He Forgot Joseph," *The Watchman-Examiner* (4 July 1946), 702–3; correspondence, "Latvian Baptists in Germany," *The Watchman-Examiner* (21 November 1946), 1187.

123. Editorial, "Baptist Relief Policy," *The Watchman-Examiner* (21 March 1946), 274–75; Letter, "Baptist Relief in Europe," *The Watchman-Examiner* (21 March 1946), 285–86.

124. J. H. Rushbrooke, "Baptists and European Relief," *The Watchman-Examiner* (4 April 1946), 331; see also Dexter G. Whitwinghill, "Baptist Relief Policy," *The Watchman-Examiner* (11 April 1946), 366.

125. See, for example, Alfred Arthur Cierpke, "Europe's Haunted Millions," *The Watchman-Examiner* (13 March 1947), 250–51. Cierpke was a German Baptist minister who stayed in the United States after the Atlanta BWA congress.

126. Editorial, "Heroic Dutch Baptists," *The Watchman-Examiner* (14 February 1946), 153; and J. W. Weenink, "The Baptists of Holland and the Nazis," *The Watchman-Examiner* (14 February 1946), 156–58.

127. Edith G. Traver, "How They Stood by the Jews in Europe," *The Watchman-Examiner* (27 June 1946), 681–82.

128. Edwin T. Dahlberg, "The Unfailing Lamp of God," *The Watchman-Examiner* (5 September 1946), 920.

129. J. H. Rushbrooke, "Baptists in Germany," *The Watchman-Examiner* (10 October 1946), 1038. In Rushbrooke's personal unpublished papers and correspondence (at the Regent's Park College Archive, Oxford), it is clear he knew much more than he admitted in this article about aspects of German Baptist complicity with the Nazis. Gilbert Laws alluded to this in his letter regarding Rushbrooke's death: "He often knew more than he could say. . . . He has often, moreover, prevented our own Baptist people from making unwise accusations and adopting an extreme position under provocation, when such an outreach could only have made bad worse." *The Watchman-Examiner* (27 February 1947), 203.

130. "Conditions in Germany," *The Watchman-Examiner* (13 March 1947), 258–59.

131. Jakob Meister, "The German Scene," *The Watchman-Examiner* (11 September 1947), 929.

132. Editorial, "The Gospel for the Jews," *The Watchman-Examiner* (10 January 10, 1946), 31.

133. Editorial, "The Gospel and the Jews," *The Watchman-Examiner* (15 January 1948), 56–57.

134. Editorial, "Need for Brotherhood," *The Watchman-Examiner* (12 February 1948), 152.

135. John Stuart Conning, "What We May Learn from Christian Jews," *The Watchman-Examiner* (7 March 1946), 227; see also John Stuart Conning, "Jews at the Church Door," *The Watchman-Examiner* (5 September 1946), 918–19.

Chapter 6

Southern Baptist Periodicals

At the beginning of the Nazi era, the Southern Baptist Convention's counterpart to the Northern Baptist Convention's *Missions* magazine was *Home and Foreign Fields*. In 1938, the magazine was replaced by separate magazines published by the Home and Foreign Mission boards.

Home and Foreign Fields (1933–1937)

The monthly *Home and Foreign Fields* focused on promoting Southern Baptist domestic and international missionary efforts, but secular news was included in missionaries' field reports. The April 1933 issue highlighted the work of Palestine-based missionary Elsie Clor. After joyously sharing that fifteen Jewish and Arab converts were baptized, Clor observed, "When we see the condition of the world and especially in Palestine, the return of the Jews and their untiring efforts in the building up of their land, it is a reminder that the Lord's coming is very close at hand."[1]

Everett Gill analyzed the changes taking place throughout Europe in August 1933. He observed that "Fascism, Hitlerism, chauvinism, Socialism, Anarchism and Bolshevism cannot but have an effect on the religious life of European peoples," and that at a 1931 Baptist Youth Congress, "the majority of the students for the ministry were Hitlerites." Nevertheless, he asserted that pessimistic premillennialism and Pentecostalism were the most "disturbing" trends in European religion and ignored Hitler's initial round of persecution of Germany's Jewish population.[2] The editors spoke appreciatively of the Nazi government's hospitality to those who attended the Berlin congress but did not mention the racialism resolution that condemned anti-Semitism.[3]

Una Roberts Lawrence, a contributing editor, composed the first clear reference to the plight of Jews under Hitler's regime. In her May 1935 column, she wryly noted: "London holds hurried cabinet meetings and sends by airplane a softly talking emissary to interview Hitler while the headlines scream of Ludendorff being called from obscurity to head the German war machine and the full-blood Jews being thrown into a labor gang to do the work behind the army lines. And from our great world statesman, Doctor Rushbrooke, there comes a grave and troubled warning that no one can tell the outcome of the continued suppression of church leadership within the German Reich."[4] In September 1937, Lawrence reviewed *The Heart of the Levant* by James McKee Adams, a Southern Baptist Theological Seminary professor. She referenced "German and Italian influence" in the political estrangement of Jews and Arabs in Palestine, acknowledged Zionism in a positive way, and concluded that evangelistic missionary activity was warranted by current political events.[5] Aside from Lawrence's columns, *Home and Foreign Fields* occasionally referred to Jews in the context of Southern Baptist evangelistic efforts. These articles, usually testimonies of conversion, did not mention the Nazi campaign against the Jews in Germany.[6]

The editors of *Home and Foreign Fields* were certainly aware of totalitarian movements. In one editorial, they asked, "How much do you know about Communism, Socialism, Fascism? Has the Bible a word on the problems with which they deal? Can the menace of the Nazis be met with God's truth?"[7] They answered their own questions in the affirmative but did not see fit to provide a prophetic critique of Nazism between 1933 and 1937. Instead, they offered a rationale for their lack of coverage: "We know a little bit about Communism, Socialism, Nazism, Fascism . . . but we see no reason why mention of one or more of these should be made from every pulpit or appear on every page; we are not blind to the terrible inequalities and the glaring evils that obtain in the social order, but we would not make emphasis of such an obsession to the exclusion of every other consideration."[8]

Southern Baptist Home Missions (1938–1948)

As the successor to *Home and Foreign Fields*, *Southern Baptist Home Missions* focused on denominational ministries in the United States. One of its contributors was Jacob Gartenhaus, the Home Missions Board's Director of Jewish Evangelism. He published an article in virtually every issue, including accounts of his evangelistic experiences, testimonies of converts, and exhortations for Southern Baptists to support sharing the gospel with Jews. In March 1938, Gartenhaus argued that evangelism was impaired when Christians exhibited anti-Semitism. He did not specifically mention Nazism, but he stated cryptically that anti-Semitism "exists today among the nations." He categorically denounced anti-Semitism as being "born of the devil and responsible in large measure for the misunderstanding and obstinacy that prevail among the Jews" in regards to Christ.[9]

It fell to Gartenhaus to explain the significance of Kristallnacht to Southern Baptists. Before Kristallnacht, "some denied many of the happenings there"—a polite criticism of Southern Baptist leaders who minimized or excused early Nazi campaigns against Jews. However, Kristallnacht's agenda could not be denied and exposed the Nazis' true aims: "But now with the brazen utterances of German officials, shocking as they are, one dares not deny some of the mad, inhuman, barbaric treatment of a helpless people." Gartenhaus advocated for the Jews suffering persecution. Declaring that "to Jewish suffering there seems to be no end, and to vile persecution, no limit," Gartenhaus quoted a story from a Jewish newspaper that pictured a Jewish refugee considering his prospects for resettlement: "Russia—I am not wanted there. Germany—not wanted there. France—not wanted there. England—not wanted there. America—not really wanted there. . . . This is a large and beautiful world, but no place for me."[10]

In May 1939, Gartenhaus highlighted his efforts to help a Viennese Jewish family that wished to escape Nazi persecution. He also hoped that God might somehow use the sufferings of the Jewish people to bring about the conversion of individual Jews: "If the persecution through which the Jewish people are passing is bringing them closer to their God, it may yet be a blessing to them and to the world."[11] Such hope was hard to maintain; even *Southern Baptist*

Home Missions published sobering statistics on the Jewish plight in Nazi-controlled Germany and Austria:

> IN 1903 THERE were 650,000 Jews living in Germany. Today, so we are told, only 300,000 of these are at liberty; 200,000 have emigrated; 30,000 are detained in prisons and concentration camps; 20,000 have committed suicide; 8,000, it is alleged, were murdered; and 90,000 died. . . . Of the 300,000 Jews in Austria, only 140,000 are still at liberty; 130,000 have emigrated; 10,000 are in concentration camps and prisons; 10,000 have committed suicide; and 5,000, so it is alleged, have been murdered. This is evidently the day of Israel's trouble.[12]

Some Jewish refugees were fortunate enough to arrive in the United States. Gartenhaus reported that the "present European situation upheaval has brought to our shores thousands of refugees, among whom are found the flower of the Jewish race"—some of whom he personally was able to meet.[13] A poem, "He Was a Jew," reminded Southern Baptists that Jesus was Jewish and that they were called "to save and bless the Jew."[14] When a reader inquired about the living conditions of the Jews in Europe, the periodical replied, "Their condition is beyond description."[15] Gartenhaus lamented, "Even surpassing the sorrows about which the prophet Jeremiah lamented are the persecutions of the Jews especially in Europe." He described the movement of Jews across Europe as "a migration born of despair and nurtured by misery with not a strip of land upon which they can rest their weary bodies . . . and nothing short of a miracle will save the millions who remain." His supporters were exhorted to display "loving sympathy" and a "spirit of kindness" to Jews.[16] Another poem admonished the readers: "Say not a Christian ere would persecute a Jew; a Gentile might, but not a Christian true. . . . You cannot persecute—whatever else you do—the race who gave Him—Jesus was a Jew."[17]

Gartenhaus highlighted the experience of Leo Stein, a German Jew who was incarcerated alongside Martin Niemöller.[18] Stein claimed that the famous German pastor said: "Jesus Christ, the founder of Christendom was a Jew. I love the Old Testament. Hitler is trying to denounce this Testament as 'Jewish' but there is no Christianity without it. Whoever is an anti-Semite and persecutes the Jews can never be a real Christian. Hitler is anti-Christ."[19] In May 1942, Gartenhaus claimed that "Jews have been forced to dig their own graves and then have been buried in them alive." He summarized the misery in stark terms: "Satanic fury has burst forth in all its intensity seeking to wipe the Jews from the face of the earth. . . . Cold, hunger and murder have been their lot, children dying in the arms of their mothers."[20]

A month before Rabbi Stephen Wise held his press conference confirming that the Nazis were exterminating Jews, Gartenhaus presented a synopsis of Nazi campaigns against Jews throughout Europe, in response to persistent interest expressed by his Baptist constituents "in the conditions of the Jews." Based on Jewish sources, he mentioned Nazi concentration camps operating in several countries:

> "OVER 30,000 JEWS" in the Baltic states "are now in labor camps and the remainder have either been interned or executed."
>
> Belgium—"A new concentration camp has been established near Antwerp."
>
> Czechoslovakia—"Mass deportations of Jews are continuing. The spread of epidemics is reported in the concentration camps, and more than ten thousand Jews are reported held incommunicado in the prisons. There is an unparalleled wave of persecution."
>
> The Netherlands—"Jews are huddled together in ghettos. . . . Others are being constantly shipped to concentration camps."
>
> Poland—"Horror is continuous without relief here. . . . In one city 13,000 Jews have been executed."
>
> Roumania—"Two hundred thousand Jews have been isolated. . . . In Bessarabia where there was once a population of 200,000 Jews, there is not one left."
>
> Yugoslavia—"Many are being driven to nearby forests and executed. Typhus has broken out in some of the concentration camps."[21]

Gartenhaus also mentioned the difficulties faced by "Jewish Christian refugees in concentration [camps] where they have nearly starved to death and have been beaten into insensibility."[22] In May 1943, Gartenhaus shared how he assisted a German Jewish Christian refugee who had escaped to Havana, Cuba.[23] Admitting that assistance to individual Jewish refugees was an inadequate response, Gartenhaus encouraged Southern Baptists to contemplate a future for the survivors of the Nazi persecution. He quoted Secretary of State Cordell Hull: "The Jews have long sought a refuge. I believe that we must have an even wider objective; we must have a world in which Jews, like every other race, are free to abide in peace and honor. . . . Of all the inhuman and tyrannical acts of Hitler and his Nazi lieutenants, their systematic persecution of the Jewish people is the most debased."

Furthermore, Gartenhaus rejected the classic Christian charge of deicide—that the persecution of Jews was justified by their collective rejection of Jesus. Although he did not oppose the return of the surviving Jews to Palestine, he did not believe the fruition of the Zionist dream would end the Jews' problems in a Gentile-dominated world. Jewish suffering would cease only when his own people "realize that in Jesus, the Jewish Messiah, lies her only hope."[24]

Gartenhaus consistently expressed respect and love for the Jewish people while hoping that they would find a spiritual home in his messianic faith. He did not understand these two positions to be antithetical or contradictory. The Nazis' attempted extermination of the Jews was evil and Jews suffered as innocent victims. In response, Christians should express solidarity with these victims and provide spiritual solace to them in their time of suffering. Convicted that Jesus was the Jewish Messiah, Gartenhaus sincerely believed in convincing Jews that embracing Jesus would provide them with spiritual comfort and peace. He wrote:

> IT IS UNTHINKABLE to have the love for Christ and at the same time not have a yearning to bring deliverances and peace to His people at a time when they are facing the greatest crisis in their long and tragic history. Christian people cannot stand aside and refuse to listen to their pathetic plea. If ever the Jews needed sympathy it is now. These trials through which they are passing have softened them to the Gospel message and many of them are really beginning to wonder if after all Jesus is not the solution to their eternal problem.[25]

Gartenhaus, through his numerous articles in *Home and Foreign Fields* and *Southern Baptist Home Missions*, was the preeminent Southern Baptist advocate for the Jewish people during the Nazi era. He consistently opposed Nazism, advocated for Jews who were persecuted, and encouraged Southern Baptists to identify with the plight of his people. No reader of these periodicals could claim ignorance of the Nazi aggression against the Jews.

The Commission (1938–1948)

The Commission was a monthly publication that served as the voice of the Southern Baptist Foreign Missions Board. Since its missionaries served both Jews and Arabs, the magazine promoted a delicate balance between the perspectives of these communities.[26] Before Pearl Harbor, the magazine supported a "sane and just neutrality" for the United States, mirroring the isolationist sentiment of the larger Southern Baptist social context.[27] However, this did not prevent the periodical from critiquing Germany's "rape of Austria" in July 1938 (without referring to its Jewish citizens).[28]

The Commission reprinted Rushbrooke's speech delivered at the 1938 Southern Baptist annual convention. He affirmed that Baptists were "as deeply concerned over the cruel treatment meted out to the heroic Pastor Niemöller by the Nazi Government of Germany as if we ourselves were the sufferers," and he insisted that totalitarianism was in conflict with the democratic values Baptists prized.[29]

W. O. Carver, professor of mission at the Southern Baptist Theological Seminary, wrote a column for *The Commission* just prior to Kristallnacht. Carver began by acknowledging the problem of Jewish suffering: "Germany continues to devise new iniquities in her persecution of her Jewish population. In mid-July Italy stiffens her trend toward repression and bolsters her increasing Nordic Aryanism with a manufactured rationalizing by a group of professors who are willing to debauch their scholarship to serve the unholy ambition of a dictator increasingly drunk with insane ambition. In other parts of Europe there are ominous expressions of anti-Semitism."[30] However, instead of expressing compassion and solidarity with persecuted Jews, Carver placed at least partial responsibility on the shoulders of the victims: "In utmost sympathy and consideration it is suggested that the Jews must themselves assume much more of the burden for solving their problem than has been evident in the modern difficulties which have arisen concerning them. . . . The Jews are fully justified in proclaiming the wrongs inflicted upon them, and in appealing for sympathy and help. But this is not enough."[31]

In February 1939, *The Commission* published a lengthy editorial on Kristallnacht written by Charles E. Maddry, the executive secretary of the Southern Baptist Foreign Mission Board. He described the unthinkable magnitude of the Nazi assault against the Jews:

> THE HALF MILLION Jews in Germany are now passing through an orgy of persecution, the like of which the world has not seen in a thousand years. For sheer brutality and fiendish ingenuity, it surpasses anything the chosen people of God have ever been called upon to suffer. . . . For a crime committed by one irresponsible Jewish youth in Paris, the whole body of the Jewish people of Germany have been fined the staggering sum of *four hundred million dollars*. Thousands of Jews have been arrested and thrown into concentration camps throughout Germany.[32]

Maddry next warned Germany of God's judgment for this injustice: "What the Jews of Germany are suffering surpasses the power of words to express; but Germany's suffering will be far greater. In all history no nation which has persecuted the Jews has escaped punishment from God." He then encouraged Southern Baptists to contribute funds for Jewish relief and offer them asylum: "What can God's people do for the suffering Jews of Germany in this fateful hour? We can contribute toward their relief and, in every possible way help to remove them from the clutches of German tyranny. This means that for these oppressed people funds must be provided and doors opened in democratic lands."[33]

The scale of the Nazi campaign against Jews was hard for Americans to grasp, and so *The Commission* illustrated the plight of a single Jew in a remarkable poem by Robert D. Abrahams, "A Shopkeeper Dies—Vienna, 1938." It revealed the inner turmoil of a Jewish shopkeeper who knew his life would soon be taken even though he had been a faithful Austrian citizen. He realized that resistance was futile, and so he resolved to die as a Jew in a tragic situation in which he will be "crucified." Nevertheless, he hoped some Jews would "survive the years that are to come."[34]

The Nazi persecution of the Jews did not change the Foreign Mission Board's ambivalence toward Zionism. A July 1939 editorial noted that "the deplorable plight of more than half the Jews in the world today because of vicious, inhuman attitudes and oppressions arouses feelings of sympathy or, alas, of antagonism and injustice, which makes difficult objective and just judgment upon events as they transpire." Specifically, the magazine recognized the "contradictory" pledges Great Britain had made to Jews and Arabs in Palestine and observed that Arab rights should not be short-changed in response to alleviating Jewish needs for safety and a homeland. The editorial offered only a general solution to this dilemma, calling upon Jews to empower "competent" leaders, and concluded, "There needs to be a deep and frank consideration of the actual desperate situation and need of eight or ten million human beings whose glory and shame are in the fact that they are Jews."[35]

Southern Baptist consideration of the plight of persecuted Jews occasionally led to self-criticism. Milledge Theron Rankin, who had responsibility for the missionary enterprise in Japan and China,[36] recounted conversations he had with Jewish exiles en route to Shanghai, China. Listening to their stories, he felt "despair" which turned into disappointment when they were reticent to continue discussions with him after they discovered he was a Christian missionary. Rankin reflected: "What should be our attitude toward the Jews? . . . We must involve ourselves more fully in the miseries and sufferings of men before we can herald to all mankind the peace of Christmas. The door which seemed to close between me and the Jew when he said, 'Oh, a Christian missionary' is a haunting challenge."[37]

The Commission occasionally published positive articles about Jewish emigration to Palestine. In September 1940, Southern Baptist missionary Kate Ellen Gruver felt "privileged to witness . . . the mighty return of the Jews to 'Eretz Israel.'" The new settlers were "tortured, persecuted, deprived of home and life in other countries" but were now "finding new life, new incentive, new hope in the land of their fathers."[38] An editorial pictured Europe in the darkest of terms, as the light of liberty was being extinguished by the march of Nazi armies.[39] Carver described the darkness confronting European Jews: "Almost every turn of the rapidly developing drama of Europe brings fresh distress to the Jews. Germany's barbaric policy passes over into each new subjugated area. France, long a place of safety and honorable citizenship, begins her chapter of shame in this tragic story of inhumanity to 'the ancient people.' Now Rumania takes up the cudgels of inhumanity to oppress this important element of her population." In response, he called upon his readers to "practice active kindness and true spiritual love toward Jews as human beings and common heirs to the grace of God."[40] He did not, however, explain how this would prevent the Nazis from destroying the Jewish population in Europe.

Maddry provided a more effective example of Christian solidarity with persecuted Jews: "The persecution of the Jews has been carried to extreme lengths by the Germans. . . . This brutal treatment has provoked a vigorous reaction on the part of the kindly Dutch people. It led to the strike at Amsterdam, which was a spontaneous act of resistance to the persecution of the Jews."[41] He reported that in light of the tragic news out of France and Poland, the very existence of European Jewry at stake:

> THERE IS SCARCELY a village in Occupied France in which some Jews have not been put to death. Sometimes it is an individual victim, but more often there is wholesale slaughter. The sadistic brutality with which these executions are carried out staggers the imagination. In the city of Lodz, Poland, there were 250,000 Jews. Now there are 80,000 left, and these are confined like animals in a ghetto that means slow death. All of the suffering and sorrow and death visited upon "God's People" for two thousand years cannot equal the suffering and tragedy inflicted upon this race in Europe during the past decade.[42]

After the entry of the United States into the war, Carver focused on the Nazis' ire against its Christian churches.[43] In contrast, *The Commission* asked Gartenhaus to imagine how Jews might participate in a post-Hitler world. He hoped that Jews (the "first victim of dictators and the greatest sufferer") might place their faith in Jesus and discover "hope, peace and security."[44] Southern Baptists also felt called to address practical issues such as hunger relief, even before the war ended. In an article "foreseeing the desperate need for relief in the war ravaged lands of Europe and Asia," the plight of Jews was highlighted: "The order has gone forth from Hitler that the remaining five million Jews still alive in Europe must be put to death as rapidly as the order can be carried out."[45] Hitler's Final Solution was acknowledged by *The Commission* and made known to its readers.

Even as the Holocaust raged, Carver opined on whether the Jews (and Romans) of the first century were collectively responsible for Jesus' death. While he believed they did hold some responsibility, he concluded that "in crucifying Jesus, Romans and Jews represented all of us"—the entire human race.[46] Carver also challenged the notion that the Jewish people continued to be "chosen." He stated, "Jesus repudiated the racial concept of election. He substituted a trans-racial and super-racial spiritual people as the 'election of faith'"—in essence, adopting a supersessionist position.[47]

An editorial on racism in September 1944 admitted that "racial prejudice" in the United States "is based primarily on differences in color, but grows also out of ancient ethnic antagonisms as, for example, anti-Semitism." However, instead of opposing Nazism, the editorial criticized "bitter prejudice, akin to the prejudice of the old-time Jew against the Gentiles . . . a spirit which in our day finds expression in an intense nationalism with a corresponding claim of superiority over other races and ranks." Similarly, troubling comments were made about African American hopes for civic and political equality.[48]

Following the ending of hostilities in Europe, *The Commission* remained silent about the liberation of Nazi concentration camps and the full extent of the Holocaust. In September 1945, Gartenhaus wrote an article on Jews in Mexico.[49] George Sadler's article on Baptist relief efforts in Europe did not mention Jewish survivors or displaced persons.[50] Even an article on the United Nations Relief and Rehabilitation Administration (UNRRA) refrained from mentioning refugees of Jewish background.[51]

The Jewish-Arab struggle in Palestine was described by Sadler, the regional secretary for Europe and the Middle East, in terms reminiscent of the periodical's position in 1938. He sought a balance between the two sides, though the Jewish community was painted in a more negative light. Reference was made to "Jewish terrorists," and Sadler claimed that "Jews were protesting against a temporary stalemate which had been reached with reference to the admission of members of their race into Palestine."[52]

The first postwar reference to the full horror of the Holocaust in *The Commission* was buried in Baptist World Alliance general secretary Walter O. Lewis's report on the Baptist movement in Europe. He surveyed the damage done to Baptist churches and ministries in each country: "Switzerland also received Jews who were being hunted like wild animals. The Nazis killed, mostly outside Germany, 6,000,000 Jews."[53] An editorial praising the United States speaking tour of Danish Baptist leader Bredahl Petersen blamed the Holocaust on "pagan philosophies which asserted that might makes right and that the weak should be destroyed. Six million Jews were annihilated."[54] An April 1948 editorial erroneously stated, "Seven million Jews were killed in Germany alone."[55]

Two and a half years after the conclusion of World War II, *The Commission* finally recognized that Jewish concentration camp survivors were part of the displaced persons (DP) population in Europe. Marjorie Moore toured DP camps throughout the continent and noted that one camp "was the temporary home of 4,300 Jews from Poland living four to six to a room." The Jewish residents were demanding passage to Palestine, in fulfillment of their Zionist yearnings. Moore's guides disparaged the Jews as lethargic and lazy, but Moore expressed some sympathy for these victims: "I saw a few of the sole survivors of seven to ten years of concentration camps. To expect European Jews to want to work, to be ambitious and cooperative, to show initiative in making quarters habitable is to expect the impossible."

Others sought to downplay or minimize the tragedy of the post-Holocaust Jewish community. The Department of Refugees of the World Council of Churches indicated that "the Jewish refugee problem has been over publicized in the United States. . . . Today Jews constitute only two per cent of the total refugee problem." Furthermore, Moore was told that only 25 percent of the displaced persons in Europe were Jewish.[56]

In 1948, *The Commission* published several articles on Palestine. It covered the tour of sixty-two African American Baptists who also attended the BWA world congress in Copenhagen. They experienced several manifestations of the Arab-Jewish conflict.[57] Southern Baptist missionary R. L. Lindsey documented the joyous celebrations of the Palestinian Jewish community following the United Nations Assembly vote in favor of partition.[58] However, *The Commission* did not acknowledge the actual birth of Israel as an independent Jewish state in 1948.

Notes

1. Elsie B. Clor, "In Old Jerusalem," *Home and Foreign Fields* (April 1933), 10–11.

2. Everett Gill, "European Christianity and the Present Crisis," *Home and Foreign Fields* (August 1933), 1–3.

3. Editorial, "Baptist World Alliance," *Home and Foreign Fields* (October 1934), 4–5.

4. Una Roberts Lawrence, "My Missionary Bookshelf," *Home and Foreign Fields* (May 1935), 21. Lawrence revisited her concern about Europe's struggle with totalitarianism in a second column in the November 1936 issue of *Home and Foreign Fields* (24). In the April 1937 edition of *Home and Foreign Fields*, she reviewed Gill's new book, *Europe: Christ or Chaos?* (26).

5. Lawrence, "My Missionary Bookshelf," *Home and Foreign Fields* (September 1937), 29.

6. See, for example, Jacob Gartenhaus, "More Jewish Trophies of Grace," *Home and Foreign Fields* (December 1933), 9, 25; and Morris Gordin, "From Communism to Christ (A Personal Testimony)," *Home and Foreign Fields* (February 1937), 1–2; "From Communism to Christ (Part II)," *Home and Foreign Fields* (March 1937), 14–15, 25, 32.

7. Editorial, "The Modern Message," *Home and Foreign Fields* (September 1934), 4.

8. Editorial, Home and Foreign Fields (July 1936), 4.

9. Jacob Gartenhaus, "Treatment of Jews," *Southern Baptist Home Missions* (March 1938), 9.

10. Jacob Gartenhaus, "The Jewish Tragedy . . . A Christian Challenge," *Southern Baptist Home Missions* (January 1939), 10.

11. Jacob Gartenhaus, "Christians and Jews Unite to Establish Better Relationships," *Southern Baptist Home Missions* (May 1939), 10.

12. "Jews in Germany," *Southern Baptist Home Missions* (May 1940), 2. The year 1903 is in the original article, but it is likely that Gartenhaus wanted to reference 1933.

13. Jacob Gartenhaus, "The Jew in Our Midst," *Southern Baptist Home Missions* (August 1940), 12.

14. "He Was a Jew," *Southern Baptist Home Missions* (August 1940), 12.

15. "How Many Jews Are Now in Europe?" *Southern Baptist Home Missions* (July 1941), 5.

16. Joe W. Burton, "New Graves Increase Israel's Sorrow," *Southern Baptist Home Missions* (July 1941), 7–8.

17. "Christian and Jew," *Southern Baptist Home Missions* (August 1941), 13.

18. Stein's account of his ordeal and his encounters with Niemöller can be found in *I Was in Hell with Niemoeller* (New York: Revell, 1942).

19. Jacob Gartenhaus, "Niemoeller—A Christian Friend of the Jews," *Southern Baptist Home Missions* (October 1941), 14.

20. Jacob Gartenhaus, "Tragedy and Triumph Mark Thrilling Year among Jews," *Southern Baptist Home Missions* (May 1942), 8.

21. Jacob Gartenhaus, "Jews in Today's World," *Southern Baptist Home Missions* (October 1942), 13.

22. Ibid.

23. "Jewish Refugee in Havana Helped by Jacob Gartenhaus," *Southern Baptist Home Missions* (May 1943), 6.

24. Jacob Gartenhaus, "Seeking the Solution for Suffering Israel," *Southern Baptist Home Missions* (August 1943), 9.

25. Jacob Gartenhaus, "Am I My Brother's Keeper?" *Southern Baptist Home Missions* (March 1944), 12.

26. See Clyde H. DuBose, "Echoes of My Visit to Palestine," *The Commission* (March 1938), 50–52; Roswell E. Owens, "Searchlights in Palestine," *The Commission* (November 1938), 230; R. L. Lindsey, "Palestine—Experiences and Expectations," *The Commission* (October 1944), 10.

27. Editorial, "A World Gone Mad with Fear," *The Commission* (March 1938), 56–57.

28. Editorial, "Germany Has Learned Nothing," *The Commission* (July 1938), 155.

29. J. H. Rushbrooke, "The Message of Baptists in the Present World Situation," *The Commission* (July 1938), 142–45; see W. O. Carver, "Niemoeller," *The Commission* (September 1939), 301.

30. W. O. Carver, "More Trouble for the Jews," *The Commission* (September 1938), 172.

31. Ibid.

32. Charles E. Maddry, "A Ghastly Business," *The Commission* (February 1939), 50–51. Italics are in the original text.

33. Ibid.

34. Robert D. Abrahams, "A Shopkeeper Dies—Vienna, 1938," *The Commission* (March 1939), 65. See also "A Jew," *The Commission* (February 1942), 63.

35. Editorial, "Palestine," *The Commission* (July 1939), 221.

36. See Milledge Theron Rankin Collection, Southern Baptist Historical Library Archive, Nashville, Tennessee.

37. M. T. Rankin, "Why Think of the Jews at Christmas Time?" *The Commission* (December 1939), 411–12; see also a children's story, "He Was a Jew," *The Commission* (December 1939), 420–21. The arrival of German Jewish refugees in China was also noted in "Refugee Jews in China," *The Commission* (August 1939), 296.

38. Kate Ellen Gruver, "A Divine Promise," *The Commission* (September 1940), 243.

39. Editorial, "Black-Out over Europe," *The Commission* (September 1940), 258–59.

40. W. O. Carver, "New Woes for the Jews," *The Commission* (November 1940), 312.

41. Charles E. Maddry, "The Dutch Unconquered," *The Commission* (September 1941), 251–52; and Charles E. Maddry, "Appalling Brutality of Nazism in Poland," *The Commission* (January 1943), 13. *The Commission* highlighted the protest of the Swedish church in "Protest against Persecution of Jews," (March 1943), 39.

42. Charles E. Maddry, "The Plight of the Jews," *The Commission* (November 1941), 318. See also Charles E. Maddry, "When Will It End?" *The Commission* (October 1942), 335: "Seven million Jews are confronted with annihilation in East Europe. It is estimated that 40,000 a month have been killed in Poland."

43. W. O. Carver, "The Nazis and Christianity," *The Commission* (June 1942), 222–23; see also W. O. Carver, "In All Europe," and Charles E. Maddry, "The New Paganism in Germany," *The Commission* (July–August 1942), 255–56, 259.

44. Jacob Gartenhaus, "Post War Europe and the Jew," *The Commission* (June 1942), 238.

45. "Southern Baptists and Relief," *The Commission* (March 1943), 33–34.

46. W. O. Carver, "Who Crucified Jesus?" *The Commission* (September 1943), 12.

47. W. O. Carver, "God's 'Chosen People,'" *The Commission* (February 1944), 13.

48. Editorial, "The Race Question," *The Commission* (September 1944), 15–16.

49. Jacob Gartenhaus, "I Found Jews in Mexico," *The Commission* (September 1945), 7, 9.

50. George W. Sadler, "Relief Needs in Europe," *The Commission* (October 1945), 5; see also "The Churches of Asia and Europe Need Help," *The Commission* (March 1946), 8–9.

51. John D. Hughey Jr., "What of UNRRA?" *The Commission* (April 1946), 7.

52. George W. Sadler, "Baptist Life—Jerusalem to Belgrade," *The Commission* (June 1946), 9; see also H. Leo Eddleman, "The Palestine Ferment," *The Commission* (January 1947), 9–11.

53. Walter O. Lewis, "Europe Today—As a Baptist Sees It," *The Commission* (July–August 1946), 4–5.

54. Editorial, "A Voice from Europe," *The Commission* (December 1947), 19.

55. Editorial, "Tragic World Needs," *The Commission* (May 1948), 18.

56. Marjorie E. Moore, "Misery Unrelieved," *The Commission* (December 1947), 7.

57. Marvin T. Robinson and Violet Long, "We Paid a Visit to Baptist Missions in Palestine," *The Commission* (February 1948), 8–9.

58. R. L. Lindsey, "Jerusalem Goes Wild over News of UN's Decision, Reports Missionary," *The Commission* (March 1948), 1, 22.

Chapter 7

An American Jewish Response—*The American Hebrew*

The American Jewish community in the 1930s and 1940s was a sociological paradox. It had experienced tremendous growth due to decades of immigration from central and eastern Europe since 1880, with most of the new arrivals settling in major American cities, such as New York. The pressures to assimilate took their toll on traditional Jewish observance but led to a rapid rise in education and socioeconomic status. In many ways, however, Jewish communities often operated as self-sufficient entities. Entire neighborhoods in areas like Manhattan and Brooklyn were overwhelmingly Jewish, giving rise to Jewish institutions such as the garment industry, restaurants, banks, schools, theaters, and newspapers. *The Forward* (an influential Yiddish paper)[1] and the *American Hebrew* (published in English and geared more to the rising middle class) were two major Jewish journalistic voices. Since the latter interacted with the wider American culture, it may serve as a surrogate of American Jewish understanding of the Baptist response to the rise of Nazism and the Holocaust.

In its March 24, 1933, issue, the *American Hebrew* noted that S. Parkes Cadman, a Congregational minister and a leader in the Federal Council of the Churches of Christ in America, "stated that it is the duty of organized Christianity to take up the fight against anti-Semitism in Germany."[2] The paper appreciatively covered the protest declaration composed by Dr. Harry Emerson Fosdick, pastor of Riverside Church in New York City, and endorsed by the National Conference of Jews and Christians: "We, a group of Christian ministers, are profoundly disturbed by the plight of our Jewish brethren in Germany . . . we are constrained, alike with sorrow and indignation, to voice our protests against the present ruthless persecution of the Jews under Herr Hitler's regime. . . . For, protesting thus against Hitler's cruel anti-Semitism, we conceive ourselves to be speaking as the sincere friends of Germany."[3]

One of the signatories was Rev. Bernard G. Clausen, pastor of First Baptist Church, Syracuse, New York. Of the twelve hundred ministers who had registered their support, the paper chose to picture Clausen, with the caption characterizing him as the "foremost among the clergymen of Syracuse in the fostering of mutual endeavor,"[4] or in other words, Jewish-Christian understanding, friendship, and cooperation. In a year-end review of how Jews and Christians had cooperated in confronting Germany's anti-Semitism, the *American Hebrew* acknowledged Fosdick's leading role and once again quoted the declaration in which the clergy called themselves "the sincere friends of Germany."[5] One might wonder if J. H. Rushbrooke was aware of this expression when he stated to the Jewish community in London in 1935 that he wished to extend to them "the hand of sincere friendship."[6]

The American Jewish Committee published a pamphlet citing support from the Christian press, and *The Watchman-Examiner* and the *Baptist Courier* (South Carolina) represented the Baptists.[7] Also in October 1933, the *American Hebrew* offered a detailed and positive review of a newly published book, *The Jewish-Christian Tragedy*, by Baptist historical theologian Dr. Conrad Moehlman, professor of the history of Christianity at Colgate-Rochester Divinity School.[8] The Jewish weekly admired Moehlman's frankness in admitting that "the root of anti-Semitism has been the charge that the Jews crucified Jesus." He rejected this because it "has been perverted as an instrument of prejudice." Other scholars had asserted that the Romans and not the Jews were to blame for the crucifixion, but the paper appreciated the fact that "this broadminded historian builds thereon an eloquent argument for mutuality and concord." The review concludes: "Dr. Moehlman pleads that Israel and Christianity can, without compromise agree in many respects. He does not ask for the surrender of concept or mission by either creed, but exalts Christianity's debt to Judaism, rehearses the bigotries that extended from the old slander, and exalts the miracle that is Israel. It is an extraordinary book for a Christian clergyman to have written."[9]

When the *American Hebrew* became aware of the forthcoming Baptist world congress in Berlin, it relied on Moehlman to provide commentary and perspective. It set the stage for his comments by asserting that the congress represented an "opportunity for Christianity to make known its feelings in respect to the Nazi persecution of the Jews and the paganization of the church." If Baptists failed to do so, Moehlman declared, "for such cowardice the Baptists would be despised in every country of the world and would be compelled to pay heavier spiritual reparations than those the Allies so absurdly imposed on Germany." He then asked if the Baptists would be "bold enough to call attention to Christianity's debt to Judaism and the shame of the ghetto, the inquisition and the pogrom? Will they dare affirm their faith in democracy, brotherhood and the Kingdom of God and their opposition to propaganda, race hatred and war in Berlin in 1934? They must to survive. But if they do, it is difficult to see how they will thereby help their spiritual brothers, the German Baptists of Germany."[10]

The *American Hebrew* published several lengthy articles about the congress. A lead editorial on the first page of the weekly—an extraordinary placement for an article about a non-Jewish organization—balanced the achievement of the congress with the chilling observation that the Hitler regime censored news about the event. It also forthrightly highlighted the pro-Nazi agenda of the German Baptists, which was not emphasized in Baptist news reports:

> GERMANS DID NOT hear or read about it, because the Reich Government prohibited reports in the German press of addresses and resolutions other than those that praised and supported the Hitler government policies, but the rest of the world marked with deep satisfaction the declarations on racialism and anti-Semitism made by the fifth Congress of the Baptist World Alliance which met in Berlin last week. The Reich Government gave the Alliance the special privilege of free speech (denied to Germans) within the convention hall; this was a condition sine qua non on which the Alliance came to Berlin. The Baptist leaders from other nations made full use of the privilege. They even offered the rostrum to an ardent Nazi who attempted to justify the Hitler anti-Semitism which, according to eye witnesses, evoked acclaim from

> Germans in the audience, "but appeared to arouse no sympathy in the ranks of delegates from other countries."[11]

The editorial next focused on the specifics of the racialism debate and quoted the congress's "forthright" resolution: "This Congress deplores and condemns as a violation of the law of God, the Heavenly Father, all racial animosity and every form of oppression and unfair discrimination towards Jews, toward colored people and toward subject races in any part of the world. . . . With our fellow Christians in all the churches, we deplore the long record of ill-usage of Jews on the part of professedly Christian nations, and declare such injustice to be a violation of the teaching and the spirit of Christ." The editorial concluded with a sharp observation about the "irony" of Christians having to admonish other Christians to forsake anti-Semitism: "The Baptist World Alliance would not deem Germany's rulers 'fellow Christians.' They are not. The present Nazi government, calling itself Christian, is pathetically in need of the teaching and the spirit of the gentle Jew of Nazareth."[12]

The same issue contained a news article about the congress. The caption under a picture of Southern Baptist George Truett stated that the Baptist World Alliance had "administered a stinging rebuke to Nazism." As in the editorial, the article situated the congress within the larger political and social German context:

> THE FIFTH CONGRESS of the Baptist World Alliance meeting in Berlin closed its sessions with a plea for free speech, for equal treatment for all regardless of race or creed and for non-interference by the state in the affairs of the church. The congress, wherein sentiments contrary to Hitlerism were expressed, was a curious phenomenon in a land that knows no free speech. The explanation for this lapse is, of course, simple enough. The Hitler government was anxious, first of all, for the tourist trade that the congress would bring; second, for the false impression it would give to the world of Germany's "tolerance"; and third, for the demagogic weapon it would provide in dealing with the churches. Mr. Goebbels was well prepared to see that none of the civilized sentiments running counter to Hitlerism would appear in the German press. Only those "unobjectionable" features of the congress agenda were given space in the press.[13]

Having established that the Nazi authorities were using the Baptists for their own political and economic ends, the report quoted the full text of both the racialism and separation of church and state resolutions already cited in the editorial and included the following significant affirmation: "This congress urges the promotion of Christian teaching concerning respect for human personality,[14] regardless of race, and as the surest means of advancing the true brotherhood of all people urges the active propagation of the gospel of Christ throughout the world."[15]

Clearly, the *American Hebrew* believed the congress and its resolutions to be of significant news value. The weekly was also impressed with the global reaction the Baptist resolutions generated. Two months later, it published an update: "Following the Baptist World Congress in Berlin at which a resolution was adopted sharply condemning the persecution of Jews and other minorities, there has been a steady barrage of telegrams from Baptist communities all over the world with the result that strongly worded protests are arriving daily at Hitler's office demanding that he cease the persecution of Jews and oppressed minorities."[16] Unfortunately, the article does not cite a source for this remarkable claim.

The *American Hebrew* was particularly interested in how Baptist ministers spoke about anti-Semitism. In 1936 it published, in two parts, the full text of a sermon by Rev. Francis K. Shepherd of the North Baptist Church of New York. The sermon, based on Daniel's story, addressed anti-Semitism by asking, "Is salvation of the Aryan or of the Jew?"[17] In March 1937, the paper paid homage to Roger Williams and his ideal of civil and religious freedom in a fictional conversation between Williams and a Jew named David.[18] The paper mentioned that Dr. Albert W. Beaven, president of Colgate-Rochester, attended a goodwill dinner in celebration of the seventy-fifth anniversary of Rochester's B'nai B'rith Lodge.[19] Almost a year after the event, the newspaper noted that the Northern Baptist Convention in 1938 had acted on behalf of Jews by protesting "against 'coercion and persecutions such as those suffered by our Hebrew brethren throughout the world.' Baptists were urged to protest 'all violations of fundamental democratic rights in our own land.'"[20]

Even though he served a Southern Baptist congregation in Mobile, Alabama, Dr. Alfred J. Dickinson was admired by the *American*

Hebrew. In "A Christian Friend Speaks," excerpts of Dickinson's sermon against anti-Semitism were offered to a Jewish audience. Noteworthy not just for its content but also for its timing—four months prior to Kristallnacht—the sermon was praised for being "unusually effective because it combined clarity of thought with vigor of expression." The article summarized the sermon:

> "THE CRIME OF Christendom," is what Dr. Dickinson called the persecution of Jews, and "a story of injustice without precedent in history." The motive for anti-Semitism, he declared, is "avarice and spoliation for money to make war. The persecutors are building a powerful machine to crush all human liberties. The power of this concentrated military dictatorship holds the democratic world under a spell of terror. Democracy is on retreat on July 4, 1938. The line of retreat is under attack, and the Jews of Central Europe bear the brunt of it. The spirit of 1776 gave us the Declaration of Independence, but the spirit of 1938 calls for a defense of human liberty implied in that great document. The war on the Jews is a war against religious, political and economic liberties."[21]

Dickinson called his church to "love his fellow-man" and praised Jews as being "surpassed by none in idealism, benevolence or contributions to the cultural arts." Returning the favor, the editorial offered "our profound gratitude and the hope—in which we are convinced he must share—that his humane and liberal viewpoint will eventually become the gospel of all the peoples of the earth."[22] Following Kristallnacht, Dickinson raised his voice against anti-Semitism at the 1938 Alabama State Baptist Convention.

The *American Hebrew* reported that an African American Baptist congregation, Abyssinian Baptist Church in Harlem, expressed "Negro sensitivity for oppressed minorities in Central and Eastern Europe . . . through the contribution of $130 . . . for the aid of Christian and Jewish refugees." The church had invited Rabbi Harry Halpern to speak, and the pastor, Adam Clayton Powell Jr., "stated that this was the largest collection that the church had contributed during the past eight years."[23]

Another friend of the Jewish people was Rev. Coulson Shepherd, the pastor of First Baptist Church in Atlantic City, New Jersey. In March 1939, he proclaimed, "When I think of the appalling condition of the Jewish people throughout Europe, and hear every day that their situation is desperate, and then realize as I do that their physical needs suggest a greater need, one which affects them in both time and eternity, I am determined that for their sake I will not hold my peace." He admitted that he got his news about Jews from the *American Hebrew*.[24]

In June 1939, the paper featured a third Baptist sermon, preached by Rev. Jesse D. Franks. He called for friendship between Baptists and Jews in order to "cultivate a better understanding of each other's faiths, hopes, and programs of service. They are seeking to please the same God. Their faiths and their hopes have much in common. . . . To this end they should find fellowship in their worship and service of their God."[25]

In the September 8, 1939, issue, Moehlman asked, "Can Christianity and Judaism be good neighbors?"[26] Reprising what he covered in *The Christian-Jewish Tragedy*, Moehlman argued for the continuing viability of both Judaism and Christianity, quoted Jewish sources to argue that Jesus could be appreciated by Jews, condemned Christian anti-Semitism, and rephrased his original question: "But why may not Christian and Jew understand one another and cooperate with one another?"[27] Jews and Christians were neighbors and should be friends as well.

In December 1940, the *American Hebrew* focused on the statements against anti-Semitism that came from the Federal Council of the Churches of Christ in America. The council declared, "We deplore the existence of anti-Semitism in America and declare our opposition to it because it is contrary to the teachings and spirit of Christ."[28] In preparation for the February 1941 Race Relations Sunday, the council urged Christians to "purge their hearts and minds" by rejecting anti-Semitism.[29] In November 1941, the paper quoted in full the public statement of the Federal Council regarding "its attitude toward anti-Semitism." In part, the council proclaimed:

> WE CONDEMN ANTI-SEMITISM as un-American. . . . Anti-Semitism is an insidious evil which, if allowed to develop would poison the springs of our national life. Even more strongly we condemn anti-Semitism as unchristian. As Christians we gratefully acknowledge our ethical and spiritual indebtedness to the people of Israel. No true Christian can

> be anti-Semitic in thought, word or deed without being untrue to his own Christian inheritance. In behalf of the Christian churches which comprise the Federal Council we voice our renewed determination to unite in combating every tendency to anti-Semitism in our country.[30]

As news of the atrocities being committed by the Nazis across Europe gradually became accepted, the *American Hebrew* reported that the executive committee of the Federal Council on March 16, 1943, urged Christians to "give their moral support to whatever measures afford promise of rescuing European Jews whose lives are in jeopardy."[31]

One senses a change in attitude toward Christians in the *American Hebrew* beginning in 1943. It volunteered few articles acknowledging Christian activity on behalf of Jews and became critical of Christianity's role in promoting anti-Semitism. It published liberal Protestant writer Kenneth Leslie's broadside against Christians for fostering anti-Semitism. He criticized Christians who never mentioned "anti-Semitism which is an element of the Christian tradition itself." As a result, the "human tragedy of anti-Semitism" could not "grip" their souls. He then mocked a "cowboy evangelist" from Detroit who claimed Jesus could not have been a Jew because of his auburn hair color. Leslie's solution to American anti-Semitism was for Christians to accept responsibility for causing the problem and change: "What can Christianity do to combat anti-Semitism? The answer is Christianity can do practically all there is to be done to combat anti-Semitism. It is a job which democracy must assign to Christianity: Clean house of this anti-democratic thought and action."[32]

In a more satirical vein, Cincinnati news columnist Alfred Segal shared the story of Mr. Tompkins, a Chicago Baptist, who pointed out to Segal that he would have fewer problems in life if he converted to the Baptist faith from Judaism. Tompkins proved his case with a story. Another member of his Baptist church acted against his Baptist tenets and "wrecked a bank." The Baptist observed: "'Were all the Baptists made to suffer because of the delinquency of this one . . . Were all Baptists called a set of bank robbers? No, none of that! Every Baptist carries his own sin alone and no other Baptist is made to help him carry the load,' says Mr. Tompkins, as he presses upon me the delights of being a Christian among Christians." How should the Jew respond to the Christian's plea to convert and escape anti-Semitism? Segal concluded: "Oh rabbis, what should the generous nature of a Jew do with such an invitation to come over and help improve the morals of the Christian world by eliminating himself? I remember another Jew who let himself be eliminated by crucifixion for the sake of the world but it didn't do much good."[33]

The critical attitude toward Christians and expressions of alienation melted away in the postwar period. The *American Hebrew* summarized the resolutions adopted by the 1948 Northern Baptist convention, applauding its "admirably liberal and enlightened outlook on national and international affairs," indicating that "churches are fully alive to the issues of the day and taking an active part in the fight for peace."[34] A charitable assessment to be sure—especially since the convention was silent on the issue of Israel's recent independence.

Notes

1. *The Forward* was launched in 1897 and by the 1930s had a circulation of approximately 275,000 readers; http://forward.com/about-us/history/, accessed 1 March 2016.
2. Lionel Hill, "America Outraged by Plight of German Jews," *American Hebrew* (24 March 1933), 315.
3. "Clergy and Social Scientists Protest," *American Hebrew* (12 May 1933), 446.
4. "1,200 Church Leaders Condemn Nazi Anti-Semitism," *American Hebrew* (2 June 1933), 50–51.
5. "Christians and Jews in Mutual Endeavor," *American Hebrew* (1 December 1933), 48.
6. "The Evils of Arrogant Nationalism," *The Jewish Chronicle* (5 April 1935), 30.
7. "Christian Press and Churchmen Decry Nazi Anti-Semitism," *American Hebrew* (13 October 1933), 362.
8. Conrad Henry Moehlman, *The Christian-Jewish Tragedy: A Study in Religious Prejudice* (Rochester, NY: The Printing House of Leo Hart, 1933). Previously, Moehlman had published a book about religious liberty, *The Catholic-Protestant Mind: Some Aspects of Religious Liberty in the United States* (New York: Harper & Brothers, 1929). Later he wrote *Protestantism's Challenge: An Historical Study of the Survival Value of Protestantism* (New York: Harper & Brothers, 1939).
9. "The Conscience of Christendom," *American Hebrew* (6 October 1933), 327.
10. "Christian Resentment against Hitlerism Grows in This Country as Nazis Assault Jesus," *American Hebrew* (16 February 1934), 276.
11. Editorial, "Baptist World Alliance's Forthright Declarations," *American Hebrew* (17 August 1934), 237. Italics are in the original text.
12. Ibid.
13. "Baptist Congress Meeting in Berlin Condemns Racial Antagonism as a Violation of the Law of God," *American Hebrew* (17 August 1934), 240.
14. The Jewish community would have understood the Baptist use of the word *personality*. The *American Hebrew* cited it in 1934: "Through centuries enlightened mankind has striven to arrive at a recognition of *personality*, not of birth or race, as a true standard of the value of man. The race principle, false its fundamentals, would even if true, mark a regression from a spiritual view-point to a biological one"; "Judeans Discuss Racialism," *American Hebrew* (9 March 1934), 317. Italics are in the original article. Years later the paper published this

statement from a Protestant's speech: "For the sacredness of the individual personality they have substituted the sacredness of race, blood and soil"; "Nazism versus Americanism," *American Hebrew* (10 March 1939), 17.

15. "Baptist Congress Meeting in Berlin Condemns Racial Antagonism as a Violation of the Law of God," 240.

16. "Church Bodies Condemn Racial Persecution," *American Hebrew* (26 October 1934), 468.

17. Francis K. Shepherd, "Daniel's Windows Opened toward Jerusalem," *American Hebrew* (20 October 1936), 481–82, 488, and American Hebrew (6 November 1936), 510–12.

18. B. W. Blindfold, "In the Days of Roger Williams," *American Hebrew* (19 March 1937), 1002, 1004, 1029, 1031–32.

19. "Tolerance, Integral Aspect of Our History," *American Hebrew* (1 April 1938), 8.

20. "Christians Condemn Anti-Semitism," *American Hebrew* (14 April 1939), 12–13.

21. Editorial, "A Christian Friend Speaks," *American Hebrew* (22 July 1938), 3.

22. Ibid.

23. "Negro Church Aids Jewish Refugees," *American Hebrew* (23 December 1938), 8.

24. "An Appeal against Bigotry," *American Hebrew* (3 March 1939), 23.

25. Jesse D. Franks, "Babel and Our Confused World," *American Hebrew* (23 June 1939), 23.

26. Conrad Henry Moehlman, "Love Ye, Therefore, One Another from the Heart," *American Hebrew* (8 September 1939), 23.

27. Ibid., 75, 78–79, 82–83.

28. "Protestant Inter-Church Bodies Deplore Anti-Semitism," *American Hebrew* (20 December 1940), 18.

29. "Federal Council Race Relations Condemns Anti-Semitism," *American Hebrew* (27 December 1940), 10.

30. "Federal Council of Churches of Christ Condemns Anti-Semitism," *American Hebrew* (21 November 1941), 3.

31. "Christians Urged to Act," *American Hebrew* (26 March 1943), 8.

32. "Christianity Fights Anti-Semitism," *American Hebrew* (17 March 1944), 5, 13–14.

33. Alfred Segal, "Better Understanding," *American Hebrew* (5 October 1945), 8.

34. Editorial, "Design for Living," *American Hebrew* (4 June 1948), 3.

Contemporary Impressions

Informed Observers of Nazism and Jewish Persecution

Robert W. Ross, in his study of the American Protestant press, concluded that readers of these periodicals would have possessed sufficient knowledge of the Nazi persecution and elimination of the Jews to make informed judgments on what was occurring in Germany and across Europe: "During the latter months of 1942, there was no longer any question about the fate of the Jews in Germany and Nazi-occupied Europe. *The Christian Century*, *The Churchman*, the *Federal Council Bulletin*, and *The Watchman-Examiner* reported all or part of the full story."[1] The Protestant press was not silent: "The American Protestant press did report what was happening to the Jews in Germany . . . the press reported far more extensively than has generally been thought to be the case. The accepted view has been that the press had said little or nothing. Clearly, this was not true. It must be said, then, that American Protestant Christians did know, for, if the people read, the people knew."[2]

What Ross said of Protestants in general certainly applies to Baptists in particular. This survey of *Missions*, *The Watchman-Examiner*, *Home and Foreign Fields*, *Southern Baptist Home Missions*, and *The Commission*, just five of a network of Baptist periodicals that would have been available to Baptists across the United States, demonstrates that Baptist reporting on the persecution of the Jews and the subsequent Nazi campaign to eliminate them during World War II was covered as it unfolded, and in extensive detail. Of course, many Baptists also had access to secular news sources.

The worldview presented by *Missions* shared much in common with the American mainline Protestant establishment. It also uncritically supported the Baptist World Alliance and its general secretary,

J. H. Rushbrooke, especially in its policies toward Europe. Chastened by the lessons of World War I, the paper was confused by Hitler's intentions, agenda, and political methodology. Seeking to be journalistically fair, it sought to discount the evidence that Hitler's anti-Semitic policies were central to his ideological perspective, but as the evidence mounted, it usually sympathized with the Jewish victims. Occasionally, it would repeat anti-Semitic canards.

Especially in the case of *The Watchman-Examiner*, the coverage of the Jewish persecution rivaled, if not exceeded, that of its secular counterparts. This Baptist paper covered the anti-Semitic campaigns by the Nazis, the emigration of German Jews from their homeland, the attacks on the Jewish populations of the conquered countries, the launch of the deportations and concentration camps, and the tragic loss of life, numbering in the millions. It covered the desire of persecuted Jews to find safe haven in Palestine, and the Zionist movement was valued as well as critiqued from a Christian concern for prophetic fulfillment. Not only that, but in the journalistic style of the day, the editors interpreted the events from a Baptist perspective that encouraged them to condemn the Nazi campaign against the Jews, and indeed, to condemn all forms of anti-Semitism consistently and forthrightly. With just occasional lapses, solidarity with Jews and a desire for friendship was expressed.

The three Southern Baptist journals provided coverage that in some ways was similar to that of their northern counterparts. By and large, anti-Semitism was condemned, though there was more freedom for those who were not appreciative of Jews to express their point of view. *Southern Baptist Home Missions* provided a unique platform for the advocacy of Jacob Gartenhaus throughout the period, making him the premier Baptist voice on the subject of anti-Semitism within the Southern Baptist Convention, and perhaps, among Baptists in general, in the United States. *The Commission*, which highlighted Southern Baptist missionary endeavors among both Jews and Arabs in Palestine, sought to provide balance in its coverage of the Jewish Zionist dream and Arab aspirations for their own independent country.

The protests and activities of Baptists did not go unnoticed, and were in fact appreciated, by the American Jewish community, as evidenced in the coverage provided by the *American Hebrew*. This

English-language paper provided accurate coverage and cogent analysis of Baptist responses to Nazi anti-Semitism and the Holocaust, and its publication of Baptist sermons was rather courageous.

Paraphrasing Ross, Baptists in the United States, if they read the news sources such as the ones surveyed, possessed a thorough and detailed knowledge of the rise of Hitler, the Nazis' anti-Semitic agenda, and the campaigns that were waged to persecute and annihilate the Jewish populations of Germany and the rest of Europe. Having established that Baptist communities throughout the United States were served faithfully by its press, the question remains: *Since the Baptists in the United States were informed, did they respond, and if so, in what ways?*

Notes

1. Robert W. Ross, *So It Was True: The American Protestant Press and the Nazi Persecution of the Jews* (Minneapolis: University of Minnesota Press, 1980), 277.
2. Ibid., 300.

PART THREE

Bystanders: Northern Baptists and the Holocaust

What did the Northern Baptist Convention have to say about the rise of Adolf Hitler and his Nazi totalitarian regime, the anti-Semitic agenda the Nazis imposed upon German society, and the attempt to exterminate the Jewish population of Europe? Since its beginnings in 1907, the Northern Baptist Convention had become accustomed to deliberating about world affairs and proclaiming its convictions on a range of moral, ethical, and political problems confronting its Baptist constituency, the United States, and the world. Baptist historian William H. Brackney agrees that, following "World War I, Northern Baptists had developed permanent structures for social concerns, ecumenical relations, and theological debate"—including "human rights."[1] In the 1930s, the Northern Baptists perceived the following threats at work: the global Great Depression and a capitalistic system in which the poor were not adequately cared for, militarism, nationalism, communism, totalitarianism, moral laxity at home, a lukewarm spirit in the church, liquor (necessitating the repeal of the Eighteenth Amendment), and the salacious nature of Hollywood's movies.

Although the convention was prepared to respond to the rise of Nazi totalitarianism, Northern Baptists were uncertain regarding the momentous changes taking place in international affairs and modern society in general, and specifically about the momentous transformations taking place in Germany and elsewhere. In his 1934 presidential address to the Northern Baptist Convention, William S. Abernethy confessed: "We are but dimly conscious that what is going on today may easily have its bearing upon events centuries hence. All we know is that forces are at work before our very eyes that will in all probability make a world very different than anything we have been accustomed to."[2]

The Hitler regime was in its second year of persecuting Jews, German Protestants were about to publish the Barmen Declaration, and Baptists were preparing to wrestle with racialism issues at their world congress in Berlin. However, Abernethy did not explicitly refer to Hitler or the rise of anti-Semitism in his address, preferring instead to highlight the evils of liquor and gambling before turning to the importance of the resolutions coming before the convention. He stated, "Surely a body of nearly one and a half million Christian people ought to have something to say for such a time as this."[3] Similarly, Edwin McNeil Poteat Jr. observed, "[That] in certain European countries there is being made the effort to subsume all religious and ethical judgments and activities under the totalitarian state indicates that once again some sort of protest is needed." In response, he reiterated the question that was to haunt Baptists for the entire Nazi era: "Where are the Baptists in such a time as this?"[4]

Notes

1. William H. Brackney, ed., *Baptist Life and Thought: 1600–1980* (Valley Forge, PA: Judson Press, 1983), 16–17.
2. William S. Abernethy, "President's Address," in American Baptist Publication Society, *For Such a Time as This: Addresses at the Northern Baptist Convention 1934* (Philadelphia: Judson Press, 1934), 6.
3. Ibid., 10.
4. Edwin McNeil Poteat Jr., "Baptists for Such a Time as This," in *For Such a Time as This: Addresses at the Northern Baptist Convention 1934* (Philadelphia: Judson Press, 1934), 61.

Chapter 8

The Convictions of the Northern Baptists (1933-1938)

When Northern Baptists assembled for their annual convention in May 1933, J. H. Rushbrooke penned a letter revealing that he was very concerned about the underlying spiritual issues posed by the political revolutions that were transforming Europe and the rest of the world. He believed that in response to these changes, Baptists should reassert their core convictions—personality (the spiritual nature of human beings made in God's image),[1] soul freedom, and separation of church and state:

> IF I WERE with you in what I trust will be a historic gathering, I should seek to emphasize the challenge which the conditions of our times present to Christianity, and, I may dare say, especially to those convictions which are fundamental to our Baptist position. We see personality in many countries crushed beneath the heel of the State. Soul-freedom is scornfully denied. Common rights of manhood are withheld on the grounds of race, religious conviction, or political outlook. . . . But much has to be done in many lands and even in nominally Christian circles to overcome narrowness and prejudice, and to secure the recognition of the elementary truth that God "hath made of one blood all nations of men for to dwell on all the face of the earth" and that therefore the welfare of one nation or group of nations can never be achieved apart from the welfare of all. Who can contribute to this more powerfully than Baptists, with their emphasis on the value of personality, on religious and political freedom and equality, and, above all, on loyalty to the God whose universal redeeming purpose is revealed in the Lord Jesus Christ?[2]

Responses to the German Jewish Persecution (1933-1938)

Rushbrooke's confidence that Baptist core doctrines could speak to the issues of race and prejudice did not escape the notice of the Northern Baptists; neither did they ignore the attacks against Jews initiated by the Nazis in April 1933. The convention on May 26, 1933, approved a resolution on "Race Relations"[3] which contained the first national public response of the Northern Baptist Convention to Nazi persecution of the Jewish people: "We deplore outbreaks of race hatred and discrimination, as seen in our own country, and in the persecution of Jews in Germany, and we call upon all followers of the Son of man to show forth his Spirit of justice and good-will for all."[4]

Although brief, the statement unequivocally expressed opposition to the Nazi campaign against the Jews and implicitly called for Baptists in other countries to refrain from anti-Semitic attitudes and actions. The call to express "good-will" represented an endorsement of extending friendship to Jews. The passage of this resolution was widely shared in Northern Baptist state newsletters and papers throughout the country, including West Virginia, Kansas, Nebraska, and Montana-Idaho-Utah.[5]

The delegates to the 1934 Northern Baptist Convention in Rochester were reminded of the dramatic events taking place in Germany by Rushbrooke, who by letter urged Northern Baptists to lay aside their concerns about traveling to Berlin for the BWA congress. The Federal Council of the Churches of Christ in America sounded the alarm about the discriminatory Aryan paragraph debate among German Christians.[6] The Committee on Denominational Day reported that the theme for the 1934 Denominational Day was "Baptists and Religious Liberty." Its resource paper referred to Thomas Helwys and Roger Williams and then cited modern-day challenges to Baptist core convictions by countries such as Germany: "The government in Germany is committed to the principle of the totalitarian state" in which the "state claims the right to tell people what they may believe and what they may not, what they may practice in the way of religion and what they may not."[7] The Resolutions Committee proposed the following statement on church and state, expressing solidarity with Jewish brethren in Europe:

> WHEREAS, IT BECOMES necessary for Baptists to reaffirm from time to time their historic position on the relation of church and state, including especially complete separation of church and state, soul liberty and freedom from coercion in matters of conscience; and
>
> Whereas, our brethren, both Christian and Jewish, in some countries, and especially in Europe, are at present suffering because of the violation of these principles by the state; therefore be it
>
> *Resolved,* that we protest against the growing tendency to request financial aid of governments, on the part of churches and denominationally controlled institutions, and that we protest the part of governments of extending their authority over religion, thereby restricting the free exercise and expression thereof.[8]

The 1934 resolution's reference to Jewish "brethren" is somewhat ambiguous but most likely referred to Jewish Christians whose place in the German churches was threatened by the Aryan paragraph of April 7, 1933, and its ensuing interpretations. In the spring of 1934, the significance of the Aryan paragraph for the German church was hotly debated, with the German Christian movement calling for the expulsion of Jewish Christian pastors from office, and others, led by Dietrich Bonhoeffer and Karl Barth, opposing such measures. The famous Barmen Declaration, published just days after the close of the NBC meeting, became the standard exposition of the latter camp. In their 1934 resolution, Northern Baptists sided with the Barthian camp against the encroachment of the Nazi government into church affairs.

George W. Truett and Rushbrooke were both in attendance at the Northern Baptist convention in 1935 as the attendees considered the significance of the BWA Berlin congress and its statement on racialism. The Committee on Denominational Day report quoted Rushbrooke: "The world knows that we are not ready to compromise on the freedom of the church, nor to condone anti-Semitism, nor to abandon our witness and work for international peace, nor to surrender the Scriptures, nor to minimize the divine authority of the Lord Jesus Christ."[9]

The Committee on Resolutions addressed the religious situation in Germany in two resolutions. In Resolution IX on Religious Liberty, it acknowledged that "the relation of church and state in Germany is not in full accord with the convictions of the Baptists."[10] A second resolution endorsed the pronouncements made at the Berlin congress: "Whereas, the Fifth Baptist World Congress, held in Berlin in 1934, made pronouncements on questions of War and Peace, Nationalism, Racialism . . . that deserve the careful study of our people; Resolved, that these reports be made available to our people for study and that we urge our constituency to give careful consideration to the material presented and the issues raised."[11]

In the mid-1930s, as the Nazi government's oppression of its Jewish citizens became somewhat more low-key, the attention of the political world in general and Baptists in particular focused on the ideological competition between democracy, fascism, and communism. The 1936 NBC convention featured three addresses on this theme: "Left through Communism?" by Professor J. L. Gillin, "Right through Fascism?" by Rev. A. C. Thomas, and "Forward with Christ!" by Professor W. W. Adams.[12] The convention then passed a short statement in opposition to Nazism based on the Baptist core conviction of freedom of worship: "We reject the practices of Communism, Nazism, Fascism and other political regimes that deny such a right, and that our historic position is based on a different religious conception."[13]

A common Nazi rebuttal against those who opposed their persecution of Jewish citizens was that other nations discriminated against citizens without receiving international censure. US Baptists were sensitive to this charge in light of the history of slavery and the nation's post–Civil War suppression of African American civil rights and segregation. At the 1937 Northern Baptist convention, the Committee on Race Relations accepted the premise of the Nazi countercharge and called upon Northern Baptists to reject race prejudice:

> THERE IS LITTLE doubt that our Christian message to those in other lands is being discounted today and often utterly nullified by the unchristian treatment accorded those of other races in the homeland. We cannot consistently champion the cause of oppressed minorities elsewhere until we first set our own house in order. We in America have been

> guilty of practices so flagrantly unchristian as to bring us under severe condemnation. Before we call attention to the mote, we do well to cast out the beam.[14]

The Resolutions Committee encouraged Northern Baptists to make use of "the Christian friendliness" program of the Woman's American Baptist Home Mission Society in great industrial centers, as well as with groups in which "national and racial origins have caused conflict."[15] Agreeing with the Committee on Race Relations' spirit of self-criticism, Northern Baptists were admonished to "give prayerful attention to the removal of the unchristian aspects of our American life which cause nationals of other lands to say, 'Physician heal thyself.'"[16] Churches were asked to "make their Christian education complete and practically effective by promoting adventures in personal evangelism, interracial brotherhood, friendliness to the underprivileged and persecuted groups, missionary service in the neighborhood, peace action, and the Christianizing civic life."[17] The denomination was challenged to reject racial and ethnic prejudice: "Whereas, the New Testament teaches that God has made of one all the races of men that dwell on the face of the earth; therefore, be it Resolved, that in the spirit of Jesus we shall study the customs, life and ideals of the members of other races, nationalities, and religions in order better to understand and properly to evaluate them."[18]

Five months before Kristallnacht, the Northern Baptist Convention acknowledged again that Jews were under attack in Nazi Germany. In the final week of May 1938, the Committee on City Missions, noting that Jews were still a major component of the immigrant population arriving from Europe and that 98 percent of immigrant Jews settled in metropolitan areas, decried the existence of "fascism" in America.[19]

The Resolutions Committee turned its attention to the international scene and specifically expressed solidarity with Jews: "We raise our voice in protest against such coercions and persecutions, including those suffered by our Hebrew brethren throughout the world, and express the hope that the moral conscience of the world and particularly of our own country may become active in helping to change this condition."[20] Resolution IV asserted that "the basic principles of democracy are violated in the totalitarian state" and therefore the convention wished to "express our sympathy with all persecuted minority groups abroad."[21] The groups were not specified, but it was likely that Jews were meant to be included. Following Kristallnacht, it fell to the Northern Baptist Convention's general council to specifically advocate for Jewish exile immigration, in an extraordinary letter to President Franklin Delano Roosevelt.

The General Council Responds to Kristallnacht

The General Council of the Northern Baptist Convention possessed the authority to speak for the convention in between annual conventions and, on rare occasions, even passed resolutions of its own. Sensing that the Great Depression was creating financial stress and emotional suffering in the churches, the council penned a year-end message of encouragement in December 1933: "The dismay of the nations, the confusion of humanity, and the world-wide wistfulness for a reality of brotherhood and the blessing of peace and the warmth of security combine to offer the followers of Christ a new day of magnificent opportunity. May we not, therefore, unite with you in a great comradeship of faith, of hope, and of love toward God and all humanity."[22]

This may have been a reference to the struggles of German Jews and Christians in Germany, since later in the meeting the council discussed the question of sending delegates to the BWA congress in Berlin. There was internal controversy about the wisdom of meeting in Berlin, for the authorization for the corresponding secretary to represent Northern Baptists was accepted only on condition that he would cover his own expenses.[23] A year later, however, the council did vote to publish "an inexpensive edition of the proceedings of the Congress."[24]

The council's first clear response to the tragedy unfolding in Germany was its approval for the 1937 NBC convention to show the movie *Martyrs in Germany*.[25] The movie had been shown at the Riverside Church in New York City on April 12, 1937, and provoked an angry reaction from the Nazi press in Germany. The film focused on the persecution of Christians by Hitler's regime, and the *New York Post* published an excerpt from the movie's written program: "All the world knows that ostracization [*sic*], privation, terror and even death are the lot of tens of thousands of Jews in Nazi Germany. As yet there is no general awareness in America that almost an equal number of Christians in the Third Reich are facing the degradation of social exclusion, the threat of penniless exile and the cruelty of the concentration camp."[26]

The second, and historically most significant, General Council response to the persecutions taking place in Germany came three weeks after Kristallnacht, when they met at the Hotel Prince George on 28th Street in New York City, from Tuesday, November 29, to December 1, 1938. During the initial morning session, the General Council "voted to request E. A. Fridell to present a resolution on Wednesday, covering the anxiety of our denomination concerning the persecution of religious and racial minorities abroad."[27]

On Wednesday, November 30, Fridell returned with two lengthy resolutions. The first resolution focused on Rumania, which considering the BWA campaign Rushbrooke was leading on this issue, was not unexpected by the council members.[28] The second was a response to Kristallnacht, which was also adopted by the council. Reacting to "the rapid rise of Totalitarianism in the world today" which the council judged to be "a deadly threat to vital religion and all human freedom and is in itself an assault on the spiritual foundations of Democracy," the leaders shared their "deepest concern the unparalleled horrors and indignities now being visited upon racial and religious minorities in several parts of the world." The council

> RESOLVED that we call upon our constituency in the states of our Convention area to give themselves to self-examination and to prayer to the end that the spirit of fear and hatred which is leading to continual oppression, and in some lands even to threats of ruthless extermination, may not find lodgment in the hearts of the American people.
>
> BE IT FURTHER RESOLVED that we give ourselves to special prayer on behalf of oppressed Jews and Roman Catholics in Germany and Baptists in Rumania, and all others who during these immediate days are special victims of persecution.
>
> BE IT FURTHER RESOLVED that we express to the President of the United States of America our concern that he take the lead in calling an international conference for the purpose of dealing with the Refugee Problem on a scale commensurate with the unprecedented situation now before us.

> BE IT FURTHER RESOLVED that we place ourselves on record with authorities at Washington approving the reception into the United States of Political and Religious refugees of acceptable character up to the full limits of existing quota standards. That we further urge our authorities under the same safe-guards to take whatever additional steps will most effectively perpetuate the time honored tradition which would make the United States a haven for victims of oppression for conscience sake.
>
> BE IT FURTHER RESOLVED that we more earnestly give ourselves as Baptists to the solution of those social problems within our borders which give rise to human suffering and need and thus undermine faith in those self-governing institutions which are indispensable to effective Democracy.[29]

This second resolution was immediately relayed to the *New York Times*, which published an article entitled "Baptists Condemn Dictators' Threat" on Thursday, December 1, 1938.[30] The *Times* highlighted the denomination's opposition to totalitarianism and support for the United States to serve as a "haven" for "political and religious refugees." The article quoted the resolution's support "for oppressed Jews and Roman Catholics in Germany and Baptists in Rumania" (substituting the word *plea* for the original statement's "prayer").

The General Council also shared the November 30 resolution in the January 1939 National Supplement insert for regional publications. It revealed how the General Council wanted its constituency to understand its actions. The council endorsed "the Baptist belief that the rapid rise of totalitarianism constitutes a deadly threat to vital religion and protests against the persecution of Jews and Roman Catholics in Germany and Baptists in Rumania" and called upon President Roosevelt "to take the lead in calling an international conference to deal with the refugee problem."[31]

The General Council's resolution was a significant milestone in regards to the Northern Baptist Convention's response to the plight of the Jewish people. Although hurriedly composed, it acknowledged the Jewish plight after Kristallnacht, mentioning them before Catholics and even Baptists. It restated Baptist opposition to Hitler's totalitarianism and advocated for Jewish refugees to be admitted into the United States. However, the resolution's request for President Roosevelt to call for an international conference was peculiar, since the prior Evian Conference (July 6-15, 1938) was a failure. Furthermore, the resolution could have provided more details on the Jewish plight and stronger language in condemning it. The impact of the resolution would have been magnified if Northern Baptist leaders had followed up by expressing their personal support for persecuted Jews.

Northern Baptist Convention Responses (1939-1948)

The momentum generated by the General Council on behalf of the Jewish people carried over to the Northern Baptist Convention's 1939 annual meeting in Los Angeles. During the evening plenary session on Tuesday, June 20, Rabbi E. F. Magnin, of Congregation B'nai B'rith in Los Angeles, spoke on the subject of "The Plea of Israel to the Christian World."[32] This may have been the first time in Northern Baptist history when a leader of the Jewish community was invited to speak before its national meeting. *The Watchman-Examiner* reported that Magnin spoke about "the persecution and anti-Semitism that faces his people in the modern world."[33]

The issue of persecuted Jews received attention from several committees during the 1939 convention. The Council on Finance and Promotion no doubt had Kristallnacht in mind when it cited "the ills of the world . . . visualized in dictatorships, in race hatreds, in economic distress, in war. The fact of religious persecution on an unprecedented scale, and under conditions of government never witnessed before, is the most dangerous and disconcerting thing about this situation."[34] The Committee on Denominational Program called for "developing and enriching personality" and preaching "the kinship of all races before God."[35] The Committee on Relations with Other Religious Bodies asked for a united Protestant stand in "the struggle against rival world views, such as those of Fascism and Communism which are now being proclaimed with evangelistic ardor" and quoted Charles Evan Hughes: "When we lose the right to be different, we lose the right to be free."[36]

The Committee of Public Relations introduced the Baptist Joint Statement on Liberty, a cooperative pronouncement by Northern, Southern, and National Baptists. The joint statement recognized that the "sudden rise of European dictators to power has changed fundamentally the organic law of the governments through which they organize sovereignty, and as a result, the institutions of religion are either suppressed or made subservient to the ambitious national programs of these new totalitarian states."

In response, the Baptist bodies called for a vigorous defense of religious liberty, not just for Baptists but for all people, including Jews: "Believing religious liberty to be not only an inalienable human right but indispensable to human welfare, a Baptist must exercise himself to the utmost in the maintenance of absolute religious freedom for his Jewish neighbor, his Catholic neighbor, his Protestant neighbor, and for everybody else. Profoundly convinced that any deprivation of this right is a wrong to be challenged, Baptists condemn every form of compulsion in religion or restraint of the free consideration of the claims of religion."[37]

The Committee on Race Relations forthrightly addressed American anti-Semitism, acknowledged the persecution of European Jews, and argued that it was the responsibility of Northern Baptists to confront such prejudice in both church and culture:

> WE NOTE WITH deep concern the evident growth of antisemitic sentiment among us. This is not so marked in the church as elsewhere, but even among Christian people it is apparent and indications are that it [is] spreading. This unbrotherly, unchristian attitude forebodes disastrous results if unchecked. While the feeling toward this unfortunate race is by no means as intolerant and violent as in certain European countries, nevertheless it is here, and notice must be taken of it. Surely it is something that our pastors cannot ignore. It will be a sorry day for the churches of America if intolerance of this sort shall be allowed to enter. The churches can and must combat this growing tide of antisemitism.[38]

The Resolutions Committee also addressed the crisis Jews were facing. The committee addressed racialism issues in general terms, but the relevance to Germany's persecution of the Jews is unmistakable. The Social Issues section of the broader resolution began by affirming that "God hath made of one blood every nation of men to dwell on all the face of the earth, and that we are His offspring." The resolution opposed "unchristian attitudes, movements, and institutions that cause tensions and misunderstandings between races, nations and groups, and tend to hatreds that eventuate in bloodshed and even in war" and then condemned "without qualification every institution of discriminatory character, every discriminatory law, every anti-racial organization, and all unfair tactics on the part of either labor or capital or any other movement that inflicts injustice and suffering upon any group of any race, creed or political affiliation." It called for Northern Baptists to "lend every effort to bring justice to any minority group that is being discriminated against because of race, color, religious beliefs, or political ideologies."

In between sections applying these principles to African Americans and Asian Americans (designated as "Orientals"), the committee then specifically addressed American anti-Semitism:

> WHEREAS, THERE IS widespread propaganda against the Jew in the United States, sometimes disseminated by so-called Christian groups; and
>
> Whereas, the Jew has made such a great contribution to religious truth and to civilization; therefore, be it
>
> Resolved, that we oppose every form of discrimination against the Jew and call upon our members to work for justice for this group in every walk of life.[39]

Having established Baptist opposition to racial prejudice of all kinds, and to domestic anti-Semitism in particular, the Resolutions Committee focused on "groups suffering distress and misery" in Europe and Asia. Although mostly concerned about Christians, the Resolution on International Relations pointedly referred to Jewish victims of Nazi oppression:

> *RESOLVED*, THAT WE record our sympathy with such groups; specifically the people of China, who are victims of an undeclared war that has brought devastation and untold misery; the Christians of Japan and others there of like spirit; the people of Czecho Slovakia [*sic*], whose territory has been forcibly annexed by Germany and who are enduring the woes of a conquered people; Christians in Germany, who are suffering for their faith; our Baptist brethren and other Christian people in Russia, who suffer disabilities for religion's sake; Jews in Germany and other lands, who are enduring sore persecution. Furthermore, be it

> Resolved . . . To help in creating among our constituency such attitudes as will promote understanding and guard against propaganda in regard to the refugee problem.[40]

Northern Baptists did not believe that they could directly intervene on behalf of Jews in Germany and its occupied territories, and thus they focused on the possibility of providing aid to refugees who might escape to the United States. In the 1940 annual meeting, the Committee on Social Service highlighted the need to assist European Jewish refugees: "*Resolved*, that we require of all relief agencies that they show the same consideration to refugees from minority groups, whether Jewish or Christian, as is given to the oppressed members from state church bodies."[41] This was one of the rare occasions in which the possibility of Baptist financial support for Jewish refugees was even raised, let alone offered. The issue of Jewish refugees may also have been raised in a clinic on race relations that addressed the topic of the "Treatment of Refugees of Various Races."[42]

The discussion concerning racial issues during the 1940 meeting was more general in nature. The Committee on Race Relations admitted that initially "it seemed advisable to the members of our committee to urge churches in the Northern Baptist Convention to give special attention this year to their relationships with Negroes and Jews." However, after consultation with leaders from around the country, the committee reversed its intention and decided to encourage "every church give special attention to racial and national groups in its community with whom understanding and fellowship are most urgently required."[43]

The Resolutions Committee also issued a general statement in relation to totalitarianism, which reasonably can be interpreted as an allusion to German Jewish persecution:

> WHEREAS, THE RIGHTS of minorities recognized by free peoples are today being violently challenged throughout the world and abolished wherever totalitarianism in any of its forms gains control of government, be it
>
> *Resolved*, that we reaffirm our faith in the democratic way of life and call on our churches to encourage and support all governmental authorities, local and national, in protecting the liberties of all our racial,

> social, political and religious groups, according to the Bill of Rights in the Constitution, and to oppose all movements, of whatever name or purpose, that seek to suppress or limit freedom of speech, press, assembly or religion guaranteed under the Constitution.[44]

The situation dramatically changed in 1941, when American anti-Semitic groups were proliferating, inspired by Father Charles Coughlin, Charles Lindbergh, and others.[45] The Northern Baptist Convention felt constrained to approve a clear resolution on anti-Semitism. Although the Committee on Race Relations admitted that their "study has been confined to our relations with Negroes and Jews, and almost exclusively to Negroes,"[46] the Resolutions Committee considered the plight of the latter community:

> WHEREAS, ANTI-SEMITISM and all racial antagonisms are definitely Un-christian [*sic*]; therefore, be it
>
> *Resolved*, that we reaffirm our belief in the equal rights of man. Furthermore, be it
>
> *Resolved*, that we seek by every method of aggressive good-will to remove every practice of a discriminatory character, every discriminatory law, every anti-racial organization and all unfair tactics that inflict injustice or suffering upon any individual or group on account of race, creed or political affiliation.[47]

On December 15, 1941, the executive committee of the Ministers Council sent out a New Year's letter that said, "Let us keep in mind and before our people the conviction that hatreds of personalities must be foreign to us, and that all racial discrimination is contrary to the very genius of Christianity."[48] In 1942, the denomination specifically opposed Hitler's racial theories and policies by invoking both science to discredit racialism and the core conviction of the unity of humanity to affirm Baptist solidarity with Jews:

> WHEREAS, WE ARE contending against the theory of race superiority as expressed by the Axis powers through their leaders; and
>
> Whereas, This theory is discredited by the findings of science and is contrary to the tenets of our religion; and

> Whereas, We see mounting evidence of practices based upon acceptance of this theory in our own country; therefore be it
>
> *Resolved,* That we reaffirm our fundamental belief in the fatherhood of God and the brotherhood of man, and that we call upon our churches, our industries, and the government to be impartial in the granting of liberty and opportunity to all, regardless of race or culture. Furthermore, be it
>
> *Resolved,* That we call the attention of our constituency to the fact that scientific men state there is no difference in the blood plasma of different racial stocks and that we deplore the practice of segregation of blood plasma on any racial basis.[49]

The 1943 convention was canceled due to wartime travel restrictions. When the NBC reconvened in Atlantic City in 1944, the "Detroit riots of 1943"[50] and the continuing expressions of domestic prejudice against Jews formed the backdrop for the report of the Committee on Resolutions. Its resolution placed anti-Semitism in a racialism context, mentioning also African Americans and "other minority racial groups." Once again Acts 17:26, the principal Baptist text against anti-Semitism and race prejudice, was invoked to express Baptist opposition to prejudice of all kinds:

> WHEREAS, PRESENT CONDITIONS reveal the unjust, undemocratic, unchristian and, therefore, dangerous attitudes and practices in relation to Semitic, Negro and other minority racial groups in our country; and
>
> Whereas, We believe in the New Testament statement in Acts 17:26 that "God hath made of one blood all races of men," and commit ourselves to the lordship of Christ in all of life; therefore, be it
>
> *Resolved,* That we dedicate ourselves and seek to commit our churches to the teaching, preaching and full practice of Christian relationships with all people; that, as members of the majority racial group in our country, we seek every possible way of enlarging our fellowship without discrimination; that we actively work for equality in housing, education, economic opportunity in every field of honorable endeavor, and the unrestricted practice of the privileges and responsibilities of free citizenship with full civil and religious liberty; and that, to this end, we call upon all Northern Baptists to co-operate honestly and sincerely as

> followers of Him who came "not to be ministered unto but to minister" and as Christian citizens of our country; and
>
> Whereas, Anti-Semitism and racial antagonism are increasing in this country at an alarming rate; therefore, be it
>
> *Resolved*, That we do everything possible, through our Councils and Home Mission Societies, and from the pulpit, in the church school and in our publications, to encourage the spirit of brotherhood and good-will.[51]

The Northern Baptist Convention's annual meetings in the post-war period (1945–1948) did not produce any additional resolutions on anti-Semitism, the destruction of the Jewish community in Europe, or Zionism and the establishment of Israel. Instead, attention was focused on developing, financing, and executing ministries for displaced persons. This collective effort was coordinated by the General Council.

The General Council and Displaced Persons

Northern Baptists anticipated that there would be a tremendous need for humanitarian aid for the victims of war throughout Europe. Prior to the 1944 convention, the General Council passed a set of resolutions on both Russian and European relief. They stated that Baptists should "collect and forward to a central depot, clothing for adults and children" and "make contributions toward the cost of packing and shipping the clothing."[52] The Northern Baptist aid plan was modeled after the BWA effort following World War I and did not feature any targeted aid to Jews.

The December 1945 resolution of the Council on Christian Social Progress declared that "democratic leaders of Europe, who have languished in prison cell and concentration camp, will likewise die unless food and clothing are given by America now."[53] The General Council affirmed President Harry S Truman's humanitarian initiatives and requested that he "repeal the present restriction upon feeding former enemy peoples" and "require UNRRA to administer relief of food, clothing and medical aid to all, according to need and without regard for nationality or religion."[54]

The first reference to Jewish refugees by the General Council was in March 1947, and it was widely disseminated by the Baptist press and state conventions. The resolution assured the convention that aid to displaced persons was primarily intended to benefit Christians, not Jews. Furthermore, Baptists were going to focus on helping Baptist refugees:

> WHEREAS, there are nearly a million displaced persons composed of men, women and children, 80% of whom are Christians of various denominations, and 20% Jews, including 150,000 children below the age of 17; and . . .
>
> WHEREAS, we have a direct concern for the approximately 30,000 Baptists now in the displaced persons camps, largely from Latvia, Lithuania, and Estonia, . . . therefore, be it
>
> RESOLVED, that we urge Congress not only to support this recommendation of the senate Foreign Relations Committee, but also to provide, by an emergency act, for the admission of a total of 100,000 displaced persons during each of the next four years, this number representing less than half of the immigration quotas not used during the war years; and further be it
>
> RESOLVED, that we offer all of our available resources, through our World Relief Committee, to assist in the resettlement of these displaced persons in suitable American communities.[55]

None of the postwar resolutions specifically mentioned assisting Jewish survivors of the Holocaust. A 1947 resolution referred to "great numbers of displaced persons who suffered barbaric treatment during the war are still in camps in Europe."[56] Northern Baptists accepted responsibility to relocate twelve hundred Baptist displaced family units. In September 1949, the convention was having difficulty fulfilling its quota, and so it sent out pleas for support. The reports clearly indicated that there was an agreed-upon division of labor between Jews, Catholics, and Protestants, with each responsible for helping their own constituents: "Catholics and Jews have already given assurances for their fair share of the 215,000 Displaced Persons who may be resettled. . . . Only the Protestants have lagged behind. Dr. Beers said that 'if we do not do our part, Catholics and Jews in place of Protestants will be brought to America before the Displaced Persons Act expires next June 30, and the Protestants will be left in Europe in despair.'"[57]

More happily, the denomination was able to report in 1950 that every state convention had agreed to sponsor displaced persons and that the Northern Baptist quota was exceeded: "Northern Baptists are proud of the fact that the 1,200 goal for displaced persons assurances have been more than reached thanks to the efforts of a great many people. In addition to this number about 350 assurances were given by Northern Baptists before the goal was set. All eligible Baptists in displaced camps have received assurances. The Resettlement Office of The American Baptist Home Mission Society reports that the states with the largest number of family unit assurances from August 1, 1949 to January 13, 1950 are: Massachusetts 135, New York 134, Pennsylvania 122, Arizona 84, and New Jersey 74."[58]

Notes

1. See Arthur Temple Cadoux, *A New Orthodoxy of Jesus and Personality* (London: Ivor Nicholson and Watson Limited, 1934).

2. *Annual of the 1933 Northern Baptist Convention*, Minutes Item 136, Letter from J. H. Rushbrooke, 182–83.

3. Ibid., Minutes Items 220–21 ("International Relations") and Item 222 ("Race Relations"), 233.

4. Ibid., Minutes Item 223, Resolution VII—"Race Relations," 238–39.

5. West Virginia, *The Baptist Banner* (15 June 1933), 15; *The Kansas Baptist* (7 July 1933), 3; *Nebraska Baptist Messenger* (July 1933), 9; *Montana-Idaho-Utah Baptist Messenger* (July 1933), 11.

6. *Annual of the 1934 Northern Baptist Convention*, Minutes Item 62—Letter from J. H. Rushbrooke, 153–54; and Minutes Item 133—Report of the Members of the Federal Council of the Churches of Christ in America, 173–74.

7. Ibid., Minutes Item 303—Report of the Committee on Denominational Day, 286–89.

8. Ibid., Minutes Item 238, Resolution VI—"Church and State," 194.

9. *Annual of the 1935 Northern Baptist Convention*, Minutes Item 303, Report of the Committee on Denominational Day, 194.

10. Ibid., Minutes Item 210, Resolution IX—"Religious Liberty (b) Germany," 271.

11. Ibid., Minutes Item 210, Resolution VII—"Denominational Affairs (e) Study of Reports," 271.

12. *Annual of the 1936 Northern Baptist Convention*, Minutes Items 252, 288.

13. Ibid., Minutes Item 257, Resolution I—"The Historic Baptist Principles (b) Church and State, Section 2—Freedom of Worship," 291.

14. *Annual of the 1937 Northern Baptist Convention*, Minutes Item 30, Report of the Committee on Race Relations, 103.

15. Ibid., Minutes Item 233, Resolution III—"The Church and the Great Commission (a) In the Homeland," 273.

16. Ibid., Minutes Item 233, Resolution III—"The Church and the Great Commission (b) In Other Lands," 273.

17. Ibid., Minutes Item 233, Resolution IV—"The Church's Education Ministry (a) In the Local Church," 275.

18. Ibid., Minutes Item 233, Resolution V—"The Church Leavening the World (b) Creating World Brotherhood," 277.

19. *Annual of the 1938 Northern Baptist Convention*, Report of the Committee on City Missions," 104–6.

20. Ibid., Minutes Item 152, Resolution IV—"The Church and Its Social Task (b)," 175.

21. Ibid., Minutes Item 152, Resolution IV—"The Church and Its Social Task (g)," 176.

22. *Minutes of the General Council of the Northern Baptist Convention*, December 13, 1933, Item 3487, 5.

23. Ibid., Items 3489–91, 6.

24. *Minutes of the General Council of the Northern Baptist Convention*, December 12, 1934, Item 3645, 7.

25. *Minutes of the General Council of the Northern Baptist Convention*, May 19, 1937, Item 4208, 7.

26. "N.Y. Martyr Film Stirs Nazi Press," *New York Post* (13 April 1937), 4.

27. *Minutes of the General Council of the Northern Baptist Convention*, November 29, 1938, Item 4494, 3.

28. Ibid., November 30, 1938, Item 4545, 9.

29. Ibid., Item 4546, 9–10. Capitals are in the original document.

30. "Baptists Condemn Dictators' Threat," The *New York Times* (1 December 1938), 9.

31. "Baptists Protest against Tyranny," *The Northern Baptist Convention Supplement to The Kansas Baptist* (January 1939), 4.

32. *Annual of the 1939 Northern Baptist Convention*, Agenda Schedule, 60; see also 155–56.

33. "NBC Convention Review," *The Watchman-Examiner* (6 July 1939), 773.

34. *Annual of the 1939 Northern Baptist Convention*, Report of the Council on Finance and Promotion, "Adjustments to a Changed World," 71.

35. Ibid., Report of the Council on Denominational Program, 144–45.

36. Ibid., Report of the Committee on Relations with Other Religious Bodies, 150.

37. Ibid., Supplement to the Report of the Committee on Public Relations, "A Baptist Pronouncement upon Religious Liberty," 170, 173–74. See William H. Brackney, ed., *Baptist Life and Thought: 1600–1980* (Valley Forge, PA: Judson Press, 1983), 423; see also 424–26 for the text of the statement.

38. *Annual of the 1939 Northern Baptist Convention*, Report of the Committee on Race Relations, 181.

39. Ibid., Report of the Resolutions Committee, Item 223, Resolution V—Social Issues, Sections (c)–(f), 269–70.

40. Ibid., Report of the Resolutions Committee, Item 223, Resolution VI—International Relations, Sections (a) and (c), 271–72.

41. *Annual of the 1940 Northern Baptist Convention*, Report of the Resolutions Committee, Resolution VI—International Relations, Section (b), 355.

42. Ibid., Agenda, Clinic VI—"Race Relations in the Modern World," 76.

43. Ibid., Report of the Committee on Race Relations, 257.

44. Ibid., Report of the Resolutions Committee, Resolution III—Threats to Spiritual Freedom, Section (b), 349.

45. See Lynne Olson, *Those Angry Days: Roosevelt, Lindbergh, and America's Fight over World War II, 1939–1941* (New York: Random House, 2013).

46. *Annual of the 1941 Northern Baptist Convention*, Report of the Committee on Race Relations, 157.

47. Ibid., Report of the Resolutions Committee, Resolution V—Social Issues, Section (b), 224.

48. "A New Year Message to the Pastors of the Northern Baptist Convention," *The Baptist Observer* (1 January 1942), 12.

49. *Annual of the 1942 Northern Baptist Convention*, Report of the Resolutions Committee, Resolution V—Social Issues, Section (e) "Race Relations," 267.

50. *Annual of the 1944 Northern Baptist Convention*, Report of the Council on Christian Social Progress, 74. The Detroit race riots began on June 20, 1943, and were precipitated by worker tensions at the Packard Motor Company. It is unclear if African American tensions with the Jewish community were expressed during the riots; see Dominic J. Capaci Jr., "Black-Jewish Relations in Wartime Harlem," in *Strangers and Neighbors: Relations between Blacks*

and Jews in the United States, ed. Maurianne Adams and John Bracey (Amherst, MA: University of Massachusetts Press, 1999), 388–89.

51. *Annual of the 1944 Northern Baptist Convention*, Report of the Resolutions Committee, Resolution III—Moral and Social Issues, Section (j) "Race Relations," 275.

52. *Minutes of the General Council of the Northern Baptist Convention*, May 22, 1944, Item 6264, 3–4.

53. *Minutes of the General Council of the Northern Baptist Convention*, December 11, 1945, Item 6410, 4–5.

54. Ibid., Item 6412, 6–7.

55. *Minutes of the General Council of the Northern Baptist Convention*, March 19, 1947, Item 6685, "Displaced Persons," 3. Capitals are in the original minutes.

56. *Annual of the 1947 Northern Baptist Convention*, Report of the Resolutions Committee, Resolution III—International Affairs Section (b) "Displaced Persons," 188–89.

57. "Churches Asked to Resettle 1200 Displaced Families," *New Jersey Baptist Bulletin* (September 1949), National Supplement, 7; see also 3.

58. "Northern Baptist Quota Exceeded as Every State Sends D. Assurances," *New Jersey Baptist Bulletin* (March 1950), National Supplement, 72.

Chapter 9

The Home and Foreign Mission Societies

The Northern Baptist Convention's ministries were overseen by several autonomous mission societies, many of which existed before the convention itself was established. The American Baptist Foreign Mission Society (ABFMS), the American Baptist Home Mission Society (ABHMS), and the Woman's American Baptist Home Mission Society (WABHMS) played distinctive roles in responding to the challenge of Nazism, the persecution of European Jews, and offering friendship to Jewish refugees who sought to create new lives in the United States.

The American Baptist Foreign Mission Society

The American Baptist Foreign Mission Society's involvement in Europe can be traced back to the beginnings of the Baptist movement on that continent. Johann Gerhard Oncken, the father of both the German Baptist fellowship and wider European Baptist movement, was baptized by a representative of the American Baptist Missionary Society, Hamilton College professor Barnas Sears, on April 22, 1834.[1] In the first half of the twentieth century, Northern Baptists did not provide missionaries to its European partners, preferring instead to provide consultative services through its appointed representatives. During the 1930s and 1940s, the ABFMS representatives were Walter O. Lewis, who was later appointed to be the general secretary of the Baptist World Alliance from 1939 to 1948,[2] and his successor, Edwin Bell.

In its 1933 report, the society referred to its participation in the International Missionary Council that was held in Herrnhut, Germany, from June 23 to July 4, 1932. The "Council faced frankly the critical problems confronting the missionary enterprise including a growing racial consciousness, and increasing nationalism."[3] It also hinted that discomfort with the victory of Hitler played a role in canceling the 1933 congress in Berlin: "Although regrettable, this decision met with general approval because of the increasing economic pressure in all countries and the grave political situation in Germany."[4]

Both the economic and political issues continued to concern the board. The minutes of the September 25-26, 1933, meeting stated, "That, with its present information, the Board would also question the wisdom of the reported plan for holding a meeting of the Alliance in Berlin in 1934."[5] The ABFMS foreign secretary voted against the Berlin meeting plan when the executive committee of the BWA met; having lost the vote, he decided to support the meeting in public statements.[6] In 1934, the board's annual report indicated that there still was concern over the propriety of meeting in Berlin, and it blamed "conditions in general" as well as financial constraints for creating a situation in which it was "unfavorable to cooperate in efforts to promote attendance upon the proposed Congress at Berlin in August, 1934."[7] J. H. Rushbrooke, however, pressed the convention to support the congress in order to demonstrate "fraternal sympathy" not with Jews but with the German Baptists.[8] Following the congress, the 1935 annual report admitted:

> ALTHOUGH THE BOARD was not represented officially, individuals closely connected with the foreign mission program found it possible to attend. There had been wide difference of opinion as to whether the meeting should be held in Germany in view of the general political conditions. However, every courtesy was extended to the delegates and there was an unusually frank exchange of opinions on such vital issues as war, race, nationalism and religious freedom.[9]

In 1936[10] and 1937, the board watched with concern as the totalitarian powers in Europe gained strength. Lewis wrote two articles for *Missions* during that period, but neither mentioned persecuted Jews, even though one of the articles was focused on events in Germany.[11] Although the ABFMS annual reports did not explicitly mention the Nazi persecution of Jews, the society's concern about totalitarian control over religion and race was evident:

> COMMUNISM AND FASCISM seek the balance of power on continental Europe. . . . The rapid spread of the totalitarian philosophy, which even seeks to bring the religious sentiments of the human heart under the control of the State to be used for its own ends, is all too evident in the political processes of many great nations. . . . Industrial, class and racial strife throughout the world are acute and their inherent and basic causes challenge Christian thought and action.[12]

The board was especially concerned about Germany, and though it couched this concern in diplomatic language, Northern Baptist support for the German Baptist Union and its work was under review. Lewis, the special representative of the ABFMS, was called back to the United States for consultation concerning the "disturbed political and international conditions in Europe, the reactionary attitudes and developments to be observed in many European countries."[13] By 1938, financial support for the German Baptist Union had been cut off: "Through the modest appropriations as well as the counsel and advice of Special Representative W. O. Lewis, Northern Baptists have been able to help the cause of Christ in nine countries, France, Belgium, Denmark, Poland, Norway, and in three Baltic States, Estonia, Latvia and Lithuania, and in Czechoslovakia."[14] On September 26, 1938, the board met with Dr. A. L. Warnshuis, secretary of the International Missionary Council, in anticipation of the Madras Missions Meeting. Warnshuis remarked that one of the problems the conference would need to address was "the approach to the Jews and minority problems."[15]

Less than a week after Kristallnacht, the Foreign Mission Board voted to have "the Officers' Council give consideration to a protest on the treatment of the Jewish people in Germany and Austria."[16] However, the Foreign Mission Board did not produce its own protest over Kristallnacht, according to the minutes of the January 17, 1939, meeting: "In accordance with action taken by the Board at the November meeting the Officers' Council had given consideration to a protest on the treatment of the Jewish people in Germany and Austria and had decided that in view of the fact that the General Council of the Northern Baptist Convention had registered a protest on the Jewish question this would be sufficient."[17]

The position of the board seems at first glance to be entirely reasonable, given that the General Council did produce a strong protest about Kristallnacht. However, upon closer inspection, a discrepancy of approach becomes apparent. The board next approved its own letter on the Rumanian situation,[18] even though the General Council had also produced one at the same meeting at which it adopted the Jewish protest. This raises a question that is not answered in the minutes. Why was the General Council action "sufficient" in one case and not the other? It is reasonable to conclude that the fate of Rumanian Baptists was more important to the board than the plight of Germany's Jews.

In its 1939 annual report, the board clearly expressed concern about anti-Semitism for the first and only time between 1933 and 1948: "The number of refugees driven from their homes now runs into the hundreds of thousands. Anti-Semitism grows worse and extends to countries where it was unknown before 1933."[19] During the first half of 1939, several designated donations from individuals and churches came in to the Foreign Mission Society for "relief of distressed Jews in Germany" or similar designations, totaling $36.82 for Jewish relief, $11.50 for Jewish Christian relief, $35 for German Baptist or Protestant aid, and $5 for "persecuted people in Europe."[20] The donations were placed in Lewis's ministry account, but the record does not indicate how he disbursed the funds. He did, however, update the board on "the problems faced by Baptists in what was formerly Czechoslovakia but is now part of Germany under Hitler's rule" at the April 1939 meeting.[21]

Lewis appeared reticent to highlight the suffering of Europe's Jews. *The Nebraska Baptist Messenger* reprinted part of an interview with Lewis that revealed his perspective on the persecution of Baptists and Jews in Europe:

> BAPTISTS AS WELL as Jews and Catholics have felt the religious persecution now sweeping parts of Europe. . . . Although the sufferings of Baptists have been of a comparatively minor nature compared with the Jews and Catholics, it has become marked in recent months. . . . Baptists and members of other religious minorities find it increasingly hard to carry out normal civil functions, such as obtaining legal forms attesting birth, marriage, and death.[22]

Even though the 1940 ABFMS annual report referred to "concentration camps,"[23] Lewis wrote a five-and-a-half-page survey on what the "war has done to the hearts and minds of European Baptists," without once mentioning the plight of European Jews.[24] In a 1941 article on war prisoners, he mentions Jews once: "Yielding to German pressure, France has thrown into concentration camps many thousands of Czechs, Poles, Jews, and others who had fled to France to escape the terrors of the Nazi regime in Germany."[25] In 1942, he wrote another update on European Baptists but did not mention Jews.[26] The World Relief Committee reported that Northern Baptists raised "approximately $125,000" for several emergency needs, including "relief of Baptist pastors and churches in the invaded countries of Europe" and "aid for Christian refugees from European countries," but aid to Jews was not mentioned.[27] If he had wanted to, Lewis could have revealed that the World Relief Committee did receive $1,247.34 for "specific" needs, including "Jewish relief."[28]

Edwin A. Bell replaced Lewis as the ABFMS special representative for Europe in 1943.[29] In November 1943, Lewis, now in his capacity as the BWA's general secretary, "made a special plea for the relief of suffering in Europe, for work in Europe after the war, and for the bringing of young people to America to be educated."[30] Bell emphasized Baptist responsibility to assist distressed Baptists in Europe. He stated that "we are witnesses to the outbreak of an unbelievable cruelty," but he never mentioned Jews as the foremost victims of that cruelty. He did, however, repeatedly mention helping European Baptists.[31] The only instance in which Bell mentioned the plight of Jews was when he highlighted the heroic efforts of Henri Vincent, the leader of French Baptists, who "had some close calls with the Nazi Gestapo because of his activities in behalf of the Jews."[32]

In 1946, Lewis reached the city of Odessa in the southern part of Russia. He encountered a Jewish woman who engaged him in a conversation about the story of Joseph and the butler he met while imprisoned. He wrote: "Joseph had predicted the butler would be released and begged him to remember his fellow prisoner. . . . The Jewish woman expressed the hope that I would not forget the sufferings of the people of Russia when I returned to America."[33] The rest of Lewis's article emphasized the need of displaced persons, especially the Baptists among them: "There are thousands of Baptists in these 'displaced persons' camps."

Similarly, in Bell's postwar reports, the need for ministry on behalf of Europe's Baptists was reinforced each year. In 1946, the ABFMS report stated: "The millions of refugees and displaced peoples and the transfers of large racial minorities have created overwhelming problems. . . . Bell's special interest has been in the Baptists, who are minority groups in Europe."[34] In the 1948 report, Bell was reported to be working cooperatively with German Baptists.[35]

The American Baptist Home Mission Society

The American Baptist Home Mission Society was responsible for mission initiatives throughout the United States and Central America. It spearheaded initiatives related to new church development, evangelism, and social justice ministries, including race relations. After speaking of Northern Baptist opposition to slavery and ministry to the African American population, William Brackney stated:

> BAPTISTS DESIGNED A similar outreach for immigrants to the United States which hardly affirmed total religious liberty. Four years after its founding in 1832 the American Baptist Home Mission Society (ABHMS) began its work with foreign populations among the Welsh and successively with Germans, Scandinavians, French Canadians, Mexicans, Chinese, Poles, Italians, Jews, Slavs, and Hindus. Partially to offset the Nativist movement which discriminated against non-English speaking Americans, Baptists sought to "Christianize" and "Americanize" the immigrants. Recognizing that few of these people were Baptist, missionaries were appointed to gather congregations, start schools, and design social welfare programs to assimilate different cultural and social patterns into a sense of national unity.[36]

After failed attempts to support missions targeting the Jewish populations in cities such as Brooklyn, the Home Mission Society essentially saw its historical approach to Jewish missions come to a conclusion. In its 1933 report to the Northern Baptist Convention, the ABHMS admitted that the once promising mission initiative in Chicago had closed: "It has been a matter of distress to all friends of Jewish work that the Albany Park Friendship Center in Chicago had to be closed during the year because of lack of funds. It is our hope that when economic conditions improve we may again undertake a work for Jews in this city."[37] The Chicago Baptist Association's executive council revealed that in addition to financial concerns, there was also dissatisfaction with the leadership.

These problems led the association to rethink its strategy for evangelizing Jews in Chicago. In the future, "work for Jews should be carried on by the churches located in the areas where they reside in large numbers. Where necessary, the missionary agencies of the denomination should come to the assistance of the local churches. Special work carried on in complete separation from the local church is hard to control, and the history of institutions directed by converted Jews would seem to justify the assertion that many of them are run in the interests of organizations rather than as distinctly missionary enterprises."[38]

In its 1935 annual report, the Home Mission Society conceded that its longstanding approach to Jewish missions required reconsideration and revision. Two concerns stood out: the need for a positive witness by individual Christians characterized by friendship (as opposed to harboring and expressing anti-Semitic attitudes) and the locus of activity being the local church (as opposed to a specialized mission):

> THE JEWS CONSTITUTE one of our major foreign-speaking groups, with four and one-half million people. They are found principally in our large cities and some of their number occupy positions of importance. The Church of Christ cannot make any headway in presenting the claims of Christ until the members possess a Christ-like spirit. These people are being absorbed rapidly in our American life but cannot make their best contribution until they are won into a Christian fellowship by the churches. There is wide diversity of opinion regarding the best method of approach, but it is possible for every church with Jewish neighbors to give them Christian fellowship and strive to win them in the same way as all others in its local field. Experience has proven to many minds that this is the real strategy.[39]

The Jewish work in Buffalo, New York, which had prospered under A. B. Machlin's leadership in the 1920s, gradually diminished throughout the 1930s due to the changing of the ethnic and cultural character of the surrounding community.[40] In its annual report to the 1937 convention, the ABHMS acknowledged the closing of the Buffalo mission: "After many years of constructive work among the Jews in Buffalo, the Hebrew Christian Center of that city was discontinued in the past year. This was done because the Jewish in the neighborhood, which at one time reached nearly one hundred per cent, has moved out almost entirely."[41] The closing of the Buffalo mission effectively ended the era of nationally directed ministries to the Jewish people.

In its 1940 annual report, the Home Mission Society discussed the topic of "Christian refugees from Europe" coming into the United States, a clear indication that Jewish exiles were not included. "The newest and most baffling problem which we confront in connection with others is that of Christian refugees from Europe. Mainly they come from Germany and the countries which Germany has overrun. . . . Our denomination has organized a committee in which the Home Mission Society is represented and is largely influential. This committee will act as a connecting link between our denomination and the American Committee for Christian Refugees."[42] To its credit, the Home Mission Society ministered to Japanese Americans and advocated for their release during the 1940s.[43] Accordingly, it fell to the Woman's American Baptist Home Mission Society to minister to Jewish people, and particularly Jewish immigrants during this period, which it managed through the extraordinary efforts of its Christian Friendliness corps of mission workers.

The Christian Friendliness Missionaries

The Woman's American Baptist Home Mission Society was the sole Northern Baptist Convention–affiliated national agency to address in a practical manner the difficulties Jewish immigrants faced in fleeing Europe and beginning a new life in the United States. Following the First World War, the society created the Department of Christian Americanization to help churches reach out to immigrants and assist in their assimilation to American life through English as a Second Language classes, social events, and sharing Christian faith. In 1936, its name was changed to the Department of Christian Friendliness. A worker lauded the ministry's relational orientation:

> WE LIKE ALL that the new name implies—a knowledge of the old-world background of these new Americans; appreciation of their country's culture; sympathetic understanding of the problems they face in being transplanted into an entirely new and bewildering world; the desire to help make these adjustments as painless as possible; and the realization that there is mutual benefit from our friendships with people who have so much to contribute to American life.[44]

Mary Martin Kinney became the director of the department, and in 1938 she published *The World at My Door* to explain the philosophy behind Christian Friendliness, share stories of the ministry in action, and spread wisdom learned after almost two decades of experience in serving thousands of immigrants. The aims of the ministry were succinctly described by the tagline: "For active good will, mutual understanding and Christian fellowship between individuals and groups of different national background."[45] Jewish immigrants were befriended and served by the society's Christian Friendliness missionaries and the local churches they mobilized for this relationally based outreach.

By the 1930s, the Christian Friendliness work was actively being pursued by a significant number of the Northern Baptist congregations. The 1933 annual report indicated that in 1931–1932, 741 churches and 5,042 volunteers reached out to 6,393 "foreign homes." The following year (1932–1933) the statistics had increased to 814 churches with 5,455 volunteers serving 8,476 homes of immigrants.[46] In 1935 the department was being served by "eight full-time district missionaries, four full-time city missionaries, and two half-time," and 915 churches with 5,210 volunteers and 1,341 prayer partners reached out to 7,435 homes.[47] Growth continued throughout the mid-1930s. In 1935–1936 fewer volunteers reached more homes: 946 churches with 4,907 volunteers served 7,539 households.[48] For 1936–1937, the statistics were 964 churches with 5,705 volunteers serving 8,230 homes. For the first time, Kinney's report mentioned that the workers made 42,607 calls and taught 39,263 English lessons.[49]

The impact of the Christian Friendliness ministry was felt across the country, and much appreciated. There is no way to discern how many of the households the Christian Friendliness missionaries and volunteers visited contained Jewish families, but in her 1938 report, Kinney confirmed that this ministry interacted with Jews: "Jewish children who are just learning what 'Christian' means—these and many others told with wide smiles as well as words how acceptable were these expressions of the Crusaders' love."[50] In 1939, Kinney stated that the convention had asked her department to help resettle "Christian German refugees."[51] For the 1938–1939 ministry year, 1,180 churches with 4,682 volunteers made 46,718 calls and reached 8,412 foreign homes.[52]

Kinney also shared stories related to Christian Friendliness ministry to Jewish refugees and immigrants. In 1940, she noted that Jews attended "our first International Christmas Vesper" program in New York City and shared a testimony from Chicago that was a perfect illustration of the relational dynamics encouraged by the Christian Friendliness movement:

> MRS. N., A Sunday School teacher, had gained a wide acquaintance among German-Jewish refugees simply through neighborliness. In the apartment across the hall from her lives a refugee family. They visit back and forth. Both housewives do the laundry on the same day each week and they chat together over the tubs. Mrs. N. uses the opportunity to discuss religion with Mrs. Jacob. Several blocks away lives Mrs. Jacob's brother, Mr. Suess, and his family. Mrs. Suess says, "I like Mrs. N. She is such a good friend! Other people are nice to me, too, but she is my special friend." These and others of Mrs. N.'s refugee friends have formed a Bible class which meets every Saturday afternoon in different homes, the hostess providing refreshments. The attendance runs from five to ten. For teacher, Mrs. N. secured a Christian Jewish woman who has had Bible training. Mrs. Suess is rapidly increasing her English vocabulary through regular attendance at a public school class for foreign-speaking people. The teacher who conducts the class is a member of our Chicago Christian Friendliness Committee. Her classes include many German refugees.[53]

During the war, the Christian Friendliness missionaries sought to embody the Northern Baptist conviction that racism, whether against Asian Americans, African Americans, or Jews, could best be countered by a concerted effort to relate to all people as friends. In 1942, Kinney reported: "A Jewish man who formerly owned a business in Europe has been supporting his family here with a dishwashing job. What a Christian Friendliness volunteer has accomplished in giving courage and practical assistance to this family is an illustration of what individual activity has meant. Summer holidays in the country were provided for children from these families. . . . The Christian religion has been demonstrated in various ways for the sake of these newly arrived seekers after freedom."[54] The 1944 report states: "Careful attention to Japanese-American resettlers, greater effort to draw Negro and white Baptists into closer co-operation, continued service to European refugees, and the urgently needed activity in behalf of Jewish Americans have been the main emphases of 1943–1944."[55]

One of strengths of the Christian Friendliness ministry was the partnership fostered with state conventions and city associations. In 1946, Kinney spotlighted the partnership with several judicatories: "Pennsylvania is enthusiastic over having a Christian Friendliness missionary again after spending months without such a leader. The response to the efforts of the missionary have made possible new ministry to a group of children of Jewish families in Philadelphia, increased calling in homes of foreign language background and the extension of interracial acquaintance and Christian partnership."[56]

Across the country, Christian Friendliness missionaries shared testimonies illustrating their interaction with Jewish people and encouraged Baptists to befriend Jews. On the Eastern Seaboard, no one was more energetic or determined in expressing Christian friendship with Jews than Matilda Utecht.

Matilda Utecht served as the Christian Friendliness missionary for Rhode Island and Maine. Utecht developed relationships with members of the Jewish community wherever she served. In 1940, two of her stories were highlighted in *Missions*. The first concerned a young Jewish woman: "One of our Jewish refugees, a girl—pretty, poised, and intelligent—is speaking before Christian groups and making a fine impression because of her—we would say Christian attitudes—and her beautiful philosophy of life. One wonders what effect her sitting with us—singing our hymns, hearing our readings and prayers—is having upon her thinking."

The second story is darker, for it concerned an anti-Semitic incident:

> ONE OF MY concerns has been the number of refugees we have in Rhode Island. I am appalled at the causes for fear among them. We do not say anymore, "It Can't Happen Here." Things are happening that give reason for wonder and worry. In Connecticut, according to the papers, a Hebrew cemetery was wrecked. Stones were thrown over and marked with swastikas; others were shattered. The damage ran into large figures. "Hoodlums" we say! Yes, but what may these same hoodlums do next? And where? When people come out of a background of fear they see more in such happenings than we who casually read about them in the newspapers.[57]

Utecht hoped that her stories would strengthen Baptist resolve to remain open to the ideals of the Christian Friendliness movement. She argued for compassion to overcome despair so that Christian friendship might be a blessing to European refugees:

> A YOUNG GIRL, a refugee from Europe, spoke before a group of Baptist young people recently. She told of hunger, but that, she said, was not important. She spoke of persecution of Jew and Christian in Europe, but that too, she said, was not important. The important thing is that America should not lose its ideals; that religious people should not lose their faith in God; and that somehow together we keep America a pattern for a new world. When we realized she had known hunger, persecution, loss of home and country, sufferings of which we have no comprehension, we sensed the depth and earnestness of her appreciation of the goodness of God and our need of knowing better how to live Christianity so that it may stand as the pattern for our world.[58]

In 1942, Utecht shared how Christian Friendliness missionaries could become deeply involved with their new Jewish friends:

> ONE OF OUR refugee girls had her first vacation, two weeks with pay, but where could an eighteen year old Jewish girl, who has been in America only a short time, go. We did not know so packed our suit cases and went to Ocean Park. The weather was perfect but that was not the best part of it. Reverend Scalisi, a Baptist pastor born in Italy, was there and made such a deep an impression at the Sunday service that she wanted to hear him again.... There isn't space to tell all the story but she went home with a beautiful Bible which she had picked out herself to learn

> not only her side of it but ours as well that she may know why she does not believe as we do, or, if it prove this way, why she does. We are hoping it may mean much for her.[59]

Utecht was instrumental in helping the Baptist churches in Maine serve refugees in their state. By 1942, the Maine Christian Friendliness corps of volunteers had grown to fifty women, and four churches reported "direct friendly contact with refugees."[60] John S. Pendleton, Maine's executive secretary, extolled the impact of Utecht's ministry:

> THE APPOINTMENT OF Miss Matilda Utecht last year as a Christian friendliness worker was a very happy one and proved most timely. In these days when hatreds are being cultivated and racial and class strifes are rampant how important it is that the Christian Church magnify the spirit of the Master. Surely it is for us to love our enemies and many of the people with whom we deal and perhaps treat unkindly are not our enemies at all but only have a skin of a different color or have been reared in different circumstances. The very fact that our Convention has a Christian Friendliness Department speaks clearly of our interest and love for all mankind. While Miss Utecht can spend only a limited time with us as we share her with Rhode Island she has already found her way into many of the churches in neighborhoods where there are foreign speaking people and her counsel is being followed and her influence widely felt.[61]

Utecht's love for refugees, African Americans, and Jews motivated her to reproach prejudice and anti-Semitism, although at times her attempts to elicit compassion became somewhat paternalistic. In one article, she compared the plights of African Americans and Jews:

> WE ATTENDED AN Urban League banquet and realized again how much needs to be done for our Negro friends. Dr. Tobias closed his speech with thoughts like these—"You may resent ignorance because it should be changed; you may resent lack of culture because something should be done about it; but when you resent color you resent God himself. He made us this way!" I feel the same about our Jewish friends. They are born into a group which they can't help. We can break down the resentments which rise up like dark threatenings from people who otherwise seem Christian in thinking and attitudes.[62]

Friends of the Jews on the West Coast

On the other coast, Christian Friendliness missionaries were also interacting with Jewish refugee families. In 1937, W. A. Shanks, the executive secretary of the Washington Baptist Convention, summarized the range of Christian Friendliness work in his state:

> "NO DEPARTMENT OF our work is more important than that of Christian Friendliness, and under the guidance of Miss Ruby Richardson scores of our Baptist women have deepened and enriched their own Christian experience through their ministry of friendliness to their sisters and other races, who are their neighbors here in Washington. . . . A Japanese Buddhist woman learned of Christ for the first time; a Catholic Austrian mother, who had lost her faith, discovered Christ anew; a bewildered, over-burdened Chinese mother found that someone really cared for her; a Spanish-Jewish woman, very much alone, discovered that there were American Christian women who had a genuine heart interest in her."[63]

In 1938, Richardson celebrated how many different nationalities her ministry reached out to, including Jews: "As I put down the number three hundred which represents approximately the number of foreign homes reached by our Baptist people, I wish each of you could visualize them as I do. You would see Japanese, Chinese, Greek, Austrian, Italian, Albanian, Jewish, Russian, Bulgarian and Syrian. Some of the homes are already Protestant Christian, but others are Greek Orthodox Catholic, Roman Catholic, Buddhist, and Jewish while still others profess no faith."[64] In her next report, she included a poem to emphasize the caring dimension of Christian Friendliness:

> *Lord, let not my religion be*
> *A thing of selfish ecstasy;*
> *But something warm with tender care*
> *And fellowship which I can share;*
> *Let me not walk the other side*
> *Of trouble's highway long and wide;*
> *Make me a good Samaritan,*
> *And neighbor unto every man.*[65]

In 1940, Washington Baptists passed a resolution on Christian Friendliness to "express our appreciation to the splendid work of Miss Ruby Richardson, who will soon relinquish her duties as Director of Christian Friendliness Work in our State, and that we pledge our support in counteracting racial prejudice and building human brotherhood."[66]

Washington Baptists were particularly active in promoting Christian Friendliness, especially in the Seattle area. European refugee ministry was its focus, because they needed "assistance in adjusting themselves to this new land after having gone through much suffering and hardship in Europe. Their problems are many and they need friendship." A monthly "Jewish-American" club was established in that city for "study and fellowship—possibly unique in the country. Christian Friendliness missionary Mary Zoa Annis reported, "A Jewish man said to me recently, 'If we ever needed friends, it is today.' That is the heart cry of all races in our world. May the response to it come from all of us who name the name of Christ."[67]

Ruth Beagle took over Washington's Christian Friendliness work in 1942. In *The Washington Baptist*, she cited a letter she received from a Baptist woman in Spokane who appreciated receiving Christian Friendliness materials on the following three racial groups: "First, the Jew against whom there is a widespread prejudice. Second, the Negro who is discriminated against in every walk of life. Third, American citizens of Japanese parentage, innocent victims of race hatred and a disregard of their loyalty as American citizens."[68] Beagle was, in turn, replaced by Violet Rudd, who in 1946 encouraged her followers to invite a rabbi or Jewish layperson to church.[69]

The Christian Friendliness movement was also strong in Northern California, where Isabelle M. Gates was serving. In 1940, she observed: "Northern Baptists gave to this Department responsibility for discovering ways to aid refugees from Central Europe. . . . The wives of five German Jewish doctors came to a Christian Friendliness Christmas party. Again and again in the months that have passed they have mentioned their deep gratitude for that experience. Their great need is friendship; often they have told us: 'We want to find American friends with whom we can share.'"[70] Gates also demonstrated how much the Christian Friendliness missionaries enjoyed their friendships with Jews:

> AN OLDER GERMAN Jewish refugee whom I met a few months ago has proved a constant delight. Her keen mind and discerning spirit are a never-ending source of amazement and refreshment as we read and study together. It was such a joy to have her come one day to my small new home for her lesson. I believe it was the first time she had been in an American home and she was the first of our foreign friends whom I entertained after I moved. After our lesson we had tea and open-face sandwiches. The latter proved a sensation and she pronounced them delicious! She insisted that she felt as though she were in paradise because "First you give me food for my spirit and now I have food for my body." You may know I felt overwhelming humility. She speaks of God with such great reverence and yet such familiarity that He is a vivid reality during the times we spend together. Her friendship has been a rich blessing and I shall miss her greatly when a new volunteer takes over the weekly lessons.[71]

Before Gates concluded her ministry in Northern California, she coordinated one last successful engagement with Jewish refugee families. Working with a German Jewish wife of a professor who relocated to the University of California, Gates created a summer camping vacation week in which Jewish children interacted with local Baptist families in Monterey. The warmth of a Baptist pastor impressed the Orthodox Jewish parents of the children: "When her father realised [*sic*] that the man who was driving his daughter to Monterey was a minister, he was overcome with astonishment. Again and again the Jewish father said, 'I cannot believe that that man is a minister. Why, he was so modest! And he lifted all the bags and put them into the car himself. In Germany, neither a rabbi nor a Protestant pastor would do such a thing!'"

Another Jewish family responded positively when their children brought home Bibles: "Later, that mother told us that her children not only read the Bibles, but pray before every meal. . . . Still another mother from one of these homes asked me this month to recommend a Christian church where her fifteen-year-old daughter might find a group of Christian young people."[72]

Muriel Ferguson took over the Northern California Christian Friendliness ministry after Gates moved north to serve the Oregon Baptist Convention. In 1941, Ferguson made note of a ministry to refugee children that included "German-Jewish boys and girls."[73] In 1942, she reported: "Not only has the Japanese situation been one that has caused deep concern, but among those classified as enemy aliens are the refugees from Germany and other axis countries. They are people without a country, for now it has become impossible for them to get American citizenship. Last summer we had twelve German-Jewish children in some of our Christian American homes at Salinas and Monterey. This was to strengthen the ties that had been established through a project started the previous year."[74]

A Legacy of Friendship

Christian Friendliness was the most prophetic and practical rebuke to racial prejudice and anti-Semitism within the Northern Baptist Convention. In 1945, the Northern California Christian Friendliness report began with a remarkable and passionate defense of the ministry's aims and goals, as it sought to combat all forms of racial and religious prejudice: "Christian Friendliness is built on the passion of Jesus. . . . This phrase, Christian Friendliness, suggests personal acquaintance with persons of Negro, Chinese, Japanese, Mexican, Russian, Armenian, alien German decent [*sic*] and of Jewish religion. For how else than by personal acquaintance may we acquire mutual understanding, active good will, and Christian fellowship among individuals and groups from all backgrounds?"[75]

The Woman's Baptist Mission Society report of the Illinois Baptist Convention stated in 1941 that "refugees, oil and crop migrants, the Jews, the American citizens of Japanese parentage and the American Negro compose some of the minority groups" ministered to by Christian Friendliness workers.[76] Christian Friendliness workers in Indiana asked their churches to "pray that horror over the plight of the Jews in Europe may find expression in patient effort to develop better understanding and opportunity for Jews in our own land."[77]

The Christian Friendliness movement not only engaged in personal ministry with Jews and other groups but also fought prejudice wherever it was manifested in the Baptist family and the larger American society. In 1943, Marian Gage presented a powerful argument against prejudice, including anti-Semitism:

> CHRISTIAN American or AMERICAN Christian—which are YOU? Are you like the big-hearted woman who, with her own boy on the ocean headed for an unknown destination, could still find time and inclination to assemble and mail a bundle of toys to make a merry Christmas for little Japanese-Americans in relocation camps? Or are YOU the one who was so annoyed by shortages she said, "Christmas presents! Nonsense! Children or not, they're Japs, and you can't trust Japs!" Or are you like the dear little lady who said, "It's just terrible what Hitler is doing to the Jews," and then added as an afterthought, "but we'll really have to do something about them in America, before they just push us out!"

The 1945 Christian Friendliness report for the Northern California state convention not only summed up the spirit of the movement but also tied together the German Jewish persecution, the Japanese American incarceration, and African American segregation with the spiritual life of the Baptist churches:

> JESUS WAS NOT afraid of any human being. Are we victims of paralyzing fears? . . . These fears must have been present in the hearts of German Christians at the beginning of the persecution of the Jews. The persecution extended to them in no time at all. These fears paralyzed us when pressure was allowed to uproot Japanese folk on the western strip. Only such a love as Jesus had breaks through paralyzing fear. As followers of His, we claim liberating love, liberation from love of ourselves and of the priorities of White Supremacy. The West need not accept the goal of Southern race relations: a more harmonious adjustment of the Negro to the white man's pattern.[78]

In 1948, Christian Friendliness missionary Martha Whalen articulated a vision of friendship that she hoped would define what it meant to be Northern Baptist. Commenting on a New Jersey Baptist Christian Friendliness Committee that included men as well as women, she said: "It was evident to the committee that there was a definite need for the people in the 'old-stock' Baptist churches to build friendships with foreign born, with those of other races, with migrant workers and with Jews. The job of breaking down the barriers of prejudice falls to those who have the vision of Christian Brotherhood."[79]

Notes

1. J. H. Rushbrooke, *The Baptist Movement in the Continent of Europe*, 1–7; see also Ian M. Randall, *Communities of Conviction: Baptist Beginnings in Europe* (Schwarzenfeld, Germany: Neufeld Verlag, 2009), 52–53.

2. Richard V. Pierard, ed., *Baptists Together in Christ 1905–2005: A Hundred-Year History of the Baptist World Alliance* (Birmingham, AL: Samford University Press, 2005), app. 2, 325.

3. *Annual of the 1933 Northern Baptist Convention*, Annual Report of the American Baptist Foreign Mission Society, 383–84.

4. Ibid., 392–93.

5. Minutes of the Board, American Baptist Foreign Mission Society (September 25-26, 1933, Meeting), 235.

6. Minutes of the Board, American Baptist Foreign Mission Society (November 20-22, 1933, Meeting), 263.

7. *Annual of the 1934 Northern Baptist Convention*, Annual Report of the American Baptist Foreign Mission Society, 410.

8. Ibid., 153–54.

9. *Annual of the 1935 Northern Baptist Convention*, Annual Report of the American Baptist Foreign Mission Society, "Baptist World Alliance," 395.

10. *Annual of the 1936 Northern Baptist Convention*, Annual Report of the American Baptist Foreign Mission Society, "Meeting of the World Missionary Council," 425–26: "The special factors rendering vitally necessary the calling of a such a meeting were . . . second, the startling advance of the principles of totalitarianism in state control of the life of peoples which has affected already a fifth of the population of the globe, and which threatens the root principles of the evangelical faith such as liberty of conscience and freedom of worship."

11. W. O. Lewis, "Recent Developments in Germany," *Missions* (December 1936), 604; "The Zero Hour in Europe," *Missions* (May 1937), 292.

12. *Annual of the 1937 Northern Baptist Convention*, Annual Report of the American Baptist Foreign Mission Society, "Surging Tides of Alien Forces," 381–82.

13. *Annual of the 1934 Northern Baptist Convention*, Annual Report of the American Baptist Foreign Mission Society, "Visit of Dr. W. O. Lewis," 381–82.

14. *Annual of the 1938 Northern Baptist Convention*, Annual Report of the American Baptist Foreign Mission Society, "Baptists in Europe," 385.

15. Minutes of the Board, American Baptist Foreign Mission Society (September 26, 1938, Meeting), 49.

16. Minutes of the Board, American Baptist Foreign Mission Society (November 15, 1938, Meeting), "Treatment of Jews in Europe," 113.

17. Minutes of the Board, American Baptist Foreign Mission Society (January 17, 1939, Meeting), "Treatment of Jews in Europe," 133.

18. Ibid., "Religious Freedom in Rumania," 133–34.

19. *Annual of the 1939 Northern Baptist Convention*, Annual Report of the American Baptist Foreign Mission Society, "Europe," 445.

20. Minutes of the Board, American Baptist Foreign Mission Society (February 28, 1939, Meeting), 193; (April 18, 1939, Meeting), 223.

21. Minutes of the Board, American Baptist Foreign Mission Society (April 18, 1939, Meeting), 212.

22. "Sees Anti-Baptist Drive," *Nebraska Baptist Messenger* (April 1939), 8.

23. *Annual of the 1940 Northern Baptist Convention*, Annual Report of the American Baptist Foreign Mission Society, "Europe," 522.

24. W. O. Lewis, "Europe's War and Europe's Baptists," *Missions* (February 1940), 86–91.

25. W. O. Lewis, "I Was in Prison," *The Watchman-Examiner* (10 July 1941), 740.

26. W. O. Lewis, "News from Great Britain and Europe," *The Watchman-Examiner* (23 April 1942), 402–3.

27. *Annual of the 1941 Northern Baptist Convention*, Report of the World Relief Committee, 272.

28. "War Emergency Fund Aids in War-Torn Countries," *The Washington Baptist* (November 1942), 4.

29. Minutes of the Board, American Baptist Foreign Mission Society (June 22, 1943, Meeting), "Edwin A. Bell," 388; *The Watchman-Examiner* (30 September 1943), 945.

30. Minutes of the Board, American Baptist Foreign Mission Society (November 15, 1943, Meeting), "W. O. Lewis," 453.

31. Edwin A. Bell, "Mr. Need Has Arrived for a Long Visit," *Missions* (May 1944), 282–84.

32. Edwin A. Bell, "First Impressions of Postwar France," *Missions* (October 1945), 421.

33. W. O. Lewis, "He Forgot Joseph," *The Watchman-Examiner* (4 July 1946), 702.

34. *Annual of the 1946 Northern Baptist Convention*, Annual Report of the American Baptist Foreign Mission Society, "Europe," 260; see also *Annual of the 1947 Northern Baptist Convention*, Annual Report of the American Baptist Foreign Mission Society, "Europe Relief," 279.

35. *Annual of the 1948 Northern Baptist Convention*, Annual Report of the American Baptist Foreign Mission Society, "Europe," 271.

36. William H. Brackney, *The Baptists* (New York: Greenwood Press, 1988), 102–3.

37. *Annual of the 1933 Northern Baptist Convention*, Annual Report of the American Baptist Home Mission Society, 635.

38. *1933 Annual Meeting of the Chicago Baptist Association*, Report of the Baptist Executive Council, "A Conviction Registered," 25.

39. *Annual of the 1935 Northern Baptist Convention*, Annual Report of the American Baptist Home Mission Society, 694.

40. "Buffalo Jewish Work," *The Baptist New Yorker* (December 1935), 2.

41. *Annual of the 1937 Northern Baptist Convention*, Annual Report of the American Baptist Home Mission Society, 627.

42. *Annual of the 1940 Northern Baptist Convention*, Annual Report of the American Baptist Home Mission Society, "Christian Refugees from Europe," 714.

43. *Annual of the 1943 Northern Baptist Convention*, Annual Report of the American Baptist Home Mission Society, "Special Relief for Japanese," 272; *Annual of the 1944 Northern Baptist Convention*, Annual Report of the American Baptist Home Mission Society, "Ministries for Evacuees," 377–79; *Annual of the 1946 Northern Baptist Convention*, Annual Report of the American Baptist Home Mission Society, "Japanese Americans," 322–23.

44. *Annual of the 1936 Northern Baptist Convention*, Christian Friendliness Department Report, 826.

45. Mary Martin Kinney, *The World at My Door* (Philadelphia: Judson Press, 1938), 176.

46. *Annual of the 1933 Northern Baptist Convention*, Christian Americanization Department Report, 680.

47. Ibid., 782–83.

48. *Annual of the 1936 Northern Baptist Convention*, Christian Americanization Department Report, 828.

49. *Annual of the 1937 Northern Baptist Convention*, Christian Americanization Department Report, 709.

50. *Annual of the 1938 Northern Baptist Convention*, Christian Friendliness Department Report, 713.

51. *Annual of the 1939 Northern Baptist Convention*, Woman's American Baptist Home Mission Society Report, 727.

52. Ibid., Christian Friendliness Department Report, 744.

53. *Annual of the 1940 Northern Baptist Convention*, Christian Friendliness Department Report, 803–5.

54. *Annual of the 1942 Northern Baptist Convention*, Christian Friendliness Department Report, 384.

55. *Annual of the 1944 Northern Baptist Convention*, Christian Friendliness Department Report, 404.

56. *Annual of the 1946 Northern Baptist Convention*, Christian Friendliness Department Report, 361.

57. "Christian Friendliness Meets the Refugees," *Missions* (February 1940), 112.

58. "America, a Pattern for a New World," *Missions* (November 1941), 567.

59. Letter dated 6 October 1942, WABHMS Box 32 Folder 5, in the American Baptist Historical Society Archive.

60. Meroe F. Morse, "Christian Friendliness Report," *The Maine Baptist Messenger* (July 1942), 8.

61. *United Baptist Convention of Maine—Year Book 1942*, Report of the Convention Board, 12–13.

62. "Dark Threatenings," *Missions* (October 1943), 471.

63. *1936–1937 Washington Baptist Annual*, Annual Report of the Board of Trustees by W. A. Shanks, Christian Friendliness, 34.

64. *1937–1938 Washington Baptist Annual*, Christian Friendliness Report, 43.

65. *1938–1939 Washington Baptist Annual*, Christian Friendliness Report, 51.

66. *1939–1940 Washington Baptist Annual*, Resolutions Committee Report, 51.

67. *1940–1941 Washington Baptist Annual*, Christian Friendliness Report, 44.

68. "Department of Christian Friendliness," *The Washington Baptist* (January 1943), 5.

69. "Christian Friendliness," *The Washington Baptist* (January 1946), 8.

70. *1940 Northern California and Nevada-Sierra Baptist Annual*, "Christian Friendliness Work," 29–30.

71. "Christian Friendliness Meets the Refugees," 112.

72. "Refugee Children as Summer Guests," *The Watchman-Examiner* (26 June 1941), 693.

73. *1941 Northern California and Nevada-Sierra Baptist Annual*, "Christian Friendliness Work," 28–29.

74. *1942 Northern California and Nevada-Sierra Baptist Annual*, "Christian Friendliness Work," 21–22; see also *1943 Northern California and Nevada-Sierra Baptist Annual*, "Christian Friendliness Work," 17–18.

75. *1945 Northern California and Nevada-Sierra Baptist Annual*, "Christian Friendliness," 48.

76. *1941 Annual of the Illinois Baptist Convention*, "Woman's Baptist Missionary Society," 70.

77. "Baptist Women and Kingdom Work," (Indiana) *Baptist Observer* (February 6, 1939), 12–13.

78. *1945 Northern California and Nevada-Sierra Baptist Annual*, "Christian Friendliness Work," 49–50.

79. "New Committee on Christian Friendliness Meets," *New Jersey Baptist Bulletin* (February 1948), 4.

Chapter 10

State Conventions Confront World Issues

The state conventions and city mission societies of the Northern Baptist Convention were middle-level judicatory expressions of the convention. Although essentially autonomous and self-governing, they operated in between the local churches and the national societies and governing structures. State conventions represented the grassroots perspective in national forums and were charged with the responsibility of promoting national programs to the churches and the clergy.

The annual meetings of the state conventions often featured the passing of resolutions. As on the national level, the resolutions did not have binding force on the churches or clergy but rather expressed the conviction of those in attendance at the time of the meeting. The quantity and quality of the resolutions varied widely. Some were politically sophisticated and carefully crafted; others were offered spontaneously or with little time for preparation. Nevertheless, the resolutions were taken seriously because they were circulated not just to the churches but often to political leaders and secular newspapers as well. Resolutions could provoke heated debates and sometimes were the manifestations of power politics, exposing theological, political, and racial divisions.

Moral and ethical concerns received the majority of the attention of the states' resolutions. Delegates focused on race relations, temperance, gambling, smoking, divorce, sexual immorality, and observance of the Christian Sabbath. Ecclesial issues such as Sunday school attendance, clergy education and compensation, and evangelism were addressed on a regular basis. Occasionally, local political or social issues also received attention. Political issues were popular subjects;

examples included nationalism, the morality of war, the expanding military armament race, the merits of socialism, communism, and fascism, and the Great Depression. Following Pearl Harbor, the moral temptations facing American soldiers and the rights of conscientious objectors were oft-repeated concerns.

There was at least one opportunity in which the state conventions and city societies could have articulated a common response, or provided some pastoral guidance, to their constituencies regarding the plight of the Jews under Nazism. On June 27-28, 1934, the secretaries of the state conventions met in Chicago. This meeting occurred one month after the 1934 Northern Baptist convention, which was the second annual meeting in a row to address the initial waves of Nazi persecution of Germany's Jewish population. The collective state leadership published a full-page "Proclamation" (which was unique in this time period), in order to encourage the churches to respond with courage to the challenges facing the country. It was distributed throughout the nation.[1]

The secretaries sensed that the convention and American society as a whole were "standing between two great eras of history—between the tomb of the old world and the cradle of a new one" and that Baptists "should now awake to the opportunities of the hour in which they live." They summarized the challenges of this new order: "Selfishness, greed, hate, strife, war, economic injustice, political corruption, nationalism, materialism, irreligion, rampant throughout the earth, constitute the chief obstacle to the application of Christ's ideals to our modern life. Sinister forces are at work which if unbridled will ultimately break down a wholesome home life, destroy all ideals of purity and decency, deprive us of all reverence for personality, and invalidate the plain teachings of our Lord and Saviour."[2] Totalitarianism, fascism, Nazism, and racism did not specifically appear in the list of challenges to civilization's progress. The entire world understood that Adolf Hitler and his National Socialism political movement were significant actors in this drama, and so it would be reasonable to expect the secretaries to have addressed the Nazi challenge to democracy and its racist anti-Semitic agenda. However, they let the opportunity slip away.

The Earliest Responses: Hitler's Rise and Sympathy for Jews (1933)

The 1933 National Baptist convention resolution that opposed "outbreaks of race hatred and discrimination, as seen in our own country, and in the persecution of Jews in Germany" received attention from state conventions around the country. West Virginia's *The Baptist Banner*, the *Nebraska Baptist Messenger*, *The Kansas Baptist*, and *The Baptist Observer* of Indiana quoted the paragraph that mentioned the German Jewish predicament.[3]

Two months later, *The Baptist Observer* printed an essay on the separation of church and state by Dr. E. M. Martinson. He stated, "Germany has it in this Nazi campaign to make the church a subordinate branch of the government and to command its support for the unchristian policy of promoting a spurious racial unity, in the interest of a narrow and inflamed nationalism, by the suppression of the Jews." He argued that the separation of church and state was "the inevitable corollary of the Baptist contention for the individual's competency to deal directly with God for his own soul." He then observed that the "persecution of the Jews in Germany is probably due less to racial and religious animosities and more to economic traits."[4]

One might imagine that the initial reactions to the rise of Hitler and the Nazis would have come from the state conventions and city societies with the largest populations of Jewish residents, but this was not the case. The first three state conventions to address Jewish persecution were from the heartland of the country—Wisconsin, Michigan, and Iowa. Each expressed sympathy for the Jews, while adopting a distinct line of reasoning to reach that stance.

Wisconsin Baptist State Convention

The theme of the June 20-22, 1933, Wisconsin Baptist State Convention was "Christ and the Modern World." Dr. E. Leroy Dakin gave a summary of the Northern Baptist Convention's resolutions, and a presentation was made highlighting Wisconsin's ministries for Poles, Italians, women, African Americans, and Chinese.[5] On Thursday morning, June 22, 1933, the Resolutions Committee presented the first state-level statement that specifically mentioned the Jewish plight: "Noting the assaults on democracy by the present world situation, we would affirm our belief in democratic processes, and express our conviction that there must be liberty for all groups, including minority religions and racial groups such as the Indian, the Negro, the Oriental, and the Jew, and minority political groups."[6]

It is unclear if the National Baptist Convention's resolution influenced the Wisconsin statement, but the reference to "Indians" prior to the traditional racial trinitarian formula (African Americans, Asians, Jews) argues for a local origin of authorship. Later that day, members of the First American Indian Baptist Church of Wisconsin provided special music.[7] The state convention in 1934 celebrated a most significant milestone—the one-hundredth anniversary of its first church, constituted by persecuted native Americans who fled from upstate New York to Wisconsin: "Baptist work in reality dates back to one hundred years ago and it is significant that the first Baptist work done in the state should be done among the Indians."[8] The convention hymn sought to celebrate the multiracial nature of God's people, albeit in language that is offensive to subsequent generations:

> *'Mongst Redmen on the prairie,*
> *Where black men live untaught,*
> *E'en midst our cities weary,*
> *New miracles are wrought...*
> *We pride of race must banish,*
> *Each seek the others' good.*
> *Then war and strife shall vanish,*
> *Men live in Brotherhood.*[9]

With a spiritual and historical foundation rooted in a consciousness of race, prejudice, and brotherhood, Wisconsin Baptists were predisposed to express sensitivity to contemporary Jewish suffering. L. B. Mosely, in his message "Man Is Our Brother," addressed the Aryan paragraph controversy: "How many churches do you know that offer fellowship to all races? Again in matters of leadership. Jews cannot preach in the German Evangelical church. Again in the realm of opportunity. My childhood playmate is a day laborer primarily because he was born with a black skin. . . . Our conception of brotherhood must be brought closer to Jesus' conception if we would follow him."[10] The Commission of Social Relations and Evangelism included a statement on the rise of prejudice against Jews in the United States: "Prejudice against the Jew is widespread and is growing in some quarters in our own country through the activities of certain Fascist organizations, some of which, we regret to say, appeal to Christian loyalty at the time that they deny the Christ spirit in their actions."[11]

Within state conventions, clusters of churches in geographical proximity were organized into associations. Although associations primarily existed to encourage fellowship between churches and accept new churches into the denomination, some also featured resolution making as part of their meetings. In September 1936, the Madison Association passed a resolution against racism that included a reference to Jews: "Since racial and class prejudice seem to be on the increase, and since both are contrary to the spirit of Jesus, Be it Resolved, that we strive more diligently to combat every form of race or class prejudice and hatred whether it be directed against a Jew, Negro or other minority group. Let us point out the fallacy and un-Christian spirit of applying to any group the faults of one member of that group."[12]

The Madison Association resolution focused on domestic anti-Semitism as an example of prejudice against minority races. It did not, however, explicitly protest against Nazi persecution of German Jews. The European situation posed a challenge to peace, and this subset of Wisconsin Baptists was isolationist, hoping that their country would not participate in another continent's conflicts.

Michigan Baptist State Convention

Prior to Hitler's ascension to power, Michigan State Baptist Convention President A. H. Harnley cataloged negative global trends in his 1932 keynote address: "The nations of the world bankrupting themselves to pay the cost of the last war and to prepare for the next war. Racial hatreds more bitter than ever, creating an atmosphere of suspicion and hatred that may be charged with dynamite."[13] On Thursday, October 12, 1933, the final day of the 1933 annual meeting, Michigan Baptists passed three significant resolutions on world affairs—the first on "World Peace" in support of the upcoming World Disarmament

Conference in Geneva, the second expressing disapproval of US "Naval Expansion," and the third on "Religious Liberty."[14] All three resolutions passed with a unanimous vote. The first two expressed the Michigan Baptist preference for disarmament and peacemaking through international negotiations and national restraint of ambition, based on the principles of the social gospel.

The "Religious Liberty" resolution was the first Northern Baptist state convention resolution devoted to the initial German Jewish crisis. It specifically sided with persecuted German Jews and boldly resisted the temptation to be impressed with fascism. Citing "recent developments abroad" promoting "racial intolerance," and based on their core conviction of "religious liberty and tolerance," Michigan Baptists encouraged their churches to "re-awaken interest in, and a keener appreciation for, the hard-won standards of religious and racial tolerance, exemplified in the thinking of the prophet Roger Williams, and in the practice of the Colonial community which he founded." They then resolved to "express our sympathies for the persecuted, both Jews and Christians, and that we take our stand in opposition to the popular Fascist tide, for a pulpit and a worship free from governmental restraint or discrimination."[15]

The Michigan state convention resolution, like the Wisconsin statement, rested on tradition and history. However, whereas Wisconsin's memory extended back to its own beginnings, the Michigan resolution hearkened back to the roots of the Baptist movement in America. It recognized that their contemporary political stance on Jewish persecution in Germany was not due to American nationalistic posturing or the desire to maintain the unfair terms of victory over Germany secured by World War I and the Versailles treaty, but to the core Baptist convictions of liberty and tolerance for all races, as articulated by "the prophet Roger Williams" and lived out in the formative years of the Rhode Island colony founded by him. For Michigan Baptists, the religious liberty and tolerance stance of Williams applied universally—to Germany as well as to America. Based on historic core convictions, Michigan Baptists decisively placed their movement on the side of racial and religious equality for all people, including "persecuted Jews."

In 1935, Michigan Baptists once again appealed to the teachings of Roger Williams in order to side with the Confessing Church faction. Their theological concern was over the separation of church and state, based on core convictions, but they did not reiterate their concern for the plight of the Jewish people in Germany in this resolution: "Whereas, We have today in Germany and elsewhere abundant evidence of the embarrassment growing out of the Church becoming obligated to the State, be it Resolved That we reaffirm our belief in the separation of Church and State, and warn our churches against the acceptance of concessions which would involve them in entangling obligations to the state."[16]

The 1937 Michigan Baptist convention passed a version of the resolution on the separation of church and state[17] in which they added a separate section to condemn totalitarianism and affirm democracy: "Whereas, The totalitarian state is inimical to, and destructive of the rights of men as individuals . . . Resolved, That we are unalterably opposed, under any conditions, either of war or peace, to any form of the totalitarian state; and that under any and all conditions we stand for the representative form of government."[18] Seemingly, by 1937, the Michigan Baptist convention had exhausted its interest in passing resolutions about Germany, the church struggle, and Jewish persecution. However, its application of Baptist core convictions as expressed by Roger Williams, the founder of the American Baptist tradition, was a significant contribution to the Northern Baptist response to the Nazi persecution of its Jewish population.

Iowa Baptist Convention

The Iowa Baptist Convention served the heartland of the United States, and most of its churches were in agricultural settings—hardly a state where one would expect Jewish concerns to be paramount. There were only 14,089 Jews living in Iowa in 1937—one-half of one percent of the state's population.[19] Nevertheless, the Iowa Baptist convention was the third state convention to speak to the plight of the Jewish community of Germany.

The 1933 Iowa Baptist convention met in session from October 11-15, 1933, overlapping the Michigan convention. Just one day after Michigan Baptists passed their landmark resolution about Jewish persecution based on the legacy of Roger Williams, Iowan Baptists also expressed solidarity with the Jews, based on an entirely different argument. On Friday morning, October 13, 1933, they declared:

> MODERN GERMANY PRESENTS the frightful example of perverted nationalism, ruthlessly persecuting the Jews and denying them the rights and privileges which go with orderly and impartial government. . . . In the name of God of all nations, races, and peoples, we deplore the prevalence and insidious influence of a nationalism, falsely so called, which engenders racial hate, which looks upon other nations through eyes of mistrust or hate, which expends vast sums of money on the discredited and iniquitous war system; and we challenge our people and all people to fresh adventure along the way of trust, goodwill and cooperation.[20]

The Iowan Baptist approach to the issue was primarily political in nature. The resolution differentiated between positive and destructive forms of nationalism, citing the Nazi revolution in Germany as a prime example of the latter kind. It was "frightful" and "perverted" because it rejected democratic norms, as demonstrated by the Nazi "persecuting of the Jews." For Iowa, this persecution was not religiously motivated—Jews were not being persecuted because of their faith. The Nazi campaign was emblematic of a racial prejudice that denied fundamental political privileges to a minority segment of the population. Any form of nationalistic political ideology that "engenders racial hate" must be opposed not just by Baptists but by all Americans regardless of religious affiliation.

Throughout the 1930s, Iowan Baptists focused on antiwar resolutions and did not revisit the situation of the German Jews. At their 1938 convention, an antiwar resolution mentioned "a misunderstanding in Palestine" without going into any details. The "threatened conflict in Europe" was an example of a war mentality engulfing much of the world. In response to these tensions, they resolved to "declare our belief in the adequacy of the Gospel as a basis for settling questions of International scope."[21]

Although Iowa's Baptists passed several resolutions both before and after the American entry into World War II, none of them spoke explicitly about the European Jewish peril. In October 1941, two resolutions alluded to Nazism. The first was reminiscent of Michigan's 1933 statement, because it applied core Baptist convictions of "freedom of conscience, separation of Church and State, and freedom of worship" to totalitarianism: "Resolved, that we vigilantly guard these sacred privileges and actively resist any and all infringement or curtailment of these rights whether by subtle governmental aid to sectarian denominations, social security for church workers, governmental recognition of the Vatican or by the establishment of Totalitarianism of government by any of its many names. As Baptists we believe in democracy and the freedom of the individual."[22]

The second resolution addressed persecution of minorities "enslaved under the evil principle that 'might makes right,'" and though Jews were not mentioned, the statement's relevance to their situation was clear. Once again, "freedom of the individual and of nations" was cited to justify the resolution's position: "We grieve because of the injustices and sufferings, bloodshed and mass-murder that are present on every hand in the world because of sin, selfishness and senseless strife; that we pledge ourselves to maintain our nation as a land of opportunity, a cradle of liberty, an asylum for the oppressed, a place for religious as well as political freedom, where church and state are separate, where freedom of conscience still prevails, and where we can worship God in spirit and in truth according to the dictates of our own consciences."[23]

Heading Toward War (1934–1938)

In 1938, Rev. Dr. Elbert E. Gates, the general secretary of the Connecticut Baptist Convention, described the mission of the state's churches in global terms. Connecticut Baptists sought to "extend their influence and service beyond the area of the local church and community into the state, the nation, and the world. The parish of the church is the world." In Gates's mind, the church's witness was vital to international peace: "The world is in trouble, through war, rumors of war and devastation by wind and water. The world needs Christ's compassion and the Christian ministry of helpfulness. Modern Christians need to become yoke-fellows with the 'Good Samaritans' in service to a world in need."[24]

How did this global responsibility relate to the terror faced by Jews in Germany? Most of the state conventions did not recommend or pass resolutions specifically sympathizing with the German Jewish population before Kristallnacht, despite ongoing measures taken by the Nazis to constrict and devastate Jewish communities and businesses. This was not due to a lack of information. Following the BWA congress in Berlin, speakers traveled across the Northern Baptist Convention, speaking at state convention annual meetings as well as associational gatherings. Connecticut Baptists listened to their own Rev. Lee Blanton, who "gave a most interesting report of the Baptist World Alliance at Berlin, Germany."[25] W. H. Bowler, executive secretary of the Northern Baptist Convention's Council on Finance and Promotion, spoke on the predicament facing Europe's Baptists, noting "the hatred and fear that possess Europe."[26]

Not all state conventions believed the discouraging news emanating from Germany regarding persecution. The 1934 Utah Baptist State Convention voted to "denounce the widespread propaganda designed to stir up distrust between peoples and races and that we pledge our support to all sincere efforts to promote a better understanding and good will among the nations."[27] The source of the propaganda was ambiguous in the resolution; it might refer to German government attacks against its Jewish population, or, as is more likely, arguments designed to encourage US antagonism toward Germany, repeating a mistake from the World War I era.

Several state conventions endorsed the resolutions passed at the 1934 Northern Baptist convention, with minimal comment. The Connecticut Baptist Commission on Social Relations decided to publish the resolutions in the state's newspaper.[28] The Pennsylvania Baptist Convention urged its members to "recognize and observe the Christian principles of the brotherhood of man in such practical fashion that race hatred and discrimination may be meliorated and abolished."[29] Other conventions passed resolutions addressing the struggles within the German church. The 1934 Kansas Baptist convention sided with the Confessing Church based on the Baptist conviction of freedom of conscience: "as Baptists centuries ago led in the fight to free the church and the consciences of men from the domination of the state, so now the Kansas Baptist Convention commends the efforts of the Protestant Churches of Germany to defy present efforts to destroy them by making them accountable to the state rather than to God."[30]

A number of state conventions opposed totalitarianism and contrasted it to American political and Christian religious values. The Philadelphia Baptist Association stated, "Communism, Fascism and

Nazism are today threatening the sanctity of the individual in the interest of totalitarianism" and thus are "unchristian and undemocratic."[31] The Kansas Baptist Men endorsed a resolution passed by the Northern Baptist National Men's organization in May 1937, which urged cooperation with "all Christian agencies against the introduction into America of Communism, Fascism and similar alienisms that strike at the very heart of our personal and religious liberty."[32] In 1936, Maine Baptists declared: "Whereas our historic Baptist principle insists upon the absolute competency of the individual soul under God, guaranteeing to men the right of religious liberty, the freedom of speech and the exercises of private judgment; be it Resolved that we condemn and reject absolutism in all its forces especially in its modern manifestations in Communism, Nazism and Facism [*sic*]."[33]

The point of these resolutions was not to advocate for persecuted Jews per se but to reiterate the classic Baptist political stance in favor of democratic forms of government and against all manifestations of tyranny. Even when unstated, the principles affirmed could be applied to the situation of persecuted minorities, including Jews.

Several states opposed the racist implications of totalitarianism in general and Nazism in particular. Massachusetts Baptists declared: "Race prejudice and friction arise out of an over-estimate of one's race and an under-estimate of other races" and that people "cannot worship the God and Father of our Lord Jesus Christ and the gods of racialism and boastful nationalism"[34]—surely a veiled criticism of Nazi Germany. South Dakota Baptists went on record to say, "We strive to keep our own country at peace and overcome all racial prejudice as far as it is humanly possible and that, to this end, we employ the teaching and example of Jesus."[35] The New York State Baptist Convention voted to "declare themselves opposed unalterably to the forces which would poison the mind of America against any of God's children, of whatever race, nationality or creed."[36]

In October 1938, New Hampshire Baptists rejected all forms of nationalism that espoused race hatred and prejudice because "God hath made of one blood all nations to dwell together upon the earth." They resolved to discard "all human prejudices and preconceived ideas from our minds concerning nations or their leaders" and to offer prayers for "the permanent perpetuation of peace and the bringing of the nations of the world together in one brotherhood."[37] This resolution made reference to Acts 17:26.

The Baptist advocacy of brotherhood was a logical consequence of the conviction that all individuals possessed "personality"—dignity and worth based on being made in God's image. Personality emphasized the sacredness and individual worth of all people, regardless of race; brotherhood was the corporate corollary that transcended the superficial differences that separated races and nations. Just prior to Kristallnacht, Connecticut Baptists passed a resolution condemning totalitarianism as a violation of both soul liberty and the sanctity of personality: "In view of the threat to religious freedom in the philosophy and practice of a totalitarian state, that we vigorously affirm the historic Baptist position on the separation of church and State and the priceless heritage of soul liberty . . . we recognize the religious conviction of the value and sacredness of personality as a fundamental faith inspiring our efforts. We, therefore, stand opposed to those forces within the social structure that devaluate and exploit the body and soul of man."[38]

Connecticut Baptists understood that totalitarianism was opposed to Baptist convictions regarding personality. Baptists in Southern California went further by specifically linking Nazism, fascism, and communism to racial prejudice and discrimination, while also affirming that the Christian understanding of personality was the basis for equality of all races and harmony between people. Equality could not be denied due to biology, in spite of Nazi assertions: "In the face of a growing tendency toward totalitarianism and the emergence of the three State religions of Nazism, Fascism and Communism . . . we declare ourselves in favor of the equal recognition of the rights of all races in the realm of law, and that we condemn race prejudice as unsupported by biologic fact, accepting in place of racial prejudice the stamp of infinite value placed on every human being by Jesus Christ."[39]

One noteworthy response to Kristallnacht was made by the Metropolitan Ministers Conference of New York. It also passed a strong resolution which cited core Baptist convictions, including the idea of "the sacredness of human personality":

> AS BAPTISTS WHOSE forefathers have stood valiantly for the principles of religious liberties of all peoples and the separation of church

> and state and have always proclaimed the tenets which make for good will, toleration and the recognition of the sacredness of human personality, therefore be it resolved that this conference of Baptist ministers of Greater New York and vicinity go on record as deeply deploring the increased hatreds of races and express our sympathy for the oppressed and afflicted in Europe and call upon our people to exert every influence to prevent religious and racial antipathies and antagonisms of all kinds and under all considerations and circumstances.[40]

Three state conventions struggled with the rise of Nazism and its anti-Semitic agenda in interesting ways. Illinois, the District of Columbia, and Minnesota will therefore be covered in more detail.

The Illinois Baptist Convention

In 1932 and 1933, the Illinois Baptist Convention passed resolutions reiterating its antiwar stance.[41] However, in 1934, the Department of Social Services confessed that in the midst of the pressing social and international issues, it was at a loss on how to advise the delegates: "But just how either the Christian man or the Christian church ought to do something effective is not quite clear in the minds of many."[42] The Resolutions Committee had mixed success with its set of statements, with at least one being tabled. The following resolution, which demonstrated the central role that the theme of personality played in opposing totalitarianism, did pass: "Whereas, one of the cardinal truths in the gospel of Christ is the sacredness of personality, be it therefore Resolved, that the Illinois Baptist State Convention place itself on record as being opposed to any industrial or social system which tends to degrade human life."[43]

In 1935, the Resolutions Committee lamented, "Resolutions drawn up by a committee and presented to the Convention for adoption have little practical effect in the churches,"[44] and therefore in both 1936 and 1937, the committee presented a narrative letter that opposed "all forces that tend to encourage racial discrimination; that make for war; all social and industrial systems that tend to degrade human life . . . and the trend towards a totalitarian state as expressed in Communism, Fascism and Nazism which destroys religious liberty and the opportunity of the individual to develop to his highest personal powers."[45]

Dr. Charles W. Gilkey, dean of the Rockefeller Memorial Chapel of the University of Chicago, set the stage for the 1938 Illinois Baptist convention when he asserted, "Today the totalitarian state is worshipped. All the gods of the pagan world are suddenly alive."[46] The Illinois Woman's Baptist Mission Society resolved to "to gain an understanding of racial backgrounds,"[47] and the Resolutions Committee offered an extensive discourse on the primary role the Baptist conviction of personality plays in the development of a just world.

Resolution III, "Rights of Personality," began with a general statement of principle: "We again affirm our conviction that human values are the supreme values, and that whatever tends to degrade personality, and compels men to serve the sin before God" must be rejected. Therefore, totalitarianism is antithetical to Christian convictions: "We also oppose all those systems of government that disregard human values and seek by coercive methods to use them for the ends of a totalitarian supreme state, thus reducing man to a subservient automaton, denying human will and conscience."[48] This statement could conceivably apply to communism as well as fascism, but the next paragraph made it evident that the resolution was a rebuttal to Nazism and its racist attacks on Jews:

> WE EMPHASIZE AGAIN that the way of Christ makes no distinctions in personality, and that it stands unalterably opposed to all human systems that exalt race above humanity. We believe that this error is the root of manifold evils that afflict man's life, and is a fruitful source of war and conflict. We take our stand on the ancient declaration of revealed truth that God hath made of one blood all nations of men, and that in Christ, whose way we seek, there is no distinction of race, or tribe, or nation, or sex, but that all men are one.[49]

The stage had been set for an expression of love and support for persecuted German Jews, but instead the committee's empathetic intent was focused on Christians experiencing Hitler's wrath: "Our sympathy goes out to our afflicted brethren, who, in prison, and concentration camps, and in exile, are being made to suffer for their faith . . . and suggest that our individual churches undertake to give financial aid to relieve the distress of these wandering and penniless refugees, when the appeal comes from legitimate organizations set up for that purpose."[50]

Between the years of 1933 and 1934, the Illinois Baptist State Convention struggled with how to react to Nazism. By 1936, the doctrine of personality gave them a theological and social principle by which to respond in a coherent and consistent fashion. However, even just before Kristallnacht, the Baptists in Illinois failed to explicitly identify the Jewish people as the primary victims of Hitler, preferring to reserve their compassion for fellow Christians. This omission would not be rectified until 1944.

The District of Columbia Baptist Convention and Kristallnacht

The only Northern Baptist Convention–related middle-level judicatory organization that held its annual session right after Kristallnacht was the District of Columbia Baptist Convention, which uniquely was dually aligned with the Southern Baptist Convention. The sixty-first annual meeting met on November 15-16, 1938, and remarkably featured three specific resolutions on the Jewish issue.

On Wednesday, November 16, 1938, the Resolutions Committee offered this brief resolution: "Resolved, That we deplore the ruthless and uncalled for cruelties to which the Jews are being subjected by Nazi Germany, and earnestly pray that these inexcusable persecutions may be stopped."[51] On the same day, Dr. Gove G. Johnson, representing the Baptist Ministers' Conference, presented resolutions on Rumania and the "Persecution of Jews in Germany and elsewhere."[52] The assembly adopted both statements. The text of this second resolution was as follows: "Appalled as we are by the most distressing position into which the Jewish people are now forced in Germany and elsewhere, in utter violation of the sacred principle of religious liberty and the rights of humanity, we, as Baptists of the District of Columbia in Convention assembled, do voice our most solemn protest against these outrages and our most earnest appeal to the governments involved to put an end to these cruel oppressions."[53]

A third resolution concerning Kristallnacht, submitted by E. Hilton Jackson, was then also approved, with the intent being that Baptist sympathy for the Jews might be conveyed to the government of the United States:

> *BE IT RESOLVED*, That this Convention, representing a constituency of thirty Churches and a membership of twenty thousand, express its unqualified approval of the expression of indignation of the President of the United States at his press conference on November 15, 1938, in his characterization of the ruthless and inhuman treatment of the Jews in Germany by the avowed authority of the German Government, and that copies of this resolution be sent to the President and the Secretary of State.[54]

Although other states and city societies did not immediately react to Kristallnacht because of the timing of their annual meetings, state convention newspapers were able to comment. A Wisconsin Baptist, Ethel Appel, shared a Christmas devotional expressing concern for Jews: "This month as we commemorate the birth of our Saviour, nearly 2000 years ago, shall we not look forward with confidence to the complete fulfillment of this sure word of prophecy and remember in prayer His chosen people who in these days are passing through severe persecution and tribulation?"[55] *The West Virginia Baptist Bulletin* declared, "This is a sad day for the Jewish people of the world. . . . In Germany, Italy, Poland and elsewhere in Europe, the cruel hand of persecution presses upon them. We hope and pray for a better day for the Jewish people."[56] The Indiana *Baptist Observer* published the full text of the Baptist World Alliance response.[57] *The Kansas Baptist* quoted from William B. Lipphard's article in the January 1939 edition of *Missions*: "Once across the frontier they cannot return. So this means final parting, a permanent separation. That is why those old Jews weep. They were up against it."[58]

Minnesota Baptists and the Anti-Semitism of William Bell Riley

The journey of the Minnesota Baptist Convention and its response to the plight of the Jewish people under Nazism is complicated by its close relationship with William Bell Riley (1861–1947), longtime pastor of First Baptist Church in Minneapolis. Riley was one of the most important fundamentalist ministers in the Northern Baptist Convention, and arguably, its most outspoken and brazen anti-Semite during the period from 1933 through 1948.

Riley began his ministry at First Baptist Church in Minneapolis on March 1, 1897, and served as senior pastor for forty-five years.

He was pastor emeritus for the last five years of his life. The church's obituary tribute to Riley, as might be expected, was glowing in its praise of their larger-than-life leader: "To see him—tall, white-haired commander that he is—creates admiration. To hear him speak in his own inimitable manner brings profound respect. To learn through sweet experience the kindly warmth of his truly pastor's heart, forges a bond of love and makes for that relationship whose presence is powerfully felt but for which there is no adequate expression in words."[59] The Northern Baptist Convention's obituary for Riley was noticeably more reserved and terse: "Dr. Riley was a writer, preacher, evangelist and crusader. He fought modernism, rationalism, materialism, atheism and evolution. This crusade led him into a field of his own and in 1947 he withdrew from the Northern Baptist Convention."[60]

Neither obituary referred to Riley's writings and speeches in which he expressed anti-Semitic views. Similarly, there are no references to Riley's anti-Semitism in any of the official records of the convention (such as the Annuals) or in *The Watchman-Examiner*, which was more comfortable with Riley's fundamentalism.[61] However, William Vance Trollinger Jr. has documented Riley's anti-Semitism. He argues that "in the 1930s and 1940s Riley transferred much of his intellectual energies from his failed fundamentalist crusade to the active promotion of an anti-Semitic, conspiratorial interpretation of national and international events."[62]

Influenced by the *Protocols of the Learned Elders of Zion* and the anti-Semitism of Henry Ford, Riley asserted that "many of the biggest trusts, banks, and manufacturing interests are controlled by Jews" in the United States and that even "the President Roosevelt regime is a Jewish controlled regime."[63] In 1933, Riley expressed a classical form of Christian anti-Semitism as well as approval of Hitler's attacks against Jews:

> JEWRY, FROM THE day that she crucified Jesus Christ until the present time, has given many occasions for her own rejection and for that opposition which she has politically pronounced persecution. Herr Hitler, who speaks from first-hand knowledge: "The Jew is the cause and beneficiary of our slavery. The Jew has caused our misery, and today he lives on our troubles. That is the reason that as Nationalists, we are

> enemies of the Jews. He has ruined our race, rotted our morals, corrupted our traditions, and broken our power."[64]

Riley's support of Hitler's anti-Semitic policies continued for several years, according to Trollinger: "In 1939 Riley vigorously argued against the notion that Jews in Germany were being punished for their religion (rather than for their subversive politics). . . . Only with the advent of World War II did William Bell Riley cease his defense of Adolf Hitler's Jewish policies."[65] Riley's indulgence in anti-Semitic speculation coincided with the diminution of his influence in Northern Baptist Convention politics. The fundamentalist battles Riley engaged in "isolated him from denominational leaders and kept him from attaining any positions of prominence."[66]

Furthermore, as "modernist Northern Baptists quickly became cultural insiders," Riley focused more on his relationships with various non-NBC fundamentalist organizations and networks which he helped to create.[67] This may explain why Riley was unable to secure enough support to be selected to preach the 1939 convention's sermon.[68] Although the liberal Northern Baptist leaders responded to Riley's anti-Semitism with silence, Jewish Christian leaders such as Joseph Hoffman Cohn (the son of Leopold Cohn) "accused a number of fundamentalist leaders, notably William B. Riley, of anti-Semitism."[69]

Riley's anti-Semitic proclamations were all published in journalistic organs of his own making or in non-Northern Baptist papers.[70] Since *The Watchman-Examiner* was consistently pro-Jewish and anti-Hitler, their unwillingness to provide a platform for Riley's anti-Semitism may have reflected a concern that it would harm the conservative cause within the Northern Baptist Convention. It was an embarrassment that they attempted to ignore. The only article in the paper published by Riley that mentioned Nazism concerned convention politics. Riley attacked the national leaders for making changes to the polity of the convention that he considered to be an unhealthy form of centralization, and he likened these machinations to Nazi strategies.[71]

How did Riley's anti-Semitism influence the positions taken by the Minnesota Baptist State Convention? Thomas S. Kidd and Barry Hankins note that in 1936, "'Riley's boys' took control of the

Minnesota Baptist Convention."[72] Riley exercised considerable influence even before 1936 as well. Did the convention's resolutions reflect Riley's prejudice?

The Annuals of the Minnesota Baptist Convention do not contain evidence that Riley's anti-Semitism attained policy status in the state convention. The 1934 convention adopted two resolutions. One expressed the evangelistic emphasis that Riley championed, and a second statement was representative of a more social gospel approach: "We must fulfill our social obligations—in regard to industrial and economic relationships, public morals, civil authority, international and inter-racial relations, and Christian citizenship."[73] The 1936 state convention again addressed race relations in the context of other social issues: "Expressing belief that the questions of universal peace, industrial justice, right race relations and all other perplexing problems can be solved only by the application of the principles and under guidance of the spirit of Jesus Christ, and pledging ourselves to do our utmost in making these principles effective in the world today and tomorrow."[74]

The Minnesota Baptist State Convention first mentioned Germany in 1938. Resolution IV, on "Peace," cited several examples of conflict, criticized territorial aggression, and noted the eschatological implications of current conflicts (a staple of fundamentalist writings). No reference to Jewish persecution was included.[75] The resolution was not particularly harsh on Germany, perhaps reflecting Riley's perspective. However, in 1939 Minnesota Baptists did explicitly endorse providing donations to organizations assisting Jewish refugees in a generally antiwar resolution. Baptist core convictions were also cited. This is the first recorded instance of Minnesota Baptists expressing care or concern for the persecuted Jews of Europe: "Every possible effort should be made by Christians to alleviate suffering among the victims of war, through such organizations as Church Committee for China Relief, such agencies for relief of the Jews as are endorsed by the Baptist Denominations, and other organizations as are sponsored by our churches."[76]

Apparently, although influenced by Riley's leadership and theological perspectives, the Minnesota Baptist state convention was able to distance itself from Riley's anti-Semitism.

Europe at War (1939–1941)

Following the outbreak of European hostilities in September 1939, Philadelphia Baptists lamented, "The forces of evil have become rampant, causing chaotic national conditions and suffering, sorrow and hardship to fellow men of other nations and races."[77] Baptists throughout the United States reacted with mixed emotions to the initial successes of the German military in which several countries fell under Nazi domination. They opposed America's entry into the war while sympathizing with the suffering of innocents and occasionally with persecuted Jews. Some were concerned about maintaining relationships with the Baptists residing in Axis countries. All of them worried about the future.

In October 1939, Nebraska Baptists recognized the challenges posed by "ruthless paganism in a variety of modern forms" but urged that "in the fullest exercise of brotherly love we use all means within the scope of Christian principles to maintain neutrality and to promote peace on the basis of justice and brotherhood throughout the world."[78] C. H. Walcott presented a resolution imploring the government "to use all legitimate means to keep our country out of European quarrels and from becoming an active participant in the present world war."[79] Nebraskan Baptists reiterated their isolationist position in 1940: "Regardless of our sympathies with nations suffering the tragedies and horrors of war, the United States should endeavor to keep peace with all nations, striving by example and good will toward all humanity to lead the way toward a permanent peace."[80] In October 1941, New York Baptists also demonstrated their commitment to staying out of the war: "We are reluctant to consider even the possibility of participation of the United States in a foreign war to the extent of sending our men outside our territorial possessions."[81]

Although Connecticut Baptists were firmly in the antiwar camp, they recognized the nefarious agenda of the Nazis. They noted that war "is the effect of racial and national claim to supremacy and expansion and conquest, and such claim is the deadly expression of the false doctrine of the superman deified in force, hatred and violence."[82] In a veiled reference against Nazi anti-Semitism, Michigan Baptists asserted that peace depended upon cornerstone Baptist convictions such as personality and individual liberty: "Under no circumstances will we hate individuals, but we will support every Christian means to secure and maintain world peace—a peace which safeguards the dignity of human personality, recognizes the equality of all men, as being made of one blood to dwell on all the face of the earth, and of all nations, and effectually guarantees those priceless liberties of conscience and religion which are the direct heritage of the teachings of Christ."[83]

Baptists in New Hampshire surely had the Jews of Germany in mind when they acknowledged sufferings caused by "race prejudices," but in light of their political neutrality, all they could offer in response was a vague and wistful hope for better race relations through the cultivation of a peaceful mentality: "We sympathize very greatly with the sufferings of many peoples owing to war conditions and race persecutions. . . . We would urge the cultivation of the brotherly spirit toward all races, and the will to live at peace with all nations."[84] As the tragedy continued, New Hampshire Baptists became increasingly dismayed at the "untold suffering" that was taking place, but they were unwilling to support entry into the war. They could only "encourage" their members to remain "unprejudiced and sensitive to the needs of all men, contributing to legitimate relief agencies for the help of the suffering, regardless of race, creed or nationality."[85]

There was a general concern within the Northern Baptist Convention for refugees and others who suffered because of the conflict, but rarely were Jewish victims mentioned. In 1940, Illinois Baptists confronted the low level of financial support for relief efforts and asked for more generosity to alleviate the needs of suffering Christians.[86] Similarly, Indiana recommended that their constituent churches provide "hearty and sacrificial support of the work of the Northern Baptist World Relief Committee" which gave aid to European Baptists, Chinese refugees, European Baptist missionaries who were "cut off from their bases of support," and "Christian war refugees in America."[87] In contrast, Connecticut Baptists expressed unease at the narrow focus on relief work being done by the Northern Baptist Convention: "In token of the spirit of Him in whom there is neither Samaritan nor Jew . . . we hereby recommend that . . . churches pledge a specific amount for the relief of Baptists and other world sufferers. For there is still needed, on a vast scale, amelioration of the lot of sufferers, refugees and potential refugees, of any race in the warring zones in this stricken world."[88]

Massachusetts Baptists expressed their opposition to Nazism but limited their response to promoting domestic interfaith and Christian Friendliness activities:

> IN THIS DAY when our civilization is threatened by a tyranny which thrives upon race bigotry and class domination, which roots itself in a pagan denial of Christian virtues, we want to set ourselves on record as favoring every sincere effort toward racial friendliness and understanding, the building of broader highways of co-operation and good will . . . we commend the co-operative approach to our inter-racial and interdenominational tasks. . . . We are heartened by the successful record of Miss Dorothy Bucklin in her work of Christian Friendliness.[89]

Throughout the war, Baptists sought to maintain their relationships with Baptists from the Axis countries. Indiana Baptists passed a resolution in October 1939 indicating that they "will not preach a gospel of hate but will continue to include the enemy within the family of God's children."[90] They reiterated this stance in 1940, saying, "We hold that the world-wide fellowship of Christian democracy must be maintained above and beyond all belligerent lines."[91] Similarly, the Wyoming Baptist Convention reminded its members "to pray for our Christian Brethren in all war-torn countries."[92] Southern California Baptists emphasized the "present persecutions of those loyal to our Baptist faith and Christian principles in Europe and in Asia."[93]

Although the Indiana Baptist Convention did not pass a resolution on Nazism, its newspaper paid a great deal of attention to the unfolding drama in Europe. Between September 1939 and Pearl Harbor, *The Baptist Observer* published eight articles on the German religious situation, Nazi persecutions of the Jews, and the threat of Nazism to the democratic world—including one entitled "Suppose Hitler Conquered America!" by Dr. Charles Stelzle.[94] One editorial exclaimed, "You cannot account for Hitler by any amount of human reasoning. To us he is the devil incarnate and occupies a similar position towards Christ and that which He represents today to that which Judas occupied towards Christ in his day." The writer then cited "the resurgence of hatred towards and persecution of the

Jews" as one example that the Second Coming of Jesus might be at hand.[95]

As war edged ever closer, Northern Baptists remained apprehensive. John S. Pendleton, the executive secretary of Maine's Baptists, expressed their collective anxiety in a poignant manner:

> NEVER IN MODERN times has there been such destitution, suffering and need. The cries of our starving, afflicted, persecuted brethren in China, Japan, France and central Europe are ever in our ears. The dark clouds of war are gathering over us and the war spirit is growing in our midst. Once again it appears that we shall have to face situations like those we older men faced twenty-five years ago. How shall we meet them? What way shall we turn? What ought we to do?[96]

Southern California Baptists heard Alice Brimson, the WABHMS executive secretary, speak on "Emergencies Confronting Christians Today in America." She emphasized "the rapidly rising tide of prejudice against the Negro and the Jew."[97] With an eye trained on the looming Japanese threat, the Resolutions Committee urged Baptists to display a spirit of brotherhood to minorities, including Jews: "In view of the unfortunately strained relations between Japan and the United States, we desire a more pronounced Christian attitude toward the Japanese in our own area. In this connection also, we call for a new emphasis upon the brotherhood of all who are in Christ regardless of race, nationality or color. We also urge a spirit of love toward those outside of Christian ranks, particularly our Jewish friends."[98]

Ohio Baptist Convention

The sole state convention resolution devoted to anti-Semitism between 1939 and 1941 was passed by the Ohio Baptist Convention. At the 1940 annual meeting, Ohio Baptists were called to offer prayers for countries impacted by the war.[99] At the 1941 meeting, Rev. Guy Wimmer, president of Shurtleff College, spoke on "God's Will for Christians in Our Day." He sought to encourage a spirit of compassion: "When confronted by a problem of human need some reply, 'Who cares?'; others say, 'I care.' This last should be the attitude of every true Christian, for our God is a God of love. Christ asks us to share with Him in the matter of world redemption." He was followed by Mrs. Leslie Swain, a nationally recognized Northern Baptist Convention leader, who spoke on emergencies confronting christians in the world at large.[100] Perhaps inspired by these two presentations, Ohio Baptists then passed a clear and specific resolution on anti-Semitism. It primarily focused on domestic racist activity:

> WHEREAS THERE APPEARS to be a rising tide of anti-semitism and other racial antagonisms; and
>
> Whereas we believe such racial feelings to be contrary to the Christian ideal, and to the best interests of our country; therefore
>
> Be It resolved that we urge all of our people to refrain from activities and comments which tend to fan such hatreds; that we urge the elimination of all restrictions and discriminations which tend to develop racial prejudices.[101]

South Dakota Baptist Convention's Struggles

The South Dakota Baptist Convention struggled over the issues addressed by other state conventions during this period with an unusual degree of transparency and eloquence. Reflecting the populist and isolationist perspectives of much of the Midwest, South Dakota Baptists were wary of entanglements far from the homeland. In their 1939 annual meeting, the convention endorsed an antiwar resolution that argued for neutrality in the European conflict:

> THAT WE URGE our ministers and members to be on their guard against the propaganda of either side of the present conflict that we may be Christian in our thinking. We urge the ministry to remember its failures in the World War and to speak with moderation and restraint on all questions pertaining to the present war. We charge our leadership with the responsibility of seeing that the gospel of love shall not be destroyed by sermons that provoke hate of any people.[102]

On the associational level, there was further discussion regarding the international racial crisis. In his sermon to the Northern Association, Roy Longfellow said, "A church big enough for God is a church which would have on its heart the problems of the races."[103] The

Central Association meeting in Huron passed a resolution specifically speaking about the plight of the Jews in Europe—one of the few association-level resolutions on the persecution of Jews in the whole period. It said:

> RESOLVED THAT, IN a world dominated so largely by force and racial bitterness, we reaffirm our faith in love and brotherhood as the only permanent solution to the world's problems.
>
> a. That we work hard to make brotherhood a practical thing in our world, especially remembering the people of our Lord's own race.
>
> b. That we work for peace.[104]

The racial concerns of the associations made their way up to the state level. At the 1941 annual meeting, the Resolutions Committee insisted that "dictatorship and totalitarianism is contrary to Christian principles, that hatred of men on account of race or creed is a violation of human brotherhood; and that we urge that no Christian by word or deed render aid or comfort to such nations as have publicly expressed their repudiation of these principles and doctrines for which we stand."[105] A like-minded resolution followed in 1942: "Therefore, we also call upon the peoples of the world to repent and renounce those sins which bring international strife: economic greed, the lust for power, the exploitation of weaker peoples, the glorification of race and nationalism."[106]

America at War (1942–1945)

Northern Baptist state conventions responded to the commencement of hostilities between the United States and the Axis powers following Pearl Harbor by reevaluating the generally accepted isolationist and antimilitary pronouncements that characterized earlier resolutions.[107] Even states that still objected to war endorsed military chaplaincy programs and supported their own members who entered military service. Patriotism was on the rise, and Baptist periodicals regularly published articles condemning Hitler and his attempt to exterminate the Jewish people.

Although the Indiana state convention did not mention Jews in any of its annual session resolutions, *The Baptist Observer* of Indiana consistently published pro-Jewish articles. In 1942, the paper asserted that anti-Semitism was incompatible with Christianity:

> IT IS INCONCEIVABLE that we can have anything even remotely resembling an America which is influenced by Christianity so long as anti-Semitism flourishes. As we know from good and substantial evidence the Nazis have used hatred of the Jews as a means to induce Christians to deny Christ by inciting them to hate and persecute their fellow men who are Jews. They have used anti-Semitism as the rallying point about which to build a following whose hatred of Jews has been transmuted into hatred and persecution of Christians . . . For the Christian Ministry, the Christian press, and the Christian laity have not been silent during the anti-Semitic attack by the Fascists upon Christian ideals and democratic integrity. They have used their prerogatives of freedom of speech and freedom of the press to create public opinion against anti-Semitism and they are now on the road to victory.[108]

In January 1943, *The Baptist Observer* published an article that contrasted Hitler's anti-Semitism with Paul's words on Mars Hill,[109] and the next month quoted Sumner Welles, US undersecretary of state, who decried "the persecution of the Jews" and "the torture and assassination of as yet unnumbered innocent persons in concentration camps."[110] In a May 1943 editorial, the paper made its position on Nazism quite clear, even if its support for Jews was somewhat ambivalent:

> IF THERE WERE no other reason for the defeat of the Axis powers, by their treatment of the Jews they have called down upon themselves the judgment of the God of Israel. No nation can persecute the Jews and prosper. The Germans may have good reasons for not liking the Jews and in many ways the Jews have made themselves obnoxious to Gentiles; but notwithstanding all that might be said along this line, the fact remains that there is a special providence surrounding the Jews and whoever persecutes them will suffer the consequences. . . . The unspeakably brutal persecution of the Jews by the Axis nations is nothing short of satanic and revolting in the extreme. The God of Israel will not let such atrocities go unrequited; they spell the doom of the Axis powers.[111]

Several state conventions believed that American racial practices and policies needed to conform to Christian ideals of justice and equality and love. Minnesota Baptists stated, "In view of an alarming increase of racial antipathy in America today, we urge our people to express the spirit of Christ in their attitude toward and treatment of other races."[112] The Iowa Baptist Convention passed racial justice resolutions in 1943 and 1944 that admonished Christians to "break down race barriers and create a feeling of World Brotherhood within our churches and communities so that present and future generations may build on a foundation of Christian Friendliness."[113]

In the aftermath of the Detroit riots, Ohio Baptists recognized that racial inequality in the United States aided the spread of "unwholesome propaganda widely used by the axis power in the present world-struggle," and in response, Baptists should address "race relations" by paving "the way to a new day of brotherhood."[114] Nebraska Baptists inveighed against the "weight of prejudice and the sin of racial pride" in 1944 and called on their churches to "seek every possible means of enlarging our fellowship with all racial minority groups."[115]

Montana and Nebraska Baptists linked Chinese struggles to the African American civil rights movement. Neither added the Jewish community's persecution to complete the standard racialism triangle. The Baptists of Montana resolved to support "the principle of racial equality and justice, the passage of Kennedy Bill, H.R. 1882, to grant to the Chinese the right of entry into and citizenship in the United States on the quota basis."[116] Nebraska's Baptists agreed, arguing for the "quota for Chinese immigrants" to be filled and for equal treatment for "Negro service men and women."[117]

Jews did gain the attention of the Colorado Baptist State Convention, but not in relation to the European Holocaust. In a manifestation of the internal Northern Baptist fight that ultimately led to the Conservative Baptist schism, Colorado Baptists urged Northern Baptists to pay greater attention to the conversion of Jews:

> WHEREAS, THE NORTHERN Baptist Convention does not at present support directly any specific Jewish Mission work,
>
> Therefore, Be It Resolved, That the Colorado Baptist State Convention in session recommend to the constituent churches that they

> prayerfully seek out and support some existing worthy Jewish Missionary enterprise until such a time as our unified Budget of the N. B. C. shall have in it incorporated the support of such work.
>
> Be It Further Resolved, That the Secretary of this body be authorized to write to the Home Mission Society informing them of our recommendation to consider the apportionment of funds to the support of Jewish Mission work.[118]

The Illinois Baptist Convention

The Illinois Baptist Convention had already established a pattern of expressing generalized concern regarding totalitarianism before the outbreak of the war, but during the wartime years, it paid closer attention to Jews and finally produced an explicit resolution against anti-Semitism. In 1942, the Report of the Committee on Social Action recommended that their churches emphasize "the urgent necessity for the safeguarding of the rights of all racial and religious minorities particularly as it relates to the status of the Negro and the Jew."[119] The Resolutions Committee submitted a set of "informal" resolutions in narrative form. It noted that "since the world is faced with certain sinister forces that, for selfish ends would destroy human life and values," the convention should "affirm our determination to oppose all forces that tend to encourage racial discrimination; all social and industrial systems that tend to degrade human life."[120]

In his 1943 keynote address, executive secretary R. G. Schell spoke against the "arrest and concentration of those who oppose Nazi philosophy." It was unclear if he was referring to the persecution of Jews, because his examples focused on the church's protests against Germany in occupied countries.[121] In 1944, the Resolutions Committee addressed several issues, including ministry to armed forces, social issues, and postwar peace. In the Social Issues Section, anti-Semitism as well as prejudice against non-white races was addressed:

> WE DECRY THE continued pattern of white domination of all colored peoples in whatever form it is expressed, and condemn all manifestations and practices of anti-Semitism on the grounds, that such things are contrary to the spirit and teaching of Christ, and are a violent, inexcusable repudiation of the fundamental principles of American

> constitutional democracy. We advocate the integration of colored peoples into our economic, political, educational, religious and social areas upon the basis of equality.[122]

This statement in favor of equality for both Jews and African Americans was based on American political principles of democracy and equality. The committee also recognized that the expected "victory of the sword will never bring a permanent settlement of the differences between men and races" since in countries such as Germany the world has "been confronted with disintegrating forces." Accordingly, Baptists must prepare themselves for the rectification of a world that has been broken, "ever seeking to eliminate the outrages perpetrated against down-trodden humanity by any and all earthly tyrants."[123]

The New York State Baptist Convention

The New York State Baptist Convention was one of the most forthright opponents of anti-Semitism during the wartime years. At its 1942 annual session, the delegates passed two clear resolutions regarding racial prejudice. The first, under the broad theme of social issues, utilized Acts 17:26 to argue for brotherhood across races: "We call upon our Baptist people in New York State more than ever before to teach, preach and practice the truth that God hath made of one blood all the nations of men, and in Christ's name, to exercise the spirit of brotherliness in all their human relationships."[124] In the International Relations resolution, a specific section devoted to "Jewish persecution" was included:

> WHEREAS, MORE PEOPLE today than ever before in human history are suffering the loss of freedom, and are being persecuted because of their religious loyalties; therefore, be it
>
> *Resolved,* that we as Baptists, true to our historic and Christian tradition, protest against such coercion and persecution, including those suffered by our Hebrew brethren throughout the world, and pray that the moral conscience of the world and particularly of our own country may become active in helping to change this deplorable condition.[125]

The discussion on racial and Jewish matters continued in the pages of *The Baptist New Yorker*. John R. Riley wrote an article titled "The

Urgency of the Race Question" in June 1943 and argued that Acts 17:26 was one of "the foundation stones" of the Baptist faith, especially when coupled with Acts 10:34-35—"God is no respecter of persons." He claimed that Christians "must stand for fair treatment and good will to all peoples" and applied the principle to Jews and African Americans: "Many church people need education about . . . (1) Anti-Semitism which cuts under our principle of religious liberty; (2) Racial discrimination against Negroes. Both of these attitudes are anti-Christian." Riley then completed the racialism argument by applying the principle to Japanese Americans.[126]

Riley's advocacy bore fruit when the convention reaffirmed both resolutions in October 1943. The resolution on Jewish prejudice was affirmed without any alterations.[127] The fact that it was repeated was significant because it demonstrated that the convention believed the issue to be both important and unresolved. The Race Prejudice resolution was also repeated but with an important modification—the plight of Japanese Americans was added.[128]

The Connecticut Baptist Convention

The Connecticut Baptist Convention dealt with the issue of racism throughout the war years. In 1942, it passed a general resolution that could reasonably be applied to the anti-Semitic policies of Nazi Germany. Imagining a "world-wide fellowship in Jesus Christ, transcending nation, race or class," the delegates opposed "every wanton act of aggression against a nation, race, class or individual; that we deplore any discrimination, of whatever nature it may be, against a nation, race, class or individual because of racial differences, or class distinction."[129]

In 1943, after Rev. J. Edward Harris preached a sermon based on Isaiah 1:3 and declared that the present world situation was "full of unchristian prejudices and racial injustices," Connecticut Baptists finally made it explicitly clear that they were opposed to the Nazi exposition of "race superiority" and against racial prejudice in the United States:

> WHEREAS, WE ARE contending against the theory of race superiority as expressed by the Axis powers through their leaders; and
>
> Whereas, We see mounting evidence of practices based upon acceptance of this theory in our own country, therefore, be it

> Resolved, That we call upon all churches and the government to be impartial in the granting of liberty and opportunity to all, regardless of race or culture.[130]

In 1944, the convention heard from Rev. J. Oscar Lee, associate secretary of the Connecticut Council of Churches, who reminded "his hearers of the one great desire in the hearts of all men, irrespective of race or color, – the passion for freedom, peace and opportunity. We are on the way to a rediscovery of the value of the individual. We are also coming to grips with the race question, not only the Negro but the Jew and the American Japanese."[131] In like manner, the Social Action Committee enunciated core convictions that should guide Baptist social philosophy and action, including the "Fatherhood of God, and consequently the brotherhood of man" and the "worth and value of the individual, and the dignity, integrity and sacredness of human personality."[132]

Postwar Resolutions and Actions (1945–1948)

Just months after the conclusion of the Second World War, the West Virginia state convention reiterated the Baptist perspective on racialism as a trinitarian phenomenon. The Report of the Commission on Christian Social Progress, adopted by the convention, began with Acts 17:26 and asserted that Japanese and African Americans should be embraced as equals. The commission then turned to the subject of anti-Semitism and referred to the Holocaust as "the terrible slaughter of Jews over the earth in recent years." It also warned about domestic anti-Semitism: "One of the most insidious evils of our day is the rapid spread of anti-semetism [*sic*]; one recently stated that there were approximately 200 anti-Jewish agencies, or propaganda groups, in the U.S.A. The terrible slaughter of Jews over the earth in recent years might happen here, and the church has a vital stake in the matter of protecting the rights of the 'chosen people' of God."[133]

On its 238th anniversary in 1945, the Philadelphia Baptist Association passed its first resolution identifying anti-Semitism as an evil to be repudiated: "Anti-Semitism, as Nazi as ever, flies under different flags. The 'Negro-White' problems, the Labor-Management quarrels give evidence of absence of a sense of brotherhood or a sense of common destiny."[134] Although New Jersey, Rhode Island, and West Virginia followed Philadelphia (see below), other state conventions repudiated racism only in general terms between 1945 and 1948. These included Indiana (1946),[135] Delaware (1946),[136] South Dakota (1946),[137] Iowa (1946),[138] New Hampshire (1946 and 1947),[139] and Montana (1948).[140] Baptists moved on to the challenges of the post-war new world order, which included the dawn of the atomic age and the growing challenge of Russian communism. They supported the formation of the United Nations. Baptists recognized that racism was still a major problem, but mostly in terms of the African American struggle for civil rights. Prejudice against Jews in the United States, in comparison, was a less pressing problem.

The fate of Jewish survivors of the Holocaust and their search for a home where they could live in security and peace was not paramount as a Northern Baptist concern. There was virtually complete silence regarding the Nazi concentration camps, but to place that silence in perspective, the same was true regarding the devastation caused by the atomic bombings of Hiroshima and Nagasaki.[141] Northern Baptists funneled their attention, energy, and resources toward responding to the crisis faced by European Baptist displaced persons. Resolutions expressed appreciation for the BWA's "service to our distressed brothers in Europe."[142] Kansas Baptists voted to donate "$20,000 from Convention funds to direct relief for European Baptists, same to be sent to Dr. Edwin Bell for handling."[143] Philadelphia Baptists strongly believed that the unfulfilled needs of Baptist displaced persons should be addressed:

> IN VIEW OF the three thousand Baptists who are in displaced persons' camps of Europe we urge our people to help find jobs and houses for these our distressed Baptist brethren, in order that they may find a haven of safety in the United States. In view of the fact that complaints have come in that other service organizations have neglected our Baptist brethren in the matter of relief, we urge the channeling of more relief through the Baptist World Alliance directly to our distressed brethren in Europe.[144]

Other states were less comfortable with assisting just Baptists, and they framed their concern for displaced persons in more inclusive terms. However, Jews were not mentioned as a group, even though there were approximately 250,000 Jewish displaced persons following the end of the war.[145] Indiana Baptists passed a resolution on the "World's Suffering Humanity" which stated:

> WHEREAS, OUR SINCERE sympathy and our prayers are offered for God's children whatever race, color, or creed; therefore be it
>
> Resolved, That we Baptists, believing in God, ask His guidance in the ways of truth and righteousness that we may serve these our fellowmen regardless of race, color, or creed; further be it
>
> Resolved, That we urge all Baptists everywhere to maintain a spirit of friendliness and brotherly love toward all men, and by so doing with God's help we may assist our nation to find a practical solution of the problems caused by bigotry, hatred, misunderstanding, greed and hunger; further be it
>
> Resolved, That we will cooperate with "CARE," The Relief Committee of the Baptist World Alliance, and with other religious bodies who strive to serve Him through service to their fellowmen everywhere.[146]

Several state conventions recognized that the fate of European displaced persons was tied to the immigration policies of the United States. In 1946, New Hampshire Baptists noted that "some 850,000 Displaced Persons are still kept in concentration camps" and lobbied President Harry S Truman and Congress to "make such changes in our immigration laws as are necessary to allow many more Displaced Persons to enter the U.S.A."[147] Iowa Baptists appealed to the American tradition of embracing immigrants and specifically supported Truman's immigration proposal for "admitting 400,000 of such people into our country for the next four years, at the rate of 100,000 per year."[148] Only New Jersey specifically referred to Jewish immigrants in their resolution affirming Truman for "his concern for the welfare of persecuted Jews, as revealed in his readjustment of the quota system in our own land and his desire to find security in rehabilitation of the dispossessed Jews of the world."[149] Other states, such as Vermont, pointedly noted that 80 percent of the displaced persons were Christian, and only 20 percent Jewish.[150]

A few states considered the possibility of ministering to the newcomers. New York State urged each church to "make definite plans for the resettlement of at least one person or family during the coming year."[151] Maine dedicated a "Freedom Farm" to "provide a home of mercy for the down-trodden from foreign shores."[152] By 1954, Freedom Farm had hosted twenty-seven families, presumably Baptist, and Maine Baptists had resettled thirty-one other displaced persons through the sponsorship of local congregations.[153]

Many European Jews desired to relocate to Palestine, and not the United States. Most Northern Baptist state conventions did not address the issues of Jewish immigration to Palestine, the Zionist vision for Jewish state, or the independence of Israel when it occurred in May 1948. Nevertheless, most of the rank-and-file Northern Baptists probably sympathized with the vision expressed by the prophecy conferences championed by John Bradbury, Daniel Poling, and other Baptists (see chapter 11). *The Baptist Observer* of Indiana applied an eschatological interpretation to the plight of Jews as early as 1935:

> NEXT SUNDAY, JANUARY 20, is designated as "Palestine Day," in recognition of the modern repatriation of Palestine by the Jews. The return of Jews to Palestine from all over the world, under the Zionist movement, is significant to every student of the Bible. Perhaps the present persecutions in Germany and elsewhere are part of a Divine plan to return the Jews to their ancestral home. At any rate, multitudes of Jews are going back to Palestine, the land is regaining its fertility, the multiplied wheels of industry are turning merrily, schools and colleges are being founded and the former glory is returning to God's land and people.[154]

Three resolutions were passed in the waning years of the war and the postwar period leading up to the establishment of Israel as an independent nation. Only one was unambiguously pro-Zionist. In June 1944, the Northwestern Colorado Baptist Association expressed "hearty sympathy with the Jewish people in their desire to return to and inhabit their homeland."[155] In October 1945, the New York State Baptist Convention passed a vague resolution on "The British Government and the Jews in Palestine," which appeared to favor British acceptance of more Jewish immigrants to Palestine. Offering compassion for "individuals in need anywhere regardless of race, nationality, creed or condition," they favored "the offering of asylum to persecuted minority peoples by the free countries that have pledged themselves to the securing of justice and freedom for all men."[156] Just days before Israel's declaration of independence, Vermont Baptists responded to the tense situation in Palestine by passing an ambiguous resolution focused on "the presence of racial prejudice, hatred and misunderstanding in the world." They criticized "the situation as we see it illustrated specifically in Palestine, and we see it exemplified in many cases in our own country."[157]

The New Jersey Baptist Convention

The historical record of the New Jersey Baptist Convention is incomplete, since many of the annuals did not contain the text of resolutions that were passed. The *Annuals* indicated that unspecified resolutions were passed and would be published at a later date; unfortunately, the missing resolutions cannot be found in the *New Jersey Baptist Bulletin*. Accordingly, it is not possible to pass judgment on what the state convention might have said concerning Jews between 1933 and 1944. At the October 1945 annual meeting, the Resolutions Committee proposed a resolution on racism and freedom:

> WHEREAS, WE HAVE contended for the theory of racial and religious freedom; and
>
> Whereas, We see mounting evidence of practices based on a contrary theory of racial and religious discrimination, be it
>
> *Resolved,* That we reaffirm our fundamental belief in the fatherhood of God and the brotherhood of man, and that we call upon our churches, our industries, and labor and the government to be impartial in the granting of liberty and opportunity to all, regardless of race, culture, or creed.
>
> *Furthermore, Be It Resolved,* That we gladly acknowledge to others what we have traditionally demanded for ourselves: namely, that we not merely tolerate, but actively defend those with whom we disagree in their right to hold and express their convictions, and finally we affirm that these are our convictions for all men, everywhere.[158]

The 1946 convention applied this general principle to anti-Semitism. In a resolution called "Jews of the World," New Jersey Baptists recognized the plight of Jewish refugees, definitively rejected anti-Semitism, and lauded President Truman, a Baptist, for the concern he expressed toward the Jewish people in a speech earlier in that month:

> WHEREAS, THE JEWISH people of many countries have been driven from their homes by anti-Semites, and
>
> Whereas, It is still impossible for them to return to their former homes, therefore be it
>
> *Resolved,* That as a state convention we express declarative opposition to anti-Semitism and that we approve for Jews everywhere, as for all people, their right to seek their own way of life, liberty, and the pursuit of happiness. Be it further
>
> *Resolved,* That we express to President Truman through our secretary our approval of his concern for the welfare of persecuted Jews, as revealed in his readjustment of the quota system in our own land and his desire to find security in rehabilitation for the dispossessed Jews of the world.[159]

New Jersey Baptists encouraged their congregations to "consider making definite plans for the resettlement of at least one individual or family during the coming year and assist them in becoming adjusted to the life of the community and to share the fellowship of our Churches."[160] Martha Whalen, New Jersey's Christian Friendliness missionary, urged the churches to implement the resolution's vision: "Many times people criticize resolutions because nothing is ever done about them. This is one we can do something about. These people have no homes, or jobs, or even hope for the future. They can have these things, however, if we as Christians are concerned enough to accept them as part of our responsibility. Let us carry out our resolution."

In practice, New Jersey Baptists only intended to host Baptist displaced persons, as Whalen made plain in her appeal: "It is important that we as Baptists help fellow Baptists."[161] H. O. Wyatt, the director of Missions and Church Extension, summarized the effort of all agencies involved in immigration placement work, recognizing the generally accepted principle that each religious community was responsible for helping its own members: "As would be expected, these displaced persons belong to a good many faiths or churches. Jewish and Catholic organizations are working enthusiastically to bring in people of their particular faiths. There are a great many Protestants among them, some belonging to the Baptist Church. We have a real responsibility for these."[162]

The Rhode Island Baptist Convention

Since the state was founded by Roger Williams, one would expect the Baptists of Rhode Island to have been consistent advocates of racial equality and opponents of Nazi anti-Semitism. Paradoxically, the state convention did not pass a specific resolution on anti-Semitism until 1948—just after the founding of Israel as an independent nation. Nevertheless, Rhode Island's Christian Friendliness ministry played a major role in encouraging its churches to respond to the needs of Jewish refugees. Matilda Utecht was cited as having had a significant impact within the state:

> OUR DEPARTMENT OF Christian friendliness has carried on a ministry of compassion, during the year, to the Jewish and Christian refugees, of whom there are hundreds in our State. Miss Utecht and her volunteers have met these hapless wanderers; profferred [*sic*] them our friendship; sought out suitable living quarters for them; taught them English; helped their children to adjust themselves to their surroundings. And by bringing them together with their newly found American friends in church gatherings and social events, have created many bright spots in their dark and tragic lives.[163]

After Utecht spoke on Christian Friendliness at the 1942 annual meeting, the convention passed a general resolution on racialism: "We urge upon the churches that their supreme responsibility is to reconcile men to God and to minister the Gospel of Jesus Christ, replacing hate with love, nationalism and racialism with the ideals and Spirit of Christian brotherhood."[164] In 1943, Rhode Island Baptists praised the Christian Friendliness work and affirmed racial justice:

> WE LIVE IN a world rife with a multitude of evils; myths of racial superiority and inferiority, confiscations, exploitation; economic, political and religious discrimination; prejudice, intolerance, distrust, and conflict instead of cooperation. Such a world exhibits the very antithesis of

> the Christian conception of a Kingdom of God. The Baptist Churches of Rhode Island have a responsibility for improving relations between races of people. We urge therefore:
>
> 1. That the Baptist Churches give whole-hearted support to Miss Matilda Utecht in her program of Christian Friendliness within our state.
>
> 2. That we seek every method of creative good will to remove all practices of a discriminatory character, all laws of discrimination, all anti-racial organizations and all unfair tactics that inflict injustice or suffering upon any individual or group of individuals because of race or creed.[165]

Utecht suffered an accident in February 1946, and after a lengthy recovery, she moved to Southern California. At the 1947 Rhode Island annual meeting, the delegates paid tribute to her ministry in a resolution opposing Nazism and affirming the Christian Friendliness spirit that Utecht modeled so powerfully:

> WHEREAS BAPTISTS BELIEVE strongly that the individual should be considered as the most significant unit in all government . . . be it resolved that we express ourselves as being directly opposed to all forms of dictatorship, whether identified with Communism, National Socialism, Fascism, or National Imperialism.
>
> Whereas the New Testament makes plain that "God has made of one blood all nations of men to dwell upon the face of the earth," and
>
> Whereas we firmly believe that all men, irrespective of race or religion, are essentially equal and dear to the Father's heart . . . we urge all Christians to put into practice this belief, by making friendships across racial and religious lines; and that they be urged to use their influence to see that as fully as possible no discrimination is sown to any individual in business, political and social life because of his race or creed.[166]

In 1948, Rhode Island explicitly labeled anti-Semitism as anathema in a brief resolution: "Whereas a rising tide of anti-Semitism, racial prejudice and class distinction threaten to destroy national harmony and Christian brotherhood, be it resolved that we reaffirm our faith in our Constitution's conception of man's rights, and acknowledge as Creator, One Father who is Lord over all."[167]

North Dakota and German Baptists

The only resolution North Dakota's Baptists approved that criticized the Nazis originated on the associational level. In 1941, the delegates to the Sheyenne River Association, located next to the eastern border of the state, approved a resolution on racial prejudice that implicitly indicted Hitler and Mussolini for their racial prejudice: "Whereas, the pagan leaders of the world are fanning the flame of prejudice and racial hatred, and whereas, it is evident that these are due to conceit and ignorance, therefore . . . we give ourselves to a program of self education that we may understand and appreciate our brethren of different races and nationalities."[168]

This action was more courageous than might be understood at face value, because Germans comprised a significant minority of the membership on the North Dakota convention—thirty-one churches with a membership of 3,716 people.[169] The German influence might have played a role in the resolution passed in the last week of September 1939. It called for "neutrality that will keep this country from becoming entangled in any foreign war" and looked forward to "the speedy arrival of a time when all difficulties between nations can be adjured in accordance with Christian principles."[170]

As the war progressed, tensions rose between the German-speaking and non-German Baptists in the state. The 1940 and 1941 resolution reports call for "continued loyalty to one another."[171] The Northwestern Association asked its members in 1942 to "continue to promote peaceful relations among all people and eliminate race discrimination"; it also called for "loyalty to our country and government."[172] In the postwar era, the Northwestern Association produced a bland resolution on racism, which stated: "That we strive to further the Biblical teachings of racial equality and freedom from race prejudice and race discrimination."[173]

In the North Dakota Baptists' centenary book, JoAnne Shoemaker and Don Shoemaker cited a "fall-out" that had occurred, culminating in the loss of the German-heritage churches. Three issues led to the parting of the ways: "(1) The practice of the Home Mission Society hiring missionaries for the German-language Baptists without their endorsement; (2) The continuation of the use of the German language in Sunday School and worship thereby adding to the wave of discontent between the American English and the American Germans during the two world wars; (3) The appropriation of mission money for Burma instead of for German Baptists."[174]

The reallocation of mission money from Germany to Burma was significant. The American Baptist Foreign Mission Society ceased providing funding for German Baptist projects after war broke out in 1939 and did not resume aid until after the war's conclusion. The negative reaction from the German-speaking churches of North Dakota to the society's policy may have represented the sole organized pro-German protest within the Northern Baptist Convention between 1933 and 1948.

Notes

1. See *The Ohio Baptist* (20 August 1934), 1–2; and *The Connecticut Baptist* (October 1934), 13.

2. "A Proclamation Adopted by the Secretaries of the State Conventions and Standard City Mission Societies Affiliated with the Northern Baptist Convention, at a Meeting Held in Chicago, Illinois, June 27–28, 1934," reprinted in *The Kansas Baptist* (September 1934), National Supplement, 3.

3. "Resolutions Adopted by the Northern Baptist Convention," *The Baptist Banner* (15 June 1933), 15; "Convention Resolutions," *Nebraska Baptist Messenger* (July 1933), 9; "Conventions Resolutions," *The Kansas Baptist* (July 1933), National Supplement, 3; "Resolutions Adopted by the Northern Baptist Convention," *The Baptist Observer* (1 June 1933), 6.

4. E. M. Martinson, "Patriotism and Piety," *The Baptist Observer* (3 August 1933), 13.

5. *Minutes of the 1933 Wisconsin Baptist State Convention*, 9, 13–14, 20–21.

6. Ibid., Resolutions Report, 60.

7. Ibid., Resolutions Report, 63.

8. *Minutes of the 1934 Wisconsin Baptist State Convention*, 9; see also "Report of the Board of Managers and Other Sources," 16.

9. Ibid., 10–11.

10. Ibid., 20.

11. Ibid., Report of the Commission of Social Relations and Evangelism, 40–41.

12. *Minutes of the 1936 Wisconsin Baptist State Convention*, Madison Association Annual Report, 59–60.

13. *Minutes of the 1932 Annual Meeting of the Michigan Baptist State Convention*, President's Address, 36.

14. *Minutes of the 1933 Annual Meeting of the Michigan Baptist State Convention*, Report of the Resolutions Committee, 50–52.

15. Ibid., 52.

16. *Minutes of the 1935 Annual Meeting of the Michigan Baptist State Convention*, Report of the Resolutions Committee, 46.

17. *Minutes of the 1937 Annual Meeting of the Michigan Baptist State Convention*, Report of the Resolutions Committee, Resolution V, Civic Affairs (c) "Civil Liberties" and (d) "Church and State," 77–78.

18. Ibid., Report of the Resolutions Committee, Resolution V, Civic Affairs (f) "Recognition of Individual," 78.

19. *American Jewish Yearbook 1941–1942*, 656, Table 1—"Number of Jews of United States, Principal Communities and Congregations, by States, 1937."

20. *Minutes of the 1933 Annual Meeting of the Iowa Baptist Convention*, Resolutions Committee, Resolution Six, 40. See William E. Nawyn, *American Protestantism's Response*

to Germany's Jews and Refugees: 1933–1941, Studies in American History and Culture (Ann Arbor: University of Michigan International Research Press, 1981), 212n2.

21. *Minutes of the 1938 Annual Meeting of the Iowa Baptist Convention*, Resolutions Committee, Resolution III, "Of War and Peace," 43.

22. *Minutes of the 1941 Annual Meeting of the Iowa Baptist Convention*, Resolutions Committee, Resolution III, 48.

23. Ibid., Resolutions Committee, Resolution VII, 49.

24. *Minutes of the 1938 Annual Report of the Connecticut Baptist Convention*, Report of the Board of Managers, 31–32. The reference to damage by water was an allusion to the devastating hurricane that had passed through the state.

25. *Minutes of the 1934 Annual Report of the Connecticut Baptist Convention*, New Haven Baptist Association, 102.

26. *Proceedings of the 1935 Southern California Baptist Convention*, 43.

27. *Minutes of the 1934 Annual Session of the Utah Baptist Convention*, Report of the Committee on Resolutions, Section 5, 20.

28. *Minutes of the 1934 Annual Report of the Connecticut Baptist Convention*, Report of the Committee on Social Relations, 65.

29. *Minutes of the 1934 Annual Report of the Pennsylvania Baptist Convention*, Report of the Committee on Resolutions, 172.

30. *Proceedings of the 1934 Annual Meeting of the Kansas Baptist Convention*, Report of the Committee on Resolutions, Resolution 5, 73.

31. *Minutes of the 1938 Annual Meeting of the Philadelphia Baptist Association*, Report of the Committee on Resolutions, "Reaffirmation of Our Characteristic Baptist Stand for Freedom," 60.

32. *Proceedings of the 1937 Annual Meeting of the Kansas Baptist Convention*, Report of the Kansas Council of Baptist Men, 27–28.

33. "State Convention Resolutions," *The Maine Baptist Messenger* (July 1936), Resolution 9, "Soul Liberty," 4.

34. "World Obligations," *Massachusetts Baptist Bulletin* (November 1936), 8.

35. *1937 South Dakota Annual*, Committee on Resolutions, Resolution 9, 31.

36. *Minutes of the 1938 Annual Meeting of the New York State Baptist Convention*, Report of the Committee on Resolutions, 22.

37. *Annual Report of the 1938 United Baptist Convention of New Hampshire*, Report of the Resolutions Committee, Resolution II, "Attitude toward World Affairs," 18–19.

38. *Minutes of the 1938 Annual Report of the Connecticut Baptist Convention*, Report of the Committee on Resolutions, 91.

39. *Proceedings of the 1935 Southern California Baptist Convention*, Report of the Committee on Resolutions, 80.

40. *The Watchman-Examiner* (8 December 1938), 1290–91; see also 1288.

41. *1932 Illinois Baptist Annual*, Report of Committee on Resolutions, 67; 1933 Illinois Baptist Annual, Report of Committee on Resolutions, 63.

42. *1934 Illinois Baptist Annual*, Report of Department of Social Services, 66.

43. Ibid., Report of Committee on Resolutions, Resolution V, 67.

44. *1935 Illinois Baptist Annual*, Report of Committee on Resolutions, Resolution VI, 71.

45. *1936 Illinois Baptist Annual*, Report of Committee on Resolutions, 71; 1937 Illinois Baptist Annual, Report of Committee on Resolutions, 69.

46. *1938 Illinois Baptist Annual*, 30.

47. Ibid., Minutes of the Woman's Baptist Mission Society, 43.

48. Ibid., Report of Committee on Resolutions, Resolution III, "Rights of Personality," 61.

49. Ibid., 62.

50. Ibid. Perhaps the imprisonment of Martin Niemöller was in view here.

51. *Minutes of the 1938 Annual Session of the Columbia Association of Baptist Churches*, Report of the Committee on Resolutions, 43.

52. Ibid., Report of the Committee on Resolutions, 12.

53. Ibid., Resolutions Related to the Persecution of Jews, 44. This resolution was cosigned by William E. LaRue and Randolph Gregory.

54. Ibid., Resolutions Related to the Persecution of Jews, 44–45.

55. "Wisconsin Baptist Associational," *The Wisconsin Baptist* (December 1938), 21.

56. "Persecution of Jews," *The West Virginia Baptist Bulletin* (January 1939), 4.

57. "Baptist World Alliance and Anti-Semitism," *Baptist Observer* (19 January 1939), 7.

58. "Up Against It," *The Kansas Baptist* (January 1939), 5.

59. "William Bell Riley," *The Watchman-Examiner* (3 April 1947), 318.

60. *Annual of the 1948 Northern Baptist Convention*, Obituaries—"W. B. Riley," 81–82.

61. For example, see "Minnesota—Dr. W. B. Riley's Fortieth Anniversary," *The Watchman-Examiner* (4 March 1937), 254.

62. William Vance Trollinger Jr., *God's Empire: William Bell Riley and Midwestern Fundamentalism*, History of American Thought and Culture (Madison: University of Wisconsin Press, 1991), 62–63.

63. Ibid., 72–73.

64. Ibid., 74. Trollinger's source is a column Riley wrote for a fundamentalist paper not affiliated with the Northern Baptist Convention; "The Fear of the Jew," *The Pilot* 13 (July 1933), 298–99.

65. Trollinger, *God's Empire*, 74.

66. Ibid., 60.

67. Thomas S. Kidd and Barry Hankins, *Baptists in America: A History* (Oxford: Oxford University Press, 2015), 192–93.

68. *Minutes of the General Council of the Northern Baptist Convention*, November 30, 1938, Item 4538, 8.

69. Yaakov Ariel, *Evangelizing the Chosen People: Missions to the Jews in America, 1880–2000* (Chapel Hill: University of North Carolina Press, 2000), 111–12.

70. Trollinger, *God's Empire*, 182–84.

71. William Bell Riley, "Denominational Dictatorship," *The Watchman-Examiner* (26 March 1942), 301.

72. Kidd and Hankins, *Baptists in America*, 199.

73. *Annual of the 1934 Minnesota Baptist Convention*, Report of the Committee on Resolutions, 10.

74. *Annual of the 1936 Minnesota Baptist Convention*, Report of the Committee on Resolutions, Resolution 6, 11–12.

75. *Annual of the 1938 Minnesota Baptist Convention*, Report of the Committee on Resolutions, Resolution IV, "Peace," 11.

76. *Annual of the 1939 Minnesota Baptist Convention*, Report of the Committee on Resolutions, Resolution III, 9–10.

77. *Minutes of the 1939 Philadelphia Baptist Association*, North Philadelphia Association Report of the Committee on Resolutions, 26.

78. *Minutes of the 1939 Nebraska Baptist Annual*, Report of the Committee on Resolutions, Resolution 9, 16–17.

79. Ibid., Minutes Items 47–48, 17. Dr. Walcott was the pastor of First Baptist Church in Lincoln, Nebraska.

80. *Minutes of the 1941 Nebraska Baptist Annual* (covering the 1940 meeting), Report of the Committee on Resolutions, Resolution V, "International Relations," 17–18.

81. *1941 New York Baptist Annual*, Committee on Resolutions, Resolution VI, "Social Issues," 21.

82. *Minutes of the 1940 Annual Report of the Connecticut Baptist Convention*, Report of the Committee on Resolutions, 82.

83. *Minutes of the 1940 Annual Meeting of the Michigan Baptist Convention*, Report of the Committee on Resolutions, Resolution VI, "Social Action," 24.

84. *Annual Report of the 1939 United Baptist Convention of New Hampshire*, Report of the Resolutions Committee, "World Affairs," 20.

85. *Annual Report of the 1940 United Baptist Convention of New Hampshire*, Report of the Resolutions Committee, "World Affairs," 19.

86. *Minutes of the 1940 Annual Session of the Illinois Baptist Convention*, Report of the Illinois-Wisconsin Board of Missionary Promotion, 45.

87. *Minutes of the 1940 Indiana Baptist Annual*, Report of the Resolutions Committee, Resolution 4, 20. See also *1940 New York Baptist Annual*, Committee on Resolutions, Resolution VII, 18–19.

88. *Minutes of the 1940 Annual Report of the Connecticut Baptist Convention*, Report of the Committee on Resolutions, 81.

89. "Report of the Resolutions Committee of the Massachusetts Baptist Convention, October 1941," *Massachusetts Baptist Bulletin* (November 1941), 4–5.

90. *Minutes of the 1939 Indiana Baptist Annual*, Resolutions, Resolution VI, "War and Peace," 21.

91. *Minutes of the 1940 Indiana Baptist Annual*, Report of the Resolutions Committee, Resolution 5b, 20.

92. *Minutes of the Fortieth Anniversary of the Wyoming Baptist Convention* (1941), Resolutions Committee Report, Resolution No. 4, 13.

93. *Minutes of the 1941 Annual Meeting of the Southern California Baptist Convention*, Resolutions, "International," 65.

94. Charles Stelzle, "Suppose Hitler Conquered America!" *The Baptist Observer* (20 March 1941), 16.

95. Editorial, "When the Armistice Was Signed," *The Baptist Observer* (6 March 1941), 3.

96. *1941 Year Book of the United Baptist Convention of Maine*, Report of the Convention Board, 13.

97. *Minutes of the 1941 Annual Meeting of the Southern California Baptist Convention*, 45.

98. Ibid., Resolutions, "National," 65.

99. *Minutes of the Annual Meeting of the 1940 Ohio Baptist Convention*, Report of the Findings Committee, 50.

100. *Minutes of the Annual Meeting of the 1941 Ohio Baptist Convention*, 23.

101. Ibid., Report of the Resolutions Committee, "Morals and Spiritual Interests," 52.

102. *1940 South Dakota Baptist Annual* (containing the minutes of the 1939 meeting), Resolutions 3 and 4, 27.

103. Ibid., Minutes of the Northern Association (May 2-3, 1940), 47.

104. Ibid., Minutes of the Central Association (May 7-8, 1940), 46.

105. *1941 South Dakota Baptist Annual* (containing the minutes of the 1940 and 1941 meetings), Resolutions, 50.

106. *1942 South Dakota Baptist Annual*, Resolutions, 26.

107. See *Minutes of the 1942 Annual Meeting of the Delaware State Baptist Convention*, Report of the Resolutions Committee, Resolutions 7 and 8, p. 8:

> 7. In this conflict for the safe-guarding of a free way of life for the freedom-loving people of the world, be it resolved, that as Baptists we endeavor to keep ourselves and others from making any man or nation the object of hatred because of race, color, or creed.
>
> 8(b). That we consider the unwisdom in ever again thinking of the United States' relation to the rest of the world in terms of Isolationalism.

108. "Mr. Ford and Anti-Semitism," *The Baptist Observer* (4 June 1942), 16.

109. William Mather, "Paul vs. Hitler," *The Baptist Observer* (7 January 1943), 11.

110. "Ten Tragic Years," *The Baptist Observer* (18 February 1943), 11.

111. Editorial, "The Jews, the Chosen People of God," *The Baptist Observer* (6 May 1943), 3.

112. *Minutes of the 1943 Annual Meeting of Minnesota Baptists*, Report of the Committee on Resolutions, Resolution 6, 8.

113. *Minutes of the 1943 Annual Meeting of the Iowa Baptist Convention*, Resolutions Committee, 34; *Minutes of the 1944 Annual Meeting of the Iowa Baptist Convention*, Resolutions Committee, 35.

114. *Proceedings of the 1943 Annual Meeting of the Ohio Baptist Convention*, Report of the Resolutions Committee, Resolution III—"Deep Wounds of the World," Section E, 55–56.

115. *Minutes of the 1944 Annual Meeting of the Nebraska State Convention*, Report of the Committee on Resolutions, Resolution 11—"Social Issues" (c) "Racial Discrimination," 45.

116. *The 1943 Montana Baptist Annual*, Report of the Committee on Resolutions, 17.

117. *Minutes of the 1943 Annual Meeting of the Nebraska State Convention*, Report of the Committee on Resolutions, Resolution XI—"International Affairs," 19.

118. *Minutes of the Annual Meeting of the Colorado Baptist State Convention*, Report on the Committee on Resolutions, Resolution 10—"Resolution on Jewish Missions," 54.

119. *1942 Illinois Baptist Annual, Report of Committee on Social Action*, Recommendation 2, 48.

120. Ibid., Report of the Resolutions Committee, 55.

121. *1943 Illinois Baptist Annual*, The Keynote Address, 35–36.

122. *1944 Illinois Baptist Annual*, Report of the Resolutions Committee, Resolution V, "Social Issues," 66.

123. Ibid., Resolution VI, "World Order and Baptist Responsibility," 66–67.

124. *Minutes of the 1942 Annual Meeting of the New York State Baptist Convention*, Report of the Committee on Resolutions, Resolution III, Social Issues—"Race Prejudice," 21.

125. Ibid., Resolution IV, International Relations—B. "Jewish Persecution," 22.

126. John R. Riley, "Social Service Column—The Urgency of the Race Question," *The Baptist New Yorker* (June 1943), 12.

127. *Minutes of the 1943 Annual Meeting of the New York State Baptist Convention*, Report of the Committee on Resolutions, Resolution IV, International Relations—B. "Jewish Persecution," 21.

128. Ibid., Resolution III, Social Issues—"Race Prejudice," 20.

129. *Minutes of the 1942 Annual Meeting of the Connecticut Baptist Convention*, Report of the Committee on Resolutions, Resolution 4, 55.

130. *Minutes of the 1943 Annual Meeting of the Connecticut Baptist Convention*, Minutes, 19; and Report of the Committee on Resolutions, 69.

131. *Minutes of the 1944 Annual Meeting of the Connecticut Baptist Convention*, Minutes, 21.

132. Ibid., Report of the Social Action Committee, 58.

133. *Minutes of the 1945 Annual Session of the West Virginia State Convention*, Report on the Commission of Social Progress, 39–40.

134. *Minutes of the 1945 Annual Meeting of the Philadelphia Baptist Association*, Report of the Resolutions Committee, 27.

135. *Proceedings of the 1946 Indiana Baptist Annual Convention*, Department of Race Relations–Social Righteousness, 45.

136. *Minutes of the 1946 Annual Meeting of the Delaware State Baptist Convention*, Resolutions, "Racial," 14.

137. *Proceedings of the 1946 South Dakota Convention*, Board of Managers Report, 27–28.

138. *Minutes of the 1946 Annual Meeting of the Iowa Baptist Convention*, Resolution 5, 49.

139. *Minutes of the 1946 Annual Report of the United Convention of New Hampshire*, Resolutions Committee Report, Resolution IV World Affairs, "Race Relations," 25; *Minutes of the 1947 Annual Report of the United Convention of New Hampshire*, Resolutions Committee Report, Resolution IV World Affairs, "Race Prejudice," 23.

140. *Minutes of the 1948 Montana Annual, Resolutions Committee*, "Race," 19–20.

141. See, for example, *Annual Report of the 1946 Annual Report of the United Baptist Convention of New Hampshire*, 17, where an anti-Hiroshima resolution was defeated.

142. *Minutes of the 1947 Indiana Baptist Annual, Resolutions*, Resolution II, "Baptist World Alliance," 22.

143. *Proceedings of the 1947 Annual Meeting of the Kansas Baptist Convention*, 22.

144. *Minutes of the 1948 Annual Meeting of the Philadelphia Baptist Association*, Report of the Resolutions Committee, Resolutions VI and VII, 29.

145. "Displaced Persons," *Holocaust Encyclopedia* (online), United States Holocaust Memorial Museum, http://www.ushmm.org/wlc/en/article.php?ModuleId=10005462, accessed 31 December 2015.

146. *Minutes of the 1947 Indiana Baptist Annual, Resolutions*, Resolution III, "World's Suffering Humanity," 23.

147. *Annual Report of the 1946 Annual Report of the United Baptist Convention of New Hampshire*, 17.

148. *Minutes of the 1947 Annual Meeting of the Iowa Baptist Convention*, Report of the Resolutions committee, Resolution 7—"Social Conditions," 50.

149. *Minutes of the 1946 New Jersey Baptist Convention*, Report of the Resolutions Committee, Resolution m, "Jews of the World," 25.

150. *Minutes of the Vermont Baptist Anniversaries for 1947*, Resolutions, 50.

151. *Minutes of the 1948 New York Baptist Annual*, Committee on Resolutions, Resolution II—"Critical Public Affairs," 19.

152. Walter L. Cook, *The Story of Maine Baptists, 1904–1954* (United Baptist Convention of Maine, 1954), 136.

153. Ibid., 138–39.

154. "Palestine Day Sunday," *The Baptist Observer* (17 January 1935), 3; see also "Jewish State in Prospect," *The West Virginia Baptist* (September 1937), 3–4.

155. *Minutes of the 1944 Colorado Baptist State Convention*, The Meeting of the Northwestern Colorado Baptist Association, Resolutions, 71.

156. *Minutes of the 1945 Annual Meeting of the New York State Baptist Convention*, Report of the Committee on Resolutions, Resolution II, Post-War Concerns—F. The British Government and the Jews in Palestine, 18.

157. *Minutes of the 1948 Vermont Baptist Convention*, Committee on Resolutions, Resolution 9, 41.

158. *Minutes of the 1945 New Jersey Baptist Convention*, Second Report of the Resolutions Committee, Resolution III, "Human Freedom," 21.

159. *Minutes of the 1946 New Jersey Baptist Convention*, Report of the Resolutions Committee, Resolution m, "Jews of the World," 25.

160. *Minutes of the 1948 New Jersey Baptist Convention*, Report of the Resolutions Committee, "Displaced Persons," 28.

161. Martha Whalen, "Baptist D.'s Need Our Help," *New Jersey Baptist Bulletin* (December 1948), 7.

162. H. O. Wyatt, "Something You Can Do and What You Can Do about It," *New Jersey Baptist Bulletin* (January 1949), 6.

163. Ibid. 35–36. See Katharine W. Johnson, *Rhode Island Baptists: Their Zeal, Their Times* (Valley Forge, PA: Judson Press, 1975), 93.

164. *1942 Yearbook of the Rhode Island Baptist State Convention*, Resolutions Report, Resolution IV, 48.

165. *1943 Yearbook of the Rhode Island Baptist State Convention*, Resolutions Report, "Christian Friendliness," 38–39.

166. *1947 Yearbook of the Rhode Island Baptist State Convention*, Resolutions Report, 34–35.

167. *1948 Yearbook of the Rhode Island Baptist State Convention*, Resolutions Report, 30–31.

168. *Minutes of the 1941 North Dakota Baptists Annual*, Sheyenne River Association Annual Meeting, Resolutions, 32.

169. *Minutes of the 1939 North Dakota Baptists Annual*, German Baptist Churches, 38–39.

170. Ibid., Resolutions, "War," 15.

171. *Minutes of the 1940 North Dakota Baptists Annual*, Resolutions, 17–18; Minutes of the 1941 North Dakota Baptists Annual, Resolutions, 20–21.

172. *Minutes of the 1942 North Dakota Baptists Annual*, Northwestern Association Annual Meeting, Resolutions 10 and 11, 24.

173. *Minutes of the 1946 North Dakota Baptists Annual*, Northwestern Association Annual Meeting, Resolutions 11, 18.

174. JoAnne Shoemaker and Don Shoemaker, *North Dakota Baptist State Convention, 1884–1984: The First Centennial, a History* (Barre, VT: Northlight Studio Press, 1984), 30–31.

Chapter 11

Jewish Friendship and Baptist Witness

The theological wars between conservatives and fundamentalists on the one side, and liberals on the other, caused significant divisions in the Northern Baptist Convention that affected its witness to the Jewish community. University of North Carolina, Chapel Hill professor Yaakov Ariel points out that the liberal influence impacted Northern Baptist ministry to Jews: "Adopting a more liberal line, devoid of premillennialist influence, the church soon abandoned its interest in the conversion of Jews."[1] The liberal leaders of the convention continued to express the good-will theme of the 1920s, especially in its commitment to the Federal Council of the Churches of Christ in America (FCCC). The statements and resolutions of the FCCC may rightly be understood as extensions of Northern Baptist social witness on racism, anti-Semitism, and the Holocaust.

Within the more conservative wing of the convention, several regions and city societies continued to promote evangelical outreach to Jews, in addition to supporting the holistic ministry of the Christian Friendliness missionaries. For example, a Jewish mission was maintained at the Euclid Avenue Baptist Church in Cleveland, Ohio.[2] In particular, the Los Angeles and Portland City Mission Societies promoted evangelistic ministry specifically focused on the Jewish community. The conservative version of ecumenical cooperation was expressed by the prophecy movement, an eschatologically focused series of conferences supported by several prominent Northern Baptist pastors.

Ecumenical Witness: Federal Council of Churches

The Northern Baptist Convention energetically supported the Federal Council of the Churches of Christ in America, an ecumenical umbrella organization for the mainline Protestant denominations. Organized in 1908, it was the forerunner of the National Council of Churches, and it focused mainly on social issues, including racism, immigration, and civil rights. Samuel McCrea Calvert, the general secretary of the FCCC, stated that "the treatment of Jews in Germany is undeniably a scandal" in May 1933.[3] In its 1934 report to Northern Baptists, the Federal Council stated that it "exercises its influence against racial prejudice" and highlighted its support of the Confessing Church faction in the German church struggle.[4]

In June 1939, the Department of Research and Education of the Federal Council published a six-page monograph on anti-Semitism that explored whether the United States was becoming increasingly receptive to the kind of anti-Semitism Nazi Germany was espousing. It recounted the history of prejudice against Jews, estimated that as many as 150 anti-Semitic organizations were disseminating hate against the Jews, exposed their techniques for spreading such propaganda, and exhorted churches to resolutely oppose such intolerance. The monograph concluded, "The Christian churches are called upon to make their own distinctive contribution by influencing the attitudes of their own members, by constant effort to the end that there shall be no anti-Semitism in the Christian Church and in the American community."[5]

The executive committee of the Federal Council produced a key statement on anti-Semitism in October 1941, which received wide press coverage.

> WE HAVE ESPECIALLY emphasized our opposition to unjust and unchristian attacks upon the Jews. In so doing we have been wholeheartedly supported by similar utterances officially made by the highest governing bodies of the great denominations cooperating in the Federal Council of Churches.
>
> Recent evidences of anti-Jewish prejudice in our own country compel us to speak again a word of solemn warning to the nation. Divisiveness on religious or racial grounds is a portentous menace to American democracy. . . .
>
> We condemn anti-Semitism as un-American. Our nation is a free fellowship of many racial and cultural stocks. It is our historic glory that they have been able to live together in mutual respect, each enjoying in

> the rich contribution which the others have made to the common good. Anti-Semitism is an insidious evil which if allowed to develop would poison the springs of our national life.
>
> Even more strongly we condemn anti-Semitism as unchristian. As Christians we gratefully acknowledge our ethical and spiritual indebtedness to the people of Israel. No true Christian can be anti-Semitic in thought, word or deed without being untrue to his own Christian inheritance.
>
> In behalf of the Christian churches which comprise the Federal Council we voice our renewed determination to unite in combating every tendency to anti-Semitism in our country.[6]

In December 1942 the council responded to reports of the mass killing of Jews with a statement offering its "deepest sympathy and indignation" and promising to help create "conditions in which such treatment of the Jews shall end."[7] In March 1943, the council "made public a program for financial assistance and havens in neutral lands for European Jews" and asked Christians to provide "their moral support to whatever measures afford promise of rescuing European Jews whose lives are in jeopardy."[8] The council also invited churches to observe a "Day of Compassion" on the first Sunday in May and encouraged prayers that God "may open the way for the deliverance of the Jewish people; that the hearts of all Christian people may be stirred to active compassion for the suffering of the Jews; that Christians in America may steadfastly oppose all tendencies to anti-Semitism in our own country."[9]

By the end of the war era, the Federal Council was able to boast that as part of its Race Relations Sundays and Brotherhood Months, "over 60,000 churches and groups in 477 cities and 46 states used special race relations literature"[10] which advocated for understanding between whites and African Americans, as well as between Christians and Jews.

West Coast City Society Jewish Initiatives

The Los Angeles City Mission Society, operating in conjunction with the Southern California Baptist Convention, conducted the most strategically intentional and extensive mission outreach to the Jews of any of the ministries affiliated with the Northern Baptist Convention between 1933 and 1948. In its 1934 annual report, the society explained its rationale for the calling of an evangelist dedicated solely to Jewish mission, Rev. E. S. Simonhoff from First Baptist Church in Hollywood:

> THE CITY MISSION Society found it possible to employ Rev. Simonhoff for part time with the understanding that the churches and the individuals who were especially interested and those who might become interested in promoting evangelistic work among the Jewish people would have an opportunity to send their gifts for the support of Mr. Simonhoff as specifics, or over and above gifts, either through the State Convention or City Mission office. It is believed that our Baptist people who have been wasting their money on independent workers will soon be sending in enough money to employ Rev. Simonhoff for full time service.[11]

Within a year, the mission society introduced two new workers. Mrs. Helen M. Steiner ("a Christian Jewess, a member of South Park Baptist Church") was called to "part-time service to promote Jewish evangelism and to arouse interest among our churches in this most important and difficult field of service in behalf of our tens of thousands of Jewish neighbors," and "Mrs. Ethel Rose, a member of Atherton Baptist Church," worked to further "evangelism and inspire interest among our churches in this—our newest venture in the evangelism of the race whom God chose as His people. We rejoice that some of these precious souls have already accepted Christ."[12]

Together these three workers held membership in local churches, indicating the desire of the City Mission Society to make this a ministry that was indigenous to the Southern California Baptist community. This was a different strategy than the American Baptist Home Mission Society (ABHMS) employed in prior efforts: "There is a wide diversity of opinion regarding the best method of approach [to Jews], but it is possible for every church with Jewish neighbors to give them Christian fellowship and strive to win them in the same way as all others in its local field. Experience has proven to many minds that this is the real strategy."[13] In 1938, the City Mission Society challenged its supporters to increase funding for the mission field of "100,000 Jews" for whom "practically nothing" was being done:

> ARE THEY NOT entitled to the Gospel message? We find them beaten by intellectual pride, robbed of their open-mindedness, and left half dead from prejudice and misunderstanding. Shall we "pass by on the other side" and leave these people, for whom Christ died, to perish? Surely, the work is exceedingly difficult, and many agencies have failed! Must we "pass by" because others have done so? Can we continue to excuse our lack of effort to bring them to a knowledge of our Savior and Lord? A definite work for these Jews could be initiated for perhaps twenty-five thousand dollars ($25,000) and the operating budget would be only about six thousand dollars ($6,000) annually. How can we escape so great an opportunity?[14]

At the 1939 state convention, Dr. Joseph Taylor, a retired missionary to China, spoke on the topic of German paganism: "Germany has substituted the Teutonic race for the living God. That is why millions of Jews have been driven from pillar to post."[15] In the mission society report, however, Simonhoff was no longer listed as a missionary.[16] The search was started for a replacement. The 1940 report rejoiced that the absence of a missionary had not hindered the pace of conversions and provided an update on the search for a new Jewish mission leader.[17] In 1941, a new director for Jewish ministry was called: "Our Jewish work is now one of our most promising activities, with Rev. Frederick J. Berger as Director of Jewish Friendship and Evangelization. Here we have a most remarkable advance."[18]

Berger's call represented a change in conviction on the part of the City Mission Society; after a national search, the society called a Gentile to lead its Jewish mission work! The society noted, "It may not be discreet to criticize what we believe are misguided methods in Jewish work in the past and even today. We do not expect Mr. Berger to devote his time to lecturing on the 'Passover' or other topics, as has been done by many missionaries to the Jews in the past. We expect him to devote his time actually to definite work in an effort to make Jesus Christ known to them as their blessed Messiah."[19]

Berger's call came at a time when the society desired to confront prejudice manifested against the trinity of groups Baptists regularly identified in its expressions of concern regarding racialism—Japanese, African Americans, and Jews: "Baptists must show a Christian consideration and an outstanding lack of prejudice for all minority groups that will reveal us to be followers of the One who loved all and gave Himself for all. Hence, we are challenged to continue with new zeal and determination our missionary interest, especially in the Japanese, Negroes, and Jews of our city."[20]

The executive secretary of the Los Angeles City Mission Society, Rev. Ralph L. Mayberry, watched over the Jewish work with care. In his 1942 report, he praised the Jewish ministry for their "commendable work" but also indicated that a change in strategy might be necessary to increase its effectiveness:

> WITH PATIENCE AND persistence we are dealing with these modern Jews who are so lacking in comprehension of spiritual truth and so devoid of background for our Christian work. How unfortunate these people are! Already we see evidences of fruitfulness. We shall continue experimenting to find the very best technique that these people may be reached with the Gospel message. We have at least one hundred thousand of them within our territory and they constitute a great responsibility that we gladly accept.[21]

Beginning in 1943, the annual ministry reports on Jewish evangelism became briefer and less informative. In that year, just one sentence was devoted to Jewish and African American ministry: "There have been developed strong missionary projects for the Jews and Negroes for our area."[22] The 1944 report merely stated, "A ministry to Jewish people through visitation, visual aid, literature distribution, a monthly publication—'The Messenger of Good Will'—and Jewish-Christian Fellowship meetings. Fifteen Jews made definite confessions of faith during the year."[23] However, the title of that last report—"Jewish Friendship and Evangelization"—hinted at the real significance of the experiment Los Angeles was attempting to live out.

Berger was convinced that in addition to mass mailed publications and special events, friendship was a key factor in Jewish evangelization. Friendship was to be expressed not only by interpersonal relationships but also through demonstrating solidarity with the Jewish community by addressing its deeply held concerns. In a message about how to share the gospel with Jews in a "tactful manner," Berger addressed the sensitive issue of Jewish suspicion of Gentiles and

Christianity—and how an emphasis on friendship might counteract that suspicion:

> THE TASK IS particularly delicate because the average Jew makes no distinction between the Christian and the Gentile; to him all Gentiles are Christian and all Hebrew-Christians are traitors. Lurking in the mind of every Jew above infancy is the remembrance that his people have been persecuted through the ages in the name of Christ. Fortunately, Baptists have never had a part in this wrong, but, on the contrary, have been the greatest champions of religious freedom both in Europe and in America. Nevertheless, while advocating religious freedom for all, Baptists have been active in presenting the claims of the One who came here nineteen hundred years ago. This presentation has always been and should always be by loving suggestion and persuasion and never by intimidation. It is with a sincere concern and love for the Jew that the Los Angeles Baptist City Society has launched a program of friendship and evangelism. It is hoped that the Jew will come to the realization that the true Christian is his friend and more important, that Jesus was and is the Christ, his Messiah.[24]

Based on the Baptist core convictions of religious freedom and liberty, Berger advocated for Christians to respect and befriend Jews. Like the Christian Friendliness missionaries, Berger loved Jews and appreciated Judaism, and thus he maintained that only tactful persuasion, practiced within the context of an authentic relationship, was a proper strategy for reaching out to the Jewish people. One of the ways in which Berger expressed his love and friendship for Jews was by enlisting Baptists in a letter-writing campaign in support of the continued immigration of European Jews to Palestine, which the British were threatening to cut off.[25] Fifteen Baptist churches responded by sending petitions to both President Franklin Delano Roosevelt and Lord Halifax, who was then serving as Great Britain's ambassador to the United States.[26]

Berger also spoke out against anti-Semitism in forceful and biblical terms, affirming the Jews as part of God's covenant:

> THE SCOURGE OF anti-Semitism is growing in America; it is based upon exaggeration and falsehood, and upon the illogic of applying to a whole people the errors of a few. Since anti-Semitism has a Satanic

> motivation, the true Christian must be on the alert so as not to become a party to it and must be mindful of God's promise to Abraham: "I will bless them that bless you, and curse him that curses you" (Gen. 12:3). Many Christians fail to appreciate the historic role which Israel had to play, including the rejection and its consequences; as Paul stated, "by their fall salvation is come to the Gentiles" (Romans 11:11).[27]

In October 1947, Berger resigned from his position to become a professor at the Bible Baptist College of San Francisco.[28] Although throughout his tenure several articles indicated that Jewish individuals accepted Christ through Berger's ministry of friendship, no comprehensive statistics were ever published to document the fruitfulness of his approach.

Berger did, however, impress the Baptists of Portland, Oregon, who attempted to duplicate his efforts. In 1943, the Portland Baptist City Mission announced that it had appointed Rev. Karl Faulkner to serve as "director of special work among the Jewish residents of the city." The society anticipated that Faulkner would live out his call in a manner "similar to that done by Rev. Fred Berger, missionary of the Baptist City Society in Los Angeles." The paper claimed that Faulkner "had experience in Poland and other European countries" and could share "a thrilling story of his wartime experiences in Europe and his escape from Nazi dominated countries."[29]

Faulkner presented his ministry to the Oregon Baptist State Convention in May 1943, and the Portland Baptist City Mission Society provided $385 for this work in the 1942–1943 fiscal year. An additional amount of $427.27 was raised for this ministry in that time period.[30] The following year, the Portland Baptist City Mission Society Financial Statement indicated that they raised $1,100.38 and spent $992.87 on Faulkner's salary of $830.13 and travel expenses totaling $162.74.[31]

In an article for *The Oregon Baptist*, Faulkner asked, "Why Should We Bother about the Jew?" With the Holocaust still going on, Faulkner noted that "even church people are indifferent to the physical plight and spiritual need of the Jew." He called upon Baptists to be concerned "for the Jewish people" in Europe: "How the Jews in Europe need our prayers. Let us pray that the Lord will use those who are left there as witnesses to Israel in the day of their great distress."[32]

Baptist Evangelicals, Anti-Semitism, and Prophecy

Theologically conservative Northern Baptists were also influenced by a premillennial prophetic interpretation of the Scriptures.[33] Premillennialism emphasized the continuing role of Israel in God's historical dealings and looked forward to its reestablishment in Palestine as a prophetic prelude to Jesus' second coming. John W. Bradbury, the successor to Curtis Lee Laws[34] as the editor of *The Watchman-Examiner*, played a leading role in popularizing premillennialism as a theological defense against anti-Semitism and Nazism.

During the Holocaust, premillennialists organized a series of conferences to promote the premillennial understanding and apply its prophetic insights to contemporary events. Calvary Baptist Church in New York City served as the site for the first New York Congress on Prophecy, which was held on November 1-8, 1942. More than thirty presentations were made by a denominationally diverse array of scholars and pastors. Besides speakers from a Baptist background, there was another connection to Northern Baptists. The American Board of Missions to the Jews, an independent mission founded by Leopold Cohn after he ended his affiliation with the American Baptist Home Mission Society, organized the conference. Bradbury was chosen to edit the conference's book, *The Sure Word of Prophecy*.

On November 5, 1942, a four-part manifesto was unanimously affirmed by the conference attendees. The manifesto focused on Israel's leading role in end-times prophecy. The return of the Jewish people to Palestine as "a separate nation," the validity of Israel's covenant with God even during the Christian era, and the need to present the gospel to individual Jews were all affirmed. The fourth section of the manifesto explicitly condemned all forms of anti-Semitism: "We believe that anti-Semitism in its present vicious world-wide manifestation, is incompatible with both the letter and the spirit of the gospel, and is to be shunned and guarded against by all who sincerely love our Lord Jesus Christ; that to do kindness and to show mercy to the seed of Abraham is a direct Christian obligation."[35]

Reflecting premillennialism's pessimism about the ability of the church to usher in the kingdom of God by human effort, the manifesto condemned Nazi anti-Semitism without advancing any solutions for its eradication or strategies to rescue Jews who were being persecuted. The only solace evangelicals could offer Jews was that the present persecution might lead them back to Palestine. William Ward Ayer, Calvary Baptist Church's pastor, stated that the church should "speak comfortingly to blind, suffering, hounded, hated Jewry. . . . The Church's prophetic message would have reminded a dispersed and suffering people of a kingdom and a King who is to occupy the throne of David in a glorious day to come when Israel is to be regathered in her own land."[36]

Bradbury prophesied against the collective Gentile world. The nations had accepted a triune "Gentile idolatry" consisting of nationalism, racism, and the totalitarian worship of government. He belittled Hitler's anti-Semitic racial doctrine as unoriginal, finding racialist ideas in both the Old and New Testaments. Nevertheless, Hitler's totalitarianism did not represent the eschatological anti-Christ of prophecy (because the rapture of the church was still in the future), but at the least it served a prophetic role; the "stage is now being set."[37]

The second New York congress was held at Calvary Baptist Church in Manhattan from December 5-12, 1943. Bradbury once again was given the assignment of editing its presentations. Ayer characterized Nazi totalitarianism as possessing "many of the elements of anti-Christ"[38] and lamented the suffering of the Jewish people in Europe. He forthrightly acknowledged that the Holocaust was under way:

> THE NATION OF Israel knows her most terrible suffering today. Stories coming out of Europe tell how Hitler, mad with Jewish hatred, plans the annihilation of all Jews, living within the boundaries of his far-flung, stolen empire. How many millions have died, God alone knows, but this much is true, the nation of Israel persecuted beyond any group of people in all the world from the days of Pharaoh, Haman, Nebuchadnezzar and Antiochus Epiphanes has probably suffered more from Europe's madman, Hitler, than in all her previous persecutions. . . . Earnest, honest leaders of Jewry today see light for their bleeding, dying people, realize that for Israel it is night.[39]

Joseph Hoffman Cohn picked up on the imagery of night and observed that Israel was "going through such a night of horror as she has not faced in all her dark history of over four thousand years.

But out of this night of insanity God has promised a daybreak for the Jews that will outshine in splendor the most brilliant scene that the human mind can imagine."[40] Cohn was referring to their restoration as a nation, but premillennialists understood the restoration of Israel in a different way than Jewish Zionists did. The latter saw the establishment of an independent Jewish homeland as the means of restoring identity, providing protection, and ensuring the equality of the Jewish people as a legitimate member of the international family of nations.[41] Dean C. Bedford, pastor of the Brighton Community Church in Rochester, New York, noted that the development of the Zionist movement and the rise of anti-Semitism in Europe took place simultaneously and wondered whether the former may have inadvertently contributed to the latter.[42] Cohn, Bradbury, and Ayer believed that Israel's restoration was a prelude to their discovering Jesus as their Messiah at the Second Coming: "For Israel, Christ's coming in power and great glory is her only hope of the cessation of anti-semitism and persecution."[43]

C. Gordon Brownsville, pastor of Tremont Baptist Temple in Boston, offered a more politically astute proposal at the 1943 conference. Based on the British Balfour Declaration of 1917 and the 1941 Atlantic Charter's articulation of "Four Freedoms" for a post-war world, he called for a "Fifth Freedom" on behalf of the Jewish people: "This freedom has to do with the United Nations' promise to the Jews, freedom from future persecution and the recognition of Palestine as a national Jewish homeland."[44]

A. B. Machlin helped found the American Association for Jewish Evangelism that sponsored a conference in 1945, which Bradbury and other Northern Baptists supported. At the conference, the nascent organization passed a statement on anti-Semitism. Its preamble affirmed that the organization was "friendly to the Jews now scattered throughout the world; and not only are we friendly to the Jewish people, but we are utterly opposed to the spirit of Anti-Semitism that is now rampant among the nations of the world."

The next paragraph condemned anti-Semitism as irrational and unfair, since the charges made against Jews, even if accurate, could just as easily be applied to other races and cultures. Therefore, the spread of anti-Semitism must have a spiritual and nefarious cause: "Anti-Semitism is a movement conceived by Satan and propagated by his servants to attain his ambition to destroy the God-conscious Jew, as part of a purpose to place Satan-controlled men in power over all the earth. We also believe that those who yield themselves to the spirit of Anti-Semitism surrender to the spirit of Satan—a spirit soon to find its incarnation in the Antichrist himself."

The closing paragraph reflected the predilection of Baptists in the United States to identify Christianity with American democracy and religious freedom, which were believed to be incompatible with anti-Semitism: "Anti-Semitism is not only unChristian, it is likewise utterly un-American. America was begotten by men and women whose lives were dedicated to founding an asylum for all the oppressed because of their religious convictions . . . the spirit of Anti-Semitism is a spirit that no born-again Christian can possibly afford to harbor." The statement concluded with a call for Christians to befriend Jews, the first half of which was reminiscent of J. H. Rushbrooke's offer to the British Jewish community in 1935: "Rather will the true Christian realize his debt to the Jew by offering him a friendly, helping hand in this hour of need, earnestly praying the while that his eyes shall be opened to behold in Jesus Christ his Messiah and the Savior of the world."[45]

The German Baptist Conference (North American Baptist Convention)

The American Baptist Home Mission Society initiated church planting campaigns among several European immigrant communities throughout the nineteenth century. It worked with German-speaking Baptists to establish and strengthen the German Baptist Conference, which in 1942 changed its name to the North American Baptist Conference. During the Holocaust period apparently no resolutions regarding the German persecution of the Jews were advanced at its Triennial meetings.

By 1935, the conference was sponsoring eighty-six workers, with the largest contingents in Poland (27), Bulgaria (22), Rumania (12), and Hungary (10), as well as three workers in Germany itself. Dr. William Kuhn, the general missionary secretary, reported that the German conference did turn over much of its European missionary work to the Baptist Union of Germany in response to Nazi aggression:

"After Germany took over Austria, we transferred the work there to the Baptist Union of Germany. When Czechoslovakia lost its independence the German Union took over the work there also."

The German Baptists in the United States, in turn, supported the German Baptist Union's Cameroon mission before war broke out, and continued to do so after the German Baptists were forced to leave when that country came under British rule. The North American Baptist Conference also engaged in relief efforts throughout Europe, in cooperation with other members of the Baptist World Alliance.[46]

The Swedish Baptist General Conference of America

The Northern Baptist Convention reached out to Swedish immigrants in the nineteenth century. By 1882 Swedish Baptists could claim 104 churches and approximately five thousand members scattered throughout the heartland of the United States and a denominational status distinct from Northern Baptists.[47] "General Conference" meetings of Swedish Baptists began in 1879.[48] By 1933, the Swedish Baptist General Conference of America had grown to 309 churches and an estimated membership of almost thirty-seven thousand members.[49]

With close ties to northern Europe, one might expect that Swedish Baptists in the United States would have expressed concerns about the political and social changes taking place in Germany. However, the resolutions passed at the Swedish Baptist annual meetings during the Nazi era scarcely refer to the social upheaval, war, and persecutions endured by Jews and others at the hands of Hitler and the Nazi regime.

In the early 1930s, Swedish Baptists endorsed a series of brief antiwar resolutions that were in step with Northern Baptist statements.[50] During the prewar period, the Resolutions Committee made no reference to Nazi totalitarianism, Hitler's ongoing measures aimed against Jews in Germany, or the activities of the Baptist World Alliance. At its 1938 general conference, delegates reiterated their opposition to "all wars of aggression" and argued for settling international disputes "through the medium of Christian diplomacy and arbitration."[51] The denomination's Executive Committee Report for the June 1939 general conference briefly acknowledged that General

Secretary Ragnar A. Arlander was empowered to represent Swedish Baptists in the United States at the 1939 Baptist world congress in Atlanta.[52]

In 1940, the Resolutions Committee presented a statement expressing opposition to the United States getting involved in any war not directly focused on defending its own national sovereignty.[53] The first mention of the flight of Jewish refugees from Germany may be found in the Russian Mission Field Report submitted for the June 1940 general conference. Missionaries Margaret Lindstedt and August Lindstedt referred first to "restrictions and irregularities" that missionaries might encounter during wartime[54] and then spoke about the Swedish Baptist mission to Jewish refugees in Shanghai: "Meetings are also being held in our church for Jewish refugees, of which there are thousands in Shanghai at present. Once again China has had to open her doors to refugees from Europe."[55]

Swedish Baptists in the United States officially expressed their opposition to Nazism for the first time in June 1941. In an antiwar and isolationist resolution, the delegates declared their disapproval "of totalitarianism" and their "sincere appreciation of the democratic peoples and our sympathy with them in their struggle against tyranny." It is unclear if the resolution's reference to "the suffering of innocent peoples" was an expression of sympathy for European Jews or a generic statement for all nationalities that were afflicted by Germany's aggression.[56]

The 1944 meeting was notable for the presence of two invited guests. Walter O. Lewis, the BWA's general secretary, provided an overview of the global Baptist movement and "assured the Conference that the application for membership which was submitted following last year's General Board meeting will no doubt receive favorable action by the World Alliance board." The conference later heard a presentation by evangelist Hyman Appelman, a Jewish Christian associated with Southern Baptists in Texas.[57]

Delegates to the 1946 general conference responded enthusiastically to a presentation on the Midwest Hebrew Mission based in St. Paul, Minnesota. Lewis returned and described the work of the BWA as "promoting religious liberty and bringing relief to the oppressed people of the world."[58] However, there were no references in the general conference records to the Holocaust, postwar Jewish concentration camp survivors, displaced persons, Zionism, or the establishment of Israel.

The General Association of Regular Baptist Churches

The modernist-fundamentalist struggles of the twentieth century featured several waves of defections from the Northern Baptist Convention. In 1932–1933, fundamentalist protest led to the formation of the General Association of Regular Baptist Churches (GARBC); a second breakaway led to the emergence of the Conservative Baptist Association in 1947–1948.[59]

Meeting in First Baptist Church in Buffalo, a Northern Baptist congregation, fundamentalists voted to "determine to do its work independent of, and separate from, the Northern Baptist Convention and all its auxiliaries."[60] Many of the resolutions the General Association of Regular Baptists passed in the 1930s featured criticisms of the Northern Baptist Convention. Prior to the entry of the United States into World War II, just one resolution (in 1934) addressed the challenge of European political ideologies, but it is more likely that Russian rather than German politics was the focus: "Regular Baptists, highly prizing our freedom of speech and liberty of conscience, call attention to the growing influence of radical socialism and Communism, both of which are more or less lawless, Godless, and unpatriotic, and we hereby express our alarm and distress at the apparent indifference of our national government to this foe of our constitution and flag."[61]

It took nine more years for the GARBC to pledge "its undying opposition to all forms of Totalism [*sic*], whether they be Nazi, Fascist, or Communist, and affirm its allegiance to principles of democratic representative government as expressed in the Constitution of the United States." The statement concluded:

> INASMUCH AS THE attitude and action of the Axis nations are demonstrably inimical to the spread of the gospel of Jesus Christ, and inasmuch as the basic opportunity to worship freely would be abridged or denied in the event of a victory by the Axis powers, the General Association of Regular Baptist Churches petitions the President of the United States to take such steps as may be required to secure the cooperation

> of all the United [Allied] Nations in a worldwide Day of Prayer for the spiritual needs and military success of the forces of the United [Allied] Nations.[62]

Anti-Semitism and the creation of Israel received attention at the fifteenth GARBC annual conference. In contrast to the silence of the Northern and Southern Baptists on the birth of Israel in 1948, the GARBC passed a brief but specific resolution on anti-Semitism, Israel's security, and sharing the gospel with Jewish people: "We declare anew our opposition to the various forms of Anti-semitism extant today, and that we express our deep concern for the People of Israel in the present distress involving the Land of Palestine, and that furthermore, we call our churches to greater endeavor to bring the Gospel to those who are Abraham's Seed according to the flesh."[63]

Despite its deep antipathy toward the Northern Baptist Convention, the General Association of Regular Baptist Churches expressed views regarding totalitarianism and anti-Semitism that would have been acceptable to the convention it left behind. The breakaway movement was officially more positive toward Israel and its Zionist philosophical aspirations than the Northern Baptist Convention, and in this respect, its position closely resembled the Baptist evangelical prophetic movement.

Notes

1. Yaakov Ariel, *Evangelizing the Chosen People: Missions to the Jews in America, 1880–2000* (Chapel Hill: University of North Carolina Press, 2000), 117.

2. The Cleveland Baptist Association, *150 Years of Mission to Greater Cleveland*, 8.

3. Michael Williams and Samuel Calvert, "Noted Churchmen Issue Statement on German-Jewish Problem," *American Hebrew* (26 March 1933), 26.

4. *Annual of the 1933 Northern Baptist Convention*, Report of the Federal Council of the Churches of Christ in America, 173–74.

5. Department of Research and Education of the Federal Council of the Churches of Christ in America, *Current Manifestations of Organized Anti-Semitism* (10 June 1939), 6.

6. *Bulletin of the Federal Council of Churches of Christ in America* (October 1941), published in "Federal Council of Churches of Christ Condemns Anti-Semitism," American Hebrew (21 November 1941), 5.

7. David S. Wyman, *The Abandonment of the Jews: America and the Holocaust, 1941–1945* (New York: The New Press, 1984), 65.

8. "Council of Churches Submits Program on Aid to European Jews to Ottawa Conference," Jewish Telegraphic Agency (18 March 1943), JTA website archive, http://www.jta.org/1943/03/18/archive/council-of-churches-submits-program-on-aid-to-european-jews-to-ottawa-conference#ixzz2aTD4i0ls, accessed 1 February 2016.

9. "Federal Council of Churches Proclaims 'Day of Compassion' for Persecuted Jews," *Jewish Telegraphic Agency* (16 April 1943), JTA website archive, http://www.jta.org/1943/04/26/archive/federal-council-of-churches-proclaims-day-of-compassion-for-persecuted-jews/, accessed 1 February 2016.

10. "February Is Brotherhood Month," *New Jersey Baptists Bulletin* (February 1946), National Supplement, 4.

11. *1934 Proceedings of the Southern California Baptist Convention*, Los Angeles City Mission Society Report, "Christ for the Jews," 138.

12. *1935 Proceedings of the Southern California Baptist Convention*, Los Angeles City Mission Society Report, "Our Jewish Neighbors," 146.

13. *1936 Proceedings of the Southern California Baptist Convention*, Los Angeles City Mission Society Report, "Our Jewish People," 171.

14. *1938 Proceedings of the Southern California Baptist Convention*, Los Angeles City Mission Society Report, "The Immediate Challenge," 175–76.

15. *1939 Proceedings of the Southern California Baptist Convention*, Minutes, 49.

16. Ibid., Los Angeles City Mission Society Report, 122. Simonhoff's resignation was reported in "Jewish Work," *Baptist News of Southern California* (September/October 1938), 37.

17. *1940 Proceedings of the Southern California Baptist Convention*, Los Angeles City Mission Society Report, "An Eventful Year," 160–61.

18. *1941 Proceedings of the Southern California Baptist Convention*, Los Angeles City Mission Society Report, "Gratifying Advance," 44.

19. "A Baptist Ministry to the Jews," *Baptist News of Southern California* (January/February 1941), 25–26.

20. *1941 Proceedings of the Southern California Baptist Convention*, Los Angeles City Mission Society Report, "Persistent Challenge," 49.

21. *1942 Proceedings of the Southern California Baptist Convention*, Los Angeles City Mission Society Report, "Losses and Gains," 89.

22. *1943 Proceedings of the Southern California Baptist Convention*, Los Angeles City Mission Society Report, 58.

23. *1944 Proceedings of the Southern California Baptist Convention*, Los Angeles City Mission Society Report, "Jewish Friendship and Evangelization," 53.

24. Frederick J. Berger, "A Desire and a Need," *Baptist News of Southern California* (March/April 1943), 21.

25. Frederick J. Berger, "Jewish Friendship," *Southern California Baptist News* (December 1943), 10.

26. Frederick J. Berger, "Jewish Friendship," *Southern California Baptist News* (February 1944), 10.

27. Frederick J. Berger, "Jewish Friendship and Evangelization," *Southern California Baptist News* (February 1945), 14.

28. Frederick J. Berger, "Department of Jewish Work," *Southern California Baptist News* (October 1947), 12.

29. "Jewish Evangelist in Portland," *The Oregon Baptist* (January–February 1943), 1.

30. *1943 Annual of the Oregon Baptist State Convention*, 30.

31. *1944 Annual of the Oregon Baptist State Convention*, 30.

32. Karl Faulkner, "Why Should We Bother about the Jew?" *The Oregon Baptist* (April–May 1944), 11.

33. See David Rausch, *Fundamentalist-Evangelicals and Anti-Semitism* (Valley Forge, PA: Trinity Press International, 1993).

34. John W. Bradbury, "Curtis Lee Laws, An Appreciation," *The Watchman-Examiner* (18 July 1946), 747–49.

35. John W. Bradbury, ed., *The Sure Word of Prophecy; Report of the New York Congress on Prophecy, Assembled in the Calvary Baptist Church, New York City, November 1-8, 1942* (New York: Revell, 1943), 11–14.

36. William Ward Ayer, "What It Has Cost the Church to Neglect the Bible's Prophetic Message," in Bradbury, *Prophecy*, 44.

37. Bradbury, "Have the Gentiles Failed?" in Bradbury, *Prophecy*, 59–62. W. H. Rogers cited Mussolini as the contemporary incarnation of Haman, the political persecutor of the Jewish people; see "A Shout, a Voice, and a Trump" in Bradbury, *Prophecy*, 124.

38. William Ward Ayer, "God's Warning through Prophecy to the Nations," in John W. Bradbury, ed., *Light for the World's Darkness: Second New York Congress on Prophecy Addresses 1943* (New York: Loizeaux Brothers, 1944), 17.

39. Ibid., 20.

40. J. Hoffman Cohn, "Disputed Passage," in Bradbury, *Light for the World's Darkness*, 29.

41. Theodor Herzl, *Old New Land*, trans. Lotta Levensohn (Princeton, NJ: Markus Wiener Publishers, 1997); Arthur Hertzberg, ed., *The Zionist Idea: A Historical Analysis and Reader* (Philadelphia: The Jewish Publication Society, 1997); and Howard M. Sachar, *The Course of Modern Jewish History*, new rev. ed. (New York: Vintage Books, 1990).

42. Dean C. Bedford, "Anti-Semitism: Its Origin, Development, and Final Doom," in Bradbury, *Light for the World's Darkness*, 183–84.

43. Rogers, "A Shout, a Voice, and a Trump," 124.

44. C. Gordon Brownville, "Calling All Jews or What about the Fifth Freedom," in Bradbury, *Light for the World's Darkness*, 209; see 219.

45. John W. Bradbury, ed., *Israel's Restoration: A Series of Lectures by Bible Expositors Interested in the Evangelization of the Jews* (New York: Iversen-Ford, 1950), 11–13.

46. Frank H. Woyke, *Heritage and Ministry of the North American Baptist Conference* (Oakbrook Terrace, IL: North American Baptist Conference, 1979), 293, 309–18, 358, 382–84.

47. Robert G. Torbet, *A History of the Baptists*, 3rd ed. (Valley Forge, PA: Judson Press, 1978), 381.

48. *Annual of the Swedish Baptist Churches of America for 1933–1934, Part I*, 104.

49. *Annual of the Swedish Baptist Churches of America for 1933–1934, Part II*, 2.

50. *Annual of the Swedish Baptist Churches of America for 1933–1934, Part I*, Committee on Resolutions Report—"Peace," 101; *Annual of the Swedish Baptist Churches of America for 1934–1935, Part I*, Committee on Resolutions Report—"War," 126; *Annual of the Swedish Baptist Churches of America for 1935–1936, Part I*, Committee on Resolutions Report—"War," 112.

51. *Annual of the Swedish Baptist Churches of America for 1938–1939, Part I*, Committee on Resolutions Report—"War," 107.

52. *Annual of the Swedish Baptist Churches of America for 1939–1940, Part I*, Executive Committee Report, 38.

53. *Annual of the Swedish Baptist Churches of America for 1940–1941, Part I*, Committee on Resolutions Report —"On Peace and National Defense," 126.

54. Ibid., "The Russian Mission Field," 52.

55. Ibid., "Shanghai," 53. Shanghai was a significant Asian refuge for European Jewish exiles; see Marcia R. Ristaino, *Port of Last Resort: The Diaspora Communities of Shanghai* (Redwood City, CA: Stanford University Press, 2003), 98–116.

56. *Annual of the Swedish Baptist Churches of America for 1941–1942, Part I*, Committee on Resolutions Report— "International Relations," 124–25.

57. *Annual of the Swedish Baptist Churches of America for 1944–1945, Part I*, Minutes, 22. For an example of his message concerning Jews, see Hyman J. Appelmann, "A Suffering People," in Bradbury, *Israel's Restoration*, 19–36.

58. *Annual of the Swedish Baptist Churches of America for 1946–1947, Part I*, Minutes, 27, 32.

59. Torbet, *History of the Baptists*, 434–37; Bill J. Leonard, *Baptist Ways: A History* (Valley Forge, PA: Judson Press, 2003), 404–6; Thomas S. Kidd and Barry Hankins, *Baptists in America: A History* (Oxford: Oxford University Press, 2015), 193, 198–201, 240.

60. "Purpose of the GARBC" Resolution, First Annual Conference of the GARBC (May 16-18, 1933), http://www.garbc.org/wp-content/uploads/2007/05/purpose-of-the-garbc-1933.pdf, accessed 11 June 2016.

61. "Communism, Socialism, and Ungodly Teaching" Resolution, Second Annual Conference of the GARBC (May 15-18, 1934); http://www.garbc.org/wp-content/uploads/2007/05/communism-socialism-and-ungodly-teaching-1934.pdf, accessed 11 June 2016.

62. "The War Effort and National Revival" Resolutions, Tenth Annual Conference of the GARBC (May 10-13, 1943), http://www.garbc.org/wp-content/uploads/2007/05/the-war-effort-and-national-revival-1943.pdf, accessed 11 June 2016.

63. Resolution Number 2, Fifteenth Annual Conference of the GARBC (May 17-20, 1948), Resolutions Committee Original Typed Report, 1. From the Historical Archived Collection of the General Association of Regular Baptist Churches, Arlington Heights, IL.

Contemporary Impressions

The Ineffectiveness of Episodic Attention

Between 1933 and 1948, the Northern Baptist Convention consistently manifested its allegiance to the historic Baptist core convictions of soul freedom, religious and civil freedom and liberty, democracy, and the sanctity of the human soul or spirit (personality). In its resolutions and statements, the convention consistently applied these convictions to the challenge posed by Hitler and Nazism by expressing opposition to all forms of totalitarianism, including fascism, and in its consideration of the plight of the Jewish people by declaring sympathy for them and opposing anti-Semitism. However, even after the general council's Kristallnacht protest, the convention never approved or undertook any practical action to assist the Jewish people in Europe and save them from extinction. Therefore, the Northern Baptist Convention was not guilty of the charge of being silent, but it did act as a corporate bystander to the Holocaust.

The American Baptist Foreign Mission Society was in the best position to mobilize activity on behalf of European Jews. It voiced in private its opposition to Berlin as the venue for the 1934 world congress. However, when J. H. Rushbrooke convinced the majority of the Baptist World Alliance's executive committee to support the German Baptist Union, the society decided upon a passive-aggressive response—denying financial support for its personnel to attend while supporting the event officially. A more principled strategy of public discomfort might have had some impact, but the Foreign Mission Society did not wish to spearhead resistance to Rushbrooke, choosing instead to place Baptist international solidarity and unity over prophetically voicing their concern for the German Jews.

In contrast, the European representatives of the Foreign Mission Society acted as bystanders. W. O. Lewis and Edwin Bell were well aware of the plight of the Jewish people, but both chose to serve in a bureaucratic manner. Displaying a curious sense of tunnel vision, they rarely spoke out against the Nazi treatment of the Jews and did not use their offices to rally Northern Baptist generosity on behalf of Jewish immigrants, or after the war, for the Jewish survivors of the Holocaust and its concentration camps. Instead, they focused on the needs of their Baptist comrades in Europe and facilitated the German Baptists' self-portrayal as victims of Hitler and the war.

During this period, the American Baptist Home Mission Society (ABHMS) also acted in a bystander mode, with the possible exception of helping exiled scholars find positions in historically African American colleges, some of which were affiliated with the society.

In stark contrast, the Woman's American Baptist Home Mission Society (WABHMS) displayed prophetic energy through its highly effective Christian Friendliness Department. The genius behind the success of the Christian Friendliness ministry was threefold. First, the society hired an amazingly dedicated and well-trained corps of professional missionaries. These women demonstrated a deep respect and admiration for the Jews they befriended, and they consistently and courageously spoke out against all forms of prejudice—whether it was expressed against Japanese Americans, African Americans, or Jews. Second, the society partnered with the state conventions and city societies, who lent moral support and organizational assistance. Third, the Christian Friendliness missionaries recruited and trained an extraordinary number of female leaders in hundreds of churches, who in turn created and maintained Christian Friendliness committees that mobilized individual women for service and relationship building with immigrants.

The WABHMS and its Christian Friendliness missionaries did more than any other Northern Baptist agency to enable Baptist individuals to transition from passive bystanders to active protagonists during the era of Nazi persecution of the Jews. The thousands of women who joined the Christian Friendliness movement may not have been rescuers in the classic sense, but it would not be unfair to characterize them as rebuilders of lives, once Jewish (and other) refugees made it to America's shores.

As the ABHMS lost interest in Jewish evangelism, the evangelical wing of the denomination filled in the void, with Los Angeles taking the leadership role. Frederick Berger's attempt to fuse traditional Baptist evangelism with a desire for authentic friendship paralleled the values of the Christian Friendliness missionaries.

Through the premillennial prophecy movement of the 1940s, evangelical Northern Baptists interacted with churches of other denominations and more fundamentalist independent Baptists. This movement provided an alternative way to express support for the Jewish people. It enthusiastically endorsed Zionist aspirations and the establishment of Israel as a Jewish homeland.

The Northern Baptist state conventions responded to the specter of Nazism from the perspective of World War I–era geopolitics.[1] In general, the states' resolutions expressed an opposition to nationalism, militarism, and war (though all were not pacifist), and opposition to totalitarianism because of the Baptist stress on the principles of soul freedom and separation of church and state. Horror about anti-Semitism and racial prejudice, Hitler's persecution of the Jews, and the Nazi campaign to systematically exterminate the Jewish population of Europe was expressed throughout the era, but not in any coordinated manner. There was no single resolution that was circulated throughout all of the states, no particular milestone received significantly more attention than other aspects of the persecution, and there is little evidence that the states were coordinating protests with each other. The state conventions did respond to the resolutions approved by the national conventions, but aside from the work of the Christian Friendliness missionaries and the displaced persons' ministry, there was no convention-wide response to the plight of the Jews on the state level.

Each state possessed its own set of theological, historical, and experiential resources by which to address the issues posed by the Nazi challenge to Jewish civil liberties and existence as a people. The individualized nature and creativity of each state's response is noteworthy. The resolutions were not templates and were not copied by each state from either a central source or from other states. Take, for example, the three state convention resolutions passed in 1933. The Wisconsin Baptists were inspired by their Native American heritage and an abiding love for liberty and democracy—core

Baptist convictions. Michigan Baptists derived their inspiration from the prophetic witness of the father of American Baptists, Roger Williams, in favor of "religious liberty and tolerance" for all. Iowan Baptists justified their opposition to Germany's persecution of Jews on a political analysis of nationalism, which the Nazis had "perverted." All three state conventions arrived at the same conclusion but via different paths.

There is little evidence that Northern Baptists advocated or tolerated anti-Semitism within their ranks. The two most significant possible exceptions were Minnesota and North Dakota. There is no doubt that William Bell Riley exercised considerable influence and control in Minnesota. It is also clear that Riley was the highest profile anti-Semite in the Northern Baptist Convention. However, there is no evidence to suggest that his anti-Semitic views gained any traction on either a national or state level. His aberrant views about Jews were quietly tolerated but apparently also largely ignored. The loss of the German Baptist churches in North Dakota deserves further research, for it is not clear to what extent anti-Semitism may have played a role in the course of events there, as opposed to heritage, commitment to missionary work in Europe and Africa, and denominational politics unrelated to the Jewish situation.

There was a broad consensus expressed by the Northern Baptist state conventions. They were opposed to Hitler's persecution of the European Jewish population, rejected anti-Semitism, and appreciated the efforts of the Christian Friendliness missionaries. At least some sought points of contact with the Jewish community to express friendship. However, beyond resolutions and supporting the local outreach of the Christian Friendliness missionaries, they engaged in very little concrete and practical action to oppose the continuing extermination of Jews, acting more like bystanders in this regard. Efforts to resettle Jewish refugees rarely happened, as Baptists preferred to focus on relocating Baptist refugees. The state conventions did not mobilize support for Jewish immigration to Palestine, and neither did they publicly support campaigns to promote the Zionist dream of an independent Israel as the Jewish homeland. Some did support changes in American immigration regulations to permit more Jewish refugees to resettle in the United States.

Northern Baptists were on the right side of history by passing resolutions that voiced support for persecuted Jews, opposing anti-Semitism as antithetical to historic Baptist core convictions, and rejecting all forms of totalitarianism, including Nazism. However, the effectiveness of these resolutions should rightly be questioned. The resolutions rarely called for any sacrifice on the part of churches and their members, except for campaigns to support humanitarian relief efforts for displaced persons. It is difficult to assess if the passing of these resolutions affected the relationship between the Jewish community and Baptist churches on a local level. With the exception of the Christian Friendliness mission work, which provided practical assistance to Jewish immigrants, the episodic attention of the Northern Baptist Convention to the suffering of Europe's Jews proved to be ineffective in countering the Nazis' destruction of the Jewish population of Europe.

Note

1. See John Milton Moore, "What ARE We Going to Do About It?" *The Connecticut Baptist* (January 1934), 7.

PART FOUR

The Ambivalence of the Southern Baptist Convention

The horrors of the Nazi persecution of its Jewish citizens and the wider Holocaust evoked many kinds of responses from Baptists: sermons, political analysis, prophetic speculation, introspective reflection, and even poetry and music. The Baptist General Convention of Oklahoma met in session one week after Kristallnacht and could not avoid what had just happened in Germany. James Wilson Storer, pastor of the First Baptist Church of Tulsa, Oklahoma (and a future president of the Southern Baptist Convention), delivered the closing sermon on "Baptists in the World Picture," which was also broadcast on radio by the Oklahoma Mutual Broadcasting Company.[1] Without specifically mentioning Jews or Kristallnacht, he said, "It would seem to some as if God had forgotten this world . . . above the lifted hand of Hitler, I see another hand and hear the voice of Martin Luther: 'A mighty fortress is our God, a bulwark never failing; Our Helper He, amid the flood of mortals ills prevailing.'"[2]

When Jacob Gartenhaus, the era's highest-ranking Jewish convert in Southern Baptist denominational work, sought to elicit compassion for Jews going to their deaths in Nazi concentration camps, he invoked the poetry of Lord Byron. Israel's oppression in Babylon was analogous to European Jewry's existential threat under Hitler and the Nazis:

> *OH, weep for those that wept by Babel's stream,*
> *Whose shrines are desolate, whose land a dream;*
> *Weep for the harp of Judah's broken shell;*
> *Mourn—where their God hath dwelt, the godless dwell! . . .*
> *Tribes of the wandering foot and weary breast,*

How shall ye flee away and be at rest!
The wild-dove hath her nest, the fox his cave,
Mankind their country,—Israel but the grave![3]

The Southern Baptist set of responses to the Nazi campaign against the Jewish people is complicated by conflicting agendas and contradictory messages. This ambivalent tone emanated from the top of the convention, where anti-Semitism was expressed even in high places.

Notes

1. *Minutes of the 1938 Annual Convention of the Baptist General Convention of Oklahoma*, Minutes Item 143, 70.
2. E. C. Routh, "The Convention," *Baptist Messenger* (24 November 1938), 5.
3. *Poems of Places: An Anthology in 31 Volumes*, ed. Henry Wadsworth Longfellow (Boston: James R. Osgood & Co., 1876–79); www.bartleby.com/270/11/179.html, accessed 12 October 2016. Gartenhaus quoted the third verse in "Israel's Unprecedented Tragedy," The North Carolina *Biblical Recorder* (25 November 1942), 20.

Chapter 12

Anti-Semitism in High Places

The Southern Baptist Convention's responses to the Nazi persecution of the Jewish people differed markedly from those of the Northern Baptist Convention. The divergences were due in part to the different social contexts of the two denominations (rural south versus urban north), as well as theological factors (the Northern Baptist Convention was more influenced by the social gospel and modernism).

However, one of the most significant factors was the role of denominational leaders in addressing the issue of anti-Semitism. While Northern Baptist leaders, with the exception of William Bell Riley, espoused varying levels of philo-Semitism, several Southern Baptist denominational officials, such as M. E. Dodd, expressed opinions and convictions that could be considered anti-Semitic.[1] These anti-Semitic prejudices were not limited to private conversations but were published in Southern Baptist newspapers and denominationally supported books. At the same time, the Southern Baptist Convention had an outstanding advocate for Jews, Jacob Gartenhaus. There was no comparable personality in Northern Baptist circles. The competition for the hearts and minds of Southern Baptists vis-à-vis Jews created an ambivalence that affected the dynamics of the Southern Baptists' responses to Nazism, the persecution of the Jews, and anti-Semitism.

Trouble at the Top: President M. E. Dodd's Anti-Semitism

Monroe Elmon Dodd served as president of the Southern Baptist Convention from 1933 to 1934. In their overview of Dodd's ministry, Emir Caner and Ergun Caner praised Dodd for his commitment to world missions and quoted a passage from his book, *Missions Our Mission* (published in 1930), which gave the impression that Dodd harbored no racial prejudice: "The God whom Jesus Christ revealed to the world is not a tribal, national, or racial God. He is for all men of all races, classes, and colors, in all nations and throughout all ages."[2] Dodd encouraged Southern Baptists to share the gospel with their Jewish neighbors, and he asserted that Jews and Baptists shared some core religious convictions as well as the historical experience of persecution:

> JEWS ARE FOUND particularly responsive to the Gospel as preached by Baptists because of some striking parallels between Jews and Baptists. They are both lovers of liberty. They are both democratic in their religion. They have both been persecuted but never persecuted others. The fore-fathers of American Jews and of American Baptists in Europe suffered religious persecutions at the hands of the same people and fled to America for its same liberty.[3]

Nevertheless, Dodd harbored anti-Semitic attitudes and was willing to leverage his leadership positions to promote anti-Semitic perspectives to millions of Southern Baptists. In 1930, prior to Hitler's rise to power, Dodd complained that there was a "type of foreigner" coming to the northern cities of the United States who possessed "utterly antagonistic religious views" that were "undermining" the Protestant-inspired American culture. Jews were among these undesirable immigrants: "We think of New York and Chicago as the two great foreign cities, and they are. They are the festering boils of the body politic. New York has 4,300,000 foreigners. As someone said, the Jews own New York, the Irish run it, and Americans pay the bills."[4]

Dodd's negative characterization of the Jews was based on cultural stereotypes and prejudices. However, he also offered criticism of Jews focused on their religious differences with Baptists: "Five hundred thousand Jews within our borders challenge our Christianity. Less than one-tenth of them have connection with any synagogue." Dodd worried that Jews, along with other immigrants, were a threat to the American way of life: "For the most part the bootleggers and criminals of each community come from these foreigners. They are the Sunday desecraters, they are the church haters, they are the God haters, they are the flag despisers. The bolsheviks and anarchists are bred and born and nurtured from this stock. How long will it take them to destroy utterly everything that is sacred in American principles and ideals?".[5]

As president of the Southern Baptist Convention, Dodd participated in the BWA congress in Berlin. He presented an address titled "The Gospel for To-Day."[6] Blending politics and religion, Dodd dismissed four political ideologies that were competing for power ("Nationalism, Bolshevism, Industrialism, Socialism") because "their appeals and proposals are geographical, sectional, racial, class." In contrast, "Communism, which does claim universal implications" was "the one supreme challenge to Christianity" and therefore was the political ideology he attacked.

This was a curious political analysis, ignoring both democracy and Nazism, the new vibrant and aggressive power in the country hosting the congress. Dodd refrained from criticizing Hitler or his Nazi regime; instead, he likened Jesus to Hitler without distinguishing how they were different: "A brilliant American journalist said the other day that Hitler and Mussolini are not only the embodiment of their regime, but they are the regime. So Christ is not simply the embodiment of Christianity, Christ is Christianity, and Christianity should be Christ." Dodd ignored the persecutions of Jews in Germany; his single reference to modern Jews concerned the Jewish heritage of Karl Marx and Jesus—a comparison often employed to charge that Jews were overrepresented in communist ranks.

Dodd published his impressions of the BWA congress and the Jewish problem in Germany in *The Alabama Baptist* and other Southern Baptist publications.[7] This analysis became the basis for chapter 1 of his 1935 book, *Girdling the Globe for God*. Dodd focused on his experiences in Germany before, during, and after the congress. He characterized Baptists who raised objections to Berlin as the congress site as advancing "vicious anti-German propaganda." Dodd praised the "German government and the German people" for how the Baptists were treated. He boasted that news reports of the congress were widespread but failed to acknowledge that the German newspapers' coverage of the congress was suppressed by the Nazis.

In the book, Dodd labeled as "false propaganda" concerns about "the Nazi program for a totalitarian state in which the state church should be all inclusive." He justified Nazi interference in the majority Lutheran Church because they accepted tax support from the government, likening it to England and the Anglican Church. He asserted that Germany's problem was not Nazism but "Atheistic Communism." He also seemed to infer that Nazism was compatible with Christianity: "The religious conflict in Germany has been between Christianity and Atheistic Communism. The German government and the German people were forced to make a choice between the two. Their choice fell on the side of Christianity and now the Atheistic Communists and their sympathizers and a few deceived people set up a howl all over the world against Germany."[8]

Dodd commented extensively on the charge of German anti-Semitism. Initially, he appeared to embrace the congress's resolution on racialism and anti-Semitism: "On the subject of racialism, all antisocial outbreaks were condemned as un-Christian. Anti-Semitism was particularly specified." Noting that German delegates voted for the resolution, Dodd then commenced his anti-Semitic attacks, which consumed the rest of the chapter—ten pages! He sought to refute "another widely circulated line of false, vicious, and anti-German propaganda relating to the persecution of the Jews in Germany." Recalling there was a "Jewish problem" in Germany prior to Hitler, Dodd admitted that it "burst forth again in the German Revolution of 1933," but that it was "very difficult to get the facts and to form an unbiased judgment on this situation for the reason that there is so much said about it, both for and against the Jews, which is pure propaganda."

An unbiased perspective involved blaming the Jewish people for their own persecution; Jews were persecuted in Germany for the crimes they had committed against the German people. The Nazi government was not to blame because "drastic measures were considered necessary in order to save the body politic" and "to save their Christianity from Communism." Jews, Dodd asserted, were supportive of communism, and Russian Jewish communists entered Germany "sowing their seed of Bolshevism, Communism and anarchy." The Nazis had every right to respond to the communist threat, and Dodd excused the excesses that occurred: "Drastic things were done. Irresponsible individuals took advantage of the situation and did worse things. There was much suffering. Some innocent people suffered, among them a few Jews."[9]

"A few Jews" may have been innocent, but Dodd proceeded to indict the entire Jewish community. Jews were unfairly represented in that country's government, college, university, medicine, and legal professions, and Jews were guilty of "using these positions of trust, responsibility and leadership for personal ends and against the public good." Therefore, Dodd justified the Nazi employment legislation that constituted the opening phase of the Nazi persecution of the Jews from 1933 through 1935: "The government, therefore, took steps to suppress these evils by equalizing the positions of public trust to Jews and Germans on a basis proportionate to the population of each. So the ax of dismissal fell upon many and they cried, 'persecution!' When they sought to turn all their goods into gold and leave the country with it, and the government passed laws forbidding this, they cried, 'confiscation!'"[10]

In Dodd's eyes, Nazi action against Germany's Jewish community was justified on the basis of "economic necessity and political expediency." Hitler and the Nazis were reasonable and Jews were self-seeking and evil, and he rejected calls for American retaliation against Germany: "If it is bad to manifest racial antipathies and hatreds it is also bad to condone the evil deeds of evil-doers simply because they belong to one particular group and to charge anti-racialism to those who condemn the evil deeds. Anti-Semitism cannot be cured by anti-Aryanism. The boycotting of Jews in Germany cannot be cured by the boycotting of Germans in America." Dodd concluded by reiterating that Germany "has stopped the tides of Russian Communism" and that "high class men and women of the Hebrew race . . . deplore as deeply as anyone else possibly can, the evil ways of many of their own race."[11]

How are we to place Dodd's views on Nazism and his anti-Semitism in historical perspective? In contrast to Dodd's acceptance of Nazi anti-Semitism, James Parkes, an Anglican observer of the same events, offered a more critical assessment: "In so far as such charges were laid at the doors of the Jewish communities of Germany *corporately*, they may be justly said to be totally false."[12] But Deborah E. Lipstadt notes that Dodd's reactions to his visit to Germany were hardly unique: "Visiting Americans, impressed by Germany's spectacular achievements, repeatedly complained to reporters about their pessimistic and critical news reports." *The Nation* observed that it was "difficult to restrain the silly people who after a week or two in Germany, during which they have seen no Jews beaten up in the streets, go back to their own countries and declare that the stories told in the papers about Germany are all untrue."[13]

However, Dodd was no mere tourist, and he was not a "silly" person. E. Earl Joiner, a Southern Baptist historian, sheepishly admitted the possibility that Dodd was simply anti-Semitic: "Apparently, Dodd had read of the political rhetoric Hitler used to justify his actions and took them at face value. The lack of critical judgment in his statement of course may reflect some ignorance of the facts. It may also, however, reflect anti-Semitism."[14]

Was Dodd an anti-Semite? His views on Jewish immigrants, his speech in Berlin, the articles he published following that event, and his subsequent chapter-length apology for Nazi Germany and his attacks on the German Jewish people justify a stronger judgment than Joiner was willing to make. Dodd's anti-Semitism appears to have derived from his virulent anti-communism. His enthusiastic defense of Hitler's initial persecution of the Jews was unmistakable; his strategy to blame the victim (the Jews) for their suffering was logically and historically unjustified; and his judgments concerning Nazi dealings with Christians and the Baptist congress in particular were naive.

The Foreign Mission Board, Jews, and Palestine

Dr. Charles E. Maddry became the executive secretary of the Southern Baptist Foreign Mission Board in 1933 and served for twelve years. In 1934, he spoke at the BWA congress and visited Southern Baptist missions throughout southern and eastern Europe. In contrast to Dodd, Maddry keenly observed that his congressional speech on the Great Commission[15] and other congress reports "were carefully censored by the German committee. All references to democracy were carefully eliminated."

After Maddry departed from Europe in 1934, he visited Baptist work in Syria and Palestine, where Southern Baptist missionaries first began serving in 1921.[16] Southern Baptists focused their work in Nazareth among Arab Christians and in Jerusalem, where "Miss Elsie Clor, a converted Jewess," was serving. She "conducted a Good Will Center, largely for Jewish children, though the work was open also to Arabs," and Saturday (Sabbath) and Sunday schools.[17] Clor discerned that Jewish émigrés were fleeing Hitler's persecution, and the dislocation was having an unanticipated spiritual effect: "The influx of German Jews within the past year has opened another and wider door of service for our Master. The sufferings of these people have made them more ready to listen to the truth. We have already come in contact with these people and feel that their hearts are good soil for the Seed."[18]

The Foreign Mission Board never launched a significant outreach to assist European Jews as they faced extermination. As the single American Baptist organization to have a significant missionary force in Europe, the prospect of a humanitarian response should have been considered. The minutes of the board do not indicate that the possibility was ever discussed. However, Dodd's disparagement of the Jewish people's experiences under Hitler indicated that the convention's leaders might not have supported such an initiative even if it had been proposed. Everett Gill, a respected and well-known senior Southern Baptist missionary based in Rumania, did not demonstrate any inclination to respond to Jewish persecution, and the Italian Baptists, an important part of the Southern Baptist presence in Europe, were supportive of Mussolini and his fascist revolution.

In 1937, Gill wrote a book entitled *Europe: Christ or Chaos?*, published by the Southern Baptist Foreign Mission Board. In Gill's racially biased worldview, Europe and the United States constituted a singular civilization, sharing a common past, a common religious heritage (Christianity; Judaism was not mentioned), and a common race ("white"). The racial purity of Europe and America was in danger from other races, creating the prospect of a dire future: "For when the white race of Europe is engulfed by some awful world-movement of enraged peoples who have suffered for centuries at the white man's hands, let America now be apprised her doom likewise will be imminent. As Europe goes, America goes. As Europe and America go, the white race goes."[19]

Jews were not recognized alongside the races of Europe (Nordic, Alpine, and Mediterranean); in fact, the millions of Jews in Europe evidently were invisible to him. He mentioned Jews once, citing a Jew who converted to Christianity and persecuted his own people. Gill devoted an entire chapter to Germany, remarking that the Nazis had been in power for four years and were dominating the political discourse of the continent. Concerning the German dream of geographical expansion, he wrote: "Fuehrer Hitler's imagination and ambition have come under its spell and once again we may witness the German '*Drang nach Osten*.'"[20] As Gill looked to the future, he feared that the injustices of World War I might lead to another war in which Germany would seek redress for the injustices of Versailles.

The Baptist understanding of personality played a role in Gill's assessment of the strengths and weaknesses of political systems. He perceived little difference between Italian fascism and Russian communism—both were dictatorships, with the exception that the latter's atheism attacked a core Baptist conviction; it violated "the inborn rights of personality."[21]

Similarly, Gill's criticism of Nazism focused on its "despotic type of government" that limited the liberty rights of individuals, and not on its anti-Semitism per se. His first specific criticism of Nazism appeared in the final chapter, which outlined the Baptist role in European politics. Baptists should defend the principle of personality in the face of ideologies that diminish individual liberty and freedom: "In the domain of personality, it is a war on the rights of the individual. It is here that Baptists are vitally interested and can make their greatest contribution by insistence on individual and democratic freedom. The new governmental system of Europe, like Fascism, Naziism [*sic*] and Communism, are making their deadly attack on the very inner citadel of human personality, not only in the domain of political, but of religious life as well."[22]

Racial prejudice played a key role in Gill's outlook. He imagined that a weakened white civilization would emerge from a future conflict between European totalitarian governments and the democracies of the Western hemisphere: "Besides all this, it must be kept in mind that this will be, as was the last, a White Man's War. The yellow and brown races will stand on the side-lines, with a faint oriental smile on their faces as they contemplate the scene of the white race butchering itself into impotency, and giving them their long hoped-for chance at world rule." He warned: "*In the realm of international relations*, as the struggle widens [beyond Europe], as it seems destined to do, it will be the conflict between the white and yellow races." Gill hoped that Christian missionary work would create a mass of believers within the "Yellow Race" before it overwhelmed the white race of Christian Europe and America.[23]

In Gill's writings, Jews (and African Americans) played no discernible role in the political, racial, and religious turmoil engulfing Europe and the United States. The Nazi persecution of Jews was ignored; for Gill, the survival of the Jews appeared to possess no geopolitical, religious, or historical significance. In stark contrast to his silence on Jews, Gill employed all of his missionary fervor in support of persecuted Rumanian Baptists.[24] Gill was in a perfect position to highlight the ongoing plight of the Jewish people during the 1930s. He knew Europe well, and other leaders, such as Maddry, relied on his judgment. Through his articles and book, he influenced the perspective of thousands of Southern Baptists. Unfortunately, he did not take advantage of his status to mobilize Baptist support for Europe's Jews.

Italy and Europe's Jews

Italian Jewish persecution has been thoroughly documented by historians.[25] American Jewish, English Baptist,[26] and US Baptist papers periodically took note of developments in Italy. The *American Hebrew* reported in July 1938 that "Jews are terror-stricken at the implications" of Mussolini's agreement with Hitler to restrict marriages between Jews and non-Jews.[27] *The Watchman-Examiner* noted at the start of 1939:

> ACCORDING TO RECENT official statistics there are 64,000 Jews resident in Italy. Since 1919 some 20,000 Jews from the lands have settled in Italy. Of this number fully 12,000 arrived after 1933, the year Hitler came into power. These are, therefore, largely German Jews. About 8,000 of the 20,000 arriving since 1919 have been naturalized as Italian citizens. In view of the new anti-Semitic laws all 20,000 Jews who have arrived since 1919 must leave Italian territory within six months.[28]

Baptists were an insignificant part of the Italian religious landscape, which was dominated by the Roman Catholic Church, but they did enjoy a deep relationship with the Foreign Mission Board and their missionaries. At the 1936 Southern Baptist Convention annual meeting, Maddry spearheaded the passing of a resolution in support of Southern Baptist missionaries and their Italian Baptist comrades, who "have been subjected to many petty persecutions, and have been hindered at every turn with hostile and unreasonable police regulations and restrictions." Protests were to be lodged with "the representative of the United States Government at Rome, Italy, to use every honorable means possible to induce the Italian Government to take prompt steps to rectify the unjust and grievous wrongs herein above mentioned and now being inflicted upon the Baptists of Italy."[29]

Maddry's concern for Italian Baptists (as well as other European Baptists such as the Rumanians) was documented in his contributions to *The Commission*. In November 1938, he was concerned that changes taking place throughout Europe were "not conducive to the growth and development of Baptist principles or to the prosperity of Baptist churches" because they required "an atmosphere of freedom and soul liberty, and this spirit is absolutely foreign to the programs and purposes of Fascist-controlled European states." In Italy, several "chapels have been closed by the government and some of our preachers have been silenced and their permits to preach taken from them."[30]

There were times, however, when Maddry did sympathize with the plight of European Jews, indicating that he was not personally anti-Semitic. Speaking of conditions in Europe during his 1938 global trip, Maddry turned his attention to the plight of Italian Jews: "Italy is beginning to treat the Jews with almost as great cruelty as Germany has shown. . . . In the past four weeks, twelve professors, because of their Semitic origin, have been turned out of the University of Rome, and similar action is being taken toward outstanding representatives of other professions."[31] In the 1939 board report, W. Dewey Moore alluded to the status of Jews in his section on "national conditions" in Italy:

> WHERE ILLITERACY IS high, and consequently bigotry dominates more readily, the State's stand on both Communism and Judaism has been taken advantage of to misinform and intimidate the public with reference to Evangelicalism also. However, during the last few months

> there is evidence of a lessening of this fear on the part of non-evangelicals, which fact may be due to the evident discord between Church and State on the current racial question.[32]

In a post-Kristallnacht passage reminiscent of Dodd's criticism of those who opposed Nazi anti-Semitism, W. O. Carver acknowledged Hitler's persecution and Italy's ties with Germany but reserved his severest judgment for those who advocated military means for opposing it: "There is growing up a powerful sentiment of unreasoning hatred toward the Berlin-Rome-Tokyo combination. At the moment, the insane abuse of the Jews is its most obvious expression. We cannot dissipate Germany's hate by hating Germany. We cannot restrain the insanity of power by ourselves going insane from fear."[33]

The Italian Baptist leaders contributed to the Southern Baptist inaction concerning Italian Jews. In a book published in 1939, the Italian Baptist executive secretary, Lodovico Paschetto, and his son Enrico, recounted the hardships Baptists faced, particularly in enduring Roman Catholic-inspired persecution, but made no mention of Jewish struggles. They focused on the impact of Mussolini's fascist revolution, which bore the marks of the patriotic defense of Italy that would be made at the 1939 BWA congress in Atlanta. Mussolini was given credit for positive changes in the country but was not held responsible for crimes against Jews. The Paschettos personally endorsed Mussolini, stating that they were confident that in Mussolini the Italian people "have a guide who really wishes good and greatness for the Italian people."[34]

After the entry of the United States into World War II, Southern Baptists faced the dilemma of having a key mission field defined as an enemy combatant. The Foreign Mission Board relayed the Italian Baptists' hope that their friendship would transcend hostilities:

> THEIR HEART'S MESSAGE to us and to their Southern Baptist brethren in America was twofold and couched in these moving and courageous words: "You are going back to your home land and to our brethren in Christ, and we want you to carry with you in your hearts two firm convictions: first, that no matter what may lie ahead for us—we may suffer; we may meet new privations, sacrifice; we may have to go into a hole in the wall to live—we are going to strive to battle through

> for Christ and His cause here, and we want your unceasing prayers for us; second, no matter what may happen between our nation and yours—between our governments war seems inevitable—it will not alter or affect our relationship in Christ with our Christian brethren. In Him we are Christian brothers! War cannot change that. God has regenerated our hearts in Christ Jesus and made them so, and mere human differences and campaigns of misunderstanding and hatred cannot change what God has wrought.[35]

Southern Baptist Middle East Missions and the Zionist Dream

The Southern Baptist Convention sponsored mission work in Syria and Palestine in the 1930s and 1940s, serving both Arab and Jewish populations. As Hitler's attacks on the Jews intensified through the mid-1930s, a Southern Baptist seminary professor, J. McKee Adams, linked Germany's anti-Semitic policies to increased immigration to Palestine: "In the wake of German anti-Semitic propaganda and persecution, aimed especially at the Jew and all Jewish interests, the flight to Palestine has been accelerated. In all probability the vast majority of these German Jews have turned their hearts to Palestine as the one remaining spot on earth for peace and security." While Adams supported Jewish immigration to Palestine, he did not believe that the Balfour Declaration should be interpreted to deny Arabs their right to political self-rule.[36] Similarly, Southern Baptist missionary to Palestine, Roswell E. Owens, observed in 1934:

> THE JEW IS returning to Palestine as fast as he can get permission to enter the country, and, of course, he is bringing his wealth with him. How this little country is booming just now! An almost unbelievable change has come about since we came five years ago. The Jew with his genius is indeed making parts of the desert to "blossom like the rose," but alas! that which he needs most of all, he does not have, and worst of all, does not want. What a glorious land Palestine will be when the Jew turns to Christ![37]

German Jews were not only bringing their wealth to Palestine; their pain held the possibility of creating a spiritual awakening: "The influx of German Jews within the past year has opened another and wider door of service for our Master. The sufferings of these people have made them more ready to listen to the truth. We have already come in contact with these people and feel that their hearts are good soil for the Seed."[38] Missionary H. Leo Eddleman, stationed in Tel Aviv, also sensed that Jewish troubles led to spiritual questioning and introspection: "We stand near the time when the British Government will begin to divide this small country that God has chosen for His own purposes into small allotments for Jews and Arabs to satisfy their nationalistic demands. Yet such troublous [*sic*] days have brought many people to think about God, life, death and destiny as never before."[39]

Both Muslims and Jews posed challenges to the Southern Baptist missionaries,[40] but the arrival of persecuted Jews from Europe evoked eschatological anticipations, as well as expressions of supersessionism:

> MOHAMMEDANISM AND JUDAISM are perhaps the two greatest hindrances to the coming of the Kingdom of God in the world today. Every knee must someday bow to Jesus, even these Arabs who almost fanatically turn toward Mecca daily in homage to Mohammed; Judaism must give way to Christianity the flower of which it is or was but the bud; and as we witness marvelous prophecy fulfillments of Jews returning to Palestine as rapidly as is physically possible.[41]

The next year, Eddleman once again shared about the difficulties in converting followers of Islam and Judaism: "Despite all the mission work that has been done among the Jews and Arabs of the world, there does not exist anywhere a Christian church composed chiefly of ex-Jews or ex-Moslems. These two monotheistic religions have rarely suffered numerical losses because their numbers have turned to Christianity through the missionary endeavor of Christ's representatives."[42] In 1942, he acknowledged that persecution of the Jewish people in a "Christian" country (Germany) and continent (Europe) negatively affected Jews' perception of the attractiveness of Christianity.[43]

Missionary Louis Hanna also noted the interrelationship between the plight of Jews in Germany and the situation in Palestine.

Unfortunately, he also resurrected the charge that Jewish suffering was due to their rejection of the messianic claims of Jesus. Speaking before Oklahoma Baptists, he "laid upon our hearts responsibility for neglect of the Jews" and said:

> NATIONAL HATRED AND religious bigotry are playing havoc in Palestine today. The condition is an offshoot of national hatred and religious bigotry in Europe. The Jew has lived by the Arab for centuries. They have no quarrel only as hate has been accentuated by European politics. . . . A large percentage of Jews going to Palestine are atheists. The Jew needs to come to Christ. As long as the Jew turns his back to Christ, he will suffer all over the world. Of the thousands who have gone from America, not one knew of Jesus. . . . Solve these questions in Europe, solve them in America, and they will be solved in Palestine.[44]

By 1940, "one hundred and fifty Jewish people of many nations" were attending classes hosted by the Jerusalem mission.[45] However, the outbreak of war forced the Southern Baptist missionaries to leave Palestine, although the mission continued under the direction of a Russian Baptist refugee, Martin Dovely, "assisted by Andrew Salzer, a converted Jew."[46] After the conclusion of the war, Palestine was consumed by the issue of the possibility of the reestablishment of a Jewish homeland. Southern Baptist missionaries were set to return, but in the annual reports of the Foreign Mission Board, there was no endorsement of Zionism: "The Palestinian problem is still unsolved. Whether the solution lies in dividing the country into Jewish and Arab areas, or whether the establishment of our International Commission will bring peace, remains to be seen."[47]

Even the Foreign Mission Board report for the 1948 convention, which met from May 18-22—days after the establishment of Israel as an independent nation—merely stated: "All well-informed peoples know that the Near East is in a state of crisis. Our hope is that our representatives may be privileged to remain at their posts. In the meantime, let us pray that the land of our Lord may become a place of peace."[48] In his personal missionary report, George W. Sadler maintained a neutral stance, with the possible exception of calling out Jews for exerting influence on the United States government:

> THE PALESTINIAN PROBLEM has been so widely publicized that most well-informed persons are reasonably familiar with it. For years, it was largely a matter of two kindred peoples' trying to occupy the same small space at the same time. Now the problem is complicated by the conflict between communism and what we customarily call democracy, the oil interests of the United States, Great Britain and Russia, and Jewish pressure upon Washington. As world citizens, we cannot separate ourselves from a situation that is fought with such far-reaching possibilities; as Christians, we are concerned with its spiritual implications.[49]

Sadler was well aware that he and other missionaries might shortly find themselves ministering in a Jewish state. He did not express enthusiasm for the establishment of Israel, and neither did he interpret it from the standpoint of biblical prophecy. His approach was matter-of-fact and pragmatic: "There are considerable possibilities that Palestine will be divided into an Arab and a Jewish state. Such a division will undoubtedly affect our work although it is not yet clear in just which way. If there is a Jewish state I am of the opinion that we will carry on, if not as missionaries, then as teachers, pastors of churches, etc. If it should be necessary I would favor our entering simply as teachers or cultural workers although I think there will be no such necessity."[50]

Notes

1. See George D. Kelsey, *Social Ethics among Southern Baptists, 1917–1969* (Metuchen, NJ: Scarecrow Press and the American Theological Library Association, 1973), 254–58. This monograph was based on Kelsey's "The Social Thought of Contemporary Southern Baptists," PhD diss., Yale University, 1946.

2. Emir Caner and Ergun Caner, *The Sacred Trust: Sketches of the Southern Baptist Convention Presidents* (Nashville: Broadman and Holman, 2003), 77–78. The Caners furthermore refer to Dodd's second book that covered the Shantung Revival in China (see 75).

3. M. E. Dodd, "The Baptists, the Jews, and World Evangelism," *Western Recorder* (29 March 1934), 10.

4. M. E. Dodd, *Missions Our Mission* (Nashville: Sunday School Board of the Southern Baptist Convention, 1930), 84.

5. Ibid., 85. Jews were often referred to as "bolsheviks and anarchists" by those who opposed their immigration into the United States. Hitler employed this charge in his anti-Semitic campaigns. Dodd's use of it indicates that he was predisposed to be sympathetic to Hitler's message.

6. M. E. Dodd, "The Gospel for To-Day," in J. H. Rushbrooke, ed., *Fifth Baptist World Congress: Berlin, August 4-10, 1934* (London: Baptist World Alliance, 1934), 165–72.

7. M. E. Dodd, "My Impressions of the Baptist World Congress," *The Alabama Baptist* (6 September 1934), 1, 8–9. See also *Western Recorder* (13 September 1934), 10–11.

8. M. E. Dodd, *Girdling the Globe for God* (Shreveport, LA: John S. Ramond, Publisher, 1935), 20–28.

9. Ibid., 29–35.

10. Ibid., 36.

11. Ibid., 37–38.

12. James Parkes, *The Jew and His Neighbor: A Study of the Causes of Antisemitism* (London: Student Christian Mission Press, 1930; rev. ed. 1938), 117.

13. Deborah E. Lipstadt, *Beyond Belief: The American Press and the Coming of the Holocaust 1933–1945* (New York: The Free Press, 1986), 33.

14. E. Earl Joiner, "Baptists and the Holocaust," a research paper presented at the International Conference on "Remembering for the Future," Oxford, England, July 10-14, 1988 (Jacksonville: Florida Baptist Historical Society, 1988), 7.

15. Charles E. Maddry, "The Great Commission," in J. H. Rushbrooke, ed., *Fifth Baptist World Congress: Berlin, August 4-10, 1934* (London: Baptist World Alliance, 1934), 146–52.

16. William R. Estep, *Whole Gospel Whole World: The Foreign Mission Board of the Southern Baptist Convention 1845–1995* (Nashville: Broadman and Holman, 1994), 419.

17. Charles E. Maddry, *Charles E. Maddry: An Autobiography* (Nashville: Broadman, 1955), 89–90.

18. *Annual of the 1934 Southern Baptist Convention*, Foreign Mission Board Report, 238.

19. Everett Gill, *Europe: Christ or Chaos?* (Richmond, VA: Foreign Mission Board, Southern Baptist Convention, 1937), 15–20.

20. Ibid., 27–33, 35–36, 59–60.

21. Ibid., 127; see 87.

22. Ibid., 185.

23. Ibid., 162, 185 (italics in original text), 188–92. Gill reiterated his biased comments regarding the "Yellow Race" in "Europe Tells the World," *The Commission* (March 1939), 78.

24. *Annual of the 1939 Southern Baptist Convention*, Report of the Foreign Mission Board, Rumania—"Persecution of Baptists," Everett Gill, 257–58.

25. Susan Zuccotti, *The Italians and the Holocaust: Persecution, Rescue, and Survival* (Lincoln: University of Nebraska Press, 1996); Renzo de Felice, *The Jews in Fascist Italy: A History*, trans. Robert L. Miller (New York: Enigma Books, 2001); and Michele Sarfatti, *The Jews in Mussolini's Italy: From Equality to Persecution*, trans. John Tedeschi and Anne C. Tedeschi, George L. Mosse Series (Madison: University of Wisconsin Press, 2006).

26. "Italy and the Jews," *The Baptist Times* (8 September 1938), 687.

27. "Italy," *The American Hebrew* (22 July 1938), 8, 13. See also "Jews in Belligerent Italy," *The American Hebrew* (21 June 1940), 4, 21.

28. "News and Notes," *The Watchman-Examiner* (26 January 1939), 83–84; see also "News and Notes," *The Watchman-Examiner* (20 June 1940), 684.

29. *Annual of the 1936 Southern Baptist Convention*, Report of the Resolutions Committee, 61–62.

30. "Charles E. Maddry, "Italian Mission Reorganized," *The Commission* (November 1938), 210; see also "Meeting of the Italian Baptist Union," *The Commission* (September 1938), 179.

31. "Dr. Maddry Returns," North Carolina *Biblical Recorder* (15 February 1939), 10.

32. *Annual of the 1939 Southern Baptist Convention*, Report of the Foreign Mission Board, 260.

33. W. O. Carver, "Germany and the Nations," *The Commission* (February 1939), 39.

34. Lodovico Paschetto and Enrico Paschetto, *They of Italy* (Nashville: Broadman, 1939), 125–96, 206–10.

35. *Annual of the 1942 Southern Baptist Convention*, Report of the Foreign Mission Board, 183–85.

36. J. McKee Adams, *The Heart of the Levant: Palestine–Syria* (Richmond, VA: The Foreign Mission Board of the Southern Baptist Convention, 1937), 86, 95.

37. *Proceedings of the 1934 Southern Baptist Convention,* Foreign Mission Board Report, Near East Report—Roswell E. Owens, 237.

38. Ibid., 238.

39. *Proceedings of the 1938 Southern Baptist Convention,* Foreign Mission Board Report, Near East Report, H. Leo Eddleman, 257.

40. For a more positive presentation regarding this challenge, see R. L. Lindsey, "We Have a Job to Do in Palestine," *The Commission* (November 1947), 8, 30.

41. *Proceedings of the 1938 Southern Baptist Convention,* Foreign Mission Board Report, Near East Report, H. Leo Eddleman, 259.

42. *Proceedings of the 1939 Southern Baptist Convention,* Foreign Mission Board Report, Near East Report, H. Leo Eddleman, 273.

43. H. Leo Eddleman, "The Land of Our Master (Part 2): The Jew and Christianity," *The Commission* (January 1942), 14–15.

44. "The Convention," Oklahoma *Baptist Messenger* (24 November 1938), 17.

45. *Proceedings of the 1940 Southern Baptist Convention,* Foreign Mission Board Report, Near East Report—Palestine and Syria, 252.

46. *Proceedings of the 1942 Southern Baptist Convention,* Foreign Mission Board Report, Near East Report—Palestine, 187.

47. *Proceedings of the 1947 Southern Baptist Convention,* Foreign Mission Board Report, On Palestine, 88.

48. *Proceedings of the 1948 Southern Baptist Convention,* Foreign Mission Board Report, On the Near East, 116.

49. Ibid., Foreign Mission Board Report, "Progress in Palestine," George W. Sadler, 125.

50. Ibid., 126.

Chapter 13

Southern Baptist National Resolutions

In the twentieth century, Southern Baptists manifested a willingness to confront social and political problems, but two factors hindered Southern Baptists in speaking out on societal issues—"the individualistic interpretation of sin and of regeneration" and the democratic structure of the convention. Nevertheless, beginning with the issue of temperance, Southern Baptists found their prophetic voice in the first half of the twentieth century on such issues as "alcohol, family problems, gambling, social sins, race relations, labor, farm tenancy, church and state, religious liberty, war, mob-violence, civil liberties, hospitals, social security."[1] Throughout the period, racism against African Americans constituted the "principal social problem affecting Southern Baptists."[2] How did Southern Baptists respond as a national body to the Nazis' racial policies against Jews? To this story, we now turn.[3]

Initial Concerns and World Peace (1933-1939)

When the Southern Baptist Convention (SBC) convened in Washington, DC, on May 19-22, 1933, the world was in turmoil. The global capitalist economic system was in distress, and political forces inimical to democracy were gaining strength. Meeting just a little more than a month after the Nazis' April 1, 1933, boycott of Jewish businesses, the convention's Social Service Commission expressed concern about "the recent counter-revolution in Germany, with its overthrow of the Republican form of government and the establishment of a Dictatorship, resulting in the unwarranted persecution of the Jews"—the first national-level Southern Baptist Convention statement on Jewish persecution during the Nazi era.[4]

The 1934 Southern Baptist convention took place two months before the BWA congress. J. H. Rushbrooke reminded the delegates of their past support of the BWA and urged them to support the Berlin meetings: "Southern Baptists have had much to do with the formation of the Alliance, and they have rendered conspicuous service at World Congresses in the past. I look forward eagerly to clasping hands with many of them in Berlin. . . . No Congress ever had a more splendid opportunity, and the witness which our great world communion is able to offer at this time is precisely what our troubled humanity needs."[5]

The needs of troubled Jews in Germany were not addressed either by Rushbrooke or the delegates in the 1934 convention, even though Southern Baptist leaders were aware that racialism was going to be a significant issue in Berlin. This omission was an opportunity lost. The Social Service Commission did mention Germany in relation to the issue of military disarmament but did not revisit the Nazis' treatment of Jews or the struggles the German churches were facing. It did, however, reaffirm "its devotion to the principles of International Peace," offering recommendations on disarmament and the need for a World Court to mediate international disputes.[6]

The 1935 convention in Memphis, Tennessee, provided a golden opportunity to revisit the plight of Jews in Germany. The BWA Berlin congress had passed a clear resolution on anti-Semitism, and Rushbrooke addressed the convention on its opening night.[7] However, in a lengthy report in which resolutions were passed on the issues of lynching, motion pictures, freedom of religion, peace, and temperance, anti-Semitism was ignored.[8]

Delegates to the 1936 Southern Baptist convention in St. Louis were presented with resolutions dealing with persecution against Baptists in Rumania and Italy, both of which were introduced by Charles E. Maddry[9] and subsequently approved. The Rumanian resolution requested that the constitutional right to "absolute religious liberty and freedom of worship" be granted to Rumanian Baptists and Southern Baptist missionaries and that Rumanian authorities put to an end "all kinds of insults, indignities and persecutions, even to the extent of throwing Baptist preachers into prison."[10] Based on "fundamental truths of the kingdom of God that distinguish us as a Baptist people," Tennessee pastor Dr. William R. Rigell forcefully railed against both Nazism and communism.[11]

The Social Service Commission declared it would "not support our government in any war except such as might be necessary to repel invasion of our land or to preserve fundamental human rights and liberties."[12] The committee made a similar point in 1937,[13] but the Southern Baptists never invoked this principle to employ military might to defend the "fundamental human rights and liberties" of European Jews. The convention did approve a single-sentence resolution on racial relationships, but it most likely was intended to address only black-white relations.[14]

In its 1938 report, the Social Service Commission expressed its regrets that World War I did not pave the way for the triumph of democracy but instead enabled "the establishment of ruthless and unrestrained dictatorships until now it seems that human freedom is imperiled in almost every government of the world." The situation in Germany was a case in point: "with truculent Naziism [*sic*] holding dominion in Germany and banishing religious freedom while it expands its borders by annexing Austria and declaring that all German people everywhere must come under its control."[15]

The committee could only offer a call to prayer as a countermeasure, but the Committee on Public Relations had another idea. It was created to represent Southern Baptists before political authorities "to demand just rights that are being threatened."[16] Northern Baptists created a similar committee, and they entered into an alliance to jointly lodge protests about treatment of Baptists in Rumania and Japan. The success of the experiment prompted the committee to ask for the convention's blessings of the historic cooperative effort, "which for the first time enables the Baptists of America to speak with a united voice when their denominational agencies are compelled to confer, to negotiate or to demand just rights that are threatened or to have other inescapable dealings with our American or other governments. United we can better defend our common, distinctive Baptist principles."[17]

Kristallnacht took place between the 1938 and 1939 conventions, and the national leaders had two options for responding to the crisis. They could have chosen to protest jointly to the German government through the Committee on Public Relations, but its chairperson, Rufus W. Weaver, was focused on Rumania. Alternatively, the executive committee could have addressed the issue, as did its counterpart in the Northern Baptist Convention. The executive committee met on December 14, 1938, in Nashville, Tennessee. With Weaver in attendance, the committee approved a set of Rumanian resolutions, one for the Rumanian government and the other for the president of the United States. They also cabled Maddry in Madras, India, to see if the mission conference he was attending might support the Rumanian campaign.[18] The minutes indicate no attention was paid to Kristallnacht.

The last Southern Baptist convention before the outbreak of hostilities in Europe was held in Oklahoma City on May 17-21, 1939. The delegates approved "A Pronouncement upon Religious Liberty" in reaction to "the sudden rise of the European dictators to power [which] has changed fundamentally the organic law of the governments through which they exercise sovereignty, and as a result, the institutions of religion are either suppressed or made subservient to the ambitious national programs of these new totalitarian states." Baptists throughout the world, the document declared, held to the complete separation of church and state: "Believing religious liberty to be not only an inalienable human right, but indispensable to human welfare, a Baptist must exercise himself to the utmost in the maintenance of absolute religious liberty for his Jewish neighbor, his Catholic neighbor, his Protestant neighbor, and for everybody else."[19]

The 1939 Pronouncement upon Religious Liberty was aimed particularly at the relationship between church and state in the United States, but the reference to the "Jewish neighbor" and the claim that religious liberty was an "inalienable human right" and hence universal in scope raised once again the issue of the Southern Baptist response to the persecution of the Jews in Germany. If the Jew in Charleston, Birmingham, or New Orleans was a neighbor, in a shrinking world was not the Jew in Berlin or Cologne a neighbor as well? Like their Northern Baptist counterparts, the Southern Baptist Convention did not offer its members any concrete responses by which they could express solidarity with the Jewish victims of Nazi persecution.

World War (1940–1945)

In 1940, the Social Service Commission reengaged with the theme of racial groups as neighbors to one another and equated American black-white relations with the Nazi ("Aryan") assault against Jews. In neither case did it take sides with the oppressed population:

> RACE RELATIONS ARE not in any sense confined to the relations of the White and Negro races here in the South, or in America. Whenever and wherever two races live along side each other or come into necessary contact with each other there is, as always in the history of the world, a race problem. Sometimes it is the Aryan and the Jew; sometimes it is the Arab and the Jew; sometimes it is the White man and the Negro, but always wherever two races have to deal with each other you have a race problem, and the race problem very often, indeed almost always, becomes one of the most acute, aggravated and aggravating problems with which any race has to deal.[20]

With the onset of military hostilities in September 1939, the ability of Southern Baptists to assist most of Germany's Jews had perhaps passed, but this paragraph at least recognized the struggle between the Germans and the Jews for the first time since 1933. Germany was specifically mentioned later in the report, but only in terms of its military aggression.[21] Southern Baptists agreed to respond to the needs of British Baptist "neighbors" and their missionary society.[22] At the 1941 convention, Powhatan W. James presented an antiwar resolution that nevertheless praised "England's heroic resistance to the Axis powers,"[23] and it was reported that $190,000 was raised for the British mission work.[24] Rushbrooke, on behalf of British Baptists, thanked the convention and framed the war in spiritual terms:

> FUNDAMENTALLY THE CONFLICT belongs to the realm of ideas. It involves a challenge to convictions of which through all their history Baptists have been champions, and to values which they have cherished—the infinite and eternal worth of the human soul, the right of all men and nations to civil and religious freedom. Over wide tracts of earth the view of man which we have learned from the Lord Jesus Christ is scornfully rejected, and liberty—both religious and civil—trampled under foot. I know that you stand unitedly and unhesitatingly with those who, prepared to sacrifice everything, are resisting the formidable forces which threaten to destroy priceless things that alone make life truly worth living.[25]

The Southern Baptist Home Mission Board agreed with Rushbrooke, stating:

> THE WAR NOW raging in Europe is not primarily a war for territory. It is a clash of ideologies. The new order which the Axis powers would establish in Europe and the world would overthrow all the things for which men have fought, bled and died for the past two thousand years. Ever since Christ preached his Sermon on the Mount there has been a continuous struggle of the individual for recognition. Out of this struggle has emerged the idea of the worth and dignity of the individual, which is the basis of democracy.[26]

The Home Mission Board asserted that the totalitarian attack against democracy was a racially inspired attack not just against Jews but also against other races and Christians as well: "When Hitler exalted racial above national ties he laid the ax at the root of the existing political structure of the world. German nationalism is racial, and German internationalism is a struggle for the domination of the Germanic tribes. . . . The new world order which Germany would establish is a racial order in which nobody but the German people would be able to live with freedom or self-respect, and millions not at all. In such a world Christianity would find no place."[27]

"We did not start this war but now it is ours," declared the Southern Baptist Social Service Commission in its 1942 report, because the war was not just about "dictators obsessed with the idea of ruling the world, but it is an effort on their part to enslave mankind."[28] The Nazi attacks against Jews, beginning in 1933, were just the first salvo against all of human civilization and therefore the struggle against totalitarianism was not primarily about saving the Jew from extermination. In response, "the Christian citizenship of our country must see to it that no racial hates enter into our thinking. . . . America must prove herself to be not only the melting but the welding pot of the remaining remnants of mankind. In the remaking of civilization it must be rebuilt around the idea of the fatherhood of God and the brotherhood of man."[29]

Although there was no convention in 1943 due to wartime travel restrictions, the report of the Social Service Commission revisited the race issue in light of the domestic racial turmoil the country was facing. For the third time since 1933 it contained a clear repudiation of Germany's persecution of the Jews: "One of the central issues in the war is the relations of races. Germany has clearly expressed the principle on which it proceeds, the principle of Germanic superiority over all other races and the right and duty of the superior race to dominate, subordinate, or exterminate the inferior race in securing its own power. Hence its anti-Semitism that has shocked the soul of mankind."

Reflecting on American racial attitudes, the commission then asked, "Have we irretrievably adopted the Germanic principle?" The answer, for both US society in general, and Baptists in particular, was no: "Germany's expression of" racial competition "has proved for the Christian American that it is untenable." Racism, whether directed against African Americans or Jews, was unjustifiable: "The illogic and irrationality of race hatred are confirmed by the teachings and the spirit of Jesus Christ. And America cannot go with Germany. We must deal with the race problem of our land on a different principle, according to which differences will not be permitted to generate bitterness, and justice will have a human and Christian, rather than a racial criterion. The mind of America is moving in this direction with respect to the Negro as well as to the Jews and other smaller groups."[30]

Again, in its 1944 report, the commission demonstrated its propensity for seeking wisdom about America's problems from the Nazi racial policies against Jews. It noted, "Hitler has shown the world the lengths to which race prejudice can go, the havoc it can work, the hate it can create, when untempered by the Spirit of Christ and unrestrained by Christian conscience. We cannot follow Hitler. We must find a way of justice that will free both races from fear and open the road for the progress of both in this our common land."[31]

The SBC executive committee appointed a committee in December 1943 to craft a strategy for a postwar era of peace. The task force submitted its report to the 1944 convention, and it included a provision on racial prejudice: "Believing in the worth of every individual, we deplore race prejudices and hatreds as undermining the respect to which every individual is entitled, and as destroying the spirit of good will, which must be the foundation of enduring peace. This is true whether we consider racial tensions in our nation or in international relationships."[32] With expectations that the European war was coming to an imminent conclusion, the Southern Baptists met in May 1945, and the Social Service Commission focused on relationships with minority groups in America, "principally the Jews, Japanese,

Indians and Negroes. By reason of religious and racial traditions of separateness, as in the case of the Jews, or of racial and physical peculiarities and their several social histories, these groups remain, and for a long time to come must remain distinct groups."[33]

By the war's end, Southern Baptists acknowledged their need to improve relationships with racial minorities, including Jews. However, they did not reach out to the remnant of the Jewish population that had survived Hitler's wrath. Racial justice primarily was a domestic problem for the Southern Baptist Convention.

Postwar Responses (1946-1948)

In the postwar period, Southern Baptists participated with others in humanitarian efforts. These efforts were based on an overarching set of principles that were adopted at the 1945 convention and then republished in 1946 and 1947. The Statement of Principles reiterated core Southern Baptist convictions on the infinite worth of human beings, soul competence, liberty, and human rights and exhorted Baptists to "resist all inequalities of basic rights and privileges in the church and in society, which arise out of racial prides and prejudices, economic greed, and class distinctions; everywhere proclaiming and practicing human brotherhood under the will and purpose of God."[34] The Committee on World Peace promoted six principles regarding how Baptists should participate in the postwar era. They included a rejection of isolationism, the superiority of democracy, the value of the United Nations, economic opportunity, full religious liberty, and "the worth of every individual respected, toward the elimination of race prejudice and hatreds which undermine respect for the individual."[35]

Southern Baptists sought to embody these principles, like their Northern counterparts, through ministry to displaced persons in Europe. Their resolutions were virtually identical to those passed by the Northern Baptist Convention, with emphasis placed on how many of the displaced persons were non-Jewish: "In camps in Germany, Italy, and Austria, nearly a million displaced persons of various denominations, composed of men, women, and children, 80 per cent of whom are Christians, and 20 per cent Jews, . . . are unable to return to their own homes because of persecution or fear of persecution by reason of their race, religion, or political beliefs."[36]

The 1948 convention met in Memphis on May 19-23—five days after the establishment of Israel. President Harry S Truman, a life-long Southern Baptist, announced on May 14 at 6:11 p.m. Eastern Time, just minutes after the Israeli declaration in Tel Aviv, that the United States would recognize Israel's existence. Scholars have since debated the reasons for Truman's support of Israel, and to what extent religious factors came alongside political considerations for the announcement of support.[37]

How did Truman's recognition of Israel affect the Southern Baptist Convention in 1948? On Wednesday afternoon, May 19, E. D. Solomon, the editor of the *Florida Baptist Witness*, "moved that the secretary of the Convention send a telegram to President Truman congratulating him on recognizing the State of Israel. The motion was lost after discussion by Dr. Solomon and L. E. Barton, Alabama."[38] Delegates who opposed Solomon's initiative "charged that such a telegram approval would be a political vote."[39] The political criticism probably referred to the fact that Truman was engaged in a presidential campaign, which he unexpectedly won. Alternatively, it might have been a response to Arab sensitivity and opposition to Israel's political moves, in light of Southern Baptist missionary work in that part of the globe.

A second attempt to secure Southern Baptist approval of Israel's birth took place the next day, when "S. G. Posey, California, presented a resolution on the State of Israel which was referred to the Committee on Resolutions."[40] When it was released by the Resolutions Committee on Friday, May 21, for a vote, it was not approved.[41] A third resolution from the floor (and not from the Resolutions Committee) was offered by Dr. William Richardson White, president of Baylor University in Texas.[42] He presented a "Resolution Concerning Baptist Concept of Freedom and Spiritual Values," which "was adopted by common consent." The text was just one sentence: "Resolved, That communism, fascism, political ecclesiasticism, and anti-Semitism are utterly contrary to the genius of our Baptist concept of freedom and spiritual values."[43]

Thus, Southern Baptists expressed concern for Jews facing anti-Semitism at the beginning (1933) and ending (1948) of the historical period under consideration. Neither resolution offered anything more than general support for the Jewish people, and the resolutions were notable for their brevity.

Affirming Silence: L. L. Gwaltney's Retrospective

L. L. Gwaltney, as the longtime editor of the influential *Alabama Baptist* newspaper, had a front-row seat from which to observe Southern Baptist responses to the Holocaust. During the Nazi/Holocaust era, Gwaltney published two books that revealed his perspective on the Nazi persecution of the Jewish people.

His 1939 work, *Heralds of Freedom*, surveyed the history of the Baptist movement from ancient to modern times. Referring to the Spanish Inquisition, he wrote: "Historians differ as to the number, but certainly as many as 250,000 were slain which makes Hitler's persecution of the Jews, by way of contrast, seem a tame affair."[44] Gwaltney viewed Kristallnacht and other Nazi attacks upon Jews in light of the battle between totalitarianism and the church. Interestingly, he did not cite any evidence that German Baptists were resisting Hitler, because they in fact were cooperating with the government:

> MEANTIME, IN GERMANY under Hitler the totalitarian state has reached its limit. The early Christians were persecuted because they would not burn incense to Caesar and worship him as God. But in Germany men have been persecuted and driven into exile because they would not bow down to and worship the state as God. Meantime, the pent-up fury of the dictator of Germany was let loose upon the Jews and every kind of repression and persecution known to the shrewd German mind has been let loose upon them. An indemnity of four hundred million dollars ($400,000,000) was exacted from them because a Jewish lad, driven to distraction by the persecution of his people, killed a petty German officer in Paris. Yet everything in Germany, except one, yielded to the will of Hitler, and that was the church.[45]

In 1947, Gwaltney wrote a curious retrospective of Baptist activity entitled *The World's Greatest Decade: The Times and the Baptists*.[46] This book uniquely provided his perspective on the entire Holocaust period. Part I covers his version of political history from World War I through the dawn of the Atomic Age. It is an idiosyncratic account, focusing on military strategy, the ideological struggle between communism, totalitarianism, and democracy, the breakdown of social morality, and the League of Nations and the United Nations. It could have served as the perfect vehicle to address Baptist responses to the Nazi persecution of the Jews, the tragedy of the Holocaust, and the possibility of the establishment of a post-Holocaust Jewish state.

It would have been quite appropriate for Gwaltney to recognize the paucity of the Southern Baptist official response to the Holocaust and to reach out to the Jewish community with a renewal of Rushbrooke's offer of sincere friendship. Instead, he chose to embrace a startling form of silence which not only betrayed his personal sense of ambivalence toward Jews but also mischaracterized the narrative of the decade.

Over ninety-four pages Gwaltney mentioned Jews only three times. In his account of atomic weaponry, he remarked that Einstein was a Jew.[47] After affirming the Balfour Declaration, he expressed disappointment that "rich American Jews" were not willing to move to Palestine:

> MY HOPES WERE raised in War I when Field Marshall Allensby, of the British army, defeated the Turks and took Palestine, and declared after its capture that it would become a home for oppressed Jews. I thought the long persecuted Jews would return to Zion with songs in their mouths. This hope was heightened by the Balfour declaration to the same effect. Then also there sprang up the Zionist movement among the Jews themselves, and all of these increased my hope that the Scripture was being fulfilled concerning the return of the Jews to their fatherland. I was terribly disillusioned when I saw that the rich American Jews had no notion of giving up their businesses, palatial homes, automobiles and servants to return to their native land and once again become shepherds of sheep and vine dressers. No, the American Jews may desire their disinherited and persecuted brothers in Europe to return to Zion but they are not going.[48]

Why did Gwaltney wish that American Jews would move to Palestine even though there was no practical way for this to happen? He maintained that races should remain separate and distinct, a belief he applied to African Americans as well as Jews:

> THE FOURTH BASIC principle is that of the consciousness of kind . . . "birds of a feather flock together." . . . Just so are men conscious of their kind, and the different kinds of folk are going to stick together. What is more, they will defend their kind if attacked by others. What then is to be the outcome of the race problem in this country, and especially in the South? Governor Ellis Arnall, of Georgia, says there is no race problem in the South, for wherever there is a problem it is based upon an assumption of a solution; but that the matter of race in the South is simply a condition for which there is no solution. This matter not only affects the white and Negro races, for the consciousness of kind is inherent in all of the races. It is evident between the Jews and the Gentiles; between the Anglo-Saxon and Latin peoples; between the Negroes, Indians and yellow races.[49]

Gwaltney's racist outlook enabled him to minimize Jewish suffering. Jews, no matter how loyal to the United States or assimilated into American society, were nevertheless outsiders who should move to the Middle East. Unless, of course, they converted to the Baptist faith.

Notes

1. William Wright Barnes, *The Southern Baptist Convention 1845–1953* (Nashville: Broadman, 1954), 245–46, 249.
2. Robert Andrew Baker, *The Southern Baptist Convention and Its People, 1607–1972* (Nashville: Broadman, 1974), 414; see also 441.
3. For a brief overview of Southern Baptist national resolutions on Jews and anti-Semitism, see Daniel E. Goodman, "Strangers, Neighbors, and Strangers Again: The History of Southern Baptist Approaches to Jews and Judaism," *Review and Expositor* 103, no. 1 (2006): 63–89.
4. *Annual of the 1933 Southern Baptist Convention*, Report of the Social Service Commission, 107–8.
5. *Annual of the 1934 Southern Baptist Convention*, Minutes Item 29, 63.
6. Ibid., Report of the Social Service Commission, 105, 113.
7. *Annual of the 1935 Southern Baptist Convention*, Order of Business and Minutes Item 18, 15, 19.
8. Ibid., Report of the Social Service Commission, 60–71.
9. *Annual of the 1936 Southern Baptist Convention*, Minutes Item 9, 19.
10. Ibid., Committee on Resolutions Report, 61–62.
11. William R. Rigell, "The Baptist Message for a Time Like This," *The Watchman-Examiner* (30 July 1936), 882.

12. *Annual of the 1936 Southern Baptist Convention*, Report of the Social Service Commission, 34–35.

13. *Annual of the 1937 Southern Baptist Convention*, Report of the Social Service Commission, 77.

14. Ibid., Committee on Resolutions Report, 100. The text is: "As a body of Christians we deplore the un-christian practices so widely prevalent in many of our racial relationships." Its placement in the set of resolutions indicates it was not meant to refer to Jewish issues in Germany (section A is about international relationships, while the racial statement is labeled section C).

15. *Annual of the 1938 Southern Baptist Convention*, Report of the Social Service Commission, 105.

16. Ibid., Report of the Committee on Public Relations, 116.

17. Ibid., 122.

18. *Minutes of the Meeting of the Executive Committee of the Southern Baptist Convention*, 103–15. The executive committee's decision on Rumania was reported in its report to the 1939 convention; see *Annual of the 1939 Southern Baptist Convention*, Executive Board Report, 33–34. Weaver made an extensive report on Rumania as well; *Annual of the 1939 Southern Baptist Convention*, Report of the Committee on Public Relations, 92–95.

19. *Annual of the 1939 Southern Baptist Convention*, "A Pronouncement upon Religious Liberty," 114–16.

20. *Annual of the 1940 Southern Baptist Convention*, Report of the Social Service Commission, 84.

21. Ibid., 87.

22. Ibid., Minutes, Item 16, 26; Item 69, 101–2.

23. *Annual of the 1941 Southern Baptist Convention*, Baptist World Emergency Committee Report, 99.

24. Ibid., Minutes Item 63, 99–100.

25. Ibid., Minutes Item 19, Baptist World Alliance Letter, 28.

26. Ibid., Home Mission Board Annual Report, 286.

27. Ibid.

28. *Annual of the 1942 Southern Baptist Convention*, Report of the Social Service Commission, 91. See also "Call to Prayer for a Just and Righteous Peace," *Annual of the 1942 Southern Baptist Convention*, Minutes Item 43, 45–46.

29. Ibid., Report of the Social Service Commission, 94.

30. *Annual of the 1943 Southern Baptist Convention*, Report of the Social Service Commission, 107.

31. *Annual of the 1944 Southern Baptist Convention*, Report of the Social Service Commission, 132.

32. *Annual of the 1945 Southern Baptist Convention*, Minutes Item 103, "Southern Baptists and World Peace," 149–50.

33. Ibid., Report of the Social Service Commission, 96–97.

34. Ibid., Statement of Principles, 60; *Annual of the 1946 Southern Baptist Convention*, Statement of Principles, 39; *Annual of the 1947 Southern Baptist Convention*, Statement of Principles, 341.

35. *Annual of the 1946 Southern Baptist Convention*, Committee on World Peace, Minutes Item 42, 39.

36. *Annual of the 1947 Southern Baptist Convention*, Committee on Resolutions, "Displaced Persons," 51. Further resolutions on displaced persons were passed at the next two conventions; see *Annual of the 1948 Southern Baptist Convention*, Committee on Resolutions, "Displaced Persons," 57; and *Annual of the 1949 Southern Baptist Convention*, Committee on Resolutions, "Displaced Persons," 55.

37. Michael J. Devine, ed. *Harry S. Truman, the State of Israel, and the Quest for Peace in the Middle East* (Kirksville, MO: Truman State University Press, 2009).

38. *Annual of the 1948 Southern Baptist Convention*, Minutes Item 22, 34.

39. "Baptists Ready to Name New Southern Head," The *Tuscaloosa News* (20 May 1948), 8.

40. *Annual of the 1948 Southern Baptist Convention*, Minutes Item 68, 48.

41. Ibid., Report of the Resolutions Committee, Minutes Item 112, 53.

42. Stephen M. Stocky, "White, William Richardson," Texas State Historical Association website, https://tshaonline.org/handbook/online/articles/fwh55, accessed 31 December 2015.

43. *Annual of the 1948 Southern Baptist Convention*, Minutes Item 129, "Resolution Concerning Baptist Concept of Freedom and Spiritual Values," 57.

44. *Heralds of Freedom* (Nashville: Broadman, 1939), 55.

45. Ibid., 128–29.

46. *The World's Greatest Decade: The Times and the Baptists* (Birmingham, AL: Birmingham Publishing Co.), 1947.

47. Ibid., 47.

48. Ibid., 16.

49. Ibid., 69–72; see also 90–91.

Chapter 14

Jacob Gartenhaus–The Southern Baptists' Jewish Voice

Jacob Gartenhaus, born in 1896 in the Austrian village of Bukowsko, was introduced to Christianity through conversations with his brother and others. Upon arriving in the United States, he experienced the world of Christian missions to Jews.[1] Eliza R. L. McGraw situated Gartenhaus's life and ministry in the context of the relationship between Baptists, Jews, and Southern culture. She observed: "Jewishness is crucial to the Southern Baptist understanding of responsibility and 'witness,' whether the Jews represent stone-throwing apostates or Jesus' brethren." Gartenhaus's call embodied this duality and ambivalence: "As she saw it, Gartenhaus never left his Jewish 'race' entirely behind, committing himself to mission work among his former coreligionists."[2]

In his 1946 report to the Southern Baptist Convention, Gartenhaus related the following story about his conversion and his relationship with his own people: "I have not changed my religion at all. Christianity is not another religion but the fulfillment of the Jewish religion. . . . Christianity does not supplant Judaism, but supplements it. I feel that I have not changed my religion but have found it. I, therefore, do not like to be known as a 'converted' Jew but as a 'completed' Jew."[3]

Daniel E. Goodman, associate professor of New Testament at Gardner-Webb University, portrayed Gartenhaus as an insensitive evangelist who "reveled in self-promotion," employed disingenuous means to present the Southern Baptist message to Jews, and exaggerated his missionary results.[4] This negative view of Gartenhaus constitutes a caricature of the man rather than a balanced assessment. Gartenhaus's personal spiritual journey and ministry should be evaluated on its own terms, in light of the times in which he lived and worked. In contrast to Goodman's approach, I propose that Jacob Gartenhaus's ministry as the highest-ranking Jewish Christian in the Southern Baptist Convention before, during, and after the Holocaust be assessed in light of the three themes that Gartenhaus himself would have recognized: mission to the American Jewish people as an expression of genuine friendship, the evil of anti-Semitism and Hitler's persecution of the Jewish people, and Zionism and the rebirth of Israel as a nation.

Mission to Jews: A Ministry of Friendship

Following his appointment as Evangelist to the Jews in May 1921, fulfilling the 1875 Southern Baptist convention resolution decades after the fact, Gartenhaus pondered the immensity of the task before him—outreach to Jews on a national level. He decided to introduce an alternative to the traditional specialized mission-focused approach to Jewish evangelism:

> THE OLD METHOD of establishing missions was very expensive, for it would have meant opening more than one hundred centers in the larger cities. Apart from this, after many years of close study and observations, my strong conviction (also the judgment of leading missionaries long in the service) was that Jewish mission centers alone could never reach all the many Jews with the gospel; each church would have to realize its individual responsibility in evangelizing its Jewish neighbors.[5]

Empowering the local church for Jewish evangelism was an inexpensive approach that could be spread through the whole country; furthermore, it appealed to "the conscience of the church" and promoted "a better understanding of true friendship between Jew and Christian."[6] For decades, Northern Baptists sponsored specialized inner-city missions, while Southern Baptists harbored a vision of creating a denominationally centralized outreach to Jews throughout the South.

Gartenhaus visualized his role as a national trainer and mobilizer of others. He centralized the vision and strategic planning work in his national office, while hoping to decentralize the administration of the actual work. He did not intend to create an office staffed by specialists,[7] but rather a vast network of churches and committees that would offer a spiritual home and hospitality for their Jewish neighbors.[8] He would be the face of Jewish evangelism and express its aims and tenets, but his goal was to have church members be the ministry's hands and feet. In his 1933 report, Gartenhaus wrote:

> FROM THE VERY beginning of our connection with the Home Mission Board twelve years ago we faced the double task of evangelizing the 500,000 Jews within our gates and enlisting the sympathy and support of Christian people, which latter task was as difficult as the former, for when the work of Jewish evangelization was first presented to our people the response was not encouraging, to say the least. Gradually Southern Baptists have come to realize more and more the Jews' real need for the gospel.[9]

Gartenhaus's vision was shared by the Woman's Missionary Union (WMU) and its affiliates throughout the convention and local congregations. By the end of the 1930s, Gartenhaus was enjoying a solid working relationship with the WMU, and they enthusiastically endorsed ministry to Jews, and in particular, Gartenhaus's work.[10] He realized there needed to be a dedicated subgroup within each congregation that would emphasize ministry to Jewish neighbors—"Friends of Israel." By 1936, Gartenhaus was sharing his dream across the country: it was through "the co-operation of Christian friends that I may multiply my usefulness and reach the teeming multitudes of my people. For this reason I have prepared a plan for the organization of Friends of Israel Groups thus seeking to reach the Jews scattered throughout the length and breadth of our territory; and it is indeed encouraging to know how many Jews have been contacted and won."[11]

In 1939, Gartenhaus was claiming success: "Some of the most encouraging communications are being received continuously from various Friends of Israel Groups who have been having marvelous experiences in contacting their Jewish friends; and it is in such communities that your servant has been permitted to render the most fruitful ministry."[12] In 1941, he expressed gratefulness that Friends of Israel groups were expanding and multiplying his ministry.[13] In

1943, Gartenhaus received the Home Mission Board's endorsement for his strategy.[14]

Gartenhaus envisioned the "Christian Friendliness" work of the church as a repudiation of anti-Semitism and as an affirmation of God's love for all of humanity, and he admonished his supporters to "keep in mind the centuries of Jewish persecution in the name of the cross, which has led many to think that all Jew haters, from Pharaoh to Hitler, were Christians. It will take much effort to convince the Jews that real Christians love them." In contrast to the Northern Baptist Christian Friendliness ministry, with its emphasis on English as a Second Language and other organized forms of social action and fellowship, the Southern Baptist approach emphasized evangelistic conversation and "social contacts with Jews" through which some might "speak a word in season for the Master."[15]

In 1945, Gartenhaus expressed satisfaction with the Woman's Missionary Union's support of the Friends of Israel groups: "Marvelous response was received from all states. Some states took almost twice the goal asked for."[16] By 1948, a year before he left the Home Mission Board to lead his own independent organization, the International Board of Jewish Missions, Gartenhaus claimed that his vision of the centrality of the local congregation in sharing the gospel with Jews had gained acceptance in other circles: "Many mission organizations are now beginning to stress the importance of the church or parish approach to the Jews, a ministry which we have advocated for many years, realizing that if the one million Jews scattered throughout the length and breadth of our Convention territory are ever to be won, the responsibility will have to be assumed by the local church."[17]

Rather than being an egotistical lone ranger who reserved the limelight just for himself as Goodman charged, Jacob Gartenhaus sought to cultivate a hospitable spirit within Southern Baptist churches so that they could befriend and share their faith in Jesus with their Jewish neighbors. He leveraged his national position to fulfill the Great Commission, as Southern Baptists understood it at the time, in relation to Jews. Gartenhaus was passionate, intense, focused, and committed to his calling. His personal journey was unique, and he never tired of sharing how he came to believe that Jesus was the Jewish Messiah through his speeches, meetings, articles, pamphlets, and books.

Anti-Semitism and the Holocaust

Jacob Gartenhaus was the most outspoken Southern Baptist opponent of the Nazi persecution of the Jews and anti-Semitism during the period of 1933 to 1948. Utilizing the "bully pulpit"[18] of his national office, he consistently brought the horrors being inflicted upon the European Jewish community to the attention of Southern Baptists, wrote numerous articles to dispel anti-Semitic prejudices, encouraged Christians to offer genuine friendship to Jews in their neighborhoods, supported the establishment of Israel as the national homeland for Jews, and at the conclusion of his tenure, authored the resolution against anti-Semitism which was passed at the 1947 Baptist World Alliance Congress which met in Copenhagen (see chapter 20).

In two 1934 articles, Gartenhaus addressed the plight of the Jews in Germany. He initially was reticent to accept the veracity of reports about Jewish persecution emanating from Hitler's Germany, because "I could not make myself believe that a civilized country in this modern age would stoop so low to seek to annihilate a whole race." He did not want to be fooled by "propaganda," and therefore he decided to "visit Germany and there get first-hand information."

Courageously, Gartenhaus rejected M. E. Dodd's published argument that Jews exercised excessive control of German professions and institutions. Jews were persecuted, Gartenhaus recounted, before they had the freedom in Germany (or elsewhere in Europe) to rise to positions of influence and power—"not a century passed that did not have its Jewish victims in Germany." The twentieth-century strain of German anti-Semitism emerged after World War I: "For thirteen years the leaders of the National Socialist party have repeatedly attacked them in speech and writing, holding them responsible for the millions who died, for the children who starved, for the Versailles, Dawes, and Young treaties, in fact, for all the ills of Europe."[19]

The second article focused on Hitler's persecution of the Jews. Gartenhaus differentiated between the troubles of the 80,000 Jews who had escaped Germany, with no clear destination before them, and the 520,000 Jews trapped under Nazi oppression. The boycotts instituted in 1933 continued to be in effect, and anti-Semitic slogans and literature rehashing false allegations against Jews (like ritual murder) were repeated without rebuttal "because the entire press is under the control of the Nazis."

Gartenhaus admitted that like everyone else, Jews were not perfect, but he adamantly maintained that it was not just or fair to "hold a whole race responsible for the misdeeds of a few." He refuted Nazi arguments related to Jewish participation in World War I and German culture, and he summarized the Jewish dilemma in Europe thusly: "All the world is now intently interested in the Jewish problem. The Jew being different from others and differently educated, is the cause of his being persecuted. He is different because God wanted him to be so." Thus, the fate of the Jews was tied to the covenant; they were chosen. They could not escape persecution through clinging to old tradition, assimilation, or even Zionism. The only path to peace for Jews, Gartenhaus contended, was their acceptance of Jesus as their Messiah—"this return to God is the only one solution."[20]

How can the Jew return to God? The most controversial aspect of Gartenhaus's thought was linking Jewish spiritual alienation, centuries of Jewish suffering and persecution at the hands of an unfriendly Gentile and Christian civilization, and intentionally targeting Jews to encourage conversions. Most importantly, Gartenhaus was not asserting a cause-effect relationship; the Jewish people were victims of the horrific persecutions, and *not* the cause of them. Christians must reject all forms of anti-Semitism, befriend Jews in the name of Christ, and share the gospel with them—just as Christians are commanded to do with people from every other race, nationality, and culture. Persecution was an evil, but if suffering opened up a person's heart to consider eternal spiritual truths, it might be used by God toward a redemptive end. This was Gartenhaus's hope for his own people, to which he dedicated his life.

Gartenhaus's ministry helped Christians understand and appreciate the Jewish people. In the foreword to Gartenhaus's booklet on *The Jew and Jesus* (1934), John Hill endorsed him as a bridge builder between Jews and Christians. Gartenhaus thought prior presentations on the subject were "proffered by prejudiced anti-Semites with a view to slandering the Jews and inciting public feelings against them," and he composed the booklet so that Christians might gain an understanding of Jewish attitudes and objections to the doctrine of Jesus' messiahship.[21] In his 1935 annual report, Gartenhaus wrote:

"We would not for a minute leave the impression that there are no difficulties and disappointments connected with the evangelization of the Jews. . . . But when we take into account the fact that for centuries the name of Christ was anathema to the Jews, we marvel at the remarkable change in their attitude today."[22]

As Nazi persecution continued to inflict suffering on the Jewish people, Gartenhaus sought to rally Southern Baptist empathy and support for the victims. Writing before Kristallnacht, Gartenhaus highlighted the tragedy of contemporary European Jewry experience:

> IF THERE WAS ever a time when Israel needed the prayers of God's people it is today. As I pen these lines they are passing through perhaps one of the greatest tragedies in their history, as if their cup of sorrow has not already been filled with the millions starving in Poland and the fate of hundreds of thousands in Germany hanging in the balance, not to mention their suffering in Rumania and Palestine. Now overnight these brutalities have extended into Austria. Complete elimination of the Jews from the life of the community is launched. "Perish Judea," is the cry heard there with increasing frequency, and perishing indeed they are. Sixty Jews committed suicide in one day; seventeen hundred Jewish suicides were reported for one week. Some assert that the long lists of suicides reported by the Vienna newspapers are really massacres. Heart-rending are the stories of events there; I shudder as I write these lines. They are destitute, undernourished, despised, afflicted, and disconsolate. "What next?" the bewildered Jew is asking.[23]

Gartenhaus continued to link Jewish persecution with evangelistic opportunity. First, Christian solidarity with persecuted Jews was an indispensable validation of the Christian message of God's love. "I have not had a single conversation with a Jew that these sad events have not come up for discussion, and unless I can assure my people of Christian sympathy, my message will be like sounding brass." Second, Christians should take all necessary steps to oppose the Nazi agenda. Gartenhaus defended the importance of resolutions and letters against anti-Semitism and persecution:

> HOW HAPPY I am that I can call their attention to the manifesto signed by several hundred clergymen calling upon Christians to oppose the "Sin of anti-Semitism." "With genuine anguish of heart," reads the

> manifesto in part, "we behold how in many places across the world today cruel forces of oppression and persecution are being released upon men and women and children of Jewish race and blood. With profound concern we note from time to time within our own beloved democratic nation the manifestation of a spirit of anti-Semitism. . . . We extend to our brethren and fellow-citizens of Jewish race and blood our solemn assurance that by the constraint of our own deepest Christian conviction we shall oppose unceasingly 'the sin of anti-Semitism,' and we shall strive continuously for the realization of that brotherhood which humanity needs, democracy requires and Christianity demands."[24]

In his 1940 and 1941 reports, Gartenhaus reiterated his belief that persecution was producing a spiritual openness on the part of Jews toward Christ. He cited two trends, the first of which he identified as the "unprecedented suffering of my people. Persecution has not relaxed in intensity. Ever increasingly Jews are being annihilated, starved and tortured." Second, he praised the response of "two of the greatest Christian democracies," in which "thousands of Jewish refugees have found shelter in their Christian homes, and the cause of Israel has been pleaded from pulpit and in the press.[25]

After the United States entered the war, Gartenhaus kept the plight of the Jews in front of Southern Baptist eyes. In 1942, he charged that "Satanic fury has burst forth in all its intensity seeking to wipe the Jews from the face of the earth. One calamity after another has befallen them." Gartenhaus quoted London's *Jewish Chronicle*, which reported that "Jews have been forced to dig their own graves and then have been buried in them alive. Whole Jewries have been uprooted and despoiled, or thrown into slavery, or locked up in ghettos, or cast adrift on the open seas in hell ships, drifting amid horrors from one inhospitable land to another, or at the end finding in the waves oblivion of their ghastly tortures."[26] Even prior to the official announcements confirming the mass extermination at Nazi concentration camps, Gartenhaus cited statistics indicating that the very survival of the Jewish people was at risk, claiming that "of the 4,000,000 of them in Nazi-occupied Europe, more than 2,000,000 . . . will be exterminated before the end of the year. An eyewitness gives an account of the massacre of 72,000 Jews in the city of Minsk, 35,000 of them in one day."[27]

In 1944, Gartenhaus published *The Influence of the Jew upon Civilization* to "counteract the widespread and poisonous anti-semitism propaganda which has found its way into many Christian circles."[28] As the war in Europe was coming to its end, Gartenhaus relayed some of the horror stories coming out of central and eastern Europe:

> ONE REPORT HAS it that the machine guns were not able to kill out these people fast enough, and Nazi doctors were called upon to assist in this gruesome task. The doctors were then killing them at the rate of more than one hundred men an hour per doctor by injecting air bubbles into their veins, . . . Some four million Jews have been disposed of in one way or another and those who have not been able to escape the clutches of the enemy await a similar fate.

Gartenhaus could never end a meditation on such a sad note; he went on to share a few general instances of Gentiles saving Jewish lives and then concluded that "these acts of heroism, Christian love, and concern" made a "great impression . . . upon world Jewry. It is this distinction between paganism of Nazi Germany and the true Spirit of Christ as demonstrated by these Christians that will in time bring the true Christ and Israel together."[29]

No other Southern Baptist leader devoted so much time and attention to the plight of the Jewish people under Nazism as Jacob Gartenhaus. He risked his career by forthrightly criticizing Hitler, even as others were praising him. He consistently reminded Baptists about Jewish suffering in the prewar period, even before Kristallnacht. As the horrors of the Final Solution became worldwide knowledge, Gartenhaus did not allow Southern Baptists to ignore the tragedy. He stood by the people of his heritage, felt their pain, and sought to bring them solace in the only way he could—by presenting the love of God through Jesus to them.

Zionism and a Future for the Jewish People

Gartenhaus was well aware of the Zionist aspirations of the Jewish people. In his autobiography, he wrote about the plight of the Jews after the war was over:

> WORLD WAR II left the Jewish people broken to pieces. Of the eighteen million Jews that existed in the world before the war, one third

(about six million) were murdered by the Nazis. Almost all of European Jewry and the teeming great Jewish centers of life and culture were wiped out. The remaining Jews, maimed in body and spirit, were wandering about aimlessly, not knowing where to lay their heads. No people wanted them in their midst. Several million Jews remained alive behind the Iron Curtain but were not permitted to practice their faith in public. . . . The Jewish race could perpetuate its identity and its very life only if it had a home of its own—and that home could be only in the Promised Land of the forefathers. . . . Thus the state of Israel came into being.[30]

Gartenhaus was a lifelong student of Zionism. In 1936, he published *The Rebirth of a Nation: Zionism in History and Prophecy*. He cited with approval the first Zionist Congress led by Theodore Herzl in 1897 and the role of Chaim Weizmann in the creation of the Balfour Declaration.[31] Gartenhaus rejected theological attempts to spiritualize the promises to Israel of a physical homeland.[32] Possibly in reference to Germany's persecution of the Jews, he maintained that the "prophets of Israel foretold not only the future restoration of the Jewish people to their promised homeland of Palestine, with blessings to themselves and ultimately to the whole world, but with astonishing accuracy portrayed the tragic history of the Jews for these two thousand years have been scattered among the Gentile nations."[33]

Although writing to a Christian audience, Gartenhaus consistently presented Jewish thought and spirituality on its own terms. He treated Jewish understandings of Zionism with respect and sympathy, acknowledging that "it is well to consider the various attitudes toward it held both by Jews in Palestine and in other lands."[34] He was also well aware that Christians were not uniform in their beliefs about Zionism:

> There are groups of Christians who, because they are uninformed as to Zionism, are indifferent to the movement. Other groups of the modern school are sympathetic with the desire of the Jews for a homeland of their own; a place which to them will be a spiritual center and reservoir of their racial genius; they desire friendly relations with the Jews because of the common root of Judaism and Christianity; the great common heritage that there is between the Jew and the Christian. They admire the gallantry and heroism not only of the leaders of Zionism, but the

> pioneers and humble people who are working out their destiny in a difficult land. They also deplore the persecution of the Jew, either in Europe or anywhere else. They perceive the difficulties of the Palestinian problem: the problem of the race relations between the Arab and Jew, the mandatory problem of government on the part of England. There are some members of Christendom who object to the return of the Jews to Palestine for fear of the desecration of the Holy places. This view smacks of superstition. Some extreme religionists, believing that God has broken off all relations with the Jews, think the whole movement is just another expression of an egotistical and nationalistic character.[35]

Gartenhaus did not consider the return of the Jews to the land of their forefathers to be just a political achievement or an end in itself. He fervently believed that the return of Israel had prophetic significance and would culminate in the Jewish people's acceptance of Jesus' messianic claims. Gartenhaus believed his fellow Jews, having returned to Zion, would "in God's own time look upon him whom they have pierced, in the days to come, proclaim him to all the worlds high priest, Savior, Redeemer, King."[36]

Notes

1. See Jacob Gartenhaus, *Traitor? A Jew, a Book, a Miracle: An Autobiography* (Nashville: Thomas Nelson, 1980).
2. Eliza R. L. McGraw, *Two Covenants: Representations of Southern Jewishness* (Baton Rouge: Louisiana State University Press, 2005), 99.
3. *Annual of the 1946 Southern Baptist Convention*, Home Mission Board Annual Report, 328.
4. Daniel E. Goodman, "Strangers, Neighbors, and Strangers Again: The History of Southern Baptist Approaches to Jews and Judaism," *Review and Expositor* 103, no. 1 (2006): 63–89.
5. Gartenhaus, *Traitor?*, 1–163.
6. Jacob Gartenhaus, *What of the Jews?* (Atlanta: Home Mission Board of the Southern Baptist Convention, 1948), 78–79.
7. From time to time, Gartenhaus would gain a short-term associate—Mollie Cohen, for work in New Orleans; *Annual of the 1940 Southern Baptist Convention*, Report of the Home Mission Board, "Jewish Evangelism," 296; and Clarke E. Burkhalter, a seminarian—*Annual of the 1945 Southern Baptist Convention*, Report of the Home Mission Board, "Jewish Evangelism," 294.
8. Gartenhaus, *What of the Jews?*, 79–83.
9. *Annual of the 1933 Southern Baptist Convention*, Report of the Home Mission Board, "Jewish Evangelism," 245.
10. *Annual of the 1939 Southern Baptist Convention*, Report of the Woman's Missionary Union, 414; see McGraw, *Two Covenants*, 98.
11. *Annual of the 1937 Southern Baptist Convention*, Report of the Home Mission Board, "Jewish Evangelism," 273.

12. *Annual of the 1939 Southern Baptist Convention*, Report of the Home Mission Board, "Jewish Evangelism," 306.

13. *Annual of the 1941 Southern Baptist Convention*, Report of the Home Mission Board, "Jewish Evangelism," 311.

14. *Annual of the 1943 Southern Baptist Convention*, Report of the Home Mission Board, "Jewish Evangelism," 247–48.

15. Gartenhaus, *What of the Jews?*, 85.

16. *Annual of the 1945 Southern Baptist Convention*, Report of the Home Mission Board, "Jewish Evangelism," 294.

17. *Annual of the 1948 Southern Baptist Convention*, Report of the Home Mission Board, "Department of Jewish Evangelism," 191.

18. "Bully pulpit" refers to leveraging one's position or office to advocate for an opinion or view. President Theodore Roosevelt is credited with originating the term; he used the presidency in this way.

19. Jacob Gartenhaus, "The German-Jewish Tragedy," *Western Recorder* (25 October 1934), 3–4. For Gartenhaus's narrative of this trip, see *Traitor?*, 200–205.

20. Jacob Gartenhaus, "The German-Jewish Tragedy," *Western Recorder* (8 November 1934), 3–4.

21. Jacob Gartenhaus, *The Jew and Jesus* (Nashville: The Sunday School Board of the Southern Baptist Convention, 1934), 5, 7.

22. *Annual of the 1935 Southern Baptist Convention*, Report of the Home Mission Board, "Jewish Evangelism," 278.

23. *Annual of the 1938 Southern Baptist Convention*, Report of the Home Mission Board, "Praying for Jerusalem," 292.

24. Ibid., 292–93.

25. *Annual of the 1941 Southern Baptist Convention*, Report of the Home Mission Board, "Jewish Work," 312. See also *Annual of the 1940 Southern Baptist Convention*, Report of the Home Mission Board, "Jewish Work," 296.

26. *Annual of the 1942 Southern Baptist Convention*, Report of the Home Mission Board, "Jewish Work," 274.

27. *Annual of the 1943 Southern Baptist Convention*, Report of the Home Mission Board, "Department of Jewish Work," 245.

28. *Annual of the 1944 Southern Baptist Convention*, Report of the Home Mission Board, "Department of Jewish Work," 306.

29. *Annual of the 1945 Southern Baptist Convention*, Report of the Home Mission Board, "Department of Jewish Work," 291–92.

30. Gartenhaus, *Traitor?*, 223–24.

31. Jacob Gartenhaus, *The Rebirth of a Nation: Zionism in History and Prophecy* (Nashville: Broadman, 1936), 12–13; see also 55–56. On Gartenhaus's appreciation for Herzl, see 68–75.

32. Ibid., 50–53.

33. Ibid., 35.

34. Ibid., 77.

35. Ibid., 89.

36. Ibid.

Chapter 15

The Conscience of Southern Baptist State Conventions

The response of the Southern Baptist state conventions to the persecution of the Jews exhibited a pattern that was quite different from that of their Northern Baptist counterparts. Only one state convention—Missouri—evidenced a period-long interest in the plight and fate of the Jews. Six states (South Carolina, Alabama, North Carolina, Georgia, Mississippi, and Tennessee) expressed some form of protest after Kristallnacht and then followed up sporadically in later years. The balance of the states expressed few or no specific convictions regarding the Holocaust between 1933 and 1948.

The Missouri Baptist General Association—A Unique Journey

Among Southern Baptist state conventions, the narrative of the Missouri Baptist General Association was unique. Whereas the other states either ignored the plight of the Jews or addressed it only after Kristallnacht, Missouri Baptists expressed concern for persecuted Jews before Kristallnacht.

In 1934, the Temperance and Social Service Committee noted that approximately 178,000 "foreigners and aliens" lived in Missouri and consequently recommended the "development of interracial friendships and the elimination of racial and religious intolerance."[1] In 1937, the Resolutions Committee challenged the delegates to reject "race prejudice which manifests itself in unchristian acts and attitudes. Remembering that God has made of one blood all the nations for to dwell on all the face of the earth, we challenge our constituency to put into practice the as-ye-would-that-men-do-to-you principle in our race relationships."[2]

One would not expect to find a Kristallnacht-related resolution from Missouri Baptists, since their 1938 meeting took place on October 18-20, three weeks before Kristallnacht. However, the Missouri Baptist General Association passed a remarkable resolution on race relations that can only be characterized as prophetic:

> IT IS WITH deep regret that we hear constantly of the race prejudice which is manifested at home and abroad. Especially are our hearts made sad when we read of the growing spirit of anti-Semitism which is spreading throughout the world, gradually seeping into our own land. Nearly two-thirds of the Jewish race has been caught in the quicksands of that unhappy continent of Europe where they seem to be rapidly and hopelessly sinking. Two of the three million in Poland are deprived of all means of subsistence. Hearts are touched by their suffering in Germany, Austria and Italy, where the slow economic annihilation of a people has become more excruciatingly cruel than annihilation by sword. To remain in these countries means sure starvation; to flee abroad they cannot, unless they are prepared to sacrifice their possessions. In the face of such a sad plight of a people, can we as followers of Christ remain silent and not voice our protests? We would not be true to our Christian heritage were we to do so, especially when we are reminded of our eternal debt to this race by the Apostle Paul who, in Romans 9:4-5, wrote, "Israelites: to whom pertaineth the adoption, and the glory, and the covenants, and the giving of the law, and the service of God and the promises; whose are the Father's, and of whom as concerning the flesh Christ came." If the Jew needs chastisement let us remember that it is God's prerogative and not man's. "Vengeance belongeth unto me; I will repay, saith the Lord." We therefore would express our deep sympathy and concern to our Jewish brethren in their hour of suffering and assure them of our love. We representatives of the Christian faith publicly condemn the oppression to which millions of Jews are being subjected as a blot on the civilization of our time.[3]

As a political document, this resolution was the most complete and detailed resolution on anti-Semitism in Europe to be found among Baptists in the United States up to that time. No other resolution specifically mentioned all of the following countries in which Jews found themselves under severe persecution: Germany, Poland,

Austria, and Italy. The reference to Italy is especially significant, since Southern Baptist mission ties to Italian Baptists made the plight of Jewish Italians invisible to many Southern Baptist leaders. The acknowledgment that the European Jews were in *Zugzwang*[4] was perceptive, and the resolution rightly called Christians to voice protest. Furthermore, the timing of the statement was remarkable; if it had been composed in late November 1938, it would still be ranked among the strongest Southern Baptist protests. To have passed it in convention before Kristallnacht gave it a prophetic dimension that was unique among Baptists in the United States.

As an expression of friendship, the Missouri resolution reached a higher plane than most Baptist statements of the time, but ultimately it was somewhat less successful as a religious testimony. The reference to Christianity's "eternal debt" to the Jews echoed J. H. Rushbrooke's expression of gratitude to the English Jewish community. The Missouri statement's "sympathy and concern for our Jewish brethren in their hour of suffering" expressed a sense of solidarity and friendship with the Jewish community. There was an emotional depth behind the words of the resolution. The Missouri Baptists felt "deep regret" and "deep sympathy and concern" for persecuted Jews. However, the inclusion of the phrase "if the Jew needs chastisement" intended to counter the argument that the victims of the persecution caused or deserved it, unintentionally may have given some credence to the unjust claim that the persecution of the Jews was due to their rejection of Jesus.

The Missouri Baptists' general secretary, E. Gobold, perhaps in response to the outpouring of empathy for persecuted Jews at the 1938 meeting, indicated support for the protest undertaken by Missouri Baptists and others. He also confirmed that Missouri Baptists were not silent. He then called for further action, but not of a political nature. He urged his members to focus on Jewish evangelism, taking spiritual advantage of the uncertain state of affairs the Jews faced: "Everybody wants to talk about the Jews. The action in Germany has increased the interest in all of us in this remarkable race of people. By all means we must not let our interests stop with a protest against the persecution of these people in Germany. Let's give them the Gospel. That is their only hope and the longer we delay about giving the gospel to the Jews the more severely they will be persecuted throughout the world. Their hearts are open now to this message as never before."[5]

The Word and Way published an editorial on December 1, 1938, focused on Kristallnacht: "Word from Germany, which we see nowhere contradicted, fills the civilized world with horror for the persecution that is being meted out to the Jews." It then quoted in its entirety a city-wide protest statement from Kansas City, which had the strong support of Baptist and other Protestant clergy. Note the reference to "personality" alongside "respect for human dignity" as being fundamental to a society's well-being:

> SHOCKED BY THE incredible persecution of minorities in Germany, the people of Kansas City join with the President and the millions of others throughout the world in protest against this developing tragedy. We feel that events in Germany are an extreme expression of an intolerance growing in many countries to a point where civilization itself is threatened. Respect for human dignity and personality is the basis of civilized living. Where it is lost there develops heart-breaking injustice and brutality.[6]

However, the editorial also lamented that Baptist persecution in Rumania was not getting equal attention and blamed Jews for Sunday commercial practices. A second editorial on December 15, 1938, once again showcased the ambivalence of Missouri Baptist leaders. On one hand, it stated, "The unspeakable persecution of the Jews in certain parts of the world, their consequent dispersion into other sections and the revolt of democracy against these outrages has focused the mind of the world on the Jew, his shortcomings, his pitiful plight, his needs and his future." This reference to "shortcomings" referred not just to the standard prejudices and anti-Semitic charges regarding supposed moral character flaws and economic advantage seeking but also supposed spiritual defects, especially lack of faith in Christianity. On the other hand, the article claimed that Jesus himself did not "lift his finger against" the Romans who oppressed the Jews of his day because "he came for another purpose." Ultimately, the article concluded that Baptists should embrace not just their civic responsibilities but also their spiritual mandate in relation to Jews: "While, as citizens of a democracy which insists upon justice to every one, we cry out against the persecution of the Jew, let us not as Christians forget to preach Christ to him."[7]

In 1943, the Missouri Baptist General Association reaffirmed a vision of racial equality based on Acts 17:26. They chronicled the tragic history of Nazi persecution of the Jews, once again with an unusual degree of specificity, and deplored the Holocaust that was taking place:

> THERE WERE 599,000 Jews in Germany in 1933, and at the end of 1942 there were less than 40,000. There were 185,000 Jews in Austria before the War, and now there are less than 13,000. It has been reported upon reliable authority that 2,000,000 Jews have perished in Europe during the past four years, in this racial war prosecuted with all the hate of a thousand hells by the German war lords. Surely, a day of reckoning is coming for those guilty of this shameless slaughter![8]

This is one of the more detailed accounts of the systematic killing of the European Jews by the Nazis to be found in Baptist committee reports for the period immediately prior to the war's conclusion, and it leaves no doubt as to the severity of the crisis the Jews faced. But the report went further still, accusing the white majority of the United States of being guilty of passing on racial prejudice to new generations: "For more than a hundred years we have instilled into the hearts of our youth a race prejudice against the Japanese, Chinese, Indians and the Negroes. This dark and satanic prejudice instilled into the hearts of our youth by supposedly Christian parents has brought forth crimes and inhuman deeds which are so hideous that we hesitate to mention."[9]

By 1944, in spite of the increasing number of revelations regarding Nazi concentration camps and the systematic extermination of the Jews in Europe, Missouri Baptists began to place greater emphasis on the racial divide between whites and African Americans at home. The Temperance and Social Service Committee reflected that priority in its report: "While there are very serious problems involved in the question regarding races—the Japanese and other nationalities, Jewish, etc.—our chief problem, as we know, is between the whites and the blacks."[10]

This brief overview demonstrates that Missouri Southern Baptists manifested the ambivalence of their denomination in an interesting way. They could express friendship and sympathy toward persecuted Jews with an unexcelled passion, but they also provided space for anti-Semitic aspersions to be vented. In the end, however, Missouri Baptists did not undertake any significant ministries on behalf of the suffering Jewish population in Europe.

Kristallnacht: Pricking the Conscience of Southern Baptists

Most Southern Baptist state conventions either ignored or paid only minimal attention to the persecution of Jews in Germany and elsewhere in Europe until Kristallnacht. The atrocities of November 9-10, 1938, provoked a number of states to respond. In part, this was due to the fact that their annual meetings were scheduled for mid-November of each year, making Kristallnacht a current news story.

The South Carolina Baptist Convention

In 1751, four congregations in South Carolina formed the second Baptist association in the United States. The Charleston association passed one of the earliest statements on Jews at its 1794 meeting, in which it called for prayers for the "propagation and success of the Gospel among the Heathen; and the conversion of the Jews to Christianity."[11] This action coincided with the dedication of the Jewish community's new synagogue building and may have represented Baptist acknowledgment of the growth of the city's Jewish population to approximately five hundred people.[12]

In the 1930s, the South Carolina Baptist Convention expressed its convictions regarding social issues through its Commission on Social Service reports. In 1935, the commission expressed concern over "the rising tides of antipathies of races and colors."[13] Meeting on November 15-17, 1938, just one week after Kristallnacht, the Commission on Social Service utilized core Baptist convictions of democracy, soul freedom, and religious liberty in opposing fascism as a political system, criticizing Hitler and Mussolini for rejecting democracy, and vigorously sympathizing with German Jews harmed during the Kristallnacht attacks:

> NO PEOPLE HAVE had more to do with the development of democracy than Baptists. The world owes a great debt to Roger Williams and those who followed in his train. Democracy is not just the rule of the majority. Fascism believes in that. It also involves the right of minority to live and to agitate for change, so long as this is advocated by peaceful means. We believe that private armies and military or semi-military organizations should not be allowed. Democracy is menaced today as it has not been in a hundred years. Hitler and Mussolini deride it. We see the trend toward fascism in the so-called democratic countries. . . . We prize the principle of soul freedom. We believe in it not only for ourselves but for others. We protest the denial of Religious Liberty in Russia, Ethiopia, Germany and elsewhere. We look with horror on the terrible persecution of the Jews in Germany. How irrational to make a whole people suffer as they are at present because of the act of a half insane boy in France. We believe world opinion and influences should be marshaled against this persecution. We must beware of being infected by this baneful tendency. It is a time when we should show special kindness to the Jews in our midst.[14]

The perspective of the state convention's newspaper, *The Baptist Courier*, was somewhat ambivalent toward Jews. A month and a half prior to Kristallnacht, three paragraph-length editorials appeared. One condemned Hitler for pressing Sudeten German rights while depriving Jews "of all rights and most of their property," noting that they are "being expelled from their homes on German soil." The second praised Chamberlain for his pact with Hitler. The third editorial sympathized with Jews who were being persecuted while also criticizing them for their attitude toward Jewish converts to Christianity:

> JEWS STRENUOUSLY COMPLAIN of mistreatment in Germany, and elsewhere, and yet when a member of their race becomes a Christian, they, in turn, administer about the same unjust treatment, depriving such a member of family connection and property rights. In fact, in most cases, they are considered as outcasts by their own people if they become Christians. It is wrong, and grievously so, that Jews have been made to suffer in various parts of the world, but it is also wrong for them to show about the same spirit towards one of their own when such accepts Christ as Saviour.[15]

After Kristallnacht, *The Baptist Courier* published the BWA's appeal for Rumanian Baptists on its cover page and mentioned the Jewish resolution, without additional comment, in its November 24, 1938, issue.[16] An editorial on December 1, 1938, noted Christian suffering in Czechoslovakia. On page 4, there was a short article that stated that German Baptists were "not immune from the sufferings of minorities, whose individuals are faithful unto Jehovah, God, whose name has been ordered erased from every page in all Germany." The statement on Kristallnacht was included as part of the Social Service Commission report.[17]

At the following two annual meetings, the Commission on Social Service restated its concern that fascist totalitarianism was opposed to Christian notions of democracy, separation of church and state, and the kingdom of God.[18] However, no specific reference was made to ongoing Jewish suffering in Germany or the countries the Nazis had recently overrun. This oversight was partially rectified in 1941. After opposing fascism and communism as alternative religions to Christianity, the commission warned Americans to treat their minorities better than the Germans had done: "We are filled with horror at the ruthless way Germany has dealt with her minorities. We must be careful to be above reproach in handling our own minority problem. We have the Oriental, the Mexican and the Negro. The main minority problem with us in South Carolina is the Negro."[19]

The 1943 annual session gave South Carolina Baptists the opportunity to deal with prejudice against Jews in particular, both in Germany and in the United States. For the first time, the term *concentration camp* was used, but it referred to the destination of those who sought to exercise freedom of speech in a totalitarian political order, not the venue for the implementation of the Final Solution.[20] Belatedly, the report lamented the failure of the German church (but not specifically German Baptists) to stand up for Christians with a Jewish heritage: "Hitler has carried this philosophy further toward its ultimate application. The descendants of Luther trying to be loyal to the state and to the church found the state was telling them even what to believe. Telling them that Jews must not be allowed to preach in the churches, nor to be members, that they had no place in the community."[21]

The Commission on Social Service called for Baptists to approach this subject with humility, because prejudice against Jews and African

Americans had reared its ugly head throughout the country. They castigated anti-Semitic leaders such as Father Charles Coughlin, Gerald Smith, and Frank Norris, warning that

> MANY OF THEM are fascist in their tendencies and most dangerous to the peace and prosperity of tomorrow. They sow intolerance and hate. It is so easy to appeal to prejudice against Jews, Negroes, etc. Recently Jewish cemeteries have been desecrated in New York. They will do all they can to stir up race prejudice and race hatred. Dr. Goebbels has counted on this as one of his strongest weapons to weaken America. . . . Beware of these who preach race or class hatred.[22]

In 1944, the Commission on Social Service condemned "the efforts of fascists to use hatred against Jews, Negroes and others." Foundational to this judgment was their understanding of the Baptist core conviction of personality: "When Jesus put supreme valuation on personality, He did not mean just white persons. He meant persons of every color and kind. Why do we find race prejudice, race hatred among Christians? Why in the so-called superior people? . . . Race prejudice undermines respect which is due to every person made in the image of God."[23]

Following the end of World War II, the Commission on Social Service surveyed the extent of human carnage that conquered countries suffered. There was no explicit acknowledgment that six million Jews died; instead, it stated that in Czechoslovakia, "the number of Jewish families killed is unknown but at least 5,000 Jewish orphans were sent" to various countries, and that in Denmark, "Jewish families were exterminated here as elsewhere."[24] In 1946, the commission connected the Ku Klux Klan to Nazism: "We note that the Ku Klux Klan seems to have linked up with German Fascism through the American Bund. Both of these organizations believe in the fundamental Nazi philosophy of the super-race."[25]

The Alabama Baptist State Convention

Alabama Baptists constituted the most important social force in that state. Dan J. Puckett, associate professor of history at Troy University, noted, "Southern Baptists, the largest Christian denomination in the state, greatly influenced, if not dominated, all aspects of life in

Alabama during the late nineteenth and most of the twentieth centuries."[26] Despite the participation of Alabama Baptists in Southern Baptist Convention and Baptist World Alliance affairs, and the persistent attention of *Alabama Baptist* editor L. L. Gwaltney to international matters, Alabama Baptists did not pass a resolution on the plight of Europe's Jews until after Kristallnacht. Puckett observed: "Kristallnacht prompted Baptists to examine more closely the plight of Jews in Germany."[27]

In 1933, the Alabama Baptist Committee on Social Conditions and Service lauded the social gospel, asserting that since "it places an infinite value on every human being," this interpretation of Christian social ethics "protests against . . . every wrong to personality."[28] In its 1937 report, the committee criticized democratic countries for standing by as "Fascist Italy and Nazi Germany" aided forces that destroyed Spain's democratic structures and religious liberty. Perhaps in a nod to Germany's Jews, it stated, "Rights of individuals are denied."[29]

The 1938 Alabama Baptist annual session on November 15-17, 1938, was the setting for the most significant protest against Nazi persecution of Jews on the state convention level of the Southern Baptist Convention. Leading up to the event, *The Alabama Baptist* columnist Charles F. Leek coupled sympathy for Jews with the insinuation that they were partly to blame for their predicament:

> THE GREATEST RACIAL question of the day concerns the problem of the Jews. Despite his denial to the Pope of Rome, that he was simply mimicing [*sic*] Hitler in his racial policy, Mussolini, the modern Nero, has issued an order to the effect that all Jews who have settled in Italy, Libya and the Aegean Isles since January 1, 1919, regardless of whether they are Italian citizens, must leave in six months. It may be that Mussolini is not monkeying Hitler after all. Maybe he wishes to get rid of all Jews Hitler has sent him since the latter began his anti-semetic [*sic*] purge. One feels sorry for the Jews, although one cannot feel that they are largely responsible for their plight.[30]

An editorial in the October 20, 1938, issue of the newspaper, after protesting against Baptist persecution in Rumania, reminded Alabama Baptists that they should also sympathize with suffering Jews: "Baptists should also remember the wail that is going up from the persecuted Jews the world over and especially in certain countries of Europe and among the countries most reprehensible in their persecution of the Jews are Germany and Italy."[31]

The message that Baptists must not be idle bystanders to the persecution of the Jews was not lost on Dr. Alfred J. Dickinson Jr., pastor of the First Baptist Church of Mobile, who at the annual convention preached an impassioned sermon attacking Nazi anti-Semitism.[32] Dickinson stated, "Today we live in a war terrorized world" in which "hate runs amuck, a ruthless and malignant force." Masterfully, he then linked this hate to anti-Semitism:

> WE BEHOLD IN Europe a war on the Jew, with the same motive as of old, hate, avarice, and spoliation to make war. Relentless hunting to death, the denial of equality in justice, exile with confiscation of property, imprisonment, homes invaded and looted, liable at any time to be at the mercy of a mob, no slander too vile to be heaped on them—this is the story of the treatment of the Jews by anti-Semitic hatred. We should expose the skeleton in the closet and unmask the hypocrisy of this vicious prejudice. The persecutors of the Jews are building a powerful military machine to strike at all human liberties. If democracy is in retreat, the Jews of Central Europe bear the brunt of the attack, and there is no peace for them.[33]

Following the sermon, Dr. John A. Davison encouraged the taking of an offering for persecuted German Jews, and $50.00 was raised,[34] comparable to approximately $815 in 2017. On November 17, 1938, the Social Service Commission responded with a set of resolutions. The commission report first provided the geopolitical context for its concerns, linking nationalism to racism. After granting some measure of praise to the appeasement agreement of Munich, it warned: "Hitler, now the dominant power of Europe, has begun his march to the East and means evidently to control everything to the Black Sea. An extreme nationalism, resulting in race hatred."[35]

After the resolution on Rumania was approved, the commission criticized Nazi treatment of Jews:

> WE NOTE WITH approval the friendly relations that have existed between our Government and the German Reich. However we have been

> saddened by the continuous persecution of Jews and other minorities. We regard persecution a violation of fundamental human rights. We believe that a great people such as the Germans are and have been false to their own well-being, and that they are justly incurring the displeasure and censure of civilized nations by their own oppression and intimidation of any groups because of religion or race. We make indignant protest against these injustices.[36]

The commission also recommended "a memorial condemning religious persecution in Rumania and in Germany be sent to the Secretary of State Hull, to the President of the United States and to the Rumanian Ambassador to Washington, [and to] the German Ambassador."[37] The resolutions passed, but not all Alabama Baptists were necessarily supportive. *The Alabama Baptist* reported that "the sermon was well received by an attentive and appreciative audience,"[38] but Leek expressed consternation about the chain of action-reaction within which Kristallnacht was enmeshed:

> THE LAW OF retaliation, an eye for an eye, and a tooth for a tooth, rules much of the world and life. Certain Jews displease Hitler. He persecutes all of them. A persecuted seventeen-year-old Polish Jew by the name of Herschel Grynszpan two weeks ago shot and killed Ernst Von Rath, secretary of the German Embassy, at Paris. Nazis in Germany, and especially in Berlin, follow with aggravated mistreatment of Jews. Aroused by this, England threatens to call off negotiations for the return of German colonies to the Reich. Now what will Germany do? This all reflects the law of the jungle. What we need is even more than the Golden Rule. The world needs more than to do unto others whatsoever we would have others do to us. The world needs the Diamond Rule, Christ's words, "That ye also should do as I have done to you."[39]

Leek noted Hitler's response to newspaper reports about Kristallnacht and wondered: "Hitler says he cannot understand why we criticise [*sic*] their treatment of the Jew when we have treated the Mormons in similar fashion. What will he say when he learns of our treatment of Indians and Negroes?"[40]

The 1939 convention may not have been as dramatic as its predecessor, but it did signify two important developments within the

Alabama Baptist State Convention. First, it represented a shift in attitudes toward pacifism, war, and American political neutrality. The Social Service Commission expressed Baptist disdain for war while admitting that force may be justified when dictators attack peace-loving people. Baptists could in good conscience oppose the Nazis: "Hitler's lying diplomacy and ruthless invasion and rape of peaceful populations became a menace to the peace and freedom of the world and so must be stopped. War is horrible and yet the right of self-defense remains. War is wholesale murder and yet men had better die than live in slavery."

Second, the commission expressed the truth about German Baptist subservience to the Nazis—a rare admission of the division that existed within the worldwide Baptist community, which was usually overlooked, denied, or covered up. Baptists "are unmolested in Germany only because their mouths are silent about the atrocities of Hitlerism against the Jews and Protestants. Italy's claims about religious freedom are only pretense, and hypocrisy."[41]

After devoting a good deal of attention to the plight of the Jews in 1938 and 1939, Alabama Baptists did not focus on the persecution of the Jews in the 1940s. The Social Service Commission continued to make general statements about racism and persecution; in 1941, it stated: "We deplore race conflicts and persecutions. We condemn the acts of those who fan the fires of race hatreds. We give our hearty approval to every effort to promote understanding and good will among all races of people. All minority racial groups should be given the same rights and privileges that the majority groups claim for themselves. We appeal for a kindly attitude and treatment of all races and colors."[42] In 1942, the commission paid tribute to the link between freedom and personality: "The very soul of freedom is the freedom of the soul. All freedoms grow out of this. The worth of the individual; the inviolable sanctity of the human personality; the responsibility of the individual before God, and his privilege of approach to God."[43]

Following the end of World War II, Alabama Baptists were unique in expressing support for holding Nazis accountable for their war crimes: "The Nuremberg trials with the conviction and execution of the leaders of the German atrocities during the war have set a new standard of war guilt and international justice."[44]

The North Carolina Baptist Convention

The delegates to the 1934 North Carolina Baptist Convention's annual meeting received just one paragraph on domestic race relations, focused on the lynching of African Americans. In the next section, the committee sought to situate the issue of non-domestic racism in the context of global geopolitics: "Nationalism, fear, suspicion, and race hatreds urge preparedness. . . . Believing that the complete acceptance and demonstration of the principles of Jesus and the cultivation of world brotherhood is the only means of assuring lasting peace, we advocate renunciation of war as a means of settling international disputes."[45] The "principles of Jesus" were the Baptist core convictions of freedom, democracy, soul liberty, respect for the personality of human beings, separation of church and state, and peacemaking.

North Carolina Baptists made this clear in 1936, in what can only be interpreted as a defense of "cardinal human rights" and a rebuke to both fascism and communism: "The body of liberty has become infected with the virus of greed, fear and lust for temporal power. Individuals, sects and nations, through ignorant expediency and armed force, are surrendering to totalitarianism. In numerous ways, tyranny is replacing democracy. Consequently, in large areas of the world it is assumed that the body, the mind and the soul of a man belong to the state rather than to him and to God."[46]

In the aftermath of Kristallnacht, the North Carolina convention's commitment to core Baptist principles provided the theological basis for the set of resolutions referencing the Jewish plight at the 1938 annual meeting. In the section on race relations, North Carolina Baptists stated: "The most flagrant expression of racial antipathy at the present time is found in the universal prejudice against the Jew and the terrible persecution now inflicted upon the Jews in Germany, Poland and other countries." They believed that "the gospel of our Lord and Savior Jesus Christ offers an adequate remedy for racial hate" and only through its acceptance "can we hope to see racial hatred disappear and to see all races living together in peace."[47]

The resolution's assertion that Jewish persecution in Germany was more "flagrant" than racial prejudice in the Jim Crow American South may have represented a temporary emotional response to Kristallnacht, an admission of the depth of the problem Jews faced, or denial on the part of the white Baptists. Following resolutions on lynching and freedom of religion, a resolution on "German Persecution" was approved in which they condemned "the present policy of the German Government which it pursues in relentless and inhuman persecution both of Christians and Jews on purely religious and racial grounds." Furthermore, they asked the American government to "modify the application" of immigration laws in order to "offer asylum to these persecuted and outraged people regardless of the immigration quotas fixed by statute."[48]

Tensions within the Baptist constituency were discernible behind both points of the resolution. The placement of Christians ahead of Jews seems insensitive so soon after Kristallnacht, but its elevation of the struggle of the German Confessing Church allayed concerns that Jews were receiving too much sympathy, to the exclusion of others; the committee's discomfort with this argument was expressed in the quote below. The openness to permitting the immigration of persecuted German Jews was not intended to signal criticism of restrictive American immigration policy; flexibility in the administration of existing regulations was all that was requested. Following a resolution on Rumania, the European refugee crisis was addressed again (containing only an indirect reference to Jews):

> THAT THE CHRISTIAN churches have a definite responsibility and a rare opportunity to act in the spirit of Jesus in caring for the castaways and refugees who wander hungry and hopeless through many lands. Among them are the seven hundred thousand persons in greater Germany, over half of them Christians—if that makes any difference; seventy thousand devotees of Democracy, Sudeten Germans who would not bow the knee to the dictator, now homeless in Czecho-Slovakia, other Czecho-Slovakians who will be homeless as Hitler tightens his grip on their land; threatened Baptists in Rumania; millions of hungry and homeless Chinese who must be fed until the harvest of 1939.[49]

Humanitarian concern was expressed in two ways at the 1943 convention. North Carolina Baptists were encouraged to provide generous humanitarian aid to allies, victims of the Nazis, and for "the Axis people as well, remembering the words of Jesus, 'If thine enemy hunger, feed him.'"[50] In a subsequent section on racial matters, no doubt influenced by the reports of Nazi concentration camps and the series of domestic riots in cities like Detroit, one of the strongest Southern Baptist protests against the Holocaust was penned:

> SINCE THE WAR began in Europe four years ago racial tensions have been acute, often blazing out in destructive ways. The treatment of Jews in many lands has been one of the most heinous crimes of history. Their utter extermination planned systematically by Nazi leaders must always call for vigorous condemnation by Christians. In this country riots between Negroes and whites in several cities are greatly deplored. The unwillingness on the part of many white people to accord Negroes full opportunity for growth in a genuine democracy, and the bitterness shown by some of the colored leaders in seeking to obtain rights denied them, are not in accord with Christian ideals for living together. The presence in this country of descendants of nations against whom we are fighting produces additional friction. In the first world war Germans, and those removed by one generation from the Fatherland, often were the objects of scorn and indifference. The bitterness expressed toward some of them at that time seems in this war to have been directed chiefly against the descendants of Japanese in the western part of the country, with the placing of a large part of the Japanese population in internment camps.[51]

In one dense paragraph, the plight of Jews in Europe, African Americans in the United States, and Japanese Americans on the west coast of the country became inextricably linked. Racial prejudice took numerous forms, but all failed the test of Christian convictions. The unequivocal condemnation of the Final Solution, noting the aim of the campaign was the systematic "extermination" of the Jewish people, was unique among Southern Baptist statements at the time. Ambivalence about white-black relations may be discerned, and the situation Japanese Americans found themselves in was most unfortunate. The committee, in response to the triune racial prejudice problem, offered specific suggestions for the Japanese and African American situations but was silent regarding how to respond to the Jews' plight:

> WE URGE UPON our people charity of feeling, that we may be able to avoid intolerance toward those of other races. Let us recognize the good in all races and in many of every nation, even as we recognize

> the undesirable in all peoples and in many of every nation. We intreat [*sic*] our people to try to learn the viewpoints of others, to temper their judgments with the attempt to put ourselves in their places, and to encourage the natural instinct of every people for freedom and self expression. We commend the move to take out of camps the interned Japanese, and place them in positions where they may pursue normal ways of living in our democracy. We endorse the efforts of some of our churches, and especially the W. M. U. of North Carolina, to assist our Negro brethren and sisters in following a worthy program of Christian activity, and express appreciation for the helpful conferences that have been conducted toward this end. We pray that our hearts may be free from all bigotry.[52]

The Georgia Baptist Convention

In 1938, the Social Service Commission of the Georgia Baptist Convention offered a fascinating critique of the situation the world was facing following Munich: "A temporary peace has been made with threatening dictators. A peace for which we are grateful, yet none can be proud. We are completely bewildered in the face of a broken league, a defeated collective security and a fading vision of disarmament." Christians should not be "indifferent to all these things, since we are concerned about the wholesomeness of personality and the health of society. Do something we must."

Just one week after Kristallnacht, Georgia Baptists took their own advice to heart and passed a resolution on Rumanian Baptists and added this message of concern for persecuted Jews: "The developments in the last few days in the renewed outbreak against the Jews leaves us appalled and speechless. We respectfully protest such discrimination and prejudice; for any man, anywhere, who is anti-Jewish in his acts or in his feelings, is at the same moment anti-Christian. Christianity, if it is real, must drive out of our hearts all prejudice and intolerance."[53]

In its repudiation of anti-Semitism, this statement affirmed that Jews and Christians must stand together in solidarity when either one was subjected to prejudice or hate. Implied as well was the point that one could not be a Nazi and a Christian at the same time. In 1939, the commission applied the 1938 stance on prejudice to the white majority culture's relationship with African Americans. To remain logically consistent, protesting against Jewish persecution in Europe necessitated an honest appraisal of the continuing struggle of African Americans to achieve social, political, and economic equality. The commission stated three basic principles to live by: "(1) The Fatherhood of God and the universal brotherhood of men; (2) The recognition of the principle of race; (3) The recognition that Christianity aims to bring each to the highest possible development. These races, and especially the Negroes, have been unjustly discriminated against."[54]

The struggle to achieve civil rights for African Americans in Georgia, and throughout the South, would not be easy. Although most of the Southern Baptist state conventions advocated equality and brotherhood in writing, the reality outside of the annual meetings was altogether different. Prejudice was widespread and strong among white Baptists, necessitating statements such as the one Georgia Baptists affirmed in 1946: "That all Christian people of Georgia, particularly Baptists, speak forth with every ounce of energy, by word, deed and thought, against the so-called patriotic groups which have so recently found birth upon the soil of our Southland; which same groups are both a counterpart of Nazi hate groups, preaching a so-called race-superiority, which is neither American nor Christian."[55] With this statement, Georgia Baptists reiterated what they had proclaimed after Kristallnacht. It was not possible to be anti-Semitic and Christian at the same time. In like manner, it was not consistent to be prejudiced against African Americans and claim to be a Christian. A racist had more in common with Nazi ideology than Baptist convictions.

The Mississippi Baptist Convention

Prior to its post-Kristallnacht convention, Mississippi Baptist annual meetings did not give attention to Jewish persecution in Germany or elsewhere. The 1938 state convention took place on November 14-17, 1938, and after passing a resolution on Rumanian Baptist persecution, the delegates registered their revulsion over Kristallnacht in a moving letter composed by J. D. Franks to German officials, including Joseph Goebbels:

> REPRESENTING 250,000 LIBERTY loving Christians, we, the Mississippi Baptist Convention, now in session in Jackson, Mississippi,

> respectfully submit to you our solemn protest against the renewed and intensified persecution of Jews in Germany.
>
> It is inconceivable to us how a great, cultured, historic people, such as the German people, could perpetuate or even tolerate the unjust, inhuman, un-Christian persecution, as have recently been reported in the American press, which your government now seems to be inflicting upon the Jews of Germany.
>
> Furthermore, we cannot understand how a responsible government could inflict horrible punishment and heavy penalties upon a highly respected race of people living within its own borders, in retaliation of a rash act committed by a lone, irresponsible, overwrought boy of the same race, living in another country. No system of civilized jurisprudence known to us could justify such retaliation.
>
> We join the Christian world in regretting and deploring the slaying of your esteemed citizen, Ernst Von Rath, German Embassy Secretary in Paris, by this misguided youth, but we must condemn as unwarranted and unjust the wholesale punishment of the Jews in Germany who had no part in instigating or executing this inexcusable crime and are therefore wholly innocent of it.
>
> Such a course as your government seems to be pursuing against the Jews of your country because of this act, we believe can only add fuel to the fires of international misunderstanding and discord that are already burning all too threateningly, and certainly cannot promote the cause of world peace.[56]

On December 8, 1938, the convention's newspaper, *The Baptist Record*, contrasted the high level of attention Kristallnacht was receiving to the lack of public interest in the Rumanian suppression of Baptists: "While the world is expressing proper sympathy for the Jews in Germany, there is little attention being paid to the Baptists in Rumania."[57] Two weeks later, Mrs. H. A. Waggoner opined that Christians should love the Jewish people because Jesus was a Jew, and accordingly, "the great wave of anti-Semiticism [*sic*] that is sweeping some of the European countries should cause the Lord's people to give themselves in prayer for them and seek untiringly their salvation."[58] The paper also quoted Jacob Gartenhaus's claim that "persecution of Jews in Europe is causing many of them to turn to the Lord; that in Czechoslovakia fifteen thousand of them are asking for baptism."[59]

Mississippi Baptists responded to Kristallnacht with an original appeal to Germany but did not revisit the issue of Jewish persecution in any subsequent convention. The Kristallnacht protest letter was filled with emotion but appeared naive in its political outlook and understanding of Nazi political calculations, intentions toward the Jews, and openness to criticism from other nations and religious bodies. The respectful tone and apparent faith in dialogue with Hitler's operatives created an impression that the Mississippi Baptists were confused by Kristallnacht, as if it were a surprising aberration and not completely in sync with German culture, which had by then become generally supportive of Nazi persecutions against Jews. Their letter, however, was noteworthy in that it represented one of the few Baptist protests to be directly sent to German officials.

The Tennessee Baptist Convention

W. Fred Kendall, a Southern Baptist leader and historian from Tennessee, observed that the resolutions of the Tennessee Baptist Convention "reflected many of the most serious and urgent current issues of the time." Prohibition, as in virtually every other state, dominated Southern Baptist attention, but other concerns also came to the fore from time to time: "Protest was made against the persecution of the Baptists in Rumania and of the Jews in Germany. Attention was called to the persecution of the Baptists in Russia, and prayer was asked for them through the year."[60] Prior to Kristallnacht, Tennessee Baptists periodically "expressed concern about military involvement"[61] in the looming war in Europe. They opposed the claims of nationalism, which asserted dominance over other aspects of life, such as religion, and encouraged racial prejudice: "Go anywhere in Europe today—in Nazi Germany, in Fascist Italy, in frightened France—and you find the radical nationalism which would make everything in the nation, including church and religion, subservient to the state."[62]

Jews were not specifically mentioned, but the reference to Nazi Germany in a paragraph mentioning race indicated that the Baptists had Jews, among other minorities, in mind. In 1936, the Temperance and Social Service Committee stated its preference for prophetic preaching—as opposed to warfare—to counteract the evils of nationalism and racism: "The sentiment of our country is at the present time predominantly against war. We can best keep it that way by keeping before the public the horrors, the tremendous cost, and the terrible aftermaths of war; and above all by cutting in two all covetousness, and selfishness, and racial and class prejudices, by means of the Sword of the Spirit."[63]

The 1938 convention took place on November 15-17, 1938, the week after Kristallnacht. Delegates created a special committee to compose protest resolutions in response to the "infringement of human rights by national governments, especially that by Rumania against Baptists and Germany against Jews and other religious minorities." Following the protest against Rumania, Tennessee Baptists expressed their view that Germany should respect the "fundamental human rights" of their Jewish citizens:

> THE TENNESSEE BAPTIST CONVENTION, in annual session assembled, representing a constituency of 375,000 white communicants, join millions of other American citizens in expressing indignation against the persecution by the German Government of Jews and other religious groups. We deplore the flagrant abridgment of human freedom and the anachronistic violation of fundamental human rights involved in all such persecution. We appeal to the Department of State of our government to use its good offices in whatever manner may be most effective in bringing the promptest end to such flagrant disregard of the rights of religious and racial minorities, and also to render whatever aid and comfort is possible to the distressed peoples of such minority groups.[64]

Tennessee Baptists hoped that their government would support the BWA's negotiating posture with the Rumanian government. Regarding Germany and the Jews, the form of "aid and comfort" to be provided was unspecified. Furthermore, Tennessee Baptists did not define a role for themselves; the protest was their sole response to the Jewish persecution, and the implementation of a solution was not their responsibility, having been referred to the State Department for subsequent action.

Following the war, Tennessee Baptists did see a role for themselves in response to the plight of displaced persons. Kendall summarized their concern and subsequent activity: "Tennessee participated in a program to aid displaced persons. . . . By 1950, when the project was completed, thirty-nine displaced persons have been sponsored by Tennessee Baptists."[65] Kendall did not indicate if any of the displaced persons welcomed by the Baptists of Tennessee were Jewish.

Conventions That Expressed Minimal Concern

While six state conventions responded with strong, or at least specific, statements following Kristallnacht, two other state conventions that met during the same time period, Kentucky and Oklahoma, were content to offer more minimal responses to Kristallnacht. Half of the state conventions of the Southern Baptist Convention did not explicitly address the issues of anti-Semitism, Nazi oppression, and the attempted extermination of the Jewish population of Europe. In differing ways, these bodies viewed the challenge of Hitler through non-Jewish-centered lenses. Some, like the Baptist Convention of Arizona, were content to pray about the world war and work to help innocent victims. In the sole resolution the Arizona Southern Baptists passed on the turmoil in Europe, they prayed for the end of the "horrible war in Europe, Japan's unholy 'undeclared' war on China, and, if it is within the present plan of God, to keep America out of the war." They also supported past President Herbert Hoover's proposal to "feed the starving women and children of occupied countries of Europe."[66]

In 1943, the Baptist Convention of New Mexico reluctantly embraced the US war effort, even though "the world's most destructive war" was "a low road, a bitter and costly road, a road of tears and blood." They did so because they saw "no future for the freedoms that we hold sacred in a world dominated by Nazism." Although the persecution of Jews under Nazism was never mentioned in the New Mexico *Annuals*, these Southern Baptists understood that racism was a significant cause and key dynamic of the Second World War: "Races are not natural enemies destined to rule or be ruled by one another as masters and servants. . . . Germany has clearly expressed the principle on which it proceeds, the principle of Germanic superiority over all other races and the right and duty of the superior race to dominate, subordinate, or exterminate the inferior race in securing its own power."

In this interpretation of the significance of the war and Hitler's racial ideology, the specific and particular Jewish struggle to survive under Nazism was not unique; Hitler was not warring solely against Jews but against "all other races." Thus, the argument continued, not with the clarion call to save the Jewish people but rather for humanity to end its "bitter race competition" and "usher in a new day of inter-racial cooperation for the common good with an abating race prejudice as between white and the colored races."[67]

Other Southern Baptist state conventions chose more sophisticated methodologies to deal with the conflict. Yet they all shared one thing in common—they ignored the specific plight of the Jewish people, and the consequence of this lack of concern was an inability to grasp fully the meaning and goals of Hitler's attempt to create a Third Reich that embodied Nazi ideals. It also closed off any possibility of providing essential aid and assistance to alleviate the sufferings of the Jewish people, six million of whom would not survive the war.

The General Association of Baptists in Kentucky

The General Association of Baptists in Kentucky[68] met in annual session on November 15-17, 1938, a week after Kristallnacht. The session endorsed resolutions on Baptist persecution in Rumania, and then Hoyt E. Porter offered a successful resolution, which offered "the deep sympathy of its members for all those religious and racial minorities that have suffered the loss of property or of civil rights because of religious loyalty or racial origin; whether in Soviet Union, the German Reich, Roumania, or other lands." Kentucky Baptists were then encouraged to "render worthy Christian service to all such people that we can reach."[69]

The *Western Recorder*, Kentucky's Baptist state newspaper, had been publishing occasional articles about the Nazi persecution of the Jews since 1934, even before the Berlin congress. Its editor declared in March 1934 that he "never had sympathy with the spirit that would persecute Jews."[70] Many of the articles were composed from an evangelical eschatological perspective[71] or were concerned with evangelization of the Jewish people within the United States.[72] Most of these articles adopted positive or benign attitudes toward Jews. From a prophetic standpoint, the Jews were God's covenant people. Evangelism was an expression of care, love, and friendship toward Jews. Some articles, however, expressed critical views about Jews.

In an editorial, "The Jew and the Persecution Complex," the editor admitted without any embarrassment:

> IF WE HAD the ear of the Jews, and thought it possible to get them to hear us dispassionately, we would suggest to them that in America any spirit that may exist among other racial strains of prejudice against Jews has been at least balanced measure for measure by equally unlovely elements in behaviour of the Jews themselves. For instance, the sense of racial solidarity and exclusiveness of the Jews has probably equaled any feeling existing among their Gentile compatriots that would lead them to discriminate against Jews.[73]

The line of argument was not uncommon. In the United States, the newspaper contended, Jews were at least partially to blame for the discrimination they had to endure. Furthermore, Jewish communal solidarity was troubling, no doubt because such exclusiveness was a hindrance to assimilation into the Protestant-dominated American social milieu. In Southern states such as Kentucky, Baptists were the dominant religious force within that Protestant majority.

Following Kristallnacht, the *Western Recorder* published an editorial, "Bitter Present Persecution of the Jews," in which Germany was criticized for persecuting not just Jews but also Christians: "The diabolical ruthlessness with which totalitarian Germany is at present persecuting the Jews has shocked the world. . . . Behold the nation whose philosophy poisoned Christian faith in America and other nations, now turned as a State policy to its one-time pagan gods, persecuting not Jews alone but in spirit and purpose all believers in the God who first of all revealed himself through the Jews." The Nazis' persecution of Jewry was relativized by placing it alongside the struggles of others.

In previous quotations, the comparison offered was between German Jews and Rumanian Baptists. To many Baptists, both persecutions should enjoy similar status. In this editorial, the real significance of the persecution of Jews was that the Nazi revolution ultimately aimed to overthrow Christianity. The real target of Hitler was not the Jewish people but Christians; the persecution of Jews was a means to an end, that being the paganization of German culture. The editorial recognized that the Jews were struggling across the continent: "Other nations in Europe were also persecuting the Jews bitterly. . . . Several millions are in lands which are now persecuting them. The diabolical fury of the Middle Ages against Jews is being enacted by boastful self-declared super-man civilizations." The editorial took comfort in the fact the United States was not among these foes of the Jews: "It is a matter of deep gratitude that there is, comparatively, a negligible fringe of this spirit in America."[74]

The Oklahoma Baptist Convention

The 1938 meeting of the Baptist General Convention of Oklahoma took place a week after Kristallnacht and focused in part on "world conditions." Pastor A. A. Duncan, while thanking the mayor of Shawnee for his welcome to the approximately twenty-three hundred attendees, proclaimed that "when persecution and racial hatred are found in the nations, I am happy to say that Baptists never persecuted and we stand unalterably against persecution. Things that are happening in Germany carry the world back to the Middle Ages. May the God of the nations put an end to the suffering of helpless people."

According to the Oklahoma Convention's *Baptist Messenger*, "At no time during the Convention could we forget the distress of millions around the world who are either being imprisoned for their faith as in Rumania, or exiled because of their race as in Germany, or suffering from the ravages of war as in China." Louis Hanna, a Southern Baptist missionary in Palestine, told the assembly, "National hate and religious bigotry are playing havoc in Palestine today. This condition is an offshoot of national hatred and religious bigotry in Europe."[75]

Oklahoma Baptists, accordingly, felt compelled to protest what was happening in Europe and elsewhere. On Wednesday, November 16, a motion was passed to empower a "special committee" whose task was "to prepare a resolution touching Religious Persecution," and J. W. Hodges (the motion's presenter), E. C. Routh (who reported on the convention for the *Baptist Messenger*), and W. R. White were drafted to serve.[76] The next evening, Hodges presented a motion that focused on the "most regrettable and vicious outbreaks of violence against various racial minorities and severe persecutions of other groups on religious grounds." It judged such persecution (and presumably Kristallnacht) as being "particularly reprehensible in the light of the teachings of Christ and of the New Testament" and condemned totalitarianism as being opposed to the Baptist core convictions, which included "freedom of speech, the principles of democracy and religious liberty—principles which Baptists have for 1900 years advocated, for which they have wrought, for which they sometimes have died."

In response, Oklahoma Baptists reaffirmed their "loyalty to the democracy of the New Testament" and their support of "freedom of conscience, of speech, and of Religious liberty." Furthermore, they forthrightly chose to "condemn this modern revival of oppression, of race hatred, and of religious persecution as undemocratic, unbaptistic, and anti-Christian."[77] Unfortunately, the resolution appeared to be more concerned with the totalitarian assault on Baptist core principles than with the suffering of the Jews of Germany; the latter played a secondary role, acting as confirmation that principles were being violated.

In contrast, the *Baptist Messenger* published an editorial on Kristallnacht in its November 17, 1938, issue, which specifically named Jews as the special victims of Kristallnacht:

> THE DAILY NEWSPAPERS are publishing the harrowing details of the persecution of the Jews by the German government. Nothing like this has happened in our time. . . . Concerning conditions in Germany we would make two observations: First, such a pogrom of persecution has elements of hate and anarchy which will sooner or later, disrupt and destroy any government which follows such a policy, and the dictators of Germany will inevitably reap what they are now sowing. Second . . . God has chastised the Jews through the centuries; but the Scriptures teach that they are a chosen people, and that the nations which persecute the Jews will pay the penalty therefor [*sic*].[78]

A subsequent editorial echoed a generally held Baptist belief about the Jews first offered in the above response to Kristallnacht. First, Germany's persecution of the Jews would fail, and if it persisted, the country's political leaders would be held accountable. The means by which the downfall would be achieved was mysterious, the implication being God would judge Germany and end the persecution of Jews. Furthermore, the Jews were still the "chosen people," and therefore any nation that persecuted them could not prosper; the Nazis would be "wrecked by their own policies." The *Baptist Messenger* expressed its horror over Kristallnacht in a level of detail that was uncommon for Baptist newspapers:

> THE ATROCITIES WHICH the Jews are suffering in Germany are almost unbelievable. Their money has been taken, their shops closed, their synagogues destroyed, their children shut out of schools, their attendance in places of public entertainment is forbidden, and now they are being herded into ghettos and treated like they are beasts. Under the domination of Hitler, Germany has reverted to the Dark Ages. One of the most disturbing facts in the world situation is the growth of anti-semitism throughout Europe and in some measure in other lands. It is impossible to forecast the outcome in Europe.[79]

Kristallnacht was not the conclusion of the Nazi campaign against the Jews but one step in a systemic line of attack. The *Baptist Messenger* may have sensed this when it worried over the spread of anti-Semitism beyond Germany's borders. Anti-Semitism was not to be restricted to Germany's prewar borders but was soon to spread throughout the European continent as Nazi troops conquered country after country.

The Baptist General Convention of Texas

It is impossible to chronicle the history of the Baptist General Convention of Texas without acknowledging the central leadership role that Rev. George W. Truett played. As the senior pastor of First Baptist Church in Dallas, one of the largest Baptist churches in the world at that time, Truett was a Southern Baptist state and national leader, and as a representative of the Southern Baptists, one of the major figures in the Baptist World Alliance.[80]

Having been elected president of the alliance at the 1934 Berlin congress, Truett returned to Texas and gave a "masterful address" on "Baptists and World Conditions" at the annual session.[81] In 1935, the convention heard from Jacob Gartenhaus on Jewish evangelism, and subsequently Truett "delivered a heart-stirring message on important matters of State and world interest at this time among Baptist people."[82] Echoing Truett, the Civic Righteousness Committee report gave implicit support to the German Confessing Church movement: "We do not believe in a totalitarian state which dictates to the churches, saying what is to be believed, and what is to be done. Neither do we believe that the state should be dominated by the church. As Baptists we believe in a free church in a free state."[83] Truett also spoke on "Baptists and the Present World Outlook" at the 1936 convention, and on the global Baptist missions work in 1937.[84]

By all accounts, Truett was considered to be a champion for liberty for all races, and for Jews specifically, as this sermon excerpt indicates:

> OH, THE PATHOS of the condition of the Jewish people in various countries and generations. The pathos of their condition now, if the newspapers are telling us one-tenth of the truth. O God, stretch forth Thy hand in Thine own way and bring to an end these inexpressible atrocities. Our Saviour was a Jew, and His mother was Jewish; the apostles were Jews, the great prophets were Jews. This great race of people, resourceful, forward looking and God-honored, have had atrocities heaped upon them throughout the world that are encugh to shock the angels, and every right-thinking nation and individual in the world should do all that is wise and worthy to put an end to such iniquity and indescribable atrocities.[85]

Nevertheless, between 1933 and 1937, Texas Baptists had not passed a resolution about German persecution of the Jews, even though Truett must have referred to the situation in these various speeches. The 1938 annual session met on November 8-11, 1938—as Kristallnacht was taking place. On Thursday evening, November 10, Truett, in his capacity as the BWA president, invited the Texas Baptists to attend the 1939 congress in Atlanta and spoke about Baptist persecution in Rumania. The minutes do not mention the night of the broken glass, and the Texans passed no resolutions of the subject, as they did on behalf of Rumanian Baptists.[86]

Why such silence? Perhaps Kristallnacht references were made by speakers but not recorded in the minutes. Or, it may be that the leaders were caught off guard by the unfolding tragedy and did not have consensus on how to respond spontaneously. However, they could not claim ignorance of what was taking place in Germany; Truett was well aware of what was transpiring in Europe, and the *Baptist Standard* previously had published an editorial on October 6, 1938, entitled "The Jews of Today." Focused mostly on the prospects of Jews settling in Palestine, it vividly described Jewish peril: "They are persecuted in many of the nations the world. In some nations the persecution is utterly heartless and cruel beyond belief. The condition appears to grow worse and the future darker rather than brighter in its prospect."[87]

The *Baptist Standard* published two editorials in reaction to Kristallnacht. In "Persecution of Jews Barbarous," the paper confessed that "language is poverty stricken to express the barbarity of persecution of Jews in Germany . . . one stands aghast at the barbarous acts of violence." It warned that "Germany will reap just punishment from such sowing of violence and robbery."[88] One week later, the second editorial decried the "German persecution of the Jews" and expressed a wish that "every Jew in the world would come to the United States."[89] As in other states, neither editorial pointed to any action approved or taken by the Baptist General Convention of Texas in support of Jews.

Regrettably, Texas Baptists remained effectively passive in subsequent years. In 1939, a nonspecific resolution was passed by the Woman's Missionary Union affirming that they believed in "racial and inter-racial equity."[90] In 1940, President J. Howard Williams noted, "In Germany and the other areas personal, academic, civil and religious liberty have been disappearing."[91] Similarly, convention secretary R. C. Campbell expressed antitotalitarian and pro-democracy views but did not specifically refer to the plight of Jews.[92]

The lack of identification with Jewish suffering under Nazism created a theological and political vacuum that permitted a new and alternative narrative to gain currency—that it was Christianity, and not Judaism, that was the central focus of Hitler's ire. In the 1940 Civic Righteousness report, J. B. Tidwell, a professor from Baylor University, asserted that the rise of totalitarian governments required that "the whole argument for a free church in a free state must be stated anew and Baptists must be in the front rank in this battle."[93] In 1941, convention President A. D. Foreman Sr. elevated the struggle to a new height, claiming that the rise of Nazi totalitarianism represented not just a political but rather a spiritual war of "Paganism against Christianity" in which the former was energized by Satan "to destroy Christianity."[94] In 1942, the Civic Righteousness report decried "pagan totalitarianism" and its "anti-Christian plans for the world."[95] The Nazi destruction of Jewish culture and religion was ignored.

Belatedly, the Woman's Missionary Union, at its annual meeting on November 9, 1943, passed a resolution that may be interpreted as containing an implicit reference to Jewish suffering. Notice the inclusion of the word *holocaust* in the resolution:

> BECAUSE ONE DICTATOR drew a line of racial superiority about himself and his people, and thus justified his aggression against other peoples, the world has experienced a holocaust, and baptism of blood, such as was never known before in history. Never would Christ have us forget that of one blood are all the nations of the earth, and that by His death on the cross, he broke down the inner wall of partition between the races. Racial prejudices belittle our profession of the belief in the brotherhood of man and the Fatherhood of God.[96]

Although Texas Baptists never passed a resolution about the Holocaust, they did engage in evangelistic ministry toward Jews. In 1944, A. C. Miller became the director of the Department of Interracial Cooperation, which conducted Jewish evangelism throughout Texas.[97] Miller denounced racial prejudice and acknowledged that "in the mind of the average gentile Christian there are unreasonable and unchristian animosities towards the Jew which make normal approach in Christian service impossible. It is of particular concern to many of us that a consistent Christian purpose shall motivate all our Baptist people with reference to these, our neighbors."[98]

In his 1947 report, Miller revisited the issue. After sections on Negroes, Japanese Americans, and Europeans, Miller devoted one-third of a page to Jews, once again emphasizing that fifty thousand Jews were "neighbors" of Texas Baptists:

> MORE THAN HALF of this number live in four Texas cities while 95 percent of them are found within sixteen [of] our Texas cities. Thus, we find them in the places where we have the best equipment in churches and in leadership. It is our opinion that we have employed about every method and plan for winning the Jew except the one used by Paul and

> the other missionaries of the first century. In our plans we set him apart and make him a distinctive person. This is the very thing the Jew of this day and America resents. . . . When we are willing to give up our preconceived notions about winning the Jew to Christ . . . we will be able to report more progress in the evangelization of the Jews.[99]

Miller's approach toward Jews ignored the trauma of the recent past that the Jewish people had experienced. Furthermore, Miller distanced himself from the evangelical prophecy movement, which highlighted the unique place of the Jewish people in human history as God's covenant people, and the Zionism that would lead to the reestablishment of Israel as a Jewish homeland a year later.

The Florida Baptist Convention

Florida Baptists, in concert with other Baptists throughout the United States, moved from a pro-war to a functionally pacifist stance following World War I. Historian E. Earl Joiner stated: "At first, Florida Baptists simply joined others in passing resolutions in favor of disarmament and of those political candidates who promised to work for disarmament. By the 1930's, however, Florida Baptists were readily approving statements opposing war rather categorically, statements indeed that bordered on pacifism."[100]

Like the Texas Baptists, the Baptists in Florida seemed unwilling to express explicit solidarity with persecuted Jews in Europe. At the January 1935 annual meeting, Rev. C. M. Brittain, the secretary of the Florida Baptists, gave a report on the Baptist World Congress in Berlin. Sounding more like a tourist than a denominational leader, Brittain said nothing about the racialism resolution or Jewish persecution in Germany, preferring instead to praise Germany: "The German people and Government officials did everything in their power to make our stay pleasant and the meetings profitable."[101]

Nevertheless, the Florida Baptist Convention was well prepared to address Kristallnacht. In September 1938, the *Florida Baptist Witness* newspaper published an article by Stetson University professor Plautus I. Lipsey Jr. He labeled the swastika a "symbol of tyrannical racial bigotry" and dramatized the pervasiveness of Nazi anti-Semitism: "Of course the indications of Jew-hating are seen everywhere. Jewish shops are marked with insults. Placards are everywhere, telling the Jews they are not wanted, that they must not enter, that they must stay away."[102] On December 1, 1938, the newspaper printed the text of a Kristallnacht resolution passed by the Baptist Pastors' Conference of Knoxville, Tennessee, precipitated by "recurrent atrocities committed against the Jews by great totalitarian powers, especially Germany." The paper quoted the resolution, which expressed "indignation at those horrible acts of inhuman injustice against the Jews, and all such acts of inhumanity to man."[103] The following week, the *Florida Baptist Witness* reprinted the *Alabama Baptist*'s editorial on German Jewish and Rumanian Baptist persecutions.[104]

Therefore, it would be a reasonable expectation that Kristallnacht would receive attention at the January 1939 annual meeting. Florida Baptists met from January 18-20, 1939, in West Palm Beach. However, the Committee on Social Service addressed the issue of morality and government without mentioning the Nazi persecution of Jews: "As Christian people, believing in the brotherhood of man, and in the universal application and sufficiency of our Gospel, we cannot always be indifferent to the decisions of governments of other nations or the welfare of other people." The committee accordingly expressed concern about "the growing power and aggression of dictators in totalitarian states where these very essentials of a free church and a free state are not only denied to their people, but are seriously threatened for all people throughout the world as the dictators reach out for one after another of the weaker nations in their mad scramble for the physical and political mastery of our modern world." In spite of the expansionist nature of the Nazi government, the committee still affirmed that they were "against war."[105]

At the 1940 meeting, Florida Baptists initially tabled but later passed resolutions sympathizing with the Finnish people, who had been invaded by the Soviet Union, protesting the shipment of war materials to Japan in light of its invasion of China, and disagreeing with the appointment of Myron Taylor as US representative to the Vatican (a commonly held Baptist position).[106] The Social Service Commission opposed "an extreme nationalism, resulting in race hatred and economic wars and boycotts," and even though the Finns were mentioned again, and Germany was criticized for its aggression against Czechoslovakia and Austria, Jewish persecution was not mentioned by name.[107]

Similarly, in 1941 the commission refrained from mentioning Jews even as it named Nazis as opponents of soul freedom and racial justice:

> THE GERMAN NATIONAL Socialist and the Italian Fascist and the Russian Communist—each deny that man as an individual is important, and attempt to assert that the welfare of the state is far more important than the welfare of any individual. It is thus easy to see that the teachings of these totalitarian systems are entirely incompatible with Baptist principles of the importance of the individual, and we can easily understand why many Baptists in these lands have preferred the concentration camp to consenting to an enslaved mind and soul.[108]

The commission reiterated its support for persecuted German Christians: "Reports from Germany tell of a great number of Christians confined in concentration camps because of their refusal to subscribe to the totalitarian scheme of life there." Ironically, German Baptists preferred submission to the Nazi totalitarian state, and few of them were confined to concentration camps. Meanwhile, German Jews, who had no such choice, were not mentioned as victims. In the single reference to a Jew—"Albert Einstein, Jewish Agnostic"—the focus was on Christian opposition to Hitler, not Jewish suffering.[109]

The Baptist General Association of Virginia

The Baptist General Association of Virginia began the period of Hitler's growing dominance over Europe by expressing its aversion to war, based on the experiences of World War I. In 1933, the Temperance–Social Service Committee proclaimed to "the world our renunciation of war."[110] In 1936, the same committee feared that events in Europe and Asia were leading nations toward renewed military conflict. It warned against giving in to war propaganda because those who did so in World War I "were victims of a cruel and selfish enterprise and a devilish hoax."[111]

The 1938 meeting took place on November 8-10, 1938, at the same time as Kristallnacht. On day one, the president of the convention, F. W. Boatwright, cited Hitler and Mussolini as examples of "rulers and statesmen" who were paying keen attention to youth.[112] A resolution on Rumania was adopted, but there was no corresponding one about German Jewish oppression.[113] The state convention's newspaper, *The Religious Herald*, posted an editorial questioning whether democracies should cooperate with Hitler in light of post-Munich incidents. The editor stated that cooperation depended upon trust and then observed: "It is hard indeed to ascribe to Mr. Hitler and his Nazi comrades any moral principles while they engage in the senseless persecution of German Jews. The civilized world is stirred again by these atrocities probably because such extreme acts cause even the most hopeful to lose hope."[114]

In his presidential address for 1939, Boatwright referred to persecutions of Christians in Rumania, Russia, and Germany but refrained from mentioning Jewish suffering.[115] The Committee on Inter-Racial Relations did focus briefly on Jews, but only in terms of domestic anti-Semitism and evangelism:

> WE ARE SURE that the members of our General Association would oppose any condition which would add to the barrier already existing between the Jews and the Savior whom we serve. If educational institutions discourage the entrance of Jews because they belong to that race; if hotels limit their hospitality to Gentile guests; if social clubs blackball Jewish applicants, we want to make it known that the Baptists of Virginia are not in sympathy with such anti-Christian, anti-American policies. We owe much to the Jew. We should like to discharge that obligation by clearing away every barrier which separates our Jewish citizens from the best that America has to offer. This best gift we believe to be salvation through Jesus Christ.[116]

The closest Virginia Baptists ever came to acknowledging Jewish persecution came in 1943, when the World Conditions Committee addressed the "reappraisal of human worth." However, the text did not contain a specific reference to Jews and may in fact have referred only to the global set of races: "We shall continue to work for better understanding between races."[117] The context of this section (human worth) reminds one of the Baptist conviction of personality, which in fact was explicitly invoked in the presidential address of 1944: "This whole world conflict centers around the interpretation of personality, the dignity and worth of the individual. That is the fundamental issue in the war between the democratic nations and the totalitarian states."[118]

The Maryland Baptist Union Association

In the early 1930s, the Maryland Baptist Union Association focused on its evangelistic mandate toward "Foreigners, Jews and Negroes in our Association territory."[119] The 1934 Social Service Committee report stated that "the problems that engage the Christian conscience" revolved around "race, war and economic justice."[120] In 1936, the committee believed that it made little sense to "condemn Communism and Fascism, social principles that are vital in the world today, but we must show that it is possible to apply Christian principles to our economic and social problems with better results."[121]

As tensions mounted in Europe and Asia, the committee expressed frustration that Christians could not achieve consensus "against war, race hatreds, economic injustice and other socially destructive forces." It also noted that among Christians, "race consciousness varies all the way from arrogant superiority to a genuine respect and Christian affection for people of all races. . . . The moral and spiritual chaos of the secular world finds its counterpart within the world community of Christians."[122]

The 1938 annual session took place on October 19-21, almost a month before Kristallnacht, and produced a resolution on Rumanian Baptist persecution.[123] *The Maryland Baptist* newspaper, a monthly, did not cover Kristallnacht. The Social Service Committee did not cite Jewish persecution in its attack on bigotry, but it did warn of the possibility of persecution against Baptists: "Once more the old bogies of bigotry, intolerance and racial prejudice raise their frightful heads. . . . We, of all people, should share in spirit the unfortunate lot of persecuted minorities. Likewise, we should heed the words of one of our great denominational leaders when he warns that within his lifetime we Baptists may again suffer persecution."[124]

As war loomed over the horizon for the United States, the 1941 annual session of the Maryland Baptist Union Association approved the report of the Committee on Social Service, which opposed racism and perhaps discreetly addressed the plight of European Jews: "The international situation is most ominous. We are utterly opposed to the pagan conceptions of the supremacy of the state over all phases of human life, the subordination and the suppression of the individual, the superiority of a single race or nation. . . . We believe, therefore, the Christian should cooperate, so far as possible, with the democratic forces of the world which are trying to stave off the enslavement of the human race."[125]

The Arkansas Baptist State Convention

Baptist historian E. Glenn Hinson accurately summarizes the political and social outlook of the Arkansas Baptist state convention in his history of the state convention. In the 1930s, temperance and gambling were dominant concerns.[126] From 1939 through 1948, Arkansas Baptists were concerned about racial issues, but the war made other priorities less urgent: "Save for concern expressed in 1943 about 'racial prejudice' toward Japanese internees of 'Relocation Centers,' Convention ethics committees did not refer to racial injustice; it was a problem which had receded into the background."[127]

Throughout the entire period, Arkansas Baptists expressed no convictions regarding Jewish persecution. In 1937, the Temperance and Social Service Committee spoke against communism, and in 1938, the convention passed the Rumanian Baptist resolution without making mention of Kristallnacht, which had taken place four weeks earlier.[128] Arkansas Baptists did express their desire that "help be given to the unfortunate of Europe in danger from want and hunger,"[129] but Jews were not expressly the objects of such aid; starving European war victims were asking for this.

Even though news about Nazi concentration camps was public knowledge, Arkansas Baptists in November 1942 looked west and spoke on behalf of Japanese Americans: "With the coming of the Japanese Colonies race prejudice again crops out and it is well for us to hear again the admonition of the great Apostle, 'Let this mind be in you which was also in Christ Jesus.'"[130]

The Louisiana Baptist Convention

With the spiritual and political influence of M. E. Dodd dominating Louisiana's Southern Baptist life, it is not surprising that this state convention did not take a clear stand in solidarity with the Jews of Europe. In 1936, the state missions report scolded the fellowship for "doing nothing in an organized way" for "Bohemians, Indians, Jews, Chinese, the Black People, etc."[131] Despite meeting a week after Kristallnacht, the Louisiana Baptists could only muster a weak protest against the "growth of 'Isms'" in which fascism is named, but communism received the bulk of its criticism.[132]

The Louisiana Baptist Convention finally addressed the issue of racism in 1944. Jews were mentioned in passing ("We believe in liberty and justice for all and that every man whether Jew, Gentile, white or black . . ."), but the focus of the statement was on prejudice against African Americans. They counseled their constituents to "do everything possible . . . for the defense and protection of all the civil rights of the race."[133]

The Illinois Baptist State Association

The 1938 annual session of the Illinois Baptist State Association[134] took place on November 1-3, one week before Kristallnacht. The delegates passed a short version of the Baptist Persecution in Rumania resolution.[135] Southern Baptists in Illinois never passed a single resolution on Jewish persecution between 1933 and 1948. They did pass a resolution promoting religious liberty for Baptists in the formerly fascist Italy.[136]

Following Kristallnacht, *The Illinois Baptist* newspaper published a set of three editorials under the rubric of "Appalling Situations" ("The Jews of Germany," "The Suffering Chinese," and "Baptists in Rumania"). The editorial clearly was sympathetic to the predicament of the oppressed German Jews:

> DAILY, THE FRONT pages of metropolitan newspapers tell us of the atrocious treatment of the Jews in Germany. Because of the killing of a German diplomat in Paris by a Polish Jew, just a boy, the German nation finds excuse to bring great suffering and humiliation to the Jews. Of course, it requires no bravery for the German government to proceed with these most violent actions. It requires no courage to plunder and persecute a helpless people. The Jews are at the mercy of Germany and it seems that Germany knows no mercy. Against the total Jewish people a fine has been levied and individuals have been fined up to $60,000. It is difficult to see what is in store for these poor unfortunate Hebrew people in Germany.[137]

In its December 30, 1938, issue, *The Illinois Baptist* published the BWA's Kristallnacht response, which restated the 1934 resolution from the Berlin congress. The BWA called upon "constituent bodies" to "take steps to furnish all possible assistance to those who are the victims of anti-Semitic action."[138]

The Illinois Baptist State Association's lack of support for persecuted Jews was somewhat surprising considering the commitment of the Illinois Baptists to evangelistic ministries for Jews in their state. Jacob Gartenhaus, who consistently raised the issue of Jewish suffering and anti-Semitism in countless articles and messages, spoke at the 1943 meeting, and it is difficult to imagine that he would refrain from raising such issues as revelations about concentration camps that were circulating throughout the country.[139] Southern Baptists in Illinois, through the Woman's Missionary Union, devoted considerable energy to Jewish evangelism and even called Mrs. Irene Hanley to serve as W.M.U. Missionary to the Jews.[140]

Notes

1. Minutes of the *1934 Annual Session of the Missouri Baptist General Association*, Temperance and Social Service Committee Report, Race Relations, 168.

2. Minutes of the *1937 Annual Session of the Missouri Baptist General Association*, Resolutions Committee Report, Resolution 3—Race Relations, 205–6.

3. Minutes of the *1938 Annual Session of the Missouri Baptist General Association*, Resolutions Committee Report, Resolution III—Race Relations, 217. The state convention's newspaper reprinted the resolutions report without further comment; see "Report of Committee on Resolutions," *The Word and Way* (3 November 1938), 11.

4. In chess, a player is in *Zugzwang* when the player has no good move to make, and so any move made will weaken one's position. The player must make a move, but there are no positive choices. This aptly described the position of the Jewish populations under Hitler's persecution.

5. E. Gobold, "On the Fly" column, *The Word and Way* (24 November 1938), 6. Gobold then warned Missouri Baptists against giving to Jewish Christian evangelists who were not connected to the denomination and endorsed the ministry of Jacob Gartenhaus. Gobold repeated his warnings about non-SBC Jewish Christian evangelists in his column two weeks later; see "On the Fly" column, *The Word and Way* (8 December 1938), 6.

6. Editorial, "Humanity Outraged," *The Word and Way* (1 December 1938), 4.

7. Editorial, "Christianity for the Jews," *The Word and Way* (15 December 1938), 4.

8. Minutes of the *1943 Annual Session of the Missouri Baptist General Association*, Temperance and Social Service Committee Report, Section IV—Interracial Problems, 141–42.

9. Ibid., 142.

10. Minutes of the *1944 Annual Session of the Missouri Baptist General Association*, Temperance and Social Service Committee Report, Race Relations, 154.

11. Joe M. King, *A History of South Carolina Baptists* (Columbia: General Board of The South Carolina Baptist Convention, 1964), 62–65.

12. Goldring/Woldenberg Institute of Southern Jewish Life website, Encyclopedia of Southern Jewish Communities—Charleston, South Carolina, http://www.isjl.org/south-carolina-charleston-encyclopedia.html, accessed 31 December 2015. The Jewish Historical Society's website states, "Charleston, South Carolina, was one of a handful of port cities where the early years of American Jewish history were played out. Jewish immigrants began arriving in the colonial capital as early as the 1690s, drawn by the promise of economic opportunity and the town's reputation for religious freedom. As late as 1820, Charleston was home to the

largest Jewish community in the United States." http://jhssc.org/charleston-history-2/, accessed 31 December 2015.

13. Minutes of the *1935 Annual Session of the State Convention of the Baptist Denomination of South Carolina*, Commission on Social Service Report, "War and Peace," 140.

14. Minutes of the *1938 Annual Session of the State Convention of the Baptist Denomination of South Carolina*, Commission on Social Service Report, 121–22.

15. Editorials, "A Jewish Error," "Hitler's Inconsistency," and "Efforts in Behalf of Peace," in *The Baptist Courier* (22 September 1938), 2–3.

16. "Religious Repression in Rumania Protest and Appeal," *The Baptist Courier* (17 November 1938), 1; "Convention News," *The Baptist Courier* (24 November 1938), 23.

17. Editorial, "Suffering in Czechoslovakia," *The Baptist Courier* (1 December 1938), 2; "How Many Baptists in Germany?" 4; "Report on Social Service," 15.

18. Minutes of the *1939 Annual Session of the State Convention of the Baptist Denomination of South Carolina*, Commission on Social Service Report, 122; Minutes of the *1940 Annual Session of the State Convention of the Baptist Denomination of South Carolina*, Commission on Social Service Report, 170–73, 184–87.

19. Minutes of the *1941 Annual Session of the State Convention of the Baptist Denomination of South Carolina*, Commission on Social Service Report, 120–21, 136.

20. Minutes of the *1943 Annual Session of the State Convention of the Baptist Denomination of South Carolina*, Commission on Social Service Report, "Freedom of Speech," 123.

21. Ibid., Commission on Social Service Report, "Freedom of Religion," 125–26.

22. Ibid., 127.

23. Minutes of the *1944 Annual Session of the State Convention of the Baptist Denomination of South Carolina*, Commission on Social Service Report, "Race Relations," 138.

24. Minutes of the *1945 Annual Session of the State Convention of the Baptist Denomination of South Carolina*, Commission on Social Service Report, 135.

25. Minutes of the *1946 Annual Session of the State Convention of the Baptist Denomination of South Carolina*, Commission on Social Service Report, 14.

26. Dan J. Puckett, *In the Shadow of Hitler: Alabama's Jews, the Second World War, and the Holocaust* (Tuscaloosa: University of Alabama Press, 2014), 76.

27. Ibid., 117. See also Wayne Flynt, *Alabama Baptists: Southern Baptists in the Heart of Dixie*, Religion and American Culture (Tuscaloosa: University of Alabama Press, 1998), 397–98.

28. *Annual of the 1933 Alabama Baptist State Convention*, Committee on Social Conditions and Service Report, 27.

29. Ibid., Committee on Social Service Report, 50.

30. Charles F. Leek, "Watching the World" column, *The Alabama Baptist* (8 September 1938), 4.

31. Editorial, "Fearful Persecutions," *The Alabama Baptist* (20 October 1938), 3.

32. *Annual of the 1938 Alabama Baptist State Convention*, Minutes Item 23, 55. See Puckett, *In the Shadow of Hitler*, 38–39; 247 cites coverage from the *Birmingham News*: "Baptists May Rap Jews' Persecution" (16 November 1938), 5; and "Alabama Baptists Condemn Nazis, War" (17 November 1938), 22.

33. Alfred J. Dickinson Jr., "A Militant Christianity and a Terrorized World," *The Alabama Baptist* (17 November 1938), 1, 9.

34. *Annual of the 1938 Alabama Baptist State Convention*, Minutes Item 24, 55.

35. Ibid., Report of Social Service Commission, 110.

36. Ibid., 112. The report was reprinted, including the Jewish resolution, in *The Alabama Baptist* (1 December 1938), 1, 9.

37. *Annual of the 1938 Alabama Baptist State Convention*, Report of Social Service Commission, 113.

38. "Proceedings of the Alabama Baptist State Convention," *The Alabama Baptist* (24 November 1938), 5.

39. Charles F. Leek, "Watching the World" column, *The Alabama Baptist* (17 November 1938), 4.

40. Charles F. Leek, "Watching the World" column, *The Alabama Baptist* (24 November 1938), 4. Leonard Dinnerstein comments: "After *Kristallnacht* in 1938, when Germans went

on a rampage against Jews in their country, *The Alabama Baptist* opined, 'While we are not party to Jewish persecutions, we believe this era of persecution can be used as an opportunity to preach repentance to Israel,'" in *Antisemitism in America* (New York: Oxford University Press, 1995), 111.

41. *Annual of the 1939 Alabama Baptist State Convention,* Report of Social Service Commission, 101–2.

42. *Annual of the 1941 Alabama Baptist State Convention,* Report of Social Service Commission, 147.

43. *Annual of the 1942 Alabama Baptist State Convention,* Report of Social Service Commission, 106.

44. *Annual of the 1946 Alabama Baptist State Convention,* Report of Social Service Commission, 87.

45. *Annual of the 1934 North Carolina Baptist State Convention*, Committee on Social Service and Civic Righteousness Report, 44.

46. *Annual of the 1936 North Carolina Baptist State Convention*, Committee on Social Service and Civic Righteousness Report, "Freedom," 48.

47. *Annual of the 1938 North Carolina Baptist State Convention*, Committee on Social Service and Civic Righteousness Report, Resolution I—"Concerning Race Relations," 37.

48. Ibid., Resolution IV—"German Persecution," 38.

49. Ibid., Resolution VI—"World Refugees," 39.

50. *Annual of the 1943 North Carolina Baptist State Convention*, Committee on Social Service and Civic Righteousness Report, Section II—"Present Humanitarian Calls," 32.

51. Ibid., Section IV—"Racial Matters," par. 1, 34.

52. Ibid., par. 2, 34.

53. *Minutes of the 1938 Baptist Convention of the State of Georgia*, Social Service Commission Report, "War" and "What Can We Do About War?" 33–34.

54. *Minutes of the 1939 Baptist Convention of the State of Georgia*, Social Service Commission Report, "The Race Question," 45.

55. *Minutes of the 1946 Baptist Convention of the State of Georgia*, Social Service Commission Report, 38.

56. "Resolution of Protest against the Persecution of the Jews in Germany," *Proceedings of the 1938 Annual Session of the Mississippi Baptist Convention*, 51–52. J. D. Franks was the pastor of First Baptist Church in Columbus, Mississippi. He represented Mississippi on the Southern Baptist Foreign Mission Board; see *Proceedings of the 1939 Annual Session of the Mississippi Baptist Convention*, 47.

57. "Sparks and Splinters," *The Baptist Record* (8 December 1938), 2.

58. H. A. Waggoner, "God's Unspeakable Gift, a Jew," *The Baptist Record* (22 December 1938), 15.

59. *The Baptist Record* (22 December 1938), 6.

60. W. Fred Kendall, *A History of the Tennessee Baptist Convention* (Brentwood: Executive Board of the Tennessee Baptist Convention, 1974), 251.

61. Ibid., 448; see 448–51 for an overview of Tennessee Baptists' views on World War II.

62. *Minutes of the Tennessee Baptist Convention 1934 Annual Session*, Christian Education Committee Report, 32.

63. *Minutes of the Tennessee Baptist Convention 1936 Annual Session*, Temperance and Social Service Committee Report, Section IV, War, 31.

64. *Minutes of the Tennessee Baptist Convention 1938 Annual Session*, 79 (capital letters in original text); see also the state's *Baptist and Reflector* newspaper (24 November 1938), 5.

65. Kendall, *History of the Tennessee Baptist Convention*, 271. The text of the 1947 resolution can be found in *Minutes of the Tennessee Baptist Convention 1947 Annual Session*, 107.

66. *1941 Annual of the Annual Session of the Baptist General Convention of Arizona*, Social Service Committee Report, 12.

67. *1943 New Mexico Baptist Annual of the Baptist Convention of New Mexico*, Social Service Report, 36–38.

68. For an overview of the history of Kentucky Baptists, see Frank M. Masters, *A History of Baptists in Kentucky* (Louisville: Kentucky Baptist Historical Society, 1953); and Leo

Taylor Crismon, ed., *Baptists in Kentucky, 1776–1976, a Bicentennial Volume* (Middletown: Kentucky Baptist Convention, 1975). Neither history provides any coverage of the Kentucky Baptists and the Jews.

69. *Proceedings of the 1938 General Association of Baptists in Kentucky*, Minutes, 53–55, 71.

70. Editorial, "The Inevitable Jew," *Western Recorder* (29 March 1934), 7.

71. See "The Jew in Prophecy and Its Fulfillment," *Western Recorder* (19 April 1934), 10.

72. See "Christians Cannot Forsake Christ to Please Jews," *Western Recorder* (13 April 1939), 10–11.

73. Editorial, "The Jew and the Persecution Complex," *Western Recorder* (26 April 1934), 8.

74. Editorial, "Bitter Present Persecution of the Jews," *Western Recorder* (8 December 1938), 8.

75. E. C. Routh, "The Convention," *Baptist Messenger* (24 November 1938), 1, 5, 17.

76. *Minutes of the 1938 Annual Convention of the Baptist General Convention of Oklahoma*, Minutes Item 111, 57.

77. Ibid., Minutes Item 124, 65.

78. Editorial, "Germany and the Jews," *Baptist Messenger* (17 November 1938), 3.

79. Editorial, "World Conditions," *Baptist Messenger* (8 December 1938), 3.

80. See Powhatan James, *George W. Truett: A Biography* (Nashville: Broadman, 1945). A more scholarly and historically sophisticated history was written by Keith E. Durso, *Thy Will Be Done: A Biography of George W. Truett* (Macon, GA: Mercer University Press, 2009). See also Harry Leon McBeth, *Texas Baptists: A Sesquicentennial History* (Dallas: Baptistway Press, 1998).

81. *Annual of the 1934 Annual Session of the Baptist General Convention of Texas*, Minutes, 23.

82. *Annual of the 1935 Annual Session of the Baptist General Convention of Texas*, Minutes, 18–19.

83. Ibid., Civic Righteousness Report, 143.

84. *Annual of the 1936 Annual Session of the Baptist General Convention of Texas*, Minutes, 18; *Annual of the 1937 Annual Session of the Baptist General Convention of Texas*, Minutes, 15.

85. George W. Truett, "The Privilege and Peril of Opportunity," in *The Prophet's Mantle* (Grand Rapids, MI: Baker Book House, 1948), 136.

86. *Annual of the 1938 Annual Session of the Baptist General Convention of Texas*, Minutes, 21–22; the full text of the Rumanian resolution can be found on 159–60. The journalistic voice of the Texas Baptists, the *Baptist Standard*, had highlighted the Rumanian situation before the annual meeting in the following issues: (29 September 1938), 1, and (24 November 1938), 2.

87. Editorial, "The Jews of Today," *Baptist Standard* (6 October 1938), 3.

88. Editorial, "Persecution of Jews Barbarous," *Baptist Standard* (24 November 1938), 3.

89. Editorial, "The Destiny of the Jews," *Baptist Standard* (1 December 1938), 3.

90. *Annual of the 1939 Annual Session of the Baptist General Convention of Texas*, Woman's Missionary Union Meeting Minutes, 65.

91. *Annual of the 1940 Annual Session of the Baptist General Convention of Texas*, President's Address, 21.

92. Ibid., Executive Board Report, 64.

93. Ibid., Civic Righteousness Report, 160.

94. *Annual of the 1941 Annual Session of the Baptist General Convention of Texas*, President's Address, 22–23.

95. *Annual of the 1942 Annual Session of the Baptist General Convention of Texas*, Civic Righteousness Report, 207.

96. *Annual of the 1943 Annual Session of the Baptist General Convention of Texas*, Woman's Missionary Union Meeting Minutes, 40–41.

97. *Annual of the 1944 Annual Session of the Baptist General Convention of Texas*, Department of Interracial Cooperation Report, 187–88; see also McBeth, *Texas Baptists*, 205, 245.

98. *Annual of the 1945 Annual Session of the Baptist General Convention of Texas*, Department of Interracial Cooperation Report, 193. Miller mentioned Jews in passing in his 1946 report as well; see *Annual of the 1946 Annual Session of the Baptist General Convention of Texas*, Department of Interracial Cooperation Report, 174–76.

99. *Annual of the 1947 Annual Session of the Baptist General Convention of Texas*, Department of Interracial Cooperation Report, 199–200.

100. E. Earl Joiner, *A History of Florida Baptists* (Jacksonville, FL: Convention Press, 1972), 165.

101. *Florida Baptist Annual 1935*, Secretary's Report, 22.

102. Plautus I. Lipsey Jr., "Looking at the World," *Florida Baptist Witness* (8 September 1938), 7.

103. "Resolutions Passed by Baptist Pastors' Conference of Knoxville, Tennessee, November 21, 1938," *Florida Baptist Witness* (1 December 1938), 14. The next resolution called for Jews to consider the claims of Jesus as Messiah.

104. "The International Situation and Persecutions," *Florida Baptist Witness* (8 December 1938), 11.

105. *Florida Baptist Annual 1939*, Committee on Social Service Report, 126–27.

106. *Florida Baptist Annual 1940*, Minutes of Meeting, 32–33. American Baptists opposed Taylor's appointment as a violation of the separation of church and state.

107. Ibid., Social Service Commission Report, 127–28.

108. *Florida Baptist Annual 1940*, Temperance and Social Service Commission Report, 133–34.

109. Ibid., 134.

110. *1933 Baptist General Association of Virginia Annual*, Temperance–Social Service Committee Report, 147.

111. *1936 Baptist General Association of Virginia Annual*, Temperance–Social Service Committee Report, 52–53.

112. *1938 Baptist General Association of Virginia Annual*, Address of President, 19–20.

113. Ibid., Resolution with Reference to Baptist Persecution in Rumania, 89–91.

114. Editorial, "Think of the End," *The Religious Herald* (17 November 1938), 10–11. In its 1 December 1938 edition, the paper also printed a brief article about President Franklin Delano Roosevelt's response to Kristallnacht (8).

115. *1939 Baptist General Association of Virginia Annual*, Address of President, 24.

116. Ibid., Report of the Committee on Inter-Racial Relationships, 88.

117. *1943 Baptist General Association of Virginia Annual*, World Conditions Committee Report, Section 3—Reappraisal of Human Worth, 98. The original statement came from the Foreign Missions Conference.

118. *1944 Baptist General Association of Virginia Annual*, Address of President, 37.

119. Minutes of the *1933 Session of the Maryland Baptist Union Association*, State Missions Report, 33; see also *Minutes of the 1934 Session of the Maryland Baptist Union Association*, State Missions Report, 21.

120. *Minutes of the 1934 Session of the Maryland Baptist Union Association*, Social Service Committee Report, 37.

121. *Minutes of the 1936 Session of the Maryland Baptist Union Association*, Social Service Committee Report, 34.

122. *Minutes of the 1937 Session of the Maryland Baptist Union Association*, Social Service Committee Report, 40.

123. *Minutes of the 1938 Session of the Maryland Baptist Union Association*, 50.

124. *Minutes of the 1939 Session of the Maryland Baptist Union Association*, Social Service Committee Report, 43.

125. *Minutes of the 1941 Session of the Maryland Baptist Union Association*, Social Service Committee Report, 38–39.

126. E. Glenn Hinson, *A History of Baptists in Arkansas, 1818–1978* (Little Rock: Arkansas Baptist State Convention, 1979), 284–86.

127. Ibid., 308; see also 289.

128. *Proceedings of the 1937 Arkansas Baptist State Convention*, Report on Temperance and Social Service, 74–75; Resolutions Committee, 81–82.

129. *Proceedings of the 1941 Arkansas Baptist State Convention*, Resolutions Committee, 84.

130. Ibid., Social Service Committee Report, 93.

131. *Annual of the 1936 Louisiana Baptist Convention*, Report on State Missions, 41.

132. *Annual of the 1938 Louisiana Baptist Convention*, Report on Social Service, 37.

133. *Annual of the 1944 Louisiana Baptist Convention*, Report on Social Service, 39–40.

134. See Lamire Holden Moore, *The History of Southern Baptists in Ohio* (Nashville: Bensen Printing Company, 1957). He makes no mention of the Illinois association's views on anti-Semitism, persecution, or Jews.

135. *1938 Annual Session of the Illinois Baptist State Association*, Resolutions, 34.

136. *1945 Annual Session of the Illinois Baptist State Association*, Resolution VII, 64.

137. Editorial, "The Jews in Germany," *The Illinois Baptist* (18 November 1938), 4.

138. "Baptist World Alliance and Anti-Semitism," *The Illinois Baptist* (30 December 1938), 6.

139. *1943 Annual Session of the Illinois Baptist State Association*, Minutes, 18. The minutes indicated that Gartenhaus's message "was a high point" of the gathering and focused on "his own experiences as a messenger of Christ."

140. *1938 Annual Session of the Illinois Baptist State Association*, Woman's Missionary Union Report, 16; *1939 Annual Session of the Illinois Baptist State Association*, Woman's Missionary Union Report, 22; *1940 Annual Session of the Illinois Baptist State Association*, Woman's Missionary Union Report, 25; *1941 Annual Session of the Illinois Baptist State Association*, Woman's Missionary Union Report, 26.

Contemporary Impressions

Southern Baptist Ambivalence toward Jews

The Southern Baptist Convention's response to the persecution of the Jews, the Nazi attempt to exterminate them, and the postwar Zionist push to create a Jewish homeland in Palestine was multidimensional. Key members of the Southern Baptist national leadership expressed anti-Semitic views and asserted that the Jewish victims of Hitler's campaign were partially responsible for their own suffering. M. E. Dodd defended Hitler in print, and others, like W. O. Carver, rationalized Baptist noninterference by demanding that Jews take responsibility for solving their own problems.

The involvement of the Southern Baptist Foreign Mission Board in Europe and the Middle East worked against Southern Baptist action on behalf of the Jewish people. The senior Southern Baptist missionary in Europe expressed a racist outlook and ignored the plight of Jews. Italian Baptist leaders, who worked closely with the Foreign Mission Board, supported Mussolini. And in the Middle East, Southern Baptist ministry to Arabs dampened their enthusiasm for the Zionist aspirations of the Jewish immigrants, even though they recognized the positive effect such immigration was having on the economic life of the region.

This lack of enthusiasm on the part of the Southern Baptist leaders may explain the lack of convention response in terms of resolutions. It would have been difficult for the delegates to pass resolutions the leaders did not support fully. The prejudice of Southern Baptist Convention leaders overcame the natural tendency to apply core convictions to the plight of the Jewish people under Hitler's domain.

Jacob Gartenhaus worked tirelessly to push the SBC in the opposite direction. He enjoyed the support of the Woman's Auxiliaries throughout the country, and he articulated concern and compassion for Jews in his lengthy annual reports to the convention. In his published books, he espoused support for Zionism, as well as for evangelization of Jewish people. He explicitly denied that there was a contradiction between advocating for Baptist friendship with Jews, opposing anti-Semitism, and being in solidarity with persecuted Jews on the one hand, and zealously seeking to convert Jews to faith in Jesus Christ on the other hand.

During the 1930s and the first half of the 1940s, Gartenhaus appears to have been marginalized by his organizational superiors, who did not share his sense of urgency in opposing Hitler. However, it may be said that at the 1947 Baptist World Alliance Congress in Copenhagen, he got in the last word (see part 6). With the passage of the resolution he composed, Gartenhaus experienced vindication, and he completed his ministry with the Southern Baptist Convention with a deep sense of satisfaction that his prophetic role in that convention had not been in vain.

The responses of Southern Baptists differed from those of their Northern Baptist counterparts in both timing and content. The Northern Baptist state conventions and city societies provided expressions of concern for Jews throughout the Nazi era, but not in any specific chronological order or coherent pattern. In contrast, Southern Baptist state conventions either produced resolutions in response to Kristallnacht or did not officially respond in a meaningful way. The cluster of responses to Kristallnacht is explained easily, since many of the state conventions took place either at the time of or within a month after the Night of Broken Glass. Missouri was the sole Southern Baptist state convention that produced a significant response to the plight of Germany's persecuted Jews before Kristallnacht.

Why did many states exhibit a lack of concern or merely offer a minimal response, and those that did respond seem unable to produce a record of consistent concern? Several reasons may help to explain the unwillingness of Southern Baptist state conventions to respond to the plight of the Jews.

On a convention level, the lack of clear leadership from the national convention inhibited responses by the state conventions. The anti-Semitism of Dodd and others, coupled with the racially prejudiced perspective of Everett Gill, discouraged Southern Baptists from expressing solidarity with Jews who were persecuted by Hitler. Similarly, the lack of enthusiasm for Zionism on the part of the missionaries serving in the Middle East may have dissuaded state conventions from addressing the subject. The attempts by Gartenhaus to keep the issues of anti-Semitism, the Jewish plight in Europe, and Zionism in front of the Southern Baptist world did not succeed in convincing a plurality of states to pass specific resolutions, let alone undertake ministries that would have alleviated the suffering of Jews in any significant manner.

On a sociological level, this lack of grassroots activity may have been due to a lack of interaction between Southern Baptist clergy and laity and Jewish religious professionals and members of the Jewish community. Many of the localities where Southern Baptists were strong, especially in the rural areas, would have had either no or a very small Jewish community.

On a racial level, despite resolutions decrying lynching and African American discrimination, white Southern Baptists did not offer a compelling and prophetic countercultural witness to the South's segregated society. Local churches were overwhelmingly segregated, Baptist politicians did not promote legislative remedies for the discriminatory and segregated practices of the Jim Crow South, and they did not as a rule provide support for African American civil rights organizations or protesters. Why would white Southern Baptists exert energy to protest anti-Semitism in Germany when they did not intend to challenge the discrimination their African American neighbors experienced on a daily basis? Some Southern Baptists felt they had no moral right to protest Hitler's anti-Semitism when American society practiced racial discrimination against African Americans and Japanese Americans. Such hypocrisy appeared self-evident and led to a stance of passive humility, which could even be justified by Scriptures such as, "Do not judge, or you too will be judged. . . . Why do you look at the speck in your brother's eye and pay no attention to the plank in your own eye?" (Matthew 7:1-3).

On a religious level, two factors encouraged Southern Baptist reticence to address the persecution Jews faced in the 1930s and 1940s. First, the Southern Baptist emphasis on evangelism as opposed to social action permitted Southern Baptists to shy away from social protest. The conversion of individual souls was the preferred pathway to societal transformation. Second, theological anti-Semitism promoted the notion that Jewish victims of Nazi persecution created the very conditions that led to their victimization. There were those within the Southern Baptist Convention who believed that the Jewish people's rejection of Jesus' messianic claims in the first century broke their covenant with God, and that outbreaks of anti-Semitism and social and political persecution of Jews were a form of judgment, or at least an expression of God's displeasure with the Jewish community's collective lack of faith in Jesus.

PART FIVE

African American Baptists

The story of African American Baptists, Jews, and the Holocaust has never been fully explored. Lunabelle Wedlock's 1942 dissertation focused on African American responses to German anti-Semitism. Although black Baptist papers were not covered in depth, Wedlock's research deserves to be acknowledged as a seminal work in African American–Jewish relations for the Holocaust period. She examined "fallacies" African American writers embraced as they responded to the Nazi persecution of Jews and concluded that "indulgence in anti-Semitism is a dangerous luxury for Negroes."[1] Following Wedlock's lead, Isabel Boiko Price's PhD dissertation in 1973 focused more precisely on the issue of African American anti-Semitism in Harlem, the veritable center of African American culture. Price identified the central dynamic that characterized Jewish-black interaction during the period—mutual sympathy lessened by a sense of competition and a resulting alienation in which African Americans felt that Jews were treated better than they were in the United States.[2]

The historical narrative of African American Baptists and the Holocaust is significant for several reasons. First, approximately 35 percent of American Baptists were African American during the period from 1933 to 1948. James Melvin Washington stated, "The history of Black Baptists is intimately interwoven with the general history of Baptists in the United States."[3]

Second, African American Baptist leaders were well aware of international politics and the Nazi persecution of the Jews in Germany. National Baptist leaders extensively commented on domestic and global issues at their national annual meetings. The National Baptist Woman's Auxiliary leaders were women of stature, and though their meetings were separate from the main proceedings of the convention, they similarly spoke to all of the key political, social, and racial issues of the day. National Baptists had actively participated in the Baptist World Alliance since its inception, and its leaders served on the executive committee. National Baptists participated in the racialism debates of the 1934 Berlin congress and helped host the 1939 congress in Atlanta.

Third, the second-class political and social status of African Americans gave that community a unique perspective on the plight of Jews suffering persecution under Hitler's campaign of disenfranchisement and then outright extermination. American participation in World War I had a profound impact on how African American Baptists understood their struggle for racial equality and acceptance. Leroy Fitts observed that the war encouraged African American Baptists to interpret their own liberation struggles from a more international perspective, recognizing that "the mob violence of the Ku Klux Klan and disfranchisement could now be viewed in the cosmopolitan milieu of dehumanizing political systems around the world designed to quench the human spirit of freedom, equality, and justice. Deprived minorities and other ethnic groups around the world were viewed by black Baptists as part of their general struggle for human dignity."[4]

African American Baptist spirituality predisposed them to be sympathetic to Jews seeking deliverance and liberty in Germany. African American Baptists gained inspiration from the Jewish Bible in general, and the narrative about the exodus in particular.[5] The cry of Moses to Pharaoh to "let my people go" was a standard refrain in black churches since they had been slaves, and even in the post–Civil War period, the Jim Crow segregationist social order functioned to perpetuate social inequality.[6] African Americans were particularly sensitive to the subjugation of minorities in general and to the German Jewish persecution in particular. Fitts observed:

> THE RISE TO power of Adolf Hitler and his political theories were perhaps the most radical international challenge to the progress of black Americans. The racial myth was given a potent international thrust with the development of Nazism as an ideology in Germany. While the Jews

> were the primary objects of this myth, black Americans realized that the world with an ideology of Nazism was not safe for their progress.[7]

In general, African Americans admired the Jewish community for its success in reaching for the American economic and social dream. Booker T. Washington advised African Americans to emulate their Jewish counterparts who manifested "unity, pride and love of race; and, as the years go on, they will be more and more influential in this country—a country where they were once despised, and looked upon with scorn and derision. It is largely because the Jewish race has had faith in itself. Unless the Negro learns more and more to imitate the Jew in these matters, to have faith in himself, he cannot expect to have any high degree of success."[8]

However, other historical realities mitigated against the formation of a cooperative alliance between Jews and African Americans, even prior to Hitler's ascension to power. In American cities, often "encounters between Afro-Americans and American Jews . . . were unequal-status, friction-generating contacts, between merchants and consumers, between landlord and tenants, between housewives and domestics. In almost every instance, the black was in a subordinate position."[9] This "bittersweet encounter"[10] between Jews and African Americans led to varying degrees of estrangement between the two communities in the 1930s and 1940s. The competition between them, and the African American perception that the relationship was not equal or mutually beneficial, influenced how African Americans responded to European Jewish persecution and gave rise to expressions of anti-Semitism. The relative affluence and greater success that Jews achieved gave license for African Americans to express both grudging admiration and anti-Semitic attitudes[11] as they protested against specific Jewish businesses and landlords that took unfair advantage of African Americans.[12]

The spirit of competition extended beyond concerns of domestic economic and social equality. The attention garnered by German Jews troubled African Americans and gave rise to expressions of jealousy. Why do Americans decry Hitler and spend so much time trying to help German Jews but then do nothing to alleviate African American suffering? African Americans observed the global protests against the Nazi persecution of Jews and wondered why their own struggle for civil rights did not engender similar expressions of solidarity and support. African Americans felt they were competing with Jews for the world's sympathy. Weisbord and Stein observed:

> SYMPATHY WAS EXTENDED to the Jew and efforts to assist him in hour of need applauded. But what about the suffering of America's black population? Whence would come their relief? . . . Shortly after Hitler came to power the *Philadelphia Tribune* recognized that it was hell to be a Jew in Germany. But, it opined, it was twice as terrible to be a black man in the United States. A 1934 editorial entitled "Germany vs. America" published in the *Tribune* succinctly observed: "The persecution of the Jews in Germany by the Nazi government is deplorable, stupid and courageous. The persecution of colored Americans by Americans is cruel, relentless, and spirit breaking."[13]

Although the African American Baptist movement was in a strong position to identify with and support persecuted Jews in the 1930s and 1940s, the negative forces of bitterness and jealousy strained the ties between the two communities. These dynamics came to a head in the 1930s, as Jews and African Americans came into close contact in the northern American cities. The country's largest Jewish community lived in New York City, while Harlem "became the center for the social and political development of black Americans. The black world looked to Harlem for inspiration and leadership," and black Baptists were a key constituency of Harlem.[14] With one of their flagship churches in Harlem—Abyssinian Baptist Church—Baptists were poised to play an influential role in the interaction between the Jewish and African American communities and affect how African Americans would respond to anti-Semitism abroad and at home.

Notes

1. Lunabelle Wedlock, "The Reaction of Negro Publications and Organizations to German Anti-Semitism," diss., Howard University, 1942, 194–207.
2. "Black Responses to Anti-Semitism: Negroes and Jews in New York, 1880 to World War II," PhD diss., University of New Mexico, 1973.
3. James Melvin Washington, *Frustrated Fellowship: The Black Quest for Social Power* (Macon, GA: Mercer University Press, 2004), 3.
4. Leroy Fitts, *A History of Black Baptists* (Nashville: Broadman, 1985), 264.
5. Hubert G. Locke, *The Black Anti-Semitism Controversy: Protestant Views and Perspectives* (Selinsgrove, PA: Susquehanna University Press, 1994), 32.

6. Jim Crow laws functioned to prevent the desegregation of the South in the late nineteenth and twentieth centuries, preventing African Americans from achieving full civil, economic, and political rights; see "Louisiana's 'Jim Crow' Law Valid," *The New York Times* (21 December 1892).

7. Fitts, *History of Black Baptists*, 266–67.

8. Booker T. Washington, *The Future of the American Negro* (Boston: Small, Maynard and Company, 1900), 182–83, quoted in Robert G. Weisbord and Arthur Stein, *Bittersweet Encounter: The Afro-American and the American Jew*, Contributions in Afro-American and African Studies (Westport, CT: Negro Universities Press, 1970), 37.

9. Weisbord and Stein, *Bittersweet Encounter*, 40.

10. Ibid., viii.

11. Marie Syrkin, "Anti-Semitic Drive in Harlem," and L. D. Roddick, "Anti-Semitism among Negroes," in *Strangers and Neighbors: Relations between Blacks and Jews in the United States*, ed. Maurianne Adams and John H. Bracey Jr. (Amherst: University of Massachusetts Press, 1999), 380–83; 449–56, respectively.

12. Ella Baker and Marvel Cooke, "The Bronx Slave Trade," in *Strangers and Neighbors,* 369–74; see also Weisbord and Stein, *Bittersweet Encounter*, 63.

13. Weisbord and Stein, *Bittersweet Encounter*, 50–51.

14. Fitts, *History of Black Baptists*, 271.

Chapter 16

The National Baptist Convention, USA, Inc.

The largest African American Baptist denomination was the National Baptist Convention, USA, Incorporated. From its founding in 1880, the convention grew steadily in spite of divisions and power struggles, which resulted in rival movements that did not achieve similar levels of membership. By the 1930s, the denomination boasted almost four million members, rivaling the Southern Baptists and far exceeding the membership of the mostly white Northern Baptist Convention. Birthed in the Jim Crow South, the denomination was a major advocate for African American civil and political rights, and it enjoyed positive working relationships with both the Northern and Southern Baptist Conventions.

National Baptist Convention leaders were involved in the Baptist World Alliance since its formation. In 1948, the denomination's historian, Dr. Sylvester Boone, recalled that Elias Camp Morris, C. H. Parrish, and D. V. Jemison represented National Baptists on the alliance level. He praised the key role Lacey Kirk Williams played within the BWA:

> THE PRINCE OF Preachers, nestor of logic, master of forensic oratory, and Christmas Evans in spiritual fervor and ardor, who served as a member of the Executive Board of the Baptist World Alliance, vice president of the Baptist World Alliance, one of the chief advisors of the Baptist World Alliance and who presented Dr. George Washington Truitt [*sic*] in 1939 to more than 60,000 people during the session of the Baptist World Alliance in Atlanta, Georgia, in such linguistic beauty that the vast host of assembled Baptists representing at least forty-two

> nations of the world, shook beneath the spell of his oratory and quivered under the sweep of his flawless speech.[1]

Williams served as the president of the National Baptist Convention, USA, Inc., from 1922 through 1940, the year of his death. As Joseph Harrison Jackson notes, "At the same time that his work with the Convention was progressing, Dr. Williams was being considered more and more as a world leader. In recognition of this, he was elected as one of the vice-presidents of the World Baptist Alliance in 1928—a position which he held with great dignity unto his death."[2] And it should not be forgotten that alongside Williams was the famous Baptist laywoman, Miss Nannie Helen Burroughs. Through the alliance, National Baptists were part of a worldwide conversation that helped to frame the global Baptist movement response to Nazism. African American Baptists brought their perspective on racialism and prejudice to the larger family and sought to enlist the BWA as an ally in its own civil rights struggle.

The National Baptist Convention was aware of the struggles of European Jews and responded through the prism of its own people's struggle to achieve equal rights in the United States during an era of oppressive and pervasive segregation. The overarching concern of African Americans to achieve full political, economic, educational, and social rights influenced how they interpreted all other political issues, including the Nazi persecution of the Jews. This led the National Baptists to articulate a unique response to the Jewish crisis that was quite unlike the positions taken by their white Baptist counterparts.

Jews, African American Baptists, and Personality

At the 1933 annual meeting of the National Baptist Convention, USA, Inc., President Williams declared, "Our churches must preach equal justice to all, the sin and folly of class and race prejudice, and the value of supremacy of love. . . . The gospel of a real practical brotherhood is the only thing that will save us. While these are crucial hours for the world and our nation, this movement has a special bearing upon, and summon for the Negro Race."[3] This was the message National Baptists brought to the 1934 Baptist world congress in Berlin.

Forty National Baptists participated, compared with approximately four hundred Southern and four hundred Northern Baptists. Martin Luther King Sr. was listed among the National Baptist leaders. J. M. Nabrit, author of the BWA report for the 1934 National Baptist Convention, reported that "the special reports of Commissions drew forth applause and discussions, especially those on Nationalism, Racialism, Marriage and Divorce. Your representative enjoyed the privilege of leading the discussion on Racialism." He also praised M. E. Dodd for his Berlin presentation and explained that the theme of the conclave was "universal brotherhood through Christ and a forward Baptist Movement against all agencies that sought to lower moral standards, destroy peace, fellowship, brotherhood, and to change the ideals of Baptists or subsidized or unify the church under state control."[4]

Surprisingly, Nabrit did not share in any depth about the racialism resolution, and neither did S. D. Ross, who also summarized the congress for the convention. Ross did mention the welcome from the German Baptists and from "Herr Hitler, the Chancellor of Germany." He also recorded J. H. Rushbrooke's response, who "assured the German people that the Baptists would adhere to their practice of enlightened courage and free speech even tho [*sic*] they were meeting in the Republic of Germany." On racialism and other issues, Ross simply recalled, "The Commission that had given study to these subjects gave their reports . . . and here is where much power of thought of presentation, and of persuasiveness was demonstrated."[5] Similarly, President Williams shared that the "Assembly registered its opposition to forms of lawlessness, race prejudice and race."[6] However, at the 1934 National Baptist Convention, no resolutions were passed that addressed the Jewish situation, even though both the Northern Baptist Convention and the Baptist World Alliance had done so.

The 1935 National Baptist convention was held in Brooklyn, New York, and dignitaries such as the state's governor, Herbert H. Lehman (a Jew), and the city's mayor, Fiorello H. La Guardia, greeted the assembly. The mayor's address reached "its highest as he evidenced his love and interest in humanity and climaxed his brilliant address with a plea for the Fatherhood of God and the brotherhood of man." This spirit of brotherhood was reinforced by the appearance of Rabbi Alexander Lyons from the Eighth Avenue Temple in Brooklyn, "who gave an inspiring and encouraging welcome."[7]

President Williams denounced Italy's aggression against Ethiopia, and in arguing for free education for African Americans, he noted "the tendency today is toward a dictatorship government, but public education and free church are inimical to that form of government." He illustrated the fight for civil rights by referring to the Jewish community: "It is reported that the Jewish people protested and had 'The Merchant of Venice' removed from a school curriculum because it gave an unfair picture of them in its drastic characterization of Shylock. Go thou and do likewise."

Making a comparison between Jews and African Americans, with the former serving as the mentor community, was a common rhetorical technique employed by African American leaders. It could engender imitation, but also it served as an expression of jealousy. Williams offered a second illustration at the conclusion of his speech—boxer Joe Louis fighting as an equal with an Italian and a Jewish competitor. Williams asked, "I wonder when the time will arrive when white preachers can meet Negro preachers" as equals?[8]

The 1936 National Baptist convention hosted the first serious discussion of the Jewish question. Convention historian L. G. Gordon presented a three-point meditation on Jewish persecution. First, Gordon claimed that the centuries of persecution that the Jewish people have endured was the result of their collective leadership's rejection of Jesus. Jews had "felt the sting of discrimination and prejudice, and have paid a fearful price for the rejection of Jesus by the leaders and many of the Jewish people. . . . Jewish leaders refused to accept the teachings of the lowly Nazarene. For that, the Jewish people suffered, and are still suffering."

Second, Gordon acknowledged the grievous circumstances Jews were facing in Germany and portrayed them as victims of discrimination at the hands of an unjust government: "I have before me an appeal urging concerted action of the nations in behalf of the defenseless Jews. Hundreds of thousands of them now are facing a terrible situation under the Nazi regime in Germany. Some of the most flagrant regulations have been imposed on them."

Third, Gordon insisted that Arab attacks on Jewish settlers in Palestine were another ramification of the Jews' lack of belief in Jesus: "Following the World War, Palestine was handed over to Great Britain as mandate and was to become once more the homeland of the Jews, but even now with this great backing, retribution for their disobeying Jehovah and rejecting Jesus still follows them. The Arabs and other nations are harassing, killing, and hoping to exterminate the Jew."[9]

It turned out that 1938 would prove to be a watershed year in the National Baptist Convention's engagement with Nazism and the Jewish persecution. Rev. J. H. Jackson, serving as the corresponding secretary of the Foreign Mission Board, advanced a penetrating critique of Nazism and fascism based on the Baptist conviction of personality:

> FASCISM AND NAZISM are demanding the loyalty and, in many instances, the sacrifice of the human personality to the orders and dictates of the State. In such political organizations man is not evaluated as an end in himself, but he is a means to an end. And that end is the existence and life of the totalitarian State. Thus the State is deified and man is called upon to worship this idol god. The totalitarian idea of man runs counter to the Christian concept of human personality and negates the sacred truths uttered by Jesus of Nazareth. Along with this development of the cult of the State there has arisen the doctrine of the supremacy of race. Especially is this true in Nazi Germany, and it has its practical expression and tangible demonstration in the expulsion of the Jewish people from Germany. To follow such a theory or view of life to its logical conclusions will naturally divide the world into many hostile camps where each race will be pitted against the other. This would not only be a denial of the basic kinship of the human family, but a concrete reaction against the old Christian belief that "God has made of one blood all nations for to dwell on the face of the earth."[10]

For Jackson, the doctrine of personality stood in opposition to totalitarianism because of the latter's deification of the state at the expense of the worth of the individual as a spiritual being. Jesus himself affirmed the personality of humanity. Jackson also rejected Nazi racialism because it would negate the doctrine of the unity of humanity. He believed that all people, regardless of racial background, were God's children. Nazi persecution of Jews served to illustrate his argument, but it was not necessarily its core concern, and thus he did not offer any tangible strategy on how to assist or protect the Jews who were suffering under Hitler's dictatorship. Nevertheless, Jackson's opposition to "the doctrine of supremacy of race" was clear.

L. K. Williams and the BWA Congress in Segregated Atlanta

President Lacey K. Williams, in a legendary oration, reviewed the history of National Baptist–Baptist World Alliance cooperation in order to garner support for National Baptist participation in the upcoming 1939 Baptist World Alliance congress in Atlanta. The controversy surrounding the choice of Atlanta was similar to the prior choice of Berlin. Selecting Berlin as a congress setting ran the risk of appearing to approve Nazi anti-Semitic racial policies, and choosing Atlanta as the 1939 congress site could be seen as ignoring or even justifying the harsh segregation and racism that African Americans endured on a daily basis. Williams countered such fears with a masterful argument—just as the Baptists opposed Hitler and sided with the Jews in Berlin, so too the BWA could provide a global prophetic voice against segregation and racism in America by holding their world congress in Atlanta.

Williams's argument contained several historically significant premises. First, he celebrated the Baptist World Alliance's historic core conviction of equality for all races: "This Body is made up of Baptists of all races and nations of the world." Williams proudly recalled that his denomination was "one of its charter members and has had continued, unbroken membership therein." Second, Williams reviewed the controversy surrounding the choice of Berlin as the congress venue, including the widely held opinion that the more prophetic Baptist rebuke to Nazi injustice would have been to boycott the city:

> WE [WERE] REPRESENTED in the last Congress held in Berlin, but prior to that session many of the Alliance's most loyal members feared that the economic, religious and civil unrest in Germany militated against holding said Congress there. Some considerations were given these objections, but it was finally decided to hold the Congress in Berlin, notwithstanding the existence of the unsavory conditions complained of. The Congress assembled in Berlin as planned. It was brought face to face with the conditions complained of before, and in a

> most courageous Christian spirit and manner it made deliverances that became classic Christian literature, that has been reechoed around the world in defense of justice and liberty. To some it appeared at first that the good discretion and practical Christianity would prevent the Alliance from holding that meeting in Germany. And, not to go to Berlin, some thought, would have been the boldest and most pungent criticism and rebuke of Germany that could have been offered. This would have been the salt seasoning and saving itself, they argued, but the majority insisted that the meeting be held in Berlin.[11]

Williams sided with Rushbrooke and the majority who embraced Berlin as the congress venue. His third point was that the Baptist witness in Berlin was indeed prophetic and righteous, and it represented a triumph of the gospel over Hitler's totalitarianism and racism:

> AND, THAT IT required a more positive and heroic type of Christianity for the Alliance to go to Berlin and execute its regular program than was required for it to abandon holding the meeting at that place. The Alliance went there, it saw, it conquered. It said to Hitler, when considering the inequalities and injustices of the Nazi reign, "Thou art the man." The Alliance at Berlin condemned tyranny, contended for the importance and reign of Baptist principles, revived the spirit of immortal Luther, and preached the claims of Christ in no uncertain language.[12]

Having justified Berlin 1934 as a prophetic stand against Nazism, Williams next dramatically revealed that the choice of Atlanta to host the 1939 congress did not originate solely with the Southern Baptists. Williams and other National Baptists were parties to the negotiations that set the terms for the congress. And just as Baptists knew they were walking into controversy by meeting in Berlin, so too Baptist leaders appreciated the challenges posed by conducting a congress in a city that typified the segregation found throughout the South:

> IN THAT MEETING the National Baptist Convention took part and by its vote and the exercise of its prerogative helped to locate the 1939 session of the Alliance in Atlanta, Georgia. This was done with a distinct understanding that the Alliance would execute its own programs and would be as it had been and act as it had done in all of its former

> meetings. At that time the people of Georgia accepted this arrangement and program, and the representatives of the National Baptist Convention then knew as well, or maybe better than anyone else there, the real status of things in America and Georgia.[13]

Williams then drove home his final point, which was the heart of the matter. The BWA would not betray its core convictions concerning the personality of humanity and the equality of all races by choosing to meet in Atlanta. To the contrary, it would be their solemn duty before God and society to oppose all manifestations of segregation and racism at the congress. The membership of the National Baptist Convention, similarly, had a duty to journey with the BWA down the road to justice and equality, with Atlanta[14] being the focal point:

> THE PLEDGE MADE by the Georgia brethren for the reception of the Alliance remains unchanged, and the requirements for said reception demanded by the Alliance then, are still unmodified and unchanged, as we understand them. Now, all of the aforesaid being true, there is no rightful alternative left the Alliance and the National Baptist Convention, except to go to Atlanta. And the National Baptist Convention should be there and take its place in that Congress of the Alliance just as it has done in the past, nothing more and nothing less. The Alliance by an open, free-voting majority, the supreme rule in Baptist procedure, decided this question. And this being true there is now no room for agitation and debate even under the guise of the right of free speech. In going to Atlanta, the Alliance should not be required to countenance any irregularities that may exist there, and on the contrary, it should be required to make in a five-day session a correction in existing disorders there which organized Christianity has failed to correct through the centuries. And all persons who would expect the Alliance to maintain a silence there on present or far-off existing wrongs, should and must be sorely disappointed. The Alliance, within its own sphere must declare the truth and condemn all wrongs, injustices and lawlessness wherever such may exist. And this it will do, nothing more and nothing less.[15]

William's argument relied on a historical precedent and a logical analogy to make a case for African American hope. Just as the BWA rallied to the cause of the Jews and courageously "spoke truth to power" in Berlin by condemning anti-Semitism in no uncertain terms in 1934, so too National Baptists could rightly expect the BWA to join them and all African Americans in the US civil rights struggle. Williams believed that a desegregated congress in the heart of the segregated South would serve as a radical challenge to the norms of white oppression. It would be a global rebuke to racism in the United States, just as the Berlin congress was interpreted as a global protest against anti-Semitism. Berlin served the Jewish community, and similarly Atlanta would serve the African American cause.

National Baptists and Kristallnacht

Before the Jewish precedent set in Berlin could affect the African American civil rights struggle, National Baptists had an opportunity to express solidarity with German Jews in response to an unanticipated crisis. Two months after the September 1938 convention, Kristallnacht rocked the world with its barbarity and hate. The National Baptist leaders, meeting in executive session on December 8, 1938, passed their first significant resolution on anti-Semitism and the persecution of the Jewish people:

> WHEREAS: THE NATIONAL Baptist Convention, Incorporated, holding an extended session in the city of Memphis, and believing in the Fatherhood of God, and the brotherhood of man, being informed thru [*sic*] the public press, of the cruel and inhuman treatment of the Jewish people by Germany and other European nations; and
>
> Whereas: the Christian world, apparently stands aghast at the awful plight of the Jews as if something new and unheard of was taking place in the treatment of a weak and defenseless people, and
>
> Whereas: We believe there is a sure remedy for these tragic ills in human society, and that remedy is the Christian religion if believed in and practiced by those who profess the same, therefore, be it
>
> Resolved, that we extend our deepest and most sincere sympathy to the Jewish people in their unfortunate plight, recognizing as we do, the great contribution made by the Jews to our civilization, thru [*sic*] business, education, literature, science, philanthropy and religion;
>
> Resolved, further, that we hereby express our earnest hope and desire that race hatred and oppression of minority groups the world over will

> soon banish from the earth and that good will and human brotherhood may prevail everywhere.[16]

The National Baptist Convention's executive committee's resolution contained none of the victim-blaming language that L. G. Gordon expressed in 1936, but it did pass judgment on the white majority Christian world, which "apparently stands aghast" at Jewish persecution and race prejudice "as if something new and unheard of was taking place in the treatment of a weak and defenseless people." The implication was clear: Jews in Europe and African Americans in the United States had been oppressed and persecuted for centuries; Hitler's attacks were nothing new. If the Christians of Germany and the United States would live up to the ideals of Christianity, persecution would cease in those cultures. The resolution affirmed National Baptist solidarity with persecuted Jews but concluded with a more general hope that "race hatred and oppression of minority groups the world over" would cease, and that persecuted peoples would gain equality and freedom.

"Suppressed, Chained Personality"

The National Baptist Convention convened its 1939 meeting a month after that year's Baptist world congress met in Atlanta. In light of the high expectations Williams set for that gathering, it was no surprise that the congress received a good deal of attention in the leadership reports provided to the convention. In his presidential address, Williams declared that the Atlanta congress "was one of the most important and significant meetings ever held by Protestants." He noted that many important resolutions were passed, including one on "The Sin of Race Oppression and Discrimination"—the resolution that dealt with anti-Semitism as well as prejudice based on skin color.

For one week, the congress did manage to create a thoroughly desegregated environment, with African Americans enjoying full equality and complete integration. This was a truly prophetic and countercultural demonstration of racial harmony that temporarily challenged Atlanta's majority white power structure. Williams was most pleased and invoked his own words about Berlin in his assessment of the Baptist witness to Atlanta: "Atlanta outdid itself and gave the Congress an unequalled, unexcelled reception. The Congress can say, 'We came, we saw, we conquered,' and 'There was great joy in that city.'"[17]

The message of the BWA congress was uppermost in Williams's mind. He noted that the international context of the congress demanded a relevant and prophetic stance on racial justice based on core Baptist convictions:

> THE CONGRESS MET when almost the entire world was a vortex of unrest and uncertainty. It was believed that the Baptists had a message and a mission for this hour. It was a message of soul freedom, liberty, equality, the only hope and redemption of oppressed, submerged minorities. From this meeting a pronounciamento was to be sent to tyrants and to the world's dictators and oppressors to let "God's people go."[18]

Williams's allusion to the exodus in the context of totalitarianism indicated that he had not just African American civil rights but also the plight of the persecuted German Jews in mind as he spoke. Both were "oppressed, submerged minorities." In a sober conclusion, Williams admitted that "race prejudice has always existed" and that African Americans should not embrace communism as an alternative to either fascism or democracy. Only a spiritual solution can decisively overturn racial prejudice and oppression:

> "TRULY THE ATLANTA Congress demonstrated that Christian people of different races and colors may meet and work together anywhere and plan a warfare against ignorance, vice, tyranny, crime, injustice, discrimination and sin, the common perils of all races and the religion of Jesus Christ. In this it was an inspiration to sincere though perplexed Christians, handicapped by a rank type of ungodly racialism. None other than a religious organization has ever dared to execute such a program in Atlanta, and none other could have done it."

However, Williams also admitted that even a global BWA witness could not eradicate racism in just one week: "But let no one of us be deceived and think that the question of color discrimination has been permanently settled. It cannot be until men everywhere and at all times realize that race antipathy and race oppression is undemocratic and unChristian."[19]

Williams's 1940 presidential address was notable for two reasons. First, it expressed Williams's concern over rival ideologies (fascism and communism) that were seeking the allegiance of African Americans. These were false options, for they are "un-American" and contrary to African American community values. The church, however, should lead the battle for authentic civil rights for all the world's minorities: "It must condemn and expose shams and false practices of current religion on inter-racial matters. It must contend for interracial justice and the freedom and opportunities of all races. It must call the race's attention to the perils and the unsettled state of minority groups the world over—that races and nations under God are never safe doing the wrong thing."[20]

Second, Williams made an original contribution to the Baptist articulation of its core conviction of personality. He coined the phrase "suppressed, chained personality" in his defense of the loyalty and patriotism of African Americans facing the prospect of serving in a future war against totalitarianism: "We have felt and known the pangs of a suppressed, chained personality, and would willingly make any sacrifices for the chance of enjoying the heritages of a free democracy and for their preservation."[21] In citing the African American experience of slavery and its denial of the fundamental recognition of humanity for African Americans, Williams created a powerful image of what oppression feels like for minorities. This evocative theological contribution was the final gift of President Williams to the National Baptist Convention, and to the worldwide Baptist movement, before his death.

Following Williams's death, the leadership mantle of the National Baptist Convention passed to Dr. David V. Jemison from Selma, Alabama, who served as president from 1940 to 1953.[22] The 1941 convention passed a resolution asking for the American military to protect its African American soldiers from brutality from white mobs, "just as would be done if Nazis, Communists, Ku Klux or Night Riders attempted to humiliate, abuse, intimidate white soldiers in the U.S. Army."[23] At the 1942 convention, the convention historian, Dr. Theodore Sylvester Boone, issued a rallying cry to African American soldiers. He framed the war as a call to arms against prejudice of all stripes, noting that the enemies of freedom and equality were in the homeland as well as in the totalitarian nations America was combatting:

> MARCH ON, NEGRO Baptists, until the shadows of hate are swept from the regions of view; march on until the meanness of prejudice is ground into the powder of love . . . march on, Negro Baptists, until the Hitlers of America, the Mussolinis of the United States, the Hirohitos of this Nation, enemies of peace, justice and fair play, friends of hate, and lovers of prejudice, are brought to an abiding realization that God is Father of all, and all are brothers.[24]

Once the war broke out, the male leaders of the National Baptist Convention focused on the domestic civil rights struggle and did not express any specific resolutions about the Holocaust. Through neglect, that responsibility was delegated to the women of the denomination.

The National Baptist Convention's Woman's Auxiliary

The National Baptist Woman's Auxiliary conducted its annual sessions alongside the National Baptist Convention's meetings. These women were well organized, and the auxiliary served as a parallel power structure through which the women could exercise leadership and express a cooperative albeit independent voice. Their sessions addressed internal organizational concerns as well as political and societal issues. The annual speeches by its key leaders were oratory masterpieces, rivaling clergy sermons. Two powerful women dominated the Woman's Auxiliary for decades—Sarah Willie Layten[25] and Nannie Helen Burroughs.[26] Both were longtime civil rights advocates.

In her 1939 presidential address, Layten reported that the Atlanta congress had "done more towards bringing about racial understanding and good will than any previous efforts in the last twenty years."[27] Corresponding secretary Burroughs noted that Baptists had a responsibility to speak on behalf of all racial groups that were enduring oppression and that the congress furthered this cause in a profound manner: "We believe God is going to make Baptists a world power if they will let him. He sent men of good will from all parts of the world to help him work miracles in Atlanta. We might as well acknowledge that we are in the midst of a new kind of revolution. It is a revolution against unchristian, unfair, unjust and unbrotherly practices against any race, anywhere. It is a Christian revolution." She also praised Rushbrooke when he said, "Let's have no more of this foolish talk about color," believing that he had "struck the world's mightiest shackle from the ankles of Christianity" when he "gave the orders, than [*sic*] were all color signs hauled down."[28]

Layten acknowledged American democracy was politically superior to Germany's Nazi regime, but she called for her country to be true to its fundamental political values because "she [America] preaches what she does not practice. Negroes are discriminated against." Layten appealed to her followers to encourage black youth to embrace democracy, because "as a minority if we cannot make it here, there is no hope elsewhere under the brutal forms of government being enforced in Europe."

The experience of European Jews under Hitler's regime did not bode well for African Americans. And although "nations are seeking substitutes for God, and Nazism is replacing old religious loyalty," Layten still believed that only Christ could satisfy humanity's desire for justice and freedom.[29] Burroughs concurred and called for wartime support of England even while demanding the end of racial discrimination at home: "If all out aid to Britain is essential to destroy Hitlerism in Europe, —all out justice for the Negro is essential to destroy race discrimination and make America safe for Democracy. Negroes and the dark races are not going to pay, sacrifice, fight and die—simply to make the world safe for Britain, and white Americans."[30]

At the 1942 Woman's Auxiliary meeting, Burroughs provided a cogent analysis of President Franklin Delano Roosevelt's "Four Freedoms," his philosophical justification for American support for Great Britain's war effort, and later, the direct involvement of the United States. Significantly, she referred to the persecution of the Jews twice:

> SEVERAL MONTHS AGO, this nation announced that it was fighting for "four freedoms—freedom of speech, freedom from want, freedom from fear and freedom of religion." White Americans with visions of the Czechs and Poles, German and Austrian Jews languishing in concentration camps or standing, unflinching, before Nazi firing squads were moved to go to battle for freedom. Negro Americans, too, have deep sympathy for these enslaved peoples. Only yesterday, our race was in the slave pen. We know what it is. But, we confess that our sympathy is mixed with sadness, fear and suspicion. We wonder if when the Czech

> and the Pole and the Jew, of all nations, eventually achieve freedom from fear, they will join the rest of the white world in appropriating and reserving for themselves this freedom for which black men, too, have fought, bled and died? Freedom for all men, everywhere, is the only thing worth fighting for.[31]

Burroughs beautifully expressed the pathos of the African American perspective regarding the war to liberate Hitler's victims in Europe. The struggle was justified, and African Americans would willingly participate and sacrifice for the cause, but with a "sadness, fear and suspicion" born of generations of experience that taught them that white civilization was unwilling to accord them the same equality that Jews and other minorities in Europe desperately desired. Why fight for the Jews, Burroughs argued, only to remain second-class citizens after the victory over Hitler had been achieved? Would the Jews of America care about African American civil rights after their families in Europe were liberated?

For Burroughs, the sacrificial service of African Americans coexisted with a sense of communal jealousy that white America gave priority to defeating Hitler's brutal racism over ending Jim Crow segregation. "What about the Negro?" she asked. Why couldn't white civilization understand that African American freedom and Jewish liberation from Hitler were equally imperative? In a conclusion reminiscent of Williams's "suppressed, chained personality," Burroughs cried: "We know that the triumph of Hitlerism means death to all freedoms. . . . But the two great democracies, Great Britain and America, must realize that the practices of undemocratic principles in so-called democracies means death to men's souls. Men cannot live even in so-called democracies half slave and half free."[32]

At its September 12, 1943, session in Chicago, the Woman's Auxiliary approved the second African American Baptist national resolution that specifically addressed the plight of persecuted Jews. The resolution not only expressed concern for the Jews but also called for the United States and other countries to provide sanctuary to them, which these countries were reluctant to consider:

> THAT NEGRO WOMEN look with horror upon the cruelties and barbarities imposed upon subjugated peoples now dominated by the

war lords of Germany and Japan, and extend to the suffering peoples heartfelt sympathy, including especially the 5,000,000 Jewish people of Europe; that the women of this Convention express the hope that at the earliest possible time the authorities of the United States and of the United Nations will give haven and succor to these people.[33]

President Layten, in her address, provided a rationale for the resolution and went beyond it in two significant ways. First, she cited reports that some two million Polish Jews had been killed by the Nazis—one of the rare references to the Holocaust in Baptist circles for the entire period under consideration. Second, she encouraged Baptists to donate to a Jewish aid organization, which was unprecedented:

THE WHOLE WORLD is alarmed about what has happened to the Jews. Since Germany has invaded Poland it is estimated that 2,000,000 Jews have been massacred. Maybe this is not altogether a Jewish question at all but a humanitarian question. What's happened to the Jews can happen to any other race that does not agree with Hitler's ideas—it could happen to Negroes in America. Certainly we do sympathize with this cry for help and should give aid to the Jewish Relief, either as an individual or as an organization. (Jewish Relief, 1 E. 44th Street, New York City)[34]

Burroughs, in her 1946 message, tied together the Baptist conviction on personality, the racialism exemplified by Hitler's persecution of the Jews, and the African American postwar ongoing struggle for civil rights in America—all in an effort to complete in the United States what was accomplished in Europe: "Let us pray. Then in sermons, addresses and by radio, movies, books, newspapers and magazines educate the people along lines that make for respect for human personality. Licking Hitler ended the war—licking Hitlerism will usher in the peace. God wants it. Are the Christians of America with Him?"[35]

Guided by Layten and Burroughs, the women of the National Baptist Convention interpreted the horrors of the Holocaust through the lens of African American suffering and patriotism. Hitler's persecution of the Jewish people was an attack on the Baptist understanding of the infinite value and worth of all people, including racial minorities. They also recognized that the struggle to uphold the personality of humanity had not ended with Hitler's defeat.

The Lott Carey Baptist Foreign Mission Convention

An internal dispute within the National Baptist Convention about the merits of cooperating with white Baptists precipitated the formation of the Lott Carey Foreign Mission Convention in 1897. Nonetheless, the two African American entities found a way to cooperate together, and many local congregations retained membership in both organizations.[36] The purpose of the Lott Carey Convention was to "go forth in the field of Foreign Missions feeding the hungering millions with the Gospel, in the Name of Christ."[37]

Primarily oriented to providing missionaries to the Caribbean islands and Africa, Lott Carey's missionaries were not deployed to Europe. Nevertheless, its leaders were well aware of the prevailing global political challenges: "The world is in the arena of a great moral and Religious conflict with 'isms' and doctrines of men, but we believe in the triumphant message of Spiritual Power and Faith."[38] In his annual report for 1940–1941, corresponding secretary Wendell Clay Somerville reiterated the long-standing policy of the convention to avoid political controversies, which he applied to the contemporary American debate over the possibility of the United States entering the European war: "Ever since its organization in 1897 the Lott Carey Foreign Mission Convention has followed a policy of non activity in economic, civic and political issues, therefore I shall not attempt to give either an official nor an individual expression at this time."[39]

However, this was not entirely accurate. At the 1935 annual session, delegates passed a resolution opposing Mussolini's invasion of Ethiopia.[40] Somerville himself believed that the faithfulness of the church "lies in the consciousness of its relationship with the big and universal issues on the outside of the four walls of our modern, well-appointed edifices."[41] Furthermore, he felt compelled to drop his neutrality stance after Pearl Harbor. The first resolution passed by the members of the Lott Carey Convention that might be interpreted as offering support for persecuted Jews in Europe came out of the 1942 annual session. They called for the church to "extend its sympathy to the oppressed peoples of every land and join with the Christians, of every faith, and nation in working and praying that the causes of war as expressed in such evils as race hatred, class distinction, national emperialism [*sic*], economic exploitation and atheistic preachments, may soon be removed from the face of the earth."[42]

Although Somerville opposed Hitler's ideological agenda in his 1943 address, he did not explicitly express solidarity with European Jews. Instead, he cited how the spirit of Nazism was being felt by African American communities:

> THE PRESENT HOLOCOUST [*sic*] is God's judgment upon the nations for their avarice and selfish pride. . . . Can't we see that this present catastrophe could not have happened if we had accepted Jesus Christ and His plan for the world. . .? The term Hitlerism has been substituted for the devil and all his satanic powers. We can see his forces at work on the battlefields of Europe, Asia, Russia and the South Pacific Island. Even here in our fair land of the free and the home of the brave we can feel his powers in Los Angeles, Beaumont, Texas, Detroit, Michigan, and in other places close at home. Our generation is certainly witnessing a world in trouble.[43]

As reports of the actual Holocaust were disturbing the conscience of all Americans, Somerville reflected on the core conviction of personality in light of the struggle between Nazism and the free societies, and he discerned a spiritual dimension to the conflict:

> IN THE CENTER of things God placed human personality as the supreme object and anything which sought to destroy or crush human personality would be regarded as sin. Christ and His way of life represent the most potent and vital force in the world. There are those among us who would say that Christianity has failed. Christianity, as Christ taught, has not failed. Christianity has not been tried. The forces of paganism and barbarism have been and are in the ascendancy today. We see its dreadful results all around us. This sinful society has no power to save itself, only the transforming power of the Spirit of Christ can give meaning to this disordered and godless world.[44]

Somerville believed that the war was a conflict between paganism, the religious force behind political Nazism, and Christianity.

The specific plight of the Jewish people was not his main concern; Somerville maintained that godlessness led to war, and he worried that evil and violence contradicted Christianity's love for personality: "Hate and war are incompatible with the teachings of Jesus. No man can be right with God who is wrong with his brother. War means the destruction of human personality and everything that destroys personality is sin."[45]

Following the conclusion of World War II, Somerville declared that the Lott Carey Convention would participate in humanitarian relief efforts, but he did not specifically mention any commitment to assist Jewish refugees or survivors of the concentration camps:

> IT IS BEYOND human imagination to depict the destructions to humanity and property which has resulted from this war. We are told that more than half of the people of Europe are hungry and homeless. Millions of children are emaciated and whose future is fraught with utter destitution. Modern warfare has completely removed all avenues for escape and defense. Women and children have been the chief victims of this fanatical slaughter. . . . The Lott Carey Baptist Foreign Mission Convention is dedicated to the task of healing the nations. During the current year we have made contributions to several world relief organizations. We keenly feel the sufferings of all humanity everywhere regardless of race, creed, or color.[46]

In the postwar period, the first explicit mention of the plight of Jewish refugees was included in the Lott Carey Convention's executive board report. W. L. Ransome stated, "The Church, then faces a double challenge, one abroad, and the other at home. We shall not neglect the one at the expense of the other. Both need us. Strife abounds between the Hindus and the Moslems, Jews wander in ships up and down the ocean, unwanted by any nation."[47]

Notes

1. Joseph Harrison Jackson, *A Story of Christian Activism: The History of the National Baptist Convention, U.S.A., Inc.* (Nashville: Townsend Press, 1980), 206–7.
2. Ibid., 157.
3. *Minutes of the 1933 Annual Session of the National Baptist Convention, U.S.A.*, President's Address, 220.
4. *Minutes of the 1934 Annual Session of the National Baptist Convention, U.S.A.*, Baptist World Alliance Report of Dr. J. M. Nabrit, 51–52.

5. Ibid., Rev. S. D. Ross's Report on Baptist World Alliance, 151–52.

6. Ibid., President's Address, 171.

7. *Minutes of the 1935 Annual Session of the National Baptist Convention, U.S.A.*, 38–39, 43.

8. Ibid., President's Address, 198–200.

9. *Minutes of the 1936 Annual Session of the National Baptist Convention, U.S.A.*, Historian's Address, 114–15.

10. *Minutes of the 1938 Annual Session of the National Baptist Convention, U.S.A.*, Foreign Mission Report, 100.

11. Ibid., President's Address, 259.

12. Ibid.

13. Ibid., 259–60.

14. See James Aaron Frith, "The Manger of the Movement: Atlanta and the Black Freedom Struggle, 1890–1950," PhD diss., Yale University, 1997.

15. *Minutes of the 1938 Annual Session of the National Baptist Convention, U.S.A.*, President's Address, 260.

16. Ibid., Extended Session, "Resolution," 311–12.

17. *Minutes of the 1939 Annual Session of the National Baptist Convention, U.S.A.*, President's Address, 69–70.

18. Ibid., 71.

19. Ibid., 71–72. For a Southern Baptist perspective on the racial implications of the Atlanta congress, see Editorial, "One Solvent for the Race Issue," *The Commission* (October 1939), 346; and "The Races at Atlanta," *The Commission* (November 1939), 389.

20. *Minutes of the 1940 Annual Session of the National Baptist Convention, U.S.A.*, President's Address, 69.

21. Ibid., 72.

22. For a review of D. V. Jemison's tenure, see Jackson, *Story of Christian Activism*, 174–214.

23. *Minutes of the 1940 Annual Session of the National Baptist Convention, U.S.A.*, Resolutions, "Resolution on Abuse of Colored Soldiers," 52.

24. *Minutes of the 1942 Annual Session of the National Baptist Convention, U.S.A.*, Historian's Report, 134.

25. For a biographical sketch of S. W. Layten, see Jessie C. Smith, ed., *Notable Black American Women, Book II* (Farmington Hills, MI: Thomson Gale, 1996), "S. Willie Layten (1863–1950)," 403–6.

26. For a biographical sketch of Nannie Helen Burroughs, see Jessie C. Smith, ed., *Notable Black American Women, Book I* (Farmington Hills, MI: Thomson Gale, 1992). See also Larry L. McSwain and William Lloyd Allen, eds., *Twentieth-Century Shapers of Baptist Social Ethics* (Macon, GA: Mercer University Press, 2008), 40–57.

27. *Minutes of the 1939 Annual Session of the National Baptist Convention, U.S.A.*, Woman's Auxiliary President's Address, 337.

28. Ibid., Nannie Burroughs's Address, 348.

29. *Minutes of the 1941 Annual Session of the National Baptist Convention, U.S.A.*, Woman's Auxiliary President's Address, 278–81.

30. Ibid., Woman's Auxiliary Corresponding Secretary Address, 290.

31. *Minutes of the 1942 Annual Session of the National Baptist Convention, U.S.A.*, Woman's Auxiliary Corresponding Secretary Address, 274–75. In her 1945 report, Burroughs advocated for a "Fifth Freedom—Freedom of Race," *Minutes of the 1945 Annual Session of the National Baptist Convention, U.S.A.*, Woman's Auxiliary Corresponding Secretary Address, 343.

32. *Minutes of the 1942 Annual Session of the National Baptist Convention, U.S.A.*, Women's Auxiliary Corresponding Secretary Address, 275.

33. *Minutes of the 1943 Annual Session of the National Baptist Convention, U.S.A.*, Woman's Auxiliary Annual Meeting, Resolutions, "Negro Women in the War and Post War World," 326–27.

34. Ibid., Woman's Auxiliary President's Address, 333.

35. *Minutes of the 1946 Annual Session of the National Baptist Convention, U.S.A.*, Women's Auxiliary Corresponding Secretary Address, 336.

36. Leroy Fitts, *A History of Black Baptists* (Nashville: Broadman, 1985), 84–89.

37. Lott Carey Foreign Mission Society of U.S.A., *Annual Report of the Corresponding Secretary 1935–1936*, 3.

38. Ibid., 7.

39. Lott Carey Foreign Mission Society of U.S.A., *Annual Report of the Corresponding Secretary 1940–1941*, 4. Also quoted in David Emmanuel Goatley, *A Divine Assignment: The Missiology of Wendell Clay Somerville* (St. Louis, MO: Lucas Park Books, 2010), 76–77.

40. *Minutes of the 1935 Annual Session of the Lott Carey Baptist Foreign Mission Convention of America*, Resolutions, 34–35.

41. Quoted in Goatley, *A Divine Assignment*, 28.

42. *Minutes of the 1942 Annual Session of the Lott Carey Baptist Foreign Mission Convention of America*, Resolutions, 36.

43. Lott Carey Foreign Mission Society of U.S.A., *Annual Report of the Corresponding Secretary 1942–1943*, 6–7.

44. Lott Carey Foreign Mission Society of U S.A., *Annual Report of the Corresponding Secretary 1943–1944*, 7.

45. Lott Carey Foreign Mission Society of U.S.A., *Annual Report of the Corresponding Secretary 1944–1945*, 7. See also the 1946 presidential address by G. O. Bullock: "Whether the white man will always rule the so called backward races of Africa, India, Burma and Java, keeping them begging for bread or whether we will recognize the supreme value of all human personality, allowing each race and nation to reap full benefit of national resources and individual ability." Cited in *Minutes of the 1946 Annual Session of the Lott Carey Baptist Foreign Mission Convention of America*, Resolutions, 23.

46. Lott Carey Foreign Mission Society of U.S.A., *Annual Report of the Corresponding Secretary 1944–1945*, 7, 9.

47. *Minutes of the 1946 Annual Session of the Lott Carey Baptist Foreign Mission Convention of America*, Executive Committee Report, 28.

Chapter 17

African American Pastors and the Jews

On the local church level, European American and African American clergy sought to address racial prejudice by hosting services with churches from other backgrounds. For example, in February 1944 the First Baptist Church of Lakewood, New Jersey (a European American congregation), invited a Jewish synagogue and an African American Baptist church to participate in a Race Relations Sunday service:

> THE PASTOR WAS assisted in the service by Dr. Louis Harrison, president of the Sons of Israel Synagogue congregation and the Rev. John L. Griffin, pastor of the Macedonia (Negro) Baptist Church. The choirs from the two churches formed a processional, with the Negro choir occupying the choir loft and singing the special numbers, while the choir of the entertaining church sat in the congregation. The pastor preached a special sermon on "God and the Conflict of Race." The entire service breathed of a fine fellowship and understanding between the Negro and Jewish neighbors.[1]

In New York, one European American church, led by the pastor's spouse, sought to encourage friendship with the African American and Jewish communities: "One way of fostering better race relations is . . . the Inter-Racial Neighborhood Club conducted by Mrs. Ward Hulburt, wife of the pastor of the First Baptist Church of Jamaica, Long Island. Jewish, Negro, and white races are represented in the membership, as well as the Catholic, Jewish, and Protestant faiths. The Club has grown so large that it now has to meet in three sections."[2]

In the African American ecclesiastical context, the leadership role of the local church pastor has long been central. Serving within a social context where African Americans have been second-class citizens and where many of the corridors of secular political and economic power have been closed to them, the local church has served as the preeminent social and political organization for African Americans. The church has represented the collective will of the people, and as its leader, the pastor was its foremost and most influential voice.[3] How then did African American pastors respond to anti-Semitism, the Nazi persecution of the Jews, and the Holocaust?

Martin Luther King Sr. and the Philo-Semitism of Martin Luther King Jr.

Rev. Martin Luther King Sr. (1899–1984) served as the pastor of the Ebenezer Baptist Church in Atlanta, Georgia. In 1934, Rev. King traveled with his family throughout the Middle East and Europe, and along with other African American Baptist leaders, participated as a delegate to the 1934 Baptist world congress in Berlin. His son was five years old at the time. In his autobiography, *Daddy King*, King recounted what it was like to experience Germany's social turmoil:

> FOR A WEEK I heard the broadcasts of a man on the radio who seemed—although I understood no German—to shriek and roar, as if he wanted everyone who heard him to rise up and follow. I heard rage in that voice; it was a sound I'd heard in my own language too many times, a sound that poured oil on roaring flames. Adolf Hitler was on the rise, and the week we spent in Germany was filled with the sight of his image on posters and of streets filled with soldiers, with the sound of his voice seemingly everywhere day and night. It was difficult to imagine, somehow, that in this same city was a huge convention of Baptists from all over the world, praying, hoping, feeling that we could take back home, some of us, a new sense of how peace was to be accomplished among men. Simultaneously the militaristic march of jackboots continued beneath unfurling flags with swastikas emblazoned on them. Perhaps both sides were convinced that they had the right answers for tomorrow.[4]

It is unclear how much King's son, Martin Luther King Jr., remembered about the Berlin congress. I have not been able to discover any references to the event in his writings and sermons, but the theme of opposition to Hitlerism and the persecution of Jews does find its analogs in his speeches, sermons, and letters. While in seminary, King Jr. developed a critical acceptance of Walter Rauschenbusch's social gospel, rejecting its "superficial optimism" and kinship with socialism, and began grappling with pacifism, in dialogue with Reinhold Niebuhr's writings.[5]

During his doctoral studies at Boston University, King was introduced to the personalistic teachings of Edgar Sheffield Brightman and L. Harold DeWolf, and under their tutelage, personalism became a significant philosophical underpinning to King's social activism:

> IT WAS MAINLY under these teachers that I studied Personalistic philosophy—the theory that the clue to the meaning of ultimate reality is found in personality. This personal idealism remains today my basic philosophical position. Personalism's insistence that only personality—finite and infinite—is ultimately real strengthened me in two convictions: it gave me metaphysical and philosophical grounding for the idea of a personal God, and it gave me a metaphysical basis for the dignity and worth of all human personality.[6]

Brightman's philosophy of personalism and religion led him to reject the Nazi temptation that so many German Christians succumbed to, and no doubt King would have been familiar with the social application of Brightman's thought. In a book published in 1937, Brightman rejected anti-Semitism as unChristian: "The treatment of Jews by Christians . . . is nothing less than scandalous. In New York City and in Germany (before Hitler too) the word 'Christian' in a newspaper often does not mean a follower of Christ, animated by his spirit. It means instead, merely, one is not a Jew."[7] The Nazi glorification of race, which relegated Jews to subhuman status, could not be reconciled with biblical faith: "But it is evident on the face of it that a positive Christianity which is limited by the ethical and moral feeling of the Germanic race is not in harmony with the Christianity of the New Testament."[8] Communism and fascism compete with Christianity for the allegiance of humanity, and so the "choice for humanity is whether it shall trust the God who has been revealed in the supreme experiences of universal human value or whether it shall turn from this God and try to make a new God out of war or race or matter."[9] For Brightman, the titanic struggle of the twentieth century was the existential struggle between authentic religious personalism and totalitarian idolatry.

King's adaptation of personality as a theological support for the dignity of humanity, coupled with his understanding of the role that love plays in human relations, enabled him to articulate Jesus' teachings in a socially constructive way: "Modern psychology recognizes what Jesus taught centuries ago: hate divides the personality and love in an amazing and inexorable way unites it."[10] It also provided him with a platform to probe the problem of God's justice in light of Jewish and African American suffering and oppression: "Why did God permit Hitler to kill six million Jews? Why did God permit slavery to continue in America for two hundred and forty years? Why does God permit blood-thirsty mobs to lynch Negro men and women at will and drown Negro boys and girls at whim? Why does God not break in and smash the evil schemes of wicked men?"[11]

In Birmingham in 1963, King criticized southern segregation by asserting that it "denies the sacredness of human personality."[12] His understanding of personality enabled him to criticize Hitler's persecution of the Jewish people and equate it with the oppression of African Americans in the United States:

> ANOTHER REASON WHY we must love our enemies is that hate scars the soul and distorts the personality. . . . We have seen its ugly consequences in the ignominious deaths brought to six million Jews by a hate-obsessed madman named Hitler, in the unspeakable violence inflicted upon Negroes by bloodthirsty mobs, in the dark horrors of war, and in the terrible indignities and injustices perpetrated against millions of God's children by unconscionable oppressors. But there is another side which we must never overlook. Hate is just as injurious to the person who hates. Like an unchecked cancer, hate corrodes the personality and eats away its vital unity.[13]

The civil rights struggle faced numerous hurdles and roadblocks, including violence promulgated by vigilante bands and police, and legal regulations designed to reinforce the restrictions of a rigorously segregated society. King's strategy of nonviolent civil disobedience directly confronted these injustices in order to foster "a substantive and positive peace, in which all men will respect the dignity and worth of human personality."[14] Although he expected persecution and incarceration, King was taken aback by the lack of support he received from white clergy and others for challenging unjust laws. While in jail in Birmingham, he invoked the memory of the Holocaust: "We should never forget that everything that Adolf Hitler did in Germany was 'legal' and everything the Hungarian freedom fighters did in Hungary was 'illegal.' It was 'illegal' to aid and comfort a Jew in Hitler's Germany. Even so, I am sure that, had I lived in Germany at the time, I would have aided and comforted my Jewish brothers."[15]

King's views on anti-Semitism and personality emboldened him to criticize Christian leaders who could not find the moral fortitude to oppose Hitler's persecution of the Jews:

> I REFUSE TO determine what is right by taking a Gallup poll of the trends of the time. I imagine that there were leaders in Germany who sincerely opposed what Hitler was doing to the Jews. But they took their poll and discovered that anti-Semitism was the prevailing trend. In order to "be in step with the times," in order to "keep in touch," they yielded to one of the most ignominious evils that history has ever known.[16]

In 1966, King confronted the issue of black anti-Semitism in the United States during the Chicago Campaign. He counterbalanced negative encounters between African Americans and Jews with examples of Jewish support of the civil rights movement. King's conclusion constituted a definitive rejection of anti-Semitism:

> NEGROES CANNOT IRRATIONALLY expect honorable Jews to curb the few who are rapacious; they have no means of disciplining or suppressing them. We can only expect them to share our disgust and disdain. Negroes cannot be expected to curb and eliminate the few who are anti-Semitic, because they are subject to no controls we can exercise. We can however, oppose them, and we have in concrete ways. There has never been an instance of articulated Negro anti-Semitism that was not swiftly condemned by virtually all Negro leaders with the support of the

> overwhelming majority. I have myself directly attacked it within the Negro community, because it is wrong. I will continue to oppose it, because it is immoral and self-destructive.[17]

Rabbi Marc Schneier chronicles the decades-long partnership between the Jewish community and Martin Luther King Jr. and offers a balanced assessment of King's position toward the Jews: "He also spoke out against anti-Semitism in the United States, especially when the virus erupted among blacks. . . . King did what he could for the Jewish people within the limits of his role as an advocate for his own people, and within the limits of his own political and moral power."[18] Schneier also notes that King considered whether his nonviolent philosophy of opposition to political injustice might have provided an effective means of protest against Nazism for the German church. He mused:

> PERHAPS IF THERE had been a broader understanding of the uses of nonviolent direct action in Germany when Hitler was rising and consolidating his power, the brutal extermination of six million Jews and millions of other war dead might have been averted and Germany might never have become totalitarian. If Protestants and Catholics had engaged in nonviolent direct action and had made the oppression of the Jews their very own oppression and had come into the streets beside the Jew to scrub the sidewalks, and had Gentiles worn the stigmatizing yellow arm bands by the millions, a unique form of mass resistance to the Nazis might have developed.[19]

Toward the end of his life, King had to confront a new permutation of African American anti-Semitism, expressed through the framework of anti-Zionism. Speaking to the more radicalized members of the African American protest movement, who rejected nonviolence, King stated:

> YOU DECLARE, MY friend, that you do not hate the Jews, you are merely "anti-Zionist." And I say, let the truth ring forth from the high mountain tops, let it echo through the valleys of God's green earth: When people criticize Zionism, they mean Jews—this is God's own truth. Anti-Semitism . . . has been and remains a blot on the soul of

> mankind. In this we are in full agreement. So know also this: anti-Zionist is inherently anti-Semitic, and ever will be so.[20]

The intergenerational ministry of the Kings and, in particular, the philo-Semitism of Martin Luther King Jr., had a counterpart in the ministries of Adam Clayton Powell Sr. and his son, Adam Clayton Powell Jr. Through their church, Abyssinian Baptist Church in Harlem, the journey of the African American Baptists would intersect with the events taking place in Germany in an unexpected manner.

Abyssinian Baptist Church in Harlem

If Harlem in New York City was the center of African American culture from the 1920s onward, then Abyssinian Baptist Church was the spiritual heart of Harlem. One of the largest Baptist churches in the country, Abyssinian practiced an activist version of the social gospel that empowered numerous effective ministries on behalf of the poor. Under the pastoral guidance of Rev. Adam Clayton Powell Sr., and his son who succeeded him, Abyssinian Baptist Church became one of the most significant African American bastions of support for Jews during the period of the Nazi persecution. The official historical account of the congregation notes that "Abyssinian Baptist Church was in the forefront among non-Jewish congregations helping to fight anti-Semitism. Both Adam Clayton Powell, Sr., and his son had participated in numerous interfaith initiatives. In 1938, Abyssinian had signed a petition urging the U.S. to admit German Jewish immigrants, and in the 1950s it had helped raise funds to stabilize Israel's economy."[21]

Abyssinian Baptist Church played a unique role in influencing the course of the Confessing Church in Germany through its discipleship of Dietrich Bonhoeffer, and in promoting African American support for Jews in the United States through the preaching and writings of its two most influential pastors.

Dietrich Bonhoeffer and Abyssinian Baptist Church

Dietrich Bonhoeffer discovered Abyssinian Baptist Church while studying at Union Seminary in 1930–1931. The church welcomed and befriended the young German scholar "as though he had never been an outsider," and his participation in the church's life was personally transformative:

> THE EXPERIENCES OF Bonhoeffer in Harlem and at Abyssinian were truly life-changing. He would later return to Germany and be martyred in the resistance against Hitler, the Nazis, and German fascism. Nevertheless, for one entire year before his return to Nazi Germany, Bonhoeffer embraced Harlem and was himself embraced by Harlem's Abyssinian Baptist Church. From a black perspective, Bonhoeffer learned about Abyssinian Baptist Church, Harlem, and race relations in the United States.[22]

Bonhoeffer's first experience in a Jewish service occurred on an Easter morning when he couldn't get into Abyssinian's Easter service; he heard Rabbi Stephen Wise at the Free Synagogue of Manhattan. Similarly, his first experience of African American spirituality was at Abyssinian, but unfortunately "Bonhoeffer never wrote an account of his Sunday mornings" at the church.[23] Nevertheless, it is apparent that he was spiritually transformed by the experience. British Baptist Keith Clements, a Bonhoeffer scholar, asserted that Bonhoeffer's immersion into black spirituality prepared him for a future in which Nazism would oppress him: "By being banned from the pulpit and joining the oppressed and eventually being imprisoned he was laicized and made Jewish and black."[24]

McCormick Theological Seminary professor Reggie L. Williams stated that at Abyssinian Baptist Church, Bonhoeffer received a revolutionary new vision of a Christianity informed by the African American experience of social injustice that "identified Jesus with the oppressed rather than with the oppressors."[25] This "black Jesus" theology enabled Bonhoeffer to move beyond traditional German Protestant theological categories and kindled a prophetic fire in his soul:

> IN HARLEM BONHOEFFER learned of a black tradition of Jesus that connected faithfulness to God, the recognition of suffering, and the presence of Christ as co-sufferer. The ministries that Bonhoeffer participated in at Abyssinian Baptist Church, coupled with the intellectual interrogation of Jesus within the Harlem Renaissance, provided Bonhoeffer with new resources to filter the nationalism from his

> Christianity and helped to develop him into an advocate of ecumenism, of peacemaking, and of social justice.[26]

Williams asserted that Bonhoeffer's Abyssinian period prepared him to confront anti-Semitism in his homeland: "Bonhoeffer returned to Germany with key developments in his faith that gave him the ability to see singular distortions in German Christianity and empowered him to push back against the emerging Nazi government racism."[27] There is no doubt that Bonhoeffer's Baptist experience influenced his understanding of the challenges the church faced, but Williams fails to address whether Abyssinian specifically influenced Bonhoeffer's views on Jews and anti-Semitism. In part, this is due to Williams's focus on the ecclesiology and social outreach of Abyssinian's senior pastor, Rev. Adam Clayton Powell Sr., while, with one exception, neglecting the question of Powell's specific views concerning anti-Semitism.[28]

Williams did cite a page from Powell's autobiography, *Against the Tide*, which summarized Powell's pastoral approach to race relations in general: "During my leadership at Abyssinia, I was criticized by some members of my race for trying to help all races understand each other better that they might love each other more. To this end we had a Jew on the Usher Board, a German teacher in the Sunday School."[29] This was the sole passage in Powell's autobiography that indicated his awareness of Bonhoeffer's attendance at Abyssinian. It does not, however, provide any insight regarding what Bonhoeffer might have learned about the African American preacher's attitudes toward anti-Semitism and Jews.

The Philo-Semitism of Adam Clayton Powell Sr.

Adam Clayton Powell Sr. revealed his respect for Jews in an illustration from a sermon that was preached in 1928. In "Progress—the Law of Life," Powell criticized the extravagant funerals of church members; the money carelessly wasted could have been spent furthering the lives of the living. In contrast, Powell pointed to the Jewish community and advised: "As Negroes we ought to learn many lessons from the Jews and one of the most important is the financial modesty which characterizes the funerals of that rich race . . . they bury very little money under the ground."[30]

After retiring from his pastorate, Powell wrote two more books in addition to *Against the Tide*, which more specifically revealed his attitudes regarding anti-Semitism and race relations. In *Palestine and Saints in Caesar's Household*, Powell chronicled his travels through the Holy Land. Although this was his primary reason for publishing this account, he confessed in the preface that he had an additional motive for sharing his travel experiences:

> THE SECOND REASON for writing the first part of this book is to help stem the world's rising tide of fierce, ungodly anti-Semitism. The author admits that it is a very feeble effort, but it is the first he has seen from a member of his race. On the other hand, he has heard whisperings of indifference to the campaign to exterminate the Jewish race—if not approval of it. The colored people should be the last, even by their silence, to give consent to the brutal persecution of the Jews. For if this campaign of inhuman cruelty against the Jews should succeed, who knows but what the same evil forces would next attempt to put the colored people on the rack.[31]

Powell linked the biblical account of Israel's servitude in ancient Egypt to the more contemporary African American experience of slavery and then criticized Hitler and Mussolini for stealing the possessions of Jews prior to permitting them to emigrate.[32] He countered the anti-Semitic prejudice that Jews cheat others in commercial dealings and pointedly passed judgment upon Gentiles, and more specifically Christians, for such prejudice:

> AS LONG AS the Gentiles have this attitude toward the Jews, we are wasting time and money trying to win them to Christianity. We cannot win people to Christ unless we love and trust them. I do not know any Christian nation among whom the Jews have lived that has given them an example which would encourage them to follow Jesus. In Germany, where Martin Luther made the fight of the centuries for religious liberty, the Jews get about as much consideration as mad dogs.[33]

In Palestine, Powell discovered that Zionism was "in no sense a religious movement, as many people seem to think, especially those who are using this as proof of the Second Coming of Christ. It is a commercial and political movement pure and simple."[34] Although he rejected fundamentalist-evangelical eschatology, Powell embraced a fully pro-Zionist analysis of the Balfour Declaration (1917) and the White Paper (1939). While acknowledging Arab opposition to Jewish immigration, Powell remained staunchly Zionist, and he even wondered whether Mussolini was the driving force behind the Arab opposition.[35] Powell's sympathy was clearly with Italy's persecuted Jewish population:

> NO ONE CAN remember the picture of 4,000 Jews trudging across the snow-clad Alps on March 12, 1939, the day on which Pope Pius XII was publicly recognized as the Christian leader of Italy and the Catholic leader of the world, without tears in his heart for the sad plight of the Jews and their senseless Italian persecutors. Why were they driven out of Italy? Because they were Jews. Why were they not wanted where they were going? Because they were Jews.[36]

Surprisingly, Powell expressed a view not shared by most other African American Baptist leaders at the time. His colleagues argued that the African Americans' plight under slavery and segregation was equal to or greater than Jewish suffering, but even before the Holocaust had reached its horrific consummation, Powell begged to differ: "The Negroes in America who are complaining about race prejudice have scarcely had a taste of it compared to the Jews."[37]

In response to the race-related riots in Detroit and other American cities, Powell published *Riots and Ruins*. Powell dedicated the book to "all those who are working for just and peaceful race relations throughout the world."[38] Powell argued that African Americans should be judged by others according to the behavioral standards exemplified by the most accomplished African Americans, as opposed to the actions of a minority of blacks who exhibited antisocial behaviors. In like manner, Powell stated, the Jewish race should be "measured by Moses, Jesus, Saint Paul, and Albert Einstein, not by Judas Iscariot and Nathan Leopold."[39]

As the conflict in Europe was concluding, Powell provided a scathing assessment of Hitler and his anti-Semitic agenda that was in full accord with his longstanding solidarity with the Jewish people:

> HITLER IS NOT hated so much for fighting England, Russia, and America. These nations can take care of themselves and they are doing a fine job of it. The thing that will make Hitler the most despicable cur and skunk in history is the cowardly and dastardly way he has treated the defenseless Jews in Europe. Ten years ago when his evil influence began to spread over the world there were eight million, three hundred thousand Jews in Europe. Today, there are only three million Jews. Five million have been killed or driven out of their homes. Because of this colossal crime committed against an unorganized, unarmed people, Germany can never again become a strong nation. She is doomed and damned. The God of the Hebrews has written Ichabod over the skies of Berlin.[40]

Powell was more than willing to condemn both anti-Semitism and racial prejudice against African Americans, no matter what country practiced discrimination. In the spirit of an Old Testament prophet, he proclaimed, "Fascists of America and of Germany, tear down your hypocritical signs in restricted areas 'Jews and Negroes not admitted' or the democratic cyclone of God Almighty's wrath will blow them with you into the sea of oblivion. Hurry up! The time is short. The storm is rising!"[41]

American Anti-Semitism and Adam Clayton Powell Jr.

Rev. Adam Clayton Powell Jr. joined the ministerial staff of Abyssinian Baptist Church in 1931, succeeded his father as senior pastor of Abyssinian Baptist Church in 1937, and served the church until his death in 1972.[42] As one of the leading voices of the African American community in New York City and later in the United States Congress, Powell had numerous opportunities to address relations between African Americans and Jews, and anti-Semitism in particular.[43]

The Harlem riot of 1935, in which protestors damaged the retail businesses of mostly Jewish merchants along 125th Street, elevated the tensions between Jews, most of whom no longer resided in Harlem, and its black residents. Anti-Semitic individuals rose to ad hoc community leadership, including Sufi Abdul Hamid, known as the "Black Hitler." Biographer Charles V. Hamilton observed that Powell Jr. associated with all segments of African American protest, even communists and anti-Semites like Hamid: "One week he would be picketing with Sufi's loud, raucous followers. Then he would make comments denouncing their more extreme anti-Semitic slogans."[44]

Following Kristallnacht, Powell Jr. took an offering for Jews at a meeting hosted by Abyssinian Baptist Church in which a rabbi was invited to speak. The *American Hebrew* reported:

> NEGRO SYMPATHY FOR oppressed minorities in Central and Eastern Europe was given concrete expression of $130 by members of the Abyssinian Baptist Church of New York City for the aid of Christian and Jewish refugees. The sum represented the total collected at a meeting in the church addressed by Rabbi Harry Halpern of the East Midwood Jewish Center of Brooklyn, NY. The sum will be equally divided between the American Jewish Joint Distribution Committee and the American Committee for Christian German refugees. In forwarding the check to the two refugee aid agencies, Rev. A. Clayton Powell, Jr., pastor of the Abyssinian Baptist Church, stated that this was the largest collection that the church had contributed during the past eight years.[45]

In his book-length political manifesto, *Marching Blacks*, Powell Jr. indicated that he did not personally embrace anti-Semitism and considered its emergence within the matrix of African American protest as an insidious import from the majority white society. He wrote:

> ANTI-SEMITISM IS A deadly virus of the American bloodstream. It is almost as deadly as anti-Negroism. In some sections it is deadlier. Just as the poor whites were told that "any white man is better than every Negro"—so the white South frequently told the black worker that "any black man was better than every Jew." Anti-Semitism among Negroes was a tragic and ironic paradox. It was deliberately instilled by those who wanted to keep the masses divided. It grew as Negro workers heard their Christian employees at home and in industry condemn the Jews. Black nationalists, especially in Harlem, found it profitable to stir up anti-Jewish feeling. Bewildered, frustrated blacks carried bitterness towards Jews in their hearts.[46]

Furthermore, Powell Jr. believed that Jewish legal support of the Scottsboro Nine defendants "was the first successful refutation of the anti-Semitic propaganda with which the Negroes had been bombarded" and was followed up by strong Jewish labor union support for African American economic rights. He minimized the existence of anti-Semitic feelings among African Americans in the 1940s: "Today while anti-Semitism flourishes and rages on the outskirts of Harlem, in downtown Manhattan and on Washington Heights, there is very little anti-Semitism among Negroes themselves."[47]

During the Second World War, Powell Jr. consistently positioned African Americans as pro-democracy and anti-Nazi. Ready and eager to serve as an equal to whites in the armed forces, the "Negro had always been an anti-Fascist."[48] However, Powell as well as other leaders, as constituents of the "Double V" campaign,[49] were not satisfied with an overseas victory over German and Italian fascism; the United States had once and for all to face the civil rights crisis of its own making and achieve full freedom for African Americans.

In a speech in 1943, Powell asserted, "We cannot divorce anti-Semitism and jimcrowism. . . . I refuse to let people call Jews Christ killers because I know that Jews were Christ creators."[50] Furthermore, he wrote: "The Negro began to shout that you cannot beat Hitler in Europe and let Hitlerism run rampant in the streets of America. There was no division now. Gone were caste and class, nationalism and internationalism. It was all out for the double V—victory at home and victory abroad."[51]

Powell Jr. reserved some of his harshest criticism for the church because of its hypocrisy: "The fundamental postulate of Christianity is equality and brotherhood. We have perverted this glorious doctrine to exclude interracial love. Religion has lost its ethical integrity and, therefore, its moral dynamic. . . . Anti-Semitism springs from the steps of cathedrals. Anti-Negroism has the implied blessing of the church."[52] He criticized the church for being unfaithful to its calling of uniting people, and thus it was a failed institution that did not represent the aspirations of its Founder. This failure manifested itself in American anti-Semitism, as well as racial prejudice against African Americans.

The Friendship of Rev. Thomas S. Harten and Rabbi Alexander Lyons

The 1935 National Baptist convention was held in Brooklyn, New York, a borough where both the Jewish and African American communities enjoyed large populations. In a display of solidarity between the two communities, the convention's vice president, Rev. Dr. T. S.

Harten, pastor of Holy Trinity Baptist Church in Brooklyn, introduced one of his clergy colleagues from the borough, Rabbi Alexander Lyons from the Eighth Avenue Temple. The rabbi's address to the assembly was positively received.[53] Harten and Lyons were personal friends and, as leaders of their respective communities, worked together to promote racial equality and justice for each other's constituency.

Rabbi Alexander Lyons was a dedicated advocate for civil rights and justice, and he enjoyed reaching out to the Christian world for support and cooperation. His obituary in *The Brooklyn Daily Eagle* stated:

> DR. LYONS, WHO was known as the "dean of Brooklyn rabbis," . . . was perhaps best known as a constant crusader for better understanding between Jew and Christian. In fact his activities along this line led to his being called the "Christian Rabbi." It is difficult to estimate the full extent of the services of this broad-minded religious leader. He will be greatly missed not only among his own people but by all Brooklynites without regard to race, creed or color.[54]

The "Christian Rabbi" sought to help his Gentile friends recognize and oppose the perversity of Hitler's anti-Semitism. In his February 1934 "Heart to Heart" column in *The Brooklyn Daily Eagle*, Lyons wrote:

> THE REAL CHRIST has again been crucified in Germany. His brethren are again the scapegoat. His real followers are ignored, insulted. Even Jews of genuine Christian conversion and loyalty are refused identification with Christianity. History has no parallel of this caricature, this contemptuous contortion of the loving righteousness of Jesus by the cruelty of the pseudo racialism of Hitler. Are Christians going to stand for this?[55]

Lyons often attended Christian gatherings, including Baptist church services. In 1935, he was the first rabbi ever to preach at Emmanuel Baptist Church (affiliated with the Northern Baptist Convention), and he spoke on the "claim of brotherhood" between Jews and Christians.[56] Later that year, he spoke at the Hanson Place Baptist

Church, calling for a joint Jewish-Christian "boycott of German goods and non participation of American athletes in the proposed Berlin Olympics."[57] He also advocated for black civil rights; just before his death in 1939 he backed calls for the appointment of an African American judge, declaring that African Americans were "entitled to a Negro magistrate in Brooklyn."[58]

The first article in *The Brooklyn Daily Eagle* that linked Harten and Lyons was a report about a tumultuous meeting Harten presided over in response to the infamous Scottsboro case, in which nine African American teenage boys were on trial for allegedly raping two white women in Alabama in 1933. Approximately four thousand people attended the protest meeting, and several dignitaries were present. After being introduced by Harten, Lyons captivated the audience as he identified with them and then employed Christian imagery to portray the plight of Hitler's victims:

> RABBI LYONS ASTONISHED many of his listeners when he recalled that he is himself a native of Alabama. He resented the Southern prosecutors' recent reference to "Jew money" raised for the defense of Patterson, Weems and their fellow prisoners. "I want to see you, and all other Christians," he said, "interpret the Resurrection properly. I am tired of a religion of mere pretense or theory. As surely as there is a God of Israel, who neither slumbers nor sleeps, there must be justice for the relatives of your Savior." He compared Southern race hatreds to Hitlerism and urged justice for all—Jew, colored, white, Gentile—on grounds of common humanity.[59]

In 1936 the progressive Jewish leader and the black Baptist pastor joined forces to combat anti-Semitism and protest against Adolf Hitler's cynical use of sports for political ends. They focused on the proposed heavyweight boxing match between the African American Joe Louis and the German Max Schmeling at Yankee Stadium. Loyola University Chicago historian Lewis Erenberg observed:

> WHILE THE POLITICAL implications of the first Louis-Schmeling fight took on greater life after the match, there were some undercurrents to suggest that boxing all along was embroiled in the international tensions of the era. Even before Schmeling's victory [in 1936] turned him

> into a full-fledged Nazi hero, Jewish and black groups had taken notice of Nazi racial philosophy, the regime's treatment of Jews, and their attitudes towards blacks. For the past year, anti-fascist groups had campaigned against American participation in the Berlin Olympics, and since the fight took place in New York, Jewish and anti-fascist groups debated whether to boycott Schmeling too. For the most part, they decided there was no need. Louis would win and that would put an end to the Nazi hero. As a result, many Jews and blacks who disapproved of the bout decided to attend.[60]

Both Harten and Lyons saw the boxing match as an opportunity to make a statement against the policies of the Nazi regime, and in the process, bring the Jewish and African American communities together in a common cause where both had interests at stake. Erenberg recounted the situation in this way:

> Rabbi Alexander Lyons of Eighth Avenue Temple and the Reverend Dr. Thomas Harten, Negro pastor of Holy Trinity Baptist Church, told an audience of six hundred gathered in Harten's chapel that they would attend the fight to protest Hitler's view that a bout between a German and a Negro was improper. They urged their audience of blacks and Jews to join with "every decent American" in boycotting all German-made goods until "Hitler comes to his senses." Rabbi Lyons declared that the Nazis were not merely anti-Semitic; they were "anti-everyone who has something they want." He pointed to several German Jews in the audience who had been forced to flee their country, and he charged that the Nazi idea of a "pure Aryan race" also discriminated against blacks. "There is no such thing as a pure race anywhere on earth," the Rabbi asserted. Both men announced, however, that they planned to attend the fight to root for Louis against Nazi racial theories. As Schmeling became more closely identified with Nazi Germany and assumed his place as the logical contender for the heavyweight throne, this sentiment would produce an organized boycott movement that would play an important role in his quest for a comeback.[61]

A month after this joint appearance, Harten invited Lyons to a meeting at his church on "the Negro's place in America." In front of some five hundred attendees, Harten "asked the Jews of America to join with the Negroes in a fight against race prejudice." In response, Lyons stated, "God did not create one human inferior to another and it is irreligious and illogical to presume that He did."[62]

Notes

1. "News from the Churches," *New Jersey Baptist Bulletin* (April 1944), 5.
2. "February Is Brotherhood Month," *New Jersey Baptist Bulletin* (February 1946), National Supplement, 1.
3. See C. Eric Lincoln and Lawrence H. Mamiya, *The Black Church in the African American Experience* (Durham, NC: Duke University Press, 1990), 115–37.
4. Martin Luther King Sr., *Daddy King: An Autobiography* (New York: William Morrow and Company, 1980), 97. I am indebted to Dr. Julian Ellison for alerting me to Rev. King's participation, which he investigated in an unpublished lecture delivered at Columbia University on February 17, 2011. It is interesting to note that King does not mention the BWA congress held in Atlanta in 1939. Ebenezer did host a guest speaker, J. B. Middlebrook, from Great Britain, who attended the BWA congress, according to J. H. Rushbrooke, *Sixth Baptist World Congress Atlanta, GA July 22-28, 1939*, 309.
5. Clayborne Carson, ed., *The Autobiography of Martin Luther King Jr.* (New York: Grand Central Publishing, 1998), 18–27.
6. Ibid., 31–32.
7. Edgar Sheffield Brightman, *The Future of Christianity* (New York: Abingdon, 1937), 79.
8. Ibid., 126.
9. Ibid., 150.
10. Martin Luther King Jr., *Strength to Love* (Philadelphia: Fortress, 1981), 52.
11. Ibid., 83.
12. Quoted in Marc Schneier, *Shared Dreams: Martin Luther King Jr. and the Jewish Community* (Woodstock, VT: Jewish Lights Publishing, 2008), 77.
13. King Jr., *Strength to Love*, 51.
14. "Letter from Birmingham Jail" (1963), in *Autobiography of Martin Luther King Jr.*, 195. King returned the theme of personality later in 1963 when he preached at the funeral of the children killed by the bombing of Birmingham's Sixteenth Street Baptist Church. Calling on the mourners to reject revenge through violence, King said, "Somehow we must believe that the most misguided among them [the assassins] can learn to respect the dignity and worth of all human personality" (232).
15. Ibid., 194.
16. Carson, ed., *Autobiography of Martin Luther King Jr.*, 331.
17. Ibid., 310.
18. Schneier, *Shared Dreams*, xiv.
19. Ibid., 34.
20. Ibid., 178.
21. Genna Rae McNeil, Houston Bryan Roberson, Quinton Hosford Dixie, and Kevin McGruder, *Witness: Two Hundred Years of African-American Faith and Practice at the Abyssinian Baptist Church of Harlem, New York* (Grand Rapids, MI: Eerdmans, 2014), 225. The church even purchased Israeli bonds; see 217.
22. Ibid., 143.
23. Charles Marsh, *A Life of Dietrich Bonhoeffer* (New York: Alfred A. Knopf, 2014), 119, 127–28.
24. Keith W. Clements, *What Freedom? The Persistent Challenge of Dietrich Bonhoeffer* (Eugene, OR: Wipf and Stock, 2011), 118.
25. Reggie L. Williams, *Bonhoeffer's Black Jesus: Harlem Renaissance Theology and an Ethic of Resistance* (Waco, TX: Baylor University Press, 2014), 2.
26. Ibid., 107.

27. Ibid., 5.
28. Ibid., 86–103.
29. Adam Clayton Powell Sr., *Against the Tide: An Autobiography* (New York: Richard R. Smith, 1938), 190. Partially cited in Williams, *Bonhoeffer's Black Jesus*, 91.
30. Powell Sr., *Against the Tide*, 167; quote on 172.
31. Adam Clayton Powell Sr., *Palestine and Saints in Caesar's Household* (New York: Richard R. Smith, 1939), viii.
32. Ibid., 13–15.
33. Ibid., 15–16.
34. Ibid., 25.
35. Ibid., 26–29.
36. Ibid., 29–30.
37. Ibid., 30.
38. Adam Clayton Powell Sr., *Riots and Ruins* (New York: Richard R. Smith, 1945), v.
39. Ibid., 77. Nathan Leopold was convicted of committing murder in 1924.
40. Ibid., 98–99.
41. Ibid., 100.
42. McNeil et al., *Witness*, 152–232. See also Leroy Fitts, *A History of Black Baptists* (Nashville: Broadman, 1985), 271–74.
43. Weisbord and Stein, *Bittersweet Encounter*, 60–62.
44. Charles V. Hamilton, *Adam Clayton Powell Jr.: The Political Biography of an American Dilemma* (New York: Atheneum, 1991), 91–93.
45. "Negro Church Aids Jewish Refugees," *American Hebrew* (23 December 1938), 8.
46. Adam Clayton Powell Jr., *Marching Blacks: An Interpretive History of the Rise of the Black Common Man* (New York: Dial Press, 1945), 66.
47. Ibid., 66–67.
48. Ibid., 117.
49. See Hamilton, *Adam Clayton Powell, Jr.*, 134.
50. Ibid., 154; original source, *The People's Voice* (24 June 1944), 5.
51. Powell Jr., *Marching Blacks*, 129. See also Hamilton, *Adam Clayton Powell, Jr.*, 119–20.
52. Powell Jr., *Marching Blacks*, 198–99.
53. *Minutes of the 1935 Annual Session of the National Baptist Convention, U.S.A.*, 39. See "Influence of U.S. Urged to Prevent War in Ethiopia," *The Brooklyn Daily Eagle* (5 September 1935), 3.
54. Obituary, *The Brooklyn Daily Eagle* (7 June 1939), 14.
55. Alexander Lyons, Heart to Heart column, *The Brooklyn Daily Eagle* (14 February 1934), 36.
56. "Asserts Brotherhood Can Be Made Reality," *The Brooklyn Daily Eagle* (11 February 1935), 4.
57. "Rabbi Lyons Asks a Modern Crusade against Nazi Rule," *The Brooklyn Daily Eagle* (12 November 1935), 11.
58. "Rabbi Backs Plea for Negro Judge," *The Brooklyn Daily Eagle* (24 May 1939), 7.
59. "Mayor Offers Moral Support in Negro Trial," *The Brooklyn Daily Eagle* (17 April 1933), 15. Lyons also spoke at a follow-up meeting in December 1933; see "Verdict Upset Is Predicted by Leibowitz," *The Brooklyn Daily Eagle* (12 December 1933), 17.
60. Lewis A. Erenberg, *The Greatest Fight of Our Generation: Louis vs. Schmeling* (Oxford: Oxford University Press, 2006), 102.
61. Ibid., 102. This quote is from "Rabbi, Negro Pastor Will Cheer for Louis in Schmeling Fight," *The Brooklyn Daily Eagle* (20 April 1936), 6.
62. "Racial Prejudices Hit in Discussion of Negro Question," *The Brooklyn Daily Eagle* (25 My 1936), 4.

Contemporary Impressions

Co-Sufferers with the Jewish People

The National Baptist Convention's response to the persecution of the Jews in Germany shared much in common with that of their white denominational counterparts. Like the Northern and Southern Baptist Conventions, the National Baptist Convention responded to the persecution of European Jews, the rising tide of anti-Semitism, and the Holocaust in three ways.

First, the leaders of the National Baptist Convention employed classic Baptist theological core convictions as they protested against Hitler's persecution of the Jewish people. The following themes predominated: the doctrine of the sacredness of human personality, the appeal to the fatherhood of God and the brotherhood of man that unites all humanity, a political philosophy that opposed totalitarianism and exalted democracy, and the charge that Nazism was fundamentally anti-Christian (it was a threat to Christianity and the liberty of the church). Yet, and quite significantly, even in this appropriation of dominant white Baptist thinking, African American clergy were able to add a creative twist from time to time. For example, L. K. Williams's brilliant coining of the phrase "suppressed, chained personality" in 1940 powerfully evoked the African American memory of American slavery and servitude.

Second, National Baptists produced a significant response to Kristallnacht. Their uniquely crafted document was not sufficiently recognized at the time, perhaps because it was not widely disseminated in the white Baptist or secular newspapers. Placed in context, it properly deserves to be compared with the Northern Baptist Convention's General Council Kristallnacht proclamation. It should also be appreciated in light of the absence of a similar Southern Baptist statement.

Third, National Baptist Convention leaders responded to the Nazi challenge in conversation with the global Baptist community through the Baptist World Alliance. National Baptist delegates participated vigorously in the racialism debates at the 1934 Berlin congress and leveraged that participation and outcome to convince the BWA to select Atlanta as the site for the next congress.

Likewise, the National Baptist Convention's response diverged from the American white Baptist response in several historically significant ways.

Whereas white Baptists viewed the Jewish plight as secondary to the survival of the Baptist churches in Europe, the National Baptist leaders interpreted the 1934 racialism resolution as a springboard for hope for African American liberation. From their perspective, if Baptists could courageously stand up to Hitler on behalf of Jews in Germany, then imagine what impact the worldwide Baptist movement might have on the discriminatory segregationist norms of the American South. Black delegates lobbied for Atlanta as the next venue precisely for this reason. Thus, the Jewish plight in Germany paved the way for a Baptist prophetic witness on behalf of African Americans five years later. It fueled the dreams of the National Baptist leaders, who hoped they had discovered a new and dramatic way to confront white Christian indifference to black claims for equality. Stated another way, whereas white American Baptists were bystanders to the Jewish tragedy in Europe, African American Baptists portrayed themselves as co-sufferers with Jews in a racially unjust world.

As a result of the Berlin deliberations and actions, National Baptists finally possessed a strategy to call white Baptists to accountability for their bystander attitude toward racial discrimination in the United States. The lesson National Baptist leaders took away from Berlin was that the white Christian churches had to live up to the demands of Jesus in Europe and in America, and that the failure of Western civilization to live according to its Christian ideals led to both the Holocaust and discrimination against blacks. Hitler could not have succeeded without German Christian complicity, support, or passive acceptance. Similarly, segregation could succeed only if white Christians in America refused to actively oppose it. Thus, the white church was the object of black prophetic critique, as much as Hitler.

Whereas white Baptists had no easy way to identify with the Jews, black Baptists, like the larger African American culture, viewed Jews as fellow sufferers. Yet this identification carried its own matrix of internal stresses. It did not lead to any large-scale denominational grassroots or practical assistance for Jewish immigrants such as the Northern Baptist Christian Friendliness movement. With the exception of sporadic local church acts of compassion, African American Baptists managed to produce only verbal expressions of sympathy. To be fair, African American poverty, which was far greater than that experienced by the majority white society, should be accepted as a mitigating factor. Yet even this sympathy was qualified by a sense of envy and a corresponding demand for attention.

When African Americans acknowledged Jewish suffering under Hitler, they also tended to compare the relative severity of Jewish and African American suffering (a form of competition) and subsequently felt justified in complaining that Jews unfairly were receiving more sympathy and support than American blacks experienced. National Baptist envy was manifested in their calls for help for Ethiopia, even in the last paragraph of the Kristallnacht resolution. The Jewish plight was not seen as significant in itself but as a kind of foil for addressing black concerns. It was more often than not addressed through the lens of black civil rights. Later on there appeared to be no National Baptist initiatives to help Jewish survivors of the Holocaust, even though the Lott Carey Baptist Mission Convention vowed to provide humanitarian aid after World War II concluded.

The National Baptist Woman's Auxiliary provided a clear and distinct female voice in this debate about Jewish persecution in Germany and its relationship to American civil rights. The reports and speeches of Sarah Willie Layten and Nannie Helen Burroughs provided insight into how African American women viewed events and demonstrated that they were very concerned with the plight of the Jewish people.

Whereas both Northern and Southern Baptist state conventions periodically passed resolutions or had presentations on the persecution of Jews, I could not discover any evidence of a corresponding level of activity within the National Baptist Convention. NBC records containing the minutes for regional country meetings indicated that these meetings were concerned with internal organizational matters, spiritual inspiration and encouragement, fellowship, and advocacy of domestic civil rights.

The apparent lack of activity on the regional level did not mean that African American Baptists were not involved in the defense of the Jewish people. On a local church level, key African American clergy were engaged in the issue, expressed strong opposition to anti-Semitism, and befriended Jewish colleagues. Abyssinian's influence on Bonhoeffer changed the trajectory of his ministry, and the Holocaust era's concern for the core Baptist conviction of personality became embedded in the theological and social outlook of Martin Luther King Jr.

PART SIX

The Baptist World Alliance and the Plight of the Jews

J. H. Rushbrooke,[1] Baptist World Alliance general secretary and later president, was the most recognizable leader of the global community of Baptists from the 1920s until his death in 1947. He endeavored to create and foster a unified international movement, and in pursuit of this dream, he was in constant communication with constituent bodies, traveling widely and composing volumes of correspondence. In his letter to the Southern Baptist Convention in 1941, Rushbrooke celebrated the central role the largest Baptist entity in the United States had played in the formation and history of the Baptist World Alliance:

> NO CONSTITUENT OF the Alliance has a stronger hold on the mind and heart of Baptists than the Southern Convention. It is the largest body in our membership; and it has a special place in our history. It was the energetic advocacy of a Southern Baptist journal that brought about the calling of the First Baptist World Congress in London, at which our Alliance was constituted. You have contributed to the Alliance two of its most influential presidents, one of whom, our beloved and honoured Doctor Truett, is happily still with you. It was your initiative that induced the World Congress of 1939 to lay its central emphasis on the task of world-evangelisation, and your recent generous gift of two hundred thousand dollars to the work of the British Baptist Missionary Society supplies irrefutable evidence that your concern for the Gospel, and you in sympathy for your brethren in their difficulties, are not in word only, but also in deed.[2]

From its inception, the three largest bodies of US Baptists (Southern, Northern, and National) assisted in the creation of the Baptist World Alliance, participated in its meetings, and provided significant leadership to and financial support for its ministries, and so it is fair to say that the history and mission of the Baptist World Alliance and the major Baptist denominations in the United States intertwined continuously. This was certainly the case on the issue of Nazi Germany and the persecution of the Jewish people from 1933 through 1945 and the postwar Allied response to hundreds of thousands of displaced persons from 1945 through 1948. At the onset of 1933, Baptists claimed to have a global membership of 10,882,279 adherents, with 9,587,826 living in North America (and most of these members lived in the United States).[3] The BWA and the three US organizations were in constant conversation, coordinating responses on issues and acting in cooperation with each other when initiatives were launched.

The identity of the Baptist World Alliance as a global fellowship of autonomous national Baptist entities was defined by its core convictions, which church historian Richard V. Pierard listed as "the authority of Scripture; salvation through faith in Christ; believers' baptism by immersion; congregational church government; and religious liberty."[4] The mission of the Baptist World Alliance was explained in the preamble of its constitution. As a global fellowship, the BWA was created to "show the essential oneness of Baptist people in the Lord Jesus Christ, to impart inspiration to the brotherhood and to promote the spirit of fellowship, service, and cooperation among its members; but this Alliance may in no way interfere with the independence of the churches or assume the administrative functions of existing organizations."[5] For the BWA, and for Rushbrooke in particular, fostering and maintaining the unity of the Baptist movement across national boundaries constituted a unique core conviction that was not necessarily shared by the constituent national or local Baptist entities. Rushbrooke's application of this core BWA-level conviction influenced how he responded to the dilemma of the German Baptists' allegiance to Hitler from 1933 through 1945 and furthermore colored his overall response to totalitarian persecution of the Jews, causing him to be more focused on Baptist persecution in Rumania than on Jewish issues and needs.

Notes

1. Ernest A. Payne, *James Henry Rushbrooke, 1870–1947: A Baptist Greatheart* (London: Carey Kingsgate Press, 1954); and Bernard Green, *Tomorrow's Man: A Biography of James Henry Rushbrooke* (London: Baptist Historical Society, 1996).

2. *Minutes of the Proceedings of the 1941 Southern Baptist Convention*, Baptist World Alliance Letter from J. H. Rushbrooke, 28.

3. J. H. Rushbrooke, "Baptist World Strength at the Opening of 1933," *The Watchman-Examiner* (2 February 1933), 106.

4. Richard V. Pierard, ed., *Baptists Together in Christ 1905–2005: A Hundred-Year History of the Baptist World Alliance* (Birmingham, AL: Samford University Press, 2005), xv.

5. Preamble to BWA constitution, in J. H. Rushbrooke, *Sixth Baptist World Congress Atlanta, GA July 22-28, 1939* (Atlanta: The Baptist World Alliance, 1939), 313.

Chapter 18

The Fifth World Congress Confronts Hitler in Berlin

The Fifth World Congress of the Baptist World Alliance originally was scheduled to be held in Berlin during July 1933, but the global economic depression made the costs of participation prohibitive, especially for American delegates. Nevertheless, in May 1932, Northern Baptist leader and BWA honorary associate secretary Clifton D. Gray hoped that the international gathering could still take place. He wrote, "My personal judgment is that at the present moment we ought to go right ahead with our plans for the Congress because we do not wish in any way to disappoint our European friends."[1] However, as he feared, the depression worsened and the BWA leaders realized that this plan was not feasible. Accordingly the BWA executive committee sadly decided to delay the congress for one year.[2]

The unexpected ascension to power by Adolf Hitler and the National Socialist Party in the first quarter of 1933, followed by the initial waves of persecution against Germany's Jewish population, prompted many Baptists, including some from the United States, to wonder whether it was wise and just to hold a congress in Berlin. They feared that it might provide some measure of political legitimacy and support to the troubling agenda of the new Nazi government. In April 1933, when Nazi discriminatory measures against Jews were first announced, even the local German Baptist steering committee members were concerned that "the political and religious situation was such as to make it difficult to carry on with any confidence preparations for a world Congress in Berlin" in 1934, and they recommended Zurich as an alternative. J. H. Rushbrooke relayed the advice of Paul Schmidt, a pro-Nazi pastor and politician who advised him that the Hitler government would be displeased about any unilateral changes in venue.[3]

A few weeks later, Gray wrote in a letter (presumably to Rushbrooke) that the administrative subcommittee had met and by consensus agreed that the congress needed to take place in 1934 and should not be held outside Berlin "unless the German Baptists felt this necessary." Gray also revealed the concern felt about German anti-Semitism:

> OUR COMMITTEE WAS influenced by what has taken place in Europe in the last ten days—Hitler's Reichstag speech, apparent agreement on Mussolini's 4-power pact, and other events which seem at this distance to give an atmosphere completely changed from what it was six weeks ago. We also felt that the present anti-Semitism and other phases of German internal policy might take on a different colour a little later, and that next Fall it might be possible to consider Berlin again.[4]

This may be the first specific BWA expression of concern that Nazi anti-Semitism represented a challenge to the holding of the fifth congress in Berlin. The subcommittee hoped that it might represent a passing phenomenon and thus not derail a Berlin setting for the international conclave.

However, the issue would not disappear so easily. At its July 1933 meeting, the subcommittee received correspondence from two member unions regarding the "anti-Jewish action of the German Government": "A letter was submitted from the Baptist Union of Scotland transmitting a copy of a resolution on this subject, together with a further letter from the Baptist Union of Australia stating that if the Alliance decided to take any action, the Australian Baptists wished to associate themselves with it." In response, the committee noted that Baptist entities were "at liberty to express themselves in any way that they consider right." Nevertheless, the committee decided that it was "inadvisable that the Alliance as such should formally adopt any resolution, since this is scarcely necessary, the Baptist attitude being well-known, and might prejudice a possible approach to the German Government in the interests of the Baptists of Germany."[5]

For the first time, the leaders of the Baptist World Alliance were confronted with the competing demands of core convictions—religious and political liberty (applied to anti-Semitism) versus preserving the unity of the international Baptist fellowship. The latter won out, in deference to German Baptist needs and sensitivities. The precedent was established, and Rushbrooke in particular promoted it throughout the Nazi period.

Journeying to Berlin (1933–1934)

Throughout the second half of 1933, Germany's ongoing political repression of individuals and parties that were not aligned with the Nazis did not escape the notice of Baptists in the United States. They were concerned that their own freedom to speak and act without interference or censorship might be curtailed.[6] Earl Barton Moyer, office editor for West Virginia's *Baptist Banner*, summarized Baptist concerns about Berlin in his editorial "Baptists May Not Go to Berlin":

> IF ANY CHANGE is made it will be a direct result of the attitude of the Hitler Government toward religious organizations and their persecution of the Jews. . . . No greater rebuke could be given to the Nazi Government than the removing of the Alliance to another country, for it would be a rebuke from all the world expressed through one body. The Baptist World Alliance is an international body. No group in the world is so fittingly qualified to rebuke Germany for religious intolerance as Baptists, due to their insistence upon personal liberty in behalf and absolute separation of the church from the state.[7]

Richard V. Pierard, a church historian, described the dynamics facing the BWA and the German Baptists, and he asserted that the Nazis had a political agenda in enticing the international Baptist community to hold its congress in Berlin:

> SINCE THE HITLER government was responding to foreign criticism of its anti-Semitic policies by limiting all kinds of international activities, the German Baptist leaders feared the Congress would expose their movement to the charge of "internationalism" and threaten their newly-gained freedom from the pressures of the established church. The Nazis, however, saw the public relations benefits of a Baptist World Congress, as it would show international guests that the new Germany was quite different from the "horror stories" about the Nazi regime. The German

> Baptists were seeking to achieve social respectability and to resist being forced into a homogenized national "Reich Church" (as some Nazi religious figures desired), and they failed to recognize they were being used.[8]

Rushbrooke responded to these concerns by waging a relentless and energetic campaign to convince Baptists that it was safe to attend the meetings in Berlin, that the German government had assured leaders the proceedings could take place without interference, and that the German Baptists desperately needed the support and encouragement they would receive as congress hosts.[9] The following explanation from the general secretary to the Southern Baptist Convention in May 1934 was illustrative of his concerns and hopes for the Berlin congress:

> TO GO TO Berlin is to stand by our brethren in a country where evangelical Christians are exposed to peculiar difficulties and perplexities. The German Baptists have appealed for a demonstration of our fraternal sympathy, and in this year—the centennial year from Oncken's baptism, when our debt to our German fellow-disciples is so powerfully brought home to us—we shall not refuse to respond to their appeal. . . . It is simply ludicrous to suppose that it is unsafe to go to Germany. I have been there repeatedly, and even within the last month, and I know. Further, there is no foundation for the idea that in Germany our Congress would be denied freedom of speech. If the World Alliance had not been fully convinced upon that point, it would never have consented to go. We shall of course show all courtesy to our hosts; but they have not asked us to suppress our principles or to come as anything other than we are—Evangelicals and Baptists. . . . No Congress ever had a more splendid opportunity, and the witness which our great world communion is able to offer at this time is precisely what our troubled humanity needs.[10]

The general secretary's justification for holding the congress in Berlin remarkably addressed every issue except one—how it might impact the persecution of Germany's Jewish population. In contrast, he made it clear that the feelings and status of the German Baptists carried much weight. In an appeal that was distributed to Baptist newspapers throughout the United States, Rushbrooke did address the issue of Nazi anti-Semitism. Arguing that Baptists from the United States and around the world must accept the invitation of German Baptists to come to Berlin, he elevated the BWA core conviction of international Baptist unity and discounted the argument that attendance in Berlin would express support for the Nazis and their anti-Semitism:

> THE SAME BRETHREN [i.e., the German Baptists] are inviting us, and in their new conditions and difficulties it is more than fitting that we make manifest our unbroken oneness in Christ. "But by going you will be endorsing Nazi policy and government!" Whoever thinks that for Baptists to hold a World Congress in Berlin implies approval of anti-Semitism, or any weakening of their view of our Lord's authority or of the Christian faith as supernatural and interracial, knows little of them and credits others with similar lack of knowledge. Baptists would show small courage if they shrank from the risk of such misunderstanding.[11]

In other articles, Rushbrooke and the BWA executive committee seemed reticent to explicitly address the issue of German Jewish persecution, even though it was understood that the issue of racialism was going to be addressed through the work of a BWA commission. In a widely circulated statement, Rushbrooke, John McNeill (BWA president) and Clifton Gray (honorary associate secretary) rebutted what they considered to be the two major objections to holding the congress in Berlin. They declared that a Berlin-based congress "offers a literally unparalleled opportunity for witness to distinctive Baptist principles" and that there would be no "cowardly silence on issues that are vital to Baptists"—including "racialism." They had more "respect" for the second argument—that "a Congress in Berlin would imperil the German Baptists." Their response was that the Germans desperately wanted it and that to cancel the event would "deny the claims of brotherhood."[12]

Berlin 1934: Repudiating Racialism and Anti-Semitism

Approximately ten thousand Baptist delegates traveled to Berlin to participate in the pageantry and deliberations of the fifth Baptist world congress from August 4-10, 1934. Each day's proceedings were reported on by the world's press, including *The New York Times* and *Time* magazine. On Saturday, August 4, the congress commenced with greetings from the hosts, the German Baptists, and from the German government.[13] Leaders from the German Christian Church spoke and extolled Hitler in a hall draped in banners with Nazi emblems including swastikas. Ominously, Professor Carl Schneider, from the Baptist Seminary in Hamburg, foreshadowed the subjugation of the German Baptists to the Nazi cause in his remarks on the centenary of the German Baptist movement:

> THE CENTENARY OF the German Baptists synchronizes with the re-birth of the German nation as a people. God the Lord has given us, in Adolf Hitler, a man who recognizes the needs of the time and its perils, and who is directing and using the forces that make for health in order to subdue those that make for decay. As a force making for health, the German Baptist community has been recognized and used by the Third Empire and actively included in the process of renewal. Never before has our movement experienced so much in the way of public recognition and support as in the Third Empire, and to-day [*sic*] in Berlin. United by speech and blood with the German people and the homeland, in love for the Fatherland and in the consciousness of sharing the responsibility for its destiny, the German Baptist movement co-operates, on the basis of the Gospel, with all its power in the work of building up a self-reliant State, in which a physically and morally healthy generation can live free and confident, contented and self-disciplined.[14]

Schneider's words are chilling in retrospect,[15] for they indicated that the seduction of the German Baptist leaders was well under way by August 1934. Schneider, and the German Baptists, embraced the dreams and aims of National Socialism with as much enthusiasm as other Germans did. He was not coerced or under undue pressure; rather, he was enthusiastic and optimistic about the future of Nazi-Baptist cooperation, and he even believed that God had sent Hitler in a politically messianic way for Germany's sake.

Schneider was not alone in his opinions or in his enthusiasm for Nazism. In his congress greeting, Dr. F. W. Simoleit, the leader of the German Baptists and a vice president of the BWA, attempted to impose a German Baptist understanding of the doctrine of separation of church and state for the purpose of insulating German Baptists from the criticism that they were participating in an event that was inimical to the Nazi government. He said, "The character of this Congress, according to its Constitution and its tradition, is throughout religious. We are not concerned with the political conditions in any land that is represented here."[16] The absurdity of this position was easy to unmask, for much of the agenda of the congress concerned itself with overtly political topics, including nationalism, militarism, peace, and of course, social justice issues such as racialism, and more specifically, anti-Semitism.

Despite Simoleit's preemptive denial, the issue of racialism was addressed in the first night's plenary. The keynote address was given by Dr. John McLaurin of Canada, who according to *The New York Times*, "declared Christianity prohibits all racial animosity and all racial prejudice and that in the church there is no place for racial distinctions. . . . He stated that no political relationship could be allowed to interfere with this principle."[17] McLaurin, against the German Christians, sided with the perspective of Karl Barth and the Barmen Declaration, which was issued in May 1934. As the congress reached its climax six days later, the international Baptist witness on racialism would be expressed more completely. They embraced the key protest points of the Barmen Declaration and furthermore asserted that the liberty of the church must be based on Baptist principles of separation of church and state and soul freedom.

With that foundation, the congress then pronounced its profound conviction that anti-Semitism and race prejudice were morally and spiritually unacceptable. On Friday, August 10, 1934, at the twelfth session, Arnold. T. Ohrn of Norway moved the following resolution on "Racialism":

> THIS CONGRESS REPRESENTING the world-wide, inter-racial fellowship of Baptists, rejoices to know that despite all differences of race, there is in Christ an all-embracing unity, so that in Him it can be claimed with deepest truth there is "neither Greek nor Jew, circumcision nor uncircumcision, barbarian, Scythian, bond nor free, but Christ is all in all."
>
> This Congress deplores and condemns as a violation of the law of God the Heavenly Father, all racial animosity, and every form of

> oppression or unfair discrimination toward the Jews, toward coloured people, or toward subject races in any part of the world.
>
> This Congress urges the promotion of Christian teaching concerning respect for human personality regardless of race, and as the surest means of advancing the true brotherhood of all people, urges the active propagation of the Gospel of Christ throughout the World.[18]

This resolution was not only dramatic in style but also comprehensive in viewpoint and full of theological and political substance. In the first paragraph, the interracial nature of the Baptist (and indeed, Christian) family was upheld; for Baptists, there could be no possibility of a church divided by race or cultural differences. It affirmed the BWA core conviction that the Baptist movement was racially united into one brotherhood; in addition, unity could not be constrained by national boundaries or political ideologies.

The second paragraph, the most important statement to emerge from all of the congress deliberations, was blatantly political and not just spiritual. It was a critique of how nations treated their racial minorities, and it specifically condemned "every form of oppression or unfair discrimination toward the Jews." Unlike the Barmen Declaration, which was limited to criticizing the government's intrusion into church polity, or the Confessing Church movement, which defended the inclusion of Jewish Christians within the church, the 1934 Berlin congress resolution approved by the Baptists addressed the situation faced by non-Christian German Jews, whose only crime was being the object of Hitler's wrath because of their heritage. This was the first such protest against German anti-Semitism by an international Christian organization on German soil, and as such, it deserves an important place in the history of the church and the Holocaust. *The New York Times* quoted the resolution in its entirety the next day.[19]

It should not be overlooked that the second paragraph also pressed for civil rights for African Americans in the United States, as well as other oppressed races. The National Baptist delegates lobbied for this, and it was this resolution that provided so much hope for the National Baptists, encouraging them to advocate for Atlanta as the next congress venue in 1939.

The final paragraph recognized the centrality of personality in the Baptist worldview, especially when the dignity and value of the individual person or soul was under consideration. All people, being made in the image of God, have personality, a soul or spiritual nature that makes each person of infinite worth. Personality not only elevates individuals; it also provides a profound basis for the social and political spheres—the "true brotherhood of all peoples"—in pointed contrast to the Nazi assertion that some races were inferior to others. For Baptists, personality trumped race prejudice and every form of narrow nationalism, including National Socialism.

Rev. C. E. Wilson of England seconded the resolution, and it was carried unanimously.[20] Wilson served as the chairperson of the Commission on Racialism, and in the commission's report, he made the theological, philosophical, and political cases for the resolution. The argument the commission made centered on the relationship between racialism and nationalism, in order to "discover what is wrong in the racial relationships of the world, and to set ourselves to destroy what is wrong." To accomplish this analysis, humanity must first appreciate "the inescapable fact of race differences": "The biological facts of race are not evil. They are natural, and we must reverently accept and acclaim them as having been ordained of God the Father of all mankind, for the actual benefit of the peoples in all the various countries and climates of this globe. God is the Lover of Variety in all He has created."[21]

Second, the commission repudiated any "biological argument for the separation or alienation of races"—a rejection of the Nazi position. Therefore, "what must be declared constantly and without any uncertainty by Baptists in every land is that race differences are no justification or excuse for any exploitation or selfish racial domination. The Golden Rule of Christ applies equally to Races as to individuals."[22]

Third, the commission offered five applications based on these positions. Race cannot be a barrier to internal church life. The current application of the caste system in India was "one of the most insidious of civilised sins." The Jewish-Arab "rivalry" in Palestine, though not truly caused by racial differences, must be peacefully defused. Economic exploitation of racial groups was unacceptable as well. Furthermore, the commission disassociated the Baptist movement from the legacy of European anti-Semitism, which the Roman

Catholic and Protestant state churches historically were unable to do. It affirmed that the Jewish origins of Christianity must be respected and honored. Anti-Semitism was not a religious but a political form of unjust prejudice:

> THE SPIRIT OF suspicion and animosity known as Anti-Semitism which exhibits itself in racial persecution is quite unassociated with questions of color and has but slight connection with religion. It is fundamentally a matter of political and economic competition. . . . If Anti-Semitism were a question of religion, then we as followers of Jesus Christ, who have been taught by St. Paul and the other Apostles, would have to declare that among all the other faiths in the world, there is none for which we have more reverent honor than for that of the Jew, and to the Jew we stand the greatest debt to show to him the grace of our Lord. With our fellow-Christians in all the Churches, we deplore the long record of ill-usage of Jews on the part of professedly Christian nations, and declare such injustice to be a violation of the teaching and the spirit of Christ. We desire for ourselves and for those we represent to express to the Jews by word and act the spirit of Jesus Christ our Lord, their Saviour and ours.[23]

The commission next turned to suggestions on how to apply the principles to "promote the cure of racial antagonism." The church should teach about human rights, cultivate friendship across racial barriers, engage in mission work "in the spirit of Christian love and respect," become humbler, and commit to "repudiating, denouncing, and opposing by every legitimate means, all racial exploitation, oppression or persecution."[24] M. E. Aubrey, the British general secretary, concurred: "We declare the equality of men and resist all those forces of the world that seek to raise barriers between races and between nations."[25]

In Wilson's oral presentation of the commission report to the congress, he said that the report should not be "interpreted as an attack upon any particular persons, parties, or governments," which was either a diplomatic attempt to provide cover for the German Baptists or an acknowledgment that many, if not most, countries were guilty of some form of racial prejudice. He then reasserted a fundamental point: every "act of racial injustice or oppression" is "a violation of the law of God," which calls us to "love our neighbor as thyself."[26]

Following the congress, Rushbrooke proudly asserted in the foreword to the official congress book, "The world knows where Baptists stand on nationalism and racialism . . . and our positions were no less definitively stated than they would have been in London or New York or Paris."[27] He later specifically cited the anti-Semitism resolution as he sought to place the achievements and significance of the congress in perspective:

> AS I READ in proof the text of speeches I heard at the Berlin Congress, I am again astonished that anyone ever imagined that Baptists would shrink from clear speaking. These utterances have evoked wide response from outside our borders. The world knows that we are not ready to compromise on the freedom of the church, nor to condone anti-Semitism, nor to abandon our witness and work for international peace, nor to surrender the Scriptures, nor to minimize the divine authority of the Lord Jesus Christ. And from multitudes of evangelical Christians outside our ranks a chorus of thankful approval has responded. We can hold up our heads and praise God that we did not miss our unique opportunity.[28]

Rushbrooke would repeat this assessment for years to come, which was not without a hint of defensiveness. From a greater distance (both chronologically and emotionally), Pierard provides the following assessment of the Berlin congress:

> THE RACIALISM COMMISSION'S report included one of the most sharply-worded attacks on anti-Semitism to be publicly aired since the inauguration of the Nazi regime, while the nationalism commission so strongly condemned chauvinistic nationalism and the unlimited sovereignty of the state that the German delegates tried unsuccessfully to tone down its wording. At Rushbrooke's insistence the Congress also adopted a strong resolution opposing war and advocating peace. The delegates left the hall with the strains of Handel's "Hallelujah Chorus" ringing in their ears, a piece that soon would be banned in Germany because of its "Jewishness." The Congress was possibly the most remarkable and controversial event in the BWA's history.[29]

Seventh Day Baptists Join the BWA

One of the unexpected positive results of the Baptist World Alliance's stance on issues such as anti-Semitism was the addition of a new denominational member from the United States. During its 1934 annual session (August 21-26, 1934), the delegates of the Seventh Day Baptist General Conference[30] voted to create a committee "to investigate the desirability and possibility of the Seventh Day Baptist denomination joining the Baptist World Alliance, and to report its findings and recommendations thereon at the next annual session of the General Conference."[31] A year prior to the congress, the denomination's newspaper, *The Sabbath Recorder*, criticized Germany's "campaign of deliberate discrimination against the Jews" in an otherwise sympathetic piece on the Nazi revolution,[32] and following the congress, the same paper praised the German government's hospitality toward Baptists in Berlin.[33]

In 1935, the Committee on Baptist World Alliance cited the 1934 BWA congress's prophetic stand on key issues as a reason for the Seventh Day Baptists to affiliate with this worldwide body:

> YOUR COMMITTEE APPOINTED at your last annual session . . . has noted with satisfaction the impact made upon the world at large, and upon the German government in particular, by the bold, fearless, and forceful manifesto issued by the Baptist World Alliance at its last meeting in the German capital of Berlin. . . . Your committee recommends that the General Conference make application for membership in the Baptist World Alliance; and that upon the acceptance of such application, an annual contribution of $40 be made to that body.[34]

The committee believed that "through this alliance of all Baptists of the world the basic principles of historic Baptist faith and policy may become better understood and appreciated by Baptists themselves, as well as more widely extended."[35]

The Seventh Day Baptists promoted the birth and initial growth of the very small German Seventh Day Baptist movement during the decade of the 1930s, and "by 1935, the German Union reported 18 churches and 500 members."[36] During the Nazi era, the foreign mission leadership of the Seventh Day Baptists reported about developments in Germany only in regards to the evangelistic and discipleship work of the German churches and pastors. The annual reports never addressed the relationship of German Seventh Day Baptists to Jews or questioned whether the Baptists there should take a stand on behalf of persecuted German Jews. They did, however, praise the efforts of the German Seventh Day Baptist leaders and churches.[37]

This is somewhat surprising, since Seventh Day Baptists did profess an affinity toward Jews and could recall a heritage in which they sought to witness to Jewish communities in the United States for more than a century. In 1834, the American Seventh-day Baptist Missionary Society passed a resolution on Jewish evangelism stating that "a committee of five be appointed by this Society, whose duty it shall be to inquire into the present condition of the Jews, and to take into consideration the expediency of our doing something to extend the gospel of Christ to that afflicted people, and to report the result of their deliberations at our next session."[38]

In 1839, the Seventh-day Baptist Society for the Promotion of Christianity among the Jews was launched, and Rev. William B. Maxson served as its first missionary. In a report, the society noted that Jews in the United States were resistant to the Christian message because of "the great suffering of their nation under Christian powers" in Europe. In general, the efforts of the Seventh Day Baptists to reach Jews in the nineteenth century produced limited results.[39] Furthermore, in regard to European missionary involvement, they had supported the evangelistic work of an extraordinary Jewish Christian mission worker who came to New York in 1882, Chaim Yedidiah Pollak, also known as Theophilus Lucky.[40]

Following Kristallnacht, *The Sabbath Recorder* first alluded to the Jewish plight in Germany in its November 28, 1938, issue. The paper admitted that "it is easy to be pessimistic in the midst of the reports of so much war news, Nazi pogroms, Palestine trouble," and it reprinted a report from the Religious News Service that spoke of "the tragedy which has overwhelmed not only Jews but also Catholics and Protestants in Germany."[41] The inclusion of Jews among other groups that were suffering continued in the December 12, 1938, issue, in which the term "warphans" (i.e., war orphans) was applied to Germany's victimized Jewish children; the columnist asked what

Jesus would do "in relation to these Warphans of Spain, Germany, China, Palestine, and America."[42]

The most detailed article related to Jewish persecution in Germany was published in the February 13, 1939, issue. *The Sabbath Recorder* specifically acknowledged "the plight of the Jews has aroused the sympathies of all democratic lands." However, the article focused on Christian refugees harmed by Hitler's aggression and called upon American Christians to respond to their needs in the same way American Jews had done so for their own people.[43]

The 1939 general conference passed a resolution on world peace that contained a general condemnation of racism that deplored "all inter-racial, inter-class, and international hatreds not only in Europe but in our own country."[44] Approved just one week before the outbreak of war in Europe and almost ten months after Kristallnacht, the resolution's rejection of "inter-racial hatreds" may justly be interpreted as implying that the Seventh Day Baptists in the United States were sympathetic toward persecuted Jews. Perhaps their unwillingness to specifically mention Jews was due to their desire to do no harm to the status of Seventh Day Baptists in Germany.

Notes

1. *Minutes of the Baptist World Alliance Administrative Sub-Committee* (20 June 1932), Item (4), Berlin Congress, 1933, 2.

2. *Minutes of the Baptist World Alliance Executive Committee* (29 November 1932), Item 6, World Congress, Berlin, 4.

3. *Minutes of the Baptist World Alliance Administrative Sub-Committee* (27 April 1933), Item (4), Fifth Baptist World Congress, 1933, 2.

4. Letter from Clifton D. Gray, Informal Record of Committee at Washington (25 May 1933), 2.

5. *Minutes of the Baptist World Alliance Administrative Sub-Committee* (20 July 1933), Item (7), Germany: Anti-Jewish Action of the Hitler Government, 4.

6. See, for example, Editorial, "Congress of Baptist World Alliance," *The Watchman-Examiner* (12 October 1933), 985.

7. Editorial, "Baptists May Not Go to Berlin," *The Baptist Banner* (2 November 1933), 3.

8. Richard V. Pierard, "The Baptist World Alliance: An Overview of Its History," *Review and Expositor* 103, no. 4 (2006): 719–20. See also Erich Geldbach, "The Years of Anxiety and World War II," which covers the Berlin congress and the Baptist World Alliance from a German-friendly perspective, in Richard V. Pierard, ed., *Baptists Together in Christ 1905–2005: A Hundred-Year History of the Baptist World Alliance* (Birmingham, AL: Samford University Press, 2005), 74–99.

9. J. H. Rushbrooke, "The Fifth Baptist World Congress," *The Watchman-Examiner* (30 November 1933), 1154; J. H. Rushbrooke, "Oncken Centenary," *The Baptist Observer* (1 March 1934), 11.

10. *Minutes of the Proceedings of the 1934 Southern Baptist Convention*, Baptist World Alliance Letter from J. H. Rushbrooke, 63.

11. J. H. Rushbrooke, "What the Berlin Congress Means for Europe," *The Alabama Baptist* (8 March 1934), 1; and Indiana's *The Baptist Observer* (1 February 1934), 10.

12. John McNeill, J. H. Rushbrooke, and Clifton D. Gray, "Baptists and Berlin: A Statement on Behalf of the Baptist World Alliance," *The Alabama Baptist* (19 April 1934), 9.

13. J. H. Rushbrooke, ed., *Fifth Baptist World Congress: Berlin, August 4-10, 1934* (London: Baptist World Alliance, 1934), Minutes, 2.

14. Ibid., Carl Schneider, "The Centenary of the German Baptists," 192–93.

15. Pierard, "Baptist World Alliance," 720: "the German Baptists soon learned that their newfound freedom was an illusion."

16. Rushbrooke, ed., *Fifth Baptist World Congress*, F. W. Simoleit, "Address of Greeting," 199.

17. "Baptists in Berlin Score Racial Hatred," *The New York Times* (5 August 1934), 2.

18. Rushbrooke, ed., *Fifth Baptist World Congress*, Minutes, Item 163, 17.

19. "Baptists Condemn Race Persecution," *The New York Times* (11 August 1934), 5.

20. Rushbrooke, ed., *Fifth Baptist World Congress*, Minutes, Items 164–65, 17.

21. Ibid., Report of Commission No. 2—"Racialism," 39.

22. Ibid., 40.

23. Ibid., 41.

24. Ibid.

25. Ibid., M. E. Aubrey, "Young Baptists and Their Tradition," 182–83; it was reprinted in *The Watchman-Examiner* (27 September 1934), 1043.

26. Ibid., Notes of Address on Report of Commission No. 2—"Racialism," 65–66.

27. Ibid., foreword, vi.

28. "Men and Things Column," *The Watchman-Examiner* (1 November 1934), 1155–56. See also J. H. Rushbrooke, "The Baptist World Alliance: Origins, Constitution, Achievements, Objects," *The Chronicle, A Baptist Historical Quarterly* 1, no. 2 (April 1938): 9–22.

29. Pierard, "Baptist World Alliance," 721.

30. See Don A. Sanford, *A Choosing People: The History of Seventh Day Baptists* (Macon, GA: Mercer University Press, 2012). He does not address the issues of the Seventh Day Baptists' attitudes toward Nazism or anti-Semitism (see 342–44).

31. *1934 Seventh Day Baptist Year Book*, Minutes, Resolution (August 25, 1934), 45.

32. Editorial, *The Sabbath Recorder* (29 May 1933), 511.

33. Editorial, *The Sabbath Recorder* (1 October 1934), 149.

34. *1935 Seventh Day Baptist Year Book*, Report of the Committee on Baptist World Alliance, 33–34.

35. *1936 Seventh Day Baptist Year Book*, Report of the Committee on Baptist World Alliance, 25.

36. Sanford, *A Choosing People*, 309. He asserted that the war essentially decimated the German Seventh Day Baptist movement: "World War II took a heavy toll from which the Germans never recovered."

37. L. R. Conradi, "Advance in Germany," *The Sabbath Recorder* (5 March 1934), 107–8; *1935 Seventh Day Baptist Year Book*, Report of the Seventh Day Baptist Missionary Society, "Germany," 128. German Seventh Day Baptists published a legally sanctioned newspaper; see *1935 Seventh Day Baptist Year Book*, Report of the Seventh Day Baptist Missionary Society, "Germany," 172; *1940 Seventh Day Baptist Year Book*, Report of the Seventh Day Baptist Missionary Society, "Germany," 119.

38. William C. Dallard, "Our Work for Jews," in Seventh Day Baptist Missionary Society, *Jubilee Papers: Historical Papers Commemorating the Fiftieth Anniversary of the Seventh-day Baptist Missionary Society, and the Centennial of the William Carey Foreign Missions Movement* (Westerly, RI: Board of Managers of the Seventh-day Baptist Missionary Society, 1892), 86.

39. Ibid., 86–90.

40. Ibid., 90. Concerning the life and ministry of Lucky, see "A Distinguished Hebrew Christian: The Late Rev. C. T. Lucky," *The Sabbath Recorder* (5 November 1917), 581–83; Raymond Lillevik, *Apostates, Hybrids, or True Jews? Jewish Christians and Jewish Identity*

in Eastern Europe, 1860–1914 (Eugene, OR: Pickwick Publications, 2014), 89–141; several articles on Lucky's life and ministry can be found in *Mishkan* 60 (2009): 4–64.

41. Editorial, "We Need Not Be Discouraged" and "Items of Interest," *The Sabbath Recorder* (28 November 1938), 382–83.

42. Charles V. Vickery, "Warphans for Christmas," *The Sabbath Recorder* (12 November 1938), 415; see also 416. Madame Chiang Kai-shek popularized the term "warphan" to refer to Chinese war orphans; see Kevin Scott Wong, *Americans First: Chinese Americans and the Second World War* (Cambridge, MA: Harvard University Press, 2005), 93–94.

43. Editorial, "Christian German Refugees," *The Sabbath Recorder* (13 February 1939), 103–4.

44. *1939 Seventh Day Baptist Year Book*, Report of the Committee on Courtesies and Resolutions, "Peace," 60.

Chapter 19

From Berlin to Atlanta (1934–1939)

In the aftermath of the Berlin congress, some feedback was positive, both within the global Baptist community and beyond. F. Townly Lord, in his history of the Baptist World Alliance, wrote:

> THE RESOLUTION ON Racialism, especially in reference to the Jews, received widespread recognition. The Jews of America and Great Britain expressed their appreciation, while in many synagogues in Eastern Europe there was thanksgiving to God for the lead the Baptists had given. Not unconnected with this was the appearance, on the platform of the next congress in Atlanta, of Rabbi David Marx, who spoke with deep feeling of the stand Baptists had taken for religious freedom.[1]

During a speech in Minneapolis, Minnesota, on September 23, 1934, Dr. David Bryn-Jones, a Northern Baptist pastor and teacher, revealed that while he was in Berlin for the congress, he spoke to a "leader" in the Nazi government, who shared with him that "its purpose was the humane annihilation of the Jewish people in Germany."[2] In contrast to Canadian Baptist John MacNeill's uncertainty over "how far" the resolutions "found publicity in the German press,"[3] the *American Hebrew* focused on the Nazi political manipulation and management of the event, censoring any criticisms that might emanate from it:

> THE CONGRESS, WHEREIN sentiments contrary to Hitlerism were expressed, was a curious phenomenon in a land that knows no free speech. The explanation for this lapse is, of course, simple enough. The Hitler government was anxious, first of all, for the tourist trade that the

> congress would bring; second, for the false impression it would give to the world of Germany's "tolerance"; and third, for the demagogue weapon it would provide in dealing with the churches. Mr. Goebbels was well prepared to see that none of the civilized sentiments running counter to Hitlerism, would appear in the German press. Only those "unobjectionable" features of the congress agenda were given space in the press.[4]

The leaders of the Baptist World Alliance were not active in lobbying for the rights and survival of the Jews suffering from Hitler's anti-Semitic persecutions, preferring to have individual Baptist national bodies respond in light of the 1934 resolution. J. H. Rushbrooke devoted much of his time between 1935 and 1938 advocating for religious liberty, especially for beleaguered Baptist conventions in Russia, Rumania, Spain, and Mexico; the plight of the Jews for him was a secondary concern at best.

On a number of occasions, however, Rushbrooke found it necessary to reiterate the Berlin congress's rejection of anti-Semitism. In July 1937, the executive committee issued a press release detailing its diplomatic initiatives on behalf of Baptists in Rumania and announcing its preliminary plans for the sixth Baptist world congress in Atlanta. Rushbrooke revealed that "attention was directed to the restrictions upon religious freedom and the prevalence of repression and persecution in various countries," and in response the executive committee approved a resolution on the issue of church and state, based on 1934's resolution. He then added: "The Committee declares the entire Baptist communion throughout the world to be resolutely opposed to religious repression of every kind, whether directed against Baptists or others, and it expresses the unwavering sympathy of all our people for the victims of persecution or repression whether belonging to our own or any other communion."[5] German Jews were not cited by name, but it is plausible to interpret the statement as alluding to their plight, even if as just one example of a more general pattern throughout the world.

The BWA and Kristallnacht

Following Kristallnacht, pressure was placed on Rushbrooke to express Baptist outrage and opposition to the events taking place in Germany. On behalf of the administrative subcommittee, he issued a press release regarding "the attitude of the Baptist World Alliance on the subject of the anti-Jewish action in the continent of Europe." The statement republished verbatim the text of the 1934 resolution on racialism and advised its "constituent bodies that the above Resolution gives a clear description of the attitude of the Alliance, which remains unchanged. Recent events have more strongly than ever justified this attitude." It then cast responsibility for acting on behalf of persecuted Jews on to the "various constituent bodies," calling upon them "at this juncture [to] reaffirm in their own way the principles set forth in the Resolution, and especially that they will take steps to furnish all possible assistance to those who are the victims of anti-Semitic action."[6]

The Kristallnacht response did not commit the BWA to any specific course of action on behalf of Jews. Kristallnacht was significant because it proved that the Baptists were on the right side of the issue, but Rushbrooke and his colleagues did not forthrightly rebuke Nazi Germany by name, express solidarity, or offer any clear words of comfort to the Jews who had just been attacked. The press release employed diplomatic language as if Kristallnacht were merely yet another political incident. Furthermore, the reluctance of the leaders to get involved was demonstrated clearly when they urged the national conventions to respond on their own.

By delegating responsibility, Rushbrooke and the administrative subcommittee signaled that the Baptist World Alliance was not going to respond to Kristallnacht in any meaningful or practical way. It certainly could have, as its ongoing political campaign against Baptist persecution in Rumania demonstrated. In that situation, Rushbrooke tirelessly lobbied European leaders, sought out new allies, and coordinated with Baptists in the United States on numerous diplomatic initiatives. For reasons Rushbrooke chose not to discuss, the Nazi persecution of the Jews did not merit or receive a similar level of intense and intentional treatment.

W. O. Lewis served as the representative of the American Baptist Foreign Mission Society in Europe, and he worked closely with Rushbrooke, the European Baptists, and the Baptist World Alliance. In 1939 he became the general secretary of the BWA, with Rushbrooke shifting to the position of president. In April 1939, the *Nebraska Baptist Messenger* reprinted excerpts from *The New York Times*'s interview with Lewis. Like Rushbrooke, he asserted that Baptists were victims of persecution and made this comparison: "Although the sufferings of Baptists has been of a comparatively minor nature compared to that of Jews and Catholics, it has become marked in recent months."[7]

Following Kristallnacht, Rushbrooke received a letter[8] from R. S. Jones, the home secretary of the Southern Baptist Foreign Mission Board, which also contained a copy of a letter from Jacob Gartenhaus. Gartenhaus noted that Alabama Baptists had taken an offering for Jews after Kristallnacht but was saddened that "nothing is being done for the Christian Jews" who were being made to "suffer more than the others."[9] Rushbrooke's reply is worth quoting at length, since it provides insight into his perspective on the persecution of Europe's Jews. After describing English Baptist efforts to aid Jewish Christian refugees through the Lord Baldwin Fund, Rushbrooke wrote:

> YOU ARE PROBABLY aware that life is made impossible in Germany for those who have any Jewish blood, even though it be but a small proportion. They are eager to leave the country. Appeals pour in daily for help; but the chief help required is in settling them outside the land and maintaining them until they can make good. All that can be done is little more than a "drop in the bucket" in view of the need. Germany is apparently making life in the land impossible for 600,000 people. Italy, with a much smaller Jewish population, is following Germany's lead. Czechoslovakia is being pressed to do the same. Hungary certainly will; Rumania has initiated some anti-Jewish measures which are as yet of a comparatively mild character; from Poland comes the report that it is quite certain to follow the policy of expulsion, and in the case of Poland some three and a half million Jews are involved. The problem is stupendous, and, apart from the actions of governments, cannot be solved.[10]

Rushbrooke's despair in the face of such a massive assault against Europe's Jews was evident. The only solution he could imagine was for governments to take responsibility for the plight of Jews; private humanitarian assistance such as he and the BWA had organized in the past was insufficient. Regarding Southern Baptist aid to Germany's Jewish refugees, Rushbrooke replied: "However, we are under obligation to do what we can for our fellow-Christians, and I suggest that your task in America would be (a) to assist any who are trying to escape from Germany to obtain permits to come to America, and (b) to take care that they are maintained until they have made good. This is the line on which we are acting in Britain."[11]

In his secretarial report prepared for the 1939 Atlanta congress, Rushbrooke provided a comprehensive review of the BWA's life and ministry during the period between the two congresses. He again defended the decision to hold the fifth congress in Berlin and balanced his criticism of the Nazi government with some praise:

> MOREOVER, FOR MONTHS afterwards, reports of the Congress, and pamphlets dealing with it, circulated freely in Germany. I think the strongest evidence of the pervasive influence of our great gathering is the fact that some eighteen months after it had taken place the authorities suppressed the further circulation of reports. They contained numerous utterances in condemnation of war, of exaggerated nationalism, and of racial discrimination—with specific reference to Jews, and also declarations on the relations of the Church and State, and other inconvenient and disturbing matter. But it redounds to the credit of the German government that its pledge to allow the Congress full freedom of discussion and decision was respected.[12]

Rushbrooke then focused on the impact of the 1934 racialism resolution: "The Jews of America and Britain and other lands publicly thanked us; in Eastern Europe they went further by thanking God in their synagogues for the witness Baptists had borne."[13] However, all he could offer in regard to subsequent actions taken by the BWA was shrouded in some mystery: "It has been the privilege of the Alliance to render manifold services to Russian refugees in Manchuria, in Sinkiang, and elsewhere; and recently, in cooperation with others, to assist the harassed Jews and other refugees from Central Europe. On these matters we cannot enlarge."[14]

Atlanta 1939—Confrontation with German and Italian Baptists

In the foreword to the 1939 world congress report, Rushbrooke admitted that the organizers were concerned about how the alliance's gathering in Atlanta would offer a living demonstration of an alternative to the American South's pervasive racial segregation. With some satisfaction and relief, he stated:

> THE ONLY ISSUE which might have marred the harmony of the Congress was the racial. The Atlanta people, white and coloured, had worked splendidly together; but it was known that outside elements might endeavour to discover or even to provoke "incidents." In the outcome, our Sixth Congress furnished a shining example of genuine Christian fraternity, and registered definite gains that will assist in the solution of race difficulties everywhere. It was a Baptist World Alliance gathering, and the Alliance knows no distinction of race. Nor can it be again insinuated, as it has often been in the past, that the Southland is intolerant of the Negro. Of the five addresses of welcome at the opening session, no less than three were delivered by Negroes, and one of these, by local choice, was spokesman for all the Baptists of Georgia.[15]

In retrospect, Rushbrooke overestimated the impact of the congress on the racist attitudes and behaviors of the white majority in the American South. For one week, and in the cloistered setting of the congress, a desegregated environment was indeed briefly created. However, there is no evidence that the demonstration of Baptist racial harmony in Atlanta precipitated any behavioral changes among Southern whites. The African American civil rights movement had to struggle for decades before there was any dismantling of the social apparatus of segregation.

Rushbrooke was also inaccurate in his claim that the white-black racial issue was the only racial challenge to the peace and harmony of the congress. The situation in Europe threatened to affect the congress, exposing a divide between the delegates from Germany and Italy, over against advocates of democracy and compassion for Jews. In a series of letters exchanged between Rushbrooke and the German Baptists months prior to the congress,[16] he categorically rejected their demand that a Jewish rabbi not be permitted to address the congress, and in fact, Rabbi David Marx did bring greetings.[17] Ernest A. Payne, writing about the congress in Atlanta, observed that Rabbi Marx "spoke out of a full heart, since these last years have been crowded with new sorrows and suffering for his oft-afflicted people. Gratefully he paid tribute to the stand which Baptists have always taken for religious liberty," and then Payne boasted: "It is our pride that our people have had their place in the van of the struggle."[18]

The Atlanta Constitution covered the BWA congress in detail, including excerpts from Marx's "hearty welcome to the Baptist brethren from many climes and many nations." Noting that "these are the days when the souls of men are troubled," the rabbi denounced militarism and welcomed the Baptist contribution to the struggle for world peace. He also paid tribute to the historic Baptist core conviction of separation of church and state:

> IT IS HEARTENING to welcome to our midst men and women from the world over whose mission is peace—peace through the instrumentalities of better human relationship and understanding. The foundations of civilization are bedded in the intangible, spiritual qualities of man. It is of supreme value that religion transcend national and racial boundaries and in its universal character strive for the full brotherhood of man. The contributions made by the Baptists to the rights of the individual to freedom of worship have become the possession of myriads of men outside the Baptist affiliation. In this country, in the politico-religious field, the principle of the separation of state is under heavy obligations to Roger Williams and his devout followers. Because of this separation, church and state can each best develop their ideals.[19]

Sectional meetings were held on Wednesday, July 26, 1939, and approximately three hundred people attended a German-language group led by Paul Schmidt. Other speakers from Germany were F. Rockschies and Hans Luckey, both of whom, like Schmidt, were submissive to the Nazis. *The Atlanta Constitution* covered the meeting and preserved important statements that cannot be found in the official congress record. The newspaper quoted Rockschies as saying: "We are convinced that the German Fuehrer has full confidence in the Baptists and their loyalty to the present government. With God Almighty still in control of human affairs, and with Adolf Hitler, who has led the German people out of a desperate situation into unity and strength, our fate is in good hands." Luckey stated, "German Baptists are experiencing a happy time. Evangelism is growing at a tremendous pace and congregations are constantly increasing. It is our great desire that peace be kept in the world, both for you and ourselves."

An attendee queried if "it is true that the German government is trying to eliminate the doctrine that Christ was a Jew," and Schmidt replied: "The German government does not concern itself about the elimination of the Jewish element in the Bible. While there are people in Germany, and other parts of the world who would not be willing to believe that Jesus was a Jew, we, as Baptists, do not consider these people to be a real danger to the Christian faith, and their number is constantly decreasing."[20]

On Thursday, July 27, 1939, during the eleventh session, the congress passed resolutions on several issues. Resolution "F" addressed "Racialism." The full text of the resolution was as follows:

> THE SIXTH BAPTIST World Congress, assembled in Atlanta, Ga., is constrained to express the judgment of Baptist people in general on the question of race relationship. The members rejoice that the preparations for the present Congress have been carried through by a joint committee of the races, and in perfect harmony.
>
> The Congress finds that the strong and unwavering convictions which govern the attitude and policy of the Baptist World Alliance are clearly and adequately expressed in the Resolution adopted by the Fifth World Congress, which met in Berlin in 1934. It therefore solemnly reaffirms what was then stated in the following terms:
>
> "This Congress representing the world-wide, inter-racial fellowship of Baptists, rejoices to know that despite all differences of race, there is in Christ an all-embracing unity, so that in Him it can be claimed with deepest truth there is 'neither Greek nor Jew, circumcision nor uncircumcision, barbarian, Scythian, bond nor free, but Christ is all in all.'
>
> "This Congress deplores and condemns as a violation of the law of God the Heavenly Father, all racial animosity, and every form of oppression or unfair discrimination toward the Jews, toward coloured people, or toward subject races in any part of the world.
>
> "This Congress urges the promotion of Christian teaching concerning respect for human personality regardless of race, and as the surest means of advancing the true brotherhood of all people, urges the active propagation of the Gospel of Christ throughout the world."[21]

The 1939 resolution merely reiterated the 1934 text, as if nothing had happened in the interim period between Berlin and Atlanta that would justify an amplification or strengthening of the earlier original statement of concern. The resolution failed to acknowledge Kristallnacht, the plight of Jewish refugees, or the viability of Palestine serving as a Jewish homeland to provide a haven of safety for dislocated European Jews. It did not offer any suggestions for action that the Baptist community might undertake, and this despite George W. Truett's assertion in his presidential address, that the "astounding fact of ghastly persecutions, both racial and religious, continues to challenge the whole world with horror, and to make a blot that is an unspeakable disgrace to civilization."[22]

Following the passage of the resolutions, the congress experienced a remarkable and heated exchange between M. E. Aubrey, the English Baptist executive secretary, and the German and Italian delegates over racialism and totalitarianism. Aubrey was the most vocal and persistent European supporter of assisting persecuted Jewish people. His choice of the topic, "Christianity and the Totalitarian State," would not have surprised any informed observer. Aubrey decried totalitarianism as inimical to Christianity, which in his view was an ally of liberty and democracy. He extolled the Baptist "dissenter" heritage and the contemporary witness of Martin Niemöller and others in Germany, and he pointedly did not mention German Baptists at all. The implication was clear to all. In capitulating to Nazism, German Baptists had failed to uphold the historic Baptist witness. They had not been faithful to the core convictions of Baptists, who were historically willing to suffer martyrdom for their faith in the face of unjust tyrannical systems.[23]

In rebuttal, the German Baptist leader, Schmidt, disagreed with Aubrey's interpretation of Christianity and the political ordering of society. In his address, "Liberalism, Collectivism and the Baptists," he deeply regretted "the fact that our Baptist brethren seem to put more trust in the reports emanating from" the state church than from German Baptists who were loyal to the Nazi government. Schmidt argued that the New Testament favored "the dual entities of worldly kingdoms and the Church's province or reign," with the latter never "making demands" of the former. Baptists could not equate any one political system, including democracy, with the gospel. Schmidt did not mention the plight of Germany's Jewish population.[24]

In his narrative of the Atlanta congress, Payne acknowledged that the congress could not "ignore the great line of cleavage in European affairs, the tension between the so-called totalitarian States and the democracies."[25] He summarized the Italian and German point of view:

> IN ATLANTA AN Italian Baptist declared that the real enemy of Baptist witness is not the Fascist State, but the Roman Catholic Church, and that the critical attitude of the former towards the latter has strengthened our position. A somewhat similar standpoint is taken by many German Baptists towards the Nazi authorities. At the Atlanta Congress German delegates drew attention to the growth of the denomination in Germany during the past few years. It has been free as long as it devotes itself to purely "spiritual" activities and in no way criticises the State, and there are wider opportunities for caravan and tent missions and similar enterprises than ever before.[26]

Payne's comment on the reception the Italian and German position received in Atlanta was a masterful understatement: "Many who heard these things and who recognize their truth felt that there is more that must be said from the Baptist standpoint regarding the totalitarian state which claims to be the final authority over its citizens."[27]

Abandoning Jews and Jewish Baptists

World War II began just weeks after the end of the sixth BWA world congress. The rift between the Baptists from democratic countries and the German Baptists grew dramatically wider, and Rushbrooke and the leaders of the BWA were powerless to heal the divide. Furthermore, the alliance felt helpless when it came to persecuted Baptists, some of whom were Jewish converts: "The distressing circumstances of many Baptists, some of Jewish extraction, seeking to escape from the continent of Europe was mentioned. Some had already been aided by advice and material help during the months preceding the war, and some had reached England or other lands. It was now obvious that under conditions of war the Alliance, deeply as its members feel for these unhappy brethren, has no means of giving them effective aid."[28]

Other organizations did not give in to such an extreme despair. At its January 1940 meeting, the BWA was invited to join an ecumenical effort coordinated by Dr. Adolf Keller, a renowned Swiss Reformed theologian who was working for Inter-Church Aid, to assist "needy evangelicals" in Poland. Rushbrooke noted that "it was difficult to ascertain either the precise position of the Baptist people or the possibilities of rendering assistance," and that he was "keeping in touch with every organization that might trace Baptists" in that country. His pessimism again found expression when he shared that "the American Quakers are finding great difficulty in rendering aid because of their insistence that needy Jews shall also be helped and their objection to control of their relief operations by the German authorities. It would appear impossible to do anything at the moment, beyond seeking information and watching developments. He was keeping in touch with Dr. Keller and with others interested."[29]

Rushbrooke's pessimism prevented the BWA leaders from considering more active participation in assisting European Baptist, Jewish, and other refugees. His assessment of the Quaker policies regarding helping "needy Jews" is also rather sad; would he have preferred that the Quakers ignore Jews in response to German Nazi pressure in order to aid Christians? His adoption of a passive bystander strategy no doubt contributed to the lack of any fund-raising campaign by the worldwide Baptist movement on behalf of Jews. In May 1940, the BWA report indicated that just two British pounds and a single US dollar had been received by the BWA for Jewish relief between July 1, 1939, and April 26, 1940.[30]

Notes

1. F. Townley Lord, *Baptist World Fellowship: A Short History of the Baptist World Alliance* (Nashville, TN: Broadman Press, 1955), 87.

2. "A List of Events in 5694," *1934 American Jewish Year Book*, 123. Following the war, Bryn-Jones published two volumes: *Toward a Democratic New Order* (Minneapolis: University of Minnesota Press, 1945) and *The Dilemma of the Idealist* (New York: Macmillan, 1950).

3. John MacNeill, "Echoes from Berlin," *The Canadian Baptist* (23 August 1934), 3.

4. "Baptist Congress Meeting in Berlin Condemns Racial Antagonism as a Violation of the Law of God," *American Hebrew* (17 August 1934), 240. See chapter 3 for a comprehensive

analysis of the *American Hebrew*'s coverage of the congress and other Baptist-related news regarding anti-Semitism and the Jews.

5. J. H. Rushbrooke, "Baptist World Alliance," *The Watchman-Examiner* (29 July 1937), 873–74.

6. *Minutes of the Baptist World Alliance Administrative Sub-Committee* (28 November 1938), Item (8), Anti-Semitism, 8–9; "Baptist World Alliance and Anti-Semitism," *Illinois Baptist* (30 December 1938), 6, and the Indiana *Baptist Observer* (19 January 1939), 7.

7. "Sees Anti-Baptist Drive," *Nebraska Baptist Messenger* (April 1939), 8.

8. Letter of R. S. Jones to J. H. Rushbrooke (dated 5 January 1939), in Baptist World Alliance Correspondence Box 15 A–L (January–June 1939), The Angus Library and Archive, Regent's Park College, Oxford, England.

9. Letter of Jacob Gartenhaus to R. S. Jones (dated 23 December 1938), in Baptist World Alliance Correspondence Box 15 A–L (January–June 1939), The Angus Library and Archive, Regent's Park College, Oxford, England.

10. Rushbrooke Correspondence to Dr. R. S. Jones (dated 25 January 1939), 1, Baptist World Alliance Correspondence Box 15 A–L (January–June 1939), The Angus Library and Archive, Regent's Park College, Oxford, England.

11. Ibid., 2.

12. J. H. Rushbrooke, ed., *Sixth Baptist World Congress Atlanta, GA July 22-28, 1939* (Atlanta: The Baptist World Alliance, 1939), Secretarial Report by Dr. J. H. Rushbrooke, 37.

13. Ibid., 38.

14. Ibid., 49.

15. Rushbrooke, ed., *Sixth Baptist World Congress*, viii.

16. Baptist World Alliance Correspondence Box, The Angus Library and Archive, Regent's Park College, Oxford, England. The exchange of letters took place between Hans Luckey and Rushbrooke: from Luckey to Rushbrooke (dated 8 December 1938), from Rushbrooke to Luckey (dated 23 December 1938), from Luckey to Rushbrooke (dated 28 December 1938), and from Rushbrooke to Luckey (dated 3 January 1939).

17. Rushbrooke, ed., *Sixth Baptist World Congress*, Minutes, Item 12, 3.

18. Ernest A. Payne, *Baptists Speak to the World: A Description and Interpretation of the Sixth Baptist World Congress, Atlanta, 1939* (London: The Carey Press, 1939), 44.

19. "Pastors from Atlanta Churches of All Denominations Express Sincere Interest and Welcome to Baptists," *The Atlanta Constitution* (23 July 1939), 10B. See also John W. Bradbury, "The Sixth Congress of the Baptist World Alliance," *The Watchman-Examiner* (10 August 1939), 898.

20. "Baptists' Status in Reich Described," *The Atlanta Constitution* (27 July 1939), 11.

21. Rushbrooke, ed., *Sixth Baptist World Congress*, Minutes, Item 99, 13; the resolution text is printed between items 103 and 104, 15.

22. Rushbrooke, ed., *Sixth Baptist World Congress*, Presidential Address by Dr. George W. Truett, 23.

23. Ibid., Rev. M. E. Aubrey, "Christianity and the Totalitarian State," 198–202.

24. Ibid., Paul Schmidt, "Liberalism, Collectivism, and the Baptists," 203–6.

25. Payne, *Baptists Speak to the World*, 36.

26. Ibid., 43.

27. Ibid.

28. *Minutes of the Baptist World Alliance Administrative Sub-Committee* (11 September 1939), Item XIV, Refugees.

29. *Minutes of the Baptist World Alliance Administrative Sub-Committee* (4 January 1940), Item VIII(b), a letter from Dr. Adolf Keller, 7–8. On Keller, see Marianne Jehle-Wildberger, *Adolf Keller: Ecumenist, World Citizen, Philanthropist* (Eugene, OR: Cascade Books, 2013).

30. *Minutes of the Baptist World Alliance Executive Committee* (21 May 1940), Item 26(c), Finance, 10.

Chapter 20

The BWA's Postwar Congresses

In the postwar period, the Baptist World Alliance held two world congresses that reflected on the Nazi era and the plight of the Jewish people. The first took place in Europe, and Copenhagen was an ideal choice of venue. The European Baptist movement had roots in that city that extended back to Julius Köbner, a Jewish convert and a friend of the German Baptist pioneer Gerhard Oncken. The 1950 congress in Cleveland symbolized the central role that the Baptists from the United States played within the Baptist global family.

Copenhagen 1947–Responding to the Holocaust

When Baptists traveled to Copenhagen, Denmark, for the seventh world congress, it was vital for the delegates to respond in some fashion to the Holocaust. And this they did; F. Townley Lord stated that the "plight of the Jews aroused the Congress to a magnificent declaration" in which they "called on Baptists everywhere to do everything in their power to alleviate the sufferings of Jews, called on the nations to open their doors to the homeless and oppressed refugees, and at the same time urged Jewry to refrain from provocative acts."[1]

After approving a resolution on international relations, the congress passed three key resolutions that related to Jews. The Resolution on Race Relations confessed the inadequacy of past attempts by Baptists to eradicate prejudice against people of other races and urged Baptists to "forthrightly" seek solutions to the "perplexing" and "grave problem" of racism. One key to the solution was the Baptist principle of personality: "Appreciation for the ideals, aspirations, and personalities of all races must be insisted upon by Christians." In a paragraph that undoubtedly referred to the German Nazi period, the congress condemned "race exterminations" as antithetical to Christianity:

> WHEREAS ONE OF the major factors in the maladjusted country, city, or state, is the improper approach to, and an illogical dealing with, the minority within their boundary; and whereas men have tried to bring about a wholesome social order by force, by bribery, and other similar plans, and failed; and whereas the basis for better race relations is dependent upon better understanding between all groups, and a desire to build a Christian order and equality for all of the children of men: therefore, be it resolved that un-Christian practices and abuses of people, such as lynchings, race extermination, economic and racial discrimination, unfair employment practices, and denial of political rights are contrary to the principles of Christianity.[2]

Jacob Gartenhaus composed the second resolution, which specifically dealt with "the unprecedented suffering through which the people of Israel have passed during recent years." It explicitly acknowledged the horror of the Holocaust, noting that "millions" of Jews were "exterminated by the most inhuman means" and that "these sufferings are not yet at an end" because "hundreds of thousands are still in concentration camps or wandering homeless from land to land." The resolution expressed the congress's "sense of sorrow and shame" that the "poisonous propaganda and destructive designs of anti-Semitism" were still alive and urged "Baptists throughout the world to manifest the Spirit of Jesus Christ, Himself a Child of Israel, and to do everything in their power to alleviate the sufferings of the Jews." Countries were encouraged to "open doors to the homeless and oppressed refugees, since there can be no abiding peace while this problem remains unsolved."

In light of the growing conflict in Palestine, the congress asked "Jewry everywhere to refrain from provocative acts and to restrain those among them who would resort to violence." Reflecting Gartenhaus's evangelical vocation, the resolution concluded with a call to share the gospel with the Jewish people:

> FURTHER, THIS CONGRESS would not be true to its convictions if it did not state its belief that the command of Jesus Christ to evangelise the world was intended to include the people of Israel. The Congress, therefore, calls upon all Baptists to do their part in supporting missionary work among the Jews. We believe that only when Christ is accepted as Lord will the Jews or any other people find salvation, peace, and freedom.[3]

This resolution represented the pinnacle of Gartenhaus's witness as a Jewish Christian, a Southern Baptist national official, and an international leader. In his autobiography, he charged that at the 1934 Berlin congress Baptist leaders refused to listen to his warnings about Nazi persecution of the Jews. He wanted the BWA to take more decisive and practical steps to confront and oppose Hitler. In contrast, the 1947 Copenhagen congress was a success in Gartenhaus's eyes because it "attempted redress and reparation to the Jewish people. There was a general and genuine feeling of repentance and a sense of duty to expiate and conciliate." With satisfaction, Gartenhaus reflected:

> I WAS NO longer a rebellious upstart. I had earned for myself a name and could no longer be silenced. Nor did anyone wish to silence me now. Many still remembered my stand thirteen years before. I went to this Baptist World Congress with the intention of soliciting the aid of the congress for the most urgent needs of the remnant of European Jewry. These remnants of the Nazi holocaust were in a very sad plight, both materially and spiritually. As they wandered about aimlessly as sheep without a shepherd, no country in the world would give them asylum and they were on the verge of despair. I sincerely and prayerfully hoped that the Baptists at that congress would heed my pleas to render assistance to my destitute people. Thank God, I was not disappointed.[4]

The third resolution, focused on ministry to displaced persons (DPs), did not specifically mention Jews but was primarily concerned with the kind of material aid Gartenhaus had dreamed would go to Jewish survivors of the Holocaust. The resolution asked that DPs and their families "should be allowed, so far as possible, to enter countries according to their own choice" and that governments "should reconsider the conditions of immigration so as to admit as large a number as possible irrespective of the national quota." It also requested that clergy be permitted to accompany DPs and counseled Baptists to be prepared to "provide for a welcome worthy of the name of Christ, and should offer and cultivate all measures making for mutual fellowship and for worship, especially to those of our own faith and order."[5]

In a speech titled "Conditions in Europe," Edwin A. Bell, the representative of the American Baptist Foreign Mission Society, did not specifically mention Jewish DPs, but he must have encountered some in the camps he visited. Their suffering illustrated "the fact that the battle for human liberties is not yet won, and that the Christian doctrine of man faces as serious a challenge in our times as it has ever faced in human history." Bell then condemned Nazism and its system of concentration camps, while also calling for compassion toward Germans and in particular, German Christians:

> NATIONAL SOCIALISM WAS, and is, a great evil. I say this in all humility, conscious of the fact that we also are sinners. But I have seen the evidences of its ugly cruelty in Dachau, in Lidice, in the Gestapo prison in Prague with its gallows and its guillotine, and the fury and bestiality of which man is capable in the almost complete destruction of Warsaw and elsewhere. The German people are drinking the bitter, bitter cup of the consequences of what prevailed in their land during these last few years. Multitudes of them are ashamed of what was there. They would not have had it so if they had seen in time where it was leading. The work of healing and reconciliation must be done quickly and thoroughly. Europe cannot live without Germany industrially, politically, or spiritually, German people must be given a chance to have a minimum level of decency at least in living. We must stand by brethren of the Christian faith in Germany and help them in the regeneration and recovery of their people, even as we strive for the regeneration of our own.[6]

The Copenhagen congress did indeed attempt to confront the needs of a devastated Europe through the gospel of Christ, in light of the destruction caused by Nazism's racialism. Rev. D. R. Sharpe, from the United States, sought to address the "race hatred and pride" Baptists confronted as they gathered in Copenhagen, and he summarized the convictions of the congress in this way: "Selfishness, greed, hate, economic injustice, race prejudice, discriminations based on race, colour or creed, political corruption, cartels, war, nationalism, Communism, Fascism, secularism, social inequalities—all these must be confronted with the redeeming Gospel of Jesus Christ."[7]

Cleveland 1950—Opposing Genocide

When the global Baptist community traveled to Cleveland, Ohio, in July 1950, the delegates assembled for the eighth world congress acknowledged the Holocaust in two important resolutions.

The first resolution focused on the United Nations' Convention for the Prevention and Punishment of the Crime of Genocide, which the United Nations General Assembly passed on December 9, 1948. It required twenty countries to ratify the agreement, and after this was achieved, it became legally effective on January 12, 1951. At the time of the eighth congress the Genocide Convention still lacked six votes for authorization. Citing the convention's definition of genocide ("the intent to destroy, in whole or part, a national, ethnical, racial, or religious group"), the congress as an expression of "Christian conscience" urged the nations of the world to ratify the convention so that it might become "part of the slowly emerging body of international law."[8]

The presentation most relevant to the genocide resolution was delivered by Dr. Culbert G. Rutenber,[9] then professor at Eastern Baptist Theological Seminary in Philadelphia, an evangelical seminary associated with the Northern Baptist Convention. Theologically a pacifist, Rutenber spoke on the theme of "The Totalitarian State and the Individual Conscience." Although he did not specifically mention Jews, he did refer to the insidious nature of totalitarianism as practiced in Germany. Echoing the classic Baptist understanding of personality, he stated, "The totalitarian state is a plunderer of the mind, a saboteur of the soul."[10] He quoted Niemöller in support of his contention that totalitarianism "denies the existence" of individual responsibility, which permitted Germans following the war to evade responsibility for the horrors inflicted upon the Jewish people:

> LISTEN TO MARTIN Niemöller as he comments upon the situation in his own country: "Nobody," writes Niemöller, "wants to take the

> responsibility of the guilt, no one of our German people is guilty, everybody shoves the guilt over to his neighbor. The local official says: I am only a little man, the whole guilt lies with you, Herr local commander; and he in turn says: I did not wrong anybody; I only obeyed orders. The whole guilt lies with you, you of the Gestapo, but the latter doesn't want it either and finally everything lands on Himmler and Hitler."[11]

The Commission on Social Justice and Human Rights proposed a second resolution on global manifestations of racial prejudice, including "discrimination against Jews in many lands, the Apartheid Movement in South Africa, the discrimination against Orientals and Mexicans in some areas, and the segregation by law of Negroes in the United States." Backed by the racialism resolutions of the 1934, 1939, and 1947 congresses, the Cleveland congress declared that "discrimination, based on religion, culture, color and race provides fertile soil for the development and spread of communism, fascism and other antisocial programs." It also confessed that Baptists were not "free from prejudice and discriminatory practices against racial and cultural groups in our worship and communities." Nevertheless, it was a Baptist conviction that "discrimination and segregation based on religion, race, color and culture are ethically and morally indefensible and contrary to the gospel of Christ and the principle of freedom for which Baptists stand."

Accordingly, the BWA called for individual Baptists to repudiate prejudice and to work toward a more just political order. Churches were asked to "examine their interracial practices and policies with a view to removing from their worship and fellowship all forms of segregation and discrimination based on race, color or culture." Politically, Baptists were encouraged to "use their influence to have discriminatory laws repealed wherever they appear in their respective countries" and to "seek where necessary the enactment of laws designed to safeguard the rights of oppressed racial groups." As a general spiritual principle, each Baptist was counseled to "sincerely and prayerfully search his own soul with a view to freeing himself from racial and cultural prejudice and embodying in his own person the mind and spirit of Christ in all human relations—in work, business, education, government, politics, recreation, social life and religion."[12]

Notes

1. F. Townley Lord, *Baptist World Fellowship: A Short History of the Baptist World Alliance*, 123–24.

2. Walter O. Lewis, ed., *Seventh Baptist World Congress: Copenhagen, Denmark July 29–August 3, 1947* (London: Baptist World Alliance, 1948), Minutes Item 154, Committee on Resolutions, "Resolution on Race Relations," 98–99.

3. Ibid., Minutes Item 155, Committee on Resolutions, "Resolution Concerning the Jews," 99.

4. Jacob Gartenhaus, *Traitor? A Jew, a Book, a Miracle: An Autobiography* (Nashville: Thomas Nelson, 1980), 205–6.

5. Lewis, ed., *Seventh Baptist World Congress*, Minutes Item 156, Committee on Resolutions, "Resolution on Displaced Persons," 99–100.

6. Ibid., Minutes Item 116, Edwin A. Bell, "Conditions in Europe," 79–80.

7. Ibid., Minutes Item 74, D. R. Sharpe, "Christianising the Social Order," 47–48.

8. Arnold T. Ohrn, ed., *Eighth Baptist World Congress Cleveland Ohio July 22-27, 1950 Official Report* (Philadelphia: Judson Press, 1950), "Resolution on Genocide," 340.

9. Larry L. McSwain and William Lloyd Allen, eds., *Twentieth-Century Shapers of Baptist Social Ethics*, Baptists Series (Macon, GA: Mercer University Press, 2008), 246. Rutenber would later serve as the president of the American Baptist Convention (Northern Baptists) from 1968 to 1969.

10. Ohrn, ed., *Eighth Baptist World Congress*, "The Totalitarian State and the Individual Conscience" by Dr. Cuthbert G. Rutenber, 140.

11. Ibid., 143.

12. Ibid., "Resolution on Race Problems," 340–41.

Contemporary Impressions

The BWA and the Holocaust

The 1934 BWA congress, controversial even before it took place, subsequently has faded from view in all but the most specialized historical treatments. However, it may be argued that its racialism resolution deserves a place alongside the universally acknowledged Barmen Declaration, due to its forthright defense of the general Jewish population and their civil rights. Barmen ignored this issue, focusing on the right of the German church to choose its leaders without interference of the state. Karl Barth's "nein" might be legendary and famous, but the Baptist "no" to anti-Semitism, declared in the German capital with the Nazi government watching, was more comprehensive.

However, it must be acknowledged that it was easier and far less costly for the delegates from the United States and the international Baptist community to express support for German Jews; after passing their resolution, they all (with the exception, of course, of the German Baptists) freely departed from Germany and did not have to worry about suffering retribution, imprisonment, or worse for their prophetic activity. Nevertheless, the 1934 Berlin resolution on racialism truly deserves to be viewed as one of the milestones in the historical Baptist defense of freedom, liberty, and human rights for all, regardless of faith or race.

The prophetic luster of the 1934 congress was tarnished by the lack of follow-up activity on behalf of the Jewish people by the Baptist World Alliance. Although he basked in the glow of the praise for the racialism resolution, J. H. Rushbrooke seemed content to interpret the passing of the resolution against anti-Semitism as the end of the matter, even though objectively, it changed nothing for the Jewish people of Germany. His primary concern was for the health and welfare of the European Baptist movement, and in particular, the German Baptists. He engineered a meeting where the politically correct stance was adopted, while not adding to the pressures German Baptists faced in trying to gain approved status as a religious movement from the Nazi authorities. He was willing to ignore German Baptist support for Hitler and his Nazi polices and thus did not press them to apply the resolution regarding the Jewish people to their own setting.

For Baptists outside of Germany, Rushbrooke offered little guidance or encouragement on how to implement the resolution. He could have spearheaded a global fund-raising campaign to assist German Jews, but he declined to do so. Following Kristallnacht, American outrage and concern set the stage for just such an initiative, but Rushbrooke did not feel compelled to organize it.

The 1939 congress in Atlanta may have produced heated debate between the British and German and Italian leaders, but it did not produce a fresh or enhanced resolution that could serve as a strong follow-up to what was achieved in 1934. Reiterating former resolutions, as if the events of the intervening five years did not require something additional to say, constituted a rather anemic response to what was developing into the crisis of the century. Once again, Rushbrooke appeared to be more concerned with ensuring the active participation and inclusion of the German and Italian Baptists than he was to chart new paths in defending Jewish rights and lives.

Thus, the Atlanta congress must be assessed as something of a disappointment. It did not reach its potential as a galvanizing prophetic event in defense of the core Baptist convictions of liberty, separation of church and state, the personality of all people, and democratic freedom for all, regardless of race and religion. Set in the segregated South of the United States, the congress could have been a clarion call for civil rights for African Americans and for oppressed minorities elsewhere, such as Jews in Germany. It could have been an intentional forum for converting Baptists from passive bystanders to the dreams of African Americans and Jews, to authentic friends of these peoples, expressed through practical deeds and progressive political stances.

Baptists missed a golden opportunity to leave Atlanta mobilized to deal a death blow to American segregation and to break through the roadblocks preventing Jewish exiles from immigrating in large numbers to the United States. Both courses of action, based on core Baptist convictions and values, had the potential to change individual lives and perhaps even to transform aspects of twentieth-century US and European history. White US Baptists, from both the Southern and Northern Conventions, bear the brunt of the responsibility for this historical miss. The 1939 congress provided the best setting imaginable for the formation of a groundbreaking alliance with the National Baptists. With a combined membership of some ten million members, they could have used Atlanta as a symbolic launching pad for a new national movement for full civil liberties in the United States. The three largest and most influential Baptist conventions in the United States could have spearheaded a campaign to assist European Jews and lobbied for their admittance into the country in substantially greater numbers.

The postwar 1947 BWA congress in Copenhagen produced a problematic legacy as well. The resolutions passed possessed much positive value, especially in their acknowledgment of the Holocaust and the sufferings of the Jewish people. However, the congress remains a disappointment in at least two respects.

First, it did not mobilize Baptists to specifically assist Jewish displaced persons. The compartmentalization of social services, in which Jews helped Jews, Catholics assisted Catholics, and Protestants took care of their own members, was well established and universally accepted, and Baptists participated within that arrangement and did not question its propriety. Nevertheless, in light of the enormity of what the Jews uniquely experienced, the application of Christian values in the social sphere should have encouraged Baptists to serve their Jewish neighbors as well as members of their own religious family.

Second, the fraternal reconciliation with German and Italian Baptists that took place at the congress was in many ways troubling and perhaps premature. There was controversy over the invitation extended to German Baptists, who themselves were concerned about what kind of reception they might receive. They were welcomed warmly and even provided clothes to wear. The value the Baptist World Alliance placed on the unity of the global Baptist movement motivated delegates to welcome the Axis Baptists back into fellowship, but in Dietrich Bonhoeffer's words, the grace offered was cheap. German and Italian Baptist leaders were not required to ask for forgiveness or express any remorse for the role they played (or as passive bystanders, did not play) during the Nazi era. No accountability was demanded, and this paved the way for Nazi-era Baptist leaders to continue in their positions in the postwar period.

By virtue of their resolutions, the global Baptist community placed itself on the right side of history throughout the Nazi period. The BWA congresses condemned anti-Semitism in 1934, 1939, and 1947, and opposed genocide in 1950. Nevertheless, the pre-1950 statements did not propose any practical mechanism or strategy for opposing the persecution and extermination of the European Jewish population, and nor did they mobilize the global Baptist community to advocate for substantial Jewish immigration to safe havens. The statements were just but not sacrificial; they cost the BWA nothing to pronounce, demanded no specific response from its people, but nevertheless garnered it some goodwill from the Jewish community in England and the United States.

The 1950 Resolution on Race Relations did ask Baptists to consider specific action strategies. It counseled Baptists to rid themselves of prejudice when they gathered corporately. It also encouraged them to challenge "discriminatory laws" and even seek to "repeal" them through engagement in the political processes of their countries. Going even further, the congress urged that Baptists proactively seek to have their countries pass laws that would prevent future discrimination.

Thus, the 1950 statement may be interpreted as a self-critique or even a confession on the part of Baptists. As they reviewed their actions as a global fellowship during the Nazi era, delegates to the 1950 congress might very well have asked themselves questions such as these: Would it have made any tangible difference if the BWA had clearly and forcefully stated to the German Baptists in 1934 that support for the Nazi regime was unacceptable, and if continued, might cost them fellowship with the rest of the international Baptist movement? What would have happened if the Baptist World Alliance had protested Germany's discrimination codes and laws and more forcefully and persistently pressed for their repeal? And how might history have been changed if the Northern, Southern, and National Baptist Conventions of the United States had rallied the BWA's global fellowship to assist persecuted Jews in practical ways, and joined forces to champion the civil rights campaign in their own country?

Conclusion

Baptists, Jews, and the Holocaust

Every account of the Holocaust aspires to answer one or more questions about the most horrific episode of the twentieth century. I have attempted to describe if, and to what extent, Baptists in the United States extended "the hand of sincere friendship" to the Jewish people during the Nazi era. However, it seems to me that Holocaust narratives inevitably end up raising as many new questions as they resolve. These questions are not just historical but political, philosophical, theological—and most importantly, personal.

Keith Clements asks: "The holocaust demands of Christians that they examine themselves, and allow others to examine them, to the roots of all their claims to be God's agents of mission in the world. It is a matter of integrity. Why have they allowed their faith—not only in the Hitler period but at other times and still today—to serve rather than challenge the abuse of power, and to be drawn into mass hatred and violence?"[1] Similarly, Walter Harrelson former dean at Vanderbilt University, and coauthor Rabbi Randall Falk assert that there continues to be a place in a post-Holocaust world for Christian denominations to review the past and put forth resolutions and statements about the events that took place between 1933 and 1948:

> EVERY GENERATION OF Christians needs to review this painful story, including its most unbearable part, the story of the Holocaust, in order to find the impulse and the strength to say to living Jews today, 'I am sorry.' Church bodies and church officials need to find ways to do the same through their own public statements, through liturgies and confessions, and in their specific statements concerning the relations of Judaism and Christianity.[2]

The point is well taken. The conscience of Christians should remain troubled in the aftermath of the Holocaust. Past denominational statements and actions need to be reassessed. Baptists need wisdom in order to be better prepared for future challenges to the core convictions we espouse and their application to religious freedom, civil liberty, democracy, human rights, and genocide.

How Well Did Baptists Respond?

How well did Baptists in the United States respond to Nazi anti-Semitism and their persecution of the Jewish people during the turbulent era of 1933 through 1948 (from Hitler's rise to power to the establishment of Israel)?

The Baptist press was not silent regarding the persecution of German Jewry or anti-Semitism. Baptists were well informed about the events unfolding in Germany and Europe. In addition to secular news sources, Baptist publications such as *The Watchman-Examiner*, *Missions*, and various Southern Baptist newspapers reported stories and offered editorials about the prewar persecutions and the wartime extermination efforts. Baptist publications did not ignore what was taking place; to the contrary, they engaged in vigorous debate regarding the significance of the Nazi persecution of Jews. Not only did informed Baptists have access to the same knowledge that the wider society enjoyed, but also they possessed sources of information from the European Baptist movement that provided a useful perspective on the religious dimensions of the Nazi curtailment of civil rights of Jews and concerning Christians who were struggling with how to relate to the new political realities of Germany.

Baptists were not silent. They produced a large collection of public statements and resolutions in reaction to the rise of Nazi totalitarianism, the initial wave of German anti-Semitic attacks, and the wartime systemic killing of the European Jewish population. These statements represented the collective voice of approximately ten million Americans and made clear that on an organizational level, Baptists in the United States opposed Hitler's destruction of European Jewry or anti-Semitism.

The statements offered a fairly uniform set of convictions regarding the religious, political, and social critique of Nazism, the civil and religious rights of the Jewish community, and the subject of anti-Semitism. With few exceptions, the resolutions passed by Baptist national and regional bodies in the United States opposed all forms of totalitarianism, including communism, fascism, and Nazism. They protested all attempts to curtail the religious, civil, and political rights of Jews. Official Baptist assemblies rejected all forms of anti-Semitism, both foreign (German) and domestic.

This uniformity in Baptist positions did not mean that they marched in lockstep with one another. Indeed, the narrative arcs of the major US Baptist conventions were quite distinct from one another.

Nationally, the Northern Baptist Convention expressed its concern about Nazism and the persecution of the Jews repeatedly. On a regional level, the various state conventions and city societies also felt compelled to offer resolutions and statements. Although there was no discernible geographical or chronological pattern to these regional responses, their random nature indicates that Northern Baptists felt compelled to reconsider new developments and revisit unresolved issues. In general, the statements and resolutions emanating from Northern Baptist Convention meetings offered sympathy but very little in terms of practical solutions or calls to concerted action. In this sense, Northern Baptists acted corporately as distant bystanders. They felt powerless to change the course of history on behalf of European Jews.

Southern Baptist Convention national resolutions were mostly silent on the Jewish persecution throughout the Nazi period. Several influential Southern Baptist leaders, such as President M. E. Dodd and senior European missionary Everett Gill, entertained anti-Semitic or racist views that would have made the passing of resolutions against Nazi anti-Semitism problematic. Southern Baptist complicity in Jim Crow culture opened them up to the charge of hypocrisy. How could Southern Baptists criticize Hitler when in their homeland African Americans were systemically discriminated against and lynching was not an uncommon practice? Furthermore, Southern Baptist missionary involvement in the Middle East diminished Southern Baptist Convention official support for the Zionist movement.

In spite of these factors, Southern Baptists also felt it necessary to sympathize with Jews. Approximately four hundred Southern Baptist delegates, including Dodd, voted for the racialism resolution that was approved at the 1934 Berlin congress. In 1939, they voted to reaffirm this stance at the Atlanta BWA congress. All across the country, national evangelist Jacob Gartenhaus tirelessly advocated on behalf of persecuted Jews and encouraged Southern Baptists to reach out in friendship to Jews.

The cumulative impact of these contradictory forces created an ambivalent Southern Baptist response to the Jewish problem which also manifested itself on the state convention level. With the extraordinary exception of Missouri, state conventions did not express explicit support in resolution form for persecuted Jews until Kristallnacht. There were Southern Baptist pastors, such as Alabama's Alfred J. Dickinson Jr., who prophetically advocated for Jews and denounced anti-Semitism before Kristallnacht, but that milestone event awakened the conscience of the entire world. Several Baptist state conventions, meeting either during the week Kristallnacht took place or shortly thereafter, were caught up in this wave of outrage and composed original resolutions in support of Jews.

In contrast to white Baptist responses to the Jewish problem, African American Baptists were not quite either bystanders or ambivalent. A more accurate characterization would be that African American Baptists experienced a competitive friendship with the Jewish community.

Two factors predisposed African American Baptists to identify positively with Jews as equals and to oppose Nazi anti-Semitism. Like African Americans, Jews in the first part of the twentieth century were part of the underclass of American society. Prejudice was the common experience of both communities. Second, African American Baptists strongly identified with the Old Testament exodus narrative. Since both Jews and blacks had experienced slavery, they could understand each other on a level not reachable by the dominant white and Christian society. This encouraged a bond between the Jewish and African American communities, in spite of the differences in religion.

However, other factors created divisions between the two communities and reduced African American Baptist enthusiasm for expressing solidarity with the Jewish victims of Nazism. Domestically, Jewish immigrants generally achieved quicker and greater progress in achieving the American dream of economic prosperity. In 1930s Harlem, Jews were generally landlords and business owners, while many African Americans from the South were unskilled employees in menial jobs who lived in rented apartments. Some African American leaders urged the black community to emulate Jews in order to achieve success, but quite naturally this inequality led to jealousy as well as admiration.

Internationally, the victimization of the Jews by the Nazis led to global expressions of protest. Even while participating in those protests, African American Baptists wondered why the world did not similarly feel compelled to support their own community's civil rights movement. African American Baptists felt like they were in competition with European Jewry for the world's compassion. This led to their plight being briefly referenced in the 1934 Berlin racialism resolution, as well as their lobbying for Atlanta to be the site for the 1939 BWA congress. Leaders such as Lacey Kirk Williams sincerely anticipated that the Baptist World Alliance would advocate for the civil rights of US blacks as they had done for the Jews in Germany.

Functioning as the international voice for US Baptists, the Baptist World Alliance's response to the Nazi destruction of European Jewry may be characterized as a complex composite of the key American responses. Like the Northern Baptists, the BWA response manifested bystander behavior. While passing resolutions that voiced Baptist opposition to Nazism, the persecution of Jews, and anti-Semitism, the BWA never developed a strategy for assisting Jewish victims of Nazism or resettling Jewish exiles in the aftermath of the Holocaust.

The Southern Baptist sense of ambivalence was also mirrored in the Baptist World Alliance. J. H. Rushbrooke rejected Nazism out of hand and harbored none of the anti-black racism that dominated the American South, and there is no evidence that he was anti-Semitic. However, his commitment to alleviating the burden the Jewish community was facing was compromised by his lifelong devotion to Germany in general and to the German Baptists in particular. Whenever the needs of Jews and German Baptists collided, the latter received the lion's share of Rushbrooke's energy and sympathy.

The African American sense of competitive friendship with Jews was also a feature of Rushbrooke's own journey. Even as the Nazi persecution of the Jews assumed massive proportions, Rushbrooke unswervingly devoted his personal and the BWA's institutional resources to fighting primarily for Rumanian Baptists' rights. Opposing the oppression of the small Rumanian Baptist community took precedence over preventing the attempted annihilation of the entire continent's Jewish population.

Philo-Semitism and Anti-Semitism

In an editorial, the *American Hebrew* made the following intriguing observation: "To be sure, not all persons who are anti-Semitic must necessarily be fascists. Nor are all fascists anti-Semitic."[3] In any community, religious or otherwise, members may exhibit of continuum of beliefs, attitudes, and prejudices. More specifically, during the Nazi era, Baptists expressed a variety of attitudes toward Jews, from extreme anti-Semitism to an enthusiastic philo-Semitism.[4]

In the United States, a few mainstream Baptist leaders expressed enthusiastic support for Hitler and Nazi policies and were also actively anti-Semitic. In Northern Baptist circles, only William Bell Riley would represent such an extremely negative position along the continuum. However, though the convention never censured him for such intolerance, Riley's anti-Semitism appears to have made no inroads, either on the national or state level. On this issue, Riley was isolated and apparently carried little or no influence, in contrast to his enormous influence on other matters, such as fundamentalist doctrine.

Within the Southern Baptist Convention, M. E. Dodd openly expressed both pro-Hitler and anti-Semitic positions for at least a decade,[5] and while holding leadership posts on the national and state levels. Unlike Riley, Dodd exercised wide influence throughout the Southern Baptist Convention, and his apology of the Nazi persecution of German Jews no doubt played a role in limiting the extent to which Southern Baptists felt free to produce national statements on this issue. Jacob Gartenhaus asserted that his advocacy for Jews was hindered, and though he did not identify Dodd by name, it is reasonable to imagine that Dodd, as president, may have sought to curtail Gartenhaus's efforts on behalf of persecuted German Jews.

Southern Baptist missionary Everett Gill exhibited a significant degree of toleration for Hitler and the Nazis, and in addition, he was passively anti-Semitic. In his book on Europe and its races, Gill raised no alarms about Nazism per se. He offered a comprehensive survey of European races and ethnic groups but omitted Jews. This would have been a remarkable omission under any circumstances, but it was extraordinary in light of the Nazi campaign against the Jews in the 1930s.

The Southern Baptist missionary corps in Palestine and the Middle East, as a group, was opposed to Hitler and the Nazi movement and yet politically anti-Semitic. Although the missionaries were aware that the immigration of Jews to Palestine was directly linked to the Nazi persecution of the Jews, the missionaries did not actively urge Southern Baptists to support the movement of Jewish exiles to Palestine. Southern Baptist aid for Jews fleeing persecution could have saved lives, but no action was taken. Southern Baptist missionaries did not express support for Zionism and essentially attempted to stay neutral in the political controversies, so as not to upset the missionary work they promoted in Arab communities.

National Baptist Convention historian L. G. Gordon expressed both opposition to Hitler and the Nazi movement as well as religious (theological) anti-Semitism. He was not in favor of the Nazi campaign to persecute Jews, but he blamed Jews for causing their own persecution. The Jews' rejection of Jesus not only led to persecution in Europe but also was to blame for the conflict they were experiencing in Palestine with the Arabs.

Both Northern and Southern Baptist leaders expressed opposition to Hitler and the Nazi movement while acting in an opportunistically evangelistic manner. Northern Baptist-supported old-style Jewish urban missions and the Los Angeles and Portland evangelism ministries leveraged the catastrophic suffering of the Jewish people as an opportunity for evangelistic witness. Gartenhaus, on behalf of Southern Baptists, exemplified this combination as well, as did the Jewish evangelism ministries connected to the evangelical prophecy movement.

These leaders and their ministries strenuously denied they were anti-Semitic; in fact, they understood themselves to be advocates for the Jewish people. However, calling attention to their plight and eliciting Christian sympathy for them in order to raise money for one's own ministry appeared ethically challenged; taking advantage of suffering to evangelize hurting people seems insensitive and contextually inappropriate. It would have been preferable for these ministries to focus on humanitarian relief, and then after the crisis was over, to resume conversion-oriented efforts.

The majority of Baptists in the United States belonged to two conventions that were in general opposed to Hitler and the Nazi movement and ambivalently pro-Jewish. The white Southern Baptist Convention and the black National Baptist Convention supported the Allied effort to defeat the Nazis while expressing conflicted attitudes toward Jews. Southern Baptists, as has been noted, expressed discomfort in criticizing the Nazis for their persecution of Jews in the 1930s due to their sensitivity about the South's systemic discrimination against African Americans. Although Southern Baptist resolutions were pro-Jewish, less positive views about Jews were published in state convention–sponsored newspapers. National Baptists identified religiously with Jews and encouraged their community to follow the Jewish pattern in achieving economic prosperity but also expressed jealousy over the attention European Jewish persecution received as opposed to the support they perceived for their own civil rights struggle.

The Baptist World Alliance, led by Rushbrooke, encompassed aspects of the preceding positions. There never was a doubt that the alliance was opposed to totalitarianism in general and Nazism in particular.[6] However, the application of the alliance's core conviction concerning the unity of the Baptist movement encouraged it to favor German Baptist sensitivities over the needs of the Jews. Furthermore, Rushbrooke's devotion to the Rumanian Baptist cause should be contrasted to his lack of energy to apply his vaunted political skills to the Jewish problem. He passively shifted responsibility for aiding Jewish refugees to either national Baptist bodies, such as the British Baptist Union, or Allied governments.

The Northern Baptist Convention and its affiliated organizations (such as the Foreign and Home Mission Societies and the state conventions), stood in opposition to Hitler and the Nazi movement while also being passively pro-Jewish. They passed a good number of resolutions but did not call for effective activity on behalf of persecuted Jews. In hindsight, these statements did place the Northern Baptist Convention on the right side of history, but Northern Baptists would have been hard pressed to point to any actions they took that made a difference.

The Christian Friendliness missionaries of the Woman's American Baptist Home Mission Society best exemplified the qualities and activities representing the extreme positive pole of the continuum. They were in opposition to Hitler and the Nazi movement and actively pro-Jewish. The Christian Friendliness missionaries sought out and ministered to Jewish émigrés fleeing from Germany, delighted in befriending Jews, portrayed Jews in a positive light, and tirelessly mobilized Northern Baptist churches and their women to reach out to Jews in friendship and love.

Within the African American Baptist community, a trio of New York–based preachers deserve to be recognized as philo-Semitic. Adam Clayton Powell Sr. and Adam Clayton Powell Jr., through their ministries at Abyssinian Baptist Church in Harlem, and T. S. Harten in neighboring Brooklyn, modeled how to cross racial boundaries in the cause of social justice. Among Anglo Southern Baptists, Alfred J. Dickinson Jr., pastor of the First Baptist Church of Mobile, consistently demonstrated a prophetic spirit in opposing Nazi totalitarianism and anti-Semitism in his sermons. Gartenhaus, a Jewish-Christian, also should be praised as philo-Semitic. Certainly, he was unalterably opposed to the Nazis, and in his mind, he was fully philo-Semitic.

In conclusion, it may be observed that there was no singular approach on the part of US Baptists to the challenge posed by Nazism and its persecution of the Jews. Even within conventions, a range of responses existed. In general, Baptist leaders and organizations tended to oppose Hitler and the Nazi movement, and the majority appeared to express philo-Semitic attitudes. Only a small minority of US Baptist leaders, mostly from the Southern Baptist Convention, were openly anti-Semitic, but it must be acknowledged that they did wield influence.

Baptist Resolutions and Core Convictions

The Baptist core convictions of soul liberty, individual and corporate democracy, and separation of church and state, and their theological derivatives of racial equality and the sanctity of personality, were clearly and consistently applied by Baptists as they responded to the rise of Adolf Hitler and National Socialism. In so doing, Baptists in the United States indicated their solidarity with the global Baptist movement, which consistently had articulated these values leading up to and during the Holocaust era.[7]

Most certainly, the application of those convictions to contemporary issues or problems through resolutions and other statements are not sufficient to solve the problems being addressed. Writing from within a Roman Catholic context, Avery Cardinal Dulles describes the role that the social teachings of the church play in relation to its theology or dogma: "In the sociopolitical area the Church's mission is not to make pronouncements on the technical aspects of politics, economics, and the social sciences, but to illuminate the moral and religious dimensions of social questions so that the faithful may better form their consciences."[8] This aptly describes the role resolutions play in the Baptist context.

Lacking any creedal, legislative, or prescriptive force by which to bind local congregations or individuals, Baptist resolutions represented the consensus of those present, as they sought "the mind of Christ" (1 Corinthians 2:16) on such matters. Even when statements call Baptists to action, the summons is not a command but an admonition or plea to recognize the existence of a significant problem and to challenge Baptists to reconsider how their theological core convictions might inform conscience and prompt a Christian reply.

Resolutions remind Baptists of who they are and what they believe so that they may remain faithful to God and true to the Baptist worldview in the midst of social change and crisis. Baptists certainly possessed "sufficient factual information" about Hitler's intentions toward the Jewish people. They engaged in analysis of the events progressed and attempted to exercise "prudence" (a term Dulles uses) in applying Baptist doctrine to the problems posed by the rise of Nazism. The convictions of Baptists in the United States were sorely tested by the unfolding drama of the Holocaust.

Baptists in the United States and the BWA responded to the challenge of fascist totalitarianism and the Nazi persecution of the Jews by reasserting fundamental Baptist convictions. From these convictions, they made judgments regarding the incompatibility of European totalitarianism and Baptist social ethics, expressed opposition to

Hitler's anti-Semitic agenda, and offered solidarity and sympathy to persecuted Jewish communities. In particular, the Baptist convictions of individual soul freedom, political liberty, and the separation of church and state logically and historically led Baptists to apply a set of secondary principles—that of personality and racialism—in order to specifically address the sociopolitical and religious issues they faced.[9]

Even Dodd stated that "the greatest contribution Jesus made to the world outside of the redemptive power of the Cross was the discovery and revelation and magnifying of personality."[10] Personality was synonymous with the biblical understanding that human beings are made in the "image of God" (Genesis 1:26) and thus individuals have infinite worth. Personality referred to the soul or spirit of a person,[11] indicating that human beings had the capacity to communicate with God, to aspire to lives of moral and ethical virtue, and to experience the full range of human emotions and appreciate creation's beauty. Furthermore, Baptists believed that personality provided a theological foundation for social justice.

In 1934, Illinois Baptists of the Northern Baptist Convention invoked personality as a key conviction to justify their opposition to totalitarianism in general (implying a rejection of Nazism): "Whereas, one of the cardinal truths in the gospel of Christ is the sacredness of personality, be it therefore Resolved, that the Illinois Baptist State Convention place itself on record as being opposed to any industrial or social system which tends to degrade human life."[12] In 1938, Connecticut Baptists voted to "affirm the historic Baptist position on the separation of church and State and the priceless heritage of soul liberty" and resolved to "pledge ourselves anew to those goals of social justice which grow out of the teachings of Jesus Christ. Varied though schemes and programs for social action may be, we recognize the religious conviction of the value and sacredness of personality as a fundamental faith inspiring our efforts. We, therefore, stand opposed to those forces within the social structure that devaluate and exploit the body and soul of man."[13] *The Watchman-Examiner* reported that in Nazi Germany, where "the propaganda machine of the Nazis is engaged in promoting *Mein Kampf*," Christian ministers were preaching biblical truth and that there was "widespread emphasis on the sacred rights of personality and the uniqueness of the Christian faith as over against the exaggerated nationalistic tendencies."[14]

The Baptist conviction that personality defines human worth provided a sound theological foundation for the development of Baptist positions regarding racialism. Racialism predated the Nazi era and had two connotations. First, it was as a categorical term for the field of study of racial relations. Second, it served as a pejorative term; an individual or political force might pursue a racialist agenda and oppress a race or ethnic group. Jews uniquely were considered both a racial group alongside Asians, Negroes, and European races, and a religious group, standing apart from Christians, Buddhists, and other religions.

Dr. J. C. Robbins, foreign secretary of the American Baptist Foreign Missions Society, in arguing against the "racial and class consciousness" of communism and fascism, affirmed: "In all this confusion and bitterness and hatred, only one institution comprises the fellowship of men of good will that can remake the world. The Church stands for the supreme value of personality."[15] Since all human beings possessed personality, people of differing races, cultures, religions, and nationalities deserved social and political equality. In Baptist thought, racial purity did not serve as a prerequisite for human rights or participation in political affairs. Baptists asserted that all racial groups deserved full individual freedom and collective political liberty.

Throughout the Nazi era, the rallying cry against Nazi persecution of the Jews (as well as support for African American civil rights and Japanese Americans imprisoned in camps) was Paul's argument to the Athenians that there exists a God who embraces all nations and values all people, regardless of racial or ethnic differences (Acts 17:24-29). The Pauline affirmation that all people are "God's offspring" led Baptists, as well as other denominations, to express social justice in terms of the "Fatherhood of God" and the "Brotherhood of Man." The Social Action Committee of the Connecticut Baptist Convention, for example, outlined three "basic principles especially applicable to social and economic affairs":

1. "The Fatherhood of God, and consequently the brotherhood of man."
2. "The worth and value of the individual, and the dignity, integrity and sacredness of human personality."
3. "The idea of fellowship and service."[16]

Core convictions could not justify political systems that sought to restrain the essential freedoms of their populations in general, or of a minority, such as Jews, in particular.[17] Rushbrooke made this clear before a Northern Baptist audience in Philadelphia in 1936:

> EQUAL HONOR BELONGS to Williams in connection with his attitude towards the Jews. That great and so often unhappy people, still victimised in many lands of the earth, had from the days of Edward I been excluded from England. Jews who came over to America found that not even the Dutch colony of New Amsterdam would allow them to worship God in their own way; in Providence they were not only unhindered but welcomed. . . . But if Williams' principle, his definite separation of the functions of Church and state, and his claim of rights for human personality as transcending and limiting the claims of the state, is accepted in English-speaking lands, it is by no means unchallenged in our day. The theory of the "totalitarian state" is asserted and applied in Russia, in Germany, and elsewhere. Russian Communism has in principle no place for free human personality. All literature and art, every cultural movement or organisation, must express the will of the State. The same is true of the National Socialism of Germany, and it is instructive to observe that the resistance which Nazism has encountered in its effort to regiment the entire life of a people springs from the same root as that of Roger Williams—the root of religious conviction, the belief in God as the final judge and lawgiver of conscience.[18]

Convictions could also hinder the Baptist response to the Jewish plight. There was consensus among the major denominations regarding war and peace until Pearl Harbor. Between 1933 and 1941, all resolutions passed by the Northern, Southern, and National Baptist Conventions affirmed that war was inconsistent with the principles of Jesus Christ. Although not all Baptists were pacifists, in practice very little room was made available for intervention in the European conflict until the United States was attacked by Japan.

Baptists opposed militarism and the arms race of the 1930s, and sympathy was expressed for political neutrality, noninterventionism, and conscientious objectors. However, once the United States was drawn into the war, patriotic support was expressed. All three conventions responded to the marshaling of their members for military service. Southern and Northern Baptists stressed chaplaincy ministries and feared for the soldiers' moral decline due to the availability of alcohol. National Baptists were quick to point out that black soldiers fought as valiantly as white Americans and therefore deserved full civil rights. Not a single resolution was passed that suggested that the United States go to war to protect, defend, or liberate European Jews.

Following the conclusion of the war, resolutions supporting ministry to displaced persons were passed, but these resolutions usually imagined that Baptists would focus their humanitarian aid on Baptist DPs. Through 1948, none of the three denominations passed resolutions supporting Zionism, advocating for the establishment of an independent Jewish homeland, or celebrating the birth of Israel as an independent nation.

The Efficacy of the Baptist Responses—Words and Deeds

Martin Luther King Jr. said, "One of the great tragedies of life is that men seldom bridge the gulf between practice and profession, between doing and saying."[19] At the 1934 Northern Baptist convention, President William Abernethy wondered aloud about the significance of the resolutions that would be passed: "Resolutions are so apt to be forgotten once they are passed. What an impressive thing it would be if, after we return to our homes, our pastors all over the land could dignify and publicize and emphasize the report of the Resolutions Committee by making it the subject of a Sunday morning service." He harbored an intuition that the report of the Resolutions Committee was "going to assume an importance this year not usually accorded it, and that from it results will accrue which may be of far-reaching importance."[20]

In similar fashion, BWA President Clifton D. Gray declared at the closing address of the 1934 Berlin congress: "Significant resolutions have been passed on the separation of church and state, on race prejudice and on peace and war. Resolutions in themselves are futile unless they lead to action."[21] Several years later, *The Watchman-Examiner* expressed frustration that convention resolutions were not taken more seriously and asked, "Would not our determinations have greater weight if we studied them more and did not write them as though we know everything about what is going on in the world and just what to do about it?"[22] Northern Baptists in New York State admitted that the passing of resolutions lacked efficacy because they did not produce deeds commensurate with their lofty ideals: "We as people repent of the sin of inactivity which has allowed us to be content in the passing of resolutions without being diligently concerned that the resolutions eventuate in action."[23]

To be sure, the passage of resolutions at a state, national, or even international level did not necessarily guarantee that the rank and file embraced the expressed positions. For example, "the white Southern Baptist Convention often supported civil rights with official resolutions, even while most Southern Baptists opposed integration."[24] German Baptists did not apply the racialism resolution they voted in favor of at the BWA congress to the "Jewish Problem" in Germany.

Nevertheless, it seems reasonable to hope that resolutions and statements applying core convictions of religious people might find some avenue of application in order to effect societal change and counteract injustices. A series in the *American Hebrew* described how the "world protest against Nazi extermination of the Jews in Europe will probably go down as one of the great outbursts of moral indignation in this war" which "has not passed without notice even in Germany."[25] In Hungary, protests by the country's Catholic cardinal and others defeated anti-Jewish laws from being passed.[26] However, it would be misguided "to assume that the world protest would be likely to lead to a change in the Nazi extermination policy of the Jews."[27]

Protests alone could not end the crisis the beleaguered Jewish people were facing: "This was one of those events which rise above protests, no matter how strong, and that sympathy, no matter how sincere, did not suffice to dispose of it."[28] Accordingly, assisting refugees was an essential example of creating "practical results of the protest against the Nazi anti-Jewish atrocities in Europe." Countries such as Portugal, France, and Spain were accepting small amounts of refugees. However, the paper noted the silence from countries like the United States, which had the capacity to accept larger number of exiles: "The real aid must come from the great overseas countries which can absorb thousands of immigrants. But these countries have not yet spoken."[29]

What actions could Baptists in the United States have taken that might have transformed their sympathetic resolutions into practical political action? Although it was extremely unlikely that any protests or actions on the part of Baptists in the United States could have halted the Nazi persecution of the Jews or prevented the extermination of a significant part of Europe's Jewish population, nevertheless some practical responses were achievable.

First, Baptists could have spearheaded, in cooperation with other religious traditions, changes in United States immigration policies in order to increase quotas for Jewish refugees and to make sure an increased number of exiles were admitted into the country. This course of action had the potential of saving the lives of tens of thousands of Jews fleeing from the Nazis.

Second, Baptists could have exerted influence on the Baptist World Alliance and Rushbrooke to be more involved in diplomatic efforts in Europe to resist Nazi efforts to marginalize and later persecute Jews. Although Baptists were a small minority in continental European countries, they could have joined with other protesters. In the early 1930s, when protests were still possible, the BWA could have given greater support to German Baptist leaders who were not sympathetic to the new Nazi regime and withdrawn support from those that did embrace the aims of the new government and its leader.

Third, Baptists could have been more positively inclined toward the dreams of the Zionists. The more fundamentalist and evangelical prophecy movement was certainly supportive of this movement for its own theological reasons and hopes, including the mass conversion of Israel to Christ and the fulfillment of the Second Coming. The conventions, however, were not limited to this kind of approach. They could have endorsed Palestine as a place for mass Jewish immigration as the best practical solution to a problem that could not be resolved otherwise. Furthermore, the Southern Baptist Convention was in a position to mediate concerns between the Jewish and Arab communities through its missionary corps.

Fourth, building on the successful model of the Christian Friendliness missionaries, Baptists could have done more to embrace and welcome European Jews into US society. Then, as a next step, Baptists could have affirmed the Jewish community as an equal partner in the struggle against all forms of social injustice, including anti-Semitism.

In a full-page editorial about the meetings of the World Council of Churches in Amsterdam, the *American Hebrew* suggested:

> IT IS A COMMON failing among all religious groups, including, of course, the Jewish, to draw up noble resolutions and the finest kinds of programs—and to let it go at that. Any suggestion rudely made that they try to implement their resolutions by actual practice is met rather with alarm . . . fighting anti-Semitism is a case in point. Perhaps they should have invited some Jewish representatives to sit with them in working out plans for this. Can anything practical be done, for example, about the splurge of anti-Semitic literature now making its rounds all over the country? Can the economic causes of anti-Jewish uprisings be tackled? Is there any practical program the churches can adopt by way of education beyond what they have already considered? You get the impression that the churches themselves, with the best will in the world, are at a loss as to what to do about it.[30]

The newspaper seemed to be implying that friendship between religious communities required more than an offer of a hand of sincere friendship; speaking with one another and learning from each other could create an environment of mutual benefit that might strengthen both communities in their quest to fulfill their pious and well-meaning resolutions about the problems the world faced.

Baptists, Jews, and Sincere Friendship

The insistence that Jews be accorded full civil rights within the framework of a tolerant British (Thomas Helwys) and colonial American (Roger Williams) society rises to the level of a core conviction for Baptists. Respect for individual conscience, the recognition that the state cannot protect the church or society through the promulgation of policies of religious or ethnic persecution, and the separation of the roles of church and state, led Baptists to extend the rights and privileges of freedom to populations that differed from the majority, within the framework of a just and tolerant civil society. In particular, Jews were to be fully included in the life of society, according to Baptists.

Nevertheless, support for the liberty rights of Jews as an abstract group (members of a minority group) did not necessarily imply that

Baptists affirmed Jewish faith or desired personal friendships with individual Jews. In other words, befriending Jews and affirming the continuing validity of Judaism as a religion was not a Baptist conviction. After vigorously defending the liberty rights of Jews, Williams felt it was prudent to clarify his own feelings about Jews; he could not "without horror think of the Jews' killing of the Lord Jesus, of their cursing themselves and their posterity; of the wrath of God upon them; of their denying the fundamentals of all our Christian worship; of some crimes alleged for which they have been so afflicted by this nation; of their known industry of enriching themselves in all places where they come."[31]

Williams's acceptance of European Christianity's anti-Semitism is not widely acknowledged. He affirmed the deicide charge, reiterated the collective and intergenerational guilt of the Jewish people for rejecting Christ, and then repeated prejudicial statements about supposed Jewish activities, ascribing them to the collective community instead of to specific individuals. Williams promoted political and social freedom for Jews as a core Baptist conviction while at the same time expressing anti-Semitic prejudice.

In contrast, Rabbi David Marx, one of the most prominent Jewish leaders in the southern United States in the first half of the twentieth century, warmly welcomed the Baptist delegates from all around the world as they converged on Atlanta, Georgia, for the 1939 Baptist World Alliance congress. In the aftermath of Kristallnacht, Rabbi Marx invoked Williams and expressed the Jewish desire for friendship with his "Baptist brethren":

> IN THIS COUNTRY, in the politico-religious field, the principle of the separation of Church and State is under heavy obligations to Roger Williams and his devout followers. Because of this separation, Church and State can best develop their ideals. A hearty welcome to our Baptist brethren from many climes and many nations. May their deliberations be laden with blessings to our common humanity and to the honor of our Universal Father.[32]

Despite Marx's idealism and hopes for Baptist-Jewish friendship, Williams's bifurcation influenced the Baptist response to the Jewish plight under Hitler's regime in a number of ways. During the Nazi era, Baptists within the United States and the BWA consistently reaffirmed Baptist core convictions regarding soul freedom, individual conscience, the separation of church and state, and the rights of minorities, including Jews, to political liberty and freedom from persecution. These principles served to promote Baptist solidarity with Jews and all other embattled minorities, but when they came into tension or conflict with other foundational convictions, solidarity for Jews was relegated to a status of secondary importance.

For example, a core conviction of the Baptist World Alliance was the promotion of Baptist unity and fellowship across national boundaries, even when nations were at odds with one another. Accordingly, Rushbrooke vigorously promoted Berlin as the site for the 1934 BWA world congress, despite misgivings from some Americans and others who were concerned about legitimatizing Hitler's initial attempts to persecute Jews, because he wanted to express support and friendship with German Baptists. Following the war, reconciliation and the resumption of fellowship with German Baptists was considered so essential that German Baptist complicity with the Nazis was in large part ignored.

Furthermore, during the Holocaust era, support for Jewish civil rights and sympathy with Jews under persecution did coexist with overt and public expressions of anti-Semitism. Prominent leaders in the Southern Baptist Convention, the Northern Baptist Convention, and the National Baptist Convention expressed anti-Semitic viewpoints and were not disciplined for such prejudice. Echoing Williams's statement, the prejudices expressed included attributing collective guilt to Jewish people for the death of Jesus, accusing Jews of exhibiting selfish and unwholesome behaviors, and exalting Christianity over Judaism. At times, the persecuted were even held responsible for their suffering, with conversion offered as the solution to their existential dilemma.

In general, Baptists felt solidarity with Jews because of their status as a persecuted minority and not because they were involved in caring relations with Jewish neighbors. Bereft of such relationships, many Baptists viewed Jews as a symbol, either through a prejudiced prism (the unscrupulous rich Jew) or as a positive stereotype (the intelligent or successful Jew). Under Hitler's persecution, the Jewish people gained sympathy from Baptists because of their persecuted status, but Baptist recognition of Jewish victimhood did not compel comprehensive, concerted, or practical action on their behalf, which friends might expect from friends.

Accordingly, Walter Harrelson and Randall Falk believe that historians should identify "more of the friends of the Jews who must surely have been active in Christian communities through the centuries."[33] There were some notable expressions of Jewish-Baptist friendship during the Nazi period. The bridge-building activities of the Christian Friendliness missionaries of the Woman's American Baptist Home Mission Society and the remarkable alliance between Dr. Thomas S. Harten and Rabbi Alexander Lyons are but two examples.

Nevertheless, generally speaking, for most Baptists, actual friendships with Jewish people were not the norm. In February 1948, the New Jersey Baptist Convention's Christian Friendliness Committee could report, "It was evident to the committee that there was a definite need for the people in the 'old-stock' Baptist churches to build friendships with foreign born, with those of other races, with migrant workers and with Jews. The job of breaking down the barriers of prejudice falls to those who have the vision of Christian Brotherhood."[34]

In the post-Holocaust era, both Christian and Jewish leaders have sought to find new ways to create bridges of communication and relationships that transcend religious affiliation. Richard Harries rightly noted that the participants in such interreligious encounters must feel free to share their "most deeply cherished convictions."[35] Of course, the convictions of Christians and Jews may not be identical or even in agreement, but true friendship can overcome such obstacles, as the Jewish scholar David Novak stated: "Jewish-Christian relationship and its attendant discourse need no longer be primarily adversarial."[36] Returning the favor, Roman Catholic Richard John Neuhaus concluded, "We can and must say that friendship between Jew and Christian can be secured in shared love for the God of Israel; we can and must say that the historical forms we call Judaism and Christianity will be transcended, but not superseded, by the fulfillment of eschatological promise. But along the way to that final fulfillment we are locked in argument. It is an argument by which—for both Jew and Christian—conscience is formed, witness is honed, and friendship is deepened."[37]

When Rushbrooke affirmed the Baptist world's desire to extend "the hand of sincere friendship" in 1935, he hoped that the gesture would be received by the Jewish community as a sign of solidarity, respect, and appreciation for the Jewish heritage. The Nazi persecution of Europe's Jews, the Holocaust and its devastating loss of Jewish life, and anti-Semitism in the United States and other countries severely tested the strength and authenticity of Baptist-Jewish friendship. Baptists in the United States have sought to learn wisdom from that trial, but only time will tell whether Rushbrooke's offer of friendship will be renewed in the twenty-first century and become strong enough to withstand future outbreaks of anti-Semitism.

Notes

1. Keith W. Clements, *What Freedom? The Persistent Challenge of Dietrich Bonhoeffer* (Eugene, OR: Wipf and Stock, 2011), 12–13.

2. Randall M. Falk and Walter Harrelson, *Jews and Christians: A Troubled Family* (Nashville: Abingdon, 1990), 194–95.

3. Editorial, "America, 1942," *American Hebrew* (8 May 1942), 3.

4. Regarding the use of the term *philo-Semitism* to represent acceptance and appreciation of Jews by non-Jewish nations, populations, and cultures, see Cecil Roth, *Essays and Portraits in Anglo-Jewish History* (Philadelphia: Jewish Publication Society of America, 1962), 10–21; and Alan Edelstein, "Philo-Semitism and the Survival of European Jewry," PhD diss., City University of New York, 1977, 24–53.

5. I own a signed copy of his notorious *Encircling the Globe* book, which he presented to someone in 1943. Even at that late date, he was not ashamed of his anti-Semitism in that work.

6. See Rushbrooke's statement: "The Nazi theory has no room for the free man, and the Nazi practice crushes and dehumanizes," in "Atlanta Hopes Disappointed: Atlanta Spirit Persists," *The Watchman-Examiner* (12 October 1939), 1123.

7. Denton Lotz, "The Baptist World Alliance: The Past as Prologue to the Future Challenges," *Review and Expositor* 103 (2006): 771–72.

8. Avery Cardinal Dulles, *Magisterium: Teacher and Guardian of the Faith* (Naples, FL: Sapientia Press of Ave Maria University, 2007), 64.

9. However, I am not claiming that all Baptists in every circumstance applied Baptist convictions and secondary principles in the same way, or even consistently. Although Baptist convictions usually led Baptists to assert that Jews should enjoy the same freedom, liberty, rights, and privileges as other citizens, there were examples of undeniable Baptist anti-Semitism, prejudice, and hostility toward Jews. Indeed, in the next paragraph I cite M. E. Dodd, who believed in personality and yet apparently was anti-Semitic.

10. M. E. Dodd, "Devotional Messages," *Baptist News of Southern California* (January-February 1940), 8.

11. See one of many articles in Baptists papers: Editorial, "Personality," *The Watchman-Examiner* (16 July 1936), 832; also see Arthur Temple Cadoux, *A New Orthodoxy of Jesus and Personality* (London: Ivor Nicholson and Watson, 1934).

12. *1934 Minutes of the Illinois Baptist State Convention,* Resolutions Committee Report, 73.

13. *1938 Minutes of the Connecticut Baptist Convention,* Report of the Resolutions Committee, 91.

14. Editorial, "Religious Conditions in Germany," *The Watchman-Examiner* (6 November 1941), 1143.

15. J. C. Robbins, "The Triumphant Church," *California-Nevada Baptist Bulletin* (October 1937), 6–7.

16. *1944 Minutes of the Connecticut Baptist Convention*, Social Action Committee Report, 58.

17. As has been noted, at the 1939 BWA congress, German and Italian Baptist leaders opposed the notions of democracy and freedom advocated by M. E. Aubrey, secretary of the British Baptists.

18. J. H. Rushbrooke, "Roger Williams: Apostle of Soul-Freedom," An Address Presented to the American Baptist Historical Society (1936), Rushbrooke Collection, [RUS7/48], Regent's Park Library Archive Collection, Oxford, England, 13–14.

19. Martin Luther King Jr., *Strength to Love* (Philadelphia: Fortress, 1981), 37.

20. William S. Abernethy, "President's Address," in *For Such a Time as This: Addresses at the Northern Baptist Convention 1934*, 10.

21. Quoted from Clifton D. Gray, "The Results of the Baptist Congress," *The Watchman-Examiner* (20 September 1934), 1020.

22. Editorial, "Baptist Convention Resolutions," *The Watchman-Examiner* (6 November 1941), 1143.

23. *New York Baptist Annual 1947–1948*, Resolutions Committee Report, 20.

24. Thomas S. Kidd and Barry Hankins, *Baptists in America: A History* (Oxford: Oxford University Press, 2015), 226.

25. William Zuckerman, "The Effect of the Protest in Germany," March of Jewish Events in Europe column, *American Hebrew* (1 January 1943), 6.

26. William Zuckerman, "Repercussions in Hungary," March of Jewish Events in Europe column, *American Hebrew* (1 January 1943), 6.

27. William Zuckerman, "The Future Nazi Policy towards the Jews," March of Jewish Events in Europe Column, *American Hebrew* (1 January 1943), 6.

28. William Zuckerman, "Sympathy Is Not Enough," March of Jewish Events in Europe column, *American Hebrew* (8 January 1943), 5.

29. William Zuckerman, "Some Practical Relief for European Jews," March of Jewish Events in Europe column, *American Hebrew* (15 January 1943), 4.

30. Editorial, "Church Council," *American Hebrew* (3 September 1948), 3.

31. Roger Williams, "The Fourth Paper Presented by Major Butler," in *On Religious Liberty: Selections from the Works of Roger Williams*, ed. James Calvin Davis (Cambridge, MA: Belknap Press of Harvard University Press, 2008), 236.

32. Rabbi David Marx, "To the Baptist World Alliance," *The Atlanta Constitution* (23 July 1939), 10B.

33. Harrelson and Falk, *Jews and Christians*, 194.

34. "New Committee on Christian Friendliness Meets," *New Jersey Baptist Bulletin* (February 1948), 4.

35. Richard Harries, *After the Evil: Christianity and Judaism in the Shadow of the Holocaust* (Oxford: Oxford University Press, 2003), 198.

36. David Novak, "From Supersessionism to Parallelism in Jewish-Christian Dialogue," in *Jews and Christians: People of God*, ed. Carl E. Braaten and Robert W. Jensen (Grand Rapids, MI: Eerdmans, 2003), 97. See also David Novak, *Jewish-Christian Dialogue: A Jewish Justification* (Oxford: Oxford University Press, 1989).

37. Richard John Neuhaus, "Salvation Is from the Jews," in *Jews and Christians*, ed. Braaten and Jensen, 72.

Bibliography

Primary and Secondary Books and Articles

Abzug, Robert H. *America Views the Holocaust, 1933–45: A Brief Documentary History*. Boston: Bedford/St. Martin's, 1999.

Adams, J. McKee. *The Heart of the Levant: Palestine—Syria*. Richmond, VA: The Foreign Mission Board of the Southern Baptist Convention, 1937.

Adams, Maurianne, and John H. Bracey Jr. *Strangers and Neighbors: Relations between Blacks and Jews in the United States*. Amherst: University of Massachusetts Press, 1999.

Alexander, Jeffrey C. *The Civil Sphere*. Oxford: Oxford University Press, 2008.

———. *Remembering the Holocaust: A Debate*. Oxford: Oxford University Press, 2009.

Allen, William Lloyd. "How Baptists Assessed Hitler." *Christian Century* (1982): 890–94.

American Baptist Publication Society. *For Such a Time as This: Addresses at the Northern Baptist Convention 1934*. Philadelphia: Judson Press, 1934.

American Jewish Committee. *The Voice of Religion: The Views of Christian Religious Leaders on the Persecution of the Jews in Germany by the National Socialists*. New York: The American Jewish Committee, 1933.

Appelman, Hyman. *From Jewish Lawyer to Baptist Preacher*. Los Angeles: Church of the Open Door, 1942.

Ariel, Yaakov. *Evangelizing the Chosen People: Missions to the Jews in America, 1880–2000*. Chapel Hill: University of North Carolina Press, 2000.

———. "Jewish Suffering and Christian Salvation: The Evangelical-Fundamentalist Holocaust Memoirs." *Holocaust and Genocide Studies* 6, no. 1 (1991): 63–78.

———. *An Unusual Relationship: Evangelical Christians and Jews*. New York: New York University Press, 2013.

Baker, Newton D., et al., eds. *The American Way: A Study of Human Relations among Protestants, Catholics, and Jews*. Chicago: Willet, Clark, 1936.

Baker, Robert Andrew. *The Southern Baptist Convention and Its People, 1607–1972*. Nashville: Broadman, 1974.

Banks, William L. *A History of Black Baptists in the United States*. West Conshohocken, PA: Infinity Publishing, 2005.

Baptist World Alliance, Second Congress, Philadelphia, June 19-25, 1911. Philadelphia: Harper and Brothers, 1911.

Barnes, William Wright. *The Southern Baptist Convention 1845–1953*. Nashville: Broadman, 1954.

Barnett, Victoria J. *Bystanders: Conscience and Complicity during the Holocaust*. Westport, CT: Praeger, 2000.

———. "Fault Lines": An Analysis of the National Conference of Christians and Jews, 1933–1948. PhD diss., George Mason University, 2012.

———. *For the Soul of the People: Protestant Protest against Hitler*. Oxford: Oxford University Press, 1992.

Barth, Karl. *Against the Stream: Shorter Post-War Writings 1946–52*. London: SCM Press, 2012.

———. *The Epistle to the Romans*. Oxford: Oxford University Press, 1968.

Berger, Alan L., ed. *Bearing Witness to the Holocaust, 1939–1989*. Symposium Series Volume 31. Lewiston, NY: The Edwin Mellen Press, 1991.

Bernheim, Mrs. Jacob (Celestine). *The Cost of Discipleship: A Jewish Experience*. Buffalo, NY: self-published, 1937.

Bonhoeffer, Dietrich. *Ethics*. New York: Macmillan, 1965.

———. *Letters and Papers from Prison*. New York: Macmillan, 1968.

———. *Life Together: The Classic Exploration of Faith in Community*. New York: Harper One, 2009.

Boyens, Armin F. C. "The Ecumenical Community and the Holocaust." *Annals of the American Academy of Political and Social Science* 450 (1980): 140–52.

Braaten, Carl E., and Robert W. Jensen, eds. *Jews and Christians: People of God*. Grand Rapids, MI: Eerdmans, 2003.

Brackney, William H., ed. *Baptist Life and Thought: 1600–1980*. Valley Forge, PA: Judson Press, 1983.

———. *The Baptists*. New York: Greenwood Press, 1988.

———. *Baptists in North America: An Historical Perspective*. Malden, MA: Blackwell, 2006.

———. *A Genetic History of Baptist Thought: With Special Reference to Baptists in Britain and North America*. Macon, GA: Mercer University Press, 2004.

Bradbury, John W. *Israel's Restoration: A Series of Lectures by Bible Expositors Interested in the Evangelization of the Jews*. New York: Iversen-Ford, 1950.

———, ed. *Light for the World's Darkness: Second New York Congress on Prophecy Addresses 1943*. New York: Loizeaux Brothers, 1944.

———, ed. *The Sure Word of Prophecy; Report of the New York Congress on Prophecy, Assembled in the Calvary Baptist Church, New York City, November 1-8, 1942*. New York: Revell, 1943.

Breitman, Richard, and Allan J. Lichtman. *FDR and the Jews*. Cambridge, MA: The Belknap Press of Harvard University Press, 2013.

Brightman, Edgar Sheffield. *The Future of Christianity*. New York: Abingdon, 1937.

Brown, Eva. "The Baptist World Congress at Berlin." *Baptist Quarterly* 7, no. 4 (1934): 154–61.

Busch, Eberhard. *Karl Barth: His Life from Letters and Autobiographical Texts*. Philadelphia: Fortress, 1977.

Cadoux, Arthur Temple. *A New Orthodoxy of Jesus and Personality*. London: Ivor Nicholson and Watson, 1934.

Caner, Emir, and Ergun Caner. *The Sacred Trust: Sketches of the Southern Baptist Convention Presidents*. Nashville: Broadman and Holman, 2003.

Canipe, Lee. *A Baptist Democracy: Separating God and Caesar in the Land of the Free*. Macon, GA: Mercer University Press, 2011.

Cannato, Vincent J. *American Passage: The History of Ellis Island*. New York: Harper Perennial, 2010.

Carenen, Caitlin. "The American Christian Palestine Committee, the Holocaust, and Mainstream Protestant Zionism, 1938–1948." *Holocaust and Genocide Studies* 24, no. 2 (2010): 273–96.

Carson, Clayborne, ed. *The Autobiography of Martin Luther King Jr.* New York: Grand Central Publishing, 1998.

Chute, Anthony, Nathan A. Finn, and Michael A. G. Haykin. *The Baptist Story: From English Sect to Global Movement.* Nashville: B&H Academic, 2015.

Clements, Keith W. *What Freedom? The Persistent Challenge of Dietrich Bonhoeffer.* Eugene, OR: Wipf and Stock, 2011.

Cohn, Joseph Hoffman. *I Have Loved Jacob.* Orangeburg, NY: American Board of Missions to the Jews, 1908; republished 1948.

Cohn, Leopold. *The Story of a Modern Missionary to an Ancient People.* Orangeburg, NY: American Board of Missions to the Jews, 1962.

Colign, Jan G., and Marcia Sachs Littell, eds. *Confronting the Holocaust: A Mandate for the 21st Century.* Lanham, MD: University Press of America, 1997.

Collins, David R. *Not Only Dreamers: The Story of Martin Luther King Sr. and Martin Luther King Jr.* Elgin, IL: Brethren Press, 1986.

Conway, John. S. *The Nazi Persecution of the Churches 1933–1945.* 1st American edition. New York: Basic Books, 1968.

Cook, Walter L. *The Story of Maine Baptists, 1904–1954.* Waterville, ME: United Baptist Convention of Maine, 1954.

Cournos, John. *An Open Letter to Jews and Christians.* Oxford: Oxford University Press, 1938.

Crismon, Leo Taylor, ed. *Baptists in Kentucky, 1776–1976, a Bicentennial Volume.* Middletown, KY: Kentucky Baptist Convention, 1975.

Cutler, Marianne. "Minority Group, Majority Space: Negotiating Jewish Identity in a Southern Christian Context." *Journal of Contemporary Ethnography* 35, no. 6 (2006): 696–728.

Davies, Alan, and Marilyn F. Nefsky. *How Silent Were the Churches?: Canadian Protestantism and the Jewish Plight during the Nazi Era.* Waterloo, ON: Wilfrid Laurier University Press, 1998.

Davis, Derek H. "Baptists and the American Tradition of Religious Liberty." *Perspectives in Religious Studies* 33, no. 1 (2006): 41–66.

Davis, James Calvin, ed. *On Religious Liberty: Selections from the Works of Roger Williams.* Cambridge, MA: The Belknap Press of Harvard University Press, 2008.

———. "A Return to Civility: Roger Williams and Public Discourse in America." *Journal of Church and State* 43, no. 4 (2001): 689–707.

Devine, Michael J., ed. *Harry S. Truman, the State of Israel, and the Quest for Peace in the Middle East.* Kirksville, MO: Truman State University Press, 2009.

Dinnerstein, Leonard. *Antisemitism in America.* New York: Oxford University Press, 1995.

Dodd, M. E. *Girdling the Globe for God: A Travelogue.* Shreveport, LA: John S. Ramond, Publisher, 1935.

———. *Missions Our Mission.* Nashville: Sunday School Board of the Southern Baptist Convention, 1930.

Dulles, Avery Cardinal. *Magisterium: Teacher and Guardian of the Faith.* Naples, FL: Sapientia Press of Ave Maria University, 2007.

Durso, Keith E. *Thy Will Be Done: A Biography of George W. Truett.* Macon, GA: Mercer University Press, 2009.

Dushaw, Amos I. *Anti-Semitism—the Voice of Folly and Fanaticism.* Brooklyn, NY: Tolerance Press, 1943.

Early, Joseph E., ed. *The Life and Writings of Thomas Helwys*. Macon, GA: Mercer University Press, 2009.

Edelstein, Alan. "Philo-Semitism and the Survival of European Jewry." PhD diss., City University of New York, 1977.

Edgcomb, Gabrielle Simon. *From Swastika to Jim Crow: Refugee Scholars at Black Colleges*. Malabar, FL: Krieger Publishing Company, 1993.

Erenberg, Lewis A. *The Greatest Fight of Our Generation: Louis vs. Schmeling*. Oxford: Oxford University Press, 2006.

Erickson, Robert P. *Complicity in the Holocaust: Churches and Universities in Nazi Germany.* Cambridge: Cambridge University Press, 2012.

Erickson, Robert P., and Susannah Heschel, eds. *Betrayal: German Churches and the Holocaust.* Minneapolis: Fortress, 1999.

Ernst, James E. *The Political Thought of Roger Williams*. Port Washington, NY: Kennikat Press, 1929; reprint 1966.

Estep, William R. *Whole Gospel Whole World: The Foreign Mission Board of the Southern Baptist Convention 1845–1995*. Nashville: Broadman and Holman, 1994.

Falk, Randall M., and Walter J. Harrelson. *Jews and Christians: A Troubled Family*. Nashville: Abingdon, 1990.

Fallin, Wilson, Jr. *Uplifting the People: Three Centuries of Black Baptists in Alabama*. Religion and American Culture. Tuscaloosa: University of Alabama Press, 2007.

Federal Council of the Churches of Christ in America. *The Churches and a Just and Durable Peace*. Chicago: The Christian Century Press, 1942.

Feldman, Egal. *Dual Destinies: The Jewish Encounter with Protestant America*. Urbana: University of Illinois Press, 1990.

Felice, Renzo de. Translated by Robert L. Miller. *The Jews in Fascist Italy: A History*. New York: Enigma Books, 2001.

Fink, Carole. "The Paris Peace Conference and the Question of Minority Rights." *Peace and Change* 21, no. 3 (1996): 273–88.

Fishman, Hertzel. *American Protestantism and a Jewish State*. Detroit: Wayne State University Press, 1973.

Fitts, Leroy. *A History of Black Baptists*. Nashville: Broadman, 1985.

Flynt, Wayne. *Alabama Baptists: Southern Baptists in the Heart of Dixie*. Religion and American Culture. Tuscaloosa: University of Alabama Press, 1998.

For Such a Time as This: Addresses Delivered before the Northern Baptist Convention Meeting at Rochester, NY, 1934. Valley Forge, PA: Judson Press, 1934.

Frankel, Jonathan, and Ezra Mendelsohn, eds. *The Protestant-Jewish Conundrum*. Oxford: Oxford University Press, 2010.

Freeman, Edward A. *The Epoch of Negro Baptists and the Foreign Mission Board National Baptists Convention, U.S.A., Inc.* Kansas City: The Central Seminary Press, 1953.

Friedländer, Saul. *The Years of Extermination: Nazi Germany and the Jews 1939–1935*. New York: Harper Perennial, 2008.

Frith-James, Aaron. "The Manger of the Movement: Atlanta and the Black Freedom Struggle, 1890–1950." PhD diss., Yale University, 1997.

Frymer-Kensky, Tikva, David Novak, Peter Ochs, David Fox Sandmeil, and Michael A. Signer, eds. *Christianity in Jewish Terms*. Boulder, CO: Westview Press, 2000.

Gartenhaus, Jacob. *The Jew and Jesus*. Nashville: The Sunday School Board of the Southern Baptist Convention, 1934.

———. *The Rebirth of a Nation: Zionism in History and Prophecy*. Nashville: Broadman, 1936.

———. *Traitor? A Jew, a Book, a Miracle: An Autobiography*. Nashville: Thomas Nelson, 1980.

———. *What of the Jews?* Atlanta: Home Mission Board of the Southern Baptist Convention, 1948.

Gaskill, Stephanie Rebekah. "Karl Barth, Missions to the Jews, and the American Response." MA thesis, Graduate College of Bowling Green University, 2010.

Gaustad, Edwin S. *Liberty of Conscience: Roger Williams in America*. Valley Forge, PA: Judson Press, 1999.

Geldbach, Erich. "Baptist-Jewish Relations: Some Observations from a German Point of View" *Baptist History and Heritage* 38, no. 2 (Spring 2003): 20–37.

Gill, Everett. *Europe: Christ or Chaos?* Richmond, VA: Foreign Mission Board, Southern Baptist Convention, 1937.

Goatley, David Emmanuel. *A Divine Assignment: The Missiology of Wendell Clay Somerville*. St. Louis, MO: Lucas Park Books, 2010.

Gold, Roberta S. "The Black Jews of Harlem: Representation, Identity, and Race, 1920–1939." *American Quarterly* 55, no. 2 (2003): 179–225.

Goldhagen, Daniel Jonah. *Hitler's Willing Executioners: Ordinary Germans and the Holocaust*. New York: Vintage Press, 1997.

Goldstein, Eric L. *The Price of Whiteness: Jews, Race, and American Identity*. Princeton, NJ: Princeton University Press, 2006.

Goodman, Daniel E. "Creating an Unknown Future: The Challenges of Partnership for Christians in Dialogue with Judaism." *Review and Expositor* 103, no. 1 (2006): 179–201.

———. "Strangers, Neighbors, and Strangers Again: The History of Southern Baptist Approaches to Jews and Judaism." *Review and Expositor* 103, no. 1 (2006): 63–89.

Green, Bernard. *European Baptists and the Third Reich*. London: Baptist Historical Society, 2008.

———. *Tomorrow's Man: A Biography of James Henry Rushbrooke*. London: Baptist Historical Society, 1996.

Greenberg, Irving. *For the Sake of Heaven and Earth: The New Encounter between Judaism and Christianity*. Philadelphia: The Jewish Publication Society, 2004.

Grose, Howard B. *Aliens or Americans?* Lexington, KY: CreateSpace Independent Publishing Platform, 1906.

Gushee, David P. *Righteous Gentiles of the Holocaust: Genocide and Moral Obligation*. 2nd ed. St. Paul: Paragon House, 2003.

Gwaltney, L. L. *Heralds of Freedom*. Nashville: Broadman, 1939.

———. *The World's Greatest Decade: The Times and the Baptists*. Birmingham, AL: Birmingham Printing Company, 1947.

Hamerow, Theodore S. *Why We Watched: Europe, America, and the Holocaust*. New York: W. W. Norton, 2008.

Hamilton, Charles V. *Adam Clayton Powell Jr.: The Political Biography of an American Dilemma*. New York: Atheneum, 1991.

Harries, Richard. *After the Evil: Christianity and Judaism in the Shadow of the Holocaust*. Oxford: Oxford University Press, 2003.

Haynes, Stephen R. *Reluctant Witnesses: Jews and the Christian Imagination*. Philadelphia: Westminster John Knox, 1995.

Heni, Clemens. *Antisemitism: A Specific Phenomenon: Holocaust Trivialization—Islamism—Post-Colonial and Cosmopolitan Anti-Zionism*. Studies in Antisemitism, Volume 3. Berlin: Edition Critic, 2013.

Hertzberg, Arthur, ed. *The Zionist Idea: A Historical Analysis and Reader*. Philadelphia: The Jewish Publication Society, 1997.

Hinson, E. Glenn. *A History of Baptists in Arkansas, 1818–1978*. Little Rock: Arkansas Baptist State Convention, 1979.

Hoadley, Frank T. *By God's Own Hand: The Story of American Baptists in Pennsylvania and Delaware*. Valley Forge, PA: ABCOPAD Press, 1986.

Hoffman, Conrad. "The Challenge of Our Jewish Neighbors." *Baptist Quarterly* 6, no. 6 (1933): 255–59.

———. *The Jews Today: A Call to Christian Action*. Study and Action Series. New York: Friendship Press, 1941.

———. *What Now for the Jews? A Challenge to the Christian Conscience*. New York: Friendship Press, 1948.

Horace, Lillian B. *"Crowned with Glory and Honor": The Life of Rev. Lacey Kirk Williams*. Hicksville, NY: Exposition Press, 1978.

Hughey, J. D., Jr. "Baptists and Religious Freedom." *Baptist Quarterly* XVII (1958): 249–55.

Hunsinger, George, ed. *For the Sake of the World: Karl Barth and the Future of Ecclesial Theology.* Grand Rapids, MI: Eerdmans, 2004.

Jackson, Joseph Harrison. *A Story of Christian Activism: The History of the National Baptist Convention, U.S.A., Inc.* Nashville: Townsend Press, 1980.

James, Powhatan. *George W. Truett: A Biography*. Nashville: Broadman, 1945.

Jenks, Philip E. *The First Fifty Years of American Baptist Men: A History of American Baptist Men, 1922–1972*. Philadelphia: American Baptist Men, 1972.

Johnson, Katharine W. *Rhode Island Baptists: Their Zeal, Their Times*. Valley Forge, PA: Judson Press, 1975.

Joiner, E. Earl. "Baptists and the Holocaust": A Research Paper Presented at the International Conference on "Remembering for the Future," at Oxford, England, July 10-14, 1988. Jacksonville: Florida Baptist Historical Society, 1988.

———. *A History of Florida Baptists*. Jacksonville: Florida Baptist Convention Press, 1972.

Kelsey, George D. *Social Ethics among Southern Baptists, 1917–1969*. Metuchen, NJ: Scarecrow Press and the American Theological Library Association, 1973.

Kendall, W. Fred. *A History of the Tennessee Baptist Convention*. Brentwood, TN: Executive Board of the Tennessee Baptist Convention, 1974.

Kidd, Thomas S., and Barry Hankins. *Baptists in America: A History*. Oxford: Oxford University Press, 2015.

King, Joe M. *A History of South Carolina Baptists*. Columbia, SC: General Board of The South Carolina Baptist Convention, 1964.

King, Martin Luther, Jr.. *Strength to Love*. Philadelphia: Fortress, 1981.

King, Martin Luther, Sr. *Daddy King: An Autobiography*. New York: William Morrow, 1980.

Kinney, Mary Martin. *The World at My Door*. Philadelphia: Judson Press, 1938.

Langmuir, Gavin I. *History, Religion, and Antisemitism*. Berkeley: University of California Press, 1990.

———. *Toward a Definition of Antisemitism*. Berkeley: University of California Press, 1990.

Leff, Laurel. *Buried by the Times: The Holocaust and America's Most Important Newspaper*. Cambridge: Cambridge University Press, 2005.

Leonard, Bill J. *Baptist Ways: A History*. Valley Forge, PA: Judson Press, 2003.

———. "Where Are You, God? Reflections on Spirituality and the Holocaust." *Review and Expositor* 108, no. 1 (2011): 13–16.

Levine, Amy-Jill. ""To All the Gentiles": A Jewish Perspective on the Great Commission." *Review and Expositor* 103, no. 1 (2006): 139–58.

Lewis, Walter O. *Seventh Baptist World Congress: Copenhagen, Denmark July 29–August 3, 1947*. London: Baptist World Alliance, 1948.

Lincoln, C. Eric, and Lawrence H. Mamiya. *The Black Church in the African American Experience*. Durham, NC: Duke University Press, 1990.

Lindsay, Mark R. *Barth, Israel, and Jesus: Karl Barth Theology of Israel*. Burlington, VT: Ashgate Publishing Company, 2007.

———. *Reading Auschwitz with Barth: The Holocaust as Problem and Promise for Barthian Theology*. Princeton Theological Monograph. Eugene, OR: Pickwick Publications, 2014.

Lipstadt, Deborah E. *Beyond Belief: The American Press and the Coming of the Holocaust 1933–1945*. New York: The Free Press, 1986.

Locke, Hubert G. *The Black Anti-Semitism Controversy: Protestant Views and Perspectives*. Selinsgrove, PA: Susquehanna University Press, 1994.

———, ed. *The Church Confronts the Nazis: Barmen Then and Now*. New York: The Edwin Mellen Press, 1984.

Lotz, Denton. "The Baptist World Alliance: The Past as Prologue to the Future Challenges." *Review and Expositor* 103, no. 4 (2006): 761–82.

———, ed. *Baptists against Racism*. McLean, VA: The Baptist World Alliance, 1999.

Lumpkin, William L., ed. *Baptist Confessions of Faith*. Valley Forge, PA: Judson Press, 1974.

Lyke, Helen B. *The Faith of Abraham: The Biography of A. B. Machlin D.D.* Winona Lake, IN: American Association for Jewish Evangelism, 1962.

Lyons, Alexander. *Heart to Heart: Frank Talks on Familiar Themes*. New York: Bloch Publishing Company, 1921.

MacCulloch, Diarmaid. *Silence: A Christian History*. New York: Penguin, 2013.

MacFarland, Charles S. *The New Church and the New Germany*. New York: Macmillan, 1934.

Maddry, Charles E. *Charles E. Maddry: An Autobiography*. Nashville: Broadman, 1955.

Maring, Norman H. *Baptists in New Jersey: A Study in Transition*. Valley Forge, PA: Judson Press, 1964.

Marsden, George M. *Fundamentalism and American Culture*. New ed. Oxford: Oxford University Press, 2006.

Marsh, Charles. *Strange Glory: A Life of Dietrich Bonhoeffer*. New York: Alfred A. Knopf, 2014.

Masters, Frank M. *A History of Baptists in Kentucky*. Louisville: Kentucky Baptist Historical Society, 1953.

Matthews, Basil. *The Jew and the World Ferment*. New York: Friendship Press, 1935.

Mazzenga, Maria, ed. *American Religious Responses to Kristallnacht*. New York: Palgrave Macmillan, 2009.

McBeth, Harry Leon. *Texas Baptists: A Sesquicentennial History*. Dallas: Baptistway Press, 1998.

McClendon, James William, Jr. *Systematic Theology*. Vol. 1: *Ethics*. Nashville: Abingdon, 2002.

———, and James M. Smith. *Convictions: Defusing Religious Relativism*. Rev. ed. Eugene, OR: Wipf and Stock, 2002.

———, and James M. Smith. *Understanding Religious Convictions*. Notre Dame: University of Notre Dame Press, 1975.

McCullough, Colin, and Nathan Wilson, eds. *Violence, Memory, and History: Western Perceptions of Kristallnacht*. New York: Routledge, 2015.

McGlothlin, William Joseph, ed. *Baptist Confessions of Faith*. Philadelphia: American Baptist Publication Society, 1911.

McGraw, Eliza Russi Lowen. "'How to Win Jews for Christ': Southern Jewishness and the Southern Baptist Convention." *The Mississippi Quarterly* 53, no. 2 (Spring 2000): 209–23.

———. *Two Covenants: Representations of Southern Jewishness*. Southern Literary Studies. Baton Rouge: Louisiana State University Press, 2005.

McNeil, Genna Rae, Houston Bryan Roberson, Quinton Hosford Dixie, and Kevin McGruder. *Witness: Two Hundred Years of African-American Faith and Practice at the Abyssinian Baptist Church of Harlem, New York*. Grand Rapids, MI: Eerdmans, 2014.

McSwain, Larry L., and William Lloyd Allen, eds. *Twentieth-Century Shapers of Baptist Social Ethics*. Baptists Series. Macon, GA: Mercer University Press, 2008.

Miller, Robert Moats. "The Attitudes of the Major Protestant Churches in America toward War and Peace, 1929–1939." *The Social Studies* XLVIII, no. 4 (1957): 120–27.

———. *Harry Emerson Fosdick: Preacher, Pastor, Prophet*. New York: Oxford University Press, 1985.

Mitchell, Beverly E. *Plantations and Death Camp: Religion, Ideology, and Human Dignity*. Innovations: African American Religious Thought. Minneapolis: Fortress, 2009.

Mittleman, Alan, Byron R. Johnson, and Nancy Isserman, eds. *Uneasy Allies? Evangelical and Jewish Relations*. Lanham, MD: Lexington Books, 2007.

Moehlman, Conrad Henry. *The Catholic-Protestant Mind: Some Aspects of Religious Liberty in the United States*. New York: Harper & Brothers, 1929.

———. *The Christian-Jewish Tragedy: A Study in Religious Prejudice*. Rochester, NY: The Printing House of Leo Hart, 1933.

———. *The First Christians and Jesus: A Study of New Testament Interpretations of Jesus*. Berne, IN: Conrad Henry Moehlman [self-published], 1938.

———. *Protestantism's Challenge: An Historical Study of the Survival Value of Protestantism*. New York: Harper & Brothers, 1939.

Moore, Lamire Holden. *The History of Southern Baptists in Ohio*. Nashville: Bensen Printing Company, 1957.

Mosher, Annette. "Roger Williams: Conviction Among the Convicted." *Baptistic Theologies* 6, no. 2 (2014): 43–52.

Mullins, Edgar Young. *The Axioms of Religion*. Nashville: Broadman & Holman, 1997.

Nawyn, William E. *American Protestantism's Response to Germany's Jews and Refugees: 1933–1941*. Studies in American History and Culture. Ann Arbor: University of Michigan International Research Press, 1981.

Novak, David. *Jewish-Christian Dialogue: A Jewish Justification*. Oxford: Oxford University Press, 1989.

Novick, Peter. *The Holocaust in American Life*. New York: Mariner Books, 2000.

Ochs, Peter. *Another Reformation: Postliberal Christianity and the Jews*. Grand Rapids, MI: Baker Academic, 2011.

Ohrn, Arnold T. *Baptist World Alliance—Golden Jubilee Congress—London, England—16th-22nd July, 1955 Official Report*. London: Kingsgate Press, 1955.

———, ed. *Eighth Baptist World Congress Cleveland Ohio July 22-27, 1950 Official Report*. Philadelphia: Judson Press, 1950.

———. *The Gospel and the Sermon on the Mount*. New York: Revell, 1948.

Oldham, J. H. *The Oxford Conference (Official Report)*. Chicago: Willett, Clark, 1937.

Olson, Adolf. *A Centenary History as Related to the Baptist General Conference of America*. Chicago: Baptist Conference Press, 1952.

Olson, Lynne. *Those Angry Days: Roosevelt, Lindbergh, and America's Fight over World War II, 1939–1941*. New York: Random House, 2013.

Parkes, James. *The Jew and His Neighbour: A Study in the Causes of Antisemitism*. London: Student Christian Movement Press, 1930; rev. ed. 1938.

Parushev, Parush R. "Jews and Christians after the *Shoah*: Christian Theological Perspectives on the Future of the Jewish-Christian Relationship." In *Reflections on Anti-Semitism: Anti-Semitism in Historical and Anthropological Perspectives*, edited by Verá Tydlitátová and Alena Hanzová, 35–44. Plzeň, Czech Republic: Fakulta Filozofická Západoceské Univerzity v Plzni, 2008.

Payne, Ernest A. *Baptists Speak to the World: A Description and Interpretation of the Sixth Baptist World Congress, Atlanta, 1939*. London: The Carey Press, 1939.

———. *James Henry Rushbrooke, 1870–1947: A Baptist Greatheart*. London: Kingsgate Press, 1954.

Phalen, William J. "But They Did Not Build This House: The Attitude of Evangelical Protestantism towards Immigration to the United States, 1800–1924." PhD diss., Rutgers University, 2010.

Phillips, J. Stephen. "Thomas Helwys and the Idea of Religious Liberty." PhD diss., Baylor University, 1998.

Pierard, Richard V. "The Baptist World Alliance: An Overview of Its History." *Review and Expositor* 103, no. 4 (2006): 707–32.

———, ed. *Baptists Together in Christ 1905–2005: A Hundred-Year History of the Baptist World Alliance*. Birmingham, AL: Samford University Press, 2005.

Powell, Adam Clayton, Jr. *Marching Blacks: An Interpretive History of the Rise of the Black Common Man*. New York: Dial Press, 1945.

Powell, Adam Clayton, Sr. *Against the Tide: An Autobiography*. New York: Richard R. Smith, 1938.

———. *Palestine and Saints in Caesar's Household*. New York: Richard R. Smith, 1939.

———. *Riots and Ruins*. New York: Richard R. Smith, 1945.

Price, Isabel Boiko. "Black Responses to Anti-Semitism: Negroes and Jews in New York, 1880 to World War II." PhD diss., University of New Mexico, 1973.

Puckett, Dan J. *In the Shadow of Hitler: Alabama's Jews, the Second World War, and the Holocaust*. Modern South. Tuscaloosa: University Alabama Press, 2014.

Railton, Nicholas M. "German Free Churches and the Nazi Regime." *The Journal of Ecclesiastical History* 19, no. 1 (January 1998): 85–139.

Randall, Ian M. *Communities of Conviction: Baptist Beginnings in Europe*. Schwarzenfeld, Germany: Neufeld Verlag, 2009.

Rausch, David A. *Fundamentalist-Evangelicals and Anti-Semitism*. Valley Forge, PA: Trinity Press International, 1993.

———. *A Legacy of Hatred: Why Christians Must Not Forget the Holocaust*. Chicago: Moody Press, 1984.

Rittner, Carol, Stephen D. Smith, and Irena Steinfeldt, eds. *The Holocaust and the Christian World: Reflections on the Past, Challenges for the Future*. London: Kuperard, 2000.

Robins, Walker. "Jacob Gartenhaus: The Southern Baptists' Jew." *Journal of Southern Religion* 19 (2017), http://jsreligion.org/vol19/robins.

Rogers, James A. *Richard Furman: Life and Legacy*. Macon, GA: Mercer University Press, 2001.

Romijn, Peter, Bart van der Boom, Pim Griffioen, Ron Zeller, Marieke Meeuwenoord, and Johannes Houwink ten Cate. *The Persecution of the Jews in the Netherlands, 1940–1945*. Amsterdam: Amsterdam University Press, 2012.

Rosenfeld, Alvin H., ed. *Resurgent Antisemitism: Global Perspectives*. Bloomington: Indiana University Press, 2013.

Ross, Robert W. *So It Was True: The American Protestant Press and the Nazi Persecution of the Jews*. Minneapolis: University of Minnesota Press, 1980.

Rushbrooke, J. H. *The Baptist Movement in the Continent of Europe*. London: The Carey Press, 1915; reprinted by BiblioLife, 2009.

———. "The Baptist World Alliance and Approaching World Congress: The Significance of Toronto." *The Baptist Quarterly* 4, no. 2 (1928): 49–52.

———. "The Baptist World Alliance: Origin, Constitution, Achievements, Objects." *The Chronicle* 1, no. 2 (1938): 9–22.

———. *Fifth Baptist World Congress: Berlin, August 4-10, 1934*. London: Baptist World Alliance, 1934.

———. *Sixth Baptist World Congress Atlanta, GA July 22-28, 1939*. Atlanta: The Baptist World Alliance, 1939.

———. "Some Thoughts on the Toronto Congress." *Baptist Quarterly* 4, no. 4 (1928): 151–54.

Sachar, Howard M. *The Course of Modern Jewish History*. New rev. ed. New York: Vintage Books, 1990.

Sanford, Don A. *A Choosing People: The History of Seventh Day Baptists*. Macon, GA: Mercer University Press, 2012.

Sarfatti, Michele. *The Jews in Mussolini's Italy: From Equality to Persecution*. Translated by John Tedeschi and Anne C. Tedeschi. George L. Mosse Series. Madison: University of Wisconsin Press, 2006.

Schneier, Marc. *Shared Dreams: Martin Luther King Jr. and the Jewish Community*. Woodstock, VT: Jewish Lights Publishing, 2008.

Seiple, Chris. "The Essence of Exceptionalism: Roger Williams and the Birth of Religious Freedom in America." *The Review of Faith and International Affairs* 10, no. 2 (2012): 13–19.

Seventh Day Baptist Missionary Society. *Jubilee Papers: Historical Papers Commemorating the Fiftieth Anniversary of the Seventh-day Baptist Missionary Society, and the Centennial of the William Carey Foreign Missions Movement*. Westerly, RI: Board of Managers of the Seventh-day Baptist Missionary Society, 1892.

Shoemaker, JoAnne, and Don Shoemaker. *North Dakota Baptist State Convention, 1884–1984: The First Centennial, a History*. Barre, VT: Northlight Studio Press, 1984.

Shurden, Walter B. *The Baptist Identity: Four Fragile Freedoms*. Macon, GA: Smyth & Helwys, 1993.

Signer, Michael A., ed. *Humanity at the Limit: The Impact of the Holocaust Experience on Jews and Christians*. Bloomington: Indiana University Press, 2000.

Smith, Jessie C., ed. *Notable Black American Women, Book I*. Farmington Hills, MI: Thomson Gale, 1992.

———. *Notable Black American Women, Book II*. Farmington Hills, MI: Thomson Gale, 1996.

Soulen, R. Kendall. *The God of Israel and Christian Theology*. Minneapolis: Fortress, 1996.

Spitzer, Lee B. "Baptists, Barth, and the Crisis of Conscience Initiated by the Emergence of Nazi Anti-Semitism," *American Baptist Quarterly* Vol. XXXIV Nos. 3–4 (Fall and Winter 2015; actually published April 2017): 343–362.

———. "The Hand of Sincere Friendship: The Responses of Baptists in the United States to Nazi Anti-Semitism and the Persecution of the Jewish People, 1933–1948," PhD dissertation, Vrije Universiteit, 2016.

Stassen, Glen H., and David P. Gushee. *Kingdom Ethics: Following Jesus in Contemporary Context*. Downers Grove, IL: InterVarsity Press, 2003.

Stein, Leo. *I Was in Hell with Niemoeller*. New York: Revell, 1942.

Strübind, Andrea. "German Baptists and National Socialism." *Journal of European Baptist Studies* 8, no. 3 (2008): 5–20.

———. *Die Unfreie Freikirche: Der Bund Der Baptistengemeinden Im "Dritten Reich."* Berlin: Neukirchener, 1991.

Sutton, Jerry. *A Matter of Conviction: A History of Southern Baptist Engagement with the Culture*. Nashville: B&H Publishing Group, 2008.

Szajkowski, Zosa. "'Reconstruction' vs. 'Palliative Relief' in American Overseas Work (1919–1939)." *Jewish Social Studies* 32, no. 1 (1970): 14–42.

Tanenbaum. Marc H., Marvin R. Wilson, and A. James Rudin, eds. *Evangelicals and Jews in Conversation on Scripture, Theology, and History*. Grand Rapids, MI: Baker Book House, 1978.

Tiller, Carl W. *The Twentieth Century Baptist: Chronicles of Baptists in the First Seventy-Five Years of the Baptist World Alliance*. Valley Forge, PA: Judson Press, 1980.

Torbet, Robert G. *A History of the Baptists*. 3rd ed. Valley Forge, PA: Judson Press, 1978.

Trollinger, William Vance, Jr. *God's Empire: William Bell Riley and Midwestern Fundamentalism*. History of American Thought and Culture. Madison: University of Wisconsin Press, 1991.

Truett, George W. *God's Call to America and Other Addresses Comprising Special Orations Delivered on Widely Varying Occasions*. Nashville: Sunday School Board of the Southern Baptist Convention, 1923.

Tulga, Chester E. *The Foreign Missions Controversy in the Northern Baptist Convention, 1919–1949: 30 Years of Struggle*. Chicago: Conservative Baptist Fellowship, 1950.

Voss, Carl Hermann, and David A. Rausch. "American Christians and Israel, 1948–1988." *American Jewish Archives* (1988): 41–81.

Wardin, Albert W., Jr. *Tennessee Baptists: A Comprehensive History, 1779–1999*. Brentwood, TN: Executive Board of the Tennessee Baptist Convention, 1999.

Washington, James Melvin. *Frustrated Fellowship: The Black Quest for Social Power*. Macon, GA: Mercer University Press, 2004.

Wedlock, Lunabelle. "The Reaction of Negro Publications and Organizations to German Anti-Semitism." PhD diss., Howard University, 1942.

Weisbord, Robert G., and Arthur Stein. *Bittersweet Encounter: The Afro-American and the American Jew*. Contributions in Afro-American and African Studies. Westport, CT: Negro Universities Press, 1970.

West, Herbert Faulkner, ed. *The Autobiography of Robert Watchorn*. Oklahoma City: Kessinger Publishing, 2007.

Whitley, W. T. *Fourth Baptist World Congress, Toronto, Canada, 23–29 June, 1928—Record of Proceedings*. Toronto: Stewart Printing Service, 1928.

———. *Third Baptist World Congress—Stockholm, July 21-27, 1923—Record of Proceedings*. London: Kingsgate Press, 1923.

Williams, Reggie L. *Bonhoeffer's Black Jesus: Harlem Renaissance Theology and an Ethic of Resistance*. Waco, TX: Baylor University Press, 2014.

Wills, Gregory A. "Progressive Theology and Southern Baptist Controversies of the 1950s and 1960s." *Southern Baptist Journal of Theology* 7, no. 1 (2003): 12–31.

Woyke, Frank H. *Heritage and Ministry of the North American Baptist Conference*. Oakbrook Terrace, IL: North American Baptist Conference, 1979.

Wyman, David S. *The Abandonment of the Jews: America and the Holocaust 1941–1945*. New York: The New Press, 2007.

Zuccotti, Susan. *The Italians and the Holocaust: Persecution, Rescue, and Survival*. Lincoln: University of Nebraska Press, 1996.

Zuurdeeg, Willem Frederik. *An Analytical Philosophy of Religion*. Nashville: Abingdon, 1958.

Additional Primary Source Collections

Northern Baptist Convention (American Baptist Churches USA)

1. *Annual Convention Books* (1907–1949), published by the American Baptist Publication Society.
2. *Home Mission Monthly* (1893–1909), published by the American Baptist Home Mission Society.
3. *Missions*, a magazine published monthly by the Northern Baptist Convention.
4. *The Watchman-Examiner*, an independent newspaper representing a more evangelical/conservative perspective.
5. *National Baptist Convention General Council Meeting Minutes* (1933–1948).
6. *American Baptist Foreign Mission Society's Board of Managers Minutes* (1933–1948).

7. *Woman's American Baptist Home Missions Society Personnel Papers.*
8. *State Convention Annual Books* (1933–1948).
9. *City Societies' Annual Convention Books* (1933–1948).
10. *Regional Newspapers and Periodicals* (1933–1948): the *Connecticut Baptist,* the *District of Columbia Baptists News Bulletin,* the *Indiana Baptist Observer,* the *Kansas Baptist,* the *Maine Baptist Messenger,* the *Massachusetts Baptist Bulletin,* the *Montana-Idaho-Utah Messenger,* the *Nebraska Baptist Messenger,* the *Baptist New Yorker,* the *California-Nevada Baptist Bulletin,* the *Ohio Baptist,* the *Oregon Baptist, Puerto Rico Evangelico,* the *Washington Baptist,* and the *West Virginia Baptist.*

Swedish Baptist General Conference of America

Annual Conference Books (1933–1948), published by the Swedish Baptist General Conference of America.

General Association of Regular Baptist Churches

Annual Conference Books (1933–1948), published by the General Association of Regular Baptist Churches.

Southern Baptist Convention

1. *Annual Convention Books* (1873–1949), published by the Southern Baptist Convention.
2. *State Convention Annual Books* (1933–1948).
3. *Minutes of the Southern Baptist Convention Executive Committee.*
4. *Minutes of the Foreign Mission Board.*
5. *Minutes of the Home Mission Board.*
6. *Home and Foreign Missions*, a publication of the SBC (1933–1937).
7. *Southern Baptist Home Missions*, a monthly publication of the Home Mission Board (1938–1948).
8. *The Commission*, a monthly publication from the Foreign Mission Board (1938–1948).
9. SBC state convention newspapers: the *Alabama Baptist* (1933–1934, 1938), the *Arkansas Baptist* (1938), Florida's *Baptist Witness* (1938), Georgia's *Christian Index* (1938), the *Illinois Baptist* (1938), Kentucky's *Western Recorder* (1938), Louisiana's *Baptist Messenger* (1938), the *Maryland Baptist* (1938), Missouri's the *Word and the Way* (1938), Mississippi's *Baptist Record* (1938), North Carolina's *Biblical Recorder* (1933–1948), the *Baptist New Mexican* (1938), Oklahoma's *Baptist Messenger* (1938), South Carolina's the *Baptist Courier* (1938), Tennessee's *Baptist and Reflector* (1938), Texas' *Baptist Standard* (1938), and Virginia's *Religious Herald* (1938).
10. Papers of Jacob Gartenhaus, Southern Baptist Archives, Nashville, TN.
11. Papers of Una Lawrence Roberts, Southern Baptist Archives, Nashville, TN.

African American Baptist Conventions

1. The Annual Session Books of the National Baptist Convention, U.S.A., Inc. (1933–1948).
2. The Lott Carey Baptist Foreign Mission Convention Annual Books.

Seventh Day Baptist General Conference

1. *Annual Seventh Day Baptist Convention Yearbooks Convention (*1933–1949), published by the Seventh Day Baptist Convention.
2. *The Sabbath Recorder*, a weekly periodical of the Seventh Day Baptist Convention, published by the American Sabbath Tract Society, Plainfield, NJ.

Baptist World Alliance

1. *Baptist World Alliance Executive Committee Minutes*, housed at the American Baptist Historical Society, Mercer University, Macon, GA.
2. *Correspondence and Papers of J. H. Rushbrooke* (1933–1947), Regent's Park College Library, University of Oxford, Oxford, England.
3. *Correspondence and Papers of Hans Luckey*, Elstal Seminary Archive Collection, Berlin, Germany.

Jewish Sources

1. *The Jewish Chronicle* (1928–1948).
2. The *American Hebrew* (1933–1948).
3. *The American Jewish Yearbook* (1933–1948).

Index